The Boys of Seelow

A Story of the Hitler Youth

Joel Connealy

Copyright © 2018 by Joel Connealy

All rights reserved. This book or any portion thereof may not be reproduced or used in any manner whatsoever without the express written permission of Joel Connealy.

First Printing, 2018

ISBN: ISBN-13: 978-0692166376 (Joel Connealy)
ISBN-10: 0692166378

Scriptor Publishing Group
7830 State Line Rd., Ste. 101
Prairie Village, KS 66208

Book layout design & eBook conversion by manuscript2ebook.com

TABLE OF CONTENTS

1936: The German Fatherland 1
    Seven German Boys 1

1939: Our Flag is the New Age 5
    The Year the War Began 5
    The Sword Forced into Our Hands 8
    Education 9
    Koby's Talent 15
    Unser deutsches Volk, Sieg Heil! 19
    Christmas on the Eve 23

1940: We are the Future Soldiers 31
    Blaz's Haircut 31
    The Hitler Youth 33
    A Day at the Range 39
    A Father's Advice 46
    Blaz's Training 47
    Hitler Youth Parade 49
    KLV Camps 53
    Over Everything in the World 55
    A Last Appeal to Reason 56
    The Game 57
    Football and Officers 61

    The Wehrmacht 72
    The War Comes to German Land 75
    Jarman Versus Blaz 77
    The Flag on High 81
    An Eleven-Year-Old Koby 86
    Cross Country 92
    The Communist Threat 94
    SS March 97
    Koby's Special Training 99
    In the Homeland Lives a Girl 102
    SS Discipline 105
    Schlusser's Instructions 113
    Die Judenfrage 115
    Forward to the West 118
    Berlin 126
    Bombs on England 134
    Back in Seelow 135
    Love of the Game 137
    Ein Volk, Ein Reich, Ein Führer 141
    Evaluations 143
    Faster and More Intense 148
    End of a Chapter 151
    Preparation 153
    A Christmas in Nazi Germany 154

1941: No Path is Too Steep **159**
    The Train Leaves 159
    Kinderlandverschickung 165
    A New Young Commander 167
    First Taste of the Cold 169

Comrade, Seek the Übermensch 179
Killing in War 182
The Truth is With Us 185
Winter March 190
How Fathers Were Doing 192
The Youth Continue Marching.. 197
The Waffen and the Allgemeine 201
Erich's Departure 204
Eve of Barbarossa 206
Forward to the East, You Storming Army 209
A Life Outside of the Military 212
No Squad for Young Boys 213
Northern Russia 215
Goodbye to Stalin, Churchill, Roosevelt................................... 216
The Last Silent Nights 217
Vertraut ihr der Führer? 218

1942: Youth Knows no Dangers 223
Topple the Jewish Throne in Russia.. 223
Personal Records.. 224
AA Guns and Artillery 225
Leningrad 228
Comrades Shot by the Red Front 234
On the Verge of Victory 245
Russian Winter... 247
A Death in the Family... 252
War is Hell 256
A Jewish SS Soldier.. 258
Nico Leipzig and Wilhelm Kramer.. 267
Across the Reich... 268

    Springtime for Hitler's Armies 271
    Night 273
    The Red Terror 280
    Russian Bear 282
    No Quick War 284
    The German Base 287
    Peace in War 289
    To Be or Not to Be 291
    An Unfortunate Discovery 294
    Reprisals 302
    A Minor Comeuppance 310
    A Run in Estonia 312
    Stalingrad 315
    Mein Führer, I Can Walk 321
    Nico's Return 323
    The Partisans 329

1943: Marches in Enemy Land 335
    A Second KLV Camp 335
    Past, Present, and Future 339
    Wollt ihr den Totalen Krieg? 343
    The Minister of Propaganda 347
    News for the Knights 351
    Hans and Tristan 353
    The Third Way 356
    A New Soldier for Hitler 364
    Tristan versus Koby 369
    A New Senft 373
    The Wehrmacht's Oath 373
    First Contact 378

Four Corners 386
   Unbreakable Spirit 390
   Back in Line 391
   Klara Hertz 392
   The Storm is Unleashed 394
   Familiar Death 399
   The Silence Will Shatter 399
   Russian Beasts 401
   Reason for Hope 403

1944: We Stand Now, Ready to Fight Against the Red Plague 409
   Not Retreating, Regrouping 409
   Barbarian Invaders, We'll Swiftly Strike Down 412
   Competition 417
   Schlusser on Leave 421
   Faith in the Führer 424
   The Red Army and the Army of the Swastika 426
   The Road of Defeat 436
   Never Saw a Father Anymore 437
   Werner von Schraeder 443
   To Fight for Freedom There 447
   Unwanted Messages 448
   Jarman's Advice 450
   The Siege Begins 453
   Der Rote Pest 457
   Jaye's Iron Cross 465
   What to do with Russian Prisoners 466
   Totenehrung (Honoring of the Dead) 469
   SS will not Rest, SS will Annihilate 472
   Our Job 473

We Hunted Them Like a Herd ... 475
Gott Mit Uns ... 478
God Save the Führer ... 480
Who Says I am not Under the Special Protection of God? ... 482
Heil Hitler ... 483
For Work and Bread ... 486
The Private on Neman's Shores ... 489
Germany's Triumph in '36 ... 497
The Darker Parts of the Sky ... 500
Kill, You Gallant Soldiers of the Red Army! ... 503
Prisoners of Their Own ... 508
Ivo: The Little Sniper ... 510
Olympia ... 511
The Third Branch of the SS ... 515
The New Guy ... 518
Washing Up ... 518
A Home Cooked Meal ... 521
A Time to Think ... 525
Heart of the Wehrmacht ... 526
Third Reich Cinema ... 528
The Reinforcements ... 530
Sanity in War ... 539
Jarman versus Jaeger ... 541
The Polish Girl ... 542
We're Young ... 548
Death in the Wind ... 551
The Church ... 553
Fußball ... 554
Allied Bombings ... 557
The Beast is on His Way ... 561

Less than Six Months...562
Hans and Wiktoria...563
Sergeant Seelenfreund's Verdict..567
Nazis..568
Hans' Confession 571
Hans is Beaten...573
The Downed Soviet Bomber 575
Red Snow 576
Sleep in Heavenly Peace 583

1945: Germany, You Must Stand, Even if We May Fall 587
The Russkies Are Ready 587
Only Girl I Know..588
The New Big City..588
That's the End of the Reich. Beyond that is Jewish Land..........594
The Seelow Heights...599
Blaz Returns Home 601
The Ninth Army Command..602
Soldiers..605
Koby Briefly Comes Back..606
Reunification 608
Deutschlandlied...616
Preparations 620
Casualties of War...625
SS Inspections 630
Bullets...633
Hellstorm 634
Germany Against All 638
Frustration at High Command..639
The Little Ones 642

When Everything Falls Apart 646
Through Life and Death 647
The Final Hours Approach 650

1945: The Battle of Seelow Heights 651
Führer Command! We Follow! 651
The Failed Artillery Strikes 652
We Stand for Germany at our Posts 654
Back to the Front 664
Koby and Blaz 665
Ten Men 667
Seelow's Finest Hour 667
The SS Meeting 681
Defenseless 683
Relief of Seelow 684
The Officer 685
The Last Awards 688
Werwolf 690
My Choice 695
Schlusser's Report 698
A Last Effort 699
The Final Conflict 702
Truth Will Triumph 707

PROLOGUE

1936: The German Fatherland

Seven German Boys

April 19, 1936

Seven boys sprinted out of the theater, grins etched on their faces. They raced down the streets of a German farm town, Seelow. It was small, they knew it by heart, and they reached a little home outside of its limits within minutes. They pretended they were cowboys and spoke with their best American accents, imitating the actors in Westerns. They ran around until nightfall, using their fingers as make-believe pistols. As they sat down for dinner, Blaz Senft mentioned the upcoming Olympics as they sat down for dinner. All the boys loved some Olympic sport, whether it was soccer, track, or one of many others. They all hoped *Deutschland* would win this year.

"*Denken Sie unser Mannschaft wird gewinnen?*" Blaz asked the group with excitement, "You think our country will win the most medals?"

"I don't know, the Americans are pretty good too," Ivo, the smallest boy in the group, said.

"No one can beat *Deutschland*," Jarman disagreed with a grin.

"If anyone wins other than us, I hope it is Italy," Koby added, appearing rather Italian himself.

"Hey," Ivo asked, "What do you guys think of *Herr* Mandel's shop getting shut down?"

"I heard he was an enemy of *Deutschland*," Erich answered. "Father told me it's because *Herr* Mandel is Jewish and their businesses haven't been doing well lately."

"I heard he was up to something," added Ivo, taking a drink of water.

"I never would've thought he was up to anything," Blaz said innocently.

"He's a Jew," Jarman said, "Our teachers say they are a big reason that we lost *Der Krieg*, The War. And why everyone struggled after it."

"*Ja*, my teacher said last week that Jews oppose a strong *Deutschland*," Koby recalled.

"Honestly, I had no idea he was Jewish until his shop went under," Ivo said, "But what do I know?"

"I didn't know he was Jewish either," Blaz concurred, combing his wavy, blond hair to the right with his fingers. "Erich, what else does *Herr* Meyer know about it? He's in the SS."

Erich answered, "My father said it didn't get shut down. It went out of business. Not enough people buying at Jewish businesses. That's what they get for boycotting German goods."

"Do you think it means anything?" asked Jurgen.

"*Nein*, I'm sure that *Herr* Mandel will be on his feet in a few months. Probably just some grown up problem with money or something."

It was almost completely dark out now, so the boys left for their homes. All of them said "*Herzlichen Glückwunschen an Hitler*" (Happy Birthday to Hitler), and goodbye to Jurgen and his family. They stayed together until they got to town and then went their separate ways. Blaz and Erich stayed side-by-side.

"Should we have wished the *Führer* an early Happy Birthday?" Blaz asked a bit nervously. "That's bad luck."

Erich laughed at this, "You think bad luck has anything on the *Führer*?"

"*Nein*," Blaz shook his head and grinned at his own silliness.

"Blaz, the *Führer* really is making Germany great. Father's been telling me about all our achievements in the last three years!"

"You always know about what's going on with stuff like that. Do you know if *Herr* Mandel was up to something?"

Erich nodded, actually looking happy to discuss this, "I do know that Mandel is against the Fatherland," Erich replied, "And the *Führer* says we must not allow anyone to stop *Deutschland* from becoming powerful again. Father says our army is becoming stronger and that it reminds him of before *Der Krieg*."

"Are we going to war?"

"*Oh, nein*! We are just prepared to keep bad countries out, that want to harm us."

"*Oh gut*," sighed Blaz.

"*Auf Wiedersehen Freund, und Heil Hitler*!" Good-bye buddy, and Hail Hitler.

"See you!" Blaz called back into the night.

"Hello Blaz," his mother said as he closed the door.

"Hello mother," Blaz greeted his mom, Cheryl.

"How was the movie, Blaz?"

"It was great! The cowboys were so brave, they can do anything," Blaz replied bouncing on the balls of his feet while he pretended to pull out pistols from his pockets. "Afterwards, we pretended that we were cowboys at Jurgen's house."

His mother tried to conceal a look of concern.

"What is it mama?" Blaz asked. Cheryl looked Blaz in the eye and smiled.

"Oh, it's nothing. You needn't worry about it." She sighed and looked back into Blaz's curious, bright blue eyes. "It's late," she said. "You should get to bed."

"Okay mama," Blaz obeyed with disappointment.

After cleaning his teeth and washing his face, Blaz walked up a steep, thin set of stairs to his room, the only room on the second level and it was quite small. He put his clothes into a basket in the closet. Blaz climbed into bed and laid his arm across his forehead.

Mandel did something bad to the Fatherland. What could it be? He seemed like such a nice man... I'll bet this is nothing. It'll all be back to normal soon, Blaz thought as he closed his eyes.

1939: Our Flag is the New Age

The Year the War Began

March 17, 1939 Friday

"Did you hear? Did you hear?" Ivo yelled, tearing down the school halls, almost tripping as he approached his friends.

"What? What?" Jurgen asked, glancing down.

"Our armies just captured Czechoslovakia!"

Doubt flashed across everyone's faces. Jarman raised an eyebrow skeptically.

"How? This quickly?" Koby said, obviously surprised, "I know the *Führer* received the land at our border, but all of Czechoslovakia? We never even declared war!"

"We conquered it without firing a shot! The Czechs just surrendered. Poland and Hungary got some land too. I found out when I was talking with *Herr* Miller about my math."

"Ivo, you're starting to act like Koby, talking to your teachers after school," laughed Jarman.

"I'd like to have his grades, he's just so smart."

"All right, all right," Koby cut in, "Who's going running with me? University scouting gets serious next year. I'm hoping that I'll be able to run at university."

"I'm coming. Koby there is no way you don't make it to university with how good you are," Blaz said. "I'm coming."

5

"I don't want to get cocky."

"So humble," Ivo commented, hand on his chest, eyes turned to heaven, "I'll come too."

"You guys?" Koby asked the rest of the group.

"Jarman, Jurgen, and I are heading to do strength training," Erich said.

"Do you want to come?" Koby asked Reinhardt.

"Sure."

"*Wunderbar!*"

Koby started out while Blaz, Ivo, and Reinhardt followed. Koby normally ran ahead but occasionally he hung back to try to push them to go faster. Blaz and Ivo were very good runners and had recently run in the school five kilometer with Koby. Koby had won for everyone under fifteen and only come second to an eighteen-year-old, while Blaz and Ivo came in third and fourth for the under-fifteens respectively.

"Once they harvest this, we can run through them instead of going around them," Koby reminded Blaz and Ivo who were struggling to keep up.

Once they'd finished their run, they stretched in the middle of the soccer field that the school was built around. After this, the four boys walked down the hallway where Erich, Jurgen, and Jarman were packing up.

"How was the training?" Blaz said.

"*Gut*, you?" Erich asked Koby.

"They did good."

"Hey, did you see Mandel's old shop is finally vacant?" Jurgen asked.

"*Ja*," Blaz answered. "I wonder what happened to him."

"That *Jew* is probably a long way from here now," Jarman said.

"He immigrated to Palestine," Erich told them, "My father saw him and his family off."

"Palestine? That sounds cool," Ivo nodded to himself.

"Hey, Jarman, I had Jewish relatives in my family like two centuries ago," Koby said somewhat sarcastically but honestly.

"Mandel was a pure Jew, you've just got a little bit of that blood and aside from that you're almost completely German."

"The teachers say they are responsible for a lot of our problems, with Jews being so rich after *Der Krieg* because they own the banks. The *Führer* has been speaking more about the problems Jews have caused our nation. Maybe we'd be better off without them," Ivo said with a hint of concern in his voice.

"The *Führer* knows what is best," Erich said.

"But what is wrong with just having some Jewish blood?" Blaz asked.

"Haven't you listened? The Jews want nothing but the death of *Deutschland*. It's our job to stop that threat," Erich said, calm as always.

Koby raised an eyebrow.

"I'm not talking about you, Koby. You're barely Jewish at all, doesn't count. The *Führer* wouldn't trace that and even if he could he wouldn't care. One of his best friends is half-Jewish, anyway. *Half.*"

"I hope you're right."

As the others dispersed, Blaz turned to his friend, "Erich, just to be on the safe side don't ever tell anyone that Koby's family has Jewish blood. I don't want him to have to leave."

"Hey, we're friends. I'd never say anything if I thought it could get you guys hurt," Erich said, "Besides, my father already knows Koby's family's genealogy. German, Jewish, and Italian."

Blaz smiled. "Your father always knows."

"With that victory over Czechoslovakia, I'm sure that Jews are the last thing on the *Führer's* mind."

"*Ja*, you're right. *Ade, Freund.*"

"See you."

The Sword Forced into Our Hands

September 1, 1939 Friday

The Hitler Youth was mandatory now, though many had sent their children into the Hitler Youth voluntarily long before it became mandatory, including Erich and Jarman's parents. Erich's hair now matched Jarman's: short on the sides, a little longer on top. These confident National Socialists were the least alarmed by the news of war. On this day, the boys looked to the sky to see squadrons of German bombers fly toward Poland. They immediately headed to Jurgen's home to find out what was happening.

"Our forces have overrun the first Polish defenses," the radio said, "Poland will be under our control before the month is out."

"Wow!" Ivo exclaimed, "That's great! *Deutschland* is going to get the land back that we lost in *Der Krieg*!"

Erich and Jarman were brimming with energy.

"Why is the *Führer* attacking Poland?" Koby asked.

Jarman answered, having been told by his older brothers, "The Poles have been attacking several positions on the border."

Koby raised his eyebrows.

"Hey," Jarman said, "What? You don't believe it? Are you doubting the *Führer*?"

"I guess I am," Koby said, nervously rubbing his forearm.

"He just wants to protect us Koby," Erich said, "The Poles have been slaughtering Germans inside their territory. Have you seen the photographs?"

"I didn't know," Koby admitted, "But do we have to attack other countries?"

"They attacked us," Jarman said through gritted teeth. Erich frowned. Koby rolled his eyes, "Jarman, come on."

"*Nein* Koby!" Jarman snapped, raising his voice to a yell and springing to his feet. Erich rose to his feet and gently held Jarman back at the elbows, just in case. "What reason has the *Führer* ever given you to doubt him?"

"Let's change the subject," Ivo suggested.

"Shut up, this is between us," Jarman shot.

"Hey!" Blaz shouted, standing up.

"This is important."

"No one loves the *Führer* more than Ivo," Blaz said with a fierce glare at Jarman, "You're taking this too far!"

"All right, let's everybody calm the hell down," Reinhardt said.

All eyes turned Reinhardt's way. Erich's lip curled into a grin. No one noticed.

"We're not even thirteen. This is why we aren't the leaders. Let's change the subject like Ivo said. We don't want to get angry at each other over this. The *Führer* is the *Führer* and he knows what he's doing."

"*Ja*, you're right," Koby said, "Sorry Jarman."

"I'm sorry too, I shouldn't have gotten so mad," Jarman said, "Let's not worry about it."

"This is the grown-ups job," Ivo said, "It'll all be done soon."

Education

September 4, 1939 Monday

Blaz woke up and rolled onto his chest to look out his single window. It was cloudy outside. A cool breeze blew leaves by his window.

First day of school is always like this, Blaz thought with a grin. He knew the Jurgen's family always welcomed rain though.

He stumbled over to his small closet, put on his school clothes, and put his running clothes into his bag. Then he walked downstairs to the table where bread, butter, jam, some meats and milk sat. His family said a prayer and started eating breakfast.

"You ready for school son?" Ottoway Senft said.

"Ready as I'll ever be," Blaz grinned as he spread jam on his bread.

"*Gut.*"

The family sat in silence for a bit. Blaz's father sipped his tea. His mother looked her husband in the eye and gestured toward Blaz who remained oblivious. Ottoway nodded his head and broke the silence.

"Blaz," he said, "I have some important things to tell you."

"*Ja*, papa?"

"After Christmas Break, you start the *Hitlerjugend*."

"Okay? Am I leaving?"

"*Nein, nein*, military training and meetings will be here in town after school."

"Oh, okay. Like Erich and Jarman."

"*Ja.*"

"That will be fun, then. Erich and Jarman talk about it all the time."

"I'm glad you think so."

Blaz turned to leave, then stopped. If he was being trained for the military, what did that mean for his father?

"What about you, papa?"

"What about me?"

"Will you be joining the army?"

His father looked up at his mother. She nodded.

"*Jawohl.*"

Blaz's mouth hung open. His papa couldn't go into battle, he would die.

"Now son, I won't be called to the front. There are many younger men who can and will be fighting. I'll only be in the reserves."

Blaz remained frozen.

"I won't be called to the front lines unless *Deutschland* begins to lose."

Blaz's shoulders relaxed.

"Have a great first day at school, Blaz," his mother said as she kissed him on the forehead. He smiled back at her, then walked briskly out the door.

The rain started to pour on his walk to school, and Blaz shifted to a run. When he reached the school, he was soaked, as were many of the other students. He jogged across the large training grounds that the schools structure surrounded. Once inside, he trudged slowly towards his classroom.

"Hey Blaz!" Blaz looked up and scanned his surroundings. Koby jogged towards him, "What's happening?"

"Oh, nothing."

"C'mon. Something's bothering you. Chin up, we have our first official running practice today. It's gonna be great, running for the Seelow Knights! So, what's bothering you?" Koby asked, still sounding excited.

Blaz smiled sadly. Koby's smile slowly disappeared, "Did your father get drafted too?"

"I'm just a bit wrapped in my thoughts, you know?"

Koby nodded. "And you found out you're being put into the *Hitlerjugend*?"

Blaz nodded, his neutral expression morphing into one of excitement.

"Hey, our fathers are old enough they won't be called on for a while," Koby reassured him, "In their thirties, *ja*?"

"True."

"But the *Hitlerjugend* will be excellent. Are you excited for it?"

"Of course, who wouldn't be?"

Blaz and Koby strolled to their first class, chatting with their friends. Girls and boys both went to the school together. Some classes were separated by gender.

"*Heil* Hitler?" Jarman asked.

"*Heil* Hitler!" Blaz answered. Koby only did the salute.

"Are you ready for training?" Erich asked them.

Koby said, "I hope they've got places in the army for runners."

"Considering all the marching they do, I'd bet so," Erich said.

"I wonder what our next move will be?" Jurgen said as he opened one of his books.

"If we didn't have a peace treaty, I'd think we'd make a move against the Soviet Union."

"The *Führer* has always said Communism is our enemy," Blaz agreed, "And Marxism."

"No one should like Communism, even the democracies understand that," Erich said, "All that 'give everyone an equal share no matter how hard they work' *Scheiße* is stupid. How is anyone going to be motivated? We have something to work for here, the Fatherland's greatness and our people's continuation."

"Noble concept," Koby reminded them, "If everyone worked equally as hard."

"But they don't," Blaz said in conclusion to that.

"Speaking of hard work," a middle-aged man with thinning blond hair, a pronounced hawk nose, and high cheekbones said from behind, "It's time to take your seats."

As the children all obeyed the order, the teacher walked to the front of the room where the bright red flag hung above the board.

"Well students, your *Realschule* has begun. My job, as well as all teachers here, is to prepare you for life in the Reich. I will be your history teacher. This will be your most important class. Any questions?"

Silence.

"Then let's begin."

As the teacher began to lecture, the class listened intently but one student put his head down. The teacher shook his head and calmly strode over to the desk. The student didn't look up. The teacher slammed his fist into the desk. The student shot up in alarm.

"There will be no sleeping in this class! You are children of the Reich and you are not only cheating yourselves by not paying attention, but you are cheating the whole Fatherland."

The class stared wide-eyed at the teacher's sudden intensity.

"The *Führer* expects well-educated young men and women. You will be these men and women who lead the Reich someday. *Heil* Hitler."

The class responded in unison, "*Heil* Hitler!"

"*Gut*, good," the teacher smiled, "Now are we ready?"

"*Ja* sir," the student said.

"*Mein Wort*," Ivo gasped as they left class, "I knew that *Deutschland* had been wronged by France.... they blamed us for *Der Krieg*? How can that be? Their side shot our ally's leader. What were we supposed to do? Let them get away with that?"

"That's why we must avenge our losses. *Deutschland* must be restored to its former greatness." Erich sounded like his father. "Poland is a good place to start. Danzig is rightful German land."

After school, Blaz, Ivo, Reinhardt, and Koby got together with their team for the first official practice. Their coach had the look of a runner but way past his prime, sporting wrinkled skin, a rough face and thick brown hair.

"*Guten tag*, Knights" their coach said, "There is really no need for introductions since we practiced all summer. No new runners I see. Koby, you met with me yesterday and ran an excellent five-kilometer. Do not run your hardest after a race. Let yourself recover. That goes for all of you. Now, on that note we will begin with a thirty-minute light run today."

"*Ja*, Coach Friederich."

Koby led Blaz, Ivo and Reinhardt towards the countryside. The rain had subsided a while ago and clouds still covered much of the sky but the sun had come out, warming the air and reflecting against the wet ground. Koby began to pull ahead but Blaz sped up alongside him.

"How good was your time?" he asked.

Koby grinned.

"Come on, how was it?"

With a big smile Koby said, "Sixteen minutes, fifteen seconds."

"*Mein Wort*! That's incredible! And you're not even thirteen!"

"*Ja*, the coach says I'll be able to run in the forty-four World Olympics for *Deutschland* if I keep improving."

"*Ja, ja*! I mean-"

"I heard the word Olympics. You know that the nineteen-forty Olympics have been canceled?" Ivo asked as he sprinted to catch up.

"Just next year in forty, and Koby wouldn't be old enough to compete anyway," Blaz said.

Ivo's eyes widened on his small face, "You're going to be in the Olympics?! *Oh mein Wort, mein Wort*!" Ivo blurted out, out of breath as they continued to run, "When are you going?"

"The coach said for the nineteen-forty-four Olympics if the war has ended and if I keep improving."

"Koby, I'm so proud of you. You are just amazing at running," Ivo exclaimed. He really had no idea what to say.

Blaz and Koby smiled. Ivo always got excited when one of them accomplished something and it was always an event to witness. The three sped up as they approached the schoolyard, Reinhardt had fallen behind early and they'd continued while he ran by himself.

"C'mon guys!" Koby yelled as he sprinted ahead.

Ivo and Blaz fell behind Koby immediately. Both of them sprinted as fast as they could, staying neck and neck until Blaz's slightly longer stride gave him the lead and he made it through the arched gate a moment before Ivo.

"*Ach, glücklich!*" Ivo panted, "Lucky!"

"Good work boys," Koby said.

Blaz bent down to catch his breath while Ivo put his hands on the back of his head. He looked at Koby, who had seemingly, already completely recovered and showed no signs of exhaustion. *He's going places,* Blaz said to himself. He stood up with his hands on his hips and squinted as he looked at the bright sky. A cloud began to block out the sun and Blaz looked back to the earth, where Ivo and Koby had started to walk back towards the school doors.

Koby's Talent

September 28, 1939 Thursday

"First running competition of the year today," Koby said as he slapped Blaz's rear. "You ready?"

"*Ja,*" Blaz said.

"And we get our *Hitlerjugend* uniforms today. *Jungvolk* is over next semester, in fact, they are combining the two. Seelow is a little behind other cities since we are so small," Koby told him, "*Hitlerjugend* will teach us how to use weapons, drive, lots of stuff we will have to do in a war. Survival techniques too, that's what Erich and Jarman are learning right now. They started *Hitlerjugend* this semester, what with them being older."

"And both their parents are members of the party," Blaz added.

"That too," Koby grinned as they walked across the schoolyard to eat their lunches. Ivo ran towards them and raised his right hand in the *Hitlergruß*, the Hitler greeting.

"*Heil* Hitler," he said.

"What's this about?" Koby asked.

"You didn't hear?"

"Obviously not."

Ivo giggled. "True. Anyway, Poland surrendered. We won!"

"*Wunderbar!*" Blaz clapped, "Then the war is over, right?"

"*Ja,*" a voice said. The three of them looked and saw Erich walking towards them, "My father told me that the *Führer* wants peace with Britain and France," he said as Jarman joined the conversation, "And the Soviet Union is running around in the east right now."

"We have our territory back and we rescued the Germans in Poland. We may as well have peace," Ivo said.

"That's the *Führer's* reasoning," Erich answered.

"Good then. Koby, looks like the next year the Olympics will happen."

"Probably not," Jarman cut in, "France and Britain won't just let us reclaim our territory. They're going to fight us. My father's division has been moved from Poland to the French border," he said, seething with anger, "Those assholes won't allow *Deutschland* to return to its glory."

"They don't want another powerful county in Europe. They call us the attackers when they have empires across the planet," Blaz agreed.

"They'll pay for that," Erich said coldly, "My father has been promoted to the *Waffen-Schutzstaffel*. He'll be leading a platoon against the French when the time for the battle comes."

"Hope he gives them hell," Jarman said to Erich with a grin.

"There is a rally in town square tonight," Reinhardt said, "Will you be there?"

"Of course."

Blaz stretched as Koby walked out of school in his uniform. They wore muscle shirts and running shorts in blue and gold color. A small Swastika was printed on the shorts.

"The coach is coming?"

"*Ja.*"

The team continued to warm up and stretch. The coach walked out and said, "All right, our meet is at the track in Bad Freienwalde, let's get in the van."

"*Ja* sir," the small group of runners obeyed and piled into the vehicle.

At the race, Blaz, Koby, and Ivo got set up to start. There were fifteen more kids from other schools there. They did some last minute stretching and jogging in place while other runners checked in. The referee walked to the starting line, pistol in hand, and gave them a quick rundown of the rules, "There will be no pushing, kicking or grabbing during the run. If you do any of these, you will be disqualified. Stay on the track. If you stray off the track you will be disqualified. I will hold up a number indicating what lap the lead runner is on. Each runner will run twelve and a half laps before finishing over there." He pointed to the far end of the track.

"*Auf die Platze! Fertig!*" Bang!

The boys bolted. Koby pulled ahead quickly. One boy stayed with him. Blaz and Ivo stayed in the middle of the pack. After the first lap, the distance between the runners began to grow. Koby's lead extended over the second place boy while the third place runner gained on second place. Blaz took a lead over Ivo but couldn't shake him. Ivo stayed close behind Blaz trying hard not to lose him. Koby was lapping competitors by the third loop. At the start of Koby's eleventh lap the timer yelled, "One thousand meters!"

Koby kicked in more speed. His face had lost all signs of emotion. Only exhaustion. Blaz had been lapped by him twice already but still was determined to finish strong. Blaz sped up and Ivo followed suite. Their speed put distance between the kids trailing them. Sweat ran down their faces as they ran with as much speed as they could muster. Koby, who'd already lapped everyone started his last six hundred and sped up to his finishing pace. As he ran ahead of them, Blaz and Ivo watched, before snapping back into race mode. As they started their last twelve hundred, Koby began his final one hundred. Blaz gritted his teeth and kept running. As he hit the last lap, Ivo made an initial attempt to overtake Blaz but Blaz fended him off. As they got closer to the finish line Blaz came even with another runner who increased his speed. They came neck and neck. As they approached the finish line, Ivo snuck through the two of them and took the lead.

Oh, no you don't, thought Blaz as he sped up, prompting the other German boy to increase his speed as well. Blaz caught up to Ivo, lowered his head and crossed right before him. The other boy crossed almost immediately after them.

"Nineteen thirty-nine, nineteen forty, nineteen forty-one!"

"*Ja!*" Blaz panted as he gasped for air. Dimples appeared on Ivo's face as he broke a smile.

"Nice run!" Koby said.

"*Danke*- how did- you do?" Blaz said in between breaths.

"Fifteen fifty-nine!"

Blaz smiled as he bent down, catching his breath. Ivo walked slowly and shakily over to them.

"*Ah, mein Wort* Blaz! You beat me by one step again!" Ivo said in a fake-angry voice.

Blaz slapped him on the back as they walked back to their coach.

"*Sehr gut, stolz auf euch*, proud of you," Friedrich congratulated them. He got down on a knee and said. "You boys are all great runners; I would never have imagined kids could run this fast for so long at your age."

"*Danke*," they all said.

"All right, get on the bus. I'll get your medals and results. We have to make it back in time for the rally."

"Can't miss that!" Ivo exclaimed.

"*Ja*, let's go!" Blaz added.

They jogged towards the small van. When they got there, the three boys stood outside the van and waited for their coach. Blaz looked up at the sunset and squinted his eyes.

"Beautiful, isn't it?" he said aloud.

"What?" Ivo asked.

"The sunset," Blaz said with a look of awe as he stared out at the red sky. Ivo glanced at Blaz with a look of confusion as to why Blaz would say something in such a serious tone.

"Makes you think about things."

Ivo turned and looked at the sun.

"There's some incredible things out there, aren't there?" Koby asked with a smile.

"*Ja*," Ivo said slowly and uncomfortably, "It is pretty."

Blaz looked at Ivo and said, "There's a plan, this isn't all just happening, the fact that we can run the way we do, that we can make all these things."

"But something's off, the world is so amazing but there's a lot of bad in it," Ivo speculated, "I guess that war is just a part of things, young people shouldn't have to die in a world as beautiful as this, but some things just aren't right," Ivo stopped, "Do you think that's why the *Führer* wanted to perfect *Deutschland*? For peace?"

"Maybe," Koby said, leaning his head on a fist.

The boys stared out at the sunset.

"We may not understand it, but there's a reason for this war. Some big reason, it's part of a plan," Blaz said, "And I'd bet that the *Führer* is a part of that, Ivo." They kept staring at horizon.

While they watched, the coach came and said, "Come on, let's get going."

Ivo walked into the van, deep in thought. Koby patted Blaz on the back and smiled at him, "You're a good kid, Blaz."

Blaz, somewhat taken off guard by the comment, didn't respond. As they got in the van, the sun vanished beyond the horizon. Blaz kept staring in silence as they drove away.

Unser deutsches Volk, Sieg Heil!

The van rolled through the country and Blaz stared out at the sky. He was still in thought from their conversation and almost wondered why he had brought it up in the first place. Blaz had been friends with Koby and Ivo for nearly as long as he could remember but deep conversations with them were few and far between. Blaz, like many Germans, was a Lutheran and so were all his friends. Only Koby, Ivo, Jurgen, and himself regularly went to church, though. Even with their religious backgrounds, God was not a topic that ever came up in their conversations. Whether it was too awkward, embarrassing, or uninteresting Blaz didn't know. The three boys had remained silent for the ride back, all thinking about their short conversation before boarding the bus. Blaz turned to Koby, who sat next to him.

"It's getting cloudy."

"So?"

"Is it going to rain?"

"I wouldn't know."

"I'm looking forward to this rally. I'm sure it'll be awesome since we just beat Poland."

Koby smiled.

"What?" Blaz asked.

"Those rallies are just about giving us a little encouragement and telling us that the Fatherland is improving."

Ivo turned his head and said while giving his chest a thump, "*Nein*, they're about pride in being German."

"They're about both," Koby said officially.

"*Ja*, that's fair," Ivo agreed, "Can you believe we're going into the real *Hitlerjugend* in three months?"

"Time flies."

Blaz nodded.

"I never thought I'd be eleven until I was," Ivo said.

Koby and Blaz glanced at each other.

Ivo turned and said, "If that makes sense."

Blaz and Koby laughed. Ivo turned towards the front as his face turned red.

When the van drove into Seelow, the boys headed to the school to get their new Hitler Youth uniforms. They walked down a hallway to a small office. A woman sat at the desk inside with large boxes full of uniforms on the floor. The boys walked in and Koby approached first.

"Koby Hertz, age twelve," he told the woman nervously.

"Ah, beginning *Hitlerjugend* next semester? *Ausgezeichnet,* excellent," the woman looked on her checklist for the name then crossed Koby's name off, "Box four," she told him.

"*Danke,*" Koby said as he turned to pick up his uniform.

Blaz stepped forward next. "Blaz Senft," he said, "Age eleven."

"Box four," the woman said as she checked yet another name off her list.

Once Ivo had gotten his uniform, the three boys walked to the changing rooms and took off their running shorts and muscle shirts. They put on white T-shirts and the Hitler Youth's light brown, long-sleeved shirts and black shorts with large pockets. Then the round hats with a small visor on the front.

"I like these uniforms, I feel invincible," Ivo said as he slid on his swastika armband.

The boys strolled out of the school towards the town square. While they drew closer they could see the light of the torches brought for the burning of books. The voices of the townspeople were loud and vibrant but as the boys arrived at the square, a man took the crowd's attention. He was tall with slicked-back blond hair, sapphire blue eyes, and a muscular build. He strode to the microphone, hands behind his back. He was clad in black pants and a coat with many medals clipped to it. He sported a cap with the nation's coat of arms in the middle and a skull below it. On his collar the symbol of the SS was on display. The SS symbol looked like two lightning bolts which stood for *Schutzstaffel*. On his right arm, he wore a Swastika armband that boasted many white stripes, indicating his high rank in the SS. On his belt was kept a Luger and several magazines for it in ammo pockets. He was flanked by two German soldiers in black with helmets which bore the SS lightning bolts on the right side and the *Hakenkreuz*

(Swastika) on the left. They held two Karabiner 98Ks, the standard infantry rifle for both the *Wehrmacht* and the SS. The crowd circled around a large pile of Jewish and Communist books. Amongst the pile was pornography, copies of the Talmud, Karl Marx's writings and other books from his supporters. There were no storybooks in the piles, no instruction books, no schoolbooks either. Many of the teenage children in the crowd wore their Hitler Youth uniforms with proud looks on their faces. The boys marched past many bright red Hitler banners as the crowd quieted down.

"Koby!" Erich said in a loud whisper, "Over here!"

He gestured towards the back of the crowd. They followed him to where Jarman, Reinhardt and Jurgen were standing with their families. The SS officer tapped the microphone and cleared his throat. The crowd stood quietly at attention, eager to hear what the officer had to say.

"That's my father up there," Erich whispered to Ivo and Blaz. Both already knew this but Erich was excited to tell someone. Blaz nodded approvingly. Their eyes returned to Erich's father.

"My fellow Germans," he began, "Our great nation has achieved a glorious victory. The losses forced on us from Versailles have been righted. A Third Reich has awakened. The old enemies will not prohibit our Reich from improving. The *Führer's* calls for peace have been ignored. The French and British only wish *Deutschland* to remain weak as in the days of the Weimar Republic. The Weimar Republic!"

A disapproving grumble made its way through the crowd at the name of the Republic they so despised. Erich's father's voice began to become louder and less restrained. He used his arms expressively in his speech. "They are nothing but tools of the Jewish bankers and the Jewish press! *Ja*, the international clique! The British Empire, the great British Empire is under the heel of the bankers. One world power on earth is not. That is our great nation. The war has come to be for this reason. We are surrounded by enemies. The Jewish elite will stop at nothing until our nation is defeated. Until we are brought back under their control. That is what they are all about. Control! As I speak, they lie to the whole world about us and our intentions! They wish our destruction, our depravity, our servitude, our slow decay into extinction! They wish this for all peoples of Europe! But we will not allow it!"

Erich's father paused. Then he raised one hand as he spoke. He pointed with one finger, while shaking his arm repeatedly, "We must cleanse our nation, we must redeem our nation, we must empower our nation! This Third Reich's prestige will surpass anything done by Germans in world history. Comrades, it is not for ideas that we live," Erich's father said, echoing Hitler, "Not for theories! Not for fantastic party programs! *Nein*! We live and fight for the German people! For the preservation of its existence!" The crowd roared in approval. Erich's father paused to let the crowd absorb his words. "The *Führer* is very proud of our advances and our progress. Your perseverance and hard work has helped this country escape the immeasurable debts the Allies demanded we repay. We were doomed to fail and wither, until the good Lord sent us a *Führer*. The *Führer's* leadership and guidance has allowed our country to go from a disempowered and weak nation to the most powerful nation ever to exist on this good earth. Nothing can stand in our way! We are great once more! And we will become greater still!"

The officer snapped his fingers. The two soldiers ran over to the pile of books and lit it on fire.

"*Unser deutsches Volk, Sieg Heil*!" Erich's father shouted triumphantly as he shot his right arm toward the sky to perform the well-known salute. "*Sieg Heil*!" echoed the crowd. They eventually lowered their arms as the flames grew. The boys watched, triumphant faces lit by fire.

Christmas on the Eve

December 24, 1939 Sunday

As time passed the town grew restless. Many seemed to think peace had been reached but uncertainty hung in the air. As the days grew colder and winter set in, it was apparent that Germany was fully prepared for war with France and Great Britain. More young men were being notified that they could be called to fight at any time including Ivo's brother, Henrik. Most of the boys' fathers received letters informing them they could be summoned to the French border as potential backups.

With training for track suspended for Christmas break and school exams completed, the boys decided to go to Jurgen's home in the country for Christmas. Clouds covered the sky, hiding the sun. A light wind blew, whipping the boys' hair around. When they arrived, Jurgen called from the barn, "*Frohe Weihnachten, meine Freunde,* Merry Christmas.

"*Frohe Weihnachten!*"

"What do you want to do?"

"Do you want to go walking in the forest?" Ivo asked.

"Sure. You've always been fond of a good hike out here," Jurgen said.

The boys agreed and headed away from the farmstead. They all instinctively began to stroll towards one of the small forests that were scattered across Seelow Heights, the hard ground littered with chaff from the wheat. When they had entered the forest, Ivo raised a question.

"Erich, do you know anything about all this inaction?" he asked.

"You mean why haven't we responded to France's pathetic attack?" Erich asked.

"*Ja,*" Ivo replied.

Erich paused but kept walking with the others, "I know that we are waiting for winter to come to an end. France doesn't seem to be able to do what it takes to win a war. You know, attack?"

They kept walking through the forest until they came to a steep hill that overlooked Seelow Heights. They slid down the hill with their feet facing sideways to keep their balance. Ivo almost fell but Erich grabbed before he went down. They crossed through a valley of tall grass between two patches of forest.

Blaz spoke up, "We're all twelve now, do you think this war will ever be our responsibility?"

The boys looked at him with mixed expressions.

"*Nein,* how can a war between us and France and England take that long?" Jarman replied. Reinhardt nodded in agreement.

Jurgen added, "We can't really be drafted for several years. Maybe helping behind the lines in two or three, but that's all."

"*Der Krieg* was only around four years long," Ivo chimed in.

"Do you hope the war is over by then?" asked Koby. After all, the war was being celebrated by many of the kids at school.

"Oh, of course," Blaz answered immediately, "War may seem exciting now, but I'm sure it becomes horrible after the initial spark, my father seems to think that."

Ivo nodded in agreement.

"Plus the warfare we used in Poland is fast-paced. We will finish France in four years, I'd be less surprised if we did it in four months," Erich said.

"You're that sure of our army?" Koby asked with an awkward smile on his face.

"You don't know my dad or the SS like I do."

Koby remained silent.

"I think we'll get an idea of how good our army is when we start the *Hitlerjugend* after the break is over," Ivo predicted, "Erich and Jarman probably know the most about it already since they've had a semester of experience."

Some of the boys nodded.

"*Mein Wort*, we're already there?" Blaz said in awe.

"I'm excited," said Ivo, "Getting the training to become fighters."

"*Ja*, and keep *Deutschland* clean from the International Jewry and their Marxism," Erich added before turning, "Hey, Koby?"

"*Ja?*"

"What was your best time again?"

Koby grinned and looked down, "Fifteen forty-nine."

"Damn."

They arrived at a wide creek and began to skip stones with the current.

"I got *funf*, five!" Ivo said excitedly.

"*Seban*, seven!" Koby said.

Erich picked up one and threw it with beautiful form. The rocked skipped several times before finally sinking into the creek.

"*Neun*, nine!"

"*Nein!*" Koby said swinging his fist at air.

"Funny how similar those two words sound," Ivo remarked.

The boys attempted to top nine for some time. Jarman, Blaz, and Koby got to eight but they failed to reach Erich's mark. Finally, they headed back as the sun set. They crossed the valley and climbed back up the hill to hike back to Jurgen's farmstead. Waiting for them was a Christmas dinner prepared by Jurgen's mother of German chicken schnitzel with gravy and mashed potatoes, green beans, bread and beer made from the Holtzer's wheat and barley.

"Let's say grace," Jurgen's father said. Jurgen's father *Herr* Holtzer, was a man who strongly resembled his son but grayer and brawnier with a beard. Though he was overweight, having a beer belly, he was strong as an ox and worked like one being whipped. All the boys admired him, as he had been one of the men who'd pulled Seelow through the depression. Quite literally. When the farmers of Seelow were forced to sell or hand over their livestock, they had no animals to pull their plows. But Holtzer and a few others organized the men and boys of the town to pull the plows themselves including Erich's father. But *Herr* Holtzer had led the way. All the boys' fathers told them this quite often. Erich's father had even tried to recruit *Herr* Holtzer for the SS twice because of this. Twice he'd been turned down. Yet it did not sour the two men's friendship.

The boys all closed their eyes, bowed their heads and folded their hands together.

"Lord, we do thank you for this good food and warm home. I thank you for the great friends that Jurgen has and that they could be with us this Christmas. You have blessed *Deutschland*, both economically and militarily and we are grateful for that. I ask, we all ask, that you would continue to bless this nation and guide the *Führer's* decisions while he leads our country to greatness. Amen."

"Amen," the boys all repeated.

"Boys, how was your hike?" *Herr* Holtzer asked the group.

"It was a good time," Ivo replied, "Nice change of pace from all the crazy stuff happening."

Erich reached for some of the beer in the center but *Frau* Holtzer saw him and scolded, "*Nein*, you are too young!"

"*Schatz*, darling," *Herr* Holtzer calmed her, "They are thirteen, they will be men soon!"

He poured a small amount into each boy's cup, "Just a little," he said with a wink. The boys all grinned.

"To *Deutschland* and to Jesus," *Herr* Holtzer said as he raised his glass gesturing for the boys to do the same. They all drank their beer. Ivo immediately spit it out into his cup. Koby and Blaz followed suite after the taste hit their mouths while Jarman, Reinhardt, and Erich all grimaced and swallowed. *Herr* Holtzer belly laughed. The boys looked down, ashamed. Seeing their faces, he told them, "Don't worry, it was my reaction the first time I had a sip. It's an acquired taste," he said with a wide smile on his face as he took a drink. Blaz looked at Jurgen questionably who raised his eyebrows and nodded as if to say, *my reaction too*. The boys went back to their food but Jurgen and his father both raised their glasses to one another and took a long swig each.

After they had eaten, the boys thanked Jurgen's mother before gathering around the fireplace. The mantle was decorated with a small nativity set, with the Baby Jesus in the center. The boys had all brought one present apiece to give to their friends. Every year the boys would pick a name of someone to buy a gift for. None of their families would be considered rich by any standard so they bought it with their own money they'd earned throughout the year. They always went in order of height, from tallest to shortest to mess with Ivo who was always holding out hope that he'd get taller than one person some year.

Reinhardt started, but first told everyone it was from Jurgen. As the brown paper was torn away, a winter hat with a swastika on it was revealed.

Reinhardt grinned, "*Danke*, Jurgen."

"*Bitte schön*." You are welcome.

Erich went next. "It's from Jarman."

Erich opened his gift and pulled a small, metal SS pin symbol.

"*Danke* Jarman. I hope that I'll be wearing this when I make it to the SS."

Jarman replied, "Thought you'd like it."

Next, Jarman read his tag aloud, "From Ivo. Aww."

Ivo rolled his eyes with a grin on his face. Jarman opened the small package and found a patch with the Swastika on it.

"Have to get our *Hitlerjugend* uniforms looking good," Ivo said.

Jarman grinned and thanked Ivo, "*Heil* Hitler."

"*Heil* Hitler."

Koby opened his from Blaz. Inside was also a red patch with black writing and white encircled the writing. It had all Koby's times on it from his five kilometer races that year with a five kilometer abbreviation (5k) centered at the top. Koby's eyes widened when he saw it.

"Blaz, this is great," Koby said, astonished, "How'd you get this?"

"I had to get the times from the coach and my mother helped me with sewing it together after I drew the design. It was fun."

"*Danke schön*. This is amazing," Koby said with an almost speechless expression.

Jurgen opened his from Reinhardt. After he tore through the wrapping he pulled out a small shovel with a Swastika on the handle. Blaz opened his next. It was from Erich. Inside he found a pocket army knife with the Swastika engraved on the hilt. Not designed for combat, but if necessary it could be.

"For the army," said Erich, "I know you'll be there someday."

"Wow," Blaz said with surprise, "This is a nice knife."

"I wanted to give you something useful, just in case."

"Well, it's great! *Danke schön*," Blaz said with a grin, "I love the hilt."

"Go ahead, Ivo," Jarman said, "Who's it from, little man?"

"It's from Koby," Ivo said.

He tore the brown packaging away and found a small, beautiful Edelweiss pin. Ivo smiled and held it up.

"If you're ever in the war or any war, that's given for survival training. I want you to earn a real one after you make it through the war," Koby explained.

"I will," Ivo replied while examining the Edelweiss.

Blaz glanced at Koby. Koby turned his head. Blaz wasn't sure, but from the look his friend gave him, he felt as though Koby knew more about Germany's predicament than any of them.

1940: We are the Future Soldiers

Blaz's Haircut

January 2, 1940 Tuesday

Blaz and his father walked down the cobblestone streets of Seelow surrounded by homes that were built almost to form a wall lining the street. Blaz pulled up his jacket against the violent wind. The German winter had set in harshly. Blaz was headed to get his required Hitler Youth haircut: a buzz on the sides and back. Blaz could get to the barber shop on his own but Ottoway had told Blaz he wanted to come to see the new look. The two turned towards the small business section of Seelow passing the lone movie theater, a couple restaurants, the local grocery store, some assorted vendors and repair shops and at the end of the block, the town hall and the church. The two walked into the barbershop and waited for Blaz's turn. Two men sat in barber chairs getting their hair cut, one by a young woman, the other by a man who looked about Blaz's father's age.

"Ottoway!"

Blaz's father looked the barber's way.

"Eldwin!"

The barber grinned. "It's been a while since you've been in here! I'm almost done here, what'll it be for you?"

"Nothing for me, we're here for Blaz," Ottoway answered with a grin.

"Blaz! Nice to see you! My you've gotten big! Must be a quarter meter taller!" Eldwin chuckled. He saw most people of Seelow walking around on a weekly basis. "Let's see. You look about twelve, say no more, buzz on the temple, and long on the top. We've had every child above ten in the town getting that cut since last year. Had several come in just this week, the Klossners, the Steiners, the Hertzes, the Kleins. So many boys for *Hitlerjugend*. Good business for me!" the barber chuckled again as he made the finishing touches on the man's hair.

"All right Blaz, hop on up here!" Eldwin said. He took out a razor and some scissors. He slowly cut away at the hair on the back of Blaz's temple with the scissors. He moved to the sides of the boy's head and snipped away at Blaz's wavy blond hair. It fell to the ground into small patches. Blaz tilted his head to watch it fall.

"Hang on, stay still," Eldwin told him.

Blaz straightened back up and faced directly forward.

"That's better."

Eldwin trimmed the hair on top of Blaz's head, before taking out his razor and beginning the buzz. Occasionally, Blaz would feel a small prick but for the most part, the haircut went smoothly. Eldwin made one last pass around Blaz's head to make sure he got any stray pieces.

"Okay, how do you like it?" Eldwin said and handed Blaz a small mirror to observe his new haircut with.

Blaz tilted his head and adjusted the mirror to get a full view of his haircut. He barely recognized himself, but there was something he liked about it. He grinned.

"I like it. *Danke*."

"I'm glad you do."

Blaz handed Eldwin back his mirror and hopped off the chair. His father paid Eldwin and exchanged a few words before he turned and gestured to Blaz to come with him. As they walked out the door Eldwin and Ottoway gave each other a wave.

"What do you think papa?" Blaz asked.

"You look good, son. You look like a soldier," his father assured him.

Blaz ran his hand through the hair on top of his scalp, slicking it to the right. *Just like Erich and Jarman*, Blaz thought, *I wonder what everyone else looks like.* Blaz and his father walked back towards their house, on the cobblestone street, the wind no longer whipping Blaz's hair around and the cold no longer bothering him.

The Hitler Youth

January 8, 1940 Monday

"*Achtung, Jugend!*"

A sizable group of children and teenagers snapped to attention. They stood outside on the field awaiting their commander's arrival. A gaunt officer, with sapphire eyes and a skeletal face, wearing a peaked cap over his straight brown hair, paced in front of the many boys and girls with insignia of the SS on his hat and coat. At last, a young man and woman strode out of the school, standing behind the officer. The young man was wearing the attire of an SS infantryman. No older than nineteen, he had the look of the ideal German: blond hair, blue eyes, lean yet strong and a height that met SS requirements. He held the Swastika flag on a pole high enough that it fluttered in the breeze. The woman wore a long-sleeved brown shirt and tie with black pants. She wore no SS insignia whatsoever.

The SS officer eyed the cadets and then began to speak, "*Guten tag*, my name is Ormand Schwinghammer. I am your *Hitlerjugend* unit evaluator. The *Jungvolk* has been combined with the *Hitlerjugend*, so ages ten to eighteen will be included in the program. Today you either return or begin your training. With the onset of war, in addition to physical training, the boys will also receive military training. You will become smart soldiers and will be taught valuable life skills while in the *Hitlerjugend*. The *Führer* wishes to have *Deutschland's* youth be trained to bring our people to its highest potential. Young men, you will be responsible for leading the Reich in the future and keeping the Fatherland safe and strong."

Schwinghammer turned to the girls. "Women, you will someday raise

Deutschland's children, take care of her homes, farm her land during war. This takes strength. We do not want weak men and women. We want strength! The *Führer* does not look on any children of *Deutschland* as having no part to play. All of you will one day be responsible for this nation's wellbeing. We will ensure you are ready for this. By the end of your training, you will be the best soldiers on the planet and be prepared to flourish in *Deutschland* and in turn contribute to *Deutschland*. *Heil* Hitler!"

"*Heil* Hitler!" the children echoed, arms raised.

"All who are joining the *Hitlerjugend* this year, step forward!" Schwinghammer shouted. The Hitler Youths lowered their arms. Blaz stepped forward, along with over one hundred and fifty new entries.

"Raise your right hand!"

The young boys all raised their arms into the air, the oldest having just turned fourteen.

"In the presence of this blood banner which represents our *Führer*, do you swear to devote all your energies and your strength to the savior of our country, Adolf Hitler? Do you swear to be willing and ready to give up your life for him, so help you God?" Schwinghammer asked, voice booming, incongruent with his gaunt features.

Blaz held his right hand in the air and proudly repeated the oath and responded positively to the questions. Affirming their loyalty to the *Führer*, the boys spoke, "In the presence of this blood banner which represents our *Führer*, I swear to devote all my energies and my strength to the savior of our country, Adolf Hitler. I am willing and ready to give up my life for him, so help me God."

"*Heil* Hitler!" Schwinghammer shouted.

"*Heil* Hitler!" the entire assembly shouted back.

Schwinghammer transitioned, "I would like to introduce those of you who are just now joining the *Hitlerjugend* to your town instructor. His name is Reynald Schlusser but you will refer to him as *Herr* Schlusser at all times. He is the manifestation of our *Führer* for you here in Seelow. Respect him and obey him as you would the *Führer*. Reynald..."

"*Guten tag* young men and women," the man said as he stepped forward, handing the flag to Schwinghammer, so that it did not touch the ground. "First, my job as your instructor is to train you to become the strongest, fittest, and hardest working youth on the earth, both boys and girls. Other nations may curse us for this. They will say, 'We work like slaves,' when in reality, it is work that is freedom. It is the sacrifices that the individual makes for their own people that shows the true character of a community. You, the youth, must stand united as Germans."

"There was indeed a time when the unity was at best defined by classes." Schlusser winced, as if this had particularly strong meaning to him, but continued, "But you, young men and women, you stand united now, whether rich or poor, farmer, working man, soldier or government. This unity will continue because the power to be united remains in each and every one of us. It is not inherited, it must be developed, it must be chosen. When we all stand together, the heart of the German people can never be broken. If, and indeed when, worlds decide to stand against us we will emerge victorious. Brotherly, we will stand together," some of them cheered and the young soldier waited to continue, letting his words sink in. The SS official seemed to like this technique, nodding to himself. Reynald Schlusser then continued on, "Second, for the boys, the Reich requires the most durable and powerful soldiers for its army. You will be put through vigorous physical training, both in endurance and strength. When your training is done, you will be in peak condition. Not only will you be tested physically, but also mentally. You must be able to react to any situation quickly. The speed of your responses could be the difference between life and death for you and your fellow soldiers. Lastly, you will participate in assisting our armies behind the front lines before you become soldiers. Many of you will be responsible for tasks in the rear such as manning artillery, reloading and outfitting guns and tanks for combat. This will help you prepare for the reality of battle. Understood?"

"*Ja* sir!"

"Boys, begin with seventy-five push-ups, followed by eight laps around the training ground."

"*Ja* sir!"

Only a few faces showed reluctance to this order, everyone else set to this task with eagerness and excitement. Some showed this in a quite obvious manner, particularly Ivo. His little body and face were shaking, and he wore a big grin.

Erich shook his head at Ivo but said nothing as they started their workout. Ivo fell behind everyone in push-ups but Koby and Blaz stood waiting for him once they'd finished.

"You two," the young soldier, *Herr* Schlusser, said while they waited for Ivo, "Why have you not started your laps?"

"We are waiting for our friend, sir, he's almost done."

The soldier paused. He knew a commander's first impression was important. He decided to take the high route. Finally, he answered, "Fine then, but from now on you must begin immediately after you are finished. No more fooling around, this is the training ground for Hitler's finest, after all."

When Ivo finished he hopped up.

"Done," he said, shaking his arms.

"Sir *ja* sir, *danke* sir," Blaz said to the young soldier as the three boys took off. The officer turned to the few remaining boys and girls.

As the boys began their laps Blaz remarked, "I think I'm going to like the *Hitlerjugend*."

"He seemed to know what he's doing." Koby agreed.

"I think I'll enjoy half of it," Ivo said shaking his arms again.

Koby and Blaz grinned.

January 9, 1940 Tuesday

The next morning, the weather turned colder and snow began to fall. The wind blew stronger, but the Hitler Youths were hardly bothered. Their minds were focused on their journey into the *Führer's* army. Some of the older cadets even sang combat songs as they marched into school. The spirit of Germany was prepared to do all that was necessary, in their minds, to ensure a lasting peace in the end. Inside, the boys began to talk about the Hitler Youth together.

"It's super, isn't it?" Jarman asked the boys who'd just entered.

"*Jawohl*," Ivo responded, "We will all be so strong after this."

"I love that we get this training," Blaz said, "And we get to do it together."

"A strong, fit generation of men ready to lead *Deutschland*," Erich said, thumping his chest, "You guys haven't scratched the surface of what you'll learn in the *Hitlerjugend*. It is so much more advanced than *Jungvolk*. Do you remember how Jarman and I were gone last semester for a few school days?"

"*Jawohl*," Koby replied as the boys put their winter clothing into their bags.

"We went to Poland," Erich revealed.

The boys' eyes lit up and questions were shot at Jarman and Erich.

"What'd you do there?"

"Did you see any soldiers?"

"Did you get to touch any guns?"

"Were there tanks?"

"Where did you go in Poland?"

"Why didn't you tell us?"

Erich quickly answered the last question first, "*Herr* Schlusser, our commander, told us not to tell anyone. Being in the *Hitlerjugend* requires a commitment. But now you're in the *Hitlerjugend*."

"In a nutshell, we saw tanks and soldiers, we got to fire guns, and we were a few kilometers inside of former Poland the first time and into Austria the second time," Jarman replied quickly.

"What else happened?" Ivo asked, clearly expecting an amazing story.

"Okay," Erich nodded with an accepting grin on his face as he looked at Ivo, "On our first trip we learned how to fire guns at a small base. But the second time we actually helped our soldiers. We got to help repair some trucks, loaded supplies and helped cook meals.

"What was the place in Austria called," Koby asked, "What was it like?"

"Ah, the second place we went was a prisoner camp called Mauthausen-Gusen, I believe. That's where we helped out all the soldiers. They were SS, actually," Jarman said.

"Really?" Blaz said, fascinated.

"*Ja*. They were pretty friendly. They chatted with us about where the supplies were headed and about what it's like to be in the SS. They've seen a lot of action. I'm hoping I become a member someday."

"What was the inside of the camp like?" Ivo asked.

"We didn't get to go inside. The camp isn't completed yet but it's going to hold Communists. We were just at the gate where all the armor and supplies go in and out. The gate had this stone arch with our *Reichsadler*, Imperial Eagle on it," Jarman described to them, "And there was a big courtyard with some of the trucks loading supplies for the camp into some stone buildings. The ones we helped unload. We stayed in one of buildings near the gate while we were there, it was a great, important trip."

"Wow."

"It's almost time for class," Koby said when he saw the clock at the end of the hallway, "See you later today guys, *Hitlerjugend* is going to be awesome."

"We want to hear more," Ivo complained.

The boys grabbed their bags, headed down the hall and split to go to their separate classes. They sat down at their desks and looked at their new class, which they hadn't taken first semester.

"School is a place that I have mixed feelings about," Ivo said to no one in particular.

"Did you see? It started snowing," Koby said.

Blaz turned and looked out the window. He watched the snow fall, something that always seemed peaceful to him. He could not imagine that bombs would fall on Germany in the same numbers as snowflakes in the years to come.

A Day at the Range

April 20, 1940 Saturday

Much time passed, and the German people became more devoted to their *Führer* than ever during these last few months of true peace. The country prospered and to many Germans, the war seemed nonexistent. In Seelow, the spring came as any other spring. The grass began to grow, the farmers started to work, their fields and flowers blossomed in the increasing amount of sunlight every day. The town was in high spirits and, like most of Germany, felt little direct effects of the war.

The boys became stronger through their hard work and appeared older after their months of Hitler Youth training. Erich became known as "The strongest son of Seelow" by his Hitler Youth commander, who loved to boast about Erich's sturdy physique and abnormal abilities to his fellow officers at command meetings. Koby, Blaz, and Ivo continued to improve in their running. Koby saw the most improvement, in endurance, education, and strength. He had a chiseled joke with Erich about being as ripped as him. Erich's strength and skill were proven during hand-to-hand combat drills when he made quick work of Koby, locking him in a stranglehold early in their practice match. The boys learned how to drive military vehicles, but the newcomers had not learned to operate a gun yet. When the Reich's war machine thundered into Denmark and Norway, *Herr* Schwinghammer decided it was time to teach the novices how to shoot. He informed Schlusser they would be going a few kilometers into Poland for target practice where the rookies would learn to fire. The morning of the excursion, as Blaz finished his breakfast and his mother told him to pay attention to instructions while he was there. "*Ja*, mother," he responded as he opened the door to leave, "*Oh, Herzlichen Glückwunschen an der Führer, mama!*"

"Happy Birthday to the *Führer*," his mother called as he turned to leave.

When Blaz got to school, several covered trucks were parked outside the school. *Herr* Schlusser wore a peaked cap, like the cap Hitler himself often wore. Some Hitler Youth cadets that Blaz did not recognize were already in the covered cargo trucks. Erich and Jarman were told to join a truck with more experienced Hitler Youth members. The others headed for a different truck, but *Herr* Schlusser split them up. Koby, Jurgen, and Reinhardt climbed into one while Ivo and Blaz hopped into the other. Most of the boys in the truck Blaz had never seen before. They all appeared eager, excited to take their next step towards becoming soldiers. When all the boys were in a truck, the armored vehicles departed.

The trucks drove east, through the German countryside of Seelow Heights. The rolling hills were dotted with pine trees. The trucks passed the near-barren German defense trenches on the sides of the hills, watchtowers just above the trees and antiaircraft guns outside of stone German bunkers. Only a handful of soldiers were occupying the Seelow Heights defenses and with no armor. Blaz leaned forward to get a look at the dormant defenses. The peacefulness of the large chain of barricades, trenches, and guns was an odd sight.

"You know when we heard all the bombers last year?" Blaz asked Ivo.

A boy turned his head their way. Both Blaz and Ivo noticed, but continued their conversation.

"*Ja*," Ivo answered shifting his eyes to Blaz.

"That base was really busy and full, now it's so quiet, like none of it ever happened," Blaz observed.

The boys looked out the back of the truck as the network of defenses began to shrink into the distance.

"The world is a big place, the fighting won't take place in one area forever," Ivo told Blaz.

"You guys could hear the attack on Poland from your town?" asked the boy who'd been listening in. Blaz and Ivo turned their focus to the boy, who looked remarkably similar to Hitler in his own youth.

"*Ja*, we could," Ivo answered the boy.

"What was it like?" the boy asked, leaning forward.

"We heard some loud noises and everyone in town was outside in moments. Some big planes flew overhead; I'd assume they were coming from Berlin. That's all we got. It wasn't anything to worry about. After all, we weren't under attack and the border is dozens of kilometers away."

"*Ja*," the boy exclaimed, "But that's really something you two! Getting to hear and see the *Luftwaffe* in action!"

"I guess it was," Ivo said, almost to humor the boy. They had barely seen a thing, other than the planes. Only heard. Still, it was locked in their memories.

"Hey, what city are all of you from?" Blaz asked the boy.

We are a unit of the *Hitlerjugend* from Fürstenwalde."

"Since you live closer to Berlin than us, well, have you ever seen the *Führer* speak in person? It is his birthday today, you know," Ivo said, pouncing on this opportunity to hear a firsthand account about their *Führer*.

"Once. A few months ago."

"What does he look like in person? Did you get a good view of him?" Blaz asked, scarcely able to contain his excitement.

"*Nein*," the boy shook his head, "There are thousands of people at his speeches, and there was no way to get close."

"What are his speeches like?" Blaz asked while Ivo listened intently, his eyes unblinking and the size of saucers. "We've only heard him on the radio."

"Oh, it's incredible. He tells you about how *Deutschland* can be bettered and by the end he's shouting about how we will make the Fatherland great," the boy responded, "I think the *Führer's* speeches are like a great story. They begin slowly, and draw you in, and then slowly get more dramatic. And then the climax is where he is loud and intense, like a final event in the story that wraps everything up. He ends it on a high note, always about our love of our country and people. He pours his heart and soul into his speeches."

This account intrigued Blaz and Ivo and they continued to talk with the boy until the truck began to slow down. Some boys at the rear of the truck leaned out to attempt to get a view of where they'd arrived. One yelled to the others, "It's a small camp, a few buildings, soldiers, a firing range. Tanks! They have *Panzers!* Two *Panzer III's!*"

At this several boys scrambled up to get a glimpse of the camp and the tanks the cadet had gotten excited over. The trucks tires kicked up dust as it drove inside the *Wehrmacht* camp.

The truck finally came to a halt while the boys eagerly waited to see the camp. *Herr* Schlusser came by each truck ordering the cadets out, but many had already jumped to the ground including Blaz and Ivo.

"Stand in formation!" *Herr* Schlusser shouted. The boys formed lines of two by seven, immediately after the words left the young soldier's mouth. "Trucks one and two follow me!" Schlusser ordered, pointing to the younger cadets, "The others follow *Herr* Heidrich!"

Schlusser gestured to another young soldier whose arms were crossed, had piercing blue eyes and brown hair in the style of the Hitler Youth. The soldier strode towards the firing range and snapped his fingers, signaling the older cadets to follow him. Schlusser pointed to Blaz's group and the second group of young cadets, Koby, Jurgen and Reinhardt among them. The two groups all proceeded to follow Schlusser towards the far right side of the range. They marched across the dusty ground, sending up tiny clouds with each step. Tank tracks and small craters from artillery were printed in the dirt. The boys walked to a small building where Schlusser ordered them to halt.

"This building houses the firearms," he told them, "You will each practice three times, once with an MP-40, once with a Walther P38, and once with a Karabiner 98K. These are the hand weapons you will likely be using in combat for the *Heer, Kriegsmarine* or *Luftwaffe*. Understood?"

"*Ja* sir!"

"Will the first seven men from truck one and truck two come forward?"

The designated cadets stepped forward Blaz, Koby and Reinhardt among them.

"Now all of you, take a Karabiner rifle and a cartridge," Schlusser said, waiting for them to do so before continuing, "Next each of you take a spot on the firing range."

The cadets marched to their positions. Blaz stepped between Koby and a medium height, brown haired boy with freckles. Koby and Blaz glanced at each other. Blaz grinned nervously but Koby gave him a reassuring nod with a steely look in his eyes.

"Insert your clip here," Schlusser told them, as he demonstrated for the young cadets, "This rifle can also be loaded with individual bullets, for future reference in case you are ever in a tight spot."

All the students mimicked him.

"Now do you see this small switch?" Schlusser asked the boys. He pointed to the top of the rifle, which was covered with metal and had a lever-like object on its right side.

"*Ja* sir."

"This is the safety. It is on right now, but if you flip it over…" he flipped it to the opposite side, "This will allow your rifle to fire. Never have this off if you are not in a battle or target practice, of course. When you are done practicing, immediately turn the safety on."

"Sir, *ja* sir!"

"Once the safety is off you will cock your rifle. This is the last step before the rifle is ready," he showed them yet another slightly larger lever-like gadget on the rifle. He pushed it upwards and the students did likewise.

"Turn towards your targets. Now pull this back until you hear a clicking noise, then push it back forward until you hear a clicking noise," Schlusser instructed them, pointing to the small, metal lever-like object that stuck out on the right side of the weapon, "The second click will indicate that your rifle is ready to fire."

The students with rifles obeyed and cocked their rifles.

"See those targets?"

Blaz looked onto the range at a several targets shaped like humans with bullseyes on them.

"Raise your rifles. Rest them under your collarbone. Do not put your face too close to the rifle. They have a bit of a kick. Close one eye to help you aim."

Blaz placed his rifle just above his right armpit and closed his left eye.

"Fingers on the trigger."

His hands were sweaty and his finger almost slipped.

"Take aim."

Blaz focused on one of the targets. He pointed his rifle directly at its head.

"*Feuer!*"

Fourteen shots rang out and a few boys were knocked off balance from their rifle's kick. Though there was smoke and many shots taken, each cadet seemed to know where his bullet had hit. Blaz lowered his rifle. Dust rose from the bullet's impact. His shot had hit the dirt to the right of his target.

Koby looked at him, "How'd you do?"

"I hit the dirt."

Koby barely seemed to notice this information and continued, "Here's some advice," he said calmly while a few shots were fired by cadets eager to continue shooting, "Aim slightly the opposite way the wind blows. And I mean slightly. The bullet's course will be affected and should hit the target. Also, aim slightly high. These targets are far away so the bullet will drop as it travels. Got it?"

"*Ja.*"

By now most of the cadets had fired a second shot while Blaz cocked his rifle. He closed his eye and took aim. He raised the Karabiner above the target's head and adjusted it opposite the wind. His finger tightened around the trigger. He pulled back and the gun let out a loud bang. He saw his target's arm fall off at the shoulder. Another shot went off and a hole appeared in the target's head.

"Nice shot, Blaz," Koby encouraged him.

Blaz fired his remaining three shots missing twice but hitting his target's leg on his final shot. They then passed their rifles onto the remaining cadets. Schlusser ordered them to remain silent while he gave more instructions. When he finished, the new cadets began firing, Blaz turned to Koby and Reinhardt.

"Reinhardt, get any hits?"

Reinhardt looked at ground and kicked at the dirt, "*Nichts.*" Nothing.

"I got two hits, one on the leg and one on the shoulder," Blaz said.

"Good job men, you'll get better! No worries," Koby said enthusiastically.

"That is why the *Führer* wants us trained, after all," Blaz remarked as several shots were fired.

"How many hits did you get Koby?" Reinhardt asked.

Koby looked down, wanting to stay humble. "Five."

"*Nein, nein.* Five??" Blaz asked, "All hits?"

Koby nodded.

"All fatal?"

Koby nodded again, his face red.

"Koby, why are you perfect at everything?" Blaz asked in an annoyed tone.

"You asked the question."

Blaz shut up now. Reinhardt chuckled to himself. Blaz joined him after a couple seconds before Koby said, "Looks like they're wrapping up. Let's get ready for round two."

On the way back from the range, Blaz, Reinhardt, Jurgen, Koby, and Ivo all got into the same truck. Dust covered their boots and pants. Ivo's face was covered in grease from the rifle.

"I shot terribly," he whined.

"We will have plenty of training by the time we are in the army," Koby reminded the group, "This was only day one."

"Ivo, you'll get better," Blaz assured him.

"Hopefully. Koby was quite the shooter today," Ivo said, trying to be positive. "That'll be Frenchmen next, *ja?*"

"*Ja,*" Koby responded, looking at the floor of the truck.

"What's wrong?" Blaz asked.

"I want to fight for the Fatherland, and I think I would die for it but

I'm not sure I can pull the trigger on another human," Koby breathed.

"If you're willing to die for the Reich you need to be willing to kill for the Reich," Jurgen said matter-of-factly.

A Father's Advice

May 4, 1940 Sunday

Blaz's father put down his newspaper as he walked past the kitchen table. *Norway and Denmark Subdued by The Führer's Blitzkrieg.*

"So, the *Führer* has done it again," Ottoway murmured to himself.

Blaz came trotting down the stairs. "*Guten Morgen,* papa. What's the paper say?"

"It says we have conquered Denmark and Norway."

Ja! Blaz thought, *The Fatherland is great again!*

"I saw several Jewish businesses closed down in Berlin while I was working this past week," his father said.

"That's good, they won't rob us Germans anymore," Blaz responded without hesitation.

His father frowned, "What have you been told about the Jews after *Der Krieg?*" he asked.

Blaz launched in, "They never even tried to help us. International Jewry actually worked against us. Promoting the breakdown of the family, men doing it with men, they demanded we pay giant sums of money; we were all on the streets, starving. What was that like, papa?"

"We certainly didn't have good times. Your mother and I struggled during the twenties and early thirties, especially after we had you. It was harder to provide for three. But I never got the impression the Jews were *solely* to blame. I know that we were forced to pay massive reparations to the Allies, but-" Ottoway looked Blaz in the eye, "What else are they teaching you at school?"

"What do you mean?"

"What are they teaching about Jews? Are you even understanding what they are saying? The Jews are not exclusively to blame for our problems, Blaz. And I don't want you to go around thinking that and destroying the livelihood of individuals who have the German people's best interests at heart."

"The Jews will get what they deserve," Blaz raised his voice aggressively, "Whether I give it to them or not."

"Don't you raise your voice at me, Blaz Adolf Senft," Ottoway said sternly, "Have we not taught you to respect your parents?"

"I've been taught to respect the *Führer*. You obviously haven't!" Blaz shouted back, "And you never respected your parents!"

Ottoway stared at Blaz, eyes narrowed at his son's harsh words, but he said nothing. He stormed off and packed his welding tools for his weekly commute to Berlin.

Blaz's Training

May 15, 1940 Wednesday

A man strode down a wide hall. He wore an SS uniform, with colored trim, indicating high rank. He entered a conference room, where several generals crowded around a map. One turned to greet the new arrival.

"*Guten Morgen*, Schwinghammer," he said, "The attack goes according to plan."

"So I've heard, Guderian. Looks like the war should be over soon."

"We have surrounded Belgian and French forces at Hannut. Belgium should fall before the month is out."

"Things certainly are going according to plan, then."

Blaz had treated his father coldly since their fight. In everyday conversations, he would respond with sarcasm and disrespect. He'd been grounded from seeing his friends several times for this, but Blaz knew he was doing the right thing.

"We captured Holland and Luxembourg," Ivo told the group at the beginning of one school day.

"*Blitzkrieg* is unstoppable," Jarman grinned.

"Erich, have you heard anything about your father?" Koby asked, showing genuine concern.

"*Nein*, he left weeks ago, and I haven't heard from him since. He didn't even tell me where his division would be," Erich explained, "My father is a great soldier, I know he will be all right."

Jurgen turned to Erich, "I've heard that there was little fighting in the Low Countries, we didn't lose many men. That's good news."

"Those countries will give up without complaint. They're weak," Erich said, "Denmark surrendered in six hours. I think they want to join us."

"Countries like that should be led by a strong nation that will protect and govern them," Jarman added, "Our occupation will benefit them."

"*Ja*," agreed Ivo.

"The *Führer* wants to unite the West to fight the Reds, France should be a part of it." Koby said.

"They're directionless nations. It's really a shame Great Britain is an ally of France and the Low Countries. The British are a strong people," Erich said.

"They should have allied themselves with us. Not those French weaklings," Jarman said without a trace of humor.

"We allied ourselves with Italy," Erich pointed out.

Koby raised his eyebrows, wincing, but grinning all the same. Soon, the bell rang and the boys headed to their classes. As Blaz, Koby and Ivo sat in their class, the teacher lectured on the importance of *Deutschland* bringing order and direction to the world. Communism worshiped the false god of equality and as a result, it had to be destroyed. If it wasn't snuffed out now it would plague the world in the future. But in different forms, not just as an aggressive army. The Reich would one day accomplish wonders. Blaz listened intently, his eyes focused on the teacher.

"You know *Deutschland's* destiny is preordained by God. Divinity is on the side you stand and fight for. One day, whether tomorrow or in a century, the Fatherland will have made the world great through our ideas. There is no stopping the power from above. As long as we are loyal to the *Führer*, that power will remain with *Deutschland*."

Blaz nodded in agreement with Ivo and the other students.

That's the plan, Blaz thought.

Hitler Youth Parade

June 8, 1940 Saturday

Herr Schlusser had decided upon holding a march through Seelow, all the Hitler Youth would be expected to attend. Blaz changed into his Hitler Youth uniform of black shorts, a light brown shirt and his armband. He almost hoped his father would try to stop him, but Ottoway simply let Blaz walk out the door.

He arrived at the school grounds early along with most of the Hitler Youth. *Herr* Schlusser was also there. Blaz ran out to meet Koby when he arrived.

"How're you doing?" he asked.

"*Gut, gut.* Why all the excitement?" Koby asked, smiling.

"I don't know. Just thought I'd run out and greet you."

The two boys walked onto the field. "You've been quiet lately, when all seven of us have been hanging out. And you haven't been coming to see us as on weekends."

"Well, you know," Blaz murmured uncomfortably.

"*Nein*, I don't," Koby shook his head, "Is something happening with your family?"

Blaz didn't answer.

"Come on, Blaz, it's me you're talking to."

"I'd rather not."

Koby sighed, "This has been going on for weeks, Blaz. What's happening?"

"Oh, okay. My papa and I had an argument. And he's been grounded me on weekends."

"What about?"

"He was disrespecting the *Führer's* decisions. And I guess I yelled at him," Blaz said, red with embarrassment.

"You yelled at your father?" Koby asked with a shocked, awkward grin.

Blaz paused before answering, "*Ja.*"

"Blaz, you can't yell at your parents," Koby told him and his tone clearly conveyed that was common sense, "The *Führer* wouldn't approve of that. Even if you were defending him."

"I know."

"You need to get that set straight," Koby advised, "You should talk to him."

"*Nein, nein,* I can't do that now," Blaz quickly shot, "I haven't had a conversation with him for weeks."

"I still think you should."

The Hitler Youth marched through the streets, holding their banners overhead. Many citizens of Seelow had come out to watch them as they passed. The Hitler Youth band marched up front followed by the flag bearers. They sang Hitler Youth songs as they marched through the streets, Blaz held his banner proudly.

"*Vorwärts! Vorwärts!*" Schlusser yelled from the front. The Hitler Youths all knew what this meant. *Vorwärts! Vorwärts!* was the Hitler Youth's anthem.

Vorwärts! Vorwärts!
Schmettern die hellen Fanfaren,
Vorwärts! Vorwärts!
Jugend kennt keine Gefahren.
Deutschland, du wirst leuchten stehn, Mögen wir auch untergehn.
Vorwärts! Vorwärts!
Schmettern die hellen Fanfaren,
Vorwärts! Vorwärts!
Jugend kennt keine Gefahren.
Ist das Ziel auch noch so hoch? Jugend zwingt es doch.

Forward! Forward!
Blare the bright fanfares,
Forward! Forward!
Youth knows no dangers.
Germany, you will stand bright, even if we may fall.
Forward! Forward!
Blare the bright fanfares,
Forward! Forward!
Youth knows no dangers.
Is the goal still so high? Youth can achieve it yet.

Unsere Fahne flattert uns voran.
In die Zukunft ziehen wir Mann für Mann.
Wir marschieren für Hitler Durch Nacht und durch Not
Mit der Fahne der Jugend für Freiheit und Brot.
Unsere Fahne flattert uns voran,
Unsere Fahne ist die neue Zeit.
Und die Fahne führt uns in die Ewigkeit!
Ja, die Fahne ist mehr als der Tod!

Our flag flutters before us.
In the future we march man for man.
We march for Hitler through night and through need
With the flag of the youth for freedom and bread.
Our flag flutters before us.
Our flag is the New Age.
And the flag leads us into eternity!
Yes, the flag means more than death!

Jugend! Jugend!
Wir sind der Zukunft Soldaten.
Jugend! Jugend!
Träger der kommenden Taten.
Ja, durch unsere Fäuste fällt, Wer sich uns entgegenstellt
Jugend! Jugend!
Wir sind der Zukunft Soldaten.
Jugend! Jugend!
Träger der kommenden Taten.
Führer, wir gehören dir, Wir Kameraden, dir!

Youth! Youth!
We are the future soldiers
Youth! Youth!
Bearer of the coming actions,
Yes, by our fists fall, Who opposes us.
Youth! Youth!
Bearer of the coming actions.
Führer, we belong to you,
We, your comrades.

Unsere Fahne flattert uns voran.
In die Zukunft ziehen wir Mann für Mann.
Wir marschieren für Hitler, Durch Nacht und durch Not,

Mit der Fahne der Jugend für Freiheit und Brot.
Unsere Fahne flattert uns voran,
Unsere Fahne ist die neue Zeit.
Und die Fahne führt uns in die Ewigkeit!

Blaz's voice cracked as he tried to hit the high notes of the song. Some boys notice but kept singing. He finished the last line quickly, to catch up with everyone else.

As they continued marching through Seelow, Blaz was surprised to see his father ahead, clapping and saluting the passing Hitler Youth banners with his right arm extended. Blaz turned his gaze ahead, still nervous to show his father any sign of recognition. He and his father made eye contact, his father smiling proudly. Blaz smiled back.

KLV Camps

June 9, 1940 Sunday

The next morning Blaz came down the stairs, still avoiding eye contact with his father, though he badly wanted to talk with him. But he was embarrassed to come crawling back at this point.

"I should tell you something," Ottoway said abruptly, after seeing Blaz wasn't ready to break the silence, "The *Hitlerjugend* has been moving into *Kinderlandverschickung* camps across *Deutschland*."

"What does that mean?"

"It means that you will be heading out of town to live at a camp since Seelow is a bombing target. There they will train you to become soldiers. You will also receive some of your education at the KLV camps," his father answered him, "Once you are at the camps you won't be doing any school sports until this war has ended."

Blaz stayed still. He stuttered, "W-when is my unit going to a KLV camp?"

"Next year, come second semester."

"When will I be able to see you and mama?" Blaz asked, forgetting his poor treatment of his father, now wishing he could undo the last few weeks.

"I don't know," His father answered honestly, "But I've been called over to defend Norway. The *Wehrmacht* doesn't expect much unrest so they have less experienced and older men like me up there."

"When do you leave?"

"This July."

"We won't see each other for a long time after school lets out?" he asked with a hint of sadness in his voice.

"*Jawohl*," Ottoway answered, trying to maintain his composure.

Blaz looked down. "Papa," he sighed, "I'm very sorry."

"What?" his father asked.

"I'm so sorry for how I've treated you. I have no excuse. I was being arrogant and disrespectful. You're my father, you've raised me, you watch out for me, you provide for me. And I repaid you for all that by treating you like-" Blaz stopped, at a loss of words. He looked back up to find his father smiling compassionately.

"I forgive you, Blaz. And I love you, son. I don't want you to grow up with unfounded hatred. You know *Herr* Meyer. He doesn't hate Jews, and he is in the SS. I believe you might me misinterpreting what your teachers are saying. The world is not so simple as 'this person is good, and this person is bad.' Know that everything I do is with my family's safety in mind. And know that I meant no disrespect to the *Führer*. He does deserve our respect."

Over Everything in the World

June 15, 1940 Saturday

"France has surrendered to the *Wehrmacht*," the radio informed the boys, who listened intently to the news of Germany's victory in France. "Several thousand troops were evacuated, but nevertheless, France is under German control. The *Führer* now intends to sue for peace with the British to end this destructive conflict."

The boys looked at one another in disbelief.

"Someone here made a good prediction," Ivo said looking at Jarman.

"Never doubt the *Führer*," he replied, raising his right arm.

"Any news of your father, Erich?" Koby asked.

"*Ja*, he wrote me a letter. He's fine, his division went through the Ardennes Forest and took the French by surprise."

"Great man, your father," Jarman said, admiration in his voice.

"He's been put in charge of an airbase in France for now," Erich finished.

"Now the war will end, right?" Blaz asked.

"The *Führer* wants peace. It's on Britain now," Erich replied.

"Do any of you really think Britain will agree to peace?" Reinhardt asked. The boys paused and turned to look at Reinhardt, who stood behind them.

"Maybe," Ivo said, "It will save them a lot of grief."

"*Bomben auf England*," Erich added. Bombs on England.

"Has anyone else's father been called into service to help the fight?" Jarman asked.

"*Ja*," Blaz answered, as well as Koby, Ivo, and Reinhardt.

"Do you know where they will be deployed?" Jarman continued, "My father is on the northern French beaches. He's defending against British aircraft."

"My father is being deployed in Norway," Blaz answered.

"Poland," Koby said.

"Same," Ivo added.

"The Netherlands," Reinhardt said.

"What about your father?" Jarman turned to Jurgen, "Why isn't he serving the country?"

"He told me he will if called," Jurgen said sternly, "But farmers are among the last to be called on, so they can keep providing for the Fatherland."

"That's fair, as they should."

A Last Appeal to Reason

June 22, 1940

"The *Führer's* offers of peace have thus far been rejected. You brave airmen now ready yourselves to embark on a great task," Heinrici said, pacing in front of a column of *Luftwaffe* pilots, "We must and shall defeat Britain. The *Führer* has ordered that our attacks be limited to military, communications, and industrial targets. No bombing of civilians. We will rise above the level of the British. You have a simple task ahead of you: take out the British fighters, so that they will be unable to defend their installations. Then our bombers will do the rest. *Heil* Hitler."

"*Heil* Hitler!"

"*Verdämmt!*" Jarman shouted when Ivo told the boys the news during a pause in a Hitler Youth meeting after school.

"The *Führer* has said the warfare will be restricted to military targets," Ivo informed them, "He says there has already been enough civilian casualties."

"*Gut*," Koby said.

"Speaking of the bombings, have you guys heard about the KLV camps?" Blaz asked the group.

"*Jawohl*, our *Hitlerjugend* are all going to one in the open country," Erich said, "North of here. *Herr* Schlusser says soldiers will fight better around their friends."

"I'll bet," Blaz said, "I would."

Koby's lip curled to a grin.

"I almost hope that we are able to fight in this war," Jarman said whimsically.

"I don't hope, but I'll be ready if we have to," Koby said, "Don't you want to, you know, do school sports, get a job, have a family someday?"

"*Ja*, but that's what soldiers fight for, all the families," Jarman replied.

"If there's no men left, there's no family," Koby said seriously.

Jarman nodded, fiddling with his belt buckle. He knew Koby was smarter than him. Blaz looked at Jarman, then Koby. They did need to be ready and willing, even excited to fight, but they couldn't lose sight of *Deutschland's* future that rested with their generation. Blaz thought about this as *Herr* Schlusser began to inform the cadets of the KLV camps they'd be sent to next year.

The Game

July 10, 1940 Wednesday

Blaz crossed the finish line drenched in sweat and gasping for air. He bent down, hands on his knees, as Koby jogged towards him.

"You did good! Eleven minutes and eleven seconds, three thousand meter!" Koby said as Blaz panted at the finish line. Ivo had his hands on the back of his head and looked at Koby.

"You too, Ivo!" Koby said, "Eleven fifteen!"

"Swell," Ivo joked as he breathed hard.

Erich walked over to the three runners. All the boys had come to watch the last track race of the school year and to cheer on their friends.

"Good running guys! I heard Blaz and Ivo's times. How'd you do Koby?" he asked.

"I got my personal best: nine minutes, seventeen seconds," Koby said, not even breathing hard.

"Wow, that's how long it'd take me to do a one mile," Erich kidded, "With this great weather do you guys want to do some capture the flag when we get back to Jurgen's?"

"Love that!" Ivo quickly answered.

"*Ja*," Koby and Blaz both agreed.

"Practice for when we're raiding Allied camps, *ja*?" Blaz joked.

"*Sicher*," Erich said, "Good practice for that. Sort of, kind of, not at all."

Koby laughed, "Okay you two, let's get in the van and talk about the teams on the way back."

Coach Friedrich approached, "Before you start talking, I'd like to tell you three how great you've done this year. I'm very proud to be your coach. Koby, we'll keep training and Blaz and Ivo are welcome to come. I get one more semester to coach you, I want to make sure you know how to keep training for the Olympics."

The boys grinned at Koby, who kept listening to the coach.

"I've already spoken to the commander of your KLV camp and he has agreed to allow you to train while there."

Koby's face lit up.

"Schwinghammer said there is a younger boy who will also train with you. His name escapes me. But he'll train with us this fall."

"*Danke* coach, *Danke schön*! I thought I wouldn't be able to keep training," Koby said with relief.

"The *Führer* wants you to become great athletes. The commander made a point of that, it's the goal of the *Hitlerjugend*. When this war is over, who knows?" the coach told him.

"*Danke* again. That is great to know!" Koby repeated.

"All right, that is all. Good season boys," the coach ended.

Later, in the forest near Jurgen's house, the boys divided up teams for capture the flag.

"Koby needs to be on the team opposite of Blaz and Ivo," Erich said.

"Jarman and you need to be split up," Jurgen told Erich.

"And you and Reinhardt should be split up," Erich replied.

"How about runners versus boxers?" Koby suggested.

There was a short silence. "*Ja*, why not?" Jarman broke the silence, "We can switch teams when we kick your butts."

Ivo widened his eyes and raised his eyebrows, "Oh, it's on!" he retorted, putting a fist in his palm.

"No changing teams now, let's go!" Erich waved to his team, "We will take the east side and you guys the west side, we'll be in the eastern clearing."

"Got it, you know, we don't do stuff like this much anymore," Blaz said.

"We're growing up, this stuff isn't fun now," Erich commented as his team walked into a thick grove of trees.

"All right, I'll go forward first with Blaz," Koby instructed his teammates, "Ivo, you are the smallest, so you flank them on the north side and when you get within sight of them, start crawling while we distract them."

Ivo nodded, and replied, "*Hitlerjugend* is coming in handy, otherwise I'd have no idea what direction that is."

Blaz smirked and then asked, "What way is it?"

Ivo pointed south, but before Blaz and Koby could respond he said, "*Nein*, just kidding," he said as he jogged north.

"Don't you just love him?" Koby said sarcastically.

"Okay, should we head into the forest now?" Blaz asked.

"*Ja*, one moment," Koby replied, "We've got to put the flag somewhere." Koby ran up a small hill to a tree and put the red towel they were using as a flag on the first branch of a tree. "Visible enough?" he asked Blaz.

"Should be," Blaz affirmed before shouting very loudly, "Okay, *wir sind bereit*!"

Erich yelled back, "READY!"

Koby jogged into the forest, hopping over brush and fallen branches. Blaz ran after him. The sunlight shone through the tops of the trees onto the forest floor.

"I just love summer!"

"One more week left until school's out," Koby replied, eyes forward.

They bent down behind a tree. Both scanned for the center of the course, which had always been a large pine tree with a large, black mark on its trunk.

"There it is," Blaz pointed out.

"Let's go," Koby whispered.

They hopped up and ran towards the clearing. As the two came in view of the clearing, Jarman strafed in between them and both narrowly avoided being tagged. Blaz sprinted to the right and Koby to the left. Without hesitation, Jarman took off after Koby, and Blaz sprinted for the flag. As he got closer he veered away, knowing there'd be a trap. Sure enough, Jurgen was waiting in the brush by the flag. Blaz lead him away to give Ivo a shot. Jurgen followed, leaving the flag unguarded. Blaz looked back to see Ivo leap off a log and bolt for the flag. Blaz spun to help him. Ivo snatched the flag and sprinted towards his home territory but didn't go unnoticed. Erich spotted him and gave chase. Erich's muscular build was deceiving as he packed a punch when it came to sprinting. He quickly gained on Ivo. As Ivo neared the crossing Erich made a desperate grab at Ivo and snagged the back of his shirt. Ivo dropped the flag as he was pulled backwards and Blaz swooped in to grab it and crossed over to claim the game for the runners.

"Good game!" Erich said, extending his hand to shake. Blaz shook his hand and called to the other boys, "We are done! It's over!"

One by one, the boys jogged to the center, "Again?" Jarman asked.

"Sure," Koby agreed.

"Beg us for a rematch," Ivo ordered.

Jarman looked at Ivo with a goofy face and said, "*Bitte*? Please?"

"Sure," Ivo replied happily while they split up on opposite ends.

"That was a lot of fun," Koby said later when they arrived back at Jurgen's farmhouse.

"Sure was," Jurgen said, wiping sweat from his forehead.

They strode between Jurgen's house and the barn and behind the stables to the farm's red water pump. Jurgen worked the pump with one arm. Reinhardt bent down and took a drink and then the rest of the boys did as well. Blaz wiped his face after and followed the others into the house. Inside, the boys made sandwiches and sat down at the table.

"We should do that again," Erich said.

"It was nice to step back and have some fun," Koby added, "Can you believe we are thirteen?"

"Almost," Blaz said, thinking of himself and Ivo.

"Time flies," Koby said.

Football and Officers

July 17, 1940 Wednesday

Blaz sat in class working on one of his exams. He finished the final problem and glanced at Ivo and Koby who were checking over their work. *May as well*, Blaz thought and began to check his answers. While he reviewed his test, the school bell rang, indicating the end of the school year. Koby, Ivo, and Blaz turned in their tests and headed into the hallway. The boys went down the hall in silence, still in thought about their finals. Many of the younger children ran out of the school, happy to begin their summer. Most of the older kids looked more worried than happy, still wondering about their final exam results. The three boys, however, went into the changing rooms to put on their Hitler Youth top for a meeting. As they undressed, Koby broke the silence, "How do you think you did?"

"I don't want to get my hopes too high, you know," Ivo responded while he buttoned his *Hitlerjugend* shirt over his narrow chest.

"Subverting expectations?" Koby asked, as he took off his school shirt and flexed his arm, "*Ja*, the *Hitlerjugend* has paid off," he grinned into a mirror.

Blaz grinned back while he combed his hair to the side with his fingers. His light blond hair had now been in an undercut for over half a year along with the rest of his friends. Ivo joined him in combing his own golden blond hair. Both combed it to the right side of their heads. Koby combed his backwards, so that it didn't lie as flat. The boys walked outside to the field and stood at attention.

Soon after, *Herr* Schlusser arrived and told the unit, "You will all continue to report here at the same time during summer break for *Hitlerjugend* sessions. As many of you know, our unit will leave Seelow next year. Artur Axmann, the new national head of the *Hitlerjugend,* wants the youth to begin playing a more active role in the military, hence we will perform substantial military training. Our unit will be joined by the unit from Neuhardenberg. That is all for now. Tonight at nineteen thirty hours, *Hitlerjugend* boys meet at town square. Dismissed!" The cadets disbanded and headed for the gate.

"Haushofer! Klein! Meyer! Hertz!" Schlusser yelled, while pointing to an older cadet, Ivo's older brother, Erich, and Koby.

Blaz and several other cadets stopped and looked to *Herr* Schlusser.

"Did I call any of your names?" Schlusser roared at them.

"Well," Ivo began before Schlusser silenced him with a cold glare. The remaining cadets funneled out. Blaz and Ivo walked towards the gate to leave. "Why do you do that? How is that going to do you any good?" Blaz asked as they walked into the street.

"I don't know. Sometimes I just have to make a comment."

"You should be careful about that."

"Maybe," Ivo replied, "But a little humor here and there goes a long way."

Blaz nodded unenthusiastically as they passed by some younger children playing soccer in the middle of the cobblestone street. He looked behind them, half-expecting to see Koby or Erich but neither had been let go by Schlusser yet. When he turned around, Jurgen and Jarman were jogging towards them.

"Blaz! Ivo!" Jurgen shouted as the two slowed to a walk, "We just went home to put our bags away, you two want to do something before the *Hitlerjugend* meeting?"

"*Ja*, that'd be great," Blaz replied, looking around, "Where's Reinhardt?"

"He's spending the rest of the day with his father before he leaves for the Netherlands," Jarman informed them.

"My father and Henrik ship out next week," Ivo said with a sad smile.

"My father too," Blaz added.

"Where is your brother heading?" Jarman asked Ivo.

"Poland with my papa."

Blaz dropped off his bag, took his Hitler Youth top off, and told his mother he'd be home before the meeting later. Ivo told them that he'd drop his bag off at home and meet them at the school gate. He jogged off while Jarman, Blaz, and Jurgen turned for the short walk back to the school. When they arrived, the four cadets who'd been speaking with *Herr* Schlusser came walking out. The older cadet seemed to be in a conversation with Ivo's brother, but Henrik gave Blaz a nod. Blaz nodded back. Erich and Koby were also in a conversation when they exited the gate. Both ended their talk after seeing their friends. Upon being recognized, Blaz asked the two, "What did *Herr* Schlusser want to speak with you about?"

"I've been made a leader of our age group at the KLV camp. *Herr* Schlusser is going to train me, a boy from each year and those two *Hitlerjugend* graduates this next half year before we ship out," Erich eagerly answered, "And when we are at the camp, Schlusser's commander will personally train me and those boys to become members of the SS."

"Wow, congratulations Erich," Jarman said glowingly.

"*Ja*, that's really impressive, not many people make it to the SS," Blaz pointed out.

"And what about you Koby?"

"He was first talking to me about training for the five thousand meter in the Olympics. No plans have changed," he assured Blaz, "And he told me that I would've been in training for the SS, but I'm not a pure German so..."

The boys' eyes widened and they stared at Koby in disbelief, who looked at the ground.

"*Nein*, he wouldn't say that," Jurgen said in disbelief.

Blaz looked at Erich for confirmation and he nodded.

"I guess the SS must remain pure, but you Koby!" Jarman exclaimed, "I can't believe that!"

"*Gut*," Koby said, trying to fight back laughter, "You shouldn't."

Erich and Koby burst out laughing. Blaz, Jurgen and Jarman glared at them but accepted they'd been fooled.

"Okay, you got us. But really, what happened?" Jarman chuckled.

"All right, I'm being trained for the SS at the KLV camps as well," Koby told them truthfully, "My family has been all Aryan since the mid-seventeen hundreds. That was the last a Jew married into the family but none since. That's the most recent you can have Jewish ancestors and still be eligible for the SS. I'm a quarter Italian but that didn't matter for the SS. Italians are Aryans too. We've heard they are loosening the restrictions anyway. They're starting to allow half-Jews. If they are proven loyal."

As he said this, Ivo came jogging into the group.

"So, what did I miss?" he asked.

"Koby and Erich are SS candidates," Jurgen told him.

Ivo's face lit up. "Sweet, good work guys!"

The boys stood around for a few seconds. Jurgen broke the silence, "Okay, we have two hours until the *Hitlerjugend* meeting. We should do something outside to celebrate the break."

"Definitely," all the boys agreed.

"How about we play some good old football?" Jarman suggested, referring to soccer.

"That sounds good, and plus we've got a field right here," Ivo said, pointing beyond the gate to the school.

They strolled back through gate. Older boys were already playing on one half of the field, but the other half was free. Jarman ran into the school to ask for a football. The boys waited outside for him. The sun was shining brightly against their tanner than normal skin and the temperature was quite hot for Germany. The weather didn't dampen their spirits or energy. It was summer! When Jarman came out he was carrying a brown ball. He dropped it and juggled with his feet before booting it over to the group. The boys separated into threes. Jarman, Erich, and Koby drifted to one side and Blaz, Ivo, and Jurgen to the other. Erich passed the ball to Koby to begin the game. Koby passed it to Jarman, who dribbled it toward Blaz, who ran towards Jarman before slowing down right as he came close to him. Blaz bent his knees and shuffled to one side, forcing Jarman the other way. Jarman cut hard to the open way and Blaz followed, only for Jarman to pull the ball back behind himself and spin back to the original direction. Blaz was knocked off balance but quickly recovered and gave chase. Ivo strafed Jarman twice, trying to get the ball back and knocked it loose the second time. Jarman slid to kick the ball to Erich who made a move past Jurgen and then hammered the ball into the back of the net.

"*Ja! Gute Arbeit,*" Koby told his team. Good work.

At that moment, over a dozen younger boys and a few girls, no older than eight, came onto the field with a ball and began to play. The boys looked at each other. Little kids being near meant no hard playing. Koby, however, ran over to the young kids and joined in with them. Looks of surprise erased disappointment. Blaz followed Koby's lead and joined. Ivo quickly jumped in and the others followed. Blaz stole the ball from a small, blond boy but let him steal it back after a few seconds of tantalizing him with the ball. Erich was passed to by a little girl and he started to show off by juggling. The children laughed, some shook their heads, grinning, as they watched Erich juggle. Mid-juggle Jarman kicked the ball away and back to the children. They ran around, passing and stealing the ball at random. Blaz and one boy began talking while jogging next to one another, waiting for the ball to come their way.

The little boy, staring at Blaz with big blue eyes under his scruffy, unkempt blond hair and oddly, no eyebrows, asked curiously, "Are you a soldier?"

"What?" Blaz asked, surprised that he could be mistaken for one.

"Are you a soldier?" the boy asked, still believing these were military men.

"*Nein*," Blaz answered, "Of course not. Do I look like one?"

"*Nein*, I guess not. But you must be something," the boy pursued the topic.

"I am a cadet."

"What's a cadet?" the little boy asked him when Blaz lunged to stop a pass.

"It's someone who's being trained to be a soldier," Blaz said, sending it to Jarman.

"You will be a soldier?"

"Probably."

"That's good, I want to be a soldier someday," the boy said.

"Fight for the Fatherland? That's always a noble goal," Blaz encouraged the kid while sending the ball over to Koby, "What's your name?"

"Alonzo Harvey, what's yours?"

"Blaz. Blaz Senft. Nice to meet you Alonzo."

The boys played with the children until the little ones began to tire out. By then, everyone was covered in sweat and the sun glinted off their faces as it descended. The little kids walked toward the gate to go home. One thanked Koby for playing with them.

"*Auf wiedersehen*, Alonzo," Blaz called to the little boy.

"*Auf wiedersehen*, Blaz," the little boy called back.

The summer sun was still out but creeping down in the sky. The boys headed back to their homes to get ready for their Hitler Youth meeting. Everyone walked off the field and towards the gate. For a minute or two they treaded silently in the streets.

"Why did we do that?" Jarman asked the group.

Blaz and the others looked at him. The group stayed silent, trying to think of an answer.

"I mean; we didn't have to do that. We just did."

"I think it was just a nice thing to do," Blaz answered, "You know, make some children happy, it's the little things in life."

"It felt pretty good," Ivo said.

"When we're soldiers, remember that's what we fight for," Koby told the group.

They nodded. Jurgen turned around at the end of the conversation to head to his farm and the others told him they'd see him later. The group broke off until it was Blaz, Ivo, Erich, and Koby. Blaz's home was the first they came to and Blaz walked over to the door. He opened the door to go in and waved to his three friends. His father was inside, packing away his welding equipment. Blaz went past him to grab his Hitler Youth cap but his father said, "How was your last day of school?"

"*Gut*, papa."

"*Gut*."

The two stood looking at each other awkwardly. There was a heaviness in Ottoway's eyes. Blaz combed his hair with his fingers to break eye contact.

"You better get ready for your meeting," his father told him.

"*Jawohl*, papa," Blaz said and jogged up the lone flight of stairs. He headed into his room and took off his dirty, sweaty school clothes and put on his Hitler Youth shorts. He then slid his arms through the sleeves of his Hitler Youth shirt and buttoned it up. He put on his boots and straightened his hair to the right again. He placed his Hitler Youth hat over his hair and slid his Swastika armband onto his left arm. The young boy then turned abruptly and marched out of his room with his legs straightened with each stride. He broke this to go down the stairs before resuming this walk.

Blaz's father watched him march out the door and he briefly waved. Blaz stepped back out into the warm evening air. He turned towards the town square and strode off in that direction. The top half of the sun peeked above the skyline, painting the sky red, pink, and orange as it set. He'd not walked far when many more boys wearing the brown shirts and black shorts joined him. They all converged on the town square. About two hundred Hitler Youth boys already stood in the square awaiting their commander's words. Schlusser waited until exactly half past seven and then raised his hand for silence. The Hitler Youth gave him their full attention.

"Members of the *Hitlerjugend* of Seelow, I have called you here to inform you more extensively of our relocation for more intense and elaborate military training. First, we will leave Seelow after this year's first semester. Seelow has been declared a likely military target for bombings by Axmann, the head of the *Hitlerjugend*. All cities in danger of bombings are being evacuated of their children to these KLV camps, or *Kinderlandverschickung*, child evacuation camps. The girls will leave to a separate camp the week after you boys. At these camps, you will all be trained with guns, hand-to-hand combat, explosives, and vehicles. In addition, selected individuals will receive extensive training for the SS. Some individuals will be trained for leadership positions in the *Wehrmacht*. Selected individuals will be trained for *Deutschland's* athletic program," Schlusser said looking Koby's way, "The war will not last forever. When this war is over the German people will abandon the production of cannons and will begin the work of peace. We will need our best athletes for international competitions with Italy, Japan, Finland, Hungary, Romania, African nations, the United States, and so forth. We will also need scientists, so those of you who show prowess in this field will be documented for it. Moving on, you will be assigned cabins by squad and will be provided proper nourishment while in training. You will help keep the camp in good condition and learn to repair military technology. While much of your time will be devoted to work and training, you will be allowed time for rest and activities to relieve any stress you might have. This will come at the end of the afternoon before evening instruction classes. Also, on Sundays you will have an almost entirely free day for exploring, sports, and religious activities. Understood?"

"Sir, *ja* sir!"

"Now, I would like to name the camp leaders and age group assistants. Klein! Haushofer!"

The two tall cadets from earlier marched to the front of the assembly. They stood by *Herr* Schlusser with stoic, unflinching expressions.

"There will be age group assistants for ages thirteen to eighteen! Age group eighteen: Raskoph! Becke! Age group seventeen: Kauffman! Glöckner! Age group sixteen: Hilderbrand! Ebner! Age group fifteen: Fleischer! Kramer! Age group fourteen: Schmid! Vogel! Age group thirteen..."

The boys glanced at Koby and Erich.

"Hertz! Meyer!"

Erich and Koby strode to the front of the many cadets and stood on the end of the other selected leaders. While Erich matched the fourteens, fifteens, and even sixteens in height and muscle, Blaz noticed Koby looked particularly shorter than all the chosen cadets. It almost made him laugh.

"Stand at attention," Schlusser told the twelve appointed trainees.

The twelve teenagers stomped one foot and pressed their arms to their sides. Their eyes locked forward, and all signs of the excitement and honor any had shown seconds earlier vanished from their faces. Blaz gazed at them, envious.

Always knew he'd go places, Blaz thought, watching Koby.

"The two oldest cadets, Klein and Haushofer, will be trained to take over command of the KLV camp when I am called to the front. If they should be deployed, the next age group will assume command. The others will be trained to be leaders of their designated squads, which will be assigned when we arrive at the camp. Each of these cadets deserves your respect and obedience. I expect you to treat their orders as you would the mine. In addition, each squad will be trained for combat in specific areas in Europe. Each commander will be taught to speak the language the locals of that area speak. These students have already been notified of this and will begin language training this summer with special teachers and myself.

You will find out what area you will be trained for at camp, likely the day of our arrival. Now, I would like to give your new commanders their designation of this title. I shouldn't tell you, but it is likely you eighteen-year-olds will be called to the front soon. The age group assistants will be trained to lead the camps in preparation for this."

Schlusser held up a box and pulled out his knife, tearing it straight down the middle of the box. Inside lay a Hitler Youth uniform with several patches attached, indicating rank. Schlusser held the winter and summer uniforms up for all to see. The summer uniform was a light khaki and the winter was black, both with several pockets like all Hitler Youth uniforms. The Swastika armband remained in its place. However, this uniform also had the *Reichsadler* clutching the Swastika in its talons. A black, triangular patch with the name of their city written in gold lay on one sleeve with their identification number in red as well. A black patch with a singular white SS lightning bolt was on the left sleeve. The hats were khaki rather than black. Klein and Haushofer, were given peaked officer's caps, while the others were given normal Hitler Youth caps in khaki. The cadets stared. Schlusser gave a box to each cadet and allowed them to return to their positions in the meeting. Koby and Erich walked back towards the group and other fourteen-year-olds, boxes in hand. Koby walked in next to Blaz and Ivo and turned back to face the front. Schlusser had one final thing to say, "You will be dismissed to return home but first we shall sing the *Hitlerjugend* banner song."

The Hitler Youth sang their anthem, Blaz's voice cracking once again during the chorus. As the song ended, everyone present raised their right arms high into the sky, fingers outstretched in the salute. "*Sieg Heil*" rang into the night as if they had already won the war. Blaz beamed, right arm raised triumphantly.

"*Heil* Hitler!" Schlusser bellowed, arms still to his sides.

"*Sieg Heil!*" Blaz shouted while many boys declared the same words in raised voices.

Schlusser removed his cap and raised his right arm into the salute. He remained there for several seconds then lowered his arm and headed towards his home. The Hitler Youths remained for a while talking, cheering and singing more of their favorite march songs. Eventually, the group thinned out and the boys left to go to their separate homes. Blaz and Erich walked back to their street with Koby and Ivo.

"Are you ready to do anything for *Deutschland*?" Ivo asked, beaming.

"*Ja*!" the others answered simultaneously.

"I cannot wait to begin training," Koby told Erich.

"It is all about *Deutschland's* glory!"

Koby started down his street before yelling, "*Auf wiedersehen, Kameraden*!" He raised his arm in the salute.

Erich and Blaz both headed into their houses when they heard Ivo exclaim, "All for *Deutschland!* Let's get to the front already!"

"*Sieg Heil!*" Blaz shouted.

Blaz closed the door as he entered his home.

"Welcome back," Blaz's mother said.

"Hello, mama," Blaz smiled.

"Here, sit down Blaz, time for dinner," she said pointing to Blaz's chair on the circular table. Blaz sat down and removed his hat.

"Blaz, you want to pray?" his mother chided him.

"Of course, mama," Blaz replied and bowed his head. "*Gott sei Dank* (Thank God) for providing for us and for letting Koby and Erich get promoted. *Danke* for our *Führer* and the success you've given our nation to carry out your will here on earth. We will try our hardest to make sure it is accomplished," Blaz finished, "Amen."

"How was the meeting?" Ottoway asked him as he took a sip of beer.

"Great, we sang *Unsere Fahne Flattert uns Voran*, *Herr* Schlusser told us about the camp we are going to, and Erich and Koby have been made leaders," Blaz said as he placed bread and sauerkraut on his plate. Meat was becoming more of an occasion since the war had started, as the price had gone up quite a bit.

"Interesting," Ottoway said quietly, "What does that mean for them?"

"Okay," Blaz started, "They got new uniforms and hats and they will have their own groups to command at camp and eventually in battle. They are going to learn some new language too!"

"Sounds exciting," his father said, raising his eyebrows, "I'm glad you're eager to serve the nation."

"That's our purpose, right? To make *Deutschland* great?"

"That's certainly part of it," his father answered, not wanting to undermine Blaz's confidence.

As Blaz lay down to sleep that night, he thought about what he might do someday when he was in the army. He imagined many places that the Hitler Youth would conquer, the great battles they would win.

The Wehrmacht

July 23, 1940 Tuesday

Through the cobblestone and dirt streets, together one last time. Blaz and his parents walked to the edge of Seelow where his father would leave for Norway. Ottoway wore a field gray *Wehrmacht* uniform with black boots and a dome-shaped helmet the same color. Blaz wore his *Hitlerjugend* uniform to see his father off. Ottoway held his wife's hand on his right. The twelve-year-old tightly gripped his father's left hand. They headed toward the beginning of the Seelow Heights defenses where the trucks were waiting, each with different destinations. Shortly after they arrived, Ivo and his family turned up. Blaz also saw Koby, whose father had been deployed weeks ago. Ottoway walked to an SS officer at a small desk to register. Ernst and Henrik Klein fell in behind him to do the same. Blaz and Ivo looked at each other, saying nothing. Koby made eye contact with Blaz and gave a nod. The officer pointed to a truck as he spoke with Ottoway.

Blaz's father walked back and said, "Now don't you worry, I'll come back."

Several tears ran down Cheryl's face before she began crying aloud. She hugged her husband and said, "I love you, Ottoway."

"I love you too, darling."

Ottoway hugged his wife fiercely but did not cry. When they let go, Ottoway got down on a knee and looked at his son.

"You're the man of the house now. Take care of her for me," Ottoway said with a smile. Cheryl smiled down at him too.

"I love you and I'm very proud of your hard work this year," his father told him, "Keep it up while I'm gone."

A few tears ran down Blaz's face as he embraced his father. His lip trembled and he closed his eyes tightly to fight back more tears while he gripped his father. Finally, Blaz let go, Ottoway stood and gave Cheryl a final kiss then told her, "*Ade, mein liebes Schatzelein.*"

With that, he strode toward his truck.

"Don't win the war until I get there," Blaz tried to say lightheartedly.

His father turned back and said, "Don't worry about it." Then he made his way to the truck. He climbed in and an officer yelled, pounding twice on the back of the truck.

Blaz's eyes welled with tears, but he breathed in, thinking, *Nein, no tears. I'm the man now, father didn't cry. I won't either.* He put an arm around his mother. She looked down and hugged him. They both looked back towards the truck. As the engine rumbled up, Blaz heard the German soldiers in the back singing, and his father too.

In der Heimat wohnt ein kleines Mägdelein
und das heißt: Erika.
Dieses Mädel ist mein treues Schätzelein
und mein Glück: Erika.
Wenn das Heidekraut rot-lila blüht,
singe ich zum Gruß ihr dieses Lied.
Auf der Heide blüht ein kleines Blümelein
und das heißt: Erika.

> *In the homeland there lives a little girl*
> *and she's called: Erika.*
> *That girl is my faithful little darling*
> *and my joy: Erika!*
> *When the heather blooms in a reddish purple,*
> *I sing her this song in greeting.*
> *On the heath, blooms a little flower*
> *and it's called: Erika.*

Slowly, the song faded into the distance and soon after, the truck disappeared into the hills. Blaz let a tear slide down his cheek after the truck was out of view. He felt the weight of having no father at this moment. *What if he never comes back?* His mother let go of him as he wandered into the grassy fields. Silent rivers wet his cheeks. *Nein, I have to be strong, I have to be a man.* He dried his eyes with his sleeve and turned around to walk back to his mother. When he got there, Koby was waiting for him.

"I'm sorry about all this."

Blaz's head snapped up, his face now showing little trace of any tears, "I just, I can't believe he's gone."

Koby stayed silent.

"All for *Deutschland, ja?*"

"We have to give up some stuff," Koby said sadly, "We're a part of something bigger than ourselves."

"At least it's only a little while," Blaz said, looking on the bright side, "And mama is still here," he paused, "And you guys too."

Koby smiled at Blaz. The two friends gave each other a hug.

"*Danke* Koby," Blaz said.

"Stay strong, *meine Freund*," Koby responded, patting Blaz on the back.

Blaz returned to his mother. She put her arm around him and they two walked back home.

The War Comes to German Land

August 26, 1940 Monday

"Berlin has been hit?" Blaz asked Ivo in disbelief.

"*Ja*, I found out this morning," Ivo panted at his doorstep before school.

"I can't believe it!" Blaz said, still shocked by the news.

"The *Führer* is furious. I'd bet that this only makes Britain fall sooner," Ivo told Blaz, hopefully.

"Let's hope," Blaz replied.

The two boys dashed down the streets to tell their other friends. Jarman swore upon hearing the news.

Later that day, they were gathered at a Hitler Youth meeting on the field. Blaz stood at attention with the other cadets. His eyes followed Schlusser. The young officer paced in front of the students and stroked his chin with his black-gloved hand. While their commander paced, the boys shot each other curious looks but no one said a word. *Herr* Schwinghammer emerged from the school building and strutted in Schlusser's direction. The SS officer whispered something to Schlusser who nodded and then turned to the boys and girls.

"I have some unfortunate news today. The British bombed Berlin last night," Schlusser told the Hitler Youth. Some gasps were heard and even those who already knew appeared a bit alarmed on hearing it from an officer.

"Seelow will now conduct air raid drills in case the British bomb us. If this should happen, you will proceed to a basement any of you might have or to the underground shelter below the school. This bombing does not change when we leave for the KLV camps. However, I have been called to the front lines and I will only be allowed to stay for the first week you are in the camp just to guide you along and get you started. The eighteen-year-olds have also been called to the front. Kauffman and Glöckner will be the second in command at the camps. Schwinghammer will be in charge. Now, give me two hundred push-ups and ten laps around the school building."

The cadets dropped down and began their push-ups without complaint. Some did all at once, others spread their push-ups out. Erich quickly finished along with many older cadets and began running around the school. Jurgen, Koby, Reinhardt, and Jarman stood up soon after. Blaz kept pumping his arms to finish up. He gritted his teeth and cranked out his final push-up. He hopped up and started running. When he looked back, he was surprised to see Ivo jumping up just then and beginning his laps too. Several laps in, Koby came alongside him and when they passed out of Schlusser's view, Koby asked, "How are you doing?"

Blaz kept running. "I've been better."

"We all have," Koby replied, "But we have to be willing to give up something for the Fatherland."

"*Wahr, ja,*" Blaz agreed.

"I'll see you when we are done," Koby said as he pulled ahead before the two came back into their commander's sight.

Blaz watched Koby run ahead of him. His brows drew together. Something had changed about his friend in the last month. Blaz didn't know what it was, Koby still took interest in Blaz's concerns and problems. He was still one of the best prospects Seelow had. He always found time to spend with his friends despite his busy schedule with the Hitler Youth, running, and SS training. Even so, something wasn't the same. Koby didn't seem himself. Blaz shook his head and kept running.

Jarman Versus Blaz

September 7, 1940 Saturday

In the following weeks, Schlusser focused more and more on military training. Target practice, hand-to-hand combat, and demolitions became more prominent for the boys in Seelow. Nearly every day since Berlin had been hit, Blaz's unit went to the base in the hills of Seelow Heights for practice with every weapon they might someday use.

On the final day of their summer break, the twelve and thirteen-year-olds were practicing hand-to-hand combat against one another. Schlusser ordered them to immobilize their opponent to claim victory. Jarman faced off against Blaz while other boys fought around them. Neither wore shoes, to prevent unnecessary injuries. The boys circled, waiting for an opportune time to strike. Their focus remained solely on each other. Blaz knew he was physically outmatched but his techniques might give him a chance. Jarman attacked first. He took a swing at Blaz's head but Blaz ducked and returned a punch that Jarman parried easily. Jarman got closer and the two soon had locked their arms to try to pull each other down. Blaz began to bend under the pressure from Jarman. Before Jarman could bring him down, Blaz pulled away from his grasp. Jarman stumbled forward and Blaz bolted behind him and wrapped his arms around Jarman's neck in a stranglehold. Jarman started to pry Blaz's arms off but Blaz kicked out Jarman's feet from underneath him and he fell to the ground. Blaz locked Jarman's arms together with his legs. Jarman moved his legs over his own head and kicked Blaz in the face. The Hitler Youth was knocked to the ground. Jarman leapt up and turned around. Blaz scrambled to his feet while wiping some blood from his nose.

"All right, no more messing around," Jarman declared.

Blaz shook his head to regain his focus. Jarman charged. Blaz swung a fist at him. He hit Jarman square on the jaw sending his opponent toppling to the ground and onto his back. Jarman slowly tried to get up to continue the fight. Blaz grabbed him by the arms and sent a knee into his stomach. Jarman fell back to the ground. This time he remained on all fours.

Schlusser walked over to the fight, appalled to see Blaz beating one of the best prospects of his age. Blaz hardly noticed and brought Jarman's head into the ground. Jarman's arms collapsed under him and his face hit the ground. He turned onto his back to fend off any more attacks. Blaz panted above him. He could easily knock Jarman out and win. By now, he knew Schlusser was watching. He walked toward Jarman and lifted him to his knees and locking his arms around his neck.

"Well done, Senft," Schlusser applauded, "You've certainly improved. Still much to work on, but I am impressed."

Blaz grinned, fiercely. There was always more to be learned, so he knew Schlusser was proud. Blaz released Jarman from his grip. Jarman slowly stood up. He looked at Blaz with contempt but then he held out a hand. Blaz took it and shook Jarman's hand.

"Good fighting, Blaz. I will get you next time," Jarman said.

"*Du auch*," Blaz replied, "You too."

The two cadets walked away and stood in formation in front of their age group leaders.

"Next we will practice firing from fifty meters. You will kneel like you are behind cover. Take your shot quickly as if you are in a battle. Move to the firing range!" Erich yelled to the other cadets.

"Front row take MP-Class. Second row, pistols. Third row, rifles. Understood?" Koby instructed them.

"*Ja* sir!" the cadets answered.

The youths marched to the range. Human silhouettes with bullseyes on them were set up and each student retrieved their weapon and ammo. Blaz grabbed a Karabiner 98K and marched to the far end of the firing range. There, he loaded his rifle and turned the safety off. He pulled back the lever and the rifle clicked, ready to fire. Blaz knelt low and held the rifle facing toward the range. He breathed in and stood up quickly to take his shot. He fired, then knelt back down below the imaginary cover. Again, he stood and fired at his target. The third time he stayed knelt and elevated himself slightly above his imaginary cover to take a shot. He repeated this twice more. With his clip spent, he stood up to observe his shooting. He gazed out at the target. All five bullets had hit where he had aimed: the heart and head.

Ja, ja!

They continued shooting until Schlusser informed them it was time to head back to Seelow. The cadets began their slow jog back. Their boots sent dust flying as they hit the ground. Blaz jogged alongside Ivo while they ascended a steep hill.

"How did you shoot?" Blaz asked Ivo.

"I didn't miss once," Ivo replied excitedly, "How about you?"

"I never missed too."

"We're getting good."

"*Ja*, we are."

"I am ready for anything the war can throw at us, Blaz," Ivo declared.

"We might get to fight soon," Blaz told Ivo, "Eighteen-year-olds are being pulled to the front. We are thirteen, you are twelve, but still we could. You know, sometimes I feel I could never fight in a battle, some days I think I could fight the entire British army myself."

"I know that feeling too," Ivo laughed as they reached the top of the hill.

"There's Seelow," Blaz said, pointing.

"*Ja.*"

They jogged in silence for a few seconds. Blaz gazed ahead. "What are you doing for your birthday, Ivo? I mean, it was very different and odd for me last week with father being gone this year."

Ivo thought for a moment. "I don't know, I will probably see you guys most of the day and maybe do something with my mother at home. It's very strange not having Father or Henrik at home, ever. Is it not?"

"It's not the same. But he was gone a lot when he was not in the army. Now he's never here though, it's weird. I miss Papa."

Ivo nodded, "The teachers and Schlusser have done a good job keeping our heads high. I miss Father and Henrik still."

As Ivo finished saying this, the two boys jogged into the town. Schlusser, who had been jogging at the front, ordered a halt. The boys stood in formation, awaiting instruction. "After this weekend, you return to school. It is your final semester before KLV. Work hard in school, be ready for more training. We will have a short meeting tomorrow and nothing more so you can get used to being back in school. This weekend we will be out at the Heights for more training. Arrive at school ten minutes early to raise the flag tomorrow. Wear your uniforms. That is all."

The youths stamped their feet and dispersed across the town. Blaz and his friends walked down the streets but turned away from their homes to head back into the country. They jogged down a hill to a small grove of trees.

"If this is our last summer, possibly ever," Koby said, "Then we've got to have some good old-fashioned fun," he pointed to a tree on the edge of the cluster, closest to the boys. A stump faced them where a large branch had once been.

"See that one?" he asked.

"*Ja,*" the boys all nodded.

"*Gut*, now see the stump where some branch used to be?" Koby asked.

They all nodded again. Koby reached to his sheath and unclipped his sheath. He slid his Hitler Youth knife out of the sheath and brought it in front of his face. He grasped the knife's handle with the tips of his fingers, ready to throw. He took a step and leaned forward while bringing his arm back. He flung the knife toward the tree hitting the stump to the left of the center.

"We are going to have a knife-throwing competition."

"Fine by me," Erich said, unsheathing his knife, "But this is old-fashioned?"

Koby laughed as he slid out his knife, "*Ja,* this feels old-fashioned."

Erich threw his knife and hit the stump slightly above the center. Jurgen and Reinhardt both hit the outer area of the stump. Jarman stepped up next. His blade went just above Erich's. Blaz stepped up next and unsheathed his knife. He twirled it between his fingers and aimed. He brought his arm back and lunged forward. The knife hit on the outside of the target, not exactly a good throw.

Ivo stepped up next and threw his with more of a parabolic motion than any of the boys but still landed a hit low on the tree. The boys threw their knives a few more times for practice, with Erich, Jarman and Koby dominating the lighthearted competition. Afterwards, they sat down on the edge of the tree cluster. Erich picked up a rock and sharpened his knife. The sun was getting low in the sky while the boys chatted and fiddled with their knives. Blaz stroked the blade.

"We have one more semester with Coach Friederich."

"*Ja*, only one," Koby said sadly.

"I'm going to try to come to more of your meets this year," Erich informed them.

"*Danke*, Erich," Koby thanked him, "We look forward to seeing you there."

Jarman stood up, "I'm going to head home, it's getting late. I'll see you tomorrow."

"Okay, see you Jarman," Erich waved.

"*Scheiße*, I better get going too," Jurgen told them.

"We all should, no reason to just sit out here," Koby hopped up headed into Seelow. The others followed.

The Flag on High

September 9, 1940 Monday

A beam of light hit Blaz's forehead, creeping down to his closed eyes, waking him. He fell out of bed, and when he stood up, he stumbled a bit. He trudged downstairs to the bathroom water pump. Blaz worked it until water slowly ran out and it maintained a steady flow. Blaz put his face under the flow and then moved his hair under it too. His hair remained in the Hitler Youth cut, his father having taught him to cut his own hair in front of a mirror. His mother would help him with the back still, though. When his hair was good and wet, Blaz took a rag from the bathroom and scampered back up the stairs. Once in his room, Blaz took off pajamas that were striped white and a faded red. He put on his Hitler Youth shorts and khaki-colored shirt in front of his mirror.

I love these, Blaz thought as he smiled at himself in the mirror, *makes me feel invincible.*

He slid on his armband then picked up his comb from on top of his dresser. The comb ran through his nearly white hair, prodding it to the right. When his hair was combed, he dried it off with the rag but was careful to keep it neatly combed. Gently, he placed the Hitler Youth cap on his head. His bright blue eyes stared back at him in the mirror.

This is it, Blaz. One semester left. Then you go to become a soldier. Are you ready? It won't be easy. Ja, I know. But I am ready to do all I can for Deutschland. Blaz shook his head. *Los! Come on! Get all of those worries out of your head.*

He turned from the mirror, out his bedroom door. He jogged down the stairs and grabbed a piece of bread before he headed out the door. When he'd eaten his bread, he lengthened his strides to impersonate a German soldier. On the way to school, he passed Erich's door. Erich exited to join Blaz, who ended his impersonation.

"*Guten tag*, Blaz! Ready for our last semester of school?"

"I am. I don't hate school at all. I'd rather be there than just be bored."

"No one with half a brain disagrees with that, Blaz."

"*Jawohl.* We have plenty of work to do at camp, and in the army, if we get there."

"We will."

"Are you excited to begin your running season?"

"I hope I'll be able to beat my time, but I'm really hoping Koby-"

"Keeps improving," they said at the same time.

"*Ja*," Blaz chuckled, "That."

Erich shook his head, grinning.

When they strode through the school gate, they both noticed the same thing. A large flagpole had been installed. Normally the school flag would fly on top of a small pole on the roof of the school. Now they had a flagpole. Schlusser was there, as well as all the teachers. In Schlusser's hands was a bright red flag, much larger than the one that had flown on the roof. In the center were a white circle and a black swastika. A smaller red and white Hitler Youth flag was placed below the Swastika banner. Erich and Blaz stood near their friends while young students, not yet in the Hitler Youth, chatted around them.

"Arrange by age group!" Schlusser shouted at the top of his lungs, "Youngest up front, oldest at back."

The entire Hitler Youth immediately made their way into rectangular formations and stood at attention. The younger students took a bit more time but obeyed unquestionably. All the students stood at attention waiting for the flag. Schlusser and Schwinghammer strode to the pole and attached the German flag first to the top rung. The Hitler Youth flag, which was red with a white stripe running horizontally which also encompassed black swastika, was placed below. Schwinghammer raised his right hand in the stiff-armed salute and began to sing the national anthem, as Schlusser raised the flags.

Deutschland, Deutschland über alles, Über alles in der Welt,

At this point many teachers and older students joined in singing.

Wenn es stets zu Schutz und Trutze, Brüderlich zusammenhält.

By now all of the Hitler Youth were singing.

Von der Maas bis an die Memel, Von der Etsch bis an den Belt,

The younger children started to sing at this point. Everyone inside the school perimeter was singing and saluting.

Deutschland, Deutschland über alles, Über alles in der Welt!
Deutschland, Deutschland über alles, Über alles in der Welt!

Germany, Germany over everything, over everything in the world,
when for protection and defense, brotherly we stand together.
From the Meuse to the Memel, from the Adige to the Belt,
Germany, Germany over everything, over everything in the world!

The masses then flawlessly transitioned into the "*Horst Wessel Lied,*" named after an early National Socialist who had lost his life at the hands of Communists. But he still marched in spirit within their ranks.

Die Fahne hoch! Die Reihen fest geschlossen!
SA marschiert mit ruhig festem Schritt.
Kameraden, die Rotfront und Reaktion erschossen,
Marschieren im Geist in unseren Reihen mit.
Kameraden, die Rotfront und Reaktion erschossen,
Marschieren im Geist in unseren Reihen mit.

The flag on high! The ranks tightly closed!
The SA marches with quiet, steady step.
Comrades shot by the Red Front and reactionaries
March in spirit within our ranks.
Comrades shot by the Red Front and reactionaries
March in spirit within our ranks.

By the time the song was over both flags flew high. The red banner with the white circle and Swastika fluttered in the breeze.

"*Sieg Heil!*" Schwinghammer shouted.

"*Sieg Heil!*" the students roared back, "*Sieg heil! Sieg Heil! Sieg Heil!*"

Following this exchange, the students headed to their classes. Blaz walked into his first class with his bag and took out his pencil and notebook. The teacher stood up from her desk. She was an older woman, in her fifties with dark blond hair, brown eyes and skin that had begun to age.

"Welcome to your German Literature class," the woman said, "In this class you will be taught advanced writing skills. I know that I only have a semester with you so we won't waste any time. Take out your notebooks. I want you all to write a story about anything you like so I can get an idea of your writing skills. It is due on the first day of next week."

The students wrote down the due date and paper name. Blaz's mind searched for an idea. *I don't know. Must have human characters, what about a story about a soldier in the army? Ja, that's it.* Blaz quickly scribbled down his idea and looked back up at the teacher.

"...aspects of writing a story are tone, characters, and plot," was what Blaz heard the teacher say. Blaz jotted the three aforementioned points down.

In study hall, Blaz's second-to-last hour this semester, he sat next to Ivo and Erich at a table in the back of the room. The three had just finished their math homework. Several students read books they'd been assigned, others worked on math or science. Blaz put his math away and took out his notebook.

"Story time?" Erich asked.

"*Ja*, did you get this assigned too?"

"Sure did," replied Erich while he reached into his bag to get his notebook. Ivo also pulled out a notebook.

"What are you going to write about?" Ivo asked the two.

"I have no idea yet," Erich answered, "I'm not very good at this kind of stuff."

"I'm going to do a story about soldiers in the army," Blaz answered Ivo.

"Ah, cool. Where will they be? What are their names?"

"Slow down, I haven't started!"

"Oh, okay," Ivo laughed.

"Got any ideas for me?" asked Erich.

"How about a guy who falls in love with a princess?" Ivo suggested.

"Ah, shut up Ivo."

"The teacher did say she wants to get a read on our abilities."

"*Ja*, so if you write a decent but unoriginal story, then the bar won't be set so high," Blaz added.

"That's a good idea, but why settle for less?"

"Not going to be lazy about it? Me neither."

Ivo started writing. Blaz also brought his pencil to paper. He didn't write though. *What was it like, the day we invaded Poland? Sunny, few clouds, warm. Ja, that will do.*

An Eleven-Year-Old Koby

September 9, 1940 Monday

The Hitler Youth stood, their arms glued to their sides on the school's field. Schlusser once again stood at the front. "I have called you hear to tell about the plans we have this semester. Nearly every other day we will jog out to the Seelow Heights for training. *Herr* Schwinghammer will evaluate our unit at the end of November. He will evaluate the boys I select per age group in sprints, shooting, hand-to-hand combat, knife, technical skills, long distance, weight lifting, and anti-aircraft operation."

He paused. The cadets remained attentive.

"This means that in our small school, most of you will be representing the unit in at least one event. How your unit performs will affect your camp's staff and conditions, so you must work hard. Is that clear?"

"*Jawohl!*"

"*Gut*, everyone may leave except leaders. Also, I want Ivo Klein, Blaz Senft, and Johann Steiner here now."

The students turned to leave, some staying for their sports. Blaz headed forward with Ivo to *Herr* Schlusser. Many taller cadets stood circled next to Schlusser. The same cadets from their summer rally wore their special uniforms except Klein and Haushofer were no longer among them. Steiner, who was average height for an eleven-year-old, with light blond hair and big, light blue eyes, walked forward as instructed. He had a thin but sturdy build and his Hitler Youth haircut was especially short on the sides, barely any hair was left. His legs barely bent as he shuffled over to *Herr* Schlusser. The young boy gazed up at Erich in admiration. Noticing this, Erich turned his head to look down at the boy. When he did this, Steiner quickly turned his head to Schlusser. Erich suppressed a grin as did the cadets that noticed this.

"On days we train at the Heights you will all run out early to make things ready. I have informed your teachers you will be dismissed with fifteen minutes left in your class period. This includes you three," Schlusser gestured to Ivo, Blaz, and Steiner, "Hertz, Senft, and Klein, I have spoken to Coach Friederich and he says this will be a light workout day for you. Every other Saturday you three are to report to him at the school for the rest of the semester."

"*Danke, Herr* Schlusser."

"Now, every day we are at the Heights each age group will focus on two different training exercises. Stay here after every meeting so I can tell you what that will be."

"*Jawohl, Herr.*"

"With all due respect, *Herr*," Blaz said, "Why are me and Ivo running out with the leaders?"

"Friederich personally asked for it."

Blaz nodded.

"Now Johann Steiner. You are our best prospect in the young age groups for running. You will be a representative for age eleven in long distance, weight lifting, and anti-aircraft for certain. I will decide on others later. That is why I want you to train with these boys when they run out to the Heights. You will also practice with Coach Friederich this semester."

"*J-jawohl.*"

"Next week on Friday we will have a five-kilometer race in the Heights with all the students so I can find three candidates for each age group. It will be divided into a few separate races for the sake of space. You will write down each time that I will yell off when you are not running. That is all for today."

The older boys turned to leave. Koby gestured for Johann Steiner to follow him and his friends into the school. Koby, Blaz, and Ivo entered the changing room while Johann waited outside.

"What about Steiner?" Ivo asked, "He can't keep up with us."

"Johann," Koby corrected him, "I'll talk with Coach Friederich."

The four boys exited the changing room. Friederich was waiting on the field with a uniform.

"Already ready," Koby breathed.

"Welcome to the team Johann," Friederich said smiling down at the nervous boy.

"*D-d-danke.*"

Ivo snickered but Blaz elbowed him. Friederich handed the uniform to the boy and instructed him to change into it.

"I am glad to have you back for one more semester," Friederich told the others, "Koby, it's time to take that next step now that you are thirteen. I'm going to work you hard this semester."

"*Bring es,*" Koby said.

"And I will give you a two-year plan for the KLV camp."

"*Danke.*"

"We hold out hope you will be able to race in the nineteen forty-four Olympics or possibly forty-eight."

"Of course," Koby said.

Johann came jogging back in his uniform at about this time.

"Okay, today I want you to run to the exit of the Heights and back here."

"All right."

The boys started at a slow jog to the gate.

"Johann, you know how to get to the Seelow Heights road exit?" Koby asked the young cadet.

Johann nodded.

"All right, see if you can stay in view of Blaz and Ivo."

"*V-verstanden.*" Understood.

Koby took off and the three boys followed. The edge of town took little time to reach. When they exited Seelow and entered the Heights the road turned from cobblestone to dirt. The Heights had many trees and tall grass, so the boys stayed on the road. There was enough open space to make it hard to lose sight of Koby, but he had pulled far ahead.

"I love running in the Heights, it's so quiet," Ivo said.

"*Ja*, it is."

"We haven't been allowed to go here alone for a long time."

"I think Coach must get permission, so we don't run here very often."

Wonder how that little kid is doing. Blaz swiveled his head. There Johann was, only a couple of meters behind the two of them.

"He's right behind us," Blaz whispered.

"Who?"

"The *Führer. Nein!* The little kid!"

"*Auf keinen Fall!* No way!" Ivo responded.

"We have to run faster, I am *not* letting coach see that we are being trailed by an eleven-year-old."

"You know we have very good times for our age, probably top ten percent."

"Who told you that?"

"Coach."

"Still, let's give this kid a run for his money."

"No pun intended?"

"What? Oh, *ja*," Blaz laughed.

Blaz increased his pace and Ivo sped up after him. Johann watched the two speed ahead. He shrugged and ran after them. They kept this pace up and eventually ran into Koby who was on his way back. Koby gave them a nod, which they returned. When they saw a surprised look flash across Koby's face, they knew they hadn't shaken Johann. They looked at each other and again increased their pace. Johann kept up.

At the exit to the Seelow Heights, the boys turned around. Johann was right behind them.

Before they started running again, Ivo asked the boy, "How in the world did you keep up with us? You are almost two years younger."

The little boy shrugged as if it was nothing.

"I guess you are just that good," Blaz admitted. He ran a loose fist through the boy's hair, before he and Ivo started running. Johann kept up with them the entire way back.

When they got back into the town Blaz murmured to Ivo, "He is worthy competition, but we are pulling into that courtyard ahead of him."

They both sprinted toward the gate and Johann took off after them. The boy gained quickly and pulled even when they passed through the gates. Blaz and Ivo tried to regain the lead. Johann kept even and almost pulled ahead himself. They slowed when they reached Coach Friederich.

"*Gute Arbeit*, especially you Johann. It appears what I have heard from *Herr* Schlusser about you is true."

Johann's big eyes lit up at this.

"How far was that, Coach?" Ivo asked.

"Ten kilometers."

"*Mein Wort.*"

"You all ran in great times, even Schwinghammer would be impressed."

"*Wunderbar.*"

"That is all for today. Go home, do your schoolwork, get some rest."

The boys walked into the school to grab their bags from Friederich's office. Koby, Blaz, and Ivo walked out of the gate and Johann went the opposite way.

"Johann!" Koby called.

Johann turned around. Blaz and Ivo did too.

"Great job today."

"*Danke!*" Johann called back, "*Du auch!*"

Johann turned his way and walked down the street but Blaz noticed there was a bit more swagger to his strides now.

"The little speedster didn't stutter!" Ivo remarked.

"He was just nervous around so many older kids," Koby explained, talking down to Ivo.

"I guess I'd be nervous too," Blaz said, "Heck, sometimes I'm nervous even now around the older *Hitlerjugend*."

"They're older, it's normal. Just imagine thinking you're on even ground older people," Koby said.

"That'd be weird," Ivo admitted, "They deserve our respect."

"It's an imperative element for a well-functioning society," Blaz stated.

Ivo laughed through his nose, "Wow, Blaz those were some big words."

Blaz looked down with slight embarrassment.

"*Nein*, it is important to use advanced vocabulary. That's something that promotes development in our collective German minds," Koby told Ivo, partially sincere but mostly sarcastic.

"Hey, are you saying I can't use big words?"

"*Nein*, but that sentence you just said was a good time to," said Koby with a grin.

"Such as?"

"Koby, are you insinuating that I am incapable of applying sophisticated, complex words into my speech?" Koby responded, doing a crude imitation of Ivo's higher-pitched voice.

Ivo stopped in the road, "That sounds smart but stupid. Who talks like that?"

"Not many people," Blaz answered.

"*Ja*, damn right," Koby said with a chuckle.

Blaz and Ivo grinned.

"Okay, I'll see you guys tomorrow," Koby smiled while he veered off onto his street.

"*Guten Nacht*, good night," Blaz called.

"*Schlaf gut!*"

Cross Country

September 10, 1940 Tuesday

Blaz jogged out to the field for the Hitler Youth meeting. By now, many children wore their Hitler Youth uniforms to school several days a week including Blaz. If he did not, he'd have to change into it every day for Hitler Youth meetings. It was easier to just wear it to school.

Schlusser gave a quick speech and called the younger students to talk with him afterwards, before dismissing everyone. Blaz changed into his running uniform and ran out to meet with Coach Friederich. He instructed them to run the five-kilometer by the Seelow farms. Koby again took the lead and lengthened it throughout the entirety of their run. Ivo and Blaz both ran their absolute hardest on this day to see how fast Johann could be. He passed them. When they got back, Koby and Johann were stretching, with Coach waiting by.

"How did we do?" Blaz asked out of breath.

"You did excellent. On pace for a five fifty-five, fifteen hundred meter. That's about your race pace last year."

Blaz and Ivo looked at each other with grins.

"How did Johann do?" Ivo asked.

"He paced a five forty-seven, fifteen hundred meter."

The boys' jaws dropped. They looked at Johann who smiled an embarrassed but proud smile. Blaz walked up to him and held out a hand.

"You are an impressive kid, Johann. I don't know much, but I know not many kids your age can do what you just did."

"*Danke,*" Johann said as he shook Blaz's hand.

Ivo walked over and shook Johann's hand too, "You make me prouder to be a German."

"All right boys, that is all for today," Friederich told them, "Enjoy your evening. Meet here tomorrow."

"*Verstanden,*" each boy responded.

The runners headed into their school to get their bags and change back into their Hitler Youth uniforms. Blaz turned to Johann.

"Johann?"

Johann glanced up.

"What does your father do?"

Johann paused at this. He slowly began, "H-he is in the navy."

"What did he do before that?"

"He was the town pastor," Johann said in a shaky voice.

"Really? Your dad is our pastor?"

"*Ja.*"

"Did he teach you all these things?"

"*Ja*, he knew how to do so many things," Johann replied but his focus was not with his teammates. His eyes wandered at nothing in particular.

Ivo entered in, "You must have a lot of skills. We saw some today and Schlusser thinks highly of you. But, you seem very quiet, even around other children your own age. Why is that?"

A tear escaped Johann's eyes and ran down his cheek. He quickly wiped it away but all the boys had noticed. Koby walked over to Johann. He got down on a knee. He put his hand on Johann's shoulder.

"Johann, your father is dead, isn't he?"

Johann let out a sob. His face was red from holding back tears. He cried quietly and shook his head '*Ja.*' The boys looked at each other with horrified expressions.

"I'm, I'm sorry, Johann," Blaz consoled the little boy.

Johann looked up at him and tried to smile but he let out another sob. He looked Koby in the eyes. Koby understood, somehow, what the boy meant and gestured for Blaz and Ivo to leave.

Outside, Blaz leaned against one of the school's stone walls. He stared blankly.

Dead. His father is dead. He'll never get to see his father while he grows up.

No advice, no encouragement, no one to comfort him the way only a father can. His father will never get to see his son grow up either. All this pain for Deutschland. Is it worth it?

Blaz blinked several times to clear his head, *Of course it is, you know that, you just wish it wasn't so.*

Blaz nodded to himself. He looked over at Ivo in his uniform. He was staring into space with his mouth half open. Blaz turned to stare down the hallway; *I will see a lot of this in the army. I cannot be fazed by this.*

Blaz didn't know how much time passed when Johann opened the door followed by Koby. He walked with the smallest of strides out to the school gate. When the young boy was out of earshot, Koby spoke, "His father died three and a half weeks ago in the *Kriegsmarine*. They only got the news just eleven days ago."

"What did you two talk about?" Blaz asked.

"I listened to him for the most part. Near the end, I told him his father would want him to be strong and power through. His father was a strong man, powerful speaker. He didn't die in vain."

"*Nein*, he didn't," Ivo said.

"How is he feeling now?" Blaz concernedly asked.

"He's still pretty depressed. I imagine this is why he's acted so shy and quiet. For a child who lost his father, he is taking it better than most. Keeping up with school and sports, he's a tough, little German."

The Communist Threat

September 12, 1940 Thursday

Blaz snapped awake as a loud screech tore through the night. He sprinted out of his room and down the stairs. He ran to his mother's room, but it opened before he reached it. They both knew what was happening: an air raid drill. Blaz held his mother's hand and they marched into the streets of the town and headed for the school. Others were already in the streets. No one ran. They had been instructed to walk quickly but refrain from running, lest they cause panic among the others. When they reached the shelter, a soldier stood guard and allowed people in, one at a time, simply ordering them to hand him any weapons they had on hand. The crowd was admitted surprisingly quickly and within minutes they were all safe in the shelter. There they sat, waiting for the drill to be completed. Sirens screamed for what seemed like hours, until they finally fell silent. Schlusser made his way to the exit of the shelter.

"*Hitlerjugend* exit first, make sure it is safe to come out. Women and younger children remain seated," Schlusser ordered.

The commanders of the Hitler Youth led the way out of the underground shelter. Blaz tagged along right behind Koby, near the front. When they exited, a hand grabbed one commander. The cadet spun and was held by the neck. A voice said in a thick Russian accent, "No one moves or call for help or I will shoot him." A pistol cocked. Two silhouettes stepped from the shadows holding machine guns. On their backs were parachutes, faintly visible in the darkness. A truck engine roared on the field. "Shut the door, no one else may exit," the voice said again.

Blaz was nearest to the door and Becke, the only eighteen-year-old commander not yet drafted translated, "Close the door." Blaz shut the door. The cadet in a stranglehold said to his comrade, "Don't worry about me, kill the bastard!"

"Silence," the Russian said in German. At this, the dozen Hitler Youth members charged at the three Russians with nothing but their fists. Blaz rushed one of the machine gunners with three other cadets. The boys tackled the soldier, each boy grabbing a limb and immobilizing the man.

"Get the gun," Koby ordered Blaz. Blaz let the soldier's leg go with one arm and reached for the gun. Before he could grab it, a spotlight shone on the scene from the truck. Schlusser ran out of the shelter.

"Stand down, boys!" he ordered.

"Sir, what's going on?" Becke demanded, with surprising ferocity at his officer.

"All a drill, which you passed," Schlusser congratulated the boys, trying to ease the tension.

"Just a drill?" Erich said in surprise, tilting his head.

"*Jawohl*, just a drill. Soldiers need to experience real fear, which I daresay you did here tonight. Fleischer, you performed excellently under that pressure, a life and death situation. All commanders performed excellently protecting our women and young children. Now, you may let our soldiers go."

The cadets realized they were still grasping the limbs of the soldiers. Each released them, the soldiers patted some youth commanders in respect as they stood up.

"Now before we open the shelter up each cadet out here, give me your name. Line up!"

"Tybalt Glöckner."

"Erwin Kauffman."

"Simon Vogel."

"Lawrence Schmid."

"Jaeger Kramer."

"Riocard Hilderbrand."

"Walter Ebner."

"Ulrich Fleischer."

"Erich Meyer."

"Hans Ristig."

"Koby Hertz."

"Blaz Senft."

"*Danke*," Schlusser said casually. Then he opened the door to the shelter. "*Austreten*, come out! All is well."

SS March

September 14, 1940 Saturday

"Beat you!" Jarman laughed.

"Good match," Blaz replied and shook his arm. They both stood up to make room for Koby and Erich. The two boys got down on their knees and clasped hands from across the small, short table.

"Ready, set, go!" Ivo exclaimed.

Both boys began to push against the other's arm. The rest all shouted for their pick to win. Erich got an early advantage. Koby's arm began to move slowly to the surface of the table.

"Koby, keep it down, please!" Koby's mother called.

"Got it, mother!" Koby gritted out. A surge of energy burst through him and he suddenly pushed Erich's arm back. Erich continued his constant barrage of pressure on Koby. Slowly, but surely, Erich kept Koby on the defensive. When he was inches away from victory, he turned his head to the window. The boys quieted down. A distant noise could be heard. A melody. Koby noticed Erich's inattentiveness and gave all the strength he had to attempt to pin his arm. Erich's arm flew back toward the table. Right before it touched, Erich swung his arm up and pinned Koby without looking back up.

"Ow! I thought I could get you," Koby muttered.

By now the melody was much closer. The boys stood. They could hear marching. They ran outside as the sound of music grew louder.

"What is that?" Ivo asked, gazing down the street.

As the sound came closer, goose-stepping German soldiers came into view. Several women and boys had come outside to see what the noise was. The soldiers marched closer onward. Blaz could see the first squad of soldiers up close: SS. Clad in black uniforms with bright red armbands, each soldier held an MP-40 as they goose-stepped down the main street of Seelow. In the middle, were the musicians. Clad in field gray, they beat drums and played a variety of brass and woodwind instruments.

"*Das ist Preußens Gloria!*" Erich exclaimed, regarding the song.

Behind the musicians marched over a hundred men wearing the field gray uniform of the *Wehrmacht* and dome-shaped helmets with curved edges. Each separate group of soldiers held guns of all kinds. Blaz recognized them all. Karabiner 98K, *Machinenpistole-40* or MP-40, *Maschinengewehr-34* or MG-34 and even Mauser anti-tank rifles were represented by the company.

The soldiers cheered, "*Sieg Heil!*" to end their song. Some of the boys and women cheered for the soldiers. Blaz watched each soldier pass and walked along with them as they goose-stepped past. One soldier on the edge of the line turned his head to Blaz. He grinned at him and winked. Blaz smiled back. The soldier returned his focus to marching. Blaz waved as he left. He'd been so mesmerized by the soldiers that he hadn't noticed a tank rolling behind them.

"A *Panzer III!*" a young voice shouted.

The soldiers marched off in the direction of the Heights. Blaz ran back to where his friends stood. They watched the soldiers march further until they were far off into The Heights, before turning back inside.

"That was so cool!" Ivo exclaimed.

"A full division!" Koby said, "And the SS!"

"Packing armor too!" Jurgen added as he knelt to the table to challenge anyone. Ivo knelt and took his hand.

"Where do you think they are headed?" Jarman asked.

"Probably to reinforce the Heights or some city in the Eastern Reich," Erich suggested.

"Why? The fighting is in the west," Blaz pointed out. Just then Ivo's arm slammed against the table.

"Darn it!"

"The *Führer* suspects the Communists may attack us, that's what we've been told in our training. Why else do you think we had that drill?" Koby told them while gesturing to Erich, "And Communism has been used by the Jews to butcher millions of Eastern Europeans."

"*Ja*, but that company, maybe even division, had a lot of offensive weapons. They had some tank rifles and rocket launchers. Not to mention, a *Panzer*!" Ivo observed.

"I don't know what the SS and *Wehrmacht* are doing here," Koby admitted, "But there's no way we would get in a tangle with the Soviet Union before we defeat Britain."

"That's the truth," Blaz agreed with repeated nods from the group.

Koby's Special Training

September 16, 1940 Monday

The age leaders were ready to go. Koby had already started running to the Heights. Blaz, Ivo, and Johann waited by the gate with Schlusser for the leaders. Schlusser kept glancing back, as if expecting each second would make a leader come out of the school. He noticed Blaz, Ivo, and Johann looking up at him for instruction.

"Senft? Klein? Steiner?" he asked.

"*Jawohl.*"

"You three may begin running to The Heights. Koby will show you where to stop. From now on you may leave when he does. And he'll give you instructions on what to ready for our training."

"As you command, *Herr*," they replied obediently.

The three Germans ran down the street and towards the hills. Johann took the lead at a fast pace. Blaz and Ivo stayed within a few dozen meters. When they reached the Heights, they scanned for the training area. On top of a hill, Johann spotted a maze of trenches, bunkers, and watchtowers inside of the hill across.

"Is that it?" he called back, pointing to the German defense network.

"*Nein*, that's part of the army's defenses," Blaz called, "We will point out the training grounds. We've been there more times than your age."

Johann turned back around and kept running. A few hundred meters along the winding dirt road they came to the grounds. Johann recognized it immediately and ran in. Blaz and Ivo followed.

"Thought he'd been here before," Ivo whispered.

Koby jogged out to meet them.

"*Gut*, you are here. How was the run?"

"*Gut*."

"I suppose I should tell you where we will be. Johann, you were given the schedule?"

Johann nodded in confirmation. The young Hitler Youth officer wandered to a grove of trees with targets on them. He unsheathed his knife and threw it at one of the targets on the lines up trees. Koby returned his focus to Blaz and Ivo.

"Today we are working the artillery and anti-aircraft guns."

This news excited the two cadets.

"Really? Sweet! This will be great!" Ivo rambled while his legs shook in excitement.

"Shut it, Ivo," Koby sighed, irritation in his voice, and he rolled his eyes, "That will be our first job in the army."

Blaz glowered at Koby, who caught this look. He stared back at Blaz trying to appear authoritarian.

"What was that glare for?" Koby asked.

"What was with your tone? Are you annoyed?"

Ivo stood still, watching the argument he seemed to have unknowingly triggered. Johann kicked at the dirt.

"I'm trying to keep us on target."

"I understand that, Koby. But you never talk like that."

"Don't talk back, cadet," Koby shot back, unintentionally awkwardly.

"Don't change yourself for this position. If you aren't able to be in the SS without changing your personality, then maybe you just aren't cut out for it," Blaz said, using the language that he rarely used to get the point across. Johann nodded multiple times at Koby.

Koby stilled. He stared at Blaz, eyes stone cold, trying to break a cadet into submission and Blaz, trying to recover his friend. Blaz steadied himself for a punch, if Koby threw one. Koby's icy expression slid into a look of shock, seeming to reclaim himself. For the first time in Blaz's life, Koby was speechless. Koby bent down and put his hands on his knees. He stayed there for a few moments. Blaz walked over to him. Koby looked up.

"I'm sorry, Blaz, I'm sorry," Koby breathed, "I… I don't know where that came from. I've never said anything like that before. It was almost like it wasn't me."

"It wasn't," Blaz agreed.

Koby stared.

"You have never had a position of this much authority over us. Now that you have it, you don't know what to do with it. It's not that you are a bad leader, you just shouldn't change your character into something… cruel, to fit into the role of a commander. It isn't for you," Blaz explained, "My papa said you should be careful about changing your principles before he left."

Koby straightened up. He took off his cap and extended a hand. Blaz took it and they shook.

"*Danke* Blaz. I am glad you caught that," Koby turned to Ivo, "Sorry for that tone I used, it was completely unnecessary and arrogant of me."

"No harm done, *Freund*," Ivo assured him. Johann grinned. Koby's attention was drawn to something behind Blaz.

"Looks like the other officers are here. Follow me to the artillery. *Bitte?*" Koby joked. Blaz shot him a smile and followed.

"Load them with these blanks," Koby told them, pointing to some ammunition crates. Koby began to load an anti-aircraft gun. Blaz and Ivo followed suite. By the time they'd finished, the other cadets had arrived. Schlusser ordered them over to the cannons where he commanded Koby to give a demonstration of how to fire one type of AA gun. Schlusser himself demonstrated another gun. Soon the cadets were firing AA guns, most of them picking it up immediately. Blaz stepped onto the AA gun and fired it several blanks and rotated the gun towards different targets. Koby nodded in approval then waved in the next cadet.

"Typical day at the farm," Ivo joked at Blaz when he came over.

"It's getting easy to do all this, like first instinct."

"Then we will be that much better in combat," Ivo said.

In the Homeland Lives a Girl

September 20, 1940 Friday

"Auf die Plätze, Fertig! Los!" Schlusser screamed at the top of his lungs. The early teen group of the Hitler Youth shot off the starting line. Koby sprinted for the lead. Blaz and Ivo dashed off behind him.

Don't get caught in the pack, Blaz thought.

The runners narrowly made it into the lead before the course thinned. Koby's lead was definitive within minutes and Blaz concentrated on second. He and Ivo kept a respectable lead over the other Hitler Youth boys but all of them were well conditioned, no one stood out as bad. Blaz and Ivo ran at their best pace to avoid any dangerous sprinters at the end. The looped course was hilly at points but it was flat stretches that they took advantage of. When the finish was in view Blaz pumped his arms and legs faster and harder. Ivo began his sprint at the same time. Ivo pulled ahead of Blaz but was clearly exhausted. Ivo swerved to try to cut Blaz off, but Blaz readjusted and reclaimed the lead. The finish line was only one hundred meters away and Ivo gave a desperate chase but was simply too tired to catch Blaz.

"Good work, Senft! You too, Klein!" Schlusser congratulated them.

"Move along, move along," one of the age group leaders instructed them.

Blaz and Ivo stumbled away from the finish to where Koby stood, already recovered.

"Good job guys, I think you got nineteen thirty-one and nineteen thirty-four."

Blaz pumped his fist.

"Ah, the other runners are coming in," Koby pointed.

Several fifteen-year-olds flew past the finish. A huge pack came behind, with Reinhardt, Jarman, and Erich. Jurgen came with the next pack, with a respectable final sprint. When the last pack passed the line Schlusser yelled the final time, "Twenty-three thirty-two!" The boys put their hands on the backs of their heads or bent down to catch a breath.

"Our three representatives for ages thirteen to fifteen at this moment would be Koby Hertz, Blaz Senft, and Ivo Klein. Today were our first tryouts. Next week we will do all the other exercises. After that we will have two more for each category. One in mid-October and one in the first week of November. That way I will know who to use that will best represent our unit. With that said, ages sixteen to eighteen, on your marks!"

While the older cadets lined up the young cadets sat down to recover.

"Good run everyone," Koby told the group.

"*Danke*," several said.

The boys rested at the foot of a hill near the starting line.

"*Auf die Plätze! Fertig! Los!*" Schlusser shouted.

The older cadets shot off from the line with much more power and flare than the younger groups.

"How has school been for everyone?" Erich asked.

"It's been fine."

"*Gut.*"

"School is school."

An awkward silence ensued.

"That went nowhere," Erich said, "What do you guys want to talk about? Politics, the war, sports?"

"Can we talk about the army's caps?" Ivo asked, "I just have been wondering what all your favorite ones are. Do you like the peaked caps officers wear? Or the ones that look like folded paper boats? I think those are cool."

The group looked at Ivo. A few smiled a bit.

"Oh, shut up, Ivo," Jarman rolled his eyes.

"I've been wondering when Erich will ask Eva out," Reinhardt began. Erich blushed when everyone looked at him.

"What's the point right now? We leave in a few months," Jurgen said.

"Who is she?" Koby said to Reinhardt.

"What?"

"Who is she?"

Reinhardt looked at Koby, "No one."

Koby raised his eyebrows and looked away with an unbelieving face.

"What? You don't believe me?"

"*Nein*," Koby admitted, "You are too quiet usually. You don't bring up things so randomly."

Reinhardt looked down and his face turned red. "Okay, but we aren't dating or anything. We just talk to each other in between classes and after school sometimes."

"Ooh," some of the boys said obnoxiously.

"What's the young lady's name?"

"Tini Vogel," Reinhardt answered, face still red.

"Ah, Tini Vogel, nice girl, cute too," Jarman teased.

"I can't believe Reinhardt got a girlfriend before any of us," Erich said, "Tini isn't quiet either."

"Probably likes men who keep their mouth shut," Ivo said.

"She does do a lot of the talking," Reinhardt smiled.

"You should ask her on a date," Erich said.

Reinhardt shook his head.

"Really," Erich persisted, "You've got a few months. Ask her out."

SS Discipline

September 23, 1940 Monday

Erich pushed the bar up for another rep on the bench press. His arms shook as he lowered it to his chest. Boys cheered for Erich and another boy of equally strong build, Marvin.

"Again!" Schlusser yelled.

Erich pushed the weight up once more. Marvin got it just halfway his chin before his arms gave out. His spotter helped him bring the weight to its place. Schlusser wrote down something onto a clipboard.

"All right! Shooting! Last event!"

The cadets, young and old, headed to the firing range.

"Rifle! Ages ten to twelve!"

The youngest cadets took their rifles. At the line, they loaded the rifles and cocked them. Each barrel rose to aim at the fresh targets.

"One shot each! *Feuer*!"

Ear-piercing shots rang out. Smoke gusted from each rifle.

"At ease!"

All the cadets lowered their rifles. Each target was unused so Schlusser could tell where the bullet had hit. The older officers and Schlusser walked by the cadets writing down where their shots had landed.

"Next age group!"

Blaz marched to the far side of the range and picked up the deserted rifle left behind by the former occupant. A click, and the safety was off. Another click and the rifle was cocked and ready to be fired.

"Ready! Aim! *Feuer*!"

Another wave of shots was fired. Once again, the older cadets wrote down evaluations.

"Oldest age group!"

The oldest children took their positions at the line. When Schlusser gave the order, they fired. Koby and Erich wrote down evaluations and reported to Schlusser.

"All cadets, aside from leaders and runners, return to Seelow!"

The cadets took off quickly and Schlusser spoke to the remaining cadets.

"For those of you who are leaders, you will remain here after each session for additional training to be field officers or SS. Senft, Klein, and Steiner. You are to assist in cleanup for today. Unload guns, replace targets, and such, starting today. Senft, unload the guns! Klein, put the empty magazines in their crates! Steiner, pick up the rifle discharges! When you are done, put the rifles in the armory. The rest of you come with me."

Blaz, Ivo, and Johann marched to the firing range and got to work. Blaz unloaded each rifle, making sure to point them down the range. One magazine at a time. He handed each to Ivo, who placed them into a wooden crate that he pushed down the range. Johann picked up each shell and put it in a small box for recycling. First, they unloaded the pistols, next rifles, and then they moved on to the machine guns. The work was slow but eventually only a few remained. Blaz picked up one of the last machine guns and tried to discharge the mag. But it wouldn't budge.

"Come on," Blaz muttered to himself. He balanced the weapon on his knee to gain leverage, keeping it aimed down the range. He pulled even harder on the machine gun to get the magazine out, but it remained stuck. Without warning, the gun fired and Blaz fell onto his back from the sudden burst. The gun landed facing away from the range, unloading bullets. Ivo and Johann both jumped back, startled. The gun fired its entire magazine, hitting trees and slicing through air before it stopped. When they had gotten over the shock, each boy looked at each other in terror.

"Oh, *nein, nein, nein,*" Blaz whimpered as he scrambled to his feet.

"What are we going to do?" Johann asked in panic, "Schlusser could be here any second."

"Or worse, just a random officer," Ivo added.

"It was my fault, I'll take the heat," Blaz shuddered, *"Oh Gott."*

At that moment, two soldiers came sprinting toward the boys. One wore the standard army uniform of field gray, the other the jet black of the SS. Blaz's heart sank.

"What the hell was that?!" the SS soldier screamed at the boys, "What were you doing with these machine guns?! Shooting away from the range too!"

"W-w-we were un-unloading them, sir," Blaz stuttered, feeling quite small.

"You certainly were! You could have killed someone! Who fired it?!" he shouted at the boys.

"I did," Blaz squeaked.

"Come with me," the SS soldier ordered.

Blaz shuffled between the two soldiers. He had no idea what they would do to him, even for an accident. When the soldiers knew Ivo and Johann couldn't see them, they stopped.

"Stand here," the SS trooper told Blaz. He took his gloves off and popped his knuckles. Before he made another move, the *Wehrmacht* soldier put a hand on the trooper's shoulder. His gaze skittered sideways. The SS soldier followed him a few meters away from Blaz.

"Emmett, he's just a little kid. Don't hurt him," the *Wehrmacht* soldier said with concern.

"Shut up, Decker. He fired a gun without permission from an officer on military grounds. We are strict in the military. If we let people fire guns all the time, then we won't know when someone is truly attacking. Mistakes must be disciplined, otherwise they'll be repeated," the SS soldier replied coldly.

"He's not in the *Wehrmacht*, he's in the *Jugend*."

"He'll be in the *Wehrmacht* soon. He needs to learn discipline and obedience."

"But he's so young!"

"Even more reason to start now."

The *Wehrmacht* trooper sighed and relented. The SS soldier nodded approvingly. Emmett strode over to the cadet and raised his fist. Blaz breathed in, ready for the punishment. The fist came fast and hard. Pain shot through Blaz's ribs and he gasped for air. The young boy stumbled backwards into a tree. He clutched his chest in agony. Never in his life had he been beaten this hard. Not even by another cadet during training. The SS soldier hit Blaz across the face, not nearly as hard as before but still with great force. Blaz collapsed to his knees. His eyes welled up, but he fought it back. Tears would get him no sympathy.

"You are tough, young man," the soldier said as he raised a fist to hit Blaz once again when a voice yelled, "*Nicht so schnell, gemeiner Soldat!*" Not so fast, trooper. Emmett and Decker looked up. Walking through the trees was *Herr* Schlusser.

"What do you want?" Emmett snapped.

"That is my cadet you are beating," Schlusser said methodically to the older soldier, "Why?"

"He fired a gun," Emmet replied.

"Did he now?" Schlusser asked with added interest, "You do know I had them practicing shooting today?"

"Don't give me that, they were done. We can't have people randomly firing guns."

"Was anyone hurt?" Schlusser asked calmly and coolly.

"*Nein*, but the gun wasn't aimed down the range."

Schlusser shot a stern look at Blaz, but continued his calm, taunting tone, "I am confused at why you took it into your own hands to beat this cadet, though. You know I am his instructor."

Emmett glared at *Herr* Schlusser. "What right do you have to lecture me?" the SS soldier challenged the instructor.

Reynald Schlusser's smile vanished. No trace of empathy or enjoyment remained. The young instructor removed his jacket. Underneath was a white, sleeveless shirt. Schlusser raised his right arm to reveal the blood group tattoo of the *Waffen-SS* near his armpit. Emmett kept a straight face. Schlusser did not stop there.

"I have every right," *Herr* Schlusser said commandingly, then showed the colored ranking on his uniform, "As a former *Waffen-SS* member during the Polish conflict and current *Allgemeine-SS Untersturmführer*, I can say what I want to you, private."

"I was giving him some discipline," Emmett explained, caught off guard by the rank of the Hitler Youth instructor.

"A man after my own heart if ever there was one," Schlusser replied with a cruel smile, "But I have my own methods of discipline that I will carry out myself for my own cadets. Next time bring them straight to me."

"You are no more qualified to deal with them than I am."

"I assure you private, only the best candidates become *Hitlerjugend* instructors. It is a monumentally important job. Now, I expect you to bring any cadets who step out of line-" he punched an unwary Blaz across the face with a gloved hand, "Straight to me."

Emmett nodded in understanding and gestured for Decker to follow him. Decker gave Schlusser a nod of respect, before striding away. Schlusser turned. He hit Blaz in the face again. But this time, Blaz noticed it was very light.

"I am sorry, Senft. I'm angrier with that private than you. But nonetheless, you will receive further discipline for firing that gun. It sets the base into an unnecessary alert, and you need to be careful with guns anyway."

Blaz stayed still.

Schlusser sighed. "Why? Why did you not aim it at the range?"

Blaz nervously did not answer.

"Answer me, Senft," Schlusser said with surprising calmness.

"I-I did aim down the range, but when it started firing all of a sudden... I dropped it."

Schlusser frowned, "Son, you can't drop a gun like that. If it had landed the wrong way... you could've shot yourself or Klein and Steiner."

Blaz looked at the ground in disgrace. Schlusser glanced down at him.

"All right, here is your punishment," the officer finally said. Schlusser reached for Blaz's Hitler Youth knife. The sheath was undone and the knife removed. Blaz looked up at it desperately. He'd already been beaten! Now this!

"You will get this back in two weeks."

Two weeks!

"*Jawohl*, sir."

"Okay, back to Klein and Steiner. I'm not finished with our older cadets," Schlusser walked away but turned around and with a smile added, "Please don't start anything."

Blaz let a cautious grin escape. Schlusser walked back to where the leaders were. Blaz followed him until they reached Ivo and Johann who were both seated under a tree. Blaz trudged over to them.

"Hey Blaz," Ivo said.

Blaz sat down. Ivo glanced his way, did a double take, then exclaimed, "*Oh Gott*! Your eye is red!"

Blaz felt just below his eye. He pressed down with two fingers. A dull pain surged through his cheekbone.

"What happened?"

"I got beaten by the SS soldier."

He lifted his uniform up. Underneath, his fair skin was marred red from the punch.

"Woah," breathed Ivo and Johann.

"Schlusser hit me twice but I bet the red eye wasn't from him."

"You've got red under the other eye. Not as much though."

Additional marks didn't surprise Blaz by now. "Schlusser told me he'd discipline me. Then, then-"

"What?"

Blaz took a deep breath, "He took my knife away."

"*Nein!*"

"*Ja.*"

"How long?"

"Two weeks."

"Wow," Ivo said, gritting his teeth briefly.

Blaz touched his empty sheath, sadly. After Blaz's first documented run, which had been impressive to Schlusser, he was awarded the knife of the Hitler Youth. It meant more to him than any object in the world.

"I'm really sorry about that, Blaz," Ivo said as he came and sat down next to his friend, "It sucks to not have your knife. The other cadets can act like real *arschlochen* when that happens. My brother told me all about when his knife got taken. Anyone who wasn't a friend treated him like a Jewish banker. Everyone just ignored him. He never had the best classmates though."

Blaz shivered, "And I thought I was starting to get somewhere in the *Jugend*."

"It is just a knife," Johann said naively.

"*Nein*, it's not. It's more than that. It's a symbol of us becoming men. It's the identity of the *Hitlerjugend*," explained Ivo, as if it was common knowledge.

Johann looked to Blaz.

"*Ja*, it is," Blaz confirmed.

The boys sat in silence, just thinking about the events that had unfolded.

Why was I the one unloading the guns? Could have happened to anyone just as easily. At least it didn't hit anyone. But that beating hurt.

The older cadets ran by without a word. Koby and Erich stayed behind to talk with Blaz and Ivo. Johann stayed near the older children but didn't speak.

"What happened to you?" Koby asked.

"I got beaten by an SS soldier for accidentally firing a gun."

"Your eyes are red!"

"I know," Blaz replied with a deep breath.

"What did he do to you?" Erich asked.

"He punched me in the ribs, and I got hit three times in the face."

"That's tough."

"Schlusser took away my knife, too," Blaz said, pointing to his empty sheath.

Koby and Erich's expressions changed from sympathy to a vague bit of disappointment in their friend, as if this revealed something about what Blaz had done. Blaz, nor Ivo, nor Johann, noticed.

"Well, it's time to head back. I will see you there, sorry about that Blaz," Koby waved as he took off.

"Try to stay in line," Erich advised, and he too ran away.

"I'd like to know what they are learning with Schlusser," Blaz commented when they were out of earshot.

"*Ja*," Ivo agreed

Blaz and Ivo locked eyes, understanding setting in. They were in an army, their friends were growing up, perhaps faster than them. Things were stricter, but it was for the greater good. They were just learning to be mature, cooperative men.

"*In die Zukunft ziehen wir Mann für Mann?*" Ivo asked.

"*Wir sind die Zukunft soldaten.*"

September 27, 1940 Friday

Ivo's prediction came true and the Hitler Youth boys began to ignore Blaz during their sessions. However, the boys were too trained and orderly to truly bully him, which Blaz had expected. Schlusser's command meant everyone would be busy nearly every second they were at the Heights. A few of his friends seemed to have an odd attitude towards him though. Jarman didn't talk with him much even when the group was in a conversation. Koby still talked with him but there was a clear barrier. Blaz's now black eye remained a reminder every time they saw him that he'd stepped out of line.

Even after I talked to him. Hopefully, at running tomorrow, Koby will open up, Blaz prayed.

During the session Blaz had hung near Ivo, Jurgen, and Reinhardt. Schlusser had announced they would be going on a three-day hike to improve marching distance the next week. Blaz hoped that before the upcoming Wednesday, his friends would be on speaking terms with him.

Schlusser's Instructions

September 30, 1940 Monday

After a rather cold session on Monday, the runners were at school preparing to go home. All the leaders and cadets had already left. Their bags were packed, and times set.

"Almost there!" Ivo said with excitement to Blaz and Koby, "Just tomorrow and then we leave!"

"It's just a hike, not the war," Koby groaned, rolling his eyes, "Don't get excited. Why do you have to act like such a child?"

Blaz closed his eyes in frustration.

"*Ja*, well, it's exciting to me," Ivo scowled.

"See you guys," Johann waved, recognizing this was not his place to interfere.

"*Auf wiedersehen*, Johann," Blaz replied.

"*Auf wiedersehen*," Ivo called.

Koby gave a wave. Blaz looked at Ivo and gestured for him to leave after pointing to Koby, who was packing his bag. Ivo nodded and walked towards the gate.

"Koby, we need to talk," Blaz said, putting a hand on his shoulder.

"What about?" Koby said without looking up.

"You," Blaz replied, "What is going on? You haven't been yourself. We talked about this a few weeks ago, even. You're still acting like that. I don't even think there was any difference, except that day."

"It's a part of being a leader," Koby answered.

"*Nein*, it's not. Erich is a leader and he's still acting like himself. I mean, we are all going to change while we get older. But you're acting completely different. You remember when you started playing with those children? And when you talked to Johann about his father?"

Koby looked up from his bag. "*Ja*, I do."

"It's good to lead, but when you abandon the people of your country, then what are you really fighting for?" Blaz asked.

Koby didn't answer. Blaz stood in front of his friend, hoping for a reply. None came. Then he turned away and walked towards the gate.

"Blaz!" Koby called.

Blaz turned around. Koby was jogging toward him. "Blaz, I will try to fix this attitude. I really will. I know that I should be able to separate training from life, but I can't yet. But, you need to accept something. We are soldiers, we are going to have to talk rough, and be, you know, jerks to each other to be effective. I'm learning to be a leader in this army. I cannot be soft on anyone, even you guys."

"But when we talk about training, you're so irritated, even disgusted with us. Why?"

Koby sighed, but not with annoyance, "Blaz, that's because I feel you, and *especially* Ivo, don't take things seriously enough. I think Jarman feels that way too. *Deutschland's* future is a serious matter."

"Believe me, I know that. I'd take a bullet for the flag."

"I know you would, but you haven't been trained as extensively as I have." He looked down, "We are National Socialists. We need to bring it to the world. That's a serious matter. We must rescue *Deutschland* from the Jewish tyranny. Also a serious matter."

"How much do you know about what we have done with the Jews? And what they've done to us for that matter?"

Koby smiled. "Listen, I have a lot to tell you. You run with me after school. It won't be a speed run because of the hike. I'll fill you in on all we've learned then."

Die Judenfrage

October 1, 1940 Tuesday

Coach Friederich assigned the boys a time and set them on their way the next day. Koby asked Ivo to run with Johann while he ran with Blaz. With initial reluctance, Ivo agreed when Blaz told him it was okay. When the two boys started running Koby asked Blaz where he wanted to go.

"Open country, how about?"

"Works for me."

They ran a few minutes. It did not take long to get out of the main town.

"Let's begin, shall we?" Koby asked Blaz.

"*Ja*. What is Schlusser teaching you about?" Blaz replied. He took a deep breath to recover some air.

"Okay. First off, in school that we all attend, we have all learned that *Deutschland* alone knows how to make the world better. Some others will listen, like the Arabs, Oswald Mosley, Mussolini, but not enough have and the ones that are responsible for this war must be defeated. National Socialism's message is being warped by the international press of the Jews. But nonetheless, more people are realizing our message. Many Britons sued for peace with us but of course that warmonger Churchill would have none of it. The war broke out in an attempt by the Jews and their allies to destroy our system. We left the world financial system. They can't have that. They must have control. They won't leave countries alone. We've been forced to fight but in doing so, we can spread National Socialism's true message to the world. And our generation will lead it to this. The *Führer* knows this, so he wants *Deutschland's* youth to be prepared to do just that."

"*Ja*, we are carrying out the Fatherland's purpose," Blaz said matter-of-factly.

"Exactly. Schlusser has been teaching us to be the leaders of the leaders. When *Deutschland* secures its Reich, we will be the heads of it. The

Reich won't run itself, it needs our help. That's why cadets like Erich and I have been selected from the German youth, we are the best of the best. That's why I have been so critical of you guys. I assure you, I don't mean to come across the way I do. I'm just very serious about this."

"Of course, as you should," Blaz agreed.

"Our job is to lead you to defeat the Jewish-controlled, enslaved nations. Some people who deliberately stand in the way of peace must be dealt with. When we have done that, *Deutschland* will have peace. We will govern it. I don't know where we will be in the rankings, but I suspect, regional governors, city leaders, and officers in the army."

Blaz took this in. "When do you think this'll happen?"

"Whenever we liberate another nation we get closer to defeating the Jewish World Order. You know we control part of North Africa now. The Arabs are very sympathetic to our views too. The Reich is already spreading. We hope that our message can one day reach the whole world. Each people should govern themselves, be free of outsiders who claim to represent them. Free from any British Empire, free from tribal warfare, free from Jewish international banks, free from Capitalist corruption, free from Jewish tyranny. Each country will unite to protect and serve its own people. What Schlusser makes sure to stress is that the enemy is not Jews so much as it is International Jewry. They are the ones in positions of influence in countries that are not their own. They want a global world with no identity, no people to love. It will just be one giant economy, with workers as little more than replaceable parts in a machine, and endless consumption by the masses. But as the *Führer* says, 'The people must not follow. The people are bound to their soil! Bound to their homeland! Bound to the possibilities of life that the state, the nation has to offer.'"

"What else are you learning?"

Koby eagerly answered, "Methods of controlling populations of occupied lands, our leaders have learned Russian. That's been a focal point of our training."

"How much do you know?"

Koby rattled something off. Blaz had no idea what he said.

"Russian? What is it you said?" he asked with a grin.

"'I know enough to speak with a Russian', that's what I said. My vocabulary could be better though. If I knew more words I could put them into sentences. We've learned words like 'I', 'we', 'the', 'that.' All the little words make a good springboard."

"While we are on the foreign topic, what about the Jews? What are we doing with them?"

"Schlusser talks with us individually about that. He has been telling me, personally, that we keep many quarantined as they would only destroy and protest our society if they were free. There would certainly be saboteurs, assassins too like the one who killed our ambassador in France a few years ago. Quarantining is a wartime measure. They are taken care of in exchange for work. We plan to deport them to Madagascar where they can set up their society and leave the world in peace. We will help them get their society running there as well."

"That's good, that actually sounds like pretty nice treatment for them. Better than I expected, based on how we talk about them in school."

"*Ja*, that's what I think," Koby agreed, "We don't want them spreading their ideas like they did in the Soviet Union. We all know how that ended up: Millions dead. That's another thing we learned about, The specifics of the Soviet Union. One of their tribe named Kaganovich exterminated ten million Ukrainians through starvation. Yezhov has murdered tens of thousands of Poles and other Slavs. The Jew Yakov Yurovksy butchered the Tsar of Russia and his whole family under orders from another member of his tribe, Yakov Sverdlov. Leon Trotsky is also a Jew. I can keep going."

"Trust me, I understand. Bolshevism *is* Judaism."

"*Ja*."

"So now that I know what's been going on we need to get things straightened out," Blaz told Koby, "Ivo and I will be serious about training and the fight ahead."

"And I won't act like an asshole for no reason."

"All right, glad we have that fixed," Blaz said as he breathed in deeply.

"*Ja*, we're friends, we can get past little things like that. And we need to stand together for *Deutschland*, not argue."

"*Unsere Fahne flattert uns voran*," Blaz began to sing the Hitler Youth banner song. Koby joined him on the next verse as they approached the gate.

Forward to the West

October 2, 1940 Wednesday

Schlusser barked out orders in the school courtyard. The day of the trek had come. Each boy was preparing his bag with the necessary provisions. However, Schlusser told them they would only be allowed to pack three meals. This was to test them when they ran out of food in the real army. Only a canteen of water was allowed. Schlusser had checked to make sure each boy had not snuck extra provisions or water in their uniforms. None had. He had also told the girls they would remain at school. The girl's female instructor gave them sessions organized by herself, generally without Schlusser's presence.

Reynald Schlusser expressed a unique interest in the boys' unit. Perhaps because he was a soldier and relished the chance at making more. The bags were heavy, not with school work but with water, food, and dead weight. Since no guns would be brought by the youth, each bag was loaded with heavy rocks or metal to give a feel for a soldier's burden.

"This will be unsupervised by myself for many of you. I will only accompany the ten, eleven, and twelve-year-olds. Each age group will obey their group leaders while hiking. I have told them which way to go. Once you have hiked one and a half days in that direction, return to Seelow."

"Now without further ado, let's be on our way," he gestured to the younger children.

Not long after the youngest children had departed, other groups began to leave, one by one. Erich took charge of his group before many groups had departed.

"March! Four rows of five!"

The boys organized into this formation.

"Let's go!" Koby yelled to the group when the church bells tolled eight o'clock. The boys marched out of the school gate and into the streets. Many women smiled at them. The Hitler Youth looked ahead proudly. Every step was professional. Marching like the *Wehrmacht*. Outside of the town, Koby and Erich allowed normal walking. The two leaders conferred together. A map given to them by Schlusser would guide them around the area. However, the map was one of Seelow and her surrounding area. Not one handmade to find an objective. They had to make their own objective, which Koby and Erich did.

"This way!" Erich ordered the squads.

The boys headed west, toward Berlin. However, there was little chance the boys could make it to the capitol. Most of the boys didn't think Berlin was even a feasible goal. It was almost seventy kilometers away. Koby had other ideas. He kept up a very fast pace. For hours, the boys marched on, trying to keep pace with their leader through the tall grass and farmland. But long marches become tiring no matter what terrain if done long enough. Finally, when the group was at exhaustion from no water, Koby ordered a halt. "Rest break!" He looked down at the watch given to him that morning, "You have five minutes!"

The boys sat down and took out their canteens.

"*Was Uhr ist es?* What time is it?" one boy asked Koby.

"*Elf uhr dreißig*, eleven thirty."

The boy nodded and took a swig out of his canteen. Blaz took a drink from his canteen but put it away to save some. Ivo took a long drink before putting away his as well. Five minutes had passed. Koby and Erich got the cadets to their feet, and the march continued. Blaz felt fine for a half hour after the break, though he marched silently while other boys talked to each other. Soon, his legs weakened again. The other boys were wearing out too. They marched on with far less enthusiasm than in each boy's gait while conversations had ground to halt. Koby and Erich noticed this and started a march song.

Es zittern die morschen Knochen,
Der Welt vor dem großen Krieg,
Wir haben den Schrecken gebrochen,
Für uns war's ein großer Sieg.

The rotten bones are trembling,
Of the World before the Great War.
We have smashed this terror,
For us it was a great victory.

The boys recognized the Hitler Youth song immediately and joined their commanders.

Wir werden weiter marschieren
Wenn alles in Scherben fällt,
Denn heute da hört uns Deutschland
Und morgen die ganze Welt.

We will continue to march,
When everything falls apart;
Because today Germany hears us,
And tomorrow the whole world.

The plan worked. Everyone straightened up and marched on with renewed enthusiasm and confidence. Blaz's strides were longer and steadier. In his head, he sang the song to keep his spirits up. Eventually, the boys came to a forest. Koby and Erich kept marching into the forest, riding the wave of high morale. The leaders read the map while they marched ahead. Light came down through the tops of the trees. When they knew where the group was they put the map away. Blaz gazed around the forest. Most of the trees in his Eastern Germany home were conifers. They did not change colors but were still majestic. When they'd marched for a while they saw several deciduous trees that were turning yellow.

"Wow," one boy said in awe.

"Where did all these come from?"

"I believe those are larches," Koby told the group while ordering a halt.

"Why do these trees change colors, but others don't?" asked another cadet.

"Something to do with temperature, chlorophyll, and sunlight," Koby told him, "It's not the most interesting process to learn about."

"Say no more."

Erich looked at the watch on Koby's wrist. "You know what? I'd say it's time for break. We'll have lunch here. Twenty-five minutes."

Each boy took out a piece of bread and some cold sausage. Not much but enough to sustain more marching. Blaz took a bite out of his bread.

"This is so cool, these trees," Blaz told Ivo, "Just standing in the forest, surrounded by green. And we get to see them."

"It is cool, I wish we had more trees like this around town," Ivo said.

"Do you think Koby wants to make it to Berlin?" Blaz asked Ivo, changing the subject.

"He definitely does. I do too. I haven't been to Berlin in my life."

"*Ja*, me neither. The home of our *Führer*, we really should try to make it," Blaz realized.

The boys finished their lunch. Koby and Erich conferred with one another over which way would leave the forest quickly enough. They quickly agreed on a direction. The boys fell in behind their leaders. A few minutes into the renewed hike, the cadets started to talk among themselves. Blaz marched in silence, as he'd been doing for the past several hours.

"Hey Blaz," a dirty blond, scruffy-haired cadet said, "How has training been with Koby? You know, the Olympics?"

"What?" Blaz said, surprised a cadet was talking to him when he had no knife, "Oh, I'm not training for the Olympics. I just enjoy it and might get into University for running. Koby is making progress though. He could have been in the Olympics this year."

"What about forty-four?" the cadet asked.

"For sure," Blaz affirmed.

"He runs what, high fifteens?"

"*Ja*, our first race is next week on Tuesday, so we'll find out how much he has improved."

"Do you think our grade will get to go cheer him on?"

"I would hope so," Blaz replied, "What have you been up to, Jaye? Aren't you playing football?"

"Ah, *ja*. I think you've seen us practicing before and after your runs though?"

"*Ja, ja*. But I'm normally paying attention to coach. Plus, there are a lot of you and you are on the far end of the field. How have you done this year?"

"All the ages from ten to fourteen have to form one team, so I don't play much," Jaye explained, "I'm not the best player, really."

"Do you like the *Jugend*?"

"*Ja*, it's a team that I get to 'play on.' Aside from some of those boring meetings, I love learning all this stuff. We are all so much fitter and stronger. I used to be so skinny. We'll be ready to carry out the *Führer's* will soon. We're going to defeat anyone who will fight us, even the Soviets," Jaye said with uncanny confidence.

Blaz nodded in reluctant agreement. *Why is it that you aren't so eager to fight? I am, I am. Is it the harsh talk about the Jews? Koby told you they're being contained, don't worry about them. They only spread conflict and immorality, it's just like an animal. Worse than an animal. Nein, it's not, what am I thinking? Ja, it is. Why didn't they help our people when times were hard? They had money. They tried to make things worse. They don't care about you. And don't think that because one is nice, the entire society could be. But what about the nice ones? They could spread across the world if they are allowed freedom. They would disrupt harmony in nations. You've been shown and told what America is like. Their cultures and peoples bicker among each other. There is no peace with them, no* central loyalty. *That will lead to their downfall, whether they realize it or not. But maybe...*

"Blaz, Blaz?" Jaye kept saying while waving a hand in front of Blaz's eyes. Blaz blinked and looked at Jaye in surprise.

"*Was?* What?" Blaz asked while he shook his head.

"You kind of fazed out for a moment there. What were you doing?" Jaye asked him with a look of concern.

"I was just thinking."

"About what?"

Blaz tried to close the curtain before this could go anywhere, "Nothing, nothing."

"*Nein,* come on, what was it?" Jaye persisted.

"Fine, I was just thinking about how we are going to carry out a new order."

Jaye beamed, interested, "What are your thoughts?"

"I certainly agree something needs to be done. It seems like other races just can't get along. Even if the tables were turned, I doubt it would make a difference, probably would be worse."

"What do you mean?" Jaye inquired.

"I mean that in America the country can never be united because they have no singular culture and people that the citizens are devoted to. They are all raised differently so they are going to fight among each other. In *Deutschland,* England, Japan, there is one culture, one people. Everyone is united for that culture. If a country doesn't have an identity, a culture, a people, then what is it really? Just a strip of land with people living and working in a giant machine. That's why I think the *Führer* sees it necessary to contain Jews, since they cause division. Koby was talking about that."

"Definitely," Jaye agreed enthusiastically, "But America seems to think they are amazing or something even though they can't unite themselves from within. Sure, they have more people-"

"That's why they think they are great," Blaz cut in, "If *Deutschland* was as populated as America with that much land, can you imagine what we could do? All united under one flag, one leader, one people."

"The more Germans, the better. That's the only reason America can ever be powerful. Numbers. Strength in numbers."

"*Ja*, so if half of America shares the same views, then they match *Deutschland* in numbers."

"Fortunately, we won't be at war with them for a while if ever, we'd beat them one-on-one anyway," Jaye pointed out, "We would beat anyone one-on-one."

Hours passed. The boys hiked on chatting and laughing. They'd left the forest long ago and now hiked in open country and farmland. Blaz talked with Jaye for a long time. The two shared their experiences in the Hitler Youth, their hopes for the army, their sports careers and their hobbies. The sun began to set eventually. Koby looked at the watch. It was much too soon to stop. The cadets tramped on. Everyone was in close proximity so they wouldn't lose anyone after sunset. Minutes after all light was gone and total darkness had set in, Koby ordered the cadets to stop. They halted in the middle of a large, grassy field next to a lone tree.

"Okay men, get out your blankets. We are sleeping here tonight. Erich and I will keep watch for wildlife and whatnot. We marched about ten hours today. So tomorrow we wake up before dawn and make for Berlin," Koby informed the twelve and thirteen-year-olds. While the boys set up camp, Erich knelt down on all fours, allowing Koby to stand on his back. Koby drew his knife and started to cut away at a low branch on the tree. The boys took out their blankets and laid them on the ground. While Blaz laid his out, some kids shoved him to the outside.

"You stay out here," Marvin told him, while pointing to the outside of the encampment.

"You should obey orders better, Senft," one boy said, shoving Blaz further out.

"*Ja*, you have no knife, so we are going to have you stay outside," Ivo joined in sarcastically.

The boys taunting Blaz turned their attention to Ivo. The darkness hid Ivo's expression. Marvin put his hands up and laughed, "God," he said, slapping Ivo on the back before he turned to Blaz, "Sorry about that."

The other boys followed Marvin. Ivo set up near Blaz and Jaye.

"Humor is our best friend," he whispered to Blaz.

Koby and Erich had gotten a fire going and each boy took out his dinner. Once again, they had bread and sausage. Koby walked to the cadets and handed a piece of chocolate to each of them.

"Boy, that was a day," Jaye said, exhaling through his nose.

"Sure was," Ivo agreed.

"Even for me that was tough," Jurgen said.

"Ah, Jurgen," Blaz laughed.

Jurgen took a bite from his chocolate. "That's good, refreshing."

"By tomorrow we'll have to find water and food," Ivo reminded them.

"We've been trained for that," answered Blaz.

"It'll be good to test it out," Jaye said. A brief silence ensued. Jaye turned to one of his friends behind him and started talking. Ivo scooted closer to Blaz.

"So how is your new friend?" he asked in a whisper though he already knew Jaye.

"*Gut*. He's a good kid. We had some great conversations."

"That's swell," Jurgen said.

When dinner was finished, boys started falling asleep. One by one they drifted off to sleep. Koby and Erich remained awake, as did Blaz. Koby sat down next to him.

Blaz stayed under his blanket.

"You were a trooper today, Blaz. All of you were."

"*Danke*. You two," Blaz yawned, "You two led us great."

"I appreciate that," Koby thanked Blaz as he stood up. "You'd better get some sleep," he added, "We are going to march hard tomorrow. We're aiming for Berlin."

"I will. *Guten nacht*."

Blaz's eyes remained open. He stared up at the stars. The stars in the rural sky of Germany. Beauty, uncontested. No city lights clouding the view. Just the universe on display.

Berlin

October 3, 1940 Thursday

"Wake up, wake up!" Koby yelled in the morning. Most of the boys woke up immediately. Koby walked around and started shaking those who didn't. Blaz rubbed his eyes. Darkness was still around them.

"*Was Uhr ist es?*" one cadet asked.

"Six twenty," Koby replied.

"When are we moving out?" Jaye said.

"Right now," Erich told him, "Forget breakfast, we only have one meal apiece for the rest of the trip. We should find some water soon though."

"Now, let's go. Sunlight will be here in minutes. Follow Erich and me," Koby ordered.

The boys started to trudge along. Their eyes were still getting used to waking up and the lack of light didn't help them. Sunlight, like Koby said, shone above the skyline very early into the hike. No sun was visible, just the red, orange and yellow clouds from its light. A sunrise in the open country is a sight to behold and when the sun came up the boys all stared in awe as they marched. The sky was painted red, orange, blue, and yellow. A ball of red rose. No one said a word. All marched ahead with their eyes glued to the sky. After several minutes, someone spoke up. "That was incredible."

"There it is!" one boy yelled. It was still late morning and they had reached Berlin. The whole platoon cheered. Everyone fast walked to make it to the city. Their packs didn't slow them down.

Inside of Berlin, the country boys marveled at the capital city. At the old buildings from centuries ago, great architecture, Berliners, and swastika banners made up the scenery. Eleven soldiers; an officer and ten troopers in the black uniforms of the *Allgemeine-SS* marched up to Koby and Erich. They examined the group seeing them to be very dirty and worn out despite the enthusiastic faces.

"*Heil* Hitler," the officer said giving the salute.

"*Heil* Hitler!"

"What are the *Hitlerjugend* up to today? Shouldn't you be in school?"

"We are the *Hitlerjugend* unit of Seelow," Erich answered respectfully showing him their district number.

"Ah, the head of the *Lebus* district, Seelow. And why are you in Berlin?"

"Our officer assigned each age group three days of marching. We headed towards Berlin," Koby answered this time.

"Very good, then. Enjoy Berlin. But make sure you keep walking. Otherwise you wouldn't be following orders," the officer grinned.

"*Danke!*" Erich replied, returning the gesture.

The SS soldiers marched away. Koby gestured for the boys to follow him. "All right. If we do the same time we did today, tomorrow, we should head out of Berlin at about," he did some math in his head, "Fourteen hundred hours. That gives us over three hours to look around Berlin. Speaking of which, who here hasn't been to Berlin?"

Almost every cadet raised their hand, including Koby. Erich did not.

"Okay Erich, you lead the way," Koby told him, "Where should we head first?"

"*Neptunbrunnen*, Neptune's fountain so we can get some water. The Brandenburg gate, the Kroll Opera House, and the *Reichstag*. That's probably all we have time for."

"Isn't the *Reichstag* under reconstruction? Because of the fire?" a cadet asked.

"*Ja*, but that's inside of the building."

"Let's get to a fountain, any fountain, *verdämmt!*" Jarman interrupted.

"*Ja*, we need some water," other cadets agreed.

"Follow me," Erich said.

A few minutes later, the boys arrived at a fountain. Once they'd seen it, they sprinted to its sides and scooped water into their hands rapidly while others dunked their heads in. Blaz brought as many handfuls of water up as a boy could in a minute. Ripples went out around the fountain from so many droplets of water returning to the surface.

"Wow," Blaz breathed, "That felt like heaven."

After they had all gotten a long drink, each boy filled his canteen to the brim.

"Brandenburg first?" Erich asked.

"*Ja, sicher,*" the cadets agreed.

"Berlin is awesome!" Ivo said in wonderment to Blaz, "I never imagined it would be this, this spectacular. It's endless!"

"It's like nothing I've ever seen!"

"The Brandenburg Gate. Finally get to see it in real life."

"It's weird we have never been here in our lives. Thirteen years, never been to the capitol," Blaz said.

"We even have a two-way railroad," Ivo grimaced at the fact they'd never used that. Blaz's, Koby's, and Reinhardt's fathers all used it to get to work every week.

"I guess we were all wrapped up in other stuff."

"Well, we're here now. I wanted to go here sometime in my life."

Blaz gave Ivo a punch on the shoulder. "Was there a chance you wouldn't?"

Ivo smiled and rubbed his shoulder once. "*Nein,* I guess not. That would have been hard not to do, but we are going into the army," Ivo said seriously.

"Here we are!" Erich shouted to the group.

There it was: the Brandenburg Gate. The light tan color of its stones glimmered in the sunlight. Swastika banners hung between each pillar that held the structure up. On the top were several horses pulling a cherub, which held a staff with the Iron Cross at the top. The boys looked at the gate still amazed with the sights they had seen in the past day. All of them put a hand on the stone to say they had touched the gate.

"I didn't know the Gate had an Iron Cross, did you?" Blaz asked Jaye.

"Is there one?" Jaye asked.

"*Ja*, on top," Blaz said, pointing to the cherub.

Jaye squinted at the top of the gate, but shook his head after a long while, "I don't see an Iron Cross."

Blaz shrugged. They sat back and gazed at the marvel of architecture for a while before moving on to the Kroll Opera House and *Reichstag* which were right next to each other.

"The Kroll Opera house, this is where the government is centered," Erich told the cadets.

"Do you think the *Führer* is in there right now?"

"I can't say," Erich told him.

The boys walked around the building. It was a large building that resembled the headquarters at an old university. When they came back around to the entrance A car drove near to the large, wooden doors and stopped. The driver exited the open-top vehicle. He waited on the passenger side of the car stiffly. The doors of the Opera House swung opened. An SS officer jogged out. He headed for boys who leaned against the fence separating them from the building.

"*Jugend*! What are you doing out here?"

"We were just wondering if the *Führer* is here today," Erich responded with tact.

"I am sorry. The *Führer* is not in Berlin right now. It's mostly generals here today."

Erich hid his disappointment well and saluted the officer, telling him they'd be on their way. "Sounds like the *Führer* must be busy."

"Probably talking with Mussolini about our next move or something."

The boys stared at the building longingly. When Erich told them to move along they followed somewhat reluctantly towards the *Reichstag*. But the capitol building wiped away any regret. The first things that caught the boy's attention were large pillars supporting the Pantheon-like entrance. Glass windows lined the symmetrical front of the building. A tower rose from each of the front corners of the building, and a dome jutted up from the top of the Reichstag, giving the building a powerful, authoritative feel, more so than the Opera House. Despite being vacant, a large, bright red Swastika flag fluttered in the breeze, as the centerpiece of the capitol building.

"Here is *Deutschland*," Erich said proudly.

The massive capitol building was a marvel of architecture, a throwback to ancient Roman and Greek civilizations. Yet again, the boys were mesmerized by the sheer size and scope of the building. For boys growing up in the country, this was something they had only imagined. Now it was in front of them. The squads wandered as close to the Reichstag as they could. A home guard trooper noticed their young age and allowed them to walk to the pillars of the massive building. Each boy put a hand on the building before thanking the guard. Once they'd gathered in the street, Erich informed them it was time to leave Berlin.

Much later, they exited the outskirts of the capital, their conversations being only on Berlin.

"Okay, we have a lot of ground to cover, and we'll be getting up nice and early tomorrow," Koby yelled to the group.

"*Jawohl*," the cadets replied.

At once, the cadets set out at a brisk pace. All the boys were eager to talk about Berlin, and not long into the march, they did. As this happened, Koby gestured for Blaz and Ivo to come to the front.

"*Ja*, Koby?" Ivo asked when they jogged up beside him.

"What did you think?" Koby asked with a dimpled grin.

"Berlin?" Ivo asked.

"Of course."

"It was like nothing I could have imagined. It was so big, so many people even on a weekday. And so many buildings," Ivo said with awe.

Koby turned to Blaz.

"I loved it."

Koby nodded.

"It was everything I hoped it would be," Blaz continued, "And then some."

"It really was," Koby said, his voice higher than usual.

"I'm glad I finally saw Berlin. Because I had never seen it before," Ivo told them, "And that really gives more scope to what we are fighting for."

"*Gott, ja.* Excellent motivation."

"Worth the entire march," Blaz added.

The boys walked at a good speed for hours. Most of the talks regarded everything they had just seen that day. At a point, Koby informed the group they had to find some food, "We have about a half hour of good daylight. Spread out and find anything you can. Groups of two. Meet at the edge of that cluster of trees," he ordered, and pointed to a small group of trees a hundred meters away or so.

The boys spread out in all directions. Ivo went with Koby, Jarman with Erich, Reinhardt with Jurgen, and Blaz with Jaye. The boys all hustled at quick paced to find food of some kind. With only one meal in their packs and nothing to eat all day, their stomachs were rumbling. The Hitler Youth were trained for this and no one complained aloud.

"Quite a trek," Jaye said.

"*Ja.*"

"You tired?"

"What? *Nein,*" Blaz said, stretching his back.

"Really, this is nothing compared to the army, I'm sure."

"*Wahr.*"

"We should probably try to find something. What is edible in a field that has been harvested?"

"Don't know, but we need to find something."

They walked for a few more minutes without finding anything, "*Verdämmt.* Let's head back," Jaye told Blaz.

"All right."

As they headed back, Jaye stumbled and fell into the dirt. Blaz tripped over him.

"Ow, what happened?" Blaz asked.

"I couldn't see anything," Jaye admitted, "It's so dark out. I could only see a few feet in front of me."

It's not that dark out, Blaz thought before hopping up and extending a hand to Jaye. The rest of the walk back was without incident. At the tree line, the others stood empty-handed. There simply was nothing in the field. Erich and Jarman came back last with something in their arms. As they approached though, the boys saw it was just firewood.

"Okay, tomorrow we catch or find something," Koby said in defeat, "Let's get a fire going."

Once the fire was burning bright, the cadets broke open their last meal. Blaz put a hand on his stomach before taking a bite. *Twenty-four hour fast,* he thought, *Sure there'll be longer ones in the army.* He took a bite out of his bread. It tasted better than anything he'd ever eaten. After hours of being on his feet with little rest, he finally was receiving fuel. Each boy quickly devoured dinner. The sun had completely set, so the boys laid down to go to sleep. Koby walked around the encampment, "We start before sunrise. Everyone get a good drink in the morning. We will find water tomorrow to refill. If we keep a fast pace and take one break, we could reach Seelow by sunset," he informed everyone, "Get some sleep soon. Erich and I will split shifts again."

Most boys fell asleep quickly even with a chilly breeze in the air. Koby and Erich both remained awake. Blaz looked over at the two. Erich looked strong as ever and showed no signs of exhaustion. Koby looked very tired though. Also stressed. Blaz whispered to the two, "Do you want me to take a third shift so you guys can catch up on some sleep?"

"Would you?" Erich asked.

"*Ja.*"

"That'd be great, Blaz," Koby said gratefully, "I'm exhausted."

"How about you take the first shift?" Erich suggested. He handed Blaz the watch. "When it is twenty-three hundred wake me up."

"Okay, you guys get some rest."

"Thanks buddy," Koby said as he fell back in exhaustion.

When Koby and Erich were out, Blaz returned to his blanket and sat down. He watched around the area for any creatures or humans. He heard nothing but the wind blowing leaves and the occasional bird. His eyelids were heavy but he stayed awake. Four hours to go.

His mind was full of scattered thoughts. When alone and awake, this would happen to him, without the distractions of daytime and busywork. Blaz looked around the circle of boys. Despite not being popular, the strongest or fastest, he still had a place with his classmates. The loss of his knife wasn't as big of a deal as he thought it would.

They're good guys, thought Blaz, looking at Jaye, Marvin, Simon, Erwin, Timo, *couldn't be a better group of guys to go to war with.*

Blaz felt a surge of pride. Pride in being a German. Being a part of such a unified team. The nation was a team, all working together. Few things felt better than knowing he was a part of something meaningful. In more ways than one.

"Erich!" Blaz whispered.

"Erich, wake up. It's twenty-three hundred."

Erich's eyes opened. He stretched his arms. "Already? All right," He took the watch from Blaz.

"Get some sleep," he ordered Blaz.

Blaz crawled towards his blanket.

"Hey Blaz."

Blaz turned his head.

"Thanks, we needed the rest. Especially Koby. He's worn out, I can tell."

"No problem," Blaz grinned in the darkness. Immediately after laying down on his blanket, he fell asleep.

Bombs on England

October 4, 1940 Friday

Morning came, but still darkness surrounded the boys. They packed their blankets and stamped out the last remnants of any fire. There was no visible sunrise this morning as the countryside was blanketed in a thick layer of clouds. Light nevertheless came and they were able to see their way. The clouds did not dull their attitudes. Berlin had made its impact, and everyone was eager to discuss it. Berlin's sights, power, and glory worked their way into talks of the war and their role in it. School and sports came up plenty, as they often do among boys. The cadets' spirits remained high for hours of vigorous hiking. Koby kept the boys going at a pace that would get them home by nightfall.

"Come on, keep up," Koby called to some boys near the back.

"We are, we are!" they called back.

Blaz turned to Jaye, "Think he will make the SS?"

"Who? Koby?" Jaye asked, "I don't know, you know him better. You're pretty good friends."

"*Ja*, that's why I'm asking for your opinion."

"Okay then," Jaye said, appearing a bit confused, "Physically he is of course cut out for the SS," Jaye began, "He's a pretty good field commander, during this trek and drills. I'd see him as a field lieutenant, squad leader. But SS? They've got to be brutal. They've got to be polite. They must be able to do anything they're ordered to. *Nein*, I can't see that. Koby's reserved, he couldn't pull it off. Erich will though, for sure."

"*Ja*, I'd agree."

"Out of water," Ivo muttered as he shook his canteen over his mouth.

"Keep your eyes open for a creek," Koby instructed, "Only a few more hours."

"New song?" Erich suggested.

"*Jawohl!*"

"*Bomben auf Engelland?*"

"*Bomben auf Engelland!*" Jarman called to the front. It was a *Luftwaffe* song, but had spread like wildfire throughout the entire German armed forces. Koby started them out, singing all the through the first stanza.

Wir fühlen in Horsten und Höhen des Adlers verwegenes Glück!
Wir steigen zum Tor, der Sonne empor,
Wir lassen die Erde zurück.

We feel in the hollows and heights the eagle's daring joy!
Though the gate we rise, the sun rises high,
We leave the earth behind!

Then the Hitler Youth joined in.

Back in Seelow

"There's a creek," Jurgen pointed out, about half an hour later.

"Fill up your canteens, get a drink, quickly," Koby ordered.

The cadets filled their canteens to the top and all got a long drink.

"Water tastes so good!" Ivo said as he stood up.

"Have we got time to find some food?" one cadet asked.

"*Nein*. The faster we make it home, the faster we can have a meal," Erich told them, "We can practice trapping and scavenging at The Heights and *Kinderlandverschickung*."

"All right, enough of that. Let's get moving," Koby said waving the cadets on.

"Seelow," Blaz sighed. The boys ran up the final hill into their town. Light still shone bright enough for them to be seen coming back. Their arms and legs were covered in dust and their clothes were sweaty and filthy. They headed for the schoolyard to report to Schlusser before they could head home.

"Welcome back!" Schlusser called.

Various positive responses came from the many cadets.

"Meyer and Hertz. Report on the hike," their commander ordered.

"Marched from zero eight hundred to eighteen hundred on day one, zero six thirty to zero eighteen twenty on day two, and zero six thirty to the current time today," Erich said.

"Excellent. How far do you believe you made it?"

"Berlin, *Herr* Schlusser!"

Schlusser was clearly surprised, allowing it to show for the boys, but made no comment regarding it, "*Gut gemacht.* That is a good seventy kilometers, just to get there. Very good. That is all I need. Good work boys. Go home, get some rest, and wash up."

When Blaz got home his mother ran to the door to hug him.

"Blaz, you've been gone so long! How was it? How do you feel?"

"*Gut, Mutter.* It was fun, we made it to Berlin!"

"Oh Blaz, that's really impressive! You're growing up so fast. You are such a trooper," she patted Blaz's head. "I have dinner ready, wash your face and change out of those clothes. When was the last time you ate?"

"This morning," Blaz lied.

"Okay, be down soon."

Blaz walked up the stairs, exhausted. *And running tomorrow,* he thought with a laugh. Blaz changed quickly and glanced at himself in the mirror to see his face covered in dirt. After he had washed up and come to the table, his mother bowed her head and folded her hands.

"Ready?" She asked Blaz.

"What?"

"Ready to pray?"

"Oh, *ja,*" Blaz replied awkwardly.

Blaz bowed his head and his mother prayed, "God, I thank you that Blaz made it back safely from his hike. I thank you for keeping our town safe and that Blaz will be safe at the-" she paused, "camp." Blaz looked up. "Please continue to bless the *Führer* and *Deutschland* as we go forward. Amen."

"Amen."

Blaz put some bread, vegetables, and a big piece of the tender schnitzel his mother made for special occasions onto his plate. He wondered why she had made it for tonight.

"How were things for you?" Blaz asked.

"Very nice. I had a night with my friends."

"*Gut*, that's good."

The two sat in silence for a moment.

"Now, how was Berlin Blaz?" his mother asked with interest.

"Incredible!" Blaz replied, eager to tell someone about the marvelous city, "There were more buildings and people in one place than I've ever seen. The capitol is an amazing building. Have you seen it?"

His mother smiled and nodded. "I have."

"*Ja*, so you know how incredible it is. We saw the Brandenburg gate, too. I've never seen anything like Berlin, mama. The most amazing city I've ever seen."

Blaz talked with his mother about Berlin, the march, and their beloved Germany far into the night.

Love of the Game

October 8, 1940 Tuesday

A blue van rumbled over the dusty road into the dirt lot of a school. Inside, Blaz, Koby, Ivo, and Johann gazed out into the field while coach Friederich drove. Rest had been had. All the boys were ready for the first race. Koby popped his neck as they headed for the starting line. Blaz and Ivo set their sights on Johann. If they could beat him, they would beat their personal records for certain. At the line, Blaz leaned forward along. He shook his fingers as the referee raised his arm.

"*Los!*"

The boys shot from the line. Koby seized first. Blaz gained some separation from the back of the pack. Johann stayed four back from Koby. Ivo kept up with Blaz as best he could. As the race wore on, Koby lapped several boys twice but not Johann. Blaz continued trying to shake Ivo but with little success. Every time, Ivo seemed to have the fire to keep up. Whenever Ivo made a run to overtake his teammate, though, Blaz would sprint as fast as he could, and Ivo would fizzle out. Koby crossed the line while Blaz and Ivo still had over two laps left. Blaz breathed a long breath through his nose and started his final sprint. Ivo sped up immediately.

"Run! Run! You've got people on your tails!" Coach Friederich yelled from the side of the track, "PRs!"

Blaz kept his rapid pace going and with two hundred meters, launched into a dead sprint. His heart beat rapidly, begging for a break. His arms propelled him and his strides lengthened. The finish line grew nearer and Ivo was not challenging his place today. Blaz flew across the line with Ivo coming moments later.

"That's it, just breath, breath," Coach Friederich instructed them, "Excellent running. Personal Records, for each of you. Blaz, eighteen forty-eight and Ivo eighteen fifty-one."

Blaz put his palms on his knees and breathed heavily. Each breath sent a chilly feeling down his throat.

"How did you do?" he asked Johann, who'd been waiting for them.

"Eighteen oh nine."

Blaz shook his head with a laugh. "*Gut gemacht*, Johann. That's a good time," he turned to Ivo and mouthed, "*Mein Wort.*"

Ivo gave an eyebrow raise in agreement. The coach then herded the boys off the track.

"Koby, exceptional time, Olympic time. Fifteen thirty-three."

Koby beamed. Ivo slapped him on the backside.

"Everyone else had improved times, good work. Keep it up."

The coach turned to speak with some officials and other coaches. The boys wandered around the track while they waited for their coach to finish up. The setting sun shone brightly against the cloudy sky. Koby ran a hand through his hair and said, "The competition is getting stiffer."

"What?" Ivo exclaimed, "No one challenged you, though!"

"Well, *ja*," Koby laughed in realization, "But I normally lap everyone twice, you and Blaz normally don't have so many people trailing you."

October 16, 1940 Wednesday

"Excellent, yet again Senft and Klein!" Schlusser yelled from the finish.

Having just finished the second trial five-kilometer, Blaz raised an arm in recognition. Then put his hands on the back of his head and breathed in exhaustion. As Blaz breathed, he coughed loudly several times. When his cough stopped, he finished his breath. Ivo looked at him with concern.

"I'm fine," Blaz assured Ivo.

One-by-one more boys crossed the finish line. Some in groups, some individually. Erich arrived much sooner than Blaz expected and, judging by Ivo's expression, sooner than he had too. When all the boys had finished, Schlusser ordered the oldest to the line.

"Younger members are dismissed for today."

All cadets, fifteen and under, made for Seelow. Each boy went at a fast walk, even the ones who had just finished their run.

"You were surprising out there, Erich!" Koby commended his friend.

"I didn't see that coming, very impressive," Blaz complimented him.

"I didn't see it coming myself, I just ran as hard as my heart would allow," Erich said.

"You looked good coming in. What was your final time?" Ivo asked.

"Tybalt told me my final time was twenty even," Erich told the group.

"*Verdämmt*, Blaz!" Ivo shouted obnoxiously, "We better watch out!"

Blaz laughed, "We ought to."

"All right, enough of that," Erich tried to put talk of him aside, "How did everyone else do?"

"Blaz and I got high eighteens," Ivo told Erich.

"I got somewhere in the high twenty-ones," Jarman said.

"High twenty-twos," Jurgen said with a bit of disappointment at his mediocre time.

"Low twenty-ones," Reinhardt added.

"Hey Reinhardt, how's your girl?" Jarman asked.

"Ah, of course," Reinhardt sighed, "I asked her on a date and we went to see a movie."

"Well done," Erich applauded, "What film?"

"*The Rothschilds.*"

"Nice."

"We have been hanging out after school when we don't head to the Heights."

"You must love those days," Ivo teased.

"They're made better than they would otherwise," Reinhardt continued, "But we are just friends who happen to be a girl and a boy. Sometimes we even chat with other boys or girls in the grade together. Jurgen knows what I'm talking about."

"They're just friends, really. No making out or anything. Yet."

Reinhardt shook his head, but it morphed into a nod. "You've got to take your time with these things."

"That is something you don't have," Ivo said, pointing, "Month and a half."

"Every guy in the town is leaving. She'll wait for me," Reinhardt smiled.

Ein Volk, Ein Reich, Ein Führer

November 15, 1940 Friday

Weeks passed, weather turned cold, clouds settled above the German countryside. The boys knew nothing but training. Their bodies worked to be made worthy of a German soldier.

As Schlusser's time ran out, he implemented more mental training on top of the school's lessons. He and the oldest leaders briefed each male Hitler Youth member after school. Their questions were blunt. However, a group of *Wehrmacht* soldiers from the Heights made sure no one told those who hadn't spoken to either Schlusser or a youth leader yet anything about their conversations. The boys who had been questioned were ordered home immediately. The others waited on the field under the watch of Hitler Youth leaders and *Wehrmacht* soldiers. Blaz was told by Koby that Schlusser was waiting to talk to him personally. He walked into a room where Schlusser waited for him.

"*Heil* Hitler," were the first words out of Schlusser's mouth.

Blaz returned the greeting and gave the Roman salute.

"Have a seat, Senft."

Schlusser sat in front of a teacher's desk and a chair was placed across from him. Blaz sat down across from him, nothing obstructing their view of each other. Schlusser began, "Senft, how has your time in the *Hitlerjugend* been? What are your thoughts about it?"

Blaz promptly responded. "I love the *Hitlerjugend*. I'm becoming a strong, young soldier. Training us to perform well as soldiers is how we will excel in our lives, in the army, and after."

"Does the *Hitlerjugend* allow you time for schoolwork? Do you feel as if you are overwhelmed?"

"*Nein*, not at all."

"What have you learned to do in the *Hitlerjugend*?"

"I have learned how to shoot rifles, machine guns, pistols, to survive in the wilderness, to work cannons and artillery, and to drive."

"What have you learned about *Deutschland* and yourself?"

"I am a German. The German people are my people, which is my most precious possession. *Deutschland* is our land. Our blood, our soil."

"Why do we train, march, and fight?"

"*Deutschland* must remain strong. We must bring *Deutschland* glory, honor, and fortune. By doing this, we will spread National Socialism's message to the whole world."

"What must we all be willing to do for the Fatherland?"

"Fight and die."

"Why must we fight and die?"

"To protect *Deutschland* from the spread of the Jew and his creation of Marxism."

"How will it end?"

"With our victory."

"How do you live for the Reich?"

"I live faithfully."

"How will you fight?"

"I will fight bravely."

"And, if it comes to it, how will you die?"

"I will die laughing."

"Who are you, Senft?"

"I am a servant of the Fatherland."

"Whom do you serve?"

"I serve Adolf Hitler, my *Führer*. By serving my *Führer*, I serve *Deutschland*. And by serving *Deutschland*, I serve God."

"That is all, Senft. You are dismissed to go home," Schlusser said abruptly.

Blaz stood up, saluted, and exited the room.

Evaluations

November 27, 1940 Wednesday

Schwinghammer arrived at the Heights before most of the boys. His appearance was unchanged, including what he wore. This time he held a clipboard and pen as well. An assistant walked alongside him and two black-clad soldiers flanked him. Schlusser came minutes later with the rest of the Hitler Youth. His gait was more rigid than normal, his steps clipped.

Schlusser snapped orders to his selected representatives to separate from the group. His voice was stern but lacked the roaring power it normally did. Schwinghammer smiled at Schlusser's tone, understandingly. The cadets launched into artillery drills. Schwinghammer watched each cadet fire the blanks while his assistant held a timer. The officer scribbled notes of some kind onto his clipboard.

Shooting followed, with Koby, Erich, and Marvin representing their fellow cadets. Every group performed superbly as far as Blaz could tell.

Cadets proceeded to repair vehicles and fought the *Schutzstaffel* soldiers hand-to-hand. Blaz had no idea how *Herr* Schwinghammer could score that. Erich's number was up for hand-to-hand fighting. The *Schutzstaffel* soldier let Erich make the first move, though he did not do this with every cadet. Erich made two jabs at the trooper before hopping back out of punching range. After several accurate, but ineffective punches, Erich got up close to try to knock the soldier off his feet. Both locked arms and pushed at each other, each trying to bring down their opponent. Erich was losing ground, but when it appeared defeat was certain, he whipped his neck around, sending his head into the soldier's unprotected face. The man stumbled, and Erich went for his legs. The soldier looked up and swung a fist at Erich's face, landing a hit. Erich went down and the trooper pinned him handily. Schwinghammer wrote something down then gestured to the next cadet and second soldier.

Weight lifting came and went with Erich impressing most of the Hitler Youths, and presumably Schwinghammer. Knife throwing was quick, Johann performed exceptionally. Next, they descended into the grassy area of the Heights between two hills where the long-distance races took place. Sprints were first. Jarman got his wish and was selected for this event, and though he ran his heart out, he was almost certainly just a blip on Schwinghammer's radar.

By far the most entertaining and impressive drill of the day was jumping. Schwinghammer took both long jumps and high jumps, but also on a drill of the Hitler Youth's design. The older cadets first lined up, choosing three people of their age group to jump over using a springboard while they were standing up. After each jump, they would add a cadet. A requirement was to do a flip during the jump from the springboard. Each age group made it over at least five, but the most impressive jump came from Tybalt Glöckner when he leapt over eight cadets while doing a flip during his jump. The younger Hitler Youths cheered, including Ivo, Blaz, Koby, and Reinhardt. The rest clapped loudly.

Unexpectedly, Schwinghammer continued to the younger cadets. Schlusser's eyes widened. Erich gave him a wink, somewhat easing the officer's mind. Three cadets from their age group lined up, including Koby. They did not just want to put the shortest cadets in. That would be too simple, and Schwinghammer wouldn't be impressed. Erich made the first jump without any trouble. Jaye joined the mix. Erich did it again. Another cadet, taller than Koby, joined the line. Erich made the jump once again. Schwinghammer hid any surprise he might've had. Jurgen joined the line next. Erich did not immediately charge this line. He stared at the line of cadets, examining the length. Then he took his position. Erich sprinted forward, leaping a couple of feet before the first cadet. He cleared the first five, and then the sixth with a clean landing as well. Erich's age group called, "*Sieg!*"

"*Heil!*" Erich threw his right arm in the air.

Schwinghammer cracked a grin but motioned for a seventh cadet to take his place. The cadet nodded and took his position. This time Erich failed, knocking over the seventh cadet. Erich pulled him to his feet, and the cadet gave Erich a pat on the shoulder.

Then came long distance. Three runners from each age came to the line. Schwinghammer yelled the starting words and fired a blank into the air. The cadets shot off. Koby once again, took the lead even over the oldest boys. Blaz was surprised to find that he was better than many of the older cadets. Throughout the race, he continually passed older boys, who had little idea of strategy during a race and simply sprinted until they ran out of gas. The final stretch was different than races against his normal age group. Not only was Ivo near him but two older boys. Neither wanted to be beaten by a thirteen-year-old. They thundered after him, eyes blazing. Blaz put his head down and gave all his energy to this last sprint. He could barely see when he crossed the line but he knew he had beaten the other boys. Darkness was all he saw for a few seconds as he staggered around. Koby came and propped his friend up.

"You a little dizzy?"

"*Ja*. I couldn't see," Blaz said as he regained focus.

"That'll happen after a fast run. Here," he handed Blaz a small cup of water.

Blaz gulped it down in the blink of an eye. "*Danke*," he gasped.

"You got a personal record," Koby informed him.

"I did?" Blaz panted.

"You got an eighteen twenty-nine. Your best this year was ten seconds longer."

"I guess I was motivated to beat the older guys," Blaz said between gasps.

"You looked like you were running possessed at the end."

Blaz let out a weak laugh, "I wanted to win, what can I say?" He breathed in again, eyes crossed briefly, "Did you have any challengers?"

"If you consider a minute and a half to be a challenger then, *ja*," said Koby with a grin.

"What was your time?"

"Fifteen twenty-nine."

Blaz coughed, "Every time you run, it's just amazing. That's Olympic time."

"Those Olympic uniforms look awesome, white with the Eagle. It was pretty cool when the Olympics were in Berlin. I wonder where they'll be in forty-eight."

"Berlin," said Ivo out of nowhere.

"Again? They can't, the same city can't host it twice in a row," Blaz doubted.

"*Ja*, then Tokyo or Rome," Koby agreed.

Blaz looked back and forth at his friends with confusion for before saying. "Ah, I see where you're going with that," Blaz pointed at Koby.

"And the Finnish long distance runners will be competition, they're always good," said Ivo, "And Africa has good athletes too."

"*Ja*, I can't wait to duke it out with Höckert and Lehtinen," Koby laughed, referring to Finnish runners who'd excelled in the nineteen thirty-six Berlin Olympics.

"*Jugend!*" Schlusser shouted at the top of his lungs to the unit. "Gather, at attention!"

The boys organized themselves and stood attentively. Schwinghammer spoke with Schlusser for a moment before announcing to the cadets, "The results will be given to me in two weeks. Then I will know your KLV camp situation. The following cadets report to Schlusser and myself: Kauffmann, Glöckner, Hildebrand, Ebner, Fleischer, Kramer, Meyer, Hertz. The rest of you, dismissed!"

The boys quickly dispersed. Everyone left the Heights as their commander instructed within a matter of minutes. Blaz and his friends discussed what Schlusser must be talking to the chosen few about.

"Those are squad leaders, so I assume he will be telling them what to do when we are at the camps. It is going to be weird having our classmates basically being in charge," suggested Jarman.

"Schwinghammer will be in charge," Jurgen reminded him.

"*Ja*, that's true, but he will probably get called to fight in the war soon."

"Really?" a surprised Ivo asked, "He's no spring chicken."

"He's only a few years older than our parents. Late-thirties, maybe early forties, I'd bet," Jarman guessed, "I think he fought in the last days of *Der Krieg*, what with the Iron Cross and no swastika."

"There will be teachers there, for the education," Blaz pointed out, "And some cooks, I'd bet."

"They're women and old men," Jarman scoffed, "None of them will be training us."

"Old people are smart, they have wisdom."

"They don't know about war, honestly most of the *Der Krieg* veterans are in their forties and fifties. Our parents were almost our age when *Der Krieg* started," Jarman retorted.

"And if women were in war," Blaz said, addressing Jarman's comment about the teachers, "They wouldn't be that bad. You've got some good athletes in the Olympics. Don't you think they could help out?"

"By all means they should take up jobs when the men are at war that need to be filled, and even have duties behind the front line. You've noticed how our male and female teachers have been teaching that women can help *Deutschland* by not only having children, and raising them, but other tasks. They didn't used to teach that. They certainly shouldn't fight and in peacetime most shouldn't enter the workforce," Jarman admitted.

"Why not?" asked Blaz, not trying to be provocative, but with interest to hear Jarman's reasoning. So he quickly added, "Not that I think they should."

"Because-"

"They're the reason we fight," Reinhardt cut in.

"Exactly, exactly," Jarman concurred.

"When you sink to the level of drafting women into the army, you've probably lost the war. It's men's job to protect women, even die for them. My father fought in *Der Krieg*. He has seen what it has done to young men. They come back completely broken, if they come back at all. He would have no respect for the German men if we had women do that. A German woman who has a child has done her service to her nation as a man in the military does his," Reinhardt said.

"Well said," Jurgen agreed, eyes wide.

"Absolutely," Blaz and Ivo said almost in unison.

"You should talk more, Reinhardt. You certainly aren't staying quiet because you have nothing to say," Jarman said, giving a tap to Reinhardt's skull.

"Maybe I will."

When in Seelow, they went their separate ways. Blaz walked home, excited to continue this journey for Germany with his friends.

Faster and More Intense

November 30, 1940 Monday

"Come on, come on!"

Blaz shivered outside. The wind blew violently, and no sunlight peeked through the thick cloud cover. The chilly air bit at Blaz's ears and cheeks, which were already red. Ivo had yet to finish his push-ups before school. Physical conditioning had become even more important leading up to Schwinghammer's arrival. And *Herr* Schlusser didn't let up afterwards. Their morning strength training had been brutal for the past months but had paid off. Each boy looked significantly stronger. Even Ivo.

Blaz jogged in place to keep warm. He had worn his summer uniform today, which he now regretted. Most of the Hitler Youth had come in their black winter uniforms which included long pants rather than the shorts Blaz wore. Finally, Ivo hopped up and ran over to Blaz.

"You took a long time," Blaz teased Ivo.

"It was much faster than the beginning of this year."

"Same can be said for all of us."

In school, Blaz's eyes remained glued to the teacher. The whole class sat straight up respectfully. The tall, older male teacher paced in front of the class, "In a brief summary of this month, animals die off when they cannot compete with better adapted species. The food chain is an example of how some species are stronger than others. Who can give us a quick example? Senft?"

Blaz stood up. "A fox preying on a rabbit."

"*Gut, sehr gut*. But we are not mere animals; we have standards to abide by. But nevertheless, we must at the same time abide by nature's laws. What does this teach us about the world? Hertz?"

Blaz sat back down, and Koby rose. "The most advanced and powerful must guide the weak for their own good. The strong must guide the weak while maintaining and improving their own civilizations and people. If they were corrupted by lesser civilizations, then civilization as we know it would collapse," Koby answered, "Then the world would descend into chaos."

"*Ausgezeichnet*, excellent. Can anyone give an example of a higher civilization abusing its power. Krause?"

"King Leopold of Belgium's reign in the Congo."

"Where can we see an example of higher civilizations helping lesser civilizations? Baumann?"

"The colonization of Africa by the British and Germans," Jaye answered, "Before we colonized Africa, the Africans only lived an existence of constant tribal warfare and constant movement with no direction other than survival. They were living an existence comparable to animals just as our ancestors had been less than fifteen hundred years ago. But Europeans have advanced to a higher level of living and we brought that to Africa."

"Indeed. We have advanced beyond simply a mere fight for survival. Survival is indeed important, it is vital for our race. But to survive is neither good nor evil. It is the canvas upon which we as individuals and we as a race paint our story. Painting it with both light and dark shades, just as each man and woman does good and evil. But without a canvas, one can do neither good nor evil. If we wish to do good, we must survive."

The class nodded. Blaz glanced at Koby, whose eyes narrowed as he thought about this. Blaz just heard him breath. "But what is good?"

The teacher had apparently expected a question after this statement, but the class lay silent. Finally, he wrapped things up. "Tomorrow will be test day and I expect good grades from this class."

"*Jawohl.*"

"The bell should ring in a minute or two. Remain seated."

The weight felt a thousand times heavier than when he first picked it up. Blaz's arms felt as though they were going to snap in half, but he finished the rep. Again, he went for another. He closed his eyes and gritted his teeth as he lifted the bar slowly skyward. With a final heave, the weight soared above his head. It took all his strength to put the weight down gently.

"How many was that?" Ivo asked, curling dumbbells.

"Twenty."

"Nice, that's a heavy weight."

"Don't need to tell me that," Blaz grasped his left arm. His pulse pounded inside. Ivo lowered the dumbbells to the ground and stretched his arms behind his back.

"What else did *Herr* Schlusser tell us to do?"

"Nothing," said Koby's voice, "Just put away the rifles and ammunition and you can be on your way."

Blaz and Ivo gave Koby an obedient nod.

"And Blaz."

"*Ja?*"

"Don't fire any of them."

An annoyed grin made its way onto Blaz's face, "Ah, shut up, Koby."

The rifles did not present any difficulties for either Blaz or Ivo that day. Once the firearms were stored in the armory, the boys set off for Seelow at a brisk pace to get out of the uncomfortable temperature.

Blaz blew on his bare hands, "I should've worn my winter uniform."

"It's that cold out?"

"It is when you're wearing shorts."

"No kidding. Any news on the status of our attack on England?"

Ivo shook his head dismally, "Nothing favorable."

"I thought we'd have beaten them by now," Blaz kicked at the road. The frozen ground did not give up any dust.

End of a Chapter

December 8, 1940 Tuesday

Blaz knew it. Koby knew it. Ivo knew it. Johann knew it. Once this race was over their running careers would be over. Koby was the only exception. Each boy had come to love their sport and was excited they'd be allowed to continue at their KLV camp but nevertheless, this race was the final chapter in their sports life. When the boys took their places to run, none of those thoughts crossed their minds. Right now, it was just important to run.

"*Auf die Platze! Fertig! Los!*"

The runners blasted off the starting line. Blaz sprinted forward to grab a leading position. Johann sharply veered when Blaz tried to pass him, cutting off Blaz's momentum. Ivo wove in between competitors as he worked his way up the leader board. Koby built on his lead every lap, but one runner, a tall blonde, kept Koby within striking distance. At first, Blaz thought Koby might be having an off day. This was disproved when Blaz, Ivo, and Johann were all lapped twice by Koby with Johann narrowly being passed at the end of Koby's race for the second time. The tall blonde roared past the finish line far behind Koby. Johann came in fourth, leaving Blaz, Ivo, and two other boys within grasp of the fifth and sixth place positions. With four hundred meters to go, Blaz dug for all the stamina he possessed. His strides felt graceful and not labored. Gradually, he forged a lead over Ivo and the two closest opponents. Ivo gasped for air and sprinted with all the energy his smaller body could hold. It was his last chance to beat Blaz in the five thousand. When they began the homestretch, Ivo made a dash to overtake Blaz. Blaz kept his focus ahead, and Ivo pulled alongside him. With Ivo now in view, Blaz received newfound motivation. He cranked out the last remnants of energy he could muster and pulled ahead right as the two crossed the finish line.

"*Verdämmt!*" Ivo yelled as he collapsed to the ground in defeat, "*Nein, nein, nein!*" Blaz let out an exhausted laugh. Koby picked Ivo up from the rough track surface, "Come on now, don't fall if you don't have to. But nice work guys, you did very good."

"What was our time?" Ivo wheezed.

"Blaz had an eighteen twenty-seven, so that'd give you an eighteen twenty-eight."

Blaz pumped his fist weakly. He'd done it. On his last race, he beat his personal best A surge of emotion shot through Blaz, and he wiped his eyes. Some of his fondest memories came from this team. Koby walked over to him and gave him a pat on the back.

"I'm proud of you Blaz, I know it sounds odd coming from me, but you've trained hard. You've worked like a real German. And you got a terrific time. I'm not going to take away from that. It's a great way to go out, few people can run like that." Koby smiled a genuine smile. Blaz even thought he was fighting back some tears.

Preparation

December 18, 1940 Friday

School was done. Essays had been handed in. Any trace of the warmth of autumn had vanished. The German winter had set in. Runs to the Heights were colder with each passing day. Schlusser increased the workload as the time to depart for their KLV camp grew nearer. The boys knew Schwinghammer would be a stricter leader and so did Schlusser, who cracked down on all loose talk, technical mistakes, and other infractions.

"No one is to speak unless spoken to when I am present. When you are at training camp and in the army, this will be the case. It is about time I enforced this in a tighter manner. We leave on January Second for the camp. The *Hitlerjugend* from Neuhardenberg will join us and you will be mixed into cabins with them. To refresh your memories, you will be staying in small rooms by squad inside a warehouse. The warehouse will not be insulated so you will need blankets. You will wake up early in the morning for physical drills. Everything we have done here will be practiced at the camp. Education takes place in the middle of the day. After this, technical drills in the late afternoon. You will learn many songs of our land, recite our Reich's sayings and exercise absolute loyalty. You must be prepared to obey orders no matter what time of day or night. No 'ifs' or 'buts' about it. This camp is a military installation, not *Hitlerjugend* on the road. You have all learned to obey orders well but bear in mind this will be an entirely new experience. Once I hand the reigns to Schwinghammer, you must all obey him as you would the *Führer* himself. The same goes for youth commanders. They are the law, obey them. As you know, should Schwinghammer be called into service, Glöckner and Kauffman will assume his command of the camp. And should they be called into service, Fleischer and Kramer and so forth and so on. Glöckner, Kramer, and Hertz will lay out the expectations of the *Wehrmacht* now."

A seventeen-year-old cadet stepped forward. His buzzed blond hair under his peaked cap, blue eyes, and sturdy build made him the ideal youth for a military propaganda poster. The cadet, with steely eyes, stared across the columns of German youths before he spoke, "We have grown up together, learned together, worked together, marched together, played together, and trained together. We are friends. But when we fight we cannot put friendship above the Fatherland. We must all be willing to call our friends out when they have second thoughts regarding their service. Loyalty, not division, will bring victory. *Heil* Hitler!"

"*Heil* Hitler!"

Glöckner stepped back to where the other youth officers stood. Kramer then strode into the spotlight, "When we step onto the battlefield, we are not only there to defend *Deutschland* but to defeat those who would destroy us. No nation that makes war with us will stand in the end. They will be liberated by the Reich of freedom."

With that, Koby strode to the front of the Hitler Youths. He showed no signs of nerves to an average attendant but those who knew him knew that he had been stressed about this for the entire day. "None of us really know what is ahead for us," Koby said, taking a deep breath, "No training can prepare us for the day when we squeeze the trigger to end a life. We are the future soldiers. That will be our duty. I said no training can prepare you for killing, but the training we are soon to endure will be as close as you can get. Germans are strong, resilient, and bold. We fear no one! *Sieg Heil!*"

"*Sieg Heil!*"

A Christmas in Nazi Germany

December 24, 1940 Thursday

Blaz and his mother sat in the fourth row. Two columns of pews were divided by an aisle in the one room church. At the front of the church was the cross behind the pastor's podium. Their new pastor did not have the passion nor spirit that Johann's father did, perhaps because of his advanced age, but that was no reason to quit going to church. Ivo and his mother sat in front of them. Jurgen sat with his mother and father in the second row. Jarman, Erich, and Reinhardt were absent as usual but Koby was conspicuously missing. Blaz had noticed Koby coming less and less but never thought he would skip on Christmas. One pleasant surprise was Jaye and his family were present. When the pastor finished his message of the Christmas story, the congregation stood for a carol. A young man in a *Wehrmacht* uniform, on leave for Christmas, stepped to the front of the church. He took off his cap revealing thick blond hair on most of his head but also a deep gash on the left side of his skull where his hair was thin. It was like a canyon in the smooth surface of the young man's head. Taking no notice of any reactions from the small crowd, he began singing, his voice a bass.

> *Stille Nacht, heilige Nacht,*
> *Alles schläft; einsam wacht*
> *Nur das traute hochheilige Paar.*
> *Holder Knabe im lockigen Haar,*
> *Schlaf in himmlischer Ruh!*
> *Schlaf in himmlischer Ruh!*

> *Silent night, holy night*
> *Everything sleeps, lonely watches*
> *Only the close, most holy couple.*
> *Blessed boy in curly hair,*
> *Sleep in heavenly peace!*
> *Sleep in heavenly peace!*

The young soldier raised his arms to encourage the congregation to join him in singing. Each German joined in the carol.

Stille Nacht, heilige Nacht,
Hirten erst kundgemacht
Durch den Engel Halleluja,
Tönt es laut von fern und nah:
Christ, der Retter ist da!
Christ, der Retter ist da!

Silent night, holy night,
Shepherds just informed
By the angel's hallelujah,
It rings out far and wide:
Christ the Savior is here!
Christ the Savior is here!

Blaz's developing voice cracked as he tried to hit the high notes at the end of the verse. None of the congregants seemed to care, but Ivo turned. Blood rushed to Blaz's face.

Stille Nacht, heilige Nacht,
Gottes Sohn, o wie lacht
Lieb' aus deinem göttlichen Mund,
Da uns schlägt die rettende Stund'.
Christ, in deiner Geburt!
Christ, in deiner Geburt!

Silent night, holy night,
Son of God, oh how laughs
Love out of your divine mouth,
Because now the hour of salvation
strikes for us.
Christ, in Thy birth!
Christ, in Thy birth!

This time Blaz hit the high notes and smiled to himself. The young soldier beamed at the community. Joy radiated from his face, as if he had never experienced happiness before and was discovering it for the first time.

"*Danke* for singing with me," he said before he returned to his seat.

The pastor took the stage once more and thanked the people for coming and wished them a Merry Christmas. Gradually, the crowd trickled out of the one-room church. Blaz's mother spoke with his friends' families while Jurgen's father spoke to the young soldier. Jurgen and Ivo talked with Blaz in the back corner of the church.

"Did you see the soldier's wound?" Ivo asked the two.

"Hush, he might hear," Blaz whispered, "Of course I saw, it was hard to miss."

"Koby wasn't here tonight," Jurgen lamented with a downcast expression.

"I thought he'd come," Blaz replied, "He's always come up until this year."

"Schlusser called a special session today at the Heights for the commanders," Ivo informed them. Right then, Jaye tripped over one of the pew's legs on his way over to them. Jurgen held out a hand, which Jaye accepted but it took him a couple of tries to firmly grasp the hand.

"Really? A meeting" Jurgen asked.

"*Ja*, Koby told me."

"How did he tell you?"

"What do you mean?"

"Did he seem disappointed, excited, regretful, angry? What was his attitude about a meeting during the Christmas Eve service?"

Ivo thought for a moment. "He seemed glad for a meeting. Not too disappointed about missing the service."

Jurgen nodded. "That's too bad."

Christmas Day 1940, Wednesday

This Christmas was a cold one for Seelow. The boys shivered as they briskly marched to the Holtzer's house. The sun was setting early in the evening, darkness advanced slowly across the land. Jurgen and his father were outside when the group arrived, waiting on them.

"Felt like we should be cold too," Jurgen grinned when the group arrived. Inside, they talked about war. Nothing else was relevant anymore. War was their life. The future held war for them. *Herr* Holtzer joined the conversation after minutes of simply listening.

"Boys, what are you hoping to accomplish as soldiers?"

Jarman sprung on the question like a trap clamping on a mouse, "Nothing for me personally, I just want *Deutschland* to win. If anything, I'd like to live to see the Fatherland win."

Herr Holtzer nodded and glanced at the other boys.

"Our goals are all the same," Erich proclaimed for the group, "It is about *Deutschland*. Nothing else. We will obey orders even if they are to fight to the last man."

"Is that what they teach in the *Jugend*?" *Herr* Holtzer asked no one single boy.

"*Ja*, I've told you before father," Jurgen reminded him.

"Of course, of course. You have."

Blaz looked around at the group and played with his hat. *It doesn't seem as cheerful this year. Everything is so serious. But seriousness is maturity and maturity is adulthood. Or something like that.*

1941: No Path is Too Steep

The Train Leaves

January 2, 1941 Thursday

Blaz hugged his mother tightly. It was time to go to the camp, leaving his mother alone in Seelow.

"All right, form up!" shouted Schwinghammer.

Blaz let go of his mother. But she didn't let go. "Mama, I have to go now."

"I know, I just wish you never had to leave," his mother whispered, on the verge of tears.

"For the Fatherland, mama," Blaz smiled as she released him. No tears were shed by either son or mother this time.

All the Hitler Youth girls had come to see the boys off. Reinhardt gave Tini Vogel a kiss on the hand. Blaz would have thought it a joke, since Jarman was standing right next to Reinhardt. But Reinhardt did not do many things lightly. Tini was flattered though, and her friends made a big deal out of it. As this happened, the other Hitler Youth stood at attention with their commanders. Schlusser and Schwinghammer ordered groups into train cars by age. The youngest boarded first. Blaz climbed into the car last of his grade. The car had a wooden floor, a window on each side and a lamp held overhead. There was no furniture and the cadets sat down against the walls with their bags. Blaz sat down to the left of Ivo. Koby was sitting to Ivo's right. He raised his eyebrows at his friend when Blaz sat down.

"Here we are."

"*Ja.*"

Schlusser's voice echoed far down the train. More orders for cadets to board other cars.

"How are you feeling about this?" Koby asked Blaz and Ivo.

"About the camps?"

"Of course."

Blaz opened his mouth but no words came out. His voice was lost for a few seconds. He passed it off as a cough. "I'm just glad I don't have to go alone," as he put his arm around Ivo with a grin.

"Aww, Blaz," said Ivo, giving Blaz's hand a pat.

Koby face-palmed, shaking his head. Jarman scooted next to Blaz from across the train.

"When we are at the camp we are having a rematch," he said.

"You still haven't gotten over that, have you?" Blaz taunted.

"*Nein*! I've literally hurt my brain thinking how you could have beaten me!"

"Skill, my friend, skill," he punched Jarman's bicep, "Those muscles aren't going to do you any good without technique."

Jarman stared at him for a moment. "Oh, shut up, Blaz."

"Ha ha!" Blaz said obnoxiously.

"Come on, when you say crap like that you've got to give me a rematch."

"*Ja,* you do," agreed Koby.

"Fine then. First chance we get."

Jarman nodded with a smirk. The train's whistle blew long and loud. The wheels began to screech against the rails as the train started up. Jurgen stood up and waved out the window to the mothers and Hitler Youth girls, "*Ade Damen*! Goodbye ladies!"

The train chugged out of the town and into the countryside. Inside the dimly lit car, the boys discussed camp. There were several stops, to pick up cadets from nearby farming communities. They didn't have long to wait once the stops were done.

"Everyone out!" Schwinghammer ordered as the train stopped. When the boys climbed out, they held their hands up to block the sun's blinding light. After their eyes had adjusted, they scanned the area. No train station was there. No buildings, in fact. Only open country to one side and a forest to the other.

"Our camp is two kilometers down this way," Schwinghammer yelled, pointing down the edge of the forest.

"Form up," Schlusser ordered. Instantly the cadets formed ranks.

"*Marsch! Vorwärts!*" Schlusser shouted.

The cadets kicked their feet high into the air with each step to perform Germany's signature march. Soon into the march, Schwinghammer ordered a Hitler Youth marching song. The boys sang '*Unsere Fahne flattert uns Voran*' and by the time they had finished, they could see the camp. The KLV camp sat on the edge of the forest, with woods on two sides. German grass and farmland surrounded the other remaining borders of the large, rectangular camp. The camp itself was on a plateau at the end of a long upward slant of grassland but was on even ground with the forest. Dirt with no grass made up much of the ground inside the camp, which had two large buildings and an outhouse. Inside the first large building were housed the armory, cafeteria, and the staff sleeping quarters. The outside of the building was wooden with a massive slanted roof. The armory and sleeping quarters were underneath the cafeteria in bunker-like rooms. The wooden walls transitioned into stone. The sleeping quarters were large, much bigger than the staff needed. The extra room was used as a bomb shelter. A steel door lay between the sleeping quarters and armory in case of an explosion. The second large building resembled a warehouse and housed each cabin of boys. A few hundred feet from the camp was a firing range. Targets were lined up along with a large shed on the side of the range. Artillery also was at the range along with an old, but operational, *Panzer III*. A thin dirt trail led downward from the camp into the fields and into the forest. Koby grinned at the sight of the trail.

"*Hitlerjugend*! I have here the cabins each age group will stay in. The cabins are divided by a wall down the middle, so you will be separated by squad. This will extend beyond your time here. Should you become soldiers, they will be your squad. Commanders will be the leaders and designate a corporal in the group. If there is not a commander in a cabin, the list will have a newly selected squad leader indicated by a *Hakenkreuz*, Swastika. Each cabin has a number inscribed outside the door, designating what squad stays there. I will nail this list to the outside of the cafeteria and staff building," Schwinghammer announced, "Find your room and drop your bag inside. Make sure you know who your squad members are. You are brothers in arms now. Then meet out here. We will raise our flag over this camp. There will be a camp picture, then a workout. Then you will be debriefed on our expectations here and what you can expect."

Schwinghammer and Schlusser strode over to the camp headquarters and nailed the list into the wooden wall. The older cadets ordered the ten-year-olds to go first. Each grade of children and teenagers found their cabin and headed directly there. Blaz was the last to arrive. In the cabin were five bunk beds and nothing else. Blaz climbed to the top of the only empty bunk and placed his bag there. The boys in Blaz's cabin were Ivo, Jurgen, Reinhardt, Jarman, Erich, Koby, Jaye Baumann, and two boys from Neuhardenberg: Hans Reichmann, an average working-class German youth, but his eyes were such a light blue they almost looked silver. His gait resembled a perpetual march, and he had a "million Reichsmarks smile." The other was Tristan Rothkirch, a boy with brown hair, hazel eyes, and an oddly large scar running along the left side of his skull. He had tan skin like Koby but was much shorter, and unlike Koby's buzz on the sides and long on the top, Tristan's hair was buzzed all the way through. His uniforms hung loose: the winter ones, the summer ones, and even the athletic shirts. Once they'd acknowledged all their squad mates, the thirteen-year-olds marched into the cold January air. It did not bother them. They hadn't noticed it yet and didn't now. At the flagpole, the squad stood at attention. Arms straightened and aligned down their bodies, eyes transfixed on their commander, not a word spoken. Schwinghammer and Schlusser held the Hitler Youth flag in their hands. Schwinghammer fastened it to the pole and began to raise it. The youths followed the flags ascent. Finally, the flag flew above the camp, fluttering in the icy breeze.

"*Unsere Fahne flattert uns voran, chorus!*" Schwinghammer commanded.

Unsere Fahne flattert uns voran!
In die Zukunft ziehen wir Mann für Mann!
Wir marschieren für Hitler, Durch Nacht und durch Not
Mit der Fahne der Jugend für Freiheit und Brot
Unsere Fahne flattert uns voran!
Unsere Fahne ist die neue Zeit.
Und die Fahne führt uns in der Ewigkeit!
Ja, die Fahne ist mehr als der Tod!

When the chorus ended, Schwinghammer quickly organized the boys into age groups for pictures. As the thirteen-year-old age group stepped in front of the camera, Schlusser separated them by height. Koby, Blaz, and Ivo were all in the front, on their knees. Koby put an arm around both his friends as the cameraman told them to smile. Blaz and Koby smiled, while Ivo glanced at Koby as the camera flashed.

"You didn't smile, Ivo," Koby laughed.

"Koby, I need to be the one guy in that not smiling."

"Why?"

"Years from now, you'll look back at that photograph, and you're going to have a good chuckle when you see my face."

"I hope so, Ivo."

"All right, disperse!" Schlusser shouted above the chatter as the last picture was taken, "Twenty push-ups, thirty sit-ups, fifteen squats and do this cycle ten times for ages fourteen to eighteen. Fifteen push-ups, twenty sit-ups, ten squats for the younger ages, ten times."

All the boys obeyed and began vigorously training. Blaz finished the first five rounds with little difficulty. Then his body started to ache. His arms throbbed with pain and his abs felt like they'd been torn up by a knife. In the spirit of the Hitler Youth, he did not complain nor let anyone know of any pain. Some of the best older cadets finished first, even with a heavier workload. Erich finished first among the younger children followed by Marvin.

Once every boy had completed the workout, Schwinghammer spoke up, "Tomorrow you will begin training. Morning will be physical training, then education, and late afternoon will be technical skills. Three meals a day, and we will have a special session each night for the commanders and SS trainees. You know who you are. During the summer, you will run out to a farm that we've set up, a few kilometers away, and work there. *Deutschland* needs more farms, and this is an excellent place for one. I have been informed that we will receive a new grade this summer, as the children in Seelow get older. Now, I have just been informed that I have been called to Norway for recruitment and security. I will be leaving the week after *Herr* Schlusser. Since you will have only been here two weeks, we have dispatched a new commander for the camp. He is eighteen, *Schutzstaffel*. He will be here to train Glöckner and Kauffman until this May. He should arrive the week after I depart. The two aforementioned cadets, you will assume leadership of the camp should you not be called up for service. I should tell you this, it is likely that a female commander will assume command over the camp later this year."

The Youths remained silent, but a sense of shock was clearly in the air. A woman? Commanding men at a military camp? Albeit young men, but even so. Could Germany not muster a man to command the camp? Schwinghammer could sense the negative reception this news was doomed to endure so he continued, "Now this means nothing. I realize you have often been taught women's role is household tasks and bearing and raising children. These are profoundly important, in fact, vital to maintaining our society. However, *Deutschland* recognizes that women can aid the Fatherland militarily during these times. Their contributions give us power. Our top filmmaker is a woman and has been for years. Our top test pilot as well. The woman that will assume command has been trained to lead these camps by the SS. Schlusser and myself will not be happy to hear of any disrespect shown to her. If women can aid the Reich militarily then it makes us that much stronger. *Heil* Hitler! *Sieg Heil!*"

"*Heil* Hitler! *Sieg Heil! Sieg Heil!*" the camp shouted, throwing up stiff-armed salutes.

"Today will be a day to get used to the camp. Go on, enjoy yourselves," Schwinghammer ordered.

The formation scattered across the camp. Some stayed outside the warehouse, others walked into the fields and still some hiked into the forest, like Blaz and his friends. The forest was full of tall evergreens. The boys walked through the forest, silent for several minutes. There wasn't anything they had to say.

After walking for a short while, Jarman spoke up, "What do you think of the camp?"

Erich shrugged, "It's good enough for me."

Ivo ran up a large rock in the forest, "I don't know about you guys, but I feel ready for some action. With Koby leading us Knights, we should do some damage in the war."

"I have to say, I am too," Koby admitted, "Wait? The Knights?"

"*Ja*, the Knights," Ivo said with a grin, "You know? Our squad."

"What are you talking about?" Jarman asked.

"The squad's got to have a name, right? We're the Seelow Knights."

"I like it," Jurgen nodded.

"All right, guess we're the Knights," Koby smiled, shaking his head.

Kinderlandverschickung

January 9, 1941 Thursday

The first week consisted of shooting air guns and rifles, running, strength training and education. A handful of their teachers had come to the camp to continue educating them. School took place in the main floor of the camp headquarters. The most eventful occurrence during their first week was the departure of their commander and any remaining eighteen-year-olds. All the Hitler Youth assembled at the flagpole to see their commanding officer off. Two large, green trucks with seats in the rear, resembling a covered wagon, came to take the young men to battle. A medium-height, strongly built *Wehrmacht* officer in a field gray jacket and slate gray trousers marked off the names that had been drafted as each cadet gave him their name. Schlusser stood beside him waiting to make sure his students reported. The officer nodded at each cadet as they gave him their name.

"Riocard Becke," the eighteen-year-old officer said robotically.

"Heinz Albrecht."

"Raphael Oborowski."

"Jeremiah Hochberg." Blaz noticed this particular cadet seemed a bit nervous, due to the name, he assumed. But the *Wehrmacht* officer nodded at him with no reaction to the name.

"Benjamin Kempf." The same response from the officer.

"Alfred Geiger."

Twenty or more cadets had reported when the officer looked up. There was one more name. Before the officer could say the name Schlusser turned to face the officer, "Reynald Schlusser."

The officer nodded. Seeing Schlusser's SS uniform he said, "Not a cadet, I presume."

"*Ja* sir," Schlusser replied.

"I have special orders for you. You are to be sent to former Polish territory as soon as we arrive in Berlin. The SS is needed to quell some insurgents in Warsaw," the officer said, "Then you will report to Romania on the Soviet border."

"*Danke, Herr*," saluted Schlusser. He then gestured to the cadets, "Do we have time?"

"*Jawohl*, of course."

Schlusser strolled towards the youngest group of children. He stared blankly, not at any one cadet. When he came to the group he took off his hat and held out a hand to a little boy standing next to Johann.

"Kolten Lichtenberg, it has been an honor serving with you." The astounded little German boy shook his instructor's hand with awe. Schlusser continued this, remembering each name, stopping to think a few times. He thanked everyone for the chance to serve the Fatherland with them.

"Koby Hertz, it has been an honor serving with you." Koby grinned at his commander who returned the gesture.

"Reinhardt Weiss, it has been an honor serving with you." Reinhardt shook Schlusser's hand firmly.

"Ivo Klein, it has been an honor serving with you." Ivo gave Schlusser a wink, to which Schlusser let out a suppressed laugh.

"Blaz Senft, it has been an honor serving with you."

Blaz nodded at his officer and smiled up at him. Schlusser shook hands with every cadet. When the young SS officer boarded the truck, the youths gave him a long Hitler salute in respect. The truck started up and was out of sight in minutes.

A New Young Commander

January 16 to January 23, 1941

Training was all that made up the following week. Schwinghammer was not fazed after Schlusser's departure and worked the boys vigorously. They quickly adapted to the more rigid command of Schwinghammer but just as they did, Ormand Schwinghammer was sent to Norway. Yet another officer they'd known for some time was now gone. Tybalt Glöckner and Erwin Kauffman stepped up to the challenge of running the camp. Two seventeen-year-olds hardly reigned in the respect that *Herr* Schlusser or *Herr* Schwinghammer had but obedience was the code of the Hitler Youth and their obedience was undeniably outstanding. No one stepped out of line during the week. Ivo skated on thin ice a handful of times but always obeyed when Glöckner gave him a warning glare.

On the day their new commander arrived, the cadets once again assembled to greet him. The truck barely arrived. There was no announcement or fanfare, the commander just leapt out of the truck, and then it was on its way. This strange entrance was noted by the cadets, but they gave no reaction. Glöckner and Kauffman greeted their commander and introduced themselves. Both appeared older than him, though they were not. The new commander shook their hands and turned to face his students. While only a year younger than Schlusser, the difference in appearance was jarring. Schlusser was the epitome of a commanding officer. A good height. An intimidating stare and professional posture. His muscular build was perfectly proportional so that he never looked awkward. Not so with the new commander. His face was that of a boy three years younger than him, he had unusually broad shoulders, a pug nose, and bright red hair, an uncommon trait in Germany. Despite all this, he had a strong build proven by the machine gun slung over his back and two heavy bags he carried at his side. It was to anyone's guess what was inside. The commander placed his bags at his feet and introduced himself, "*Guten tag, Hitlerjugend*. My name is Derry Kurzmann, I have been made your interim commander. I will be here until late May, so that gives us plenty of time to train. I was briefed by your former commander, Reynald Schlusser, and he gave me some papers regarding special orders for certain cadets. Now, would all officers please step to the front?"

All officers did so.

"Now where is Koby Hertz?"

Koby raised his arm.

"You and your team will be allotted a specific hour of the day, occasionally more to train long distance, you know why."

Koby smiled sheepishly at the ground, while many heads turned his way.

"Now as I understand it, none of you will be called up into service while I am here, correct?"

Glöckner interceded for the boys, "*Ja*, that is correct."

"*Wunderbar*, that's always a hassle," the young officer chuckled to himself, "Moving on, it is nearly sixteen hundred hours, so let's get out to the range. Glöckner, Kauffman! Lead the way."

Glöckner and Kauffman immediately pointed to the cadets and shouted, "March!" The cadets fell in behind them, towards the range.

First Taste of the Cold

February 3, 1941 Monday

Blaz blew on his hands. His breath floated visibly into the air. The entire camp had left the installation for a jog, while Blaz was waiting with Koby at the entrance to the forest trail. Johann and Ivo were still changing into their uniforms, which were quite inappropriate for the freezing temperature that morning. Unfortunately, Monday was the day of their long run, which always exceeded six miles, even more for Koby. Tuesday, they would work on sprints; Wednesday was a five-kilometer run; Thursday, a medium run, four or five miles; Friday and Saturday, generally two or three miles and a rest day on Sunday, along with the rest of the camp. Koby had been given an up-to-code watch to time runs, which was quite exciting for him. Blaz was glad he wouldn't be wearing one, though. Time seemed to enter a 'no passing' zone during cold runs. And having a watch to look at would make it worse.

"*Verdämmt*, it is cold out today," Koby shivered with his hands wrapped around himself.

"It sure is," Blaz said with his hands in his shorts, "Cold enough that I'm doing this," he gestured with his eyes to his hands.

"It is that type of weather."

"Sometimes I feel I could stay out in this for hours, except my hands freeze so easy," Blaz said.

"I can sympathize with that," Koby looked to the cabins, "Ah, here they come."

Johann and Ivo trotted to their former teammates.

"All right, let's go," Koby ordered his friends.

Koby quickly gained a lead, looking faster than ever. But Johann stayed much closer to him than normal. The eleven-year-old would be a force to be reckoned with in the future. Blaz and Ivo kept a respectable pace. On freezing days like this they found the only way to get through a long run like this was to make conversation.

"How have you liked our new commander?" Ivo asked.

"He is no *Herr* Schlusser, but you can't replace him. He's not as intimidating as *Herr* Schwinghammer was. I still like him though. He seems a bit on edge about leading the camp."

"Who can blame him? He looks like he's our age," Ivo snickered.

Blaz let a laugh through his nose, "I wouldn't go that far. But he does look *really* young."

"You can say that again."

"But he knows his stuff. He was an excellent shot with all the guns, he could pilot the tank, and he made quick work of Erich and Tybalt when he demonstrated some knew techniques on them."

"Speaking of 'excellent shots,' one of our squad mates is remarkably terrible."

"Ivo," Blaz groaned, "Don't say that."

"Aw, don't want to admit that your boyfriend is a horrible soldier?"

Blaz glared at Ivo murderously.

"Sorry," Ivo backed down, "But he can't shoot to save his life."

"Go easy on Jaye," Blaz said, glancing at the ground.

"He was stuttering and pausing through that entire reading when the teacher asked him to read that paragraph."

"What are you saying?"

"I'm saying I don't think he has good eyesight."

Blaz nodded. They kept their pace and remained silent for a few seconds.

"*Verdämmt*, it's so cold!" Ivo screamed suddenly.

Blaz jumped to the side, startled.

"Sorry, I just feel warmer when I yell."

"Fair enough but give me a warning."

"You got it," Ivo replied with a grin.

Their run lasted for twenty-five. By the time they'd returned, the rest of the camp was there, already on strength training. Push-ups, sit-ups, and crunches among others. They quickly joined in and proceeded to do what Koby ordered them to: two hundred seventy-five push-ups, three hundred crunches, a five-minute plank, and then stretching. By this time, most of the Hitler Youth, including Blaz, were immune to any workout their commanders could concoct. After a long stretch, it was time for education.

A Small, Rootless International Clique

The boys went into the headquarters and underground to the classrooms. Science was an important part of their education and heavily relied on. Technological progress and improving their people was the main goal of National Socialist education. Today their history teacher was giving them a lesson on the Roman Empire and how it was defeated by none other than Germans.

"Our ancestors defeated the strongest empire in world history. Not only that, our allies repelled another great empire, the Mongols. Neither Germans nor Japanese were ever meant to be ruled by another people. We wish all people to self-govern themselves in the end. But we were made to prosper and patrol. We were made to bring our race together, therefore making the world better. National Socialism, unlike Communism and Capitalism, encourages unity while maintaining the beauty of each race of people and preserving and cultivating their culture and uniqueness. Even more, we want our people to live life and live it to the fullest. That is, live well, live with a purpose. To strive to better themselves physically and spiritually. And someday all will unite to make the earth great. When the nations unite to fight a common enemy that threatens them all, this is true unity. It respects the existence of the various peoples on earth. Internationalism does not. *Deutschland,* Scandinavia, German Americans, even Britain will fall in with us. Already, the Mediterranean nations have joined us. Italy, Spain, many Frenchmen. One day, we may even bring the Slavs under the banner of National Socialism. We've become a race of *übermenschen*, superhumans," the history teacher explained. He was a lanky man, with slick, dark brown hair, and a thin face.

The teacher continued, "Mind you, *übermenschen* and subhuman *untermenschen* can be found in any race of people, indeed even our own such as the November criminals who signed the Versailles Treaty. You breed superiority through using your talents and abilities and strength to better your people. *Untermenschen* exist in every people. When you turn your back on your people you are among the lowest creatures on earth, lower than any animal. This is an *untermensch*. It is vital you understand this. No person is born as either. Loyalty to your people does not come at the expense of the hatred of others. God has created many peoples and all should ideally live on, indeed. When an animal goes extinct, we consider it a great tragedy and a loss. Should we not do the same for the many unique humans? *Deutschland's* people were on the road to extinction before the *Führer* brought faith and hope to her again. The *untermenschen* want only destruction, anarchy, and power for themselves. *Ja*, the Marxists and Capitalists both advocate this mindset, in different ways. They are two sides of the same coin." The teacher began to pace.

"The elite control the people with money and media. They cloud the people's minds with petty, idiotic details. And they will do anything to maintain this hold. This is why the war has come to be. Our great *Führer* has defied the Marxists and Capitalists and brought about prosperity for *Deutschland*. Internationalism, or International Jewry, being the ones behind the money, have seen to it that their press set out to stop us from bringing this alternative to the world. Our very ideas are a danger to them. You see, if we succeed and spread National Socialism, the Marxists and Jews will lose their grip and their power on the world. They will no longer be able to manipulate world events for their own gain. They will no longer control the banks and world currency. They won't be allowed to continue their propaganda through their cinema. They won't be able to continue with their plans to eradicate our people, our blood. It is for this reason they are *untermenschen*. For they do not wish to allow the many diverse peoples of this earth to live on. They wish for one race on this earth, lorded over by themselves. They wish to destroy the great beauty of the unique peoples of the world. They preach equality, but what they truly speak of is an equally shared misery. This stain on the earth known as Marxism, Egalitarianism, and Communism, of Jewish creation and advocacy, must be removed from Europe. They must keep to themselves. And the Jewish International Capitalism must be destroyed as well. Capitalism and Communism focus on the material. International Capitalism's end goal is a non-binary, soul-crushing machine. The society is not for the good of the people. It is for the good of those with the monopolies. In National Socialism, the state nurses a healthy community and the community nurses the state. Both work together for the good of their nation's people." The teacher paused for a moment. All eyes were intently looking upon him.

"Even now, *Deutschland* has united with repentant and awakened Jews. Our *Führer's* good friend Emil Maurice is a Jew. Yet he serves his nation in the *Luftwaffe* and was the second member of our SS. Should those who wish to help us be denied? *Nein*! They can embrace National Socialism for their people. It is our goal that all peoples embrace National Socialism so that each people may continue to live on and live to the fullest of their potential. Your own people are your most precious possession. The world must come to understand this. We live and fight for our people, for the continuation of its existence. Unfortunately, International Jewry has not followed the example of the few. So we must expel this plague. The Jew is indeed our enemy; they have oppressed us through their use of money, media, and the banks. They are schemers and usurpers. Their ideologies in both America and Russia are a threat to not only *Deutschland*, but to the world. If the world fails to see this now, they will one day pay dearly for it. Not by our hands. But one day, the entire world will know we are right. Whether tomorrow, or in the next century, it will come. The Jewish throne must be toppled before this happens."

Following their history class, Blaz's age group went to science class. Their biology class focused on education about humans and animals.

However, experiments were outlawed. No dissections of any animals took place.

Alongside this, physics and weapons science were strongly emphasized so Germany would remain the most advanced nation on earth in these categories. Blaz was just old enough to be in biology and because of the intensifying demands of the war, younger students were rushed through courses as efficiently as possible at the camps.

"The most ambitious and greatest races on earth dwell in the Germanic nations, for their people have worked to make them so. They are not so by default but have become this way. However, you boys will learn of human biodiversity while in this class. The uniqueness in each breed of humans allows them to excel in particular fields at varying degrees." The teacher paused, surveying the room. All eyes were on him.

"With this knowledge, you boys will have the great responsibility of advancing the Third Reich when we are gone. The *Führer* has great faith in you. All will fall under the banner of National Socialism. Pride and love for one's own people will take the world to great heights. In the future, our descendants will venture out and conquer yet unknown worlds. And you boys, from the Fatherland, must lead us to this. The world will be made great. Any Communists who would wish to destroy our society will be dealt with appropriately. *Jugend*, how is it that you maintain order?"

"Through strength," they answered simultaneously.

"*Ja*! Never go easy, do not be lenient on those who wish to harm our Reich. Those who would try to destroy our people deserve no mercy. Churchill, he must pay for his shameful bombings of our civilians. He brought the war to this, beginning civilian bombings. How will we defeat this menace? Our people must bond together, must work together towards this common goal. With *Deutschland's* work ethic and determination, nothing cannot be accomplished. And as you know, the Germanic work ethic is unrivaled. We have built ourselves up over centuries, numerous times proving our importance to the world. When we stand together, no one can topple us. There are innumerable contributions *Deutschland* and her people have given humanity access to: the printing-press, the airplane, the gasoline automobile, motorcycle, sub machine gun, flamethrower. Where would Europe be without *Deutschland*? They would be trapped in the dark ages! Under the oppression of the Catholic church! Germans caused even the Pope to lose his power! And we will cause the Communist leaders to lose their power as well!"

Arithmetic had the most humorous use of rhetoric. Blaz had seen Ivo silently laughing with his head down on his desk on reading it for the first time. This class was sprinkled with questions that kept the cadets' minds on the enemy. Today Blaz worked on this problem: "A bomber takes off weighing nine metric tons and carrying one hundred and sixty bombs, each weighing twelve kilograms. The bomber's fuel weighs one hundred and ten kilograms. The airplane drops its payload on Moscow, the world's capital of Marxism. When the airplane returns triumphantly, there are two hundred kilograms left in fuel and bombs. How much does the airplane weigh?"

Let's see now, Blaz thought, *nine thousand kilograms plus...* Blaz scribbled out some calculations. *One thousand nine hundred and twenty kilograms plus one hundred and ten kilograms equals... eleven thousand and thirty kilograms. Okay, now subtract two hundred from two thousand thirty, that's one thousand eight hundred and thirty. Subtract that from eleven thousand and thirty and that is... nine thousand two hundred.* Blaz wrote down his answer.

Next question.

"A bomb is prepared to drop on a weapons factory in Poland, the European center of Jewry, from a height of two hundred and twenty meters. The bomb weighs ten kilograms. What is the bomb's gravitational potential energy?"

Two hundred and twenty times ten times nine point eighty-one, that is... Blaz wrote out the problem and worked it, *twenty-one thousand five hundred and eighty-two joules.*

After many questions resembling these, education was over for the day. Now it was time for military training. The Knights were given a schedule. They would practice shooting, knife throwing, and assorted primitive weapon handling three times a week. The other four days would consist of technical and survival skills, such as starting fires, building traps, identifying edible plants, driving, repairing vehicles and hand-to-hand combat.

Jarman took Blaz aside for a match. The boys circled, like dogs in a fight. Jarman looked quite intimidating, there was a fire in his eyes, a desire to redeem himself for being beaten earlier. Not only this, but Jarman had grown several inches since their last match. His biceps were defined and large. His chest slanted upward, giving him a proud look. His physique now certainly rivaled that of Koby, and perhaps even Erich. Blaz had not gotten noticeably taller but his scrawnier form had transformed into a lean muscular body, strong enough to pass the high standards of the Hitler Youth. Blaz watched Jarman closely, allowing his opponent to make the first move. Jarman worked his way closer to Blaz, until he was within arm's reach. The moment he was, he took an aggressive swing at Blaz's head. Blaz bent back, his spine contracted into an unnatural position. He recovered quickly and sent a punch at Jarman's chest, making contact. Jarman barely noticed and bore down on his squad mate. Blaz had never felt smaller than he did now next to Jarman. His friend seemed to block out the sun. He was in the shadow of someone he felt couldn't beat.

Nein! Nein! He's just another soldier on the battlefield. Defeat him like the rest.

Blaz sprung at Jarman, catching his friend off guard. He fired a frenzy of punches, not letting Jarman return any. His friend stumbled back but did not fall. He shook the blows off and appeared even more determined to win now. He blocked or dodged punch after punch and kick after kick that Blaz sent his way. With no way to defeat Jarman and taking a beating to the head from the punches, Blaz tried the most insane and desperate move he had left. He leapt up, sent his legs above his head and wrapped them around Jarman's neck. Jarman bent to ground still not toppling, and Blaz landed on his back. Blaz and Jarman were now in an awkward position. Blaz's legs were wrapped around Jarman's neck while he lay on the ground, and Jarman faced in between Blaz's legs.

"*Scheiße,*" Jarman muttered. Then he untwisted Blaz's legs from around his neck and split them apart.

Blaz almost let out a cry of pain but suppressed it, despite feeling like he would rip in half. Jarman turned him onto his chest, still holding his feet with one hand and forced Blaz's face into the dirt with the other. His nose hit the ground and a wave of pain shot through his head. Blaz turned his head to the side to get a view and spit out some dirt. Jarman's palm wrapped around Blaz's skull. Blaz's feet were pressed into his lower back. His arms were unable to fight back as he couldn't turn to face Jarman.

"Give up?"

"Ha ha, ow!" Blaz said when his face was pressed into the ground even harder for his snippy response.

"Come on," Jarman jeered. Blaz tried to push-up but Jarman applied more pressure and his arms collapsed. He searched his mind for a way out. Jarman scraped his face against the dirt.

"Fine! *Du gewinnst,* you win!"

Jarman released Blaz, whose legs fell the ground. He rolled onto his back. His face and shirt soiled. He shook his head and a small cloud of dust came out of his hair. When he looked up, Jarman suddenly looked concerned, "God, Blaz! You are bleeding all over; your nose is spouting blood. And it looks like I broke it."

"What?" Blaz put a hand below his nose. When he brought it to eye level, it was covered in his own blood. His eyes went wide but only for one moment. The cadet quickly recovered from the surprise. "Would you look at that?" he said, hopping up energetically to prove he was okay.

"We need to stop that bleeding, see if it's broken. Let's get a rag," Jarman said, "No reason not to when we can."

"*Ja, ja,*" Blaz agreed as he trotted after Jarman.

The doctor's building lay behind the camp's headquarters. It was tiny, with white walls and a brown, shingled roof. Inside was a single room that was divided by a curtain so there would be a waiting area. Jarman offered a hand to his friend several times on the way there but Blaz repeatedly insisted he could walk by himself, getting annoyed after the third and final time. It wasn't that big of a deal. And Jarman was the tough guy. Even the mean guy. He had shoved Tristan to the ground after his squad mate had failed to hit a single target earlier in the week.

Jarman knocked on the door. The doctor did not answer, rather *Herr* Kurzmann. Before the young officer could ask why they were here and not at the range or in the fields, Blaz looked up, revealing his bloodied face and broken nose. Kurzmann nodded to himself and let them inside. He gestured to some seats. Jarman and Blaz sat down.

Kurzmann then walked to the other side of the curtain, "Doctor Steinbeck. When you are done with *Herr* Meyer, we have another patient for you," Blaz and Jarman heard Kurzmann say.

"Erich?" Blaz whispered.

"Maybe," Jarman whispered back.

They quieted down to eavesdrop on the conversation. Kurzmann came back through the curtain, "You know what? Just come in here, both of you, Senft and Knecht. You'll hear our conversation anyway."

In the doctor's room was Erich, on the examining table, in nothing but his underwear.

"Senft take off your shirt, try not to get blood on it," the doctor said.

"I just need a rag," Blaz answered, but unbuttoned his black uniform and white undershirt.

The doctor ignored Blaz, and moved on, "*Herr* Meyer, you may put your clothes on."

Jarman stood awkwardly in the background. While Erich dressed, Kurzmann told him some news.

"Meyer, you are being sent to a special school for the SS."

Erich's eyes lit up, he almost let out a shout of joy but maintained his composure.

"You are leaving at the end of the week on Sunday morning. You will receive training until you enter SS service at age seventeen. Your birthday is in May?"

"*Jawohl*," Erich confirmed.

"You are the pride of *Deutschland*; I am proud to have been your commander, brief as it was."

Erich laughed and replied, *"Danke, Herr* Kurzmann."

Blaz's gaze was forced up at the ceiling by the doctor, who was stopping the bleeding with some tissues, but Blaz moved his eyes to Erich and Kurzmann.

"The SS, congratulations Erich," Jarman gaped.

"Ja," Blaz said with his neck still craned at the ceiling, "What an honor."

"It really is an honor to be SS, but I'll miss you guys. Koby is squad leader now. Wonder who'll be corporal?"

"I get the feeling you know," Jarman said.

"It's you," Erich grinned again.

Jarman nodded with a smirk, not surprised at all. He knew he was at least the third best soldier in the squad and commanded some authority, being the strongest in the group with Erich's departure. Another departure.

Comrade, Seek the Übermensch

February 4, 1941 Tuesday

Four boys sprinted past a tree then slowed to a stop.

"Again!" Koby yelled as he led the boys back for another sprint.

"Come on, how many more?" Ivo whined.

"Three more!"

"You know running two kilometers is easier when you just run it straight through, instead of dividing it up," Ivo pointed out.

"We need our starts to be good, whether you're in a race or not," Koby said while he stopped at the starting line, "I have no doubt you could march to Paris and back, but if you aren't quick enough, you won't make it through the first battle."

"*Verdämmt*, that conversation shifted fast," Ivo shivered.

"Ivo, Ivo," Koby groaned. "*Auf die Platze! Fertig! Los!*"

Blaz, Jaye, and Koby fired air rifles side-by-side. A light rain made the ground turn to mud. Kurzmann watched intently. Air rifles were commonly used over real rifles for target practice to save money and materials. Bullets cost more than pellets. *Herr* Kurzmann had instructed the cadets to duck down and crawl over to other targets today. Since they used air rifles for this particular drill, they could do this without risk of wounding or possibly killing each other. Jaye's confidence was reeling now. He couldn't hit targets at all anymore. Today was no exception.

Blaz took a shot at a dummy, nailing it in the head. He dove to the ground and crawled to a new place on the range. He aimed diagonally across the range and fired. The dummy's head rocked back and forth when Blaz's pellet hit. Koby aimed his rifle over Blaz's shoulder and fired a shot. The pellet hit the dummy in the temple.

"Nice shooting," Blaz said.

"Same to you."

Blaz fired off several more shots, not missing once. Few cadets missed stationary targets at all anymore. Koby led the Knights to a second miniature firing range, on the edge of the forest. Kurzmann followed. The cadets needed to be prepared to be able to use anything possible as a weapon. Therefore, they were trained to throw rocks with deadly accuracy and could build primitive bows and arrows from wood and twisted bark.

"Okay, you remember how to build a bow and arrow, I hope?" Koby said, without forgiveness, should they have forgotten.

"*Jawohl*," each Knight replied.

"*Gut*, let's get going." The boys all ran into the forest to search for suitable wood and tough bark. When each boy had found one they thought sufficient, they would take their knife out and cut away. The process took time, but no one complained. Once their bows and arrows were made, they searched for rocks that would make a suitable arrowhead. This took even longer. It was not easy to find a stone sleek and skinny enough to make an arrowhead. Blaz and Ivo searched for a good twenty-five minutes before they found one apiece. Blaz fastened his rock to the arrow with twisted bark until it was immovably in place. Then they trotted back to the small range to test out their arrows. Each boy fired his arrow, many hitting the target but missing the bullseye. Ivo stepped up and fired an arrow straight into the bullseye of his intended target.

"*Gut gemacht!*" Koby complimented Ivo, and handed him another arrow, "Shoot again."

Ivo fired one at a second target and hit the bullseye.

"Third's the charmer," remarked Jarman, implying Ivo would miss. He ran to the targets and retrieved the arrows.

"Once more?" Ivo fired again and hit the bullseye.

"And you have no experience, before *Hitlerjugend*?" asked Koby.

"*Nein*, my father knows how to use them."

"At least we know what to do when we are weaponless. I'd like to see you start shooting like that with rifles."

"Baumann!" Kurzmann called out, "Come with me. The rest of you, head to lunch."

Jaye nodded and strode over to Kurzmann, saluting him.

Jarman, Erich, and Tristan had just finished their shooting. Tristan put away his rifle, and as he headed toward the others, Jarman violently shoved him to the ground. Tristan stayed down as Jarman approached him.

"Nothing?" Jarman said, sounding disappointed, "Fine."

Tristan watched Jarman walk away before he got to his feet.

Killing in War

February 5, 1941 Wednesday

Blaz was running faster than he had since the five-kilometer in November. Trial five-kilometer time, and Glöckner had been assigned to time them to make sure they were improving, particularly Koby. Johann had improved much since November, and while he couldn't challenge Koby, Kurzmann was keeping an eye on him as a potential SS candidate. Blaz and Ivo were both running their legs off to try to compete with Johann at this point.

"*Lauf schneller*, run faster!" Glöckner shouted as Blaz approached the finish line. Blaz gritted his teeth and put his head forward. His legs were blurs as he crossed. Ivo flew across the line soon after.

"Excellent! Koby, you got a fifteen twenty-four. Johann, sixteen fifty-seven this run, *verdämmt*, little man! Blaz, eighteen twenty-one, Ivo, you got an eighteen thirty-six. That's all brilliant or exceptional. I will give these results to *Herr* Kurzmann. Now go get ready for school," Glöckner ordered.

The four boys gave Tybalt a stiff-armed salute then walked to their rooms. Johann branched off earlier in the warehouse to head to his cabin while waving to his teammates.

"Nice kid," Ivo said.

"He is," Koby said, frowning, "I can't imagine him ever being in the SS or even the army for that matter."

"There's always the *Kriegsmarine* or *Luftwaffe*," Ivo laughed.

"Oh, shut up, Ivo," Koby said, "You know what I mean."

"I do."

Blaz interjected, "I don't know, he could be an excellent soldier. He's athletic-"

"All of us are at this point," Ivo interrupted.

"He's athletic and excellent in endurance. He's smart, he takes orders well, and he has decent military skills. Why wouldn't he be a soldier?" he inquired as they walked into their cabin, where Tristan was stacking up his books to take to class.

"*Guten Morgen*, Tristan," Blaz and Koby said in unison.

"*Guten Morgen*," Tristan responded with a shy smile. Koby, Ivo, and Blaz began to take off their running clothes and put on their winter uniforms. Tristan hurried out of the cabin once they'd arrived.

"We need to integrate him into the squad better," Koby said, "Returning to your question, Blaz, I believe that Johann is too, well, nice."

"Nice? That's why? You can't be nice and be in the military?" Blaz realized how stupid the question as soon as he asked it.

"There's more to it than that. Can you see him killing someone? Even if it is in a war?"

Blaz thought for a moment. "*Nein*," he admitted, "*Ich kann nicht.*"

"He's a reserved, respectful, good-natured kid. He's just respectful of life in general," Koby said as he put on his undershirt, "I'm wondering if he gets that war is different in that respect. It's okay to kill in a war. And even if he does know that, would he care?"

"He's not in your squad, so does it affect you?" Ivo said.

"Not really."

"Then why care?"

"Just because something doesn't affect me, doesn't mean I can't have a stance on it. Poverty doesn't affect me anymore, but I'm glad that we will get to work in the field this summer to help stop what little of that *Deutschland* has."

Ivo nodded slightly, not really absorbing what Koby had said.

Blaz looked over to Ivo, and back to Koby, "He'll be ready when the time comes. And he won't be in the war as soon as we will. He's eleven, we are thirteen, Jarman and you will be fourteen this June. Erich will in May."

"*Scheiße*! We're getting to that age quick," Ivo said.

"*Ja*, we'll be the third in line after Tybalt and Erwin's groups leave this summer," Koby reminded them.

"Koby?" Blaz cut in, "I know this is a bit off topic, but do you think you will be sent to an SS academy?"

Koby looked down and grinned, "*Nein*, I doubt it. That would be another squad leader gone. I think they're training me as a *Wehrmacht* officer at this point."

"That's good. I really wouldn't want you to leave."

"Me neither," chimed in Ivo.

"I'd like to stay too," Koby said, "I think I've got a talented squad, we could do some damage in the war."

"*Heil* Hitler," the history teacher saluted.

"*Heil* Hitler," the class enthusiastically replied.

"Now, have you all finished your papers?" the teacher asked the class.

"*Jawohl*," everyone answered simultaneously.

"*Sehr gut*. Pass them to the front."

Each student passed a single paper to the front. Their handwriting was small to conserve paper. When the teacher collected the papers, he placed them on his desk, and turned to the class, "Today we are going to quickly review the war up to this point."

"*Feuer! Feuer!*" Koby yelled at his squad. Jarman fired the artillery piece and a deafening roar was emitted.

"Reloading," Koby said while he and Hans prepared the artillery to fire again. Blaz and Ivo spun the piece to aim to the right, into the fields.

"*Fertig, feuer!*"

Jarman fired the artillery.

"One more time! Reload her!"

Ivo and Blaz rotated the artillery further right.

"*Feuer!*"

A final roar crackled in the air. Once the sound faded, the boys turned and stood erect. Kurzmann nodded and waved them along.

Koby ordered the squad to make formations, which he headed. Kurzmann evaluated their efficiency, seeming to constantly look up with skepticism. The boys held fake rifles and moved in accordance to their commander's orders.

"*Heil*!" Koby finished, and all the Knights shot their right arm into the air.

"Move along," Kurzmann gestured, "Begin marching drills."

The Knights goose-stepped away doing the head turn as they pretended the *Führer* stood where they turned their heads. Koby held his hand up to halt.

"Okay, form up. Two-by-two."

"*Gut gemacht*," Erich said approvingly to Koby off to the side. Blaz ran a finger across his dirty forehead.

The Truth is With Us

February 6, 1941 Thursday

"Always coldest on our long run days, is it not?" Blaz said to Ivo while they ran through the fields.

"It wasn't bad yesterday."

"It was good, always nice to not have terribly cold weather for five-kilometer time trials." As Blaz said this he let out a coarse, rough cough, "Because that is what happens."

"Whoa, you sound like a sick horse."

"Oh, shut up, you."

Ivo smiled and turned his focus back forward. The weather had taken a turn over the night. Clouds were in the sky on this day. The sun did not even try to break through. No snow came but clouds covered the entire horizon on the frigid winter day. The boys ran through field after field, running their hardest, despite their limbs going numb the further they went. When it felt as though their fingers might become immovable, Koby ran by them. He yelled their time as he went by. That was their signal to turn around. No time was spared and Blaz and Ivo spun on their heels. They increased their pace, aiming for a negative split, meaning their time on the run back would be shorter than the run out. Once they'd finished, they stretched out with Koby quickly to warm their bodies. Koby informed them they achieved a negative split before they headed to change into their Hitler Youth uniforms. While Blaz slid his tiny running shorts off, his bare hand brushed his thigh.

"*Mein Wort*! That is cold!" he whispered.

'What?" Ivo asked.

"*Nichts*," Blaz answered, "Nothing."

"Each of you has been born into the Third Reich. The Reich has become the culmination of human civilization. What we had accomplished in six years before the sword was thrust into our hands is truly incredible. We have established the precedent that the world will soon follow. Civilizations where each people strives to perfect themselves, rid themselves of the sick immoralities that our beloved Fatherland was a haven for before our *Führer* brought back the Protestant values that Germans had held dear. Bear in mind, we changed the culture of our nation before it was too late. We were no superior people, as the *Führer* made clear in *Mein Kampf*. Certainly, we were and are superior to many primitive people, but we were in a state of decay. Each people does indeed have strengths and weaknesses that come about naturally, but the goal of National Socialism must always be to improve your people, their work ethic, their science, their creativity!

Always dream boys! One day, when this war ends, we will accomplish great things. Build magnificent buildings, drain seas to make room for our growing populace, build aircraft that will propel us to the stars! As Germans, as brothers, we shall accomplish all this. The greatest gift anyone can be given is their own people! The National Socialist fire can never be truly extinguished as long as you remain loyal. I cannot stress enough, that whether tomorrow or in one hundred years, the day will come. Know this as you fight for the *Führer* and *Deutschland*. In the end, truth will be the victor in this struggle. The truth is with us,"

Following the long-winded introduction to their history class, they studied the accomplishments of the German people and how they could continue to improve the Fatherland. Historical events were cited to back up claims. From the heroic Germanic tribes to the German states being the first to throw off the chains of Catholicism, there were many events that the Germans could turn to.

"*Schneller!* Faster!" Kauffman shouted at Koby's squad. Blaz pumped his arms, completing push-up after push-up, even as his pace slowed. Jarman and Erich appeared as if they were in fast motion. Koby and Jurgen steadily cranked out push-ups. Hans and Reinhardt kept persisting, though it was apparent they were struggling. Tristan and Ivo were stopping every five by now, but did not lower to the ground, they stayed propped on their palms. Blaz's arms were wearing out and he arched his back to give himself a quick respite. Almost as soon as he had done so, he started back up again. Another seven push-ups and his right leg began to shake as he came up for an eighth. Suddenly his left arm gave out but he recovered before he could touch the ground.

One by one, the Knights finished their allotted push-ups and Glöckner ordered them to work the tank's cannon. The tank was loaded only with blanks, and only blanks for reloading. The *Panzer III* had a crew of five so Erich and Koby were the commanders and drafted men into their squad. Erich's squad of Jarman, Hans, Reinhardt, and Tristan went first. They drove the tank forward and backward, fired some blank shots and rotated the main gun. Koby and his squad hopped in once they'd finished. Koby ordered each man to his position.

"Erich, you are the loader. Blaz, you are the gunner. Jurgen, you're the driver. Ivo, you're the bow gunner."

Koby climbed to the hatch to take command. Jurgen started it up. The tank's engine emitted a low roar then transitioned into a smooth hum. The tank crawled forward.

"All right, Erich, load a shell! Blaz, fire on my command! Ivo, give us some anti-personnel fire. Ivo's machine gun fired empty shots over and over. The loud bangs kept coming. Koby rotated the main gun to the left into the open field.

"Shell loaded!" Erich called.

"*Ein Moment*," Koby answered, "Not yet... *feuer*!"

Blaz fired the cannon. The inside of the tank was rocked by sound. The tank itself vibrated from the violent emission.

"Again!"

Erich lifted another blank shell and put it in place.

"Ready!"

"Fire her away!"

The gun sounded and crackled through the air.

"Now move her back, reverse! Reverse! They're firing back!"

Jurgen immediately backed the tank up. Koby watched through the top of the tank for anyone in the tank's way, whether he was pretending or not was up to interpretation. He kept the commander's pistol unholstered.

In the room that night the boys all undressed from the long day. It was only nine o'clock, which was the curfew at their KLV camp, so the boys normally stayed up talking until they fell asleep. None of the boys had been allowed any pajamas, as they weren't becoming of a soldier, so the boys slept in their underwear with two blankets during the cold winter nights.

When they'd all gotten in bed, Jaye entered the room. Blaz's eyes went wide when he saw his squad mate. Jaye was wearing big, round, thin-brimmed glasses and his dirty blond hair was neatly combed, something he never did.

"Jaye, you're back!" Ivo blurted out upon seeing him, "You look sharp!"

"I look like an idiot, don't I?" he asked, but not looking embarrassed.

"*Nein, nein*, you look good with glasses," Koby told him.

Jaye still looked skeptical.

"You look good with glasses, Jaye," Erich assured him. Jaye took Erich's opinion as fact and walked over to his bunk.

"I think Reinhardt would look good with them too," Hans remarked.

Reinhardt stroked his chin and pretended to smoke a pipe.

"They gave me contacts too. Two pairs of them for when we go into combat."

"Aren't those really uncomfortable?" Ivo asked.

"I didn't think so. The ones they gave me aren't glass."

"Ivo, you were having trouble with those push-ups today," Erich said with a patronizing grin.

"After one hundred, my arms feel like they're falling apart from the inside."

"Erich," Koby began, "SS? Where are you heading?"

"SS camp southwest of Seelow. Our training is going to be brutal. I'll be deployed in April of nineteen forty-four, should they need me," Erich answered, "But I'll have a lot of near combat experience before then, I've been told. You guys probably will too. *Hitlerjugend* has been performing behind the front-line tasks lately in the West."

"I can't wait for that," Ivo said.

"*Ja*," agreed Jarman.

Jurgen cut in, "What's the number one thing you miss from Seelow?"

The boys thought for a moment.

"The warmer houses," Ivo answered with wide eyes.

"It was less rigid," Blaz replied.

"The women," Hans laughed.

Some of the other boys looked at Hans in confusion, though Erich and Jarman found amusement from this.

"Gosh, I never thought I'd miss girls, and now I haven't seen one in over a month and I'm losing my mind," Hans said.

"Wait, you wouldn't count the chefs, or any teachers?" Jarman asked, on the verge of laughing.

"*Nein*," Hans replied, losing his composure, "If I did the SS would probably throw me in prison for pedophilia or something."

The boys all silently laughed at this remark. Their silent laughs became snickers until they were all laughing out loud. They did not laugh long, knowing that the cabin next door would hear them.

"I don't know why I laughed," Koby said still smiling, "It wasn't even that funny," he realized.

"We just all were ready to laugh at something, we hold laughter in all day," Ivo grinned.

"Okay, *ja*."

"I still feel like an idiot," Jurgen said.

"*Ja*," Hans agreed.

"All right, *Herr* Comedian," Koby said, "Let's cool off from that."

Blaz smiled and lay down on his top bunk above Jarman. Koby turned off the sole gas lamp they were allotted. Blaz pulled a blanket over his bare chest. His smile remained when he closed his eyes.

Winter March

February 7, 1941 Friday

Clouds blanketed the Eastern German countryside. Light snow fell as Blaz ran through the open, harvested fields. Ivo ran beside him, Koby and

Johann were far ahead. Their nearly bare legs were red and purple from the frosty, frigid air. Each exhale turned to vapor and dusted their faces. They ran in silence.

Blaz frantically studied his notes for some last minute studying before math.

"Notes away!" the teacher commanded, "Time for the quiz."

Their math teacher passed out quizzes to each student. Everyone got to work immediately. Blaz started on the first problem. He flew through the first five with ease. Then the word problems began.

A Panzer IV weighs twenty-five tonnes. A Panzer III weighs twenty-three tonnes. A Panzer II weighs eight point nine tonnes. A Panzer battalion is made up of fifteen Panzer IV's, ten Panzer III's and fifteen Panzer II's. How much is the battalion's weight?

Blaz scribbled multiplications onto his quiz. It took a little time but he finally wrote seven hundred and thirty-eight point five tonnes.

A factory employs three hundred personnel. The employees produce ten thousand bullets per day. The bullets are put into the mags of MP-40s, Karabiner 98Ks and Walther P38. Knowing these mag capacities, how many magazines for each gun could the employees fill with bullets when specializing in a given weapon?

Blaz knew the mag capacity for each gun by heart so he had little difficulty.

MP-40s: Three hundred and twelve point five magazines.

Walther P38s: One thousand two hundred and fifty magazines.

Karabiner 98Ks: Two thousand magazines.

Kurzmann's training was efficient to say the least. He looked and sounded like a cadet, but he commanded the camp with unchallenged authority.

Blaz's squad was sent into the forest to stay the night. Every cadet secretly hated this assignment during winter, though fortunately they rarely had to do it. It was still afternoon, but Kurzmann wanted a long march before the boys could rest. Then they could set up camp and find food and water for the night. The cloud cover kept any potential warmth from the sun away. Koby and Erich marched at the head of the squad. Behind them, two by two, came Hans and Reinhardt, Blaz and Tristan, Ivo and Jurgen, Jarman and Jaye. The boys marched briskly with straightened legs. Their bags slung over their shoulders, they carried an air rifle in one arm with the barrel facing to the sky. Their eyes remained locked ahead, trying to forget the cold. Blaz was glad he was marching next to Tristan. No talking was permitted on this march until the commanders ordered a halt. Had he been next to Ivo, Blaz didn't know whether he'd be able to remain quiet. Tristan was already a quiet individual, and Blaz didn't know him well. There was no bad blood between any members of the Knights. They all got along and had some good laughs in the cabin each night, but Tristan was generally in the background during those conversations. Even Reinhardt spoke more. Blaz glanced at his squad mate through the corner of his eye. Tristan's hazel eyes remained focused ahead, so Blaz returned his gaze forward, *I wonder if his father is alive. I wonder how my papa is doing.*

How Fathers Were Doing

Ottoway Senft stood stiffly in front of a stone building. The weather was frigid but he toughed it out. The building was the largest in the small northern Norwegian town. It housed the *Wehrmacht* headquarters. The stone building had the appearance of a middle age structure but had a rough wooden roof. Inside lay the office of the *Wehrmacht* Second Lieutenant in charge of the town and the sleeping quarters of the *Wehrmacht* soldiers. There were very few jobs to do in this town, which thirty-nine-year-old Ottoway was just fine with. Two guards always stood at the entrance to their headquarters though no incidents ever happened. A guard was posted at the back of headquarters at all times. At least five soldiers were required to be patrolling the few streets of the city during the day. When curfew occurred, all the men but two would sweep through the town to make sure everyone had returned home. Two guards always patrolled around headquarters at night. Only sixteen soldiers had been selected to stay in this small town not including the Lieutenant. They were all over thirty, most of them fathers like Ottoway. All had been drafted, save the lieutenant, who was a veteran of *Der Krieg*. The Norwegians were quite compliant and Ottoway had learned some Norwegian through talking with them every day. He had also taught some of them German. Norway had been so cooperative that Ottoway's squad was pulling out next month, only leaving the Lieutenant and four other men. Ottoway had been fortunate to avoid combat thus far, and he prayed it would remain this way for the duration of the war.

Far south of Ottoway's town, in the Norwegian port city of Bodø, Ormand Schwinghammer directed Norwegians down a wide street lined with destroyed buildings. They held tools, pushed wheelbarrows full of stone and two large trucks rolled behind them carrying mortar to the blasted out of buildings.

"*Ja*, that's it. Let's get your city rebuilt!" he shouted to them in their own language while holding a map of the city. Schwinghammer had been made *Standartenführer* of Bodø. The forty-year-old SS officer was to rebuild the city while recruiting Norwegians and Swedes into the *Wehrmacht* and SS. His company numbered two-hundred-and-fifty soldiers and new men were added each week from the locals. The *Standartenführer* he'd replaced had been sent to prepare younger troops in case of a Soviet attack. Schwinghammer looked over his papers with his lieutenant and pointed to a building, one that was especially gutted. A little girl sat amongst the wreckage with a boy who looked to be her slightly younger brother. The two watched the workforce begin to repair the town.

"Such a pity that we had to bomb these great nations," the *Standartenführer* lamented, "We will make it up to them."

"*Jawohl, Standartenführer*," the lieutenant concurred.

In The Hague, The Netherlands, Reinhardt's father, Albert, patrolled the cobblestone streets with his rifle gripped tightly. The forty-year-old walked in a loose formation with three other men, about his age. The streets were lined with colorful houses all connected together. Reinhardt's father hadn't seen any combat yet, and like Ottoway, he prayed it would remain that way.

To the east, Jarman's father, Rudolf, was already preparing for action in the east. While the plans were secret, the German soldiers had a good idea that the USSR would not be their ally for much longer. German intelligence suspected a Soviet attack was coming. Jarman's father had been in Southern Poland and had seen combat during the opening days of the war. Other than a short six-week stint in the attack on France, combat had been scarce for the last year. The thirty-eight-year-old would soon be designated to be part of Army Group South.

Koby's father looked like his son. Older, but he had the same runner's body, even more so after months of service in the army. Jakob was not the best shot but the thirty-five-year-old had accepted that he would probably die in service and like many Germans, was willing to. It was no longer up to him if he survived.

In Warsaw, a city never willing to submit whether to Germans or Soviets, Erich's father was constantly quelling insurrectionists and reactionaries. The thirty-four-year-old was frustrated by some of his SS superiors' attitudes toward Jews, who he was often in combat against. The ghettos were necessary: the Jews had too many violent partisan movements in the Reich. But he hated that he was often kept from the front to quell uprisings. Erich's father had been successful in recruiting German Jews and Poles into the *Wehrmacht* and SS. While many in the SS congratulated him on this, there were those who were disgusted by it. Ulrich Meyer did not care what anyone thought as long as Germany won in the end.

A group of young soldiers sat around a large wooden crate. Each young man held several cards in their shivering hands. Their breaths turned into clouds at each exhale. An MP-40 was slung around Henrik Klein by a strap. Each young man was eager to see action, ignoring their instincts of self-preservation.

Reynald Schlusser held his dagger in his hand. Blood dripped off the tip of the sharp blade. The young officer's life for the last weeks had been drastically different than his time training the Hitler Youth. He had just killed two Polish insurgents who attacked him while he investigated a building. The twenty-year-old officer had been searching houses for weapons that the Reich would confiscate. This was not the first time they'd been attacked while searching a building. Two days earlier, an elderly Pole fired a pistol at Schlusser when his two guards had gone into the back of the shop, where they found a stash of weapons for the Polish resistance. The man knew he would be found out and attempted to kill Schlusser. And he should have hit him. But fate and the old man's unstable arm gave Schlusser his life back. The bullet flew past Schlusser's head right above his shoulder. With uncanny speed, the young officer drew his Luger and sent a bullet through the old man's chest. His soldiers were in the room seconds later and reported their findings.

Today, Schlusser had been questioning a young man and his business partner, both about his own age. He'd ordered his men to wait outside a room, giving the Poles some form of trust. Schlusser searched the area for weapons, particularly where the Poles would be seated. While he was doing so, he heard a dagger being unsheathed. Both men pulled knives on Schlusser and charged him. Schlusser was bent down, so rather than pulling a weapon he kicked out the legs from under the attacker. He parried an attack from the second Pole, giving him time to draw his own dagger. His men had heard the commotion and ran in, rifles raised. One Pole fell immediately. But the second was too close to Schlusser to take a shot. The Pole knew he was doomed now, but a dead SS officer would be a worthy sacrifice. He took a stab at Schlusser's heart. Schlusser sidestepped the attack with speed, grabbed the wrist of his attacker, and tightened his grip on a nerve. The Pole dropped his knife.

"You're coming with us now," Schlusser said in Polish, one of many languages he knew, as he looked into the man's eyes.

The Pole spat, "Go to hell, Nazi," and swung his free fist at Schlusser.

Schlusser ducked, spun behind the Pole, and stabbed him in the back. The young man gasped. Schlusser pulled his dagger out and let the Pole collapse to the ground, as he bled out. Schlusser shook the blood from the blade as best he could before sheathing it and ordered his two men to dispose of the bodies. A shot rang out and Schlusser looked at one of the soldiers who shrugged.

"He wasn't dying fast enough," the soldier said, ejecting the empty shell from his rifle.

When they got into their car bound for headquarters, one of the SS soldiers turned to Schlusser who sat in the back of the open top car.

"How many have you killed?" the young soldier asked.

"Poles?"

"People in general."

"None," Schlusser laughed.

"Come on now. They're people."

"Have a sense of humor. I've killed as many as you've seen, at least in this year. I don't know how many in thirty-nine."

"So four?"

"*Jawohl*. Can we agree that Marxists aren't people?"

"Sure," the soldier laughed, before turning serious, "That was the first person I've killed."

"Doesn't surprise me," Schlusser replied, "You are one of the younger in the SS, at seventeen. How did it feel?"

"It felt so... sudden. It was so easy. I just pulled the trigger and BANG! He was gone."

"Trust me, it won't feel like that when we go into combat. Each kill is earned and it's hard. We'll be lucky to survive a single battle."

The young soldier pulled at his collar. He'd heard this, but he hadn't yet killed anyone when he had been told before.

The Youth Continue Marching

Finally, the freezing march was over and done with. At least until the next morning. Koby sent Reinhardt and Jurgen to find some firewood, Blaz and Tristan to find some dry grass, Hans, Ivo, and Jaye to search of water, while he, Erich and Jarman spread out to find food. Blaz and Tristan accomplished their task and set about gathering quickly in silence until Blaz asked, "Why are you so shy, Tristan?"

Tristan looked up from looking down at the grass with an emotionless expression. Blaz swallowed and reworded his question, "I mean, so quiet, so reserved?"

Tristan looked Blaz in the eye. His normally tanner face had paled from the little sunlight Germany saw in winter. He slowly opened his mouth, as if he was hesitant to reply, "I-I honestly don't know. You know, since it's just the two of us, I don't feel pressured to say the right things," Tristan explained, "I feel that around groups, I know I shouldn't. Were you ever quiet around groups?"

Blaz thought for a moment. He'd been friends with the boys from Seelow for as long as he could remember. He wasn't the most social boy, but he wasn't shy by any standards, so he answered, "Not really."

"I-"

"What?" Blaz asked quickly.

"Nothing," Tristan said.

"*Nein*, what is it?" Blaz persisted. Tristan shook his head and looked away.

"*Kamerad*?"

At this, Tristan turned back, "I used to be in the *Swingjugend*, back in Cologne before we moved to Neuhardenburg. Hans helped me to leave that lifestyle behind. I met him when the *Swingjugend* and I were out at night beating up Hitler Youths. I stayed behind after we beat Hans up."

"Why?"

"Why'd we beat them up or why did I stay behind?"

"I know that the *Swingjugend* were degenerate leftovers from the Weimar Republic. Why'd you stay behind?"

"I didn't at first. I walked about twenty meters with everyone else, out of the alley where we'd beaten him up. But I stopped. I heard Hans groan and I walked back to him. We'd given it to him real good. His arm was broken, you could see it jutting out under the skin. I sat down next to him and he glanced up at me. No hatred at all, no thirst for revenge. He smiled, tried to smile, and asked me, 'Why do you hate me?' I told him it was because he was a National Socialist and National Socialists are, well, too constricting. He stood and asked me if I wanted to go to the mountains with his detachment the next weekend. For some reason, I found myself walking home with him, and taking him to the doctor. We became fast friends after the little trip to the mountains."

"Awesome."

Tristan nodded. "I was put in Hans' squad. I was the smallest kid in my squad and we weren't all buddies. A few of them had come across the *Swingjugend* before and weren't as forgiving as Hans. Hans got along well enough with everybody, he probably would've gotten along better if he hadn't stood up for me all the time."

"*Ja?*"

Tristan smiled slightly. "I was the odd one out. They always were always," Tristan seemed at a loss of words now. Though appropriate words were there he didn't, or wouldn't, use them. But he continued after a long pause, "They would dominate me, I guess," Tristan lowered his voice so only Blaz could hear even if someone was nearby, "They'd beat me up a lot whenever I failed at our drills or said something that was stupid. I used to say a lot of stupid things. I still fail at our drills a lot too."

"Tristan-" Blaz tried to object, though he knew it was true. Tristan's weaknesses far outnumbered his strengths. He wasn't just weak and scrawny, he wasn't very fast and he was horrible at school.

"Blaz, don't try to sugarcoat it. I'm a terrible soldier," Tristan said bluntly, "And I'm stupid." Blaz looked at the ground for a moment and picked up some dry grass. Tristan waited for him to look back up, almost for his approval because when Blaz made eye contact, he continued, "Whenever they did that, Hans would try to talk them out of it, but they ignored him."

"What happened? I feel like this is going somewhere."

"It is," Tristan nodded, "One day, after drills we were at my old squad mate's home. His father is an automobile mechanic, so we were in the shop where he works. There were some cars there with their wheels off. We were just talking at first, but then I said something and the mood kind of changed. A few minutes later they told me to hold this plywood, so they could take punches and try to break it. I was holding it, back to one of the cars. They started punching it and every time I would take a few steps back then step back forward. Hans didn't throw any punches, I'm glad he didn't. But most of my squad was strong and one of them broke through the board. His fist hit me in the face and I stumbled backwards, and my head scraped against the underside of... you know the wheels, the part right above it?"

"*Ja?*"

"It was pretty rusty and it caused this," Tristan pointed to his scar.

"*Mein Wort*," Blaz murmured.

"I guess that's why I don't talk all that much," Tristan admitted and picked up some dry grass.

Blaz glanced at the ground, then back to Tristan who looked up from the grass, "You should talk more. After all, we will be in the *Wehrmacht* together as squad mates."

"I guess I should," Tristan nodded.

"How much longer until we head to battle, do you think?"

"When we are sixteen, I bet. We will probably be helping out behind the lines sometime next year, if the war is still happening then."

"That will be great. Being a soldier."

"That's what I've been living for. It will be an honor to fight for *Deutschland*."

Blaz and Tristan grinned at each other and hurried back to the campsite.

The squad shivered miserably in the cold night. They were grouped around the fire, trying to get more warmth. Snow had begun to fall and the boys now stood up and moved around to keep warm.

"*Verdämmt*, I hope it's not this cold wherever we fight," Ivo shivered. Ivo and Tristan seemed to be the coldest of the group, as they were shivering much faster.

"Me too," Tristan said and wrapped around his shoulders. Blaz let a smile curl on one side of his mouth.

"We all do. Now, let's not talk about the weather," Jarman suggested.

"*Ja, ja*," Hans agreed, "I don't want to think about the cold. We have to be here all night anyway."

"Speaking of which, what time is it?" Jaye asked Koby.

Koby held the watch closer to the fire.

"It's twenty-one hundred."

"And what time did they say we can head back?"

"Oh seven thirty, tomorrow morning."

"Jesus," Jaye sighed.

"Before we change the subject, I think we all know that we aren't getting sleep tonight," Koby said, "We are going to have to keep moving to keep from freezing."

"So, we walk in circles for the next nine and a half hours?" Ivo asked.

"Pretty much."

"*Scheiße*," Hans swore.

The Waffen and the Allgemeine

February 8, 1941 Saturday

The Knights trudged through a new blanket of snow that covered the earth, their faces expressionless from a night of absolute misery. No one spoke. Hans and Ivo remained silent. Koby did not bother to keep them in formation. Blaz's eyelids felt like lead. His legs felt weak, and he had to focus hard to walk straight. He stumbled several times while they made their way through the snow, which made it even more difficult to walk. For what felt like days, they hiked.

"Good job squad," Koby said with a yawn.

Herr Kurzmann trotted over to the exhausted squad, "Well done boys. Now I know you'll hate to hear this but it will be a normal day for you still. The enemy certainly won't let you have a rest. Koby, Ivo, Blaz, you know what to do. The rest of you come with me."

Koby led the two back to their cabin where they changed into their running uniforms.

"Koby, if I die on this run, will you pick my body up?" Ivo said, only half-joking.

"*Nein*, I don't have the energy. I couldn't lift up a piece of paper right now. So on second thought, *ja*, I'll pick your body up."

"Oh *nein*!" Ivo pointed at Koby, "You shut up, *arschloch*."

"Just kidding *freund*."

"Ready?" the high, child voice of Johann said from the cabin entrance, "Ready to run in the snow?"

"What?" Blaz looked towards the entrance. "Hey! Johann!"

"*Ja*, we're ready," Koby smiled. He turned to Blaz and Ivo, "Johann would be a good fit for our squad."

They walked out of the cabin and eased into a run. Soon, Koby got his usual lead but Johann was tailing him closely. Blaz and Ivo kept a competent speed but lacked any spark. They could tell that Koby was staying ahead of Johann through sheer willpower. The snow weighed them down, making each stride difficult. They pushed through the run and came back completely exhausted. Johann was as energetic as before, though he'd run as fast as he ever had trying to catch Koby, this being his only chance. Koby had to be spent, but being an officer, did a fine job concealing it.

That day of school was one of the most brutal of Blaz's life. He, nor Koby, nor anyone in their squad had eaten in twelve hours, they'd stayed up walking around all night, had a morning workout and still had to wait for three more hours. Their stomachs felt nonexistent. And worse yet, the teachers had picked today to have lectures. Trying to stay awake during a lecture after such a night was difficult but none of the boys dozed off, for fear of the consequences.

"The *Schutzstaffel*, or SS, are the best trained and most elite German troops," explained the history teacher, "They fight for *Deutschland*, and for National Socialism. As I've heard, we have one student in here that will become an SS trainee tomorrow. He knows who he is, but I must emphasize the honor it is to be drafted into the SS. Furthermore, there are different divisions of the SS. The *Waffen-SS* and the *Allgemeine-SS*. The *Waffen-SS* fights alongside our great *Wehrmacht* soldiers, many of you will be a part of the *Wehrmacht's* army branch. The *Allgemeine-SS* acts as a police force for the Reich's territories."

There were more branches of the SS, these known notably for running internment camps, battling the partisan fighters and the *Gestapo*. The *Allgemeine-SS* was tightly connected to these minor branches, to be sure.

One last time at the firing range. Erich shipped out for an SS academy the next morning. Blaz took his practice shots, striking his mark with each. He then stepped out and walked over to Erich and his friends. A depressed, smile if ever there was one worked its way onto his face. The whole squad would miss Erich, but the SS was the ultimate honor one could receive. Their friend was taking a step forward, and they were proud and happy for him.

After more drills and a better than usual dinner, the boys were dismissed to their cabins. They were exhausted but felt the need to stay up and talk with Erich.

"Last night with us," Koby said.

"*Ja,*" Erich said sadly, "I can't believe it."

"You're going to make the *Führer* proud," Jarman told him, "I'll miss you though."

"You really have earned this honor," Blaz said, "I just wish you didn't have to leave for it."

"Me too," Ivo added.

"I didn't know you that well before this last month or so," Jaye chimed in, "But I'm glad that I got to know you. You are the best soldier in Seelow."

Erich nodded. "*Danke,* guys. I'll make *Deutschland* proud. It's been great being squad mates with all of you. And I couldn't have asked for better friends to grow up with," he said, glancing at the boys of Seelow. "Keep working hard. With luck, we'll meet in the war someday."

Erich's Departure

February 9, 1941 Sunday

At the crack of dawn, Kurzmann knocked on the cabin door. Today was the day off for the Hitler Youth, and so most were allowed to sleep in, but, the SS had arrived early this morning, so Koby's squad and the rest of their age group quickly changed into their winter uniforms and followed *Herr* Kurzmann. The morning was frigid, with fresh snow on the ground. A short distance outside the camp, sat a truck bearing the *Balkenkreuz*, a straight-armed cross, resembling a black addition symbol with a white outlining. Two officers stood waiting for their new recruit. One was perhaps in his early thirties; the other looked to be fifty and was decorated with many different awards, including an Iron Cross for service in *Der Krieg*. Several young *Waffen-SS* soldiers stood around the truck, chatting with one another in their obsidian uniforms. Kurzmann approached the officers and raised his right arm. The officers looked up. Both were strongly built, the younger had dark brown hair, which was barely visible under his cap and a had neck like a tree trunk. The older had white hair and a scar from previous service, running down his mandible.

"*Heil* Hitler!"

"*Heil* Hitler!" the officers responded.

"I have brought your newest cadet. I assume you will be needing these papers." Kurzmann said as he held up a folder with papers recording Erich's accomplishments in the Hitler Youth, his ancestry, and identification.

"*Jawohl*, of course," the older officer replied. He flipped the folder open and examined the papers. After a few minutes, he looked up again.

"Everything seems to be fine," the officer said smoothly, "Now, Erich Meyer. Step forward."

Erich did so. The officer walked over to Erich. He looked him up and down. No emotion was readable from the officer's expression. The boys watched him closely. Finally, the officer stepped back.

"Erich, you certainly look to be what they say you are. We are excited to train you at our school. You will be a great soldier," the officer complimented his young prospect. "If you have any parting words, now is the time to say them."

Erich nodded and turned around. He made his way over to his friends, hands behind his back. First, he came to Koby. He gave him a hug. "I love you, Koby. Take care of them for me. They're going to need a good leader to take them through the war," Erich said, his eyes misty, "And if this war ends soon, good luck at the Olympics."

Koby patted Erich on the shoulder, "Good luck in the SS. Bring *Deutschland* glory. I'll miss you, *Brüder*."

Erich gave Hans, Jaye, and Tristan some quicker hugs and goodbyes.

"Jurgen, keep everyone together. You're the peacekeeper."

Erich walked over to Jarman, but before he could do anything, Jarman wrapped his arms around Erich's shoulders and neck.

"God, I'm going to miss you. Make the *Führer* proud. I wish you didn't have to go so soon," Jarman said through gritted teeth, eyes shut tight.

"I'm going to miss you too, Jarman. Keep working the way you've been, maybe see me at the academy?"

Jarman laughed a bit. "Maybe."

Erich reached into his pocket and pulled out the SS pin that Jarman had given him at Christmas over a year before.

"Now I can put this on," he told his friend, clipping the pin to his uniform.

Erich moved to Blaz and bent down to give him a hug.

"Blaz, you're extremely thoughtful, you consider things. You don't need to, we already have it figured out, but you're a good kid. Be ready for war, Blaz. Don't let it take you off guard."

"Don't worry, I won't. Godspeed, *Kamerad*," Blaz nodded firmly.

Erich didn't bother bending down for Ivo. He picked him up and set him back down, "Ivo, don't let the war take away your sense of humor. Stay positive. Keep the Knights together."

Ivo returned tight-lipped grin.

"Reinhardt, when you have something to tell them during the war, tell them. You're smart, they're going to need some of that, I know."

Reinhardt gave him a reassuring nod, "Take care, Erich."

"You too."

"All right," the officer called to the soldiers, "Load up! We are moving out! We have more camps to stop at! Let's go!"

Erich turned and strode toward the truck. The SS soldiers climbed into the truck. Erich hoisted himself in by the handgrip. One SS soldier chuckled at the young boy's eagerness. As the truck revved up, Erich glanced back at his friends and waved. Jarman and Koby extended their right arms into the air. The rest of the squad and entire age group joined in the salute. Kurzmann himself extended his arm as the truck pulled further away into the distance. They watched until the truck was out of sight, then, one-by-one, turned back to the camp. Kurzmann, Marvin's squad, Hans, Jaye, Tristan, Ivo, Blaz, Reinhardt, Jurgen, Koby, and finally Jarman.

Eve of Barbarossa

June 4, 1941 Wednesday

Kurzmann had departed, leaving Glöckner and Kauffman back in command. The boys anxiously waited for their next commander, some skeptical as to whether a woman would really lead their camp. They received their answer within days. During the morning after an endurance workout, the boys were singing their daily anthem at the flagpole. Three armored trucks thundered into the camp without warning near the end of the anthem. The passenger door of one truck opened. Out stepped a blue-eyed woman with long blond hair, done in a ponytail. She wore the formal black SS uniform, bearing the Swastika armband. She did not wear a peaked cap, rather, a field cap with death's skull in the middle. The officer was very pretty, with a slim build. She appeared to be in her early twenties. The only weapon she carried was a dagger. Glöckner and Kauffman saluted her as she strode towards them.

She returned the salute. "Are you the commanders?"

"*Jawohl*," they replied in unison.

"*Wunderbar*," she murmured before turning to the formation of boys. She then shouted in a loud, authoritative voice, "All of you who will turn seventeen by August fifteenth and older step forward!" Glöckner, Kauffman and their cabins all stepped forward along with four more cabins. Sixty-seven boys in total.

The woman continued, "You are leaving for service. Those of you that are eighteen or turning eighteen soon will be sent into service. The age group below, for now, you will be operating anti-aircraft guns. You will be leaving in twenty minutes. Now, go pack up."

The older boys were stunned. Some appeared visibly frightened, jaws dropped, eyes wide. Nevertheless, they all marched to their cabins and prepared to depart from the camp.

The woman then turned to the now smaller group. "My name is Loraine Vogel, but you will refer to me as '*Untersturmführer*' or '*Frau* Vogel.' You boys are under my command now. I want absolute obedience. You will be near the front sooner than you may think. I have no doubt that your former commanders have prepared you well, but many of you will be operating weapons, being fire fighters, or moving supplies close to the front by next year. Age groups sixteen, fifteen, and fourteen will all likely ship out of this camp in the next year. Now, it's time for your education, as I understand it. Get your books, go to class. *Jetzt*, now!"

"*Jawohl!*"

The remaining squads hurried back to their cabins to retrieve their schoolbooks. The older boys were almost done loading into trucks when Blaz came out. He, and many other boys paused to watch. The trucks hummed loudly, ready to leave at any moment.

"Did I tell you to watch the trucks? Get to school!" their commander shouted at them.

Some boys saluted then obeyed, some shouted "*Jawohl*," but Blaz simply turned towards the headquarters without a word. If there was anything to say about a change in their education, it was the increasing amount of attention being directed towards the conquest and National Socialization of the lands to the east.

"The land the Communists possess must be conquered by Germans. Aside from our growing population's need for room and land, Communism is a disease that must be stopped before it spreads to every corner of the globe. Capitalism lacks the convictions to stand up to this plague, so we must take the initiative. You young men know that nothing in life comes easily, especially to us. *Deutschland* has had to fight for all that we have since Bismarck united our great people and long before then. Communism gives no incentive; it encourages laziness, an incompetent workforce, and a dysfunctional economy. Germans must never rely on anyone; everything we need lies in ourselves, in our own work. This is why other peoples come to our way of thinking, as many are realizing. From the Middle East to South America, our movement spreads. We have many obstacles in our way. The Jews, the Reds, the Capitalists. If it comes to a war of annihilation with Russia, so be it. Otherwise, they will attempt to infect our nation and the world with their false ideologies. Already, they have killed millions in the Ukraine and hundreds of thousands of our German brothers in the Volga regions."

Forward to the East, You Storming Army

June 22, 1941 Sunday

Schlusser stood only a few feet away from the Soviet border in Romania. Dozens of tanks and thousands of men were amassed behind him. His commander strode to his side.

"The attack is underway in the north. I have just been informed. It is time." He placed a flare gun in Schlusser's right hand. "Do the honors."

"This is it," Schlusser said, turning to his squad, "No turning back."

"We're with you, sir," Schlusser's youngest soldier said, "To the end."

Schlusser raised the flare. "*Gott mit uns*! For the movement, for the *Führer*, and for *Deutschland*!" He fired, sending a bright red light into the air. The Germans charged forward, into enemy land.

"*Jugend*, our country has invaded the Soviet Union. Our great nation has embarked on a crusade to rid the earth of the Red Plague and its oppression. May God be with our forces as they fight for freedom. Communism must meet its end by our fists. *Möge Sieg unsere sein*!" May victory be ours!

Krämer stepped forward from behind Vogel, raised his right arm, and roared at the top of his lungs, "*Sieg*!"

"*Heil*!" the boys shouted back.

"*Sieg*!"

"*Heil*!"

"*Sieg*!"

"*Heil*!"

"*Sieg Heil*!" they all shouted at once to finish the chant.

"Form up into squads. We march in formation to the farm," their commander ordered, "Oldest age groups first. Rows of three."

The boys formed up, with Blaz's cabin behind six other cabins. On *Frau* Vogel's command, they began marching. They marched enthusiastically, fueled by their chant with the feeling that they could conquer worlds. The now commanding youth officers, Fleischer and Krämer, began a march song. A tried-and-true Hitler Youth march.

Die Jugend marschiert mit Frohem Gesang bei Sonnenschein und Regen!
Die Jugend marschiert mit sieghaften Drang
Dem großes Ziel entgegen!
Wir stürmen die Welt
Gehen fest unsere Schritt,
Wer jung ist der fügt sich freilich mit!
Die Jugend marschiert, kein Pfad ist zu steil, dem Siege entgegen zu eilen.
Sieg Heil!

The youth marches with cheerful song, by sunshine and rain.
The youth marches with a victorious urge, towards the great goal.
We storm the world, going steady in our steps.
Who is young gives themselves up freely!
The youth marches, no path is too steep, to stand against the rush to victory!
Sieg Heil!

Blaz grinned at the triumphant ending of the chorus. Invincibility. The cadets marched on with firm steps after the end of the song, some still humming its tune. The farm was a good mile at least so it took time. Throughout the summer, they operated the farm as a replacement for school. Their physical workouts were less demanding during the summer, mainly because of farm work. The Hitler Youth were completely prepared for Germany's bright future now. They could survive in the wilderness, grow their own food, hunt, and had a fair education.

Blaz walked through the field with Ivo watering the wheat they were growing. Blaz pushed a wheelbarrow full of water, and Ivo carried. The soil was pleasantly soft but not muddy so Blaz was able to push the wheelbarrow and maneuver well. The weather was bright and sunny, but a light breeze kept the temperature cool.

"Ivo?" Blaz asked.

"*Ja?*"

"Do you think we can beat the Communists?" Blaz asked, "Because I feel invincible right now."

"I think we can, I can't be sure if we will."

"You have cold feet about this attack?" Blaz breathed with relief.

Ivo assured him, "There's plenty of people who are nervous about this attack. Though from what I've heard from the older guys whispering, we've scored some early victories."

"That's good news, but don't you think we should've defeated Britain, and then attacked the USSR?"

"Actually, I think we should've attacked in late April or early May, not late June this year, but I'm not in charge. We had to attack the Reds sometime."

The two headed back to refill the wheelbarrow and start on the next column.

"You know, Erich will probably be in combat later than us because of how strict the SS is with age," Ivo told Blaz.

"*Frau* Vogel said we'd be out of here sometime next year. And then we will be doing everything except actual combat."

"*Ja*," Ivo grinned while he pumped water into the wheelbarrow, "It'll be scary. But I want to fight."

A Life Outside of the Military

August 8, 1941 Friday

Throughout the continuous training, no complaint was heard from even the new young cadets that had come in July. *Frau* Vogel had done away with any whining hours after their arrival. Blaz continued running with Koby who never seemed to get tired of training.

"Koby, how do you keep this up?" Blaz panted after their workout.

"Maybe I'll get to do this instead of the military someday," was all Koby said.

The sun hung low in the sky. Most of the boys had retired to their cabins. Only the officers were allowed out past nine, but most boys were ready for sleep by the time nine o'clock rolled around due to the fact they got up at five-thirty, so staying out wasn't considered much of a privilege. The highest-ranking officers were now Vogel, Schmid, and a new officer for the large fifteen-year-old group, Krauss. Koby used his rank to allow himself some alone time at night. He often would come back to the cabin past nine thirty. What he did exactly was to anyone's guess. Johann had laid low for much of his time at the KLV camp. He had no rank, was quiet, had no incidents; good or bad, but was consistently a fine cadet. Koby often commented that he wished Johann could be in their squad. He and Johann had become good friends through their running. And Johann had improved at quite a fast rate, more than Koby could've imagined, outshining Blaz and Ivo.

Blaz lay awake face-up on this warm, summer night. His blanket lay at the other end of the bed next to his feet. The dim lamp shone against his light blond hair. He was shirtless and lay in his underwear. The Knights had mostly dozed off to sleep, some with their blankets, some not in the hot and humid warehouse room. Blaz looked down his chest and flexed his now well-defined abs. He pounded them with a fist, testing their solidity. He looked at his arms, which were much stronger, demonstrated by what Blaz could lift now. Veins ran down them, giving him a lanky but sturdy look. The entire squad, save Jarman and Jurgen was a lanky, lean squad built for endurance and long marching. Jarman and Jurgen were the muscle of the group. They'd worked hard to become strong, powerful soldiers and both were excellent at hand-to-hand fighting. Only Koby could challenge them among their squad mates. Nevertheless, all the boys looked healthy, fit and strong. The young boy pulled his blanket over his body and closed his eyes, ready for much needed rest.

No Squad for Young Boys

August 10, 1941 Friday

Frau Vogel had just announced that the squads above Blaz would be leaving in October to work behind the lines and utilize the flak guns. There was little doubt Blaz's squad would be next. However, *Frau* Vogel gave boys under Blaz's age a reassurance they would receive much more training before they were deployed. Despite Germany winning the war, it was clear there was going to be a great demand for soldiers. The Fatherland simply did not have a big enough population to turn anywhere else other than their youth.

While the boys worked at the farm in the heat, Blaz chatted with Ivo, Tristan, Jurgen, and Jaye while the others worked elsewhere. Each one held a hoe to keep the ground loose during the torrid summer before they laid down fertilizer. Ivo swung his over his head and almost smacked Blaz in the face.

"Whoa! Watch it!"

"Oh, sorry, sorry."

"We are definitely leaving around the New Year?" Jaye asked, adjusting his glasses.

"For sure," Jurgen said, "They've been recruiting from this camp every couple months. We won't be any different."

Tristan added shyly, "Koby has been talking about getting a tenth man for the squad lately."

"We probably won't get one. No younger kids will leave the camp until they're drafted. He'll have to file a request once they're drafted," Blaz said.

Later during the work in the field, Blaz and Ivo found Koby, who was working alongside Johann.

"How's work going?" Blaz smiled, holding his tool the way a German soldier held a rifle when marching.

"*Gut, gut,*" Koby grinned back. Johann smiled at his friends.

"We finished up over there," Ivo said while pointing closer to the farmhouse, "So we decided to come and help you guys out."

"*Danke,*" said Koby and hammered his tool into the ground, "I thought that run was pretty good this morning. We all clocked in a personal record. Must be the cooler mornings."

"I don't know how you keep improving, with how fast you are to begin with," Ivo awed.

"I've got the right motivation."

"And you've got Johann chasing you," Ivo added.

"*Ja,*" Koby laughed, "And I've got Johann chasing me."

"You two have been getting faster too," Johann complimented Blaz and Ivo, not really understanding the point of the conversation.

"*Danke*, Johann," Blaz said, "But you've been really outstanding."

The four runners got to work. They hammered the ground, making it softer, since there'd been little rain. When Johann was out of earshot, Blaz quietly said to Koby, "You've been saying you want to add another squad member. You want to add Johann?"

Koby nodded, "*Ja*, he would be in our squad if I had a say."

"What makes you want to add him so much?"

"He's calm, reserved, and takes orders well. And I like him. He's a good kid," Koby answered, keeping a straight, sincere face. Somewhat to Blaz's surprise.

"And?" Blaz persisted.

"And what?"

"Come on, I know there's a little more to it."

Koby didn't bother resisting and replied, "He's been talking with me a lot. About stuff, life. He's a good listener but when he needs to be he's a good talker. He's been getting me to think."

Blaz smiled, knowing Koby wasn't going to say anymore, so he backed off. But knowing Johann, he could tell what Koby had been thinking about.

Northern Russia

September 1, 1941 Monday

Stretching after running was a key component of the routine Koby had the four runners go through. It prevented muscle injuries, and since Koby liked mixing speed workouts in, they worked all types of muscles. While they stretched, Koby made an announcement.

"I found out what date we are leaving. Our squad ships out for Northern Russia on January tenth," he told them seriously, "We won't be fighting, they don't plan on using us to fight. Mainly menial tasks and operating artillery and such."

Blaz and Ivo nodded solemnly, though they were both very excited for a change and had been eager to fight for months. It seemed so early. Could this be happening across the Fatherland? Or were they a select few? Only Koby knew the seriousness of Germany's position was immense. The Russians had begun using child soldiers out of desperation. Germany had to retaliate with a generation of boys who were ready and eager to fight. For the Russians, it didn't matter your paperwork. You just fought. Right now, for the Germans, an officer just misfiled your age in his paperwork and you were in the military. It was not a disregard for life by either side necessarily, but an act of desperation to push the war in their favor. Losing the war would be much worse.

"Well," Johann began a bit sadly, "I will miss you guys."

"I will miss you too," Koby responded quickly but genuinely.

"I will too," Blaz smiled, trying to be positive with Johann.

"Me too," Ivo said.

Goodbye to Stalin, Churchill, Roosevelt

December 9, 1941 Tuesday

The news that Germany now had declared war on America was jarring, to say the least to the many cadets. *Frau* Vogel did not announce it at the morning pledge but allowed the cabin leaders to inform their squad mates themselves. That night, in their small room, the boys went about business as usual. Changing, taking care of their teeth, deodorant. They'd all climbed into bed and were talking about the recent news that Germany was at the gates of Moscow.

"The war will be over soon. Once Moscow falls, we can concentrate on capturing their resources. Then we'll crush Britain," Jarman visualized aloud, "I just hope the *Führer* doesn't give them another peace offer. They have it coming."

"You know he doesn't want to fight the British," Tristan said quietly.

"Then what?" Hans asked.

Jarman began, "Churchill and Roosevelt will probably try to drag America into the war."

Koby trudged into the room. He pushed his hair back into its combed position, put a hand on his forehead while looking down, and murmured, "America has entered the war. With the Allies."

Mixed expressions filled the room. A look of terror formed on Tristan's face, Jaye pounded a fist angrily into his bed, Reinhardt put his face into his palms, Blaz ran his hands through his hair multiple times, Hans rubbed his right arm with a blank look, Ivo shoved his pillow into his face, and Jurgen stared straight ahead.

But Jarman smiled and popped his knuckles. "Goodbye to Stalin, Churchill, Roosevelt."

The Last Silent Nights

December 23, 1941 Tuesday

Johann had asked Blaz, Ivo, and Koby if he could talk to them on Christmas Eve. Though *Frau* Vogel personally seemed indignant about Christmas, she allowed the boys to celebrate it in their own way, giving them the evenings of the twenty-fourth and twenty fifth off. So the boys had free reign to go where they wanted those nights. While Johann and Koby talked, Jarman smirked as he listened to the conversation but said nothing. Johann noticed, but didn't understand that Jarman was smirking because he thought it was pathetic. "Do you want to talk with us on Christmas?" Johann asked him.

Blaz turned immediately to Jarman, "*Ja*, come on Jarman. Show some Christmas spirit. You'd love it."

"*Nein*, not interested."

"Come on."

Jarman opened his mouth to respond but Ivo had started already, "Come on now, don't snub us," he said.

"*Nein, nein,*" Jarman said, irritated, "I'm not doing this."

"You should," Ivo quickly said.

"*Nein,*" Jarman said calmly this time.

"Twenty hundred hours," Koby smiled then ushered the runners out of the cabin.

"What? How's that going to change his mind?" Blaz asked.

Koby raised his eyebrows, "He'll be there. I guarantee it."

Vertraut ihr der Führer?

December 24, 1941 Wednesday

The day began with a run. Koby wouldn't take off Christmas Eve. He had followed Coach Friedrich's instructions to a fault, and Friedrich hadn't said Christmas Eve was a time to slack off. He did, however, have Christmas Day marked off, so Koby worked himself extra hard on the Twenty-fourth in his timed five-kilometer, which he had convinced *Frau* Vogel to time. Yet another best time for Koby: Fourteen fifty-nine. *Frau* Vogel was actually smiling when Blaz flew by. A smile of awe. Of Koby. *He is impressive*, Blaz thought as he cracked a smile himself between breaths.

"What did you want to talk to us about?" Koby asked Johann that night. The other boys around them were talking among each other, not paying attention to Koby, Johann, Blaz, and Ivo's conversation. Jarman sat as far away from them as he could.

"You guys are leaving soon," Johann said, while pulling on one thumb with his other hand, "What do you think of the *Führer?*"

Blaz and Ivo glanced at each other. Jarman's attention was captured for good. Koby looked back at Johann, and said, "What?"

"The *Führer*," Johann restated, "Who is the *Führer*?"

The four boys were confused by the question.

"The *Führer* is the *Führer*," Ivo answered, as if the term "*Führer*" was completely self-explanatory.

"And that's all?"

"The *Führer* is *Deutschland's* savior," Blaz said without a second thought.

"The Party is Hitler. But Hitler is *Deutschland*, as *Deutschland* is Hitler," Koby echoed Rudolf Hess.

"The *Führer* is God on earth," Jarman said instantaneously.

"*Ja, ja*," Koby nodded. Blaz frowned at this one.

Johann nodded, expecting these responses, "Why? Why is he all these things?"

"He's brought freedom and prosperity to *Deutschland*," Koby said.

"He's made *Deutschland* great," Ivo added.

Blaz said, "He's rescued *Deutschland* from International Capitalism and Communism."

"He's made us free of eternal debt and servitude to the banks," Jarman answered.

"And that makes him God? What about to the rest of the world?" Johann asked with more maturity than he had ever exhibited.

"The rest of the world?" Jarman smirked, "He will be to them what he is to us soon."

Blaz sighed at Jarman's grandiose fantasies.

"Is the *Führer* good?"

"Of course," everyone said at once.

"Why were people in Seelow disappearing last year? And why don't any of us care? We don't even notice it," Johann asked though he'd clearly taken notice of it but refrained from provoking his friends.

"You think that doesn't happen in other countries?" Jarman answered, "You don't think the Americans and Soviets imprison possible threats?"

"We're the good guys, right? We shouldn't be taking away good people."

"Johann, what are you trying to say?" Ivo asked, glaring, "You can't question the *Führer*, you know that. What reason is there to? And we've sworn oaths to him."

"Does that mean we're not allowed to think for ourselves?" Johann answered with a question.

"You're just thinking what your father taught you," Jarman shot back, standing up and looking down on Johann. He knew who Johann's father had been.

"I've also been taught the opposite by everyone else. And there came a time when I had to make a decision for myself," Johann said calmly, but stood his ground across from Jarman, not shrinking back.

Koby ran a hand through his hair nervously, "Okay, I think we're done with that. Johann, follow me."

Johann obediently and trustfully followed Koby out of the cabin. Blaz glanced around the cabin and ran out after them. Koby took Johann out of the warehouse, Blaz continued to follow.

"Johann. What are you doing?" Koby asked. His tone was vexed.

"I'm asking questions. And answering," Johann put simply.

"Why are you dissenting with our *Führer*? *Deutschland* is the greatest nation on earth. All because of the *Führer*."

"We worship him. It's not right, I'm worried about how much our, well, entire nation has become so admiring of him. We can't even disagree with him anymore," Johann explained, "Have you heard what we've been being taught in school?"

Koby stood still for a moment, wondering what Johann was playing at, "Of course. What about it?"

"The *Führer* doesn't like the Jews. And I'm worried about what could happen to them," Johann said. Blaz stepped outside, showing himself. Koby and Johann noticed but continued.

"Johann, have *you* heard what we've been taught in school? Put the pieces together! Marx, Kaganovich, Kamenev, Trotsky, Yezhov! They are our enemies! They've butchered millions of people in the east!"

"That's just Communist Jews."

"Which they happen to dominate that ideology. Johann, we have thousands of Jews in our armed forces. Jews who want each people to have the right to self-determination. But Jewish ideologies are a plague. That's what we must get rid of," Koby said, hoping this would set Johann's conscience at ease, "But we're quarantining them. We've even allowed them to immigrate to Palestine. Only Marxists get the bullet."

"Who are we to say who's a Marxist or not?" Johann interrupted, looking to Blaz for support, "Do you really think all Jews are Marxists? If that were being done to German National Socialists, I'd be just as against it."

"Of course I don't believe all Jews are Marxists, but a lot are. And Johann, we are at war! It's a substantial number of Marxist Jews that want to destroy the German people anyway." Johann looked to Blaz again, but Blaz stayed silent. He agreed with Koby.

Johann shook his head, "I don't want any of us to be angry at each other when you leave. I'll leave it if you leave it."

Koby didn't answer immediately. Blaz nodded '*ja*' rapidly when Koby looked to him.

"Okay, no harm done," Koby agreed, putting a hand out, "We'll forget this conversation ever happened."

Johann shook Koby's hand with a relieved smile but said, "*Nein*, we won't."

1942: Youth Knows no Dangers

Topple the Jewish Throne in Russia

January 7, 1942 Wednesday

Wir sind des Geyers schwarzer Haufen, heia-hoho!
Und wollen mit Tyrannen raufen, heia-hoho!
Spieß voran, drauf und dran,
setzt auf's Klosterdach den roten Hahn!

We are the Geyer's black-clad band, heia-hoho!
And want to fight with tyrants, heia-hoho!
Lance ahead, on the verge (of victory),
Set on the monastery roof the Red Rooster (set on fire).

The boys sang the old Germanic song as they marched through the woods, which were dusted with a light snow.

Koby led the squad ahead, as they marched at a brisk pace, all trying their best to imitate a real soldier. The song was written about the peasant's war during the times before Germany became a nation. The war was for freedom against the Lords and Vassals. Florian Geyer was the great leader who led the rebellion.

Once their song was done, Koby began a new one only a few minutes after. The German regiments' favorite way to pass time while marching was singing as a group, and the youth were brought up in that tradition. After their march had brought them several kilometers away from camp, Koby ordered them to halt and set up for the night. The boys quickly and efficiently got a fire going and found a source of water. And this time they caught a rabbit and found some edible plants. That night was a cold one, and the Knights stayed very close to the fire. They talked over their dinner, mainly about their upcoming departure.

"*Scheiße*, can you believe it?" Jarman asked the group, "We are finally leaving and getting to help out the front lines."

"We are going to turn the tide against the Russians for good!" Ivo said sarcastically, though he meant part of his comment.

"*Ja*, we are! Goodbye to Stalin," Blaz grinned while punching the air.

"Freedom is coming to Russia. I bet Ukraine is so happy to be liberated from the Bolshevik butchers," Hans added.

"I'd be happy, assuming I knew what Communism was like," Blaz said, beaming.

"Same here," Ivo agreed.

"*Deutschland* and the world can't have any of that Jewish Bolshevik plague," Koby said.

"It won't remain for much longer," Jarman said, thumping his chest.

"Since the Knights are coming to slay the Soviet dragon," Ivo remarked, holding his arm at length, pretending to hold a sword.

Personal Records

January 9, 1942 Friday

Blaz sprinted toward the finish line. He wore his old track uniform, though he was freezing in it. Ivo was about ten meters behind him, sprinting as fast as he could. Koby had crossed the finish line minutes ago. Blaz had come over a small hill in time to see Johann slow to a stop. Blaz was determined to get his personal best, knowing it would probably be his last, maybe ever. He closed his eyes and put his head down, trying to use every last bit of energy in his small, fourteen-year-old body. He flew across the finish line and spread his arms apart after he'd crossed. Ivo zoomed past moments later and stumbled over to Blaz, Koby and Johann.

"Times?" Ivo panted to Koby, as he put his hands behind his head.

"All personal records," *Frau* Vogel said, "Congratulations. If this war ends anytime soon, Koby, you are in the Olympics."

Koby pumped his fist.

"Now get ready for your last day at the camp," Vogel ordered, "And today won't be easy, I assure you."

The four boys saluted their commander and walked back to the warehouse.

"We all did it!" Ivo addressed the others, "All got personal bests."

"I knew I was going to get it the moment we started," Koby said matter-of-factly, "I wanted it bad, I felt good, everything was in place."

"You're not the only one," Blaz said as buttoned up his black Hitler Youth uniform.

AA Guns and Artillery

January 10, 1942 Saturday

Two dark green trucks rolled through the countryside. They headed in the direction of the sun. The boys had just left their camp. Johann had given Ivo and Blaz big hugs, as big as the little Hitler Youth boy could make them.

"Stay on guard, fight hard guys," Johann told them, "*Ade, meine Freunde. Gott mit uns,*" he finished, quoting the *Wehrmacht* motto.

"You too," Blaz and Ivo returned with smiles of farewell. Koby and Johann looked each other in the eye for a long time. Johann smiled farewell and walked to his friend. Koby kicked at the dirt and walked toward Johann. They both gave each other a hug, Johann whispering to Koby, "Stay strong. And stay you."

"*Danke* for being my friend," Koby whispered back, "I love you Johann. Don't get in trouble while I'm gone, promise?" Koby asked, referring to Christmas.

Johann smiled, and shook his head, "Can't promise."

Koby nodded and stood up. He gave Johann a playful pat on the head then turned and climbed into the truck. And when their truck headed out they saw the remaining Hitler Youth members, so very young at this point, raise their arms in salute.

Their truck rumbled through fields and forests before arriving at a train that was seemingly stopped in the middle of nowhere. When the trucks came to a stop, the boys unloaded, and stood at attention. An officer with platinum blond hair wearing a field gray *Wehrmacht* uniform waited for them next to a large wooden crate. He looked about thirty and wore gloves. He frowned when he saw the Hitler Youths, whispering something irritably to his adjutant, "They told me these boys would be seventeen! They don't look older than fourteen!"

The adjutant nodded quickly, but motioned with his piercing, sky blue eyes to the Youths. The officer returned the nod. The boys all handed him their identification papers, which he handed to his adjutant, who began to skim through them, "Says here they're seventeen, sir."

"Bullshit," the commander said, looking his new troops up and down. "Welcome to the *Wehrmacht*, young men." The boys grinned at hearing themselves being referred to as young men. The officer continued on, "I'm sure you are excited to fight, most of the recruits seem to be, but you'll have to wait for that. My name is Aldric Steinhoff, but you will refer to me as *Herr* Steinhoff. I will be your commander from now on. This train will take you to outside of Leningrad, on the eastern side of the city. You will be working anti-aircraft guns and artillery, moving the wounded, preparing meals for the soldiers and unloading supplies from trains and trucks," he pointed to the train, "You'll be unloading this when you arrive. Right now, I have a few things you will need, just in case." He opened the wooden crate, revealing several Walther P-38s.

"Standard issue, better to give them to you now than later. We will need to find your squad another man by the time you graduate to combat in the army," the officer said, gesturing to Koby, "but later. Once you make it to the army, you will be given your primary weapon, likely many of you will be rifleman. Line up, take one pistol, and four magazines. The pistols already have one magazine in them."

The boys each took their new weapons and examined them, fascinated. Though they'd seen these dozens of times at the KLV camp, these were special. Blaz slid his magazine into the pistol and turned the safety on. He placed his pistol into the new holster. He then strapped his sheath and dagger to his belt.

"Load up, all in this car," the officer pointed to a car like the one they'd been in on the way to the KLV camp. The boys eagerly climbed into the car, some with their hands still on their sheaths and holsters. The officer and his assistant slid the doors shut and the boys were off to Leningrad.

"*Dämmt*, it's getting colder," one of the boys shivered inside the car.

Everyone had noticed this a while ago, but no one had mentioned it. They curled up against the walls. They wrapped their arms around their legs, shivering in the poorly insulated car. It was night as far as they could tell from the line window. They had one gas lamp to light the car at night. Koby eventually spoke up, "We should get some rest. The train isn't going to reach Leningrad while we're sleeping."

"You sure?" Ivo asked seriously.

"I'm positive," Koby assured him. The cadets moved to lie down on the wooden surface of the car and were soon fast asleep.

January 11, 1942 Sunday

Koby was right. The train stopped that morning to pick up more supplies, which the boys loaded onto their car.

"Koby, how much further do you think Leningrad will be?" Blaz asked curiously.

"I'd say we've got another night, at least," Koby answered, "Just an estimate, though."

"Okay. Are you nervous?"

"Me?" Koby laughed, "*Nein*, of course not. You?"

"A little bit," replied Blaz, "Can't lie. I'm nervous about that time when I have to pull this trigger on someone," the fourteen-year-old said, while giving his Walther a pat.

"*Verdämmt*, you better be ready when it comes. You can't give the Reds any mercy, they will use a second chance to kill you."

Blaz heart felt like it skipped a beat, and a shiver went down his spine, "*Ja*, I know."

Leningrad

January 12, 1942 Monday

After much time on the train, the boys arrived outside of Leningrad. They could just see the silhouette of the city on the horizon even through the frigid, cloudy morning. Still kilometers away, but close enough that if the city were abandoned, all would be conquered within several hours. Smoke from constant artillery barrages and attacks shrouded part of the city in darkness. To the east the boys could see a lake where more of the German army was positioned. They were perhaps only a kilometer from the lake. The boys' train had stopped next to a massive artillery piece that was mounted on a train car. They recognized it as a rail gun, capable of firing across the English Channel, meaning it could easily hit Leningrad. Steinhoff immediately ordered the boys to begin unloading supplies from their train. The boys got right to it. They loaded the supplies onto trucks that were headed a kilometer or two closer to Leningrad to distribute them to the front.

"Good work, boys. Keep it up. Once you're done there, I will get each of your squads set up at your artillery."

Hearing this, the boys worked even faster. Jarman and Marvin lifted the wooden crates from each car and handed them to the rest of the boys who carried them into the waiting trucks. Pairs of *Wehrmacht* soldiers hopped into the back of each truck to guard the weapons as the trucks drove off to the near front.

The boys worked for hours unloading car after car, until they had finally completed their job. Steinhoff immediately ordered them to follow him. He set up Marvin's squad then Koby's squad followed him over to an anti-aircraft position near the rail gun. In front of the rail gun were artillery pieces, not as long of range as the massive weapon but capable of firing at counter attacking Russian armies.

"Here," the *Wehrmacht* officer pointed to anti-aircraft guns behind the artillery and rail gun, "You boys split up into groups of three and operate our flak guns protecting the rail gun. I'm in charge of this entire area as captain. Should I not be here, my lieutenant will give orders to fire." He gestured to his assistant who nodded. The officer continued, "If neither of us are here then you are in command, Sergeant Hertz."

"As you command," Koby answered.

The officer and his lieutenant turned away to direct many other young troopers working behind the front lines. When the officer turned, Koby immediately ordered the boys into groups, and gave them their positions on each flak gun.

"Jarman: operator, Blaz: loader, Jaye: gunner. Go!" Koby turned to three more of his squad mates, "Reinhardt: operator. Hans: loader, Ivo: gunner. Go! I'll operate, Jurgen: loader, Tristan: gunner. Disperse!"

The groups ran to their guns several meters away from each other, so they'd have to yell to communicate with their other squad mates. Jarman and Jaye adjusted their gun in the direction of Leningrad, while Jurgen's gun aimed south to protect the rear. Koby also adjusted his gun to aim in Leningrad's direction. Blaz loaded the flak gun to maximum capacity. Then the boys waited. They didn't have to wait long. They had arrived as the Soviets were launching a massive counterattack: Lyuban Offensive Operation.

A few hours later, in the afternoon, the attack came. It was on the front lines so the boys still couldn't see it. But their commander ordered the artillery to fire on the Russians. He knew the enemy artillery was coming.

"Artillery, hit their infantry. Rail gun, fire on the city!" Steinhoff shouted as he sprinted across the line giving orders.

"*Jugend*, be ready for aircraft!"

Jaye jumped into the flak gun's 'chair,' though it scarcely resembled one. He cleaned off his glasses hastily. Jarman and Blaz readied themselves to rotate the loaded gun. They waited, watching the skies for enemy aircraft.

"Incoming!" they heard a voice scream. Several shells hit the ground around the boys' position. The Russians had unleashed a wave of artillery fire on the southern German front.

"What do we do?" screamed Blaz over the thunderous explosions to Jarman.

"We don't fire, that's the artillery's job!" Jarman shouted back.

"This is some heavy stuff!" Blaz yelled, replying to distract himself from the fear he felt. A shell hit the ground only meters away from their gun. Blaz put a hand over one ear. There was no ringing, but the explosion had been loud. Loud enough to cause pain in his ear.

"Jaye, do you see any planes?" Jarman yelled over the screeching of incoming shells.

"None!" Jaye responded with panic in his tone.

Blaz held onto the flak gun, as if being closer to it would protect him. Even Jarman did this. Steinhoff's lieutenant ran by the boys, and shouted over the artillery, "No planes yet, stay sharp!" He then turned to the artillery, shouting the coordinates they were to fire on. The artillery then unleashed their power on the Soviets. The shells had begun to stop falling as frequently but still an occasional one hit ground near them.

"Blaz!" Jarman shouted over the explosions "We've got two Russian fighters coming from the lake area! Get over to Reinhardt and tell him, they're still focused on the rear!"

"*Jawohl!*" Blaz darted towards Reinhardt's flak gun, about half a football field away. He leapt over the craters left from Soviet artillery after stumbling into the first one he came to. He safely made his way over to Reinhardt and slowed to a jog at about fifteen meters away.

"Reinhardt! We've got fighters!" and as he said this, Jarman and Jaye fired on the fighters that flew overhead, "Adjust the gun away from the-" Blaz was thrown off his feet and into the air. Dust rose all around him. He landed hard on his back and his head flew back against the solid, frozen dirt. His legs flew into the air, as if they were weightless, causing him to do a backwards somersault. He was several meters behind the flak gun now, not unconscious but in shock. He tried to get up, but when he did his vision became blurry and he collapsed again. When he opened his eyes, Reinhardt was knelt over him, trying to wake him up.

"Blaz! Blaz!" Reinhardt yelled, louder than he'd ever spoken.

Blaz put a hand on his forehead, not fully remembering what had just happened but recognizing his friend.

"Where are we?" he asked blissfully.

"What?!" Reinhardt asked at a yell. He was clearly shocked by the question but a quick smile flashed across his face, when he realized his friend was talking. "Blaz, we're in Leningrad! Come on, Blaz!" Reinhardt shouted, realizing Blaz had hit his head, "Who am I?"

"You are Reinhardt."

Reinhardt breathed a brief sigh of relief. His friend could either see or hear. "How many fingers am I holding up?" he asked, holding up four; three on one hand, one on the other.

Blaz looked down, as his vision went black for a few seconds. When it returned, he looked back up, "Ah, I-" he stammered, "Seven?"

"*Nein!*" Reinhardt said desperately, "Come on, Blaz!"

"Ha ha!" Jarman's voice shouted, "That'll teach them!"

Reinhardt looked up to see a fighter trailing smoke and barreling toward the ground in the distance.

"Blaz, we're fighting Soviets. Soviets!" Reinhardt yelled, but tried to have his tone remain calm, "You remember that? What do you remember?"

"The train, where's the train?" Blaz asked, starting to panic, "We were on a train!"

"*Ja*, but we got off the train and now we are fighting Soviets in Russia," Reinhardt said slowly.

"W-we are in Russia?"

"*Ja*," Reinhardt lifted Blaz to his feet, "*Kommen sie*, come on," Reinhardt helped Blaz a few steps toward Jarman then let him go. Blaz took a few steps then stumbled sideways and almost fell down, but Reinhardt caught him. The two proceeded slowly toward Jarman and Jaye, with Reinhardt supporting Blaz so he wouldn't fall. Jarman ran over to help and thanked Reinhardt, who sprinted back to his flak gun.

"Blaz, we beat them! We beat those fighters!" Jaye squealed as he jumped down from the gun.

Reinhardt turned around and called, "I should tell you, he's a little out of it. He took quite a hit to the head!"

Jarman nodded. "Blaz, how are you feeling? Can you see?"

"I can see."

"Can you walk?" He let Blaz go. Blaz put a foot forward and walked over to the flak gun, stumbling a few times but regained his balance each time.

"*Gut.* Now here," Jarman unscrewed Blaz's canteen and gave him some water. "Now just sit down and rest, you'll be better in no time."

The next few hours were quieter, yet the Germans fired several times from the boys' position, each shot making Blaz's head pound with pain. Koby came over to talk briefly to his friend, during a stretch of silence as the sun set.

"How are you feeling?" Koby asked, putting a hand on Blaz's shoulder.

"*Gut, gut.*"

"What was it like? Being thrown into the air like that?"

"I don't remember anything but the feeling right when it hit," Blaz shivered, "My heart just skipped a few beats, it was terrifying. Absolutely terrifying."

"I'm glad you're okay. *Gott sei Dank* it didn't hit you," Koby pointed to his *Wehrmacht* belt, the only piece of the uniform they'd been given so they could attach their weapons to it. The belt was inscribed with the words of the *Wehrmacht* motto, '*Gott mit uns*,' God with us. Koby raised his eyebrows and grinned.

Blaz nodded before another headache caused his eyes to blacken. Steinhoff's assistant jogged over to the flak cannon.

"Is everything all right over here?" the lieutenant inquired.

"Fine, *Herr*. Private Senft got thrown by an artillery strike during the shelling. He's still getting headaches, but he should be all right," Koby replied.

"Luck has smiled on you today, kid," the lieutenant said briefly before turning to Koby, "Sergeant Hertz, I'd prefer you and your shell-shocked trooper stay here, but our scouts have reported that the Russians may be mounting another attack tonight. We need you all at your flak guns."

"Of course, sir," Koby saluted.

Blaz stood up and leaned against the flak gun. He looked at the ground and smiled awkwardly.

Boy, this will be a long war.

Comrades Shot by the Red Front

January 13, 1942 Tuesday

That night was a cold one, but the rest was needed. Freezing winds bit at the boys as the *Wehrmacht* soldiers took shifts, watching for Russian counterattacks. Blaz had one of the best sleeps he'd had in a while, though. His headache kept him from noticing the cold until he was fast asleep. Jarman shook him awake the next morning, "Blaz, are you feeling better?"

Blaz put an icy hand on his head, "*Ja*, I am. Did you have a good rest, Jarman?"

"As good as I could in this frigid temperature. Woke up a couple times hearing artillery. It was really far away, though."

The boys sat and stood and paced at their guns for hours that day. The sun had come out but that did little to warm them in the freezing Russian winter. Koby paced furiously, whether he was anxious for something to happen or just freezing was up for debate. In the afternoon, Captain Steinhoff walked over to Koby's flak gun. Neither Blaz, nor Jarman, nor Jaye knew what he said, all they saw was Koby, with something in his hands, go running towards the front.

"Where do you suppose he's heading?" Jaye asked with boredom.

"Maybe they're giving him some message to send to the front," suggested Jarman, while he examined his knife. Blaz straightened up.

"Probably."

"Does anybody have some cards?"

Jaye checked his pockets out of hopes that he might have some. Blaz did the same.

"*Verdämmt*," Jarman swore, seeing them hold out empty hands.

"Hey," Blaz remembered, "Did you guys hit any of the planes yesterday?"

A smile returned to Jarman's face, "*Ja*, we hit the second fighter. Someone else hit the first one."

"What was it like?" Blaz asked with genuine interest.

Jaye answered. "Awesome, it was exhilarating. Shooting down the Reds, it was almost like we were in a different world when we were shooting at them. I was just completely ignoring the artillery, just focusing on the one target. And it worked." He grinned to himself.

"Wish I could've been helping," Blaz commented, "But I'm sure there'll be more than that in the war. I guess you got your first kill."

Jaye's smile vanished, as if he just realized he'd killed someone.

"Come on, look alert!" yelled Captain Steinhoff, "The Reds are trying to break the siege. Our front lines are holding their counterattack off at the moment. Give them some cover fire!"

The artillery opened fire again. The boys watched the guns light up the sky while keeping an eye out for any planes. None came.

Koby came dashing into the German artillery line, with yet another object in his hands. This time Blaz could tell it was a letter of some kind. Koby handed it to Steinhoff, who gave him instructions before the sergeant headed to his squad mates. He told the first two crews something, then came to Blaz, Jarman, and Jaye.

"We're going behind the front lines to evacuate the wounded. Steinhoff says we will be going around the lines of Leningrad today and tomorrow. This'll be one of our jobs from now on, so don't get too comfortable at the flak guns."

"Don't worry, we weren't comfortable," Blaz joked.

Jaye grinned while he opened his bag. He safely stowed his glasses and put in contacts with some difficulty.

"No kidding," Koby admitted, "Come on now, let's go!"

The boys set off at a jog toward the front, which was only about a kilometer away. With them went replacement soldiers and a medic to take care of the more critically injured. They all stayed alert for artillery fire from the Russians. Koby led the group ahead towards the lines, passing some

German artillery positions and tanks on the way. Some soldiers waved to them as they passed by.

They arrived at the front, where Germans were defending their position with new MG-42 nests. A decent number of trees provided good cover for the German forces. Not only that, but the front of their lines was just outside a city block of a suburb of Leningrad. Germans were encamped inside the buildings, on top of the buildings, in trenches next to trees, and in the wreckage of bombarded buildings. An officer ran over to the Knights.

"*Gut*, you are here," the officer said at volume, "We have some wounded that need to be taken away from the front. And I see you have replacements. *Gut.* Can you carry the more critically injured into those trucks?" he asked, though it was an order, and pointed to two large troop transports.

"Of course, sir," Koby said and turned to the Knights, "Time to use our training. Get to work."

The boys spread out, heading over to the positions where the German soldiers were encamped. Most were *Wehrmacht*, but some were *Schutzstaffel*, of the *Waffen-SS*. Blaz jogged with Jaye over to a machine gun nest that a soldier was waving them to. Inside the nest were five soldiers, wearing gray-green uniforms. One operating the massive machine gun, one feeding bullets into the weapon, and two lookouts holding Karabiner 98K rifles. The fifth was lying on the ground, with blood soaking through his uniform at the shoulder. The soldier with the rifle was trying to stop the bleeding.

"Can you boys get him to a medic? He's lost a lot of blood," the soldier pleaded.

"*Jawohl*," Blaz answered, trying not to stare at the injured soldier's bloody arm. The boys jumped into the nest and crawled to the wounded man's side.

"Here," Jaye said and grabbed some bandages out of his bag. He wrapped the soldier's arm up to try and stop the bleeding.

"Now let's get him up." The boys and the rifleman lifted the injured soldier to his feet. When the soldier was up, it revealed much blood on the ground beneath him and on his back. Blaz got under the man's good shoulder and let the man lean on him. Jaye held the soldier's other hand

and told him, "It'll be all right, we're going to get you better." They hoisted the man into the truck with some difficulty.

"*Danke Hitlerjugend*," the soldier said weakly, as he leaned against the back of the truck closing his eyes.

"Our honor," the boys saluted. Immediately they headed back through the suburban streets and wooded field. A soldier with SS insignia on his camouflage uniform and a *Wehrmacht* soldier on top of a flat-roofed building waved the boys over. The building gave them decent cover behind a wall that lined the roof. The boys ran into the building and up the stairs. On the roof were three *Wehrmacht* soldiers, one manning a machine gun. The other two had rifles, and one was helping the soldier who'd waved the boys over with an injured *Waffen-SS* soldier. The injured SS soldier was leaned against the wall, next to the stairs. His head had a gash running across the left side of his head and blood ran down from it. Blaz took his bandages out, wrapping them around the man's head.

"How did he get this wound?" Jaye asked the other SS soldier.

"We were repelling a Russian attack here. Their artillery impacted right next us, we both were sent flying. I landed in some grass, but he banged his head against the street," the SS soldier answered, gritting his teeth at the last part.

"Can he walk?" Blaz asked.

"I was able to help him walk over here, though I was almost carrying him. I think he has a concussion. Not to mention all the blood he's lost. These men said I could nurse him on the roof until the medics arrived. Do you have medics?"

"We're taking them to the medics, *ja*," Jaye answered.

"*Danke*," the soldier said while giving each boy a quick pat on the head. Blaz and Jaye positioned themselves under the injured man's armpits and lifted him up. They were helped down the stairs by the healthy SS soldier. While they walked through the streets with the SS trooper an explosion sounded in the trees outside the town.

"Artillery! Russian troops, in range!" screamed a German, "*Feuer erwidern!*"

"*Scheiße*," Jaye shouted, "Let's get him out of here!" They quickened their pace, helping the soldier towards the truck. The soldier tried to get in himself, but the boys insisted that he allow them to help.

"Keep bringing more wounded!" Koby yelled to them from the second truck, while he and Hans helped a soldier in. Blaz and Jaye headed back into the town, gunfire drawing nearer with every step. They jogged into the trees just outside of the town, where the German machine guns and tanks fired into the thin forest. While the two boys scanned for wounded men, bullets splintered the trees behind them, bark bits scattered into the air. They ducked down behind a wide tree, as more bullets flew by. The Russians were charging.

"Oh God," Jaye whimpered, terrified, "Oh God, we're gonna die."

Blaz stayed behind the tree with Jaye, just as terrified as his friend. His arms shook as he put a hand on his pistol.

Help us, help us, someone. What are we going to do? Oh God. Blaz's mind raced in desperation. *Come on! Pull it together, there are soldiers fighting for Deutschland that need your help. Go, you coward!*

Blaz turned to Jaye and put a hand on his shoulder, "Come on, we've got to do our jobs! The flag means more than death?"

Jaye looked into Blaz's eyes in terror. "*N-nein*, I c-can't," he stammered.

"*Ja*, you can," Blaz shouted over the gunfire, "These men are fighting for our people, they're being killed and wounded. We have to help them, come on!"

Blaz stood up and sprinted. Bullets flew by, hitting trees behind him. He did not look to see whether Jaye followed.

"Medic! Medic!" a soldier shouted. Blaz leapt into a small, round trench, and went to his hands and knees in his landing. Four *Wehrmacht* soldiers were in the trench; one operating the machine gun, with two holding rifles. The fourth was laying at the back of the trench with a bullet wound in his chest. One soldier shouted, "Get this man out of here! Quick! Get him behind the trees and work your way into the-" A bullet hole appeared in the soldier's helmet, and he fell backwards. Blaz jumped back in shock. The soldier on the machine gun swore in anger and fired another burst into the charging Russians. The Russians were getting closer to their position, not quite close enough to lob a grenade into the trench though. Blaz put his hand on his cap, not knowing what else to do. The second *Wehrmacht* soldier emerged from the trench and dove for cover. He dashed from tree to tree, until he was fifteen meters away from the trench. The soldier took his stick grenade and chucked it towards a large tree where several Russians stood behind. All Blaz heard was a faint scream, and an explosion. That was all. The *Wehrmacht* soldier took his rifle off his back, and shouted something to the machine gunner, while giving hand signals.

"Lay down fire! Left-" the soldier was cut short and fell to the ground. A bullet had torn through his leg. The soldier screamed in pain while grasping the leg with one arm. Blaz peeked above the trench, now at the front of it, next to the last fighting soldier who manned the machine gun. The soldier screamed curses at seeing his comrades fall while he fired away at the Russians. A bullet flew through his arm, and he stopped firing. His grip loosened on the mounted machine gun, but he pulled himself back up in a surge of adrenaline and resumed shooting. Blaz scrambled out of the trench and sprinted towards the wounded soldier who'd thrown the grenade. He unholstered his pistol and turned the safety off. Cautiously, he worked closer to the wounded man. When he peeked out from behind cover bullets immediately hit the tree behind him. He got a look at the shooter, who stood across from him, behind yet another tree. Blaz snapped a low hanging limb off and placed his black cap on the end of it. The tree was thin enough for him to be able to reach to both sides easily, but fortunately he was small enough for it to provide sufficient cover. He poked the cap out on the left side, while moving his body and pistol to the right, ready to fire. As the cap peeked further out a barrage of bullets flew through it. Blaz dropped the stick, leaned to the right and fired off three shots at his attacker who had exposed himself. His aim was good, and the soldier collapsed. Blaz barely saw the soldier begin his fall before he hastily concealed himself again. He then rolled over to the tree where the wounded soldier was. The soldier had propped himself up so he couldn't be seen easily behind the thick tree.

"*Danke*, kid," the soldier smiled with gratitude and pride. Almost as if it were his own son who had come to rescue him, "Here, take my rifle."

Blaz holstered his pistol with lightning speed and took the rifle. The German soldier pulled out his pistol. They heard some shouts in Russian. Blaz looked for half a moment. Three Russians were charging at the tree.

"Take that side!" Blaz shouted to the soldier even though he had no authority. Blaz raised the rifle, turned around the tree, and fired. The first Russian soldier fell. The *Wehrmacht* soldier shot a second only moments later. By now there was no time to cock the rifle for a third shot. The final Russian raised his bayonet to run Blaz through. Blaz sprang up and raised his rifle to block the weapon. The Russian knocked the rifle out of Blaz's arms with the bayonet, then hit Blaz's head with the back end of his rifle. The boy toppled backward to the forest floor. The enemy soldier spun around the tree and immediately cut the German soldier's hand with his bayonet, causing the soldier to drop his pistol. Then he raised the rifle over his head to finish the German soldier. Blaz leapt up and onto the Russian's back moments after he had hit the ground. The Soviet stumbled forward, missing the killing blow. Blaz was sent hurling over the enemy's head as he fell. The wounded *Wehrmacht* soldier grabbed the Russian by the leg when he lunged at Blaz. When the young German turned around, the Russian was furiously choking the *Wehrmacht* soldier, who kicked and swung desperately to escape the stranglehold. Blaz unholstered his pistol, raised it at the Russian's head, and fired. The unwary Soviet crumpled to the ground as the bullet flew through his skull.

"Ingal!" the *Wehrmacht* gunner screamed, "Our *Panzers* have arrived!"

Two tanks rumbled by Blaz and Ingal. Their machine guns fired, making sure no Russians were still alive to counterattack. Blaz stood up and helped Ingal up too. The soldier could put no weight on his injured leg, and Blaz had trouble helping him walk. The man did his best to hop on his good leg, and they made it to the town with no falls. Jaye jogged over to help them through the town. Blaz glared at him. Jaye looked down, face red with embarrassment more than cold. Blaz looked back ahead. Three soldiers ran by in a hurry to reinforce the position. Blaz turned to Jaye,

"There's another wounded man in that trench. Make yourself useful and go get him."

Jaye obeyed without hesitation. Once he'd left, the soldier asked Blaz, "What was that all about?"

Blaz answered Ingal with fire and contempt. "We were assigned to rescue injured soldiers. We arrived up where you were right when the Russians charged. And he didn't do anything, dirty coward."

Ingal smiled at the boy's attitude. "He certainly missed an opportunity. But I can't say you should treat him this way for long. This will motivate him to do something next time," Ingal replied as he limped along, "Was this your first time in a firefight?"

"*Jawohl.*"

"Everyone reacts differently to battle. No training can prepare you for this. Just be glad he's not in the army yet. That reaction would've warranted some punishment if he was," Ingal sighed, "You boys will have hands on experience before you're in the army. Not many get that. I certainly didn't."

They'd arrived at the truck now. An SS officer lifted the man into the truck, and thanked Blaz. Ingal leaned over to the officer and whispered something into his ear.

The man listened, nodding his head, several surprised expressions appearing. Finally, Ingal leaned back into the truck. The SS officer looked at Blaz with a smile. "What's your name, son?" he asked.

"Blaz Senft," the fourteen-year-old answered nervously.

"Private Senft, I'd like you to stay here after your squad mates have left. Once we have this area cleared up, you and several other men will be awarded," the officer said warmly.

Blaz couldn't believe it. An SS officer, the toughest of the tough, the best of the best, was awarding him for service.

"*Danke, Herr. Danke,*" he stuttered.

"Now, finish your job then report back to me," the officer ordered.

"Right away sir," Blaz said with strength in his voice. He turned and ran back into the town. An SS soldier soon waved him over to a balcony. Blaz sprinted up the stairs. He was greeted by the SS soldier, who asked him to take another *Waffen-SS* soldier down to the medics. The first SS soldier helped the injured man to his feet. The camouflage uniform was red with blood, on the chest and left arm. Blaz walked the man down the stairs, then the first soldier thanked Blaz before turning and sprinting up to his position. The injured soldier clumsily stumbled along with Blaz's guidance. He was clearly lightheaded from loss of blood. Blaz hurried him to the transport then sprinted back into the town and to the tree line just outside of it. A machine gun position waved him over. One soldier made his way to Blaz. The soldier wore the field gray *Wehrmacht* uniform, though the uniform's colors were barely visible through the filth. The solider appeared fine initially, but Blaz noticed right away that he was clutching his arm and letting it hang limp. Something jutted out inside the sleeve at the elbow that looked suspiciously like a bone.

"Where are the medical trucks, son? I think my arm is broken."

Blaz looked at the injured man sadly. He'd seen so many dead and injured countrymen today. He quickly gave the man instructions, and the soldier walked off. The machine gun position was behind a mound of dirt and grass that provided decent cover.

"Young man!" an officer called. Blaz jogged over to find him nursing yet another injured man. The man bled from his chest very badly. His field gray uniform appeared black where the blood darkened it.

"*Ja*, sir?" Blaz respectfully answered, while staring at the wounded man and breathing rapidly.

"This man needs a medic really badly," the soldier said quickly, "Can you get him to the medic?"

"It would be my honor," Blaz replied while getting the man to his feet. He tried to walk with the soldier leaning on him, but the man was too injured to lend any help. Blaz tried again but couldn't get far with the soldier. Fortunately, Reinhardt came running towards him from the town, "Need some help? We've gotten as many men as we can load."

"*Ja*."

The two boys together were able to carry the man to the trucks and were aided by Koby in loading him in. At least ten *Wehrmacht* soldiers stood in a line before the SS officer who had spoken earlier to Blaz. Mixed with them were two young SS soldiers. They stood erect, awaiting the officer's words.

"Move the trucks out! Get them to the medics!" the officer shouted. The trucks started up and rolled off to the back lines. Koby ordered his squad to follow him.

"Wait. Private Senft, remain here. The rest, head back."

Blaz stepped out of the formation and strode briskly over to the line of German soldiers. He stood on the left end. Koby knew better than to question an SS officer, especially one so decorated. The squad marched off. The officer examined the troopers, then turned to his assistant, who held a briefcase. He opened it, revealing many Second-Class Iron Crosses; black, symmetric, curved crosses with silver lining along the outside. The colors of Germany made up the design of the fabric that attached the crosses to the uniforms: red, white and black. The officer took one at a time, pinning them onto each soldier's uniform and gave each of them brief words of praise. Each soldier remained in an upright stance, some cracking smiles, particularly the younger ones. The officer finally came to Blaz, knelt down on one knee, and pinned the Iron Cross onto Blaz's black uniform, just to the left of his heart. The soldiers leaned over, staring at Blaz in amazement at such a little boy receiving such an award.

"Private Senft, I award you the Iron Cross for your bravery in rescuing many of our men today, while holding off the enemy to save your countrymen. You have displayed great bravery, even though you are not yet in the army," the officer smiled at him, and Blaz returned the gesture, "You are a hero today, Senft. Thank you for your brave service and going beyond the call of duty."

The officer turned and stomped a foot. "*Heil*, to you. *Sieg Heil!*"

"*Sieg Heil!*"

"Dismissed," the officer said, saluting.

The many soldiers dispersed to their positions. Blaz watched them go, before returning to the back lines. He walked back through the fields of grass and trees. The cold weather wasn't bothering him at all. He felt invincible. Blaz smiled the entire way back. He'd never felt so good in all his life.

Blaz approached the German artillery position still wearing a smile. Jarman greeted him at their flak cannon.

"Blaz! What was that about?" Jarman asked, "Not in trouble, *ja?*"

Blaz shook his head, grinning, "It was about this," he answered, and pointed to the medal. Jarman's eyes went wide. He reached out and fingered the medal on Blaz's uniform.

"Wow," he awed, mouth wide open, "The Iron Cross," Jarman stared at the medal, something he wanted to earn more than anything. "Jaye," Jarman called, "Blaz was awarded the Iron Cross!" Jaye simply shuffled over to them, still ashamed of his failure up front with Blaz. He looked at the medal.

"Congratulations," Jaye said sincerely, "You earned it," the cadet glanced down, playing with his fingers. He then looked back up, into Blaz's eyes, "Blaz, I swear, that will never happen again. I completely forgot everything I'd learned, the *Führer* would be ashamed of me, *Deutschland* is ashamed of me," he said through gritted teeth, "I swear I'll have your back."

Blaz had really wanted to light into Jaye for deserting him. But they weren't soldiers yet, and Jaye was angry with himself already. He knew what he'd done was dishonorable. "Make sure you do," Blaz answered and gave his friend a punch on the shoulder.

"I will."

The other boys admired Blaz's Iron Cross as they ate their dinner that night. There was little light, but everyone managed to see it well enough. Question after question came; about how he got it, what he did to earn it, how he managed to even stay alive. Blaz explained everything, though he did not smile while explaining it.

"So many men were dying and screaming up there," Blaz thought aloud, "It was awful, that's why I felt I had to go help that soldier," he paused, in thought, "Now, come on, you guys have some stories from today."

The boys talked for hours about the day, even as they separated to their flak guns.

On the Verge of Victory

January 18, 1942

The boys were moved around the back lines over the course of the week. They ran into Marvin's squad once but had little time to talk. The Russian offensive was not as fierce, though there were continued pushes in places along the southern front where the boys were. Their medical runs were not under fire like the first time and they did not encounter as many wounded troopers. Leningrad was under constant artillery barrage.

While this happened, Blaz followed behind his squad mates, as they headed to a new position to protect it from potential Soviet aircraft. They arrived on top of a flat hill where a massive German position was encamped. Two *Panzers IV's* waited to be given the order to attack. Artillery and flak guns were on the hill, and many *Wehrmacht* personnel walked around the camp. The boys headed to the open flak guns and assumed their positions. There they waited, some dogmatically hoping someone would attack. The boys were out of luck on this count.

"When are we going to attack the city?" Jarman asked Blaz and Jaye as he paced by their flak gun, "I can see it from here, *Gott verdämmt*! What are we waiting for?"

"Maybe trying to force a surrender?" Jaye suggested.

"We can't break through to the city?" Blaz threw into the mix.

"Look at this, though," Jarman said, "We have positions like this for miles and miles. We could take the city."

"Heck, if I know," Blaz shrugged, "That's why we aren't the generals. They've done well so far, I'd say. We're outnumbered in this war, but we're winning."

"Numbers don't matter for us," Jarman scoffed.

Jaye's eyes widened at the shortsighted statement and he held in a laugh.

"Okay, not true," Jarman said, "I'm just really wondering why we're halted here. The generals do know what they're doing, that's why numbers don't matter as much, the generals know how to use each man," he said with a grin.

January 23, 1942

Letters arrived from their mothers and fathers. They'd received them at KLV camp, but this was different. Their parents were eager to hear back from them to make sure they were all right. Blaz could not wait to tell his parents he'd been awarded the Iron Cross. He opened his father's letter first. The handwriting was sloppy, not his father's normal fine print. It read:

Lieber Blaz,

Hope you've had safe travels to the front. Were your last days at the KLV camp fine? Are you all right? Where are you now? I am in Norway right now, but I will be shipping out for Northern France. How are Ivo and Koby doing? Stay strong, Blaz. The war won't last forever. God be with us, in our fight. Heil Hitler.

Liebe, Father

Blaz smiled to himself and wiped his eyes so the paper wouldn't get wet. He glanced over to Jarman, who had torn open one of his letter. Jarman read through the letter, folded it up, and put it into one of his uniform's pockets. He stared ahead blankly. Finally, after minutes of staring straight ahead, he stood up. Both Blaz and Jaye were afraid to ask.

"*Mein Vater ist tote*," Jarman said with his voice giving out, "My father is dead." He held back until rivers ran down his face, freezing quickly after. "Damn it, father, why'd you die? You could make it through anything, you always did," Jarman said. His shoulders shook. Blaz tried to think of something to say. He sat down next to Jarman and put a hand on his shoulder. Jarman looked up at Blaz. He smiled amidst his tears and gripped his friend. "Blaz, I don't know, I don't know. I'll never see him again."

Blaz had to say something. "He was a soldier before our *Führer* was the *Führer*?"

"*Ja*," Jarman replied with sniffle. It was odd to see the strongest, toughest boy in the squad in such a state.

"Did he die fighting?"

Jarman nodded with another tear streaming down his cheek.

"He died doing what he loved, for the country that he loved, for the people he loved," Blaz comforted Jarman, "He died for a noble cause."

Jarman nodded with a sniff, "He did, I know. No cause could be better. And he died doing his favorite thing. I only wish I could've seen him one last time. Damn it, father, I love you…"

Mama, Papa, please don't die, Blaz thought as Jarman continued to weep. *No one die.*

Russian Winter

January 24, 1942

The weather became colder, as if to add insult to injury. It was already colder than anything the boys had experienced in Germany, but now the cold began to visibly take its toll on them and the entire *Wehrmacht*. It was unbelievably cold. The wind picked up, and waves of snow would shower the German troops. By now gloves had been distributed, but many of the German soldiers lacked winter coats and pants. The boys were in nothing but their winter Hitler Youth uniforms and gloves. They remained huddled around their flak guns or pacing furiously to stay warm. Thick clouds blocked the sun all day, and no warmth made it through. Steinhoff kept telling his garrison that warm clothes were on their way, but the German army's morale was plummeting. They had expected Moscow to be captured, and yet the news said their attack had stalled. Much of the army at Leningrad had been there for months and little progress had been made. Poor attitude was weakness. Still, their illnesses threatened their morale every day. The longer they were at the front, the more they put their training into effect. Jaye had changed, refusing to complain or show any signs of weakness, even when his squad mates did.

Blaz paced by the flak gun, hoping against hope that one minute the weather would become warmer. Each breath let a cloud into the air that blew back into his face. He couldn't smell anything, his nose was constantly stuffed up, and he had a horrible cough. His throat felt like it would rip open each time he hacked into the frigid air. Koby ran over from his gun, and paced beside Blaz, unwilling to stay still in the freezing cold.

"Boy, this is cold," Blaz said miserably.

Koby laughed weakly, "*Ja*, you bet it is. We'll get winter clothing soon, I'm sure."

"*Gut*. Then my face," he paused to hold back a cough, "Will return to normal color," he commented before coughing uncontrollably, drawing Jaye's attention.

Koby continued pacing, "What do you plan on doing after the war, Blaz?"

"Wow," Blaz let out a hacking cough, "I," he coughed again, "That seems like a way off now, I'm not sure right now. I'd like to get married."

"*Ja*," Koby said, his tone indicating for Blaz to continue.

"What about you?" Blaz rasped. He felt some blood come up his throat and turned away from Koby to spit it out.

"Blaz, are you okay? You've been coughing ever since it got colder. And it sounds awful," Koby said with concern. Then he saw the blood on the ground. "Blaz! You're really sick! That's bad, really bad that you're coughing up blood."

"Even if I'm not okay, what are we going to do about it?" Blaz asked through another cough.

Koby stayed quiet for a moment, shaking his head, "Nothing, I guess. The medics already have enough to do, and they couldn't do anything for a cough. But God, Blaz. You sound terrible."

January 31, 1942

The weather stayed frigid, worse than anything the boys had ever experienced. Each night was a struggle to sleep. They'd had left their dignity behind by now, doing whatever they could to stay warm. At night, they slept together for body heat but even then, they thought they'd freeze every night. Reinhardt and Ivo had horrible, rasping coughs too. The entire *Wehrmacht* was at the breaking point and still had to repel the Russian counterattacks in the ungodly weather.

Every day they were sent to the front lines to bring sick soldiers to medics, and worse still, what they were doing today: clearing dead bodies. Soldiers froze at night at the front with no protection from the cold, so the boys had to remove the bodies. Each face frozen in sleep, the soldiers died peacefully during the night. Trench by trench, the boys hauled the bodies of their countrymen away. Miserable faces were everywhere, the German soldiers would give their fallen friends and comrades one final glance. Blaz and Ivo picked up one dead German and tried to walk away with him, but one soldier wouldn't let go of the dead man's hand.

"Joseph, he's gone, you can't help him," another soldier said.

"*Nein, nein*, he's not dead!" the soldier shouted desperately, "He's going to be all right, I'm going to help him!"

The soldier pried away the screaming soldier's hand from the dead man. He then gestured to the boys to get out of there. Blaz and Ivo quickly hurried away and brought the dead man to an SS officer who bore a strong resemblance to SS Deputy Reinhard Heydrich.

"Put him here," he told them, pointing to a line of dead bodies next to a truck. The officer did not even look their way. He stared ahead blankly. No joy or life lay in those eyes. Any happiness that had once been in him had left. They laid the man at the end of the line and trudged back into the forest. Blaz looked around at all the miserable men, with nothing to stay warm. But still they remained at their posts, on guard against the Russians. Ivo coughed violently, drawing attention from surrounding soldiers. They watched the Hitler Youths at work, they had nothing else to do. Anything to take their minds off how cold they were. The boys couldn't smile. They'd never seen anything worse than Leningrad. No one spoke. Koby gave orders by pointing. They returned to the SS officer with body after body, some appearing to have been dead longer than others. After what felt like hours of work, the Heydrich SS officer allowed them to return to their flak guns. It very well may have been hours of work, but no one could tell since the sun was almost always blotted out by thick, dark clouds.

Each boy felt like they were going to fall flat on their face on the march back, but they soldiered on. Steinhoff was the only man who didn't have a look of misery on his face. He tried to keep his *Wehrmacht* company's morale up, as a commander would. For days and nights, the boys slept almost nearly in piles, half of them now sick. Every shred of dignity had disappeared. Blaz's sense of humor was lost during the long, miserable months of frigid, dismal weather. No more laughter could be heard among the encampments of the Germans.

February 9, 1942

The cold weather persisted, and so did the *Wehrmacht*. The Russian counterattack was somehow held at bay. Jarman, Blaz, and Jaye were adjusting their flak gun, aiming it into the sky of dark gray. A mixture of clouds and smoke.

"When are winter clothes going to be here?" a soldier demanded of Aldric Steinhoff.

"I don't know," the commander admitted. The boys looked up as the men walked by their gun.

"My squad is freezing. I've lost two good men at the front, not from Russians but from this damned weather," the man growled, almost at a shout, "We've been here for months. It's February, and we've seen other companies with proper winter clothing."

Steinhoff stopped and turned to the soldier, "Son, if it was up to me, we would have had those winter clothes at the start of December," Steinhoff frustratedly shot back.

"Does the *Führer* not care about us? Damn him!" The soldier rattled of several other words, some that the boys had never heard before. But they knew their Führer was being insulted. Jarman took a step in the direction of the soldier. Blaz and Jaye grabbed him.

"Let the officer handle him," Jaye whispered.

When the soldier finished swearing, Steinhoff stared calmly at him. None of the anger the boys had expected was expressed. "Are you finished?" Steinhoff asked.

The soldier quietly muttered something else. All the boys picked up was the end, "...the *Führer*."

"Back to your post," Steinhoff said, "Swearing won't bring the supplies any faster. And don't go spreading your attitude. Just keep silent."

The soldier turned away muttering more words as he walked away. Steinhoff watched the soldier disappear towards the front. The commander turned to the boys. He looked ready to say something, but after a long pause, he simply marched away. The boys watched him with looks of confusion. Why had he tolerated the soldier's remarks? Surely he was not fine with disrespecting the *Führer*.

A Death in the Family

February 13, 1942

At long last, the clothes arrived. No one in the squad had ever been so happy to receive anything in all their lives. Koby, Jurgen, Hans, and Jarman brought the clothes back from the trucks. The rest of the Knights was sick and leaning on the flak guns. They couldn't lay down or they would freeze in the snow that grew higher and higher with every storm. Blaz and Jaye supported themselves alone, but they coughed so hard that they bent over each time a fit came. Ivo, Tristan, and Reinhardt's coughs were even worse. Everyone remained at their own flak guns though. Steinhoff had told them if fighters came, that they were too sick to make it back to their flak guns in enough time if they all stayed at one gun. *Wehrmacht* soldiers passing by them often had coughs, but none as bad as the fourteen-year-olds. Spring couldn't come soon enough for the boys. Blaz felt weaker than he ever had in a Hitler Youth uniform. He had little appetite, but he somehow kept going each day. But Death was busy during the war.

February 17, 1942

The boys grabbed sleep whenever they could, even preferring to stay moving at night when it was coldest and sleep during the day. Everyone fell into sickness one by one. The winter clothing was overdue, but it perhaps saved the German army. The Russians had a saying, "There's no such thing as cold weather, only the wrong clothing."

For now, sickness was still their main enemy. Koby took up his role as leader and did his best to nurse his sick squad mates back to health. Ivo, Reinhardt, and Blaz's sickness was peaking, and something had to give. Either the boys or the sickness. Desperation for anything that could cure his friends clouded Koby's mind. Finally, he brought them to the medical shelter; a slapped-together wooden building that housed fifty cots. All were full around the clock. The building was not much warmer than outside, but the boys stayed in their winter clothing and under blankets. Blaz leaned over to Ivo, who was laying on his back.

"Ivo," he whispered, "Ivo?"

Ivo turned to Blaz. He smiled weakly, "*Ja?*"

"How are you feeling?"

Ivo coughed as Blaz said this, "Does that answer?" he tried to joke.

"*Ja,*" Blaz said with a violent cough. "Can you see how Reinhardt is doing?"

"All right," Ivo leaned to the other side of his cot, "Reinhardt," Ivo whispered, with a clogged throat, "Reinhardt," he said, louder this time. No response. Ivo kept trying to wake him up, "Come on, Reinhardt. Are you awake?"

Blaz straightened up to see Reinhardt, taking off his coat. His friend lay flat on the cot, eyes closed. Ivo got up. He shook Reinhardt. Blaz came over next to Ivo.

"Reinhardt!" Ivo said, at nearly a shout, desperate for some response. Blaz put his ear on Reinhardt's chest, and his fingers onto his neck. He looked up in shock. There was no pulse.

"Medic!" he screamed weakly with one of his loud coughs interrupting him. He stood up and started running for a medic, "Medic, we need a medic!"

A man ran over immediately.

"He doesn't have a pulse!" Blaz told the doctor, on the verge of tears. The doctor got on a knee and felt for Reinhardt's pulse. He stayed there for well over a minute. Finally, the doctor turned to Blaz.

"I'm sorry, son. He's gone," the doctor said. Blaz's jaw dropped and he shook his head in disbelief. Ivo whispered, "*Nein.*" Blaz shook his friend in a last act of desperation. Reinhardt's skin felt like ice.

"*Nein,* come on Reinhardt. Wake up, will you?" Tears flowed from Blaz's eyes, and down his face. "Wake up! Please? Don't be dead, Reinhardt. Don't be dead."

Ivo stayed beside Blaz, shell-shocked. His tears froze before they reached his chin. Blaz buried his head next to his dead friend. Why Reinhardt? Reinhardt didn't deserve to die like this.

There was no funeral. No goodbye to Reinhardt. He died without warning, without a word. Silence and tears. Koby tried not to cry. He tried to be a strong commander but couldn't fight back silent tears. The medics carried Reinhardt's body out of the little hospital building to send back to his mother. Steinhoff himself signed the condolence letter. He did so in embittered silence. Nothing but a dismal expression. He was a commander, but this was undoubtedly the first fourteen-year-old to die under his command.

The boys watched their friend's body being carried away, until Steinhoff's assistant told them to get back to their positions. Blaz and Ivo returned to their cots. Blaz silently cried himself to sleep that night amid the endless coughing. The Hitler Youth had been trained to deal with this. When it happened, Blaz forgot all of it.

February 23, 1942

The boys did not speak for much of the following week. Blaz and Ivo did recover and were back on the flak guns. Steinhoff needed to send more men to the front and ordered the boys to split into groups of two, with three going to artillery. Blaz and Ivo were now on a flak gun together. The artillery was two hundred feet in front of the flak guns. Blaz and Ivo stood silently by their flak gun, in their winter clothes but the weather was still dismally cold. At least the sun was finally out. They had been silent for days, still thinking about Reinhardt. Their recovering voices were hoarse, and they could not speak clearly. While they stood in the cold, Steinhoff sprinted by them, yelling orders to the flak guns.

"The *Luftwaffe* is coming, do not fire. They're coming from our airbase south of here to bomb Leningrad. Hold fire, our scouts have reported the Russians are too weak in this region to launch an effective defense."

The boys turned their gaze south waiting for the Luftwaffe. Blaz wondered for a moment whether the flak guns would even be capable of firing in the weather. Then a low humming noise occupied his ears. Next, a vast number of airplanes glided over the horizon, making their way in the direction of Leningrad. The aircraft flew over the German position; fast, little fighters and gigantic, elegant bombers. A dozen Soviet planes rose to meet them. The German fighters accelerated towards Leningrad to destroy their only resistance. The Soviets flew fearlessly into the jaws of death. The German soldiers cheered to see their fighters rout the enemy aircraft which plummeted to the ground like moths around a flame.

"Keep pounding them guys," Ivo applauded hoarsely. Flak fire came in the distance, firing at the *Luftwaffe*. The fighters swooped down, firing their machine guns at the flak guns. The boys kept their eyes on the bombers, as they approached Leningrad. They were too far too see the bombs, but they heard faint explosions in the distance.

"Artillery! Artillery!" Steinhoff screamed, "Lay down fire! Russian infantry is attacking."

The artillery blasted away, drowning out the *Luftwaffe*. The two *Panzer IV's* rolled out towards the front. On their turrets were painted "*Stahlfaust*" and "*Deutschlands Glorie*" or "Steel Fist" and "Germany's Glory." Steinhoff yelled at the three other tank commanders. Blaz watched with interest, it was the first thing that had taken his mind off Reinhardt. Two *Panzer III's*, "*Blut und Eisen*" and "*Waffe der Hakenkreuz*" or "Blood and Iron" and "Weapon of the Swastika" rolled behind them, each flanking one on the *Panzer IV's*. Blaz continued to watch the tanks. The last he'd seen one move was when two saved him and Ingal the day he'd been awarded the Iron Cross.

"Go get them boys," he muttered.

War is Hell

February 26, 1942

The Russian attack failed. The Germans advanced forward, preparing to form a pincer movement around the Soviet shock army. The squad was once again sent to help evacuate the wounded from the front. The replacements lead them to the positions. Koby and Blaz went in together on this one. No Soviets expected this time.

While Blaz trudged through the defenses, he again saw dozens of maimed and disfigured bodies. Grown men whimpering like children as they grasped their bleeding chest or held up an arm that no longer had a hand on the end of it. Young men, not yet in their twenties, frozen to death in the snow. Men, whose eyes had no life or warmth in them. They only knew cold, miserable nights, brothers gone, and constant death. Every time Blaz saw one of his dead or suffering countrymen, more hatred was built in his heart for the Russians. He said nothing as they helped the wounded and hauled away the dead that day. Anger burned on his face every time he carried away a dead soldier.

By the end of the day their coats were covered in the blood of their wounded and fallen comrades. As the sun set, Blaz and Ivo sat at their flak positions. Blaz put a palm on the gun. It was colder than the air.

"God, Ivo," Blaz rasped, "How many Germans have to die before these Russians just surrender? We have their city surrounded, they are being hammered by our artillery, raided by our bombers, and we beat back all their counterattacks. Why don't they give up?"

Ivo coughed, and asked, "Would you?"

Blaz paused at this unexpected reply, though he'd heard this question before in the same context, "*Nein,*" he admitted.

"Until our flag flies over the city, they'll fight to the last man."

March 1, 1942

"*Gleiche Ziel!*" Ivo shouted to Blaz.

Blaz rotated the flak gun to remain on a Russian fighter. Ivo opened fire as it swooped low and unleashed a barrage of bullets on their position. The plane's shots sent dust flying into the air around the boys.

"Hurry Ivo!" Blaz shouted.

Ivo fired again, and this time his aim was true. Blaz saw a small explosion on the plane's wing. The aircraft continued to plummet towards the earth. "*Scheiße!*" Ivo shouted and jumped off the flak gun. Blaz sprinted away and dove to the ground, covering his head with his hands. The plane landed mere meters behind their flak gun. The explosion was not as big as they thought it would be. Nonetheless, it was lucky they'd bailed out. The flak gun was fine, but flames and debris had rained down on it when the plane exploded.

Ivo and Blaz looked at each other with wide eyes. They grinned awkwardly, scared but relieved. Both quickly ran back to their flak gun, and Blaz moved it to follow another Russian fighter. Their artillery fired away, hammering both attacking Russians and Leningrad itself.

"Blaz!" Ivo shouted the artillery, flak and airplanes, "He's heading southeast, get me ahead of him!"

Blaz rotated and lowered the gun slightly, "Ready?"

"*Gut*! Hold there!" Ivo yelled back. The pilot flew his plane right into their line of fire. Ivo made him pay for that.

Steinhoff shouted to the flak guns, "Concentrate fire on the fighters, quickly! We have a squadron coming to finish them off!"

Blaz and Ivo kept hammering the Russian airplanes, landing another hit, but not a fatal one. It made a difference though. Twelve *Luftwaffe* Messerschmitt fighters arrived and strafed through the unwary Russian fighters bringing down the rest of them.

"*Ja!*" Blaz shouted and threw a fist into the air. It seemed Germany was on the verge of victory. Germany had lost many men, but the boys had seen nothing but declared "victories." But they were still no closer to breaking Leningrad.

A Jewish SS Soldier

March 7, 1942

Food never tasted so good. The squad ate their lunch quickly, enjoying every bite. Blaz's health had returned, and with it his appetite. They'd begun to sound and look healthier again. The Knights were dirty and worn out though. The entire *Wehrmacht* was. Sallow eyes were everywhere and few smiles, and the weather stayed unrelenting. The squad had been sent to yet another place to carry away bodies and the wounded.

Their truck drove them to the location. The boys exited to see nothing but *Waffen-SS* soldiers. To the boys, it was just another company of their countrymen though. Elite, but countrymen.

"Come on, divide up," Koby ordered. Blaz paired with Koby. The boys spread out across the SS defenses to find the wounded and dead. Though they were soldiers, Blaz noticed something different about the SS. It wasn't their camouflage uniforms. It wasn't the SS insignia. It was the men themselves. The men did not have looks of misery on their faces. No fear. No worries. The SS was all smiles today. Not smiles of happiness, but of pride and determination. After helping several wounded men into the truck, Koby and Blaz ventured further into the SS camp. Several minutes of walking brought them into a thick grove of trees. The SS soldiers appeared more and more infrequently. A clearing came into view. Ten men were on their knees with their hands behind their heads. Koby and Blaz knelt behind a tree to watch.

They could hear a pacing man in a black uniform saying in German, "I am required to treat you as prisoners of war, *ja?*"

Two SS soldiers stood behind what seemed to be Russian soldiers on their knees. One appeared to be a veteran, the other a teenager.

The Russians were facing the boys, with sheer terror on their faces. Many were only the age of Reynald Schlusser. One man stood out. He had no fear on his face, and his uniform indicated rank. The Russian replied in

German, "If you and your SS men expect to be treated well when you lose this war, I advise you to treat us respectfully."

Koby and Blaz heard the SS officer chuckle. "I would be more worried about what happens when we win the war," the officer answered, again in German. "Now, down to business," he said nonchalantly. The SS officer knelt to look at the Russian officer at eye level, "Your men have been continuously raiding our company and killing our troops from the north. You can tell us where they are hiding out and we will allow you and all your men to live. You will be sent to a prison camp, but you will receive special treatment, as I am in the power of granting you this."

The Russian looked back to his men. He then looked back to the SS officer. Hatred burned in his eyes. This was not the first time either of the boys had seen this look. They'd slipped it a couple of times themselves.

"You can't expect me to give you this information. How could I ever look one of my countrymen in the eye again, after putting so many in danger?" the Russian calmly said, despite his apparent anger.

The officer stood up. He unholstered his pistol and began stroking it as one strokes a cat, "You will put ten Russians in danger if you do not give me this information."

The Russian turned to his men, speaking in his native tongue, "Would any of you like to answer the man's question?"

Koby understood what the man said, because of his extensive officer training. Blaz shot him a questioning look, so Koby told him what the Russian had said. Several Russians shook their heads "no," some kept their heads down.

"No one?" the German officer said in Russian. Koby once again translated, quietly of course. "How much worse can your lives become? Are you really happy living here? Has Stalin given you the lives Communism promises? Do you have land of your own? Are you equal?"

The Soviets did not respond. The officer reached into his coat. When his hand came out, he was holding a picture. The officer swaggered over to the first Russian.

"Here, pass it down," the officer instructed him. "This is my wife, my children, and my farm. I own this farm. It is mine." The Russians looked at the picture, one by one. Koby and Blaz continued to watch the interrogation. "The one who gives me this information, I swear to you on my life, I will personally make certain that he receives a five-hundred-acre farm for himself and his family when the Reich has won the war," the officer pressed. The Russians stayed silent, though most were clearly conflicted. The officer waited a few minutes for a response.

"Last chance," the officer finally said. Koby repeated this to Blaz. He was horrified by his countryman. The officer raised his pistol to the Russian commander's head and fired. The commander slumped to the ground, in a lifeless heap.

"Now that you know I am not bluffing, are any of you more willing now?" the Russians looked up at him, not in terror but defiance. The officer stared down at them with merciless eyes. He finally looked up, and said to the young SS soldier, "Kill them."

The young soldier eyes widened. "But *Gruppenführer* Krüger, they are prisoners of war," the soldier protested, "We can't-"

"Put a bullet through each of their heads," the officer said sternly.

"*Gruppenführer*, they are defenseless men-"

The officer cut him off, "They are not men. They fight for Communism. Surely you haven't forgotten that. How did you get into the SS with this weakness?"

The officer strode over to the young SS soldier and took his rifle. He walked to the side of the line of Russians. He knelt, cocked the rifle, raised it, and fired. Five of the nine Russians fell to the ground.

"Excellent," the officer smiled, in the way a teacher congratulates a student on answering a question correctly. Blaz's mouth hung open.

The officer used the four remaining rounds to kill the last four Soviet soldiers, then gestured for the two guards to follow him away. When all was clear, Koby and Blaz crept over to the bodies. One Russian was breathing, presumably being hit by the first rifle shot. He was bleeding, in the lower chest. Koby turned him over. A face stared back at the boys. A young man with pleading eyes. No malice. He even looked a bit like Koby. Once tan skin that had paled in the winter and long, dark brown hair and green eyes. The Soviet slowly said with difficulty in Russian, "Aren't you going to kill me?" gesturing to the boys' armbands.

Koby looked into the Soviet's eyes, "We should kill you," and he took out his pistol. Blaz kept his eyes on the Soviet as he unholstered his instinctively. Then the young man pulled his coat and shirt down, revealing a tattoo of a Jewish star on his upper chest, as if to speed up the process of them killing him. The Russian was a Jew, and a Soviet Jew as well. Public enemy number one in the Reich.

Blaz looked at Koby. All his hatred he felt for the Russians could be taken out on this man right now. He could avenge Reinhardt. Yet he didn't pull the trigger. He instead turned to Koby and said something that even surprised himself, "Koby, we have to help him."

"Blaz, he's a," Koby lowered his voice, "A Jew. And a Red."

Nearly everything Blaz had ever been taught told him Koby was right.

"Damn it, Koby," he swore, "He's a wounded, defenseless man. They're not monsters. They're men. Men!"

Koby glanced back at the Soviet Jew. The Soviet stared, not knowing what the boys were saying. Ever so slowly, and to Blaz's surprise, Koby said, "But what can we do?"

"Let's carry him deeper into the woods," Blaz suggested, "Hurry."

The boys lifted the Soviet up and got under his armpits, helping the man limp along. After they'd gone a way into the forest, they laid him down.

"We need to take off your coat," Koby instructed him, "It gives you away."

The boys took off the Soviet's coat with no protest. Blaz took out some bandages and wrapped the young man's chest in them, damming the bleeding.

"Here," Blaz said, putting his cap, onto the Russians head. Koby slid off his armband and put it on the Soviet Jew's arm. Blaz took his knife out and carved a Swastika as high as he could into a nearby tree.

"Tell him to stay here," Blaz told Koby.

"Stay here," Koby ordered the Soviet, "And don't take that off," he added, pointing to the armband. Koby and Blaz jogged back through the forest. "Now what?" Koby whispered.

"We go get a dead soldier. We bring him back here and dress the Soviet in his uniform. Then we pretend he's a wounded SS soldier. We get in the truck with him. Then when we get back, we tell the medics he is doing well enough. They only treat those who are dealing with life-threatening wounds and sicknesses. Then we get him to the edge of our defenses. He can make his way out of the war zone. An SS uniform could buy him some time," Blaz explained.

"That's disrespectful to the dead," Koby frowned.

"Is a dead man worth a live man?"

Koby reluctantly gave in, "I guess we don't have another option."

The Russian Jew put on the SS uniform and stood up with some difficulty. He returned Koby's armband and Blaz's cap before sliding on the SS armband and putting on the SS helmet.

"Great," Blaz smiled, "You could pass for an SS soldier. Except the haircut maybe. Koby, tell him if he is asked any questions by a German when we're with him, pretend he's deaf."

Koby translated, and the Jew nodded. The boys again got under the young man and helped him limp off. A burning feeling shot through Blaz's stomach every time they passed an SS soldier on the way back to the truck. Even when the soldiers waved and smiled at the boys, the burning, tingling sensation slithered up Blaz's spine from his stomach. His face felt like it was on fire. But the Soviet wisely returned the grins and waves. Koby whispered urgently to Blaz, who kept looking at the ground when anyone passed, "Calm down."

Blaz took deep breaths, praying no one would notice the Soviet. After what felt like an eternity, they arrived at the truck. The squad had been waiting for them to come back, having collected as many bodies as they could load into the truck. Jarman helped Blaz and Koby lift the soldier into the truck, unaware that he was helping a Soviet soldier.

On the short ride back to the camp, Blaz remained silent. He felt the best way to keep the secret safe was to say nothing. Jarman leaned forward and kneaded his fingers together. For most of the drive, he stared at the ground. Occasionally, he glanced up at Blaz or Koby. They always looked away when he looked up. When the truck slowed to a stop, Jarman glanced over to his friends. Normally they would have spoken. Fortunately for Blaz, Koby, and the Soviet, Jarman did not give it a second thought.

The medics admitted patients, examining their wounds quickly to decide whether they needed immediate attention. Koby stood nearby, watching the Soviet soldier. Blaz stood with the squad, glancing over, perhaps a little too often. Right before the doctors could examine the Soviet, Koby strode over to the doctor.

"Sir, this soldier is fine enough for now. My squad and I have patched him up good. He can wait. You have many more serious injuries, I'm sure," Koby said professionally.

The doctor looked from Koby to the Soviet, "What do you have to say about this soldier?"

Koby froze. Blaz's face burned again. The Jew looked at the doctor and stuttered, "*I-ich werde g-gut sein.*" I will be fine.

The doctor didn't notice anything. The soldier was just in a bit of shell-shock. Nonetheless, he asked, "You sure?"

"*Ich werde gut sein,*" the Jew said with a charming smile to the doctor.

The doctor smiled back and waved him along. Blaz felt the burning feeling disappear. Koby led the Soviet back to Blaz's flak gun. The rest of the squad stayed put, assuming Koby and Blaz were speaking with an officer. Blaz realized he didn't know the Jew's name yet while he walked to the flak gun.

"*Was ist ihre Name?*" Blaz asked the young man, "What is your name?"

The Jew turned to Koby in confusion, asking something in Russian.

"*Ach, ja,*" Koby remembered to translate, and repeated Blaz's question in Russian.

The Jew grinned and nodded, "Lukov Rosovsky."

Blaz only heard Koby respond in Russian, then Lukov respond in Russian.

"Koby Hertz," Koby told Lukov, then turned to Blaz in German, "Tell him your name."

"Blaz Senft," Blaz said, looking up at Lukov.

"Blaz," Koby said in a low tone, "What the hell are we going to do? He's going to be found out if he stays long. We can't send him back to Leningrad. What are we going to do?"

Blaz leaned on the flak cannon. He put his hands over his eyes in frustration, "Let me think." his mind raced furiously, he felt as if he was at gunpoint. He raised a hand, then put it down again. Koby glanced behind them. That was when Blaz came up with a plan. "He's got the SS uniform, *ja?*"

"*Ja,*" Koby answered, impatiently.

"We get him to a vehicle. He can use that to go further away from Leningrad, maybe even back into Russian land," Blaz said, knowing it sounded like a long-shot. Koby thought for a moment. By his body language, he didn't like this plan. But he couldn't think of anything else.

"Fine," Koby finally said, "But, we need to teach him to say some things if he needs gasoline or is stopped on the road."

"*Ja,*" Blaz agreed.

Koby turned to Lukov. He rattled off some Russian, and Lukov nodded. Koby began to teach him.

"Say, '*Ich brauche Benzin,*' Koby pronounced very clearly then said in Russian, "I need gasoline."

"*Ick brauhuh Benzeen,*" Lukov stuttered.

"*Gut,*" Koby encouraged him, "*Ich brauche Benzin.*"

"*Ich brauche Benzin,*" Lukov repeated.

"Say it again," Koby ordered him in Russian.

"*Ich brauche Benzin.*"

"One more time, let me hear the music," Koby said in Russian, holding up a prompting hand.

"*Ich brauche Benzin.*"

"Now say, '*Ich gehe nach Moskau,*' I am going to Moscow."

Lukov repeated this much faster.

"*Ich gehe nach Moscow,*" Koby said again.

"*Ich gehe nach Moscow,*" Lukov repeated.

"Good, good."

Koby gave Lukov one or two more phrases to remember. Then he provided him instructions in Russian. Blaz wished he could understand the conversation. Koby finally gestured to both Blaz and Lukov, "*Folgen sie mir,* follow me." Koby led them near the tanks, where many German vehicles were parked. Steinhoff sat on a tank with several papers he was examining thoroughly.

"*Scheiße,*" Koby murmured, "How do we get the keys to the vehicles?"

"Teach him how to say, 'Give me the keys to that motorcycle,'" Blaz whispered. Koby and Lukov exchanged the same words, over and over. Lukov eventually strode towards Steinhoff. He glanced back at the boys as if to say, "Wish me luck."

"Give me the keys to that motorcycle," the Jewish SS soldier ordered Steinhoff, not aggressively, but assertively. Steinhoff looked at Lukov. The *Wehrmacht* commander did not appear suspicious at all. The SS insignia signified prestige that these super soldiers possessed. Steinhoff didn't dare question the SS soldier. He handed the keys to Lukov and returned to his papers. The Soviet smiled with relief at Blaz and Koby as he headed to the vehicle. The tension was over. The Soviet mounted the motorcycle and started it up. Blaz and Koby ran to meet him a way down the road.

Lukov stopped his bike and said to Koby, in Russian, "God bless you two. Thank you for your mercy. I would never have expected that from any German."

Koby smiled and nodded. Blaz stood to the side awkwardly, feeling a bit out of place since he couldn't understand what Lukov had just said. Koby turned to Blaz and repeated what Lukov had said. Blaz held out a hand to Lukov, "I wish you luck in the war."

Koby translated.

Lukov took Blaz's hand, "God bless you in the war as well," Lukov said. "One question. What do you Germans," Lukov pointed to the Iron Cross on Blaz's Hitler Youth uniform, "Get that for?"

Koby again translated.

"Bravery," Blaz answered with a straight face. Koby translated once more.

Lukov nodded with a smile, taking this in as if he'd thought it was awarded for something else before. He then started the motorcycle. Koby said something before Lukov rode away. Lukov nodded in understanding at Koby's words. The motorcycle drove away, with its Jewish SS driver.

"Not a word to anyone," Koby warned Blaz, "Not a word."

Sleeping didn't come easily to Blaz. He woke up every fifteen minutes and each time he opened his eyes his heart jumped at the first voice he heard. It was an awful feeling. Worse still, they'd told the Jew their names. Something told him he'd done the right thing, but his training told him he had betrayed Germany. And he knew if anyone found out what he'd done, they would agree with his training.

March 9, 1942

What were the consequences of helping a Russian escape on the front lines? The question rang in Blaz's head every day. Not so much that he was a Jew. He just knew they had helped an enemy soldier who happened to be Jewish, which only made things worse. Point being, it had been an enemy soldier. He shouldn't have helped. Would he be executed? Koby kept Blaz calm, telling him to just act normal.

"If they knew, they would have come by now."

Nico Leipzig and Wilhelm Kramer

March 21, 1942

The first day of spring had arrived in the Soviet Union. A time when the world comes back to life. But soldiers don't come back to life. Nothing was turning green. The weather was as cold as it always was. Spring meant nothing in Russia. Ivo brought it up anyway.

"First day of spring," he told them while they ate breakfast. He rolled up his sleeves, exposing his bare skin to the cold.

"Roll your sleeves down, Ivo," Koby said scowling at Ivo's stupidity, "I'm not going to see another man die of this damned weather."

Ivo rolled his sleeves down.

April 1, 1942

The wintry weather persisted. Negative temperatures were commonplace. Somehow, the *Wehrmacht* held on. Soon, soon they would capture Leningrad and Moscow.

New Hitler Youth members arrived now, to operate artillery. Two loners broke off from the other new arrivals. One looked younger than anyone in Koby's squad. He was shorter than Blaz but just taller than Ivo and hadn't matured yet. This young-looking kid strutted up to Koby and saluted. He had scruffy blond hair, big eyes, a childish face and small chest, "I am Nico Leipzig. Are you Sergeant Hertz?"

"I am. It looks like you are our new squad member. Who's the tall one?"

"That is Wilhelm Kramer. We just met. I'm from Berlin, he's from Dresden," Nico answered respectfully.

Wilhelm, a tall, built cadet with brown hair, an aquiline nose, and dark blue eyes, strode over to Koby and extended a hand.

"Wilhelm Kramer."

"Koby Hertz."

"I've been instructed to join your squad. What's my job?" Wilhelm asked with no emotion.

"Take that flak gun with Nico," Koby instructed, pointing to his left.

"As you wish," said Nico, who hurried over with a spring in his step to the gun. Wilhelm followed over, but without Nico's strange enthusiasm.

Koby turned to the squad, "All right, get back to your posts."

Blaz and Ivo walked back to their flak gun.

"They are getting younger, *nein?*" Blaz asked Ivo, desperate for conversation, "Or just smaller."

Ivo mumbled, *"Ja."*

The whole squad their cannons, dying of boredom, but by now, they knew they didn't want anyone to attack.

Blaz put his hand over his face, and just began to think. *Father. I wonder how father is. Gott sei Dank he was sent to France. And Lukov, where could he be? I wish, I knew what was going on with him.*

Across the Reich

Ottoway Senft's transfer to France had been wonderful for him. Norway's cold was long forgotten, replaced by France's cool, mild weather. France was the safest place for a German to be. Though Ottoway was still on guard against unruly French individuals, his army experience had been much more enjoyable than Blaz's thus far. Blaz's last letter had told him of Reinhardt's death. This did not come as comforting news to Ottoway, to say the least. He, like the boys, had thought they'd be safe at the back lines. Now he worried for his son's safety.

The moon was bright, the weather was frigid, and the sky was cloudless. A menacing figure in a black trench coat and a peaked cap bearing death's skull strode through the streets of a Russian town. A second man followed behind him dressed the same. Men clad in black, carrying machine guns and rifles trailed them. The leader in the trench coat shouted orders to the soldiers following him and pairs of the black-clad men ran to homes, breaking down the doors. They all emerged, moments later with exclusively men held at gunpoint.

"What is this? What are you doing?" a voice yelled in Russian. An old man hobbled into the streets and to the man in the black trench coat.

"What do you mean?" the man in the trench coat inquired.

"What are you doing to our townsfolk? Killing them? Why?"

"Twenty SS soldiers were found dead outside the town! Bodies mutilated, arms sawed off, tongues torn out of their mouths! Reprisals must be made. Had we done anything to provoke this from you?" the man in the trench coat roared back, taking off his peaked cap. The second man with no trench coat also removed his peaked cap, revealing himself to be Reynald Schlusser.

The old man struggled to reply to the surprising answer, but at last spoke up, "We welcomed you into our town only days ago! Your men talked with us and treated us well," the old man pleaded to both officers, desperate that they might call this off.

The SS leader fired into the air. It was no bullet, but a flare. The SS all looked his way, down the main street. "Old man, if you tell us the renegades responsible," he switched to a commanding shout, "If anyone here knows of the renegades who murdered our men and divulges their location, we will leave your town in peace, your men will be spared!"

No one spoke up. Schlusser left the commander's side and walked down the street. He suspected some knew but simply wouldn't speak up. The commander finally, raised the gun again, firing a second flare. The SS soldiers raised their weapons and began marching the men to the edge of the village. Schlusser drew his pistol and aimed it at the old man.

"Tell us their location," he said calmly, "We don't want to do this."

"If I knew I would tell you," the old man said.

Schlusser gritted his teeth. "Perhaps you would." He flicked his pistol, gesturing for the old man to move along. The old man obeyed in defeat. One man spun on the SS, attempting to seize a weapon, but was shot dead immediately.

The men lined up at the edge of town after this. The SS raised their rifles.

"Last chance," the SS leader said, surveying the Russians. None said a thing. The SS guard raised his arm, then dropped it. "Fire!"

Lukov's motorcycle was gone. A Russian Jew in enemy land. The cold bit at his skin. He was making his way west, hoping to find a town where he could lay low. He was nervous he might be killed by Russian partisans, but the SS uniform had saved him more than once from German troops, so he kept it. Lukov stubbornly fought on, through each night. He didn't think any Russians knew that he was even still alive. The Germans weren't looking for him either, which was a gift.

He eventually did make it to a town, half dead, though. At every home, he begged the Russians to help him, but none would. They all thought he was the enemy. Door after door was shut in his face. Finally, he came to a small house, where a child opened the door.

"Little boy, can you help me?" was all he could think to say, while he grasped his stomach and leaned on the outside of the house. Not only was he bandaged here but he also hadn't eaten for days. The little boy stared at him in fear.

"I am actually a Soviet soldier," Lukov told the boy.

"No, you're not," the little boy said.

"Please?"

"Alexander!" a voice called from inside the house. Footsteps made their way towards the door. A thin, older man, about fifty-five, walked toward Lukov. "What do you want?" he growled.

"I am not a German, I am not a German," Lukov repeated, sliding down the door frame, "Please help me. I've been walking for days with no food and I am hurt bad." he slid up his SS jacket. His bandage was a dark shade of red, rather than white.

The older man looked at Lukov. He sighed and ushered the Russian Jew inside.

"Fine. I won't turn away a wounded man."

"God bless you, sir," Lukov limped inside, embellishing his injuries slightly.

"Sit down, I want to talk with you," the man instructed Lukov. The man and Lukov talked for hours, ending with the father finally being convinced not only that Lukov was not SS, but that all Germans were not killers when he heard of Hitler Youth helping a Russian soldier.

Springtime for Hitler's Armies

April 16, 1942

Sunlight warmed the ground. Standing water could be seen in some places. Snow still fell occasionally, but the weather felt like heaven for the German army. For the first time in what seemed an eternity, the boys felt actual, natural warmth. The *Wehrmacht* was putting the finishing touches on the destruction of an enormous Soviet army. The boys had been awarded that morning with 'Eastern Front Medals' for over sixty days of service in combat zone. Due to the frigid and unbearable conditions, soldiers were awarded for being present and surviving at their posts.

"I will never take anything for granted ever again," Ivo said thankfully, taking off his heavy coat for the first time in months.

"Same here," Blaz grinned.

"I feel like I'm on a different planet. It's a new beginning."

"I hope this war ends. There has been enough death."

Ivo tilted his head and frowned at Blaz. "Only if it ends in victory."

"*Natürlich*," Blaz quickly answered, "But Jarman has already lost his father. Reinhardt is dead," he paused and took a deep breath, "Someone else is going to die, Ivo. If we end up in a battle, someone will die. Maybe all of us. I know, I was in one. And I still don't know how I'm alive."

April 29, 1942

"We have them! Artillery! Open fire!" Steinhoff yelled at the top of his lungs.

Artillery shots rang into the air, raining death from above.

"Steinhoff sounds like he senses a victory!" Blaz shouted over the artillery.

"*Ja!*" Ivo shouted back, "You think the Russians are done?"

"*Nein*, they'll never be done. They're too tough to surrender."

"You seem to be a little sympathetic to Russians as of late," Ivo said.

"I-I don't think they're all murderers. Think about it. Who knows how many there are? There must be a few good men."

"We can't worry about that right now," Ivo said, rolling his eyes, "We can talk about the morality of this later, right now we're fighting to survive. If we don't kill them, they'll kill us."

Ivo brought his attention back at the artillery. Blaz glanced out of the corner of his eye at his friend. The artillery kept firing.

Night

April 30, 1942

The ending of a song woke Blaz. He had dozed off in the later part of the day, after a night and morning of watching the skies and artillery fire. He looked in the direction of the fading tune. Two SS soldiers appeared, marching over a hill. Following them were men. Men beyond count. All had their hands on the backs of their heads.

"Ivo, Russians!" Blaz whispered.

Another song began. More SS soldiers came into view carrying machine guns and their lips moving in harmony.

Wir standen für Deutschland auf Posten, Und hielten die Große Wacht!
Nun hebt sich die Sonne im Osten, Und ruft Millionen zur Schlacht!
Von Finnland bis zum Schwarzen Meer...
Vorwärts! Vorwärts! Vorwärts nach Osten du sturmen'd Heer!
Freiheit das Ziel! Sieg das Panier! Führer befiehl, wir folgen dir!
Führer befiehl, wir folgen dir!

We stood for Germany at posts, and kept up the great watch.
Now rises the sun in the east, and calls millions to battle!
From Finland to the Black Sea...
Forward! Forward! Forward to the east, you storming army!
Freedom the goal! Victory the banner! Führer command, we follow you!
Führer command, we follow you!

Blaz and Ivo grinned at each other, recognizing a great victory had been won. This song not only sounded happy, but soldiers rarely sang when their spirits were low. The Russian soldiers looked humiliated, not knowing what their opponents were saying. They could only imagine the horrible things the enemy must be singing about.

As the song ended, Koby approached Blaz and Ivo. "Come with me."

"What's happening?" Blaz asked while they followed their squad leader.

"Those soldiers, the Russians," Koby pointed to the still oncoming line of prisoners, "That is the Second Shock Army, or what's left of it. We've captured them. This leaves a closer route to Leningrad itself. I have to assemble five members of the Knights, plus myself, to scout out the enemy territory in sets of two."

"*Ach, Scheiße,*" Ivo murmured.

Koby led them under a temporary shelter where Steinhoff had his maps and meetings. Jarman, Hans, and Nico nodded when their squad mates arrived. Steinhoff stood behind a table, where a map was laid out. He wasn't the only officer in the room. An SS officer stood behind Steinhoff, not so much as glancing the boys' way.

"Young men," Steinhoff acknowledged, "I assume Koby has given you the basics of this mission?" The Knights nodded in assent. The SS officer still did not look up, he kept his eyes fixed on Steinhoff. "Excellent. Now," Steinhoff pointed to the map, "We are a kilometer from Lake Ladoga. You will split up, exploring defenses near the lake to two kilometers away from her beaches. Two of you will head directly north, two northwest and two northeast. You will scout the Soviet defenses; guns, vehicles, artillery, manpower, cover, terrain. Leave nothing out of your report. Anything to add?" Steinhoff ended, turning to the officer.

"*Jawohl,*" the SS officer said, finally looking at the boys, "If you should come across Russians, you kill them. We will provide you each with a grenade, and three of you with a time bomb, for any vehicles."

Steinhoff's lieutenant drove them closer to the Russian lines. As he dropped them off, he wished the Knights good luck. Koby and Nico set out for the central defenses, Hans and Ivo headed west, while Jarman and

Blaz took to the east, nearest to the lake. Darkness had fallen, and the boys crept ever so slowly along the still snowy ground. The trees were barely visible in the moonlight. It felt like they covered one hundred meters in an hour. Jarman kept his right hand on his pistol, holding binoculars in his left. Blaz followed behind, also keeping a hand near his pistol.

"Shh," Jarman shushed Blaz, holding one hand up, "Do you hear that?"

Blaz paused. There was a noise. A faint sound of laughter.

Probably the Russians.

Jarman gazed through his binoculars, in the direction of the noise. Substantial light was emitted from Russian vehicles and the occasional fire.

"Can you tell what they've got?" Blaz whispered.

"They've got only a few tanks, several trucks, hell of a lot of men, machine guns. They're encamped across a field we'd have to go through."

Blaz turned back to observe the faint lights from the Russian outpost. He had only just done so, when a gunshot sounded in the distance, nowhere near them, but close enough to be heard.

"*Scheiße*," Jarman muttered.

A couple minutes after, two more shots rang out, still in the distance. There was no return fire after these.

"Check it out, Blaz," Jarman handed Blaz the binoculars, "See if you can see anything that I missed."

Blaz looked through the binoculars, in the direction of the Russians. He saw everything Jarman described but could tell the defenses did not end here.

"Let's go scout out the lake area," he suggested.

"*Ja*, we should," Jarman agreed.

Making their way through the thinning forest, they arrived at its edge, only dozens of meters from the lake. Blaz stepped out into the sand, but Jarman pulled him back.

"Stay in the forest, idiot," he warned.

"Sorry, sorry."

Jarman looked down the beach, from the cover of a wild bush. He stared through the binoculars for a while, making mental notes. It was so quiet, just for a few seconds. Then artillery would fire somewhere in the distance. After some time, he handed the binoculars off. Blaz crouched behind the bush, scanning down the beach. While he observed the Soviet defenses, a shot from a rifle flashed in his binoculars. Immediately after, a bullet hit the tree behind him.

"Time to go," Jarman shout-whispered. Another bullet whistled by, hitting another tree. Jarman sprinted deeper into the woods, with Blaz hot on his heels. Another shot rang out, and Jarman let out a shout of pain and clutched his left arm. He did not stop running though.

"Jarman!" Blaz yelled.

"I'm fine!" Jarman said through gritted teeth.

Blaz jumped over a hill and slid down a steep ravine. Jarman landed hard, meters away. If it weren't for the snow, the repercussions would have been worse. Blaz moaned with dull pain throughout his body. He crawled over to Jarman, who was still clutching his arm.

"Are you okay?" Blaz asked.

"Banged up," Jarman repeated, "You?"

"Good enough."

"We have to get out of here," Jarman said, forcing himself to his feet. Blaz pushed himself up by his arms. They set out as fast as they could but Jarman lagged behind. Blaz slowed down for him. "Hurry! Up this hill should be some German troops." Jarman limped up the hill.

"*Hände hoch! Hände oben den Kopf!*" a voice yelled, "Hands high! Hands above your head!"

"Don't shoot!" Blaz shouted, "We are German!"

Jarman and Blaz walked out of the forest, with their hands above their heads. A German soldier ran over to them, with his machine gun slung around his back. He patted them up and down, taking their grenades and time bomb.

"*Hitlerjugend?*" he asked.

"We are *Hitlerjugend* from Seelow. We were sent in as scouts."

"Ah," the soldier nodded under his helmet, "We were told to expect some scouts. Follow me."

Further east, they were taken to meet up with Steinhoff, the SS officer, and their squad for a report. The soldier led them to their commanding officer who was under a tent with many papers and maps, who they saluted then stood at attention. The soldier remained. Hans and Ivo came in minutes later.

"Where is Koby?" Blaz whispered to Ivo.

"How should I know?"

Blaz shut up. Steinhoff waited for several minutes, before taking a seat.

"Knecht, report," Steinhoff ordered.

Jarman still had a wound in his arm, but he began, "Eastern shore defenses. Many men, too many to count, they have trenches, but no vehicles right on the lake."

"*Sehr gut*," Steinhoff wrote down notes, "Continue."

"Farther inland they have minimal tanks, but they are there. Trucks and cars, plenty of them. Some are transports and some have machine gun mounts. There are tons of troopers, but they've mostly got rifles. Not too many machine guns in the trenches."

"Senft?" Steinhoff asked, "Have you anything to add?"

"*Ja* sir," Blaz answered, trying his best to add something of relevance, "I wouldn't recommend using tanks. Or at least not heavy tanks. The forested terrain is uneven and closer to the lake, it is swampy. The ground will sink underneath a tank."

"*Danke*. Klein and Reichmann, report on their far eastern defenses."

Hans began to explain the Russian defenses, but Blaz turned to look toward the forest. *Where is Koby?*

Blaz turned back away from the forest.

"Hands high!" a German soldier yelled. Blaz, Jarman and everyone with Steinhoff turned. Two German soldiers' guns were raised, and they inched closer to two side-by-side figures in the darkness.

"Don't fire! We are *Hitlerjugend*!"

Blaz immediately recognized the voice as Koby's. The German soldiers also recognized the authentic German accents coupled with developing voices and jogged over to Koby. Blaz followed, Steinhoff did nothing to stop him.

"We need a medic!" Koby yelled to the approaching men. Blaz skidded to a stop next to the soldiers. Nico was hunched over and clutching his stomach. Blaz got a glimpse of it. A gash was visible. His black uniform was tattered around the wound.

"We need a medic!" Koby looked to the *Wehrmacht* privates with pleading, pitiful, youthful eyes, "Please!"

The two soldiers looked from Koby to each other, trained soldiers melting under the pressure of seeing such a young boy bleeding to death in front of them. Fortunately, Steinhoff came sprinting over with a medic. The SS officer followed.

"Here, lay him down on his back." Koby laid Nico down for the medic. The doctor instantly attempted to plug up the bleeding. "Knife? Bayonet?" The doctor asked Koby.

"Knife," Koby answered quickly.

The doctor nodded and began working again on Nico. Steinhoff turned to the two German soldiers, Koby, Blaz and their squad mates.

"Wait under the tent. The medic needs his space. I'll brief you later."

They turned away without a word.

In the tent's light, Blaz noticed the skin around one of Koby's eyes was reddened.

"What happened to you and Nico?" he asked the moment they were under the tent. Jarman was on the other side of the tent. He took off his uniform to finally get a view of his own wound. Blaz and Koby attention was captured on him momentarily. His arm was covered in dry blood. The bullet had not gone through his arm. It had grazed him, slicing his arm open. He looked up at his squad mates, who were still staring at him. With a disheartened smile, he waved them off. Koby turned to Blaz, Ivo, and Hans, who had come over to the standing circle.

"We were heading towards the Russians, trying to get a closer view, you know."

The others nodded.

"We were climbing up this steep hill, and at the top we ran right into a Russian. He had a rifle, I went for that, got a good grip on it. He fired a shot while I had my hands on it. The Russian looked only a year or two older than us, probably. Nico helped me wrestle the rifle out of his hands. He tackled Nico, I guess he saw we had pistols. They went sliding down the hill, and I chased after them. Nico was able to slip away from the Russian for a second. I could've shot him! But I kept running at him, I tried to fight him with my fists. I don't know why. He was stronger than me. He beat the shit out of me," Koby threw a hand up toward his red-skinned eyes. "Nico tried to get him off me. That Russian just shook him off and he slammed my head against the ground. Then he went after Nico. He fought well. No match for that Russian though. I saw him pull a knife, and he stabbed Nico. I heard him gasp and then groan. Then he just collapsed to the ground, clutching his stomach. Poor Nico," Koby said almost to himself, "That's when I pulled my gun out. I shot the Russian twice. God, he was so young. It felt," Koby paused, "Awful."

"How can you feel like that's awful?" Jarman called, "He stabbed your squad mate. He tried to kill you."

"Both sides try to kill each other, but he was only a kid like us. I don't want to kill people so young."

"*Ja*," Hans said, "It sounds a little like you're sympathizing with the enemy."

"I'd shoot Stalin or Kaganovich in a heartbeat, but unfortunately, you have to fight through a lot of good men to get to the leaders," Koby answered. The two German soldiers turned to the boys.

Jarman let an exhale out of his nose, "You are thinking about this too much, Koby."

The argument ended there.

"You're thinking about it just enough," Blaz whispered to Koby.

A grateful smile escaped Koby's downcast face, "*Danke*, Blaz."

Nico survived the night but was deemed too wounded to remain at Leningrad. The next train took him back to Berlin.

The Red Terror

The snow fell. Dark clouds blotted out the sun. The thick forest kept out nearly all light that made it through the clouds. Schlusser led his men along the dirt road that cut through the forest. Ten soldiers marched on foot behind him. An eleventh man carrying an MG-42 marched alongside the officer.

"The town is two kilometers up ahead men! Almost there!" Schlusser called back.

"*Heil!*" his soldiers replied.

"You are lucky to have grown up in such an extraordinary time, Reynald," the soldier next to him said.

"I consider it a blessing from the Lord," Schlusser said, "To serve as great a man as the *Führer*."

"I can't begin to say how little we have to live for here."

"What do you have to live for now, Nikita?"

The Ukrainian SS soldier smiled, "A future. A future where there are no Communists."

Schlusser nearly laughed out loud, but suppressed it to a chuckle, "That certainly is something worth living for. But what else?"

"I want to see Ukraine become a nation like your Third Reich one day. I want us Ukrainians to live for our people, our families but also to pursue art, projects, and improvement. Ukraine hasn't had a chance to really live and fight for anything other than an empire we have no stake in."

"As long as we get some *Lebensraum*, we will be honored to see your people follow our example."

A shot rang out, a scream, then the sound of a body collapsing. Schlusser and Nikita sprang into action. "Ambush!" one soldier shouted before being cut down. Schlusser raised his machine gun and sprayed fire in the direction of the shots. Nikita opened fire on the partisans who surrounded the Germans. He seemed to know exactly where they hid. Behind trees, in trees, in the snow.

"Get some! Get some you Bolshevik bastards!" he bellowed.

German after German was shot down, some dying, some screaming on the ground. Schlusser remained on his feet before taking a bullet to the chest. He collapsed to his knees. Nikita continued to fire, felling three partisans who had emerged to finish the Germans. Schlusser reloaded his weapon then tried to rise to his feet. As he did, two grenades landed near him.

"Get down!" Nikita roared, shoved Schlusser to the ground, then leapt onto one grenade. Moments later, both grenades exploded. Nikita was gone. Schlusser was thrown through the air. When he hit the ground some fifteen feet away, he rolled onto his back to face his men. Five of his soldiers stirred on the ground. One glanced to his commanding officer in fear. Schlusser put a finger to his mouth. The soldier nodded, ever so slightly. Schlusser froze as the partisans approached. They grinned amongst each other. One partisan handed his machine gun to his comrade, strode over to one of the Germans, and knelt at his side. He took out a cigarette and lit it. The German soldier coughed up blood as he did this. A second partisan jogged over. He grabbed the German's jaw, forcing his mouth open. The first man pulled the man's tongue from his mouth and pressed his cigarette into it. The German screamed as the fire burnt his tongue. He kicked and bucked, trying to get his torturers off. But to no avail. Schlusser remained still. Six more partisans entered his vision. One drew his knife as two more men held a German up. The knife-wielding partisan spat in the SS soldier's face. The German did not flinch.

"Do you think you know pain?" the partisan asked.

The SS soldier, who knew Russian, answered, "I know that whatever pain I experience at your hands will fulfill my oath to my *Führer*."

The partisan scowled. He slammed the man into the dirt road, holding him down by the neck. The other partisans held the soldier's arms down. The first raised his knife into the air. He brought it down hard, into the center of the man's right hand.

The soldier let out a wail of pain as the knife pierced his flesh. He screamed all the louder as the Soviet twisted the knife inside of his hand. Schlusser's heart raced. His men were being tortured while he did nothing. He felt for his pistol on his belt. It was not there. Yet another German screamed as he was shot in the ankle while the Soviets simply laughed. Eventually, the Soviets grew tired of their torture. But they would not shoot them. Schlusser closed his eyes as he heard his men's throats being slit. He was alone. And the snow fell.

Russian Bear

A young man charged into the lone bedroom of a small home. A boy was vomiting blood onto his small bed. His father was at his side, holding his hand tight. Lukov pushed a warm rag down on the boy's forehead.

"Come on Alexander," the father answered, "Come on."

Alexander closed his eyes. His father drew nearer to him and put his head on the boy's chest. He rose to his feet. Lukov looked to him questioningly.

"He's alive, just asleep," the father said. Both of them went into the only other room in the house, where there were three wooden chairs, a stove and a table. The two men sat down in apparent distress. "What are we going to do?" the father murmured, "My only son…" Lukov only sat with his fingers kneaded together. The older man wiped his eyes. "He's only twelve, Rosovsky," the old man wept. As he quietly cried, there was a loud, urgent knock on the door. Lukov sprung up and answered. A bearlike, bearded man stood outside, wearing a big, brown coat and hat.

"Is Alexander here?" the man asked.

"Yes," Lukov said, "Who are you?"

"Vladimir," the man said and shook Lukov's hand then walked into the house without any further invitation.

Lukov hurried after him, "Vladimir? Anything else?"

"Nothing that's important."

Alexander's father rose to meet this man. He seemed to know who this was.

"Vladimir! Good to see you," he said, embracing the man, "Did you recover from your wound? How is Maria?"

"I'm getting better. Maria is doing quite well," Vladimir said, then added with added with a laugh, "Moving out of the city has been hard on her." Lukov saw the older man crack a small smile as Vladimir chuckled. "Ah! What the hell am I thinking? Alexander! He's sick, isn't he?"

"You always seem to know," the boy's father nodded.

"I'm going to have to take him now," Vladimir said.

"*Nyet*," the older man shook his head, "When he dies, I want him to be with me."

"If you give him to me, you will have many more years with your son. I beg you, comrade. You will not regret it."

The older man hesitated. Alexander coughed violently from the other room. Everyone heard him spitting out blood onto the ground. "Very well," the older man agreed, "Take him."

Vladimir rushed over to Alexander's side. He felt the boy's forehead.

"Shit," he muttered, before picking up Alexander with relative ease. He did not say another word as he headed out the door with Alexander in his arms.

No Quick War

June 4, 1942

Blaz and the squad marched across the wet, muddy ground. In front and behind them, German soldiers marched along. Tanks rolled at the front and men had stopped to set up artillery at the rear. The time had come to push for Leningrad. Orders had been given to set up the artillery. On a small incline, overlooking the forest, the Germans readied their artillery and defenses. While Blaz set up artillery, he glanced at the soldiers beginning to disperse into the woods. They were working on new defenses. Trenches, machine gun nests, and anti-tank nests. This time, they would overcome the Russians.

"Koby!" Jarman yelled, "We have the artillery set up!"

"Load it up. Wait for the commander's order to fire."

Blaz and Ivo ran over to an artillery piece and waited.

Ivo glanced at Blaz, "Do you think other children our age have done this? You know, fight in a war?"

"*Nein*," Blaz said almost immediately.

Another conversation died. There was little that was new. Blaz leaned on the artillery, without a thought.

June 7, 1942

"*In die Zukunft ziehen wir Mann für Mann,*" Blaz sang to himself, pacing with no direction, "*Wir marschieren für Hitler, durch Nacht-*"

"What are you singing, Blaz?" Ivo asked as he returned to the cannon.

"*Wie bitte*? I'm sorry," Blaz returned from his trance, "Oh, I was just singing the *Hitlerjugend* anthem."

"You're losing it."

"Maybe."

Ivo chuckled.

"But, have to fight on."

"If not us then who?" Ivo proclaimed melodramatically.

"Exactly."

"Have you heard from your father?"

"I have," Blaz said, "He's doing fine. Yours?"

"Haven't heard," Ivo lied. His father was a spy, and he had heard from him. "Will we get to go home for Christmas maybe?" he asked, subtly steering the conversation a new way.

Blaz sighed and shook his head, "No way."

"Blaz, Ivo!" Koby called as he ran towards them. He was running the same way he had during training. His long, graceful yet quick strides.

"*Ja!*" Blaz and Ivo snapped to attention, hoping for a new order.

"Steinhoff and his division advanced past the Russian defenses and have encircled them all the way to Ladoga. We are to fire on the Russian positions behind Steinhoff for the next five minutes. Next, aim ahead of Steinhoff's troops, and make sure you get distance beyond the first Russian position. Then Steinhoff and his men will be there to crush them from the front and the rear."

"*Jawohl!*" Blaz answered, cranking the artillery slightly toward the lake, "Fire on the Russian positions, Ivo."

Ivo nodded and opened fire.

"Hold!" Blaz called, "*Neue Ziel*, new target. One moment," Blaz said and rotated the gun, gritting his teeth as he did so. The rest of the German artillery boomed and screeched as they rained hellfire on the Russian positions.

"Cease fire!" an officer yelled after five minutes had passed.

"Stop!" Blaz yelled to Ivo.

Ivo loosened his hold on the controls, his hands shaking for a brief few seconds after his grip had slackened.

June 8, 1942

"Getting closer to Leningrad, *ja*?" Jarman asked, as the squad unloaded ammunition from a truck.

"*Jawohl*," Koby said.

Blaz lifted a crate out of the truck and handed it to Koby.

"Will we have more ammunition?" Blaz asked, "Yesterday we couldn't fire too much artillery, we had to spread it out over a lot of time."

"We'll figure out a way," said Hans.

"Hertz! Sergeant Hertz!"

The Knights looked toward the direction the voice had come. A young, helmeted soldier walked briskly toward them.

"*Heil* Hitler!"

"*Heil* Hitler," Koby dispassionately responded, throwing up a brief salute.

"*Brigadeführer* Faust orders you to report to him immediately. *Unteroffizier* Knecht. You too."

Koby and Jarman followed the officer out of sight.

"Wonder what our *SS-Brigadeführer* wants," Jurgen commented.

"He told us that he and Steinhoff wish to move our squad out of here to a town away from the front. We will mainly be loading transportation that will send supplies to the front," Koby informed the squad, "We were never supposed to have seen as much action as we have anyway. They hope to get us to a military training camp by next year, maybe earlier."

"*Ja?*" Wilhelm asked, "And who will operate this artillery?"

"None of our business," Jarman answered harshly.

The German Base

June 12, 1942

When Blaz climbed off the truck, he put his hand up to shield his eyes. His new home was in view. The base was a made of dark stone, composed of several buildings that bordered the Baltic Sea. One central, trapezoidal building with a flak gun on the top stood out from the rest. Blaz recognized the other buildings to be mostly barracks, and presumably an armory. There was an open-air warehouse on the sea, with a dock for boats.

"We are back in civilization," Blaz whispered to himself, so grateful to see a building, knowing he'd be sleeping inside, in a room, for the first time in months.

June 19, 1942

Just as everyone hoped, life at the German base was much more enjoyable when compared to the abysmal conditions at Leningrad. The Estonian seaside base was quite peaceful, as well as the town. The squad had free time for the first time in half a year. They slept inside and finally were fed well. Routines returned; they had physical training with the two other squads there. The relaxed command even allowed Koby to resume his running training in the town. Julian Knernschield, their new commander, had one very strict requirement; the raising of the flag in the morning of every day, as they sang the *Horst Wessel Lied*. He also had the Hitler Youth begin with their anthem preceding the national anthem. News about the war was frequent now.

"Newspaper!" Ivo said, tossing it onto the table that the boys were eating supper around in the mess hall. Hans snatched the paper and scanned through the headlines.

"What's happening?" Jurgen asked.

Hans kept reading, then answered, "Reinhard Heydrich has been assassinated." The boys glanced at each other in shock. Heydrich was a big name in their minds. A major leader in the Third Reich. Only Hitler, Himmler, Goering, Goebbels and perhaps Rommel were better known than him.

"And Cologne has been bombed!" Hans exclaimed, his hands trembling.

"So?" Wilhelm shrugged with little concern, "Plenty of towns have been bombed. The Brits do that. Berlin has even been hit."

"*Nein, nein*! This time it's different. Over one thousand bombers hit Cologne!"

Jarman choked on a bite of food. He coughed several times, and blurted out, "You're kidding!"

"Unfortunately, *nein*."

"How many dead?" Jaye asked.

"Hundreds."

Tristan sighed and put his head in his hands.

"No one was supposed to be able to hit the Fatherland like that," Jarman gasped in astonishment.

"Well, you better be ready for more of it," one of the twenty other men at the base said from the table next to them.

"Why?" Ivo inquired.

The soldier looked around, then leaned toward the boys, "I shouldn't tell you this, I don't want to hurt the morale."

"Go on," Koby prodded him.

"The war is balancing out; we aren't advancing as fast as we used to. We need to win some battles on the Eastern Front, especially near Stalingrad," the soldier said matter-of-factly.

"Is Stalingrad important?" Jaye asked ignorantly. So much so, it drew an eye roll from both Koby and Jarman.

"Jesus Christ, *ja*!" the soldier exclaimed in astonishment, "It's the gateway to the Caucasus oil fields and Eastern Russia's food supplies. If we capture those, then the war will shift in our favor again. Probably for good."

"There's nothing to worry about?" Ivo pressed.

The soldier opened his mouth then hesitated, "Nothing to worry about," he answered.

Ivo nodded, glad for the reassurance. Most of the boys accepted the answer as honest, but Koby frowned to himself, seeing through the disingenuous response.

Peace in War

June 27, 1942

"How was the run, Koby?" Blaz asked when Koby jogged into the bright, open courtyard where the twenty-eight boys and men at the base kept fit each day.

"*Wunderbar*, it feels great to be running again. It lets me forget about the war, for a little bit of the day."

"Are you feeling fast? Strong?" Ivo joined in.

"*Ja*, now I am. Boy, those first few days though I didn't. I felt weak and worn down."

"We all felt weak the first few days here."

"We didn't realize how physically taxing Leningrad was on us, *ja*," Koby concurred.

"Nobody should have to go through what us and our soldiers did this past winter," Ivo thought aloud.

"That'd be the worst, to have to endure that again. Wow," Blaz said with a shiver.

"I guarantee we'll have to do something of that nature again," Koby said.

"As long as it's not that cold, and we have more food, and better clothing," Ivo joked.

"Well, that somewhat defeats the nature of that experience," Koby smiled.

"*Ja*, I know," Ivo grinned, "Just not as cold then, if I had to choose one."

"We are about done here, what do you want to do? We've got free time," Blaz asked Koby and Ivo.

"Have they got a football? We could pass that around, it's beautiful out today," Ivo suggested.

"*Ja*, let's go see," Blaz agreed, and the Knights ran into the base.

"You really think they'd have a football?" Ivo asked.

"Doesn't have to be a football, just something like that," Blaz said.

After searching for some time, Koby spoke up, "There's not a ball here, so let's crush all the old newspapers together and use that as a ball."

"Sounds good," agreed Blaz.

"Better than nothing," Ivo added.

They gathered all the old newspapers and crushed them together into a ball.

"Okay, it's dry out, this should hold up fine," Koby declared. He started with the newspaper ball and juggled it in the air. He lost control after fifteen, which was low for any of the boys normally.

Koby looked up in mild embarrassment. "Guess I'm rusty."

"Here, let me see what I can do," Ivo said.

Koby kicked the ball over to Ivo, who spun it off his foot into the air. He started off well. He bounced the ball from left to right foot. He got to fifteen and lost it. Then he kicked it towards Blaz, who bounced it off his head, and started juggling with the makeshift ball. He used his feet, chest, and thighs to keep the ball in the air. He got to thirty-four, then sent it over to Koby. Koby received it in midair and juggled it.

"*Danke*," he said.

Blaz nodded in response. Koby did better this time, getting into the high twenties.

"Do you remember when we could get it into the hundreds?" Koby asked.

"*Ja,*" Blaz answered, "But I bet we could get it there if we do this for a couple of hours."

"I have no plans," Ivo remarked.

"All right then, let's shoot for one hundred."

"We still have some of it," Koby smiled, as he threw the ball into their barracks.

"*Ja, Deutscher Fussball,*" Ivo said, and thumped his chest.

"*Deutscher Fussball,*" Koby said to himself, as if to test how an unfamiliar word sounded in a new language.

Blaz looked up, "You know what that soldier said about the war?"

"*Ja?*" Koby and Ivo said almost simultaneously.

"I'm have a feeling, just on how he said it, that if we don't win these eastern battles soon," he paused nervously, "I think *Deutschland* might lose."

"You shouldn't worry so much," Ivo tried to calm Blaz, "What makes you think that we can lose?"

"Leningrad."

"Stow that talk," Koby snapped, shooting a stern look at Blaz.

To Be or Not to Be

September 1, 1942

Heinrici dialed in numbers on the rotary phone. His staff waited around him. Hundreds of troops were just outside the doors.

"General von Manstein? I have received word the attack has begun."

"It has. Your orders are to hold in the center until Stalingrad is secured. Once Stalingrad is under our control, the Caucasus oilfields will be ours. Then we will resume the push towards Moscow. *Sieg Heil.*"

"*Sieg Heil.*" Heinrici hung up and turned to his staff. "The battle of Stalingrad has begun. We must defend the center. Once Stalingrad is secured, we will win the war. *Heil* Hitler."

"*Heil* Hitler!"

The weather was still pleasant, only a bit nippy in the mornings. Koby sat in the mess hall, waiting for his squad to come to breakfast after their morning workouts. He'd just gotten back from his run, and he sat oddly straightened up while he tapped his right foot rapidly on the floor. Jarman sat on Koby's right, Blaz and the soldier sat to his left, respectively.

"How was it?" Koby asked.

"What? The training?"

Koby simply nodded.

"Fine," Blaz kept his sights on Koby, who looked straight ahead, with dead eyes.

"What is it?" Blaz asked his entranced sergeant. Koby snapped up, just fast enough that it appeared be odd.

"*Nichts.*"

"*Nein*, what is it?" Jarman reinforced Blaz, turning a serious face to Koby.

"Nothing," Koby repeated sternly, glaring at both of them. Blaz backed off. Jarman stared back for a few seconds then let Koby be.

September 9, 1942

The squad was left alone at the base for several hours, a few days a week. On other days, they would patrol, while one of the other two squads remained at the base. Five adult soldiers always patrolled at night. Today, the *Wehrmacht* soldiers were patrolling the Estonian town and the boys were left to guard the base.

"Here's the letters," Blaz said to the group and passed them out to the Knights. Everyone who'd received a letter tore it open eagerly.

"Ah, Erich wrote us," Koby said, happily.

"Go on," Jarman urged.

"Okay, here we are."

Meine Freunde, it has been too long. I apologize for my not writing, but the SS school restricts how often I can send letters. I am very sorry to hear about Reinhardt. I still can't even believe it. Are you still in Leningrad? I hope you will be able to move out of there after that. What is going on wherever you are? Are you all doing okay? Are all your families fine?

The school has been tough, tough physical training and mental training. We even train with live bullets being fired above us. But I'm not to see combat until I turn seventeen in May of 1944. Counting down the days to that. I do feel bad about you having been in battle and my not. I'll have to make up for that when I am finally on the battlefield. On that note, congratulations to Blaz for earning the Iron Cross.

Though I have not seen actual combat, I've been on many marches and non-combat missions. It will be a real honor to fight for the Reich. I have learned that I will be in the Waffen-SS, not the Allgemeine-SS, thank God. Koby, lead them well, Jarman, keep them fighting. You guys continue persevering, better times are ahead!

Sincerely, Erich Meyer

Koby folded the letter and passed it to Jarman who slid it into his uniform pocket, "All right, now we had better get to defensive positions. I think *Herr* Knernschield would prefer that."

Koby and Tristan went to the roof of the base, with a rifle each. Ivo and Jurgen trotted to the front of the base. Jurgen retrieved an MP-40 from the armory to guard the entrance with. Jaye and Hans took the base interior and courtyard, carrying only their pistols and knives. Jarman and Blaz took to the supply docks. Jarman took a rifle from the armory and held it tightly across his chest. Blaz let his arms relax and swing, while he patrolled the docks.

"And the docks are secure," Blaz reported over-dramatically to Jarman. "*Gut.*"

Blaz took his cap off and spun it around on a finger.

"Any news from your father?" Jarman asked Blaz about the letters they'd received.

"*Ja*, he's been in France and he's doing just fine. He hasn't had to kill anyone yet."

They remained quiet for a long time, indulging in thought. Jarman gazed out at the sea. Blaz snapped his fingers, "I'm going to get a rifle, Jarman."

"Okay."

Blaz jogged into the base, and to the armory. He did not pause to look at the guns. He just took a rifle and headed back out to the docks. When he got back to the docks behind Jarman, he could hear singing.

"*Bald flattern Hitlerfahnen über allen Straßen. Die Knechtschaft dauert nur noch kurze Zeit,*" Jarman sang softly. Blaz wasn't sure if Jarman even knew he had come back. Because he kept singing, repeating the line, as the song dictated, "*Soon flutter Hitler's banners over all streets. The bondage will last only a short time now.*"

Blaz smiled, "Nice."

Jarman jumped a bit, startled. He glanced over his shoulder and his face turned red. He marched off the dock he was on, and to another. Blaz sighed and gazed out to the sea.

An Unfortunate Discovery

September 15, 1942

The squad marched down the main street of the Estonian town, rifles held in hand. It was a perfectly symmetrical formation; each rifle held across its bearer's chest, their steps synchronized and heads facing forward. Estonians went about their daily business, taking little notice of the patrolling youths. Some children watched them with their eyes alight.

The squad sang march songs as they patrolled the Estonian town. Spirits high, they marched along in the cloudless sky, with a light breeze blowing.

> *Die Jugend marschiert mit frohem Gesang*
> *bei Sonnenschein und Regen;*
> *die Jugend marschiert mit sieghaftem Drang*
> *dem großen Ziel entgegen.*
> *Wir stürmen die Welt, geh'n fest unser'n Schritt*
> *wer jung ist der fügt sich freilich mit,*
> *die Jugend marschiert, kein Pfad ist zu steil,*
> *dem Siege entgegen zu eil'n.*
> *Sieg Heil!*

Some civilians turned at the shout of "*Sieg Heil,*" the only words they consistently heard from Germans, but quickly turned back to their work.

"*Sieg Heil Viktoria?*" Koby called back to the marching youth.

"*Ja!*" came the reply.

"Begin!"

The squad burst forth singing the *Waffen-SS* song they'd heard time and time again over the past year. When the song ended, Koby ordered, "Spread out! Two-by-two. Cover backstreets especially."

Each pair of Hitler Youths dispersed down separate streets. Jarman and Blaz teamed up and he threw Jarman a smirk. Jarman blushed as they marched down a street lined with tall, connected, wooden buildings on the outside and distinct colors painted within the wooden boards to distinguish separate houses. Most were white, gray, brown or black, but there were occasional dark blues as well.

"You take right, I'll go left," Jarman commanded at a crossroads, "Come back here when this road leads to a major street."

Jarman turned to the left and Blaz marched away to the right. The road was windy and the tall, connected homes prevented the Hitler Youth from seeing down the entire thin street. When he came around one of the winding corners, there was a man hoisting up a large crate about seventy meters down the road. Blaz noticed the box to have, in large print, the German words, "**Diese Seite Oben**." This side up. The box looked suspiciously similar, if not identical to what the *Wehrmacht* received their ammunition and weapons in at Leningrad. The man looked in Blaz's direction and quickly hoisted the crate up and carried into the home he was next to. Blaz quickened his pace and approached the home.

He raised a hand and knocked on the door. No answer. Blaz banged on the door with a fist. There still was no answer. Blaz was about to bang on the door again, but it swung open. A man stood before Blaz, who looked surprisingly Germanic. Blond hair, blue eyes, tall, but also had facial features like that of Germans in addition to these characteristics. Blaz glanced behind the man to see if anyone else was in the vicinity. There was no one in view. The man looked down at Blaz with a condescending gaze. Blaz ignored it.

"Can I help you?" the man said, in German.

"*Sprechen sie Deutsch?*" Blaz asked cheerfully. This would make things much easier. The man nodded. "That's an interesting accent. German isn't your first language, is it?"

The man nodded again.

"May I come in?" Blaz asked.

"I suppose so," the man sighed with boredom. He turned and left the door open. Blaz took off his cap and laid it on the ground at the door. It was never wise to go into a potential enemy home alone, so he left his hat and knife for Jarman who would undoubtedly grow impatient at the crossroads. Then he walked in, gripping his rifle tightly. The first floor was one room, a large round table sat in the middle, with two closets on opposite sides of the room. There was an oven, a handpump sink with a cupboard above it. Aside from the cupboards, the wooded walls were bare and painted a dark blue. At the back of the room was a staircase leading up somewhere else within the home.

"I saw a man bringing a large, wooden crate into this house. Has anything of that description entered your home in the last five minutes?" Blaz asked the man who took a seat at the table.

"*Nein*," the man denied immediately with disinterest.

Blaz raised an eyebrow. "Now come on, I know it was this home."

The man shrugged.

"All right then. In that case would you be okay with me searching your house?" Blaz persisted, keeping his tone polite.

"That is fine," the man answered, as if Blaz's presence was merely a minor annoyance. Blaz gripped his rifle with one arm and walked around the room. He opened both closets, searching them thoroughly and feeling the floor for any boards that might be hiding anything. The man remained at the table. He'd even taken out a cigarette and begun smoking. Blaz rose in frustration at finding nothing.

He couldn't have had much time to hide that crate. Blaz strode over to the stairs, feeling each floorboard and trying to lift them up. The first four stairs then came to a small flat area before turning to the left and continuing twelve stairs upward. At the top, after every stair had been checked, Blaz looked around the top floor at the end of the twelve stairs. There was a short hallway with a lower ceiling than the first floor, and two doors, on each side of the hall. Blaz cautiously opened the door on the right. Once he'd entered the dimly lit room; which contained a bed and a wardrobe, nothing else, Blaz gripped his rifle tightly with two hands. The room had one window which allowed more light into the room near the bed. His first instinct was to look under the bed. And, of course nothing was there. He opened the wardrobe to find only clothing.

Damn it, he thought to himself.

He turned around to search the next room. The new room looked much more promising. It was a storage room, with many assorted items. Most were junk, but Blaz searched beneath them, nonetheless. While he was squatted on the ground, looking under a sheet, the man walked into the room. Blaz looked up.

"You almost done?" the man asked, though not in his tone from before. He sounded more eager for Blaz to leave. This time, Blaz noticed.

"*Ja*, of course," Blaz answered and stood up, "Just one minute or two and I should be done."

Blaz strode to the back of the room, where a large table was outlined by the white sheet over it. He yanked the sheet off and pushed the table away. Underneath was wooden floor but a clear outline of a hatch and a disguised handle. One that looked like a piece of a crowbar. It could almost be mistaken for debris.

"What have we here?" Blaz asked the man, proud with himself for finding this. The man did not answer. He stepped forward. Blaz raised his rifle. The man halted at this.

"Not another step," Blaz warned, "Open this hatch." He moved further from the hatch as the man walked towards it. The man pulled the hatch open, Blaz stayed in his place, rifle raised.

"You go in first, and don't say a word," Blaz ordered the man, starting to get nervous. The man climbed down what Blaz soon saw to be a short ladder. Blaz removed the ammunition from his rifle then laid his weapon on the ground above the hatch. He slid the ammo into his shirt pocket. He unholstered his pistol, keeping it trained on the man as he slid down the ladder. At the bottom was the black crate he had seen. Two pale teenagers stood next to it, one a seventeen-year-old boy, the other a girl about Blaz's age, though taller than him.

"Open the crate," Blaz ordered.

The teenage boy stared back at the Hitler Youth with contempt. Blaz raised his pistol higher, toward their heads. The boy opened the crate, revealing grenades, ammunition, and machine guns. All German manufacturers. Blaz put a second hand on the Walther, even more prepared to fire.

"What are these for?" Blaz shouted this time, looking from the teens to the man, "What were you going to do?"

The boy and girl remained silent. Slowly, reluctantly, the man answered, "We-we were going to form a resistance here."

"They are Jews, then?" Blaz asked quickly, "A Jewish resistance?"

"*Ja.*"

"How many more of you are there?"

No response.

"How many?!" Blaz shouted, his voice cracking.

Still, they stubbornly refused to answer.

"You realize I can't let you go now?" Blaz stammered with both his hands trembling on his pistol, "You'll kill my brothers! There's only one way this can end!"

"Two," the Jewish boy whispered. He bolted for the crate, Blaz pulled the trigger, and the boy slumped to the ground. The man charged while yelling something in Estonian. Blaz scrambled away and fired another shot. The man fell at his feet but lunged for his leg. Blaz shot the man again, this time in the head. He glanced up at the sound of a click. The girl had a machine gun pointed at him and had just put in the magazine. Blaz's pistol was still lowered and he was at her mercy. The girl gestured with her eyes for Blaz to drop the gun, with a nervous grip on her own weapon.

She's bluffing.

Hoping for luck, he slowly raised his pistol at the girl. The girl's fingers tightened on the trigger. Blaz closed his eyes. But no bullet came. He opened his eyes to find the girl desperately pulling the trigger. She'd never turned the safety off. A shot sounded and the girl collapsed to the ground, hands still on the gun. Blaz approached with his pistol still trained on her. The girl inhaled a labored breath. Her fingers relaxed on the gun and it slid down her side. Blaz knelt next to her and looked her in the eye.

"I'm sorry," he said, "I had to."

The girl raised her hand and put her fingers under Blaz's armband. She tightened her grip around it and breathed her last breath. Her hand went limp dragging the armband down to his elbow. Blaz stared at the dead girl, oblivious to everything.

Then he noticed his armband. He pulled it back up to his bicep. Blaz picked up the gun that was supposed to kill him and ejected the magazine. Then he removed the first bullet in the chamber and slid it into his shirt pocket.

Outside on the streets, Jarman frantically searched for Blaz. He would not shout though; he didn't want to look weak or vulnerable in front of the Estonian population. Calmly, he knocked on doors and casually ask if the residents had seen a Hitler Youth.

"He is about one and six-tenth meters tall, fifty kilograms," Jarman communicated using his fingers and the similar words for kilograms and meters in the two languages. He also pointed to his blond hair and blue eyes to indicate Blaz had those same traits.

But all the citizens shook their heads, presumably saying they did not know where Blaz could be. Jarman paced up and down the street, looking for a clue as to where his squad mate had gone. As he passed a home, the door opened and Blaz shuffled out.

"Blaz!" Jarman exclaimed, giving his friend a short hug. "Where have you been? What's going on? We're long overdue."

"That's fine. I just killed three people who were hiding weapons."

Jarman gave Blaz a pat on the shoulder and said with a grin, "Good job, Blaz! What were they packing?"

"They were hiding grenades and German machine guns."

"They were probably going to ambush us sometime if you hadn't caught them," Jarman assured Blaz, who had not reigned in much solace from the congratulations of killing three people.

Blaz nodded, "We should get *Herr* Knernschield. And collect up the weapons."

September 16, 1942

Knernschield personally investigated the bodies and interrogated Blaz, so that he would not need to be court-marshaled for shooting civilians. The weapons were the proof needed to exculpate Blaz. The bodies were inconspicuously disposed of, to avoid any reaction from the town.

"What was it like?" Ivo asked from the flak gun, while he and Blaz guarded the roof, "I mean, you shot a girl. And she was our age."

"You know, Ivo," Blaz said bitterly, "I don't really want to talk about it."

Ivo wanted to hear more but fell silent.

They stared in separate directions at the town and the sea. Ivo looked at Blaz, who looked down at the stone roof.

"Ivo, why do I care? I shouldn't care that I killed those people. We aren't supposed to feel for the enemy. And they would've killed us too."

Ivo leaned forward in the flak gun, took off his hat and scratched his head. "I haven't killed anyone face-to-face, so I can't say for sure. But if you look into their eyes, you can see it. They feel fear, they feel pity, they also feel hatred. And killing isn't enjoyable. Even if it is the enemy."

Blaz kneaded a pebble between his fingers and glanced around at Ivo. His eyes looked wet but he wasn't crying.

"Blaz, come on. What happened back there? They won't be the last people you kill, talking will make you feel better."

"I've told you what happened, I've talked about it already. To you, Koby, *Herr* Knernschield."

"What was different? Different from the Russians at Leningrad, different from the AA guns?"

Blaz inhaled, "It wasn't the killing. I've done that before. But every person I have shot has stared at me with hatred. And they all died quickly. But the girl just looked at me with, with none of that. Even after I shot her and knelt next to her, instead of punching me or something, she just touched my armband."

Ivo looked at Blaz with eyebrows raised, "That's odd. Why'd she do that?"

"I don't know. All I know is she didn't look at me the way everyone else has. I wish she had."

September 19, 1942

"The SS is coming to the town," *Herr* Knernschield informed his troops, "After the incident with the weapons and Jews, our district *Gruppenführer* has decided to send a detachment here to find any other conspirators and teach the town their place."

Blaz examined the reactions of the other soldiers after Knernschield had finished. The older ones appeared troubled by this news, while the younger ones were eager for a visit from the SS. Blaz's squad saw nothing if not mixed reactions.

Reprisals

September 21, 1942

The SS came marching into the city, late in the afternoon before sunset. But they did not come to meet with Knernschield. Not at first. They marched through the city, singing a gloomy song.

Und uns kann die ganze Welt,
Verfluchen oder auch Loben. Grad wie es ihnen gefällt!
Wo wir sind da geht's immer vorwärts!
Der Teufel der lacht nur dazu:
Ha ha ha ha ha ha!

And us can the whole world,
Curse or praise. Grade us as they choose.

> *Where we are we always go forward!*
> *And devil only laughs:*
> *Ha ha ha ha ha ha!*

The march song traveled across the town and slowly dispersed as each soldier branched out into houses around the town. Knernschield ordered his soldiers to stay in the base while the SS did their work. No one heard gunshots, so that was a good sign. But after a time, a voice came shouting from outside, "Open up, we need you out here!" Knernschield ordered everyone, including the Hitler Youths, to grab a rifle and come with him. Knernschield himself followed an SS soldier to the edge of town and over a hill into a large open field. Dozens of men, and a few women were digging a massive hole. Easily thirty were there. Dozens more townspeople had followed and watched at a distance. An *Allgemeine-SS* officer paced around the area where the people dug. About thirty SS soldiers were with him. Knernschield marched up to the officer, exclaiming, "*Heil* Hitler!"

The officer responded, in the same way, then began instructing Knernschield. He pointed to the hole and the people around it. Knernschield looked at the officer questioningly but turned around to his soldiers without any further words.

"Ready your rifles," he ordered.

Several troopers cocked their rifles immediately, but one older soldier stuttered, "Excuse me, sir?"

"READY YOUR RIFLES."

"For what?"

"To execute these people."

The soldier opened his mouth to object again but Knernschield had moved on. But he turned around moments later and said, "There is a good chance they are partisans, comrade. Many of them probably knew about the plot."

The soldier nodded solemnly, then Knernschield moved on to the Hitler Youth. "Are all your rifles ready?"

"*Ja* sir," Koby answered with no hesitation.

"*Sehr gut*," Knernschield nodded. When he had turned away, Ivo ejected the cartridge from his rifle and put it into his pocket.

"What are you doing, son?" Ivo froze at the sound of another German voice. An SS private walked over to him and put a hand on his shoulder, "What's your name?"

"I-I-vo K-klein."

"Why did you eject your cartridge?"

"W-well, I-"

The SS soldier stared down at Ivo, shaking his head. "Come with me," the soldier scowled, grabbing Ivo by the arm and dragging him towards the pit.

"You come along as well," a second soldier told the rest of the Hitler Youth. Koby led his squad after the SS soldier.

"Cock your pistol," the soldier ordered Ivo.

Ivo inhaled angrily, and unholstered his pistol. Another SS soldier grabbed an older teen, about nineteen, and carried him over in front of him. The young man did not struggle, perhaps he'd already tried before and knew it was pointless. The young man was forced to stand in front of the pit by the SS soldier, who then backed away. The first SS soldier turned to Ivo and said, "Shoot him."

Blaz's heart jumped. Ivo's hand shook on his pistol. But it remained at his side. Koby stepped forward and said in a trembling voice, "Sir, I cannot allow you to order my soldier to shoot that man." The soldier spun to face Koby. The other soldier by the Jewish man walked toward Koby, with a look of anger and disgust with a dissenter.

"Repeat that," he ordered.

"I cannot allow you to order *my* soldier to shoot that man," Koby replied with newfound confidence and a cold glare.

"You forget your place little boy," the soldier smirked at Koby's emboldened tone. He shoved Koby to the ground, with hardly any effort. Koby scrambled back up only to be punched in the face by the soldier. He stumbled back to the earth.

"Don't get back up, little boy," the soldier taunted, "Partisans must be dealt with. No mercy."

The first SS soldier grabbed Ivo's arm and forced him to aim at the young man's chest, seeing that the issue had been dealt with.

"Wait!" the second SS soldier shouted, "Have the squad leader do it."

"*Nein*, we'll have him do the next one," the soldier said, as if he were assigning chores to separate children. Now knowing he had two Hitler Youths to kill people with, he forced Ivo's finger down on the trigger. It happened so fast, Blaz couldn't believe it. The young man had no time to even let out a cry of pain. He just fell lifelessly into the hole.

The first SS soldier released Ivo, who didn't move. He stood still with the gun in his hand, pointed at the ground. The second soldier dragged Koby over to the first soldier who'd forced Ivo to shoot.

"Get another prisoner," the first soldier said, and the second obeyed.

"Holster your pistol," the soldier ordered Ivo. Ivo did so.

"Now walk back into your formation."

This time, Ivo refused. He did not even recognize the soldier had spoken. The SS soldier's patience wore out before it had begun, and he punched Ivo in the face. Ivo went to the ground grasping his cheek. The soldier had hit him hard. SS soldiers knew how to punch.

"That was from the Jews," the soldier glared, "Back in line."

As the soldier turned his attention to Koby, Blaz saw Ivo look up at the soldier with his eyes red with anger, and a glare of pure hatred. He held this look for an awkwardly long amount of time, until he had to be exaggerating the hatred on his face. The soldier either did not notice or knew that glancing at Ivo would be a minor defeat for him. He began talking to Koby, and Ivo finally stood up and strode away, with the hate on his face replaced with capitulation and failure. More prisoners were shot. Jaye turned away from where the shootings were taking place. Blaz saw him on his hands and knees, vomiting. He felt a little jolt in his stomach after this. After another round of prisoners was shot, Blaz threw up, putting a shaking hand on his forehead. Some SS soldiers began backing away and shaking uncontrollably or vomiting themselves on all fours or leaning over with their hands on their knees.

But the two soldiers who'd taken Ivo seemed unaffected. The second soldier forced a second man to his knees in front of the pit. About the same age as the first.

"Now, you are going to pull that trigger and put a hole in his chest," the soldier told Koby, but very indiscreetly. The Hitler Youth heard every word.

"*Nein*," Koby whispered, "I can't shoot him, sir."

"Why not?" the soldier angrily shot back.

"I just can't. It's not right."

"These are partisans. They were going to fight us. There is no mercy for them."

"Why don't you shoot him then?"

The SS soldier drew his pistol and shot the young man in the heart. The shot sent him falling into the hole. Blaz gasped in shock. He felt as if all the air in the world had disappeared.

"Bring another one over," the *Allgemeine-SS* soldier yelled.

A woman was brought over to the same position the first boy had been. The SS soldier grabbed Koby's arm again. He forced it upwards again. Koby fought back this time. Though Koby was much stronger than he'd been since Leningrad, he was no match for a fully-grown SS soldier hellbent on vengeance.

When Koby's gun was pointed at the woman, the soldier calmly looked at Koby, "Now, you are going to shoot her, here and now," then suddenly changing his tone that of a father giving a child an important life lesson, "This is all a part of becoming a real soldier. You have to obey orders, no matter how harsh it may seem."

The woman stared at Koby with pleading eyes. Koby's hand wavered while the SS soldier slowly released his grip. The soldier warmly said, "I wouldn't have you do this if it wasn't necessary, Koby."

Koby glanced up at the soldier. The soldier smiled at him and put a hand on his shoulder. Blaz saw Koby recoil as the gloved hand touched him. "*Fik dich*," Koby whispered to the SS soldier, the meaning being exactly what one would think.

The SS soldier's warmness disappeared, "All right then." He drew his dagger slowly, "Would you rather be killed by a knife or a gun, Koby?"

Koby looked at the soldier, both confused and scared by this insinuation. He stuttered, which was odd for Koby to do, "A-A gun, s-sir."

"I would think that she would answer the same way, only an idiot would choose the knife if given the chance," the soldier smirked, "I'd ask, but I don't speak Estonian."

Blaz felt a shiver go down his spine. A third SS soldier glared at his two comrades.

"You understand what I'm saying?" the soldier said condescendingly. Koby gave no reply. "I'm going to make her suffer, and you will hear her suffer. Or you can end all that before it starts."

Koby stared in shock. The soldier stared back unflinchingly. Then the third SS soldier intervened, "Georgy, stop this."

Blaz's eyes went wide on hearing a Russian name being spoken to this SS soldier.

"*Nein*, Jakob! These Jewish swine are responsible for all the suffering my people have gone through in Stalin's Russia. They led the revolution. I have no pity left for them."

"Surely-"

"They drove my people to madness! Cannibalism! My father was driven to that! The Jews deserve no mercy for Russia."

"These ones did not-"

Jakob backed away when Georgy took a step toward him with his knife. The Russian SS soldier then ordered Koby to fire. Koby looked back to the girl. His hand wavered on the pistol. But he did not fire. The soldier took two threatening steps towards the woman. Koby fired. The woman fell into the pit. The soldier smiled triumphantly.

"Took you long enough," he said mockingly, shoving a tearful Koby down, and had turned away before Koby had even hit the ground.

"*Nein*! Don't tell me it is all right! It is not!" Koby shouted in anger at Jarman.

Knernschield and the men at the base remained quiet, all listening to the exchange. The rest of the Hitler Youth also stayed quiet. Many of them had their hands on their foreheads deep in thought.

"Koby, you did what you had to do," Jarman consoled him.

"You say that, of course you would! You have no problem gunning down anyone if it's in the name of the *Führer*. Even kids!" Koby screamed.

Jarman moved back at Koby's harsh accusation. Hans' eyes widened. Knernschield knew enough was enough and stepped in, "Hertz, I think it's time for you and your squad to retire for tonight. Get to the barracks. Immediately."

"By your command, sir," Hans answered, leading the squad away.

As they came to the entrance of the barracks outside, Hans grabbed Koby by the lapels with both hands and slammed him against the barrack's stone wall in a surprising surge of strength. Koby was surprised too, by his rapid change of expression.

"What were you thinking?" Hans whispered, but in a commanding tone, "Questioning the *Führer* in front of our superior officer? You should know better!" Hans released Koby, then said in disgust, "Here, get in the barracks."

Koby obeyed and ducked into the ten-man structure. Hans shook his head at Koby when everyone was in the building. "You need to get a hold of yourself, Hertz," Hans criticized his sergeant, "We've sworn oaths to the *Führer*, and we'll be taking the ultimate oath when we graduate into the army. And the ones we've taken are binding. As long as the *Führer* lives, we are all bound to obey. Even if it violates what we believe to be right. And how do you know the *Führer* would condone that? The SS could just be acting alone. It could be Himmler or one of his underlings. Did you notice how most of them were repulsed by those two men's behavior? Some were vomiting, taking bad shots. Obviously, there will be some form of punishment for a town that is found to have a resistance movement. This could've been them disobeying a command. You know the *Führer*, you know he doesn't want innocents dead. He wants each people and nation to strive to perfect themselves. It is not in the *Führer's* character to condone their behavior. And Koby, they probably were partisans."

"Did you see how much that soldier enjoyed it?"

"*Ja*, it was revolting," Hans said, "But the reality is, they probably were involved in that planned uprising."

Koby sat down on a bunk bed and ran his hands through his hair, "I don't know. Maybe they were partisans. God, it didn't feel good though."

Blaz shuffled over to Koby, who sat in the corner of their barracks with his arms on his knees, and his head on his arms. He stared blankly when Blaz sat down next to him. He sat quietly, trying to think of what to say. Koby broke the silence first though.

"I could have stopped that from happening," Koby said, "I could have."

"Koby, it was more my fault than yours." Koby turned to look at Blaz with a confused expression. "I found the weapons and reported it. Then Knernschield called the SS here."

Koby shook his head, glancing down, "You had to do that Blaz. If you didn't they would've killed a lot of us. You did what any soldier should do. I let a woman get killed, that's not soldierly."

Blaz nodded in agreement, then said bluntly, "He was stronger than you, and he was a son of a bitch."

Koby looked up in in surprise. "Blaz, you've never sworn like that in your life."

"I figure if I'm going to, it ought to be for someone who deserves it."

Koby nodded, staring ahead.

A Minor Comeuppance

September 22, 1942

Knernschield ordered the Hitler Youth to guard the base the next morning, hoping to avoid any rash decisions on patrol from the youths. Koby assigned everyone their stations, telling Blaz and Ivo to guard the entrance with him. Rifles in hand, they headed to the gate, and stood outside of it. Koby held his rifle at his side, Blaz across his chest in an upward position and Ivo in a downward position across his chest. Their black Hitler Youth uniforms were still dirty from the day before, they rarely had the chance to wash them.

"Why'd you order us out to the gate?" Ivo asked randomly.

"I don't want any trigger-happy people out here today. Like Jarman."

"You think there'll be backlash then, *ja*?" Blaz suggested.

"I'd be mad; they will be too."

Ivo was clearly eager to steer the conversation away from the massacre, "You remember training? I wonder what's going on with *Herr* Schlusser."

"*Herr* Schlusser, *ja*. I hope he's doing okay," Blaz reminisced.

"Here's one: can you name all of our commanders we've had from the start of our training to now?" Ivo asked.

"Oh, that's tough," Blaz answered. Koby remained gazing at the road. "Let's see, *Herr* Schlusser, *Herr* Schwinghammer, *Herr* Kurzmann," Blaz looked up at the sky, "There was *Herr* Steinhoff, *Frau* Vogel, and now *Herr* Knernschiel-" At that moment, a rock hit Blaz on the right side of his temple. He stumbled back into the gate and put one hand up to his head. He did not drop his rifle. Ivo raised his rifle to display force but was hit in the nose by another rock. Koby spotted the perpetrators. A group of pre-teens stood next to a shop and one boy shouted an enraged insult in Estonian at Koby. The boy hurled another rock at the Hitler Youths. Koby let this one hit him in the shoulder, out of guilt. He grunted at the pain but shook it off. Blaz scrambled to Koby's side and Ivo joined him.

When it became apparent that the boys did not intend to stop, Koby raised his rifle and fired a warning shot. This was met with a barrage of rocks, one hitting Ivo right on the forehead. He fell, losing his grip on his rifle. He put both his hands on his forehead, breathing rapidly through gritted teeth.

"*Voltreffer!*" one boy laughed, meaning 'Bullseye!' in German. It was to Blaz and Koby's guess where he'd picked that up.

"What do we do?" Blaz asked. It didn't seem prudent to fire on young children, considering how the town must feel towards them after the day before.

"We grin and bear it," Koby replied, "Make sure Ivo is okay. These little guys are bold."

Blaz turned his back to the taunting boys and knelt next to his friend. Ivo was still clutching his forehead. Blaz could see some blood trickling down onto the side of his scalp and on his ear and hair. Blaz forced Ivo's hands away, revealing a massive gash.

"All right," Blaz scowled and stood up, "He's hurt Koby, let's run these kids off."

"Fine, fine."

Blaz sprinted at the boys, bayonet raised. The Estonian children scattered and ran away. Blaz gave chase but gave it up quickly.

Inside the base, Koby gave Ivo a rag to soak up the bleeding, "That's a really big gash. They were hurling those hard," Koby told Ivo.

"You're telling me?"

"We have to wrap this up, then we have to get back out there."

Blaz wrapped Ivo's head in gauze, around the back of his head and to his forehead in several circles.

"All right Ivo," Blaz grinned, "Good as new."

"*Ja, ja,*" Ivo rolled his eyes, "Now I've got a permanent scar on my forehead and when people ask how I got it, I have to say, 'A twelve-year-old hit me in the head with a rock.' That'll be fun."

Knernschield and his patrol returned that evening. Ivo's bandaging attracted attention immediately and Knernschield remained at the gate to inquire what had happened.

"I hit the corner of the stone part of the gate. I turned right into it, hit my forehead and I was bleeding pretty bad, so they bandaged me up."

"You don't expect me to actually believe that," Knernschield said. But then he smiled, "But so we don't have to bring back any *friendly* comrades, we will just gloss this over."

"*Danke*, commander," Koby sighed.

A Run in Estonia

September 23, 1942

"Good luck on your run today, Koby," Blaz said, while Koby stretched.

"*Danke.* You know, when the war is over, are Olympics going to exist anymore?"

"Sure they will, once the war is over, everything will go on like normal. Unless you're the losers," Blaz smirked, clearly thinking one of Germany's best competitors; both in the war and in the Olympics, the USA, would be gone after the war.

"Hang on," Knernschield called.

"*Ja* sir," Blaz and Koby saluted.

"In light of yesterday's events, someone is going to have to go with you and bring a Walther. Keep it holstered. Senft, you may as well go."

"*Ja* sir."

Koby and Blaz ran off into the town, heading for the countryside.

"It is good to be back," Blaz said, taking a deep breath.

"Good to have you back," Koby grinned, giving Blaz a slap on the butt, "We'll head out for a long one today, so you can keep up easier."

"Outside the town?"

"*Sicher*, sure. I don't want to be in this town right now."

It only took minutes to emerge out of the town and into the countryside. Open, wheat fields and rolling hills lay before them.

"Can you believe that we were at track races just two years ago? We were in school, playing capture the flag."

"That's the first thing we are doing when we go back to Seelow!" Blaz exclaimed.

Koby burst into laughter. "The way you said that, you sounded so happy about capture the flag."

"It was fun, okay," Blaz defended his overreaction. After a sprint up a steep hill they came to an overlook of the sea and of rocky cliffs at the seaside.

"Wow, look at the view," Koby loftily murmured, "Incredible. I've never seen the sea like that."

"I wonder how far we're seeing right now. And not a boat on the horizon."

Blaz and Koby sped up and stayed quiet for a while, just enjoying the pure silence. Only the distant crash of waves into the limestone cliffs, and an occasional gust of wind that blew through their hair. Eventually, Koby broke the silence, "How is your father?" he asked out of the blue.

"He has been all right. He says France has been quiet enough, at least where he is. So far, I would wager he's had the better deal of the two of us. He even got to go on leave for his anniversary this summer. And how is your father getting along?"

"He's near Kharkov, last I heard. Not in Stalingrad, *Gott sei Dank*. But I was talking with Ivo recently; his brother was saying he'll be moving into Stalingrad. Pray that he will be all right."

"I will. How old is Henrik again?" Blaz asked.

"Since he was in the *Hitlerjugend* with us, I think he is twenty or twenty-one."

"God, that doesn't seem old at all."

"*Nein*, it doesn't."

"Jarman's brothers are also moving into Stalingrad, at least Jarman told me that. And he wouldn't be kidding."

"They're all older than twenty, *ja*?"

"I think so, Helmut, Karl, and Heinrich. They weren't in the *Jugend* with us, though."

"They have to be all right. That family has already lost the man of the house. I don't want Jarman to have to go through anything like that again. And he has two younger sisters who'd have to go through that. And *Frau* Knecht*,*" Koby thought aloud, "You know, I don't like Jarman's attitude for killing, and his approval for it, but he's been through a lot. He'll come around."

"I hope so," Blaz nodded and looked a couple hundred meters ahead. There was a small lake on the horizon.

"It's kind of nice for September," Koby said, as a light breeze blew through their hair.

"*Ja*, it is. Do you think it will last?"

"That would be nice," Koby said. The dirt road passed by the lake. The lake began quickly, there were no rocks where they were, just a small slope into the lake, "Kind of like Lake Weinbergssee."

"*Ja*," Blaz nodded. The next thing he knew, he was falling toward the water with no way to stop. The lake wasn't that deep so once he'd gone underwater, he shot up, "Wow, that's cold!"

Koby laughed hysterically at the top of the little slope.

"What was that for?" Blaz asked, holding his arms out.

"I don't know," Koby shrugged, beaming, while Blaz climbed out of the water, "Just a bit of fun."

"Fun? I'll show you fun," Blaz grinned and dove at Koby's legs. Koby tried to jump away but Blaz got a hold of him. They wrestled each other into the water, stopping once they'd both gone under.

"Was that fun?" Blaz asked with a big smile.

"That is cold," Koby shivered. He laughed and tackled Blaz deeper into the lake.

"How are we?" Ivo asked, when Blaz and Koby arrived back at the base, still soaking wet, "What happened?"

"Koby shoved me into a lake," Blaz said with a playful glare at Koby.

"Then you got some revenge," Koby remarked.

"You want to take me on this next time?" Ivo asked, excited by this.

"I'll see what I can do."

Stalingrad

November 19, 1942

Schlusser stood, buffeted by the wind that the gutted buildings did nothing to stop. A particularly strong gust blew into him, sending ash into his eyes. Schlusser wiped them with his sleeve and blinked several times. He tightened his scarf, which blended in well with his *Wehrmacht* uniform. He breathed in through his nose. The air smelled of smoke and a hint of gasoline. His squad advanced behind a tank through the rubble of Stalingrad. A Romanian squad followed behind them.

Schlusser had been removed from the *Waffen-SS* soon after the reprisals in Russia. For not carrying out a similar order. He had been sent to the *Wehrmacht* and demoted. He retained a fair rank nonetheless. His new squad did not know why he had been assigned or about his history in the *Waffen-SS*. He didn't talk about it. In Stalingrad, he had no time to talk at all amidst the endless sounds of gunshots, near and far. And there seemed to be ash eternally floating through the air.

"Sir?" one of his soldiers whispered.

"What Max?"

"Willi thinks he spotted a Russian nest. Up on the third floor of the building ahead. At the end of this street."

"We'll hold fire," Schlusser answered, "But stay close to the tank."

The soldiers stayed near their tank as ordered and the tank slowly rumbled toward the building. They made it within one hundred meters with no shots. That would be as far as they would advance in peace. A bazooka fired from the building, and a rocket hurdled toward the tank, hitting directly in front of its treads.

"Take cover!" Schlusser roared, as bullets rained down on the tank, and the troops behind it. Some soldiers rushed closer to the tank's rear, while most of the thirty or so men sprinted for buildings. Schlusser among them. Max followed close behind. A few Axis soldiers were cut down by rifle fire. The tank's machine gun returned shots, aiming for windows.

"Sir!" Max yelled over the gunfire, "We need to get to that building quick!"

A Romanian across the street went down as he said this. The tank's cannon fired, blowing a massive hole in the building's side. The bazooka fired again. The tank took a hit this time, but the rocket did not pierce the armor.

"Back up!" Schlusser both yelled and waved to the tank commander, violently swinging an outstretched arm. The *Panzer III* responded quickly and shifted into reverse, to get out of the bazooka's range.

"Rudi! Valerian!" Schlusser yelled to two soldiers a building behind them, "With me!" Schlusser crept through the blasted-out skeletons of buildings toward the Russian position. Three soldiers with him. Two Germans, one Romanian.

"*Scheiße*! Now we have to get across an open street," Rudi murmured as they made it near the building.

"I'll go first, you follow, one at a time," Schlusser ordered. The young officer crouched slightly, then sprinted. No Russians fired at him. He knelt below a window of the house, signaling to his other troops to hold fire on him. Max sprinted next, this time a desperate, last second shot was fired at him. Johannes went next, with Rudi aiming where he saw the shot come from. The Russian was ready but so was Rudi. As the enemy emerged, Rudi fired his rifle, sending the Russian tumbling out of the window.

"*Los! Los!*" Schlusser mouthed to Rudi. The soldier sprinted across the street to his comrades.

Schlusser smashed the window nearest to him, and vaulted in. No Russians were in the room. The three other Germans climbed in after him. Schlusser raised his machine gun and began creeping to the door. Once there, he kicked the door open, immediately spraying fire across the room. Three of four Russians were cut down, but the fourth dove to the ground and raised his rifle at Schlusser. Max was on him though. He fired a shot, hitting the man in the head.

"Come on, quick!" Schlusser waved to the four soldiers. The men scrambled up the stairs, guns raised. As he rounded a bend, Schlusser ran into a Russian, who'd been coming down the stairs. He knocked the gun out of the Russian's hands before putting a round through his skull. Schlusser booked it to the top of stairs where a machine gun nest was. He mowed down the Russians, while the other three soldiers advanced to the next room. Valerian entered first, then backpedaled out, clutching his bloody chest.

Schlusser ran to his side, "Valerian!"

Valerian groaned through gritted teeth but waved his allies to advance. Schlusser didn't hesitate to move along. Max and Rudi had taken down two more Soviets.

"*Weiter!*"

The door of the next room swung open, and Schlusser was looking down the barrel of a bazooka.

He flung himself to the side. The bazooka fired, and the rocket flew across the room, slamming into the wall. Rudi collapsed after being hit in the head by a beam. Schlusser fired his gun into the Soviet as he skidded to a stop. He drew his pistol and headed towards the door. As he took a step toward the opening, a grenade rolled to his feet. He bolted through the door and fired to his left side. It was a lucky guess and he hit the Russian in the chest. The Russian fired back, hitting Schlusser's leg. Schlusser fired again and the Soviet's head snapped back. Then the grenade exploded. Wood and rock from the walls near the grenade were blown into him. The young officer felt a sharp pain in his left arm and the side of his head but let out no cry of pain. Max came sprinting into the room, right in front of his commander.

"Sir!" Max shouted, waving a hand in front of Schlusser's eyes. The young officer's vision was blurry, but he tried to rise to his feet. Max caught him as he fell back down, "Sir, your arm and leg and head are bleeding really bad! Let's get you out of here!"

Schlusser didn't respond.

November 23, 1942

Letters arrived. Soldiers and Hitler Youth tore them open, some with excitement, others with dread. Everyone had received at least one letter. Most soldiers were overjoyed to find that their families at home and brothers in the war were all right, but hid it, only smiling in nothing short of relief, sometimes telling their closest friend. Blaz sat alone. Before he opened his letters, one from both his parents, he glanced around at members of his squad and thankfully, he only saw looks of relief and even a few laughs. With that in mind, Blaz opened his letter from his father, only a bit nervously. Once he recognized his father's handwriting his mind was put at ease. His father was fine, no wounds, nothing.

Still in France, still all right.

Blaz tore open his mother's letter.

Dear son, dear Blaz

Blaz was embarrassed at first at his mother's affection, but it turned into a smile of appreciation.

Have you been well, son? I worry about you every day, but I am very proud of you. From what your friends have written to their mothers, they say you've been quite the trooper. Be safe, Blaz. You and all your friends. We are all behind you here in Seelow. Everyone cannot wait to see you boys again. I have so many more things I would like to tell and ask you,

But I have wonderful news for you. This spring you will be a brother.

Liebe, Mütter

Blaz finished reading. His jaw dropped in astonishment. His eyes welled up and rubbed one with a fist. Was he crying over this? Koby approached Blaz, seeing the light tears streaming down his friend's face.

"*Ist alles gut?*" Koby asked, hoping for the best, in what appeared to him as what could only be bad news. And to his surprise, Blaz looked up with overwhelming joy written on his tear-stained face. Koby relaxed, now confused.

"What is it? What's the news?"

"I'm going to be a brother!"

"You're going to be a brother!"

"*Ja!* My mother's having a baby!"

"How? Your father's been away," Koby checked.

"My father was on leave this summer, remember?"

"*Ach ja.* When will the baby be born?"

"Some time in spring next year."

"Wow, that's incredible. You're going to be a brother."

"I know, I can't wait to see him."

"More motivation to finish the war."

"As if we needed more."

"Ivo!" Koby shouted across the mess hall. Ivo looked up. Koby jerked his head towards Blaz, so Ivo hopped off the bench next to his table and scampered over.

"What's happening?" he raptly asked.

Koby looked to Blaz, who extended his hand to give Koby the pleasure.

"Guess what?" Koby began, making it seem like he had world-changing news.

"What?" Ivo said, eyes lighting up.

"Come on, guess."

"Oh, why do you do this?" Ivo complained, putting his hands atop of his head and leaning back to think of something that could be so worthy of Koby's hyped tone. "Let's see, um, Stalingrad has been captured? Henrik didn't mention that."

"*Nein*, one more time. Guess something more confined. It doesn't have to do with the war."

"Ah, okay," Ivo put his hand on his forehead, searching for something unrelated to the war. "I can't think of anything."

"Blaz is going to be a brother!" Koby finally told Ivo, sounding excited himself.

"No way!" Ivo blurted out, at a yell. The rest of the Youth started heading over at this.

"What is it?" Jarman said, more nonchalantly than Ivo.

"Blaz is going to be a brother!" Ivo exclaimed.

Jarman's newfound interest immediately became apparent, "Really Blaz? That's great!"

"*Ja*, really."

"Congratulations Blaz," Jurgen grinned.

"Graduating from the single child family. Siblings are the best," Hans smiled.

"You hoping for a boy or a girl?" Wilhelm asked.

Blaz looked back at him and winked. He wanted a little brother.

"That's what I thought," he chuckled.

"Either will be great."

The squad discussed name ideas and eventually started talking about their own siblings. But when Knernschield strode over, he collected their attention.

"According to my contacts at command, you will be receiving two additional young men for your squad. They should arrive in November, and shortly after you will head back to the Reich for further training." Knernschield said nothing else, leaving the Knights to return to their conversation

Mein Führer, I Can Walk

Schlusser woke up in a hospital, next to Rudolf. Max was sitting between their beds, not in a field gray *Wehrmacht* uniform, but the jet black of the *Waffen-SS*.

"Sir, you're back!" Max exclaimed when he saw Schlusser open his eyes.

Schlusser put a hand on his forehead as he scanned around the room. A pair of crutches leaned against his bed within arm's reach, his pistol was on the desk between his bed and the next, his head was wrapped, and his left arm was in a sling, "Where am I?"

"Hospital," Max answered, then seeing Schlusser's displeasure with this answer, added, "Oh, in Berlin."

"Berlin?" Schlusser asked, "How long have I been out?"

"About four days," Max replied.

"How about Rudi? And Valerian?"

"Rudi is sleeping. He was awake on the train back here. Valerian was dropped off in Romania. Oh, and sir, I have good news for you. Our whole squad has been promoted to the *Waffen-SS*. For our tenacity in Stalingrad up until your injury. Our squad will undergo the training while you recover."

Schlusser smiled in satisfaction and leaned back, "Why am I back in Berlin? Could they not have done anything in Stalingrad?"

Max shook his head, "*Nein* sir, your leg would've been lost for sure. They thought it'd be best to bring you back."

"For sure?" Schlusser asked, regarding Max's comment about his leg.

"We made an attempt to save your leg, they got the bullet out. But-"

"But what?" Schlusser rose to a sitting position.

"They're removing your leg today, sir. The doctor will be here any minute."

"What?!" Schlusser roared, "*Nein*, that isn't going to happen!"

Max and Schlusser met eyes for a moment. Schlusser glanced to the pistol. Max did too. They looked back to each other, then both lunged for the weapon. Schlusser was quicker. He cocked the weapon, and put it under his blanket, keeping it in his hand.

"Sir, don't do anything-"

"I'm not losing my leg."

"But-"

"Shut up, Max."

The dark-haired, now SS soldier, obeyed his commander. He stared at the ground, fiddling with his fingers. Five minutes of silence passed, and a doctor, with his equipment, entered the room full of beds and wounded German men.

"Soldier," the doctor said, "I'm afraid you're going to have to lose your leg. You lost a lot of-"

Schlusser whipped out the pistol and aimed it at the doctor, "No one's losing a leg. Get the hell out of here, take your shit with you," he commanded, gesturing to the doctor's equipment.

The doctor held his hands up, "Your chances of recovery are very slim. It's best for you to lose your leg."

Schlusser fired a shot into the floor tiles, "You get the hell out of here. I'll be better by Christmas."

The doctor did not hesitate to leave and took his equipment with him. Max looked at Schlusser, eyes unnaturally wide, and he wore an idiotic smile. An admiring smile. Schlusser adopted a stoic expression, lowered his pistol, and clicked the safety on.

Nico's Return

December 5, 1942

A light snow fell on the Estonian town, slowly settling on the cobblestone streets and dirt roads. The town went about its business as usual as possible. There was no shortage of foot traffic. People were getting ready for Christmas. Koby stood out by the entrance to the base with *Herr* Knernschield; Jarman, Blaz and Ivo behind them. Today their new recruits arrived.

Koby and Knernschield conversed by themselves. Blaz swung back and forth on his heels and toes with his shirt slung over one shoulder. Jarman had challenged everyone to stand out in the snow shirtless. Knernschield had turned him down, but Koby had accepted. Blaz and Ivo had too.

"Hertz, you will undoubtedly be moving out by spring. My squads will be moving to the Leningrad front," Knernschield explained, drawing attention from Blaz, Ivo and Jarman, "I've done my best to get you into a training camp. Once you turn sixteen, you'll be in the *Wehrmacht*."

"*Danke*," Koby nodded, "Who'll be watching the base?"

Lowering his voice, Knernschield answered, "Another squad of *Hitlerjugend* and two or three older *Wehrmacht* soldiers."

Jarman, Blaz, and Ivo went back to their own chat.

"That bad?"

"*Ja*, I must say, Hertz, I've met many *Hitlerjugend* in my tenure in the army. And you personally have the greatest grip on the reality of the war."

"Where were you stationed before here?"

"I fought in France, and then I fought in the early days of Barbarossa until we made it here. Since my squad was older than many of the soldiers we were told to guard the base. And then we received a second squad, and finally you boys."

"You said I have a grip on the reality of the war. I know Stalingrad is important, but what do you mean by that?"

"Most *Hitlerjugend* I've met are fervently believing in victory. Actually, it seems all the younger soldiers are the ones with more faith in final victory. And nothing can change their perspective."

"You don't believe we will win the war, sir?"

"*Nein*, I wouldn't say that. As a commander, it's not my place to suggest anything that could lower morale. Lead by example, troops respect that. However, between you and me, with the situation in North Africa turning against us, even with Rommel in command there, if we do not eliminate the Soviet Union from the war in the next few months, we shall probably lose it. It all comes down to Stalingrad."

"I can't imagine us losing the war, though. Would National Socialism still exist? The *Hitlerjugend*? I want my kids to be trained the way I've been. We all have skills to go into life with now. Safe streets, tight community, loyalty, and honor."

Knernschield sighed. "Should we make peace with the democracies, then it would be us and the Bolsheviks. That's a best-case scenario for us, I suppose."

While this conversation was happening, Jarman asked Blaz and Ivo, "Have you heard about any of the new weapons? Rumor is that there will soon be a tank bigger and stronger than the Tiger Tank. The Tiger Tank!"

"That's good, you know, I don't understand why they aren't making more of the Tigers. Every soldier says their great," Blaz wondered.

"Probably cost, that's always the reason," Ivo said.

"If we can get some better equipment up here, the Reds will surely fall apart."

"They'll fall anyway, but better weapons can only help," Jarman agreed.

"Hey, over there!" Ivo shouted, "Looks like a military truck!"

Knernschield and Koby halted their conversation. A green truck arrived, with a covered back.

"There will be supplies for us too," Knernschield told the Youth. The boys nodded in understanding: he meant, "Unload the truck."

The truck slowed to a stop, leaving tire tracks in the snow behind it. The driver opened the door, and saluted Knernschield. The boys hurried to the back of the truck. At the back corner Koby nearly ran into one of their new recruits. They stopped right in front of each other, face-to-face, with the new cadet standing just above Koby in height.

"Sorry Koby," the cadet said in a deep voice.

"Nico?" Koby said in astonishment, "Is that you?"

"*Ja*, it's me," Nico said shyly, differently than his former excitement. Nico's face appeared almost the same but more mature. He was thinner, his eyes sallow, partially due to him growing several inches so quickly.

"Wow, you sure got taller!" Ivo said, as this is what everyone was thinking.

Nico smiled and kicked at the snow, "*Danke*, it's been weird, getting so much taller so quick. I was shorter than you last time I was with you guys," he said pointing to Blaz, "You've gotten taller too."

Another cadet stood next to Nico, he was about Nico's new height with light brown hair, blue eyes, and a smooth, unblemished face. He was lean but clearly stronger than Nico.

"We haven't seen you since Leningrad. Guess the army knew what squad to send you to," Blaz said, "Any news in Berlin?"

"*Jawohl*, but first I'd like to introduce you to Gunther Schütz," Nico gestured to the other cadet, "He's from my *Hitlerjugend* unit, he got injured overseeing a KLV camp. He was sent to Berlin and they decided to send us back up together," Nico turned to Gunther, "This is Koby Hertz, Blaz, Ivo, and Jarman. Sorry, I can't remember your last names."

"Understandable," Jarman dismissed his faulty memory, "Jarman Knecht."

"Blaz Senft."

"Ivo Klein."

"*Schön, sie zu treffen*," Gunther said politely, extending a hand to Koby then to Jarman, Ivo, and Blaz, saying all their names, "Nice to meet you."

"Nice to meet you, Gunther," each one replied.

"Welcome back to the Knights," Ivo told them.

"The Knights?"

"Squad name," Koby said quickly, "Any news from Berlin? Bombings?"

"I can say we ended up in bomb shelters several times."

"Plenty," Nico agreed.

"The *Führer* has assured us that victory is on the horizon. They say we are making a super bomb, but that we will only use it as a last resort because of its power."

"Has the *Führer* appeared in public lately?" Koby asked.

"Several times," Gunther answered.

"*Sehr gut.*"

The cadets stood in the snow, each wondering about this so-called super bomb. Jarman broke the silence, "Why were you hospitalized, Gunther? And why did you get to oversee a KLV camp?"

Gunther lifted his shirt up revealing a sewed-up bullet hole in his side, "I got hit by friendly fire during drills. I oversaw a KLV camp because I grew up on a farm outside Berlin, I've grown up around guns, I know a lot of that stuff they want all German youth to know. When A.H. took power-"

"A.H.?" Ivo interrupted.

"Adolf Hitler."

Oh, the *Führer.*"

"My papa just calls him A.H. He's met him before. When the *Führer* took power, my papa bought a bunch of rifles since firearm licenses were extended, so I grew up hunting and shooting clay pigeons. Not to mention all the things you learn growing up on a farm."

"He's a jack-of-all-trades," Nico said.

Jarman pressed to hear how Gunther was wounded, "All right, but how'd you get shot?"

"A cadet was at the range for the first time. I was overseeing the younger kids, and let's just say he turned around and pulled the trigger. I think he thought there was no more ammo. But I had enough luck that it didn't hit me anywhere too serious."

"*Verdämmt,*" Ivo sighed, "Friendly fire."

"Lots of guys were crowding around me. The cadet who fired apologized so many times, I started to feel sorry for him. But the medics kept me from bleeding out, then I got sent back," he said, nodding his head at the memory. "Koby, may I ask you a question?"

"Shoot."

"Why?" he asked, pointing at Koby's bare chest.

"Oh," Koby laughed, "Jarman challenged us to stand out and wait with our shirts off."

"How fun," Gunther grinned, yanking his shirt off. Nico followed suit.

"Oh God, we better unload these supplies," Koby remembered, snapping his fingers, "I'll be back in a second."

Blaz, Ivo, and Nico vaulted into the back of the truck, handing down crates to the three stronger cadets who carried them into the base. Koby came back with the rest of the Knights. With the whole squad now working, the job was finished quickly.

The mess hall that evening was filled with the soldiers of the whole base. The wind howled as snow blew violently outside. Knernschield and his corporal debated in the back of the room, their arms becoming more active in their communication as the conversation went on. The other soldiers chatted away, enjoying their night together as comrades. Some were very interested in talking with the Hitler Youth.

"*Ja*, I was in the *Hitlerjugend*," one told Nico, Blaz, Gunther, and Koby, while he and his friend lit their cigarettes, "Then I graduated from that, worked in a factory as a mechanic, then the war started so I joined the army."

The soldier next to him held a packet of cigarettes out to the boys, "Want one?" Gunther, Nico, and Blaz reached for the cigarettes, but the first soldier shook his head, and told the boys, "You are too young for this."

"Okay mother," the second soldier sarcastically remarked, retracting his offer.

"On that note," the first soldier said, rolling his eyes, "How has the *Hitlerjugend* training changed since thirty-seven?"

"You are twenty-three, Jan?" Blaz asked the soldier upon hearing the year he'd graduated from the Hitler Youth.

"*Ja*, I look older?"

"Younger, actually."

"Ah, well thank you," the soldier laughed, "Anyway-"

Knowing that Jan meant to repeat his aforementioned question, Koby cut him off, "Our *Hitlerjugend* instructor liked variety, I believe. I guess all instructors do that but he seemed to be aiming for balance. If you had an obvious natural talent, he would try to electrify that to its best potential though. We did strength, endurance, shooting, boxing, and fighting hand-to-hand. Technicalities as well."

"And individual briefings, teaching us our mandate," Blaz added to Koby's description.

Jan nodded as if he already knew all this. He exhaled a puff of smoke then continued, "What was your instructor's name?"

"We had multiple, but mainly one named Reynald Schlusser," answered Koby.

"*Schutzstaffel*?" the second soldier asked, the one who'd offered them cigarettes.

"*Jawohl*," Blaz answered instantaneously.

"Your *Hitlerjugend* commander? What was he like?" Koby asked the soldier.

Jan laughed to himself, "He was an asshole, if I say so myself. He had a strict mindset, not much else. We didn't do military work though. We learned how to shoot, but no tanks or marching drills. A lot of hiking, remaining silent, and beatings if we were caught stepping out of line. I was beaten several times myself."

"That sucks," Blaz said, "With the right commander, the *Hitlerjugend* can be great. It's still damn hard, but that's part of becoming a man."

"Most of my enjoyment, or appreciation, has come looking back," Jan said, putting his feet on the table and leaning back into his chair. He put his cigarette to his lips and breathed in, "It's important to have a strong, durable youth. After all, they are the future adults."

"Our commander sounds a lot like yours," Nico told Jan, "Especially at *Kinderlandverschickung*. I had trouble meeting the *Hitlerjugend* standards while I was there but when I did, whenever any of us did, we felt invincible. And in our rallies, we would feel invincible."

"Not anymore we don't," Gunther laughed.

"*Nein*, not anymore."

Jan's friend spoke up, "These *Kinderlandverschickung* camps? Who goes to these? What are they, my child is only two, so I haven't heard anything about that."

"Everyone I know was evacuated," Gunther said, "Those in the *Hitlerjugend*, that is. Ten to eighteen. Only for cities and towns that are deemed possible targets for bombing raids."

The Partisans

December 6, 1942

Lukov and Alexander made their way through the forest. Alexander in a deep brown coat and Lukov in the German uniform, in case they were caught by the SS. The sun was setting, the snow was deep, they both carried several logs of firewood. Alexander had recovered. Two weeks after being taken away, Vladimir had come back, with Alexander walking alongside him, looking better than ever.

"Xander, are we nearly there?" Lukov asked, as the sun descended below the horizon, "If we're out here-"

"We're almost there Lukov," Alexander said, "Don't worry, I know where it is."

"Even-"

"Even in the dark."

Lukov shut up. Alexander led him along. Minutes kept passing, light kept leaving. The sky was almost black, Lukov could see countless stars already. As they trudged through the darkness, Lukov shortened his steps. He started to lose Alexander after this. Soon the young boy was out of sight. Lukov transitioned into a frantic pace. He didn't need to be stuck in the woods on a winter night in Russia.

"Xander!" he shout-whispered.

"Lukov!" Alexander yelled and came running back, "Come on now, keep up. Don't want to get lost."

"Yes, of course. Lead on."

"The *Führer* leads; you follow him?" Alexander joked.

"Don't say that again," Lukov scolded the twelve-year-old Russian. Alexander paid Lukov no mind and began humming a German song Lukov had heard before. The *Wehrmacht* had sung it several times as they marched eastward through the small farm town: Forward to the East.

"There it is," Alexander stopped and pointed. Lukov couldn't see what Alexander could but followed anyway. Moments later, Lukov saw the home. A log cabin. Alexander dropped his firewood off on the rough, wooden porch where a large pile already was. Lukov proceeded to follow suit as Alexander knocked on the door. Seconds later the door swung open and Lukov was staring down the barrel of a shotgun. He and Alexander raised their hands above their heads. Alexander remained astoundingly composed. An older woman in her sixties was at the door aiming the shotgun at Lukov's chest. The woman gestured for them to come inside. Alexander casually dropped his arms down to his sides and walked in. Lukov kept his hands up as he followed the twelve-year-old in. The gun remained on him.

The home was cozy, if anything. It was one open room that included a bed, a stove, a table and chairs, and three couches. Clearly made by their owners, they were coated in animal fur and were set up around a fireplace. Alexander plopped down on one of the couches. A bear fur rug lay in the middle of the three couches that were positioned next to the fireplace. An old man hobbled over with a cane and handed Alexander and Lukov a piece of warm bread. Alexander scarfed his bread down in the blink of an eye. Lukov took a bit longer to savor the taste. The elderly couple sat down next to each other, across from Alexander and Lukov. The man had a medal around his neck.

"That's a Second Patriotic War medal!" Lukov blurted out. The man simply nodded. The woman still had the shotgun in her arms and eyed Lukov's SS uniform. Alexander started chatting with them, as if they were his grandparents. Eventually, the woman cut him off, "Alexander, who is this? And why is he wearing an SS uniform?"

"This is Lukov Rosovsky," Alexander said, "He's the Soviet soldier I told you about. He was captured by the SS and some Hitler Youths helped him esca-"

"Alexander, I told you that no Hitler Youth would help a Soviet escape," the old man interrupted, "None."

"That's what happened," Lukov replied, "Do you think I'd make up such an improbable story?"

"That uniform doesn't help your standing with me," the old man retorted.

Lukov unbuttoned the uniform halfway down and pulled down his undershirt to reveal his tattoo of the Star of David. The Soviet couple's eyes went wide. The woman's hands seemed to relax on the shotgun. The couple seemed to come to a mutual understanding on seeing this.

"Why did you come in an SS uniform?"

"In case we were seen by the SS," Alexander explained, "It's a long way from here to the town."

"True enough." The old woman smiled and stood up, putting another log into the fireplace. "But why did you bring him here in the first place?"

Alexander looked at Lukov, "I told him about our group."

"I figured you did," the woman said. The old man glared at Alexander and, to Lukov's shock, drew his pistol and aimed it at the boy.

"It was the only way I could've gotten him to come this far with me!" Alexander nervously exclaimed.

"Alexander, we have allowed you into this partisan group on your word that you would not speak of it to anyone else outside of this home. You broke your word. We can't have any more of that," the man said.

"I'm sorry. But Lukov is on our side, trust me."

"I believe you. But this is serious business you have become involved in. And you have to play by our rules... you know very well why. Do you not?"

Alexander nodded, staring at the ground.

"No more of this, Alexander," the man said sternly, before turning to Lukov, "You came here wanting to join the partisans? The resistance to the invaders?"

"Yes."

"You think we are too old to be part of any resistance?" the old man asked.

"There are jobs you could do, I'm sure," Lukov answered tactfully.

"Indeed, but fighting is not one of them. That's why we need young people like you."

"Pardon me for asking, but what can a boy Alexander's age do for the partisans?" Lukov interrupted.

"What can some Hitler Youths do for Germany?" the old man replied.

Lukov remained silent. The woman put her shotgun down. She and Alexander took one end of the bear rug. They pulled it away, revealing a hatch in the floor. The old man opened it. Alexander ran to the open hatch and waved down into the basement. A familiar voice called back up, "Good evening, Alexander!"

"Hi Vladimir," Alexander smiled, then climbed down the short, wooden ladder into the basement. Lukov followed. Four men and a woman were waiting at the bottom. The hatch above them clicked shut.

"Welcome Xander," the bearded Russian said rather affectionately and hugged the scrawny twelve-year-old with one arm. His other was in a sling and his chest was tightly wrapped.

"Good to see you, Vladimir," Alexander grinned up at him, "Maria," he added, glancing to the woman.

"Lukov Rosovsky," Vladimir said, eyeing the new arrival he'd seen many months before, "Xander has told us about you. It was a pleasure to meet you this past winter. Why do you want to join the partisans?"

"I want to do my duty to the Motherland."

"Very good," Vladimir said, "You fought at Leningrad, correct?"

"Yes."

"Damn," one Russian murmured, "Heard it's been like hell over there."

"It's not looking good."

"We're here to ease the pressure, anyway we can," the woman said.

One Russian blew smoke from his nose, and then stamped out his homemade cigarette, "Rosovsky, you're here to bring down as many Germans as you can before you get a bullet put through your head."

"Same deal as in the Red Army?"

Vladimir nodded, and added, "I'm going to teach you German as long as we're both alive. It will come in handy."

With that, he held out a knife to Lukov. Inscribed on its handle was the Hammer and Sickle. Lukov accepted it.

1943: Marches in Enemy Land

A Second KLV Camp

January 7, 1943

"Clear away! Get the roads clear!" Knernschield shouted, "The new guards come today, make sure the snow is all cleared."

"*Ja* sir! *Ja* sir!" the soldiers and Hitler Youths answered quickly, continuing their work. Knernschield had taken the lead in shoveling snow away. Whenever an area was complete, Knernschield would move to another area. The adult soldiers would follow him immediately, but the Youths would stay behind and clear away snow until the pavement or cobblestones were clearly visible. Then they would follow Knernschield.

While they still worked away, two trucks rolled into the base. An SS officer leapt out of the passenger seat, and strode toward Knernschield, whose peaked cap made him the clear commanding officer.

"*Heil* Hitler," the SS soldier saluted.

"*Heil* Hitler," returned Knernschield.

Ten Hitler Youths climbed out of the back of the second truck, all about Koby's squad's age. Two SS soldiers jumped out of the back of the first truck, hands on their guns.

"We have come to replace you here," the SS officer informed Knernschield, "Get your stuff, your trains are at the nearest station to move you to your new posts."

"*Jawohl.*"

January 8, 1943

Blaz opened his eyes at the sound of sleet hammering the train's roof. The steady rumble of the train did not drown out the steady downpour any longer. On the splintered, wooden floor of the train car around Blaz, lay his squad mates, all sleeping peacefully. Scarce light made it into the car, especially with clouds covering the area. Blaz scooted over to the wall, staring into the darkness. The train slowed, and the other boys awoke at the change of speed, rubbing their eyes.

"Where are we?" Ivo asked loudly over the sleet. No one answered.

Finally, Blaz gave everyone's answer for them, "I don't know."

The train at last came to a halt. Sleet continued to pound the train, making it deafening inside the car. The massive doors, and some of the boys shielded their eyes from the light they expected. But they were greeted by dark skies, full of nearly black clouds. No blinding light at all. Two soldiers peeked in and one said, "*Du folgst uns, schnell*! Follow us, quick!"

The Hitler Youths jumped out of the train car and ran after the soldiers. They were led across a small stretch of prairie in between two forested areas. The soldiers ran ahead, every few seconds glancing back to make sure the youths kept up. They entered the forest quickly, and only a few dozen meters in, a tall, imposing building made of darkly colored stone became visible. Surrounding the building were partly cleared areas, making way for firing ranges, artillery, tanks, trucks and obstacle courses. At first the boys thought it was simply a military base. But when the soldiers led them inside the base it became apparent that it was also a training camp. Thirty-three more Hitler Youths were inside the base's mess hall. All looked about their age: fifteen.

"Sir," Koby asked one soldier, "May I ask where we are?"

"The German Reich, Posen, formerly Poland. Five hundred kilometers southwest of Leningrad, one hundred and fifteen kilometers east of the Seelow Heights defenses. Now, you are the squad leader, I assume?" one of the soldiers said.

"*Ja* sir."

"You and your squad, check in to barrack five with *Hauptsturmführer* Müller. *Heil* Hitler."

"*Heil* Hitler!" the squad echoed, shooting their right arms into the air.

January 9, 1943

"And I will expect you to finish this course in a reasonable time. I will inform you if your time is satisfactory. Between now and September, you will improve in speed, strength, agility, shooting, and coordination until you are fit to be soldiers in the best military on earth: The German *Wehrmacht*. As members of the Hitler Youth until age eighteen, your black and red uniforms will designate your ranking to the army. This year, your squads will be shipped out to fight against the Red Plague!" the Hitler Youth saluted their *SS-Hauptsturmführer* then turned to face the course. They were expected to complete the course with a rifle on them. Obstacles included nets and rocks to climb, barbed wire to crawl under and several open stretches to sprint.

"*Auf die Plätze! Fertig! Los!*" shouted *Hauptsturmführer* Müller.

For the rest of the day, the boys were evaluated for their ability in shooting, running, lifting, and fighting. All forty-four Hitler Youths completed their drills in satisfactory time. Their shooting was satisfactory. All were satisfactory. But none of them were sure if they had pleased *Hauptsturmführer* Müller. Except Koby.

"We all did good," Koby assured everyone that night, "Now the Knights are going to build on this," he added, grinning at Ivo.

"What's your personal assessment?" Hans asked, "How did we all do?"

"Hans; you need to work on your shooting, your endurance and strength is good. Tristan; strength must, *must* improve. Blaz and Nico; same for you. Wilhelm; endurance must improve. Jaye; strength could be better as could your shooting. Jurgen; endurance needs improvement. Ivo; you shot good, strength must be better. Gunther and Jarman; try to build on everything from today. We all looked decent, I think we were all stronger at the beginning before Leningrad. We'll be ready for the army, though. On that note, any criticism of myself?"

Jarman immediately answered, "Your hand-to-hand combat."

"I think that goes without saying, for everyone."

"Your endurance," Ivo joked.

"Shut up, Ivo," Hans rolled his eyes, while shaking his head, "But seriously, you did great, but knife-throwing could be better. And maybe speed in reloading and drawing."

"*Gut, gut,*" Koby said, clapping his hands together, "*Hauptsturmführer* Müller will assign us our positions that we will train for in the army tomorrow. Based on our performance. Most of us will be riflemen, each squad will get at least two machine gunners, and then the one that is designated for heavy machine guns, a sniper and of course our heavy weapons man."

"We're still going to train with other weapons?" Nico asked.

"*Ja*, but each private, has a designated position within the squad. Their weapon is bound to change throughout the war of course though," Koby explained, "They want to make sure you're an expert with at least one weapon."

January 11, 1943

Hauptsturmführer Müller completed assigning positions to the first three squads. He now came to Koby's squad with his papers in hand. The boys stood in a row, with Koby and Jarman, the ranking officers, furthest to the right, where Müller approached from.

"Hertz's squad, very good," Müller said to himself, "Let's see, Hertz, as squad leader, you will receive our new weapon the *Sturmgewehr-44*. It has the range of a Karabiner and a better firing rate than the MP-40. All of you will keep your Walther pistols. That will go without saying from now on."

Müller moved on to Jarman, whom he stood eye-to-eye with, "Knecht, you will also be a machine gunner using the STG-44. The Stig will be ready by the time your squad moves out and we will receive a shipment. That will be your weapon. For now, we will train you heavily on large machine guns and sub machine guns until they arrive."

"*Ja* sir."

"The sub-machine gunner will be Baumann. MP-40."

"*Ja* sir."

"Kramer, you will be the heavy weapons man. *Panzerschrecks* and *Panzerfausts*, anti-tank weapons. The *Panzerschreck* will likely be your issued weapon."

"*Ja* sir."

"Riflemen will be Schütz, Leipzig, Holtzer, Rothkirch, Senft, and Reichmann. Klein will be trained with a scoped Karabiner."

"*Ja* sir."

Past, Present, and Future

February 4, 1943

It was frigid, but nothing compared to the Russian winter a year before. Most days were cloudy, with snowfall once a week. Upon hearing of the German defeat at Stalingrad, *Hauptsturmführer* Müller became determined to keep morale high, which wasn't hard with most Hitler Youths. Müller kept their focus on drills, distracting them from the reality that the war was indeed taking a bad turn.

"I want a twenty-kilometer march today; you boys will undoubtedly be in a unit that will need endurance. All forty-four of you. March in four rows. One of my men will lead you. Rifles loaded."

"*Heil!*"

"Come on, *schnell!*"

The cadets ran for the armory, everyone grabbing a weapon. Each squad lined up, and an aging soldier strode to the front of their formation in his camouflaged uniform and SS insignia on his collar.

"All right boys. March."

The SS soldier set a fast pace, with the boys marching behind him. They marched through the forest, no road, only wilderness. The SS soldier allowed the boys to make conversation as long as they stayed in formation and kept up. Blaz was on the edge of the formation.

"Where are you from?" the boy next to him asked. He was taller and stronger than Blaz, his hair was black, his eyes blue, and he had freckles.

"Seelow."

"Seelow? Where is that?"

"It's a few dozen kilometers east of the capital. It's the gates to Berlin. Where are you from?"

"Nuremberg."

"Nuremberg? How many rallies have you been too?"

The boy grinned in remembrance of the glory days. "I went to the ones from nineteen-thirty-four to thirty-eight. My family and me. Everyone in Nuremberg goes to those."

"You were there when Leni Riefenstahl was filming *Triumph of the Will*? You've seen that, right?"

"God, *ja*. Best movie I've ever seen. She knows how to shoot a movie. And my brother was singing in the *Hitlerjugend* rally scene."

"That's the best, when tens of thousands of *Hitlerjugend* were singing all at once."

"Incredible. I still remember the *Führer's* speeches vividly."

"The *Führer's* speeches are the best."

"He gets so emotional and into them, no one on earth can speak the way he can," the boy said, "Once you see and hear the *Führer* speak, you can only ever want to make *Deutschland* great."

Blaz nodded, "I wish I could see him in person."

"Maybe someday. Once the war is won, you should go to one of his speeches. I'm sure he'll have a massive rally once we win the war. Maybe a million people at one speech."

"That'll be something to see. I can only imagine how amazing that would be. Our flags everywhere, people celebrating across *Deutschland*, it'll be spectacular."

"*Ja*, you just have to see the *Führer* speak," he paused, "What's your name? I forgot to ask."

"I forgot to ask too. My name's Blaz Senft."

"I'm Dietrich Himmler."

"Pleased to meet you," they both said simultaneously.

"Himmler?" Blaz asked, "That's really your last name?"

"*Ja*, that's a lot of people's first reaction."

"Well hey, the leader of the SS is a big deal. Hitler, Himmler, Göring, Goebbels, and Rommel are names that would draw most people's attention."

"Goebbels, you know it's incredible that a cripple like him is one of the most powerful men in *Deutschland*."

"I know, it is. But he's very intelligent."

"I'd be too if I couldn't do athletics, I would do nothing but learn. But I'd rather be athletic if I had to pick one."

"Same here."

Kilometers passed, march songs killed time while the SS soldier kept going at an unreal pace. The freezing weather didn't seem to matter to him. If anything, it fueled him. He even took off his gloves at a point.

"Dietrich?" Blaz asked during a long period of silence.

"*Ja?*"

"How long have you been here?"

"At the base?"

Blaz nodded.

"I've been here a since early December."

"Oh, so not that much longer?"

Dietrich shook his head, "*Nein*, not too much."

"Where've you been before here?"

"I've been stationed in Latvia at a factory. We were anti-aircraft men for most of last year. I was in a KLV camp for all of the year before that."

"Any action?"

"Had to fire on a few Russian planes."

"Hit any?"

"*Nein*. What about your squad? Have you fought yet?"

"We haven't been sent to fight actually. We have just happened to be in situations where we had to."

"Where have you been?" Dietrich asked with added interest.

"Leningrad and a village in Estonia."

"Leningrad? What'd you do there?"

"Flak guns."

"How did you end up fighting?"

"Our job was to bring injured soldiers back to trucks so they could be moved out. My friend and I wandered up to the front line, right when a Russian counterattack was happening. We were getting shot at and I ran into a machine gun nest to help them. Some of the men in there got killed," Blaz paused, remembering that day, "One man tried to get a better shot and left the hole, he got hit in the leg and I ran out to save him."

"Keep going," Dietrich told him with increased interest.

"Then I had to shoot a Russian. He fired at me, but I used my hat to draw him out. When he exposed himself, I shot him. I was able to get over to the soldier; I think his name was Ingal. Three Russians charged at us, we beat them."

"Is that why you have the Iron Cross?"

"*Ja*."

"Wow, what was it like being shot at?"

"Honestly, I was terrified at first. But I wasn't going to be a coward, and after I charged into that nest and to Ingal, I didn't feel anything. My body just took control; I don't know if I would've felt a bullet hitting me."

"Wow," Dietrich gaped, "You've been through that? What else? What else?"

"If you can imagine, we spent months in weather that is negative five times colder than what it is now. We were sick and weak, you should've seen our squad then. We really recovered when we left that freezing hellhole."

"Your squad looks pretty strong," Dietrich assured him.

"*Danke.*"

"Go on."

"Aside from that, sleeping in those conditions was terrible. We'd all curl up together in groups to conserve body heat. Half of us were sick at a point. One of us didn't make it."

Dietrich's fascination turned to horror. He stammered in shock, "One, one of your friends died? But how?"

Blaz gritted his teeth briefly and continued, "He just couldn't go on. It was too cold, he wasn't the only one to die from the weather. I saw so many bodies, just frozen. Their faces were as white as snow, and miserable. But my friend looked so peaceful when he died. Just like he was sleeping."

"At least he died fighting for a worthy cause."

Wollt ihr den Totalen Krieg?

February 18, 1943

Reynald Schlusser sat among several soldiers, from all branches of the *Wehrmacht*, *Luftwaffe*, *Kriegsmarine*, and the *Heer*. As well as the SS. He was in an indoor arena, with thousands of Germans crowding the stadium known as the Sportpalast. A constant low roar occupied the air in the arena from the thousands of voices. Schlusser's left arm was in a sling. He'd received the wound badge for when shrapnel had nearly taken his arm off and *had* taken his left ear off. True to his claim, Schlusser had been walking by

Christmas, albeit with a crutch. But now his leg was completely better. All soldiers surrounding him had wounds of some kind. From broken arms, to lost legs, to brutal burns on their bodies. Schlusser sat quietly, unlike many, waiting for the big moment. Joseph Goebbels was speaking today. Stalingrad had been lost. The German war effort was beginning to look grim. Goebbels was here to put rumors the English had started to rest.

As Goebbels walked to the podium with a slight limp from his clubfoot, the crowd fell silent. The minister looked out over the audience, dark hair slicked back, wearing a light brown uniform with a red armband. He began, "Only three weeks ago I stood in this place to read the *Führer's* proclamation on the tenth anniversary of the party's winning of power and to speak to you and to the German people."

Schlusser settled in for the speech. It would be seen by the thousands at the arena and millions more would hear it broadcasted. Schlusser doubted how much of an impact the minister could make on the war effort. He simply was no Hitler when it came to speeches.

Goebbels had gotten to the crux of his speech. He was now to ask the German people what they wanted, "To make the truth plain, however, my German comrades, I would like to ask you a series of questions, which you must answer them to the best of your knowledge and convictions. When my audience indicated their spontaneous approval of my demands on January thirtieth, the English press reported the next day that it was all a propaganda show that did not represent the true opinion of the German people."

The audience booed and grumbled at this. "Let them come here!" men around Schlusser roared and bellowed.

"Lies! Nothing but lies!" a Hitler Youth screamed several rows behind Schlusser. The young officer couldn't help but smile at the enthusiasm.

Goebbels continued, stating he had invited a cross-section of the German people, which he had indeed. Soldiers from the eastern front, officers, thousands of German women, youth and those of venerable age, farmers, civil servants, artists, architects, engineers, teachers, and the working man. No estate, no profession, no age group had been left out.

"The English maintain that the German people have lost their faith in victory." The crowd grumbled in disapproval. "I ask you," Goebbels shouted, "Do you believe with the *Führer* and with us in the final, total victory of the German armed forces?"

"*Ja!*" the crowd roared, thousands standing up, including Schlusser.

"Second. The English maintain that the German people are tired of the struggle!"

"*Nein!*" the crowd refuted.

"I ask you: Are you prepared to follow the *Führer* as the phalanx of the Fatherland and to stand behind the army with grim determination through all turns of fate until victory is ours?"

"*Ja!*" came the thunderous reply.

"The English maintain that the German people have no desire any longer to accept the government's growing demands for war work. I ask you: Are you and the German people willing to work, if the *Führer* should command it, ten, twelve and if necessary fourteen or sixteen hours a day and to give everything for victory?"

"*Ja!*" the crowd cheered, especially the women, who would be filling these roles.

"The English maintain that the German people are against the government's total war measures. That what it wants is not total war, but capitulation!"

Schlusser rose to his feet, declaring, "Never surrender!" the entire crowd rumbled loudly in disapproval, "Never!"

"I ask you," the minister said, ever so briefly pausing. Then he shouted at the top of his lungs, "*Wollt ihr den Totalen Krieg?!*" Do you want total war?

The crowd leapt to its feet, even as Goebbels continued, roaring an indisputable, "*Ja!*" The Germans' blood was boiling. Schlusser's heart thumped fast. It pounded on his sternum. He put his right hand on his chest and took a deep breath. The crowd quieted, while Goebbels went on with utter determination, reaching what had to be the climax. The energy was incredible. The crowd seemed ready to erupt. Goebbels could feel the crowd's spirit. And it powered him. "The English maintain that the German people have lost their trust in the *Führer*!"

The most outraged reaction came at this. The crowd roared in furious disapproval, some screaming, "*Führer befiehl, wir folgen!*"

"I ask you-" Goebbels began before he was interrupted by the clamoring masses.

"*Führer befiehl, wir folgen! Führer befiehl, wir folgen! Führer befiehl, wir folgen! Führer befiehl, wir folgen! Führer befiehl, wir folgen!*" the crowd chanted in unison. Goebbels himself looked amazed, even touched, by the crowd's patriotism and loyalty to the *Führer*.

"I ask you: do you trust the *Führer*? Is your willingness to follow the *Führer* through thick and thin absolute and unlimited?!"

"*Ja!*" the crowd replied.

Goebbels continued, asking five more questions to which the crowd promptly answered, "*Ja!*"

"You have told the enemy exactly what they need to hear, so they have no illusions or false ideas. Because behind us stands the strongest ally on earth: the people themselves, who are ready to follow the *Führer* despite what dangers may come our way!" Goebbels shouted in an impassioned and exasperated voice. On several occasions, his voice sounded nearly ready to crack. "The *Führer* has commanded, and we will follow him. In this hour of national reflection and contemplation, we believe firmly and unshakably in victory. We see it before us, we need only reach for it! We must resolve to subordinate everything to it. That is the duty of the hour. Henceforth, let the slogan be: People rise up and let the storm break loose!" The crowd erupted in applause and fanatical shouts. Every soul in the stadium stood up, cheering madly. Schlusser sprung to his feet, threw his good arm up and screamed as loud as he could, "*Heil* Hitler!"

"Never surrender!"

"*Wollt ihr den Totalen Sieg?!*"

"*Sieg Heil!*"

"*Heil mein Führer!*"

A song began prevailing over the rapturous shouts. Schlusser recognized it immediately. "*Deutschland über alles, über alles in der Welt,*" the crowd began. More joined in the singing, one by one, until the only words uttered by anyone in the stadium were those of the anthem, "*Wenn es stets zu Schutz und Trutze, brüderlich zusammenhält. Von der Maas bis an die Memel, von der Etsch bis an den Belt! Deutschland, Deutschland über alles, über alles in der Welt! Deutschland, Deutschland über alles, über alles in der Welt!*"

Schlusser and the soldier next to him met eyes. They both smiled. Nothing could stop them now.

The Minister of Propaganda

Schlusser soon strode away from the raucous crowds. He needed to speak with Goebbels. He had never met a member of the High Command. It was a moment where his admiration was getting the better of him. But maybe he would be allowed to speak with the minister. Goebbels was making his way through the crowds, shaking hands with the smallest children while heading for the back rooms of the stadium. Schlusser followed. The people, at this moment, revered Goebbels as much as Hitler. He was being smothered with applause and was barely able to make his way through the crowd. The minister seemed to have no fear of an assassination attempt. Schlusser came to within ten meters of the minister. The rest of the walk to the back rooms, he kept this distance. Goebbels hailed the guard at the door, then proceeded to open it.

"*Herr* Minister!" Schlusser called.

The guard stepped forward, blocking Schlusser's path to Goebbels, "I'm sorry soldier. The minister cannot speak with anyone right now."

"Nonsense," a voice said from behind the guard, belonging to none other than the minister himself. The short, thin man hobbled over to

Schlusser. He put a hand on Schlusser's sling, "Where were you wounded, soldier?"

"Stalingrad, sir," Schlusser answered, a stupid, admiring expression on his face.

"Stalingrad," the minister repeated, "What is it you want, soldier?"

"I wanted to speak with you, sir," Schlusser replied, with more composure but still sounding awestruck. The guard glared skeptically at Schlusser. Goebbels did not.

"Anything for our wounded warriors," Goebbels said, waving Schlusser into the back room. A couch and two armchairs sat waiting. Another door was on the opposite side of the room, presumably opening to a garage of some kind.

Goebbels gestured for Schlusser to take a seat. Schlusser sat down in an armchair and Goebbels sat down diagonally from him on the couch. The minister did not lean back but sat on the edge. It was only now that Schlusser noticed the pistol Goebbels had on his belt. A waiter brought the two men wine. Goebbels declined, but Schlusser accepted. He never got wine at the front.

"What is your name?" Goebbels asked. Schlusser glanced up to make eye contact with the minister.

"Ah, Reynald Schlusser, sir," he answered, taking off his cap and placing it on his lap.

"Reynald, what is it you wanted to talk with me about? I would actually like to ask you a few questions about yourself," Goebbels said.

"Oh," Schlusser said, a bit surprised Goebbels would have interest in what he had to say, "Well sir, as minister of propaganda, what exactly is your job?"

Goebbels smiled warmly, like any man asked about explaining his profession, "Reynald, my job is to interpret news in a way the people can understand."

"Do you alter what the news is? Do you ever tell lies?" Schlusser challenged the minister, knowing other countries to use propaganda that were simply lies. And knowing of questionable actions made by the SS so far.

But as the question left his lips, Schlusser felt his heart skip. He shouldn't be questioning his leaders. Of course they told the truth.

To his amazement though, Goebbels smiled again, "*Nein*, why would I do that?"

"I don't know. Other countries do it. Why would we be different?"

"Reynald, my goal is not to deceive our people into following us. It's not about the following, it's about the truth. That is why we have united our great nation. A lie cannot unite people the way the truth does. Certainly, there are those who will deny the truth but with lies, one day their weight becomes too great for the state to maintain and the truth triumphs. That is why I have made it a goal of mine to tell the truth," Goebbels said looking Schlusser in the eye the whole time, "The truth is the only way we may combat the Jews. They have the presses of America, Britain, and Russia. All to export lying propaganda across the world. The Jews, as you know, want Europe and indeed the world, to become a single racial state devoid of the unique qualities each people possesses. And they will lord over it. Particularly, they have a vendetta with our Aryan race of Europe. They will ferment foreign wars to cause the mass exodus of peoples into Europe to accomplish this. They will make the public docile to the violence and misery this will cause through their lying press. They will push practices that us Christians should revile. We were given a glimpse of their plans for *Deutschland* during the Weimar Republic. Our Fatherland had given up on the family in a generation, art was neglected and given into the hands of the wicked, we were the center of homosexuality in Europe, birth rates plummeted, prostitution was rampant. You are old enough to remember these days, *ja*?"

Schlusser nodded. "My best friend committed suicide after selling himself."

Goebbels shook his head at the memory of such times. "Those results were no accident, Reynald. They accomplished this using the degenerate movies and music, which promoted it. It was a great mistake to let this happen. We must run the press and media of our own nation, naturally. It is unfortunate that we must fight Britain. Britain is a natural enemy of

America. America exports some of the worst ideas, practices, and lifestyles I have ever come across in my study of the arts, of propaganda, and the press. Their movies and music promote everything that is immoral and amoral. It is quite appalling. Of course, this is because the Jews have an iron grip on that nation. If Europe, and indeed the world, are ever to know peace and freedom, American Jewry must fall. It is a bastion of corruption, filth, and villainy. The Jew is quite strong there. They own it all. The root of evil. The people are utterly brainwashed. These things will escalate should we lose. Worse things than Weimar even. It is fortunate we woke up when we did. The truth was what we needed."

"Why won't the rest of the world recognize it sir?"

"They can think no other way. They are in the pocket of the Jewish mass press. Sometimes, something more than truth is needed. Presentation also matters. The presentation of the truth must be entertaining to keep the attention of the masses."

"Perhaps the people can't handle the truth."

Goebbels rapidly shook his head at this, his eyes widening, "It is a mistake to think they can't. They can. The German people demonstrate that more than anything. It is only a matter of presenting the truth in a way they can understand," the minister claimed, "I assume you are religious Reynald? You may tell me."

"I am Catholic," Schlusser answered, taking a sip of wine.

"Ah," Goebbels nodded, raising his eyebrows then rattling something off in a language Schlusser did not understand.

"I'm sorry?" Schlusser chuckled, "I only speak German, Polish, Russian, Ukrainian, and English. And some Dutch."

Goebbels' eyes widened and he laughed out loud, much merrier than Schlusser, "You put me to shame, Reynald."

"What language was that? Spanish? Italian?" Schlusser asked, "My expertise is Slavic and Germanic tongues, not Mediterranean."

"Latin," Goebbels answered, "I speak Latin and German."

"Latin is a dead language," Schlusser pointed out, sipping his wine.

"I've found use for it, you know how much Hitler admires the Roman civilization," the minister replied, with a chuckle himself. He leaned forward, his fingers kneaded together, "Tell me Reynald. Tell me about your experiences at the front."

Schlusser nodded, "Of course sir."

News for the Knights

February 26, 1943

As the weeks passed, the Knights did all the training they'd done at Seelow Heights and the KLV camp. But this time there was nothing else. Only training. In a few short weeks, their shooting was noticeably better, their hand-to-hand combat was exceptional, and they could sprint faster than ever. Müller showed great interest in their training. Behind doors, he was terribly nervous about the war. But keeping the Youth morale high was vital to what chance Germany had at winning the war.

"Has your brother or sister been born yet?" Koby asked next to Blaz outside. The Hitler Youth crowded the courtyard by their flag, which the wind beat violently on the bitterly cold February day.

"Not when mother wrote this. But she says she thinks it will be soon," Blaz grinned while bouncing one of his knees excitedly, "Ooh, I can't wait to see him- or her."

"Calm down there," Koby smirked.

"Koby, you'd be excited if you were about to have a sibling," Blaz assured him.

"Maybe," Koby said as he tore open his letter. He read it through, his eyes widening as he went on. By the end, he had tears in his eyes too, but looked like he was about to start laughing.

"What is it?" Blaz asked in concern.

"My mother is going to have a baby. Father was on leave over Christmas," Koby said, breathless.

"Hey, that's awesome!" Blaz grinned. He and Koby looked up to find several Hitler Youths with dismal expressions and heads buried in their heads. Hans and Nico among them. Their squad mates congregated around them, one-by-one. Hans' eyes were red with tears.

"Hey Hans," Jurgen said calmly.

"Hey Jurgen," Hans replied, with no animosity, "My mother, little brother, and little sisters are all dead," he said with a weak voice, "Berlin was bombed. They'd moved there for work. Father just told me," he waved the letter.

The boys stood stock-still.

"I-I'm sorry," Jurgen sincerely said, "I can't imagine."

"*Ja, ja*," Hans said in between sobs. Suddenly he quit crying. He shot to his feet, "*Gott verdämmt!*" he screamed in rage, "Why'd this happen! Damn it, damn this war! Damn those Brits!"

Hans breathed in violently, no one could tell whether he would continue raging or begin sobbing. Hans went to his knees with gritted teeth, looking down, hands over his face. He began crying again, yet they were sobs mixed with shouts of anger. The boys didn't know what to say. Jarman tried his best, though.

"I know how it feels," Jarman said, taking a knee next to Hans.

"I know you do. God, how can you deal with this?" Hans cried, "*Gott verdämmt.*"

"Always think about what you have left," Jarman advised, "I'll come home to my mother, my brothers and sisters. You still have your father."

Hans breathed in, "*Ja*, I do. But I love my family so much. I just can't-" Hans stopped mid-sentence and began crying again.

Hans and Tristan

March 4, 1943

The next days were silent. Not only for Blaz's squad, but for all Hitler Youth present at the training camp. Many more had lost family members. Nico had lost his older brother in North Africa. Ivo later opened his letter to find his older brother Henrik had gone missing in action.

"Where was he last?" Blaz asked from a lower bunk.

"He said he was going into Stalingrad in his last letter," Ivo sighed, pulling a letter from his only bag, "The Sixth Army."

"They captured Stalingrad, didn't they?"

"They almost did. Then they were surrounded by the Russians and, apparently, they had to surrender. And I don't get the feeling the Reds treat prisoners well. They nail German prisoners to boards by their tongues, brand them with hot rods, beat them to death with their fists, horrible things he told me about," Ivo shuddered, "All I want, I just want to see my whole family again, altogether. One day, I want to come up that hill into town, and walk down the street to see my mother and father and brother. My father would pick me up like he used to, and mother would hug Henrik and me."

"You think Henrik can survive, wherever the Russians hold him?"

"You don't think he will?" Ivo asked with sudden aggression in his voice.

"*Nein*," Blaz reluctantly retracted, irritated at Ivo's eagerness to accuse, "But I'm worried about anyone captured by the Reds."

"At least he's still alive. He's tough, like papa. I know he'll survive."

At night, after the squad washed up, Blaz changed into his athletic uniform at the showers. Tristan and Hans were the only ones left, and Blaz could hear them as they exited the showers and started changing.

"I'll see you there, Ivo," Blaz said as Ivo left for the barracks.

"See you," Ivo echoed. Blaz walked closer to Tristan and Hans, making sure he looked busy changing until he ducked behind a wall. Hans didn't notice him anyway.

"Hans, I'm really sorry about it," Tristan said, Blaz could tell he was desperate to calm Hans.

"A lot of good that does!" Hans nearly shouted.

"Hans, we're friends. Don't shut me down. You've been quiet for the last few days. I've seen you playing with your pistol, giving it looks. I'm worried about you. You don't smile, you've got to stay strong."

"Damn it, Tristan, I don't give a shit about that. You've done the same for the last three years," Hans said, with a murderous glare at Tristan, "You God damn weakling, don't tell me who needs to be strong, you damn, little-"

"Hey!" Tristan shouted at Hans. It was the first time Blaz had seen Tristan stand up to anyone, or shout. It was almost comical. "Don't call me a weakling! I know you're hurting, but you ought to stop feeling sorry for yourself."

Hans swung wildly at Tristan and hammered him in the nose. The next thing Blaz knew, Hans had knocked Tristan to the ground and was repeatedly and brutally punching him in the face. Each time he threw a punch, he muttered some indiscernible words. Tristan tried to fight back, but he was simply too weak to even handle Hans.

"Hans!" Blaz finally shouted, when it became apparent Hans wasn't stopping. Hans spun to face Blaz, and back down to Tristan. He let go of Tristan's loose athletic shirt, stood up, and backed away. Blaz stepped over Tristan, in between the two fifteen-year-olds from Neuhardenberg. Hans' arms and legs were shaking, his breathing rapid and unsteady.

"What did I just do?" Hans asked Blaz, his whole body shaking.

"You just attacked Tristan! What were you thinking?" Blaz yelled.

"I-I," Hans stammered, "I don't know, I was just so mad, I-" Hans looked behind Blaz to see Tristan still on the ground. The two made eye contact. Blaz stepped out of the way and held a hand out. Tristan knocked it away. Blaz smiled at this though. Tristan was acting tough. He had never acted tough in all the years Blaz had known him thus far. He wiped blood away from below his nose. One of his eyes was swelling shut.

"Tristan, are you all right?" Hans asked, his tone pleading.

Tristan nodded.

"I didn't mean-"

"I know, Hans. I am a weakling. I'm the weakest. I don't have any right to tell you to suck it up, after me walking around doing the same for years." Tristan gave Blaz a nod and walked out of shower facilities. Blaz watched him leave, then turned back to Hans who had sat down with his head in his hands.

Blaz shook his head, "Why did you do that?"

Hans' right leg still twitched as he stared ahead at the wall with his silver-blue eyes, "I lost it. I lost it with him."

"What do you mean?" Blaz asked quickly, "Lost it with Tristan? He's a good kid."

"But he's weak Blaz! So damn weak! That's what I mean! I know that I'm no Jarman, but Tristan is weak physically and in spirit. He's let himself be pushed around for years. Ever since I've known him. I've put up with that, only because he *is* a good kid, at least at heart. Blaz, he is the kind of kid that needs National Socialism. He needs high expectations and he needs quality people around him, otherwise he'd be ruining himself, on drugs, you know. I really thought the *Hitlerjugend* would boost his confidence. He entered a year later than me. I bragged to him about all the stuff we did, I was pretty into working out and guns. I got into great shape," Hans said, "I thought when he got a good squad who didn't beat up on him, that he'd maybe man up. Well, *nein*. He's as weak as ever. And when he told me that, I just lost it. I've kind of wanted to beat him up for a long time, toughen him up."

Blaz's lip twitched. He took a seat next to Hans. "You know you're the best friend he's got."

Hans turned to Blaz and smiled, "He thinks highly of you. I doubt you know it, but he thinks you are maybe his best friend next to me."

Blaz almost laughed. "Why? We don't talk all that much."

"I know that. He even knows that. But does Tristan talk with anyone in our squad more than he does with me?"

"*Nein.*"

"He's spoken with you more than anyone besides me," Hans told Blaz.

"Really?" Blaz asked in surprise. Hans nodded. Blaz leaned forward and put his chin in his palms, "I had no idea," he murmured, "Why me?"

"Maybe you've given more of your time than anyone else."

Blaz ran a hand through his hair. *Have I?*

The Third Way

March 15, 1943

Blaz sprinted through the forest, with a rifle and backpack, near the middle of his squad. The course was designed to simulate obstacles on the battlefield. There was no trail; they simply followed the people in front of them. Müller had led the way, one cadet following him ten seconds later and so forth and so on. They were told when they finished climbing the nets at the end, to wait on the platform at the top, about eight meters high.

"*Scheiße!*" Wilhelm's voice yelled from ahead in the woods. Blaz ran around a corner to find barbed-wire waiting. A good twenty meters of it to crawl under. Wilhelm's backpack was caught. Blaz dropped down and crawled under the barbed wire. He used his forearms and elbows to drag himself forward while holding onto his rifle. His backpack caught on the barbed wire hastily. Tristan came crawling past him, with his backpack ahead of him, and rifle slung over his shoulder.

Damn it. Blaz crawled backward out of his backpack. He carefully brought his rifle up over the bag, just missing the barbed wire. He slung it over his shoulder so it lay across his back. Then he resumed crawling forward.

"Hurry up!" Ivo yelled from behind.

Blaz pushed his backpack forward, easily making it under the barbed wire now. But he was also behind everyone else, save Ivo. Once he made it out of wire, he switched his rifle and backpack mid sprint and kept running. He was only a few meters behind Nico still as he approached a large leap over a trench filled with more barbed wire. Nico jumped, with a long stride and planted his right foot on the other side. His left foot slipped though, and the weight of his backpack caused him to fall backwards into the sharp metal.

"Ow!"

Blaz stayed focused, and gave all he had into his jump, angling his head forward first. He just made it and stumbled to the ground after he'd landed. Nico crawled out of the trench, hands and face bloody. Blaz pushed himself to his feet and kept sprinting through the forest. Soon, he came to a clearing, where the nets and platform lay. Blaz dropped his rifle and backpack and started climbing up the net. The net swayed, it was a lot harder to climb than he thought. But he made it to the top where Gunther, Hans, and Tristan were waiting. Below, the other squads and *Hauptsturmführer* Müller held a large gray sheet with an orange circle in the middle. Jarman, Wilhelm and Koby also held the sheet too.

"Schütz! Now!" Gunther closed his eyes and jumped off the platform. He landed to the left of the circle, but the boys caught him easily. Gunther sat up, and the boys began bouncing the sheet. All the boys laughed and smiled as they threw him into the air. Even Müller. While the boys had fun below, Nico and Ivo climbed to the top. Finally, Müller signaled to prepare for the next boy.

"Reichmann! Go!"

Hans didn't pause and jumped smack into the middle. Then it was Tristan's turn.

"Rothkirch!" Müller shouted, "Go!"

Tristan gulped. He looked down at the sheet. His tan face went pale. The other boys glanced at each other and smirked. Jarman among them. Koby stared up at Tristan with concern. Hans looked disappointed and shook his head. Ivo rolled his eyes. Several seconds passed.

Blaz put his hand on his face and dragged it down. "Come on, Tristan," he whispered, "Be a man."

Tristan took one tiny step forward. He took a deep breath. He closed his eyes. Then leapt off the platform. Some of the cadets' jaws dropped. Blaz's eyes went wide. Ivo gasped. Tristan landed in the middle of the sheet, safely. Müller and Tristan made eye contact for a moment. Hans beamed at his friend. Tristan nodded to him.

March 18, 1943

Blaz and Ivo spotted each other during weight lifting. The base didn't have actual weights, they only had the metal rods. But Müller found a way around that. He drilled or hammered holes into the sides of boxes containing bullets and put them on each end of the rods. Blaz made twelve reps before he started slowing down.

"Come on Blaz! Keep going!" Ivo said, looking over to Hans and Tristan. Tristan was still going strong. Blaz glanced over and thrust the bar over his head. He brought it back down, then sent it up again. Tristan noticed and sped up as best he could. Blaz started to outlast him a few reps later. But Tristan kept trying. He managed another rep. Blaz did as well. Tristan gritted his teeth as he tried to get to fifteen. His arms were shaking, he was red in the face, but he sucked in and threw his arms skyward. The weight went up too. Blaz quickly pumped out three more to counter Tristan's one. Tristan lowered the weight but didn't stop. He sent it up again. Blaz responded. Tristan brought it back down and tried again, but this time he couldn't do it. Hans helped him lower it down safely. Blaz finished out with six more, before Ivo helped him lower it as well.

Blaz spun to face Tristan on the bench, "Tristan, that was good! Better than you've ever done. And right after we did chin-ups and running!"

"What happened?" Ivo asked him in amazement. It was only an exceptional performance by Tristan's poor standards.

"Just had motivation to try and beat you," Tristan shrugged, tucking in his shirt.

Blaz raised his eyebrows, "That was good, keep it up."

"What's happening Koby?" Jarman asked while they ate dinner.

"What?"

"What's happening? Any news?"

"Nothing we haven't already heard. We keep losing ground in North Africa, but the Desert Fox has kept us going. We may yet keep our foothold there," Koby informed them. Jarman took a bite of cold chicken. Most of their meals were cold at this point.

"Blaz," Wilhelm said, "Has your mother had the baby yet?"

Blaz shook his head and grinned, "*Nein*, not yet. A little early still."

"Hans, we need a rematch against your football team," Gunther said, "We were the better team. And we almost had you in that last minute."

Hans took a drink of water, and shook his head, "What is it called when you almost win?" He looked around at everyone, then back to Gunther, "Oh *ja*, losing."

Gunther smacked the table with his fist, "Damn it, I knew you were gonna say that."

"We do need a rematch though," Tristan chimed in, specifically speaking to Gunther.

"*Ja*, so I can beat at least you again," Gunther laughed.

Hans split his fingers apart at the run and middle finger to form a "V" at Gunther, signaling *verlieren* or "lose".

"Hans," Gunther growled, "I should beat you up sometime."

"Hey, we box tomorrow. I'll take you."

"You're on."

"Koby, can I box you?" Tristan asked abruptly.

Koby turned quickly at this question, "Well, we're supposed to fight people near our skill level so that we improve."

"Just this once. I won't ask again if you fight me tomorrow."

Koby sighed, "All right fine."

"Awesome," Tristan said, and stood up to return his empty plate.

Gunther leaned into the group, as he sat at the outside, "What's going in with him? He's terrified of fighting half of us."

"Has he ever fought you?" Jarman asked Gunther.

"*Nein*," Gunther shook his head, "You?"

"*Nein*," Jarman almost laughed.

"How many of you has he beaten in a fight? At this camp or the last one?" Jaye asked, pushing his dirty blond hair back into place.

No one raised their hands.

"He beat me once," Ivo admitted, "The day after our march and after I'd gotten back from a run."

"Okay just one," Jaye said.

"Hang on he's coming back," Wilhelm said. Tristan walked over and sat back down. He had gotten seconds. He took a bite of chicken, then took a drink of water.

Jarman raised his eyebrows at Blaz and Koby and stood up to get seconds himself. Which Jarman did more often than anyone. This was the first time Tristan had though.

March 19, 1943

"Stay down, damn it!" Jaye swore.

"Give me something I can't take," Blaz gasped, having just been pummeled with a barrage of punches. His mouth and nose were both bleeding and one eye was swollen shut. In contrast, Jaye had no blood on his face. He advanced. He hammered Blaz with relentless punches. Blaz was no longer able to defend effectively. He took punch after punch, blocking about half, while only landing one solid punch.

"Go down!" Jaye shouted in frustration, swinging even harder. Blaz shook his head wearily, and advanced at Jaye. The Hitler Youth raised his gloves for Blaz's attack. Blaz bared down on Jaye and sent punches both at his face and chest. Jaye was surprised by the quickness of the attacks and didn't defend as well as before. Blaz landed some hard punches, but Jaye sent a rocket into his jaw, and he fell. Müller counted down. Blaz tried to get up, and nearly had made it to an upright position when his eyes went spotty and he fell back to the ground. Müller finished counting, then announced Jaye the victor. Ivo and Jarman got Blaz's armpits over their shoulders and helped him off. Tristan and Koby were next.

"What happened to you there?" Jarman asked Blaz and held his bloody head up.

"I don't know," Blaz said, shaking his head, "He came out-"

"*Nein, nein,* Blaz! You can beat Jaye. You weren't aggressive enough until the end."

"I'll do better next time."

"You better. That was just shit."

Koby was already on the attack against Tristan. The smaller Hitler Youth parried many punches, frustrating Koby. He took jabs at his sergeant, landing a few. Koby shook them off and kept focusing on landing a decisive blow. His punches were fast and powerful, and Tristan was being battered. Koby finally landed what appeared would be the final blow. Tristan landed hard in the dirt. Koby watched Tristan struggle to get up, and at five seconds turned around and winked at his friends. When Koby turned around, a gloved hand slammed into his face. He backpedaled, more out of shock than anything.

"Hertz! Don't ever let your guard down!" Müller roared. Koby nodded quickly, knowing better than to ask why Müller had let Tristan bend the rules. He raised his gloves to defend against another barrage of punches from Tristan, regaining his composure hastily. Tristan's punches began to grow slower, and Koby returned some of his own. Tristan took a hard one to the mouth, drawing some reaction from the other boys.

"*Mein Gott!*" Jarman exclaimed.

Tristan shook his head, and blood spun in all directions. He swung his arms around in a stretching motion. Koby moved forward.

"Come on Tristan!" one boy shouted.

Tristan smiled and put his gloves up. Koby pounded him now. Tristan took punches to the ribs, nose, and mouth, while he desperately tried to hit back. Finally, Koby landed the decisive blow, right in the jaw. Tristan went down, and blood began flowing as Müller counted. Tristan tried to get back up, but to no avail. Blaz jogged out to help Tristan off. Hans came over as well. Several boys from other squads did too.

"Good work, Tristan!" one boy congratulated him while Hans and Blaz lifted Tristan up.

"*Danke*," Tristan said, exhausted. Everything below his nose was covered in blood.

"How?" another boy asked, "Koby's an SS caliber boxer!"

"Where there's a will there's a way," Tristan answered as he was helped off by Hans and Blaz.

"Have you talked with him lately?" Blaz asked Hans as the two walked around the base's exterior that night.

"A couple days ago I had a long conversation with him," Hans replied, "He's been trying really hard in drills. Not just trying but trying to be the best."

"He's been eating more lately too."

"About time. He's really, really skinny, you can see right through him. Hey, there he is!" Hans pointed. Tristan was doing jumps onto a bench, then back down, and back up again.

"Tristan!" Hans called. Tristan turned his head to them and waved. Hans started jogging over, and Blaz sped up his walk.

"How's it going?" Hans asked.

"*Gut*," Tristan answered, and kept jumping.

"Excited for the rematch this weekend?"

"Oh *ja*," Tristan nodded, as he jumped up onto the bench. Hans sat down on one end. Blaz sat down next to him.

"Hans!" a voice called. Hans and Blaz both looked the way the voice had come. Koby jogged toward them. "Hans, I need to talk to you."

Hans nodded, and followed Koby away. Tristan kept doing his exercises.

"Tristan?"

"*Ja?*"

"What changed?" Blaz asked.

"What changed?"

"You're working hard in drills and doing the extra work Müller told you to. You never would've done that before."

"I thought it was time I made something of myself. Instead of being a weakling."

Blaz rubbed his eyes. Tristan stopped jumping and sat down next to him.

"Blaz, have you heard from your father?"

"Not for a while, you?"

"I don't have a father," Tristan answered.

"You don't? But you told me-"

"Well, not for a long time anyway."

"What happened to your papa?"

"He died a long time ago. When I was ten years old."

"How?"

"He and my brother had joined the brownshirts. They were early party members," Tristan explained, folding his hands, "Before the *Führer* was the *Führer*. And he was raising me to be a party member. My papa was in the brownshirts until thirty-six, and then he became a member of the *Wehrmacht*. He died in the war in Spain a year later."

"I'm sorry."

"It's okay," Tristan said, "It was a long time ago. You know, I think that's what happened. I don't think papa would have been proud of me over the last few years. And I just now realized that."

"As long as I've known you-"

"I'm not anything to be proud of?"

"Well-"

"Come on."

"*Ja*, you aren't."

Tristan nodded. Blaz looked up through the trees. Tristan did too.

"Weather's been getting warmer," Tristan said.

"It has."

"Blaz, thanks for being my friend," Tristan smiled.

"Same to you, Tristan," Blaz smiled back.

A New Soldier for Hitler

April 20, 1943

Bald flattern Hitlerfahnen über allen Straßen, die Knechtschaft dauert nur noch kurze Zeit!

"*Sieg!*" Müller roared.

"*Heil!*"

"*Sieg!*"

"*Heil!*"

"*Sieg!*"

"*Heil!*"

"My Youth, you have very much improved since your arrival. The *Führer* would be proud." Blaz could've sworn he saw Müller look Tristan's way. "But there is much to improve on. You must be the best soldiers on earth. The German *Wehrmacht* has made great strides in our fight against the International Clique! We have suffered a setback at Stalingrad, *ja*. But we maintain our foothold in North Africa, we have subdued all of Europe! Only because we have the best soldiers on earth! You, my Youth, must continue this excellence! On our *Führer's* birthday let us prepare to embark on a great undertaking. We will carry on this fight for the future of Europe, despite what trials may come our way! Let us rise up and show the whole world, that our courage and honor are like an indestructible fortress! *Heil* Hitler!"

"*Heil* Hitler!" the boys shouted back, extending their right arms into the air.

The Knights began their drill, a fifteen-mile run while wearing backpacks stuffed with equipment. Müller told them to run west and turn around at the large lake. Koby led the way, with Blaz and Ivo right behind him. Tristan ran to Blaz's side prompting Hans to run up to the front too.

"Feeling good?" Blaz asked both.

"Better than I ever have on a run," Tristan answered.

"Feeling fine," Hans winked, "Hey Tristan, you've been looking a lot better lately. At everything."

"*Danke*," Tristan blushed.

"Give us a flex," Ivo said from behind Hans. Tristan looked down, embarrassed.

"Come on," Ivo said again, "I'll flex." He moved his backpack and flexed his arm. They were wearing the Hitler Youth tanks, so he didn't need to pull up a sleeve.

"Not bad," Hans grinned, then flexed his arm himself.

"Better," Ivo admitted, gesturing to Hans.

"Much," Blaz snickered.

Ivo gave him an animated glare, "All right then, let's see yours."

"With pleasure," Blaz said, and flexed his arm.

Hans raised his eyebrows at Ivo, "Better than yours," he smirked, "But not mine."

"You're both pretty good," Tristan said.

Hans pulled one arm out of the backpack straps, pulled his shirt over his head, and put it in his backpack, "Shirtless?"

"*Ja*," Blaz agreed. Ivo followed suit.

"Tristan?" Hans said.

"I'll do it at the turnaround point, okay? Keep you in suspense."

"Come on now," Hans ribbed him.

Tristan shook his head with a grin.

Over an hour later, the boys arrived at the lake. They put down their backpacks and caught their breath. Ivo went to Blaz and punched him in the abs while he recovered. Blaz jumped back in surprise, "Ow!"

Ivo shook his head, grinning, "You think we'll ever be in better shape than we are now?"

"God, it'll be tough to be better than now," Hans said.

"Not if we stay in the *Wehrmacht*," Jarman said from behind them.

"*Ja, ja*," Hans nodded, then turned to Tristan, "Come on."

"All right," Tristan said, and took his tank off. Even though Blaz knew what was coming, he was still surprised. Tristan finally had a six pack, his shoulders were broader, his neck thicker, and his chest slanted upwards. He looked as soldierly as any of the boys now. Not the odd man out. That was Ivo now and Ivo looked like he knew it.

"Wow!" Jurgen exclaimed, "Is that you Tristan?"

"Damn, you've really been working."

"Good birthday present for the *Führer*. A new soldier."

Tristan's face turned red. So he ran with the subject of the holiday, Hitler's Birthday: "*Heil mein Führer!*"

"What say we put those arms to the test?" Jarman suggested looking at Hans, "Tristan?"

"*Ja*," Tristan nodded.

"What did you have in mind?" Hans asked, starting to wonder if Jarman knew he'd beaten up Tristan a month and a half ago.

"You two lay on the ground, facing each other."

Tristan and Hans lay down.

"Arm wrestle," Jarman said, "I'll monitor, so there's no lifting your arms up."

"*Natürlich*," Tristan grinned as the two locked hands.

"*Wunderbar. Drei, Zwei, Ein, Los!*" Jarman signaled. Hans immediately went on the offensive. He made quick advances and had Tristan's arm to about a forty-five-degree angle. But then he stalled. Tristan kept him halted for a good five seconds. Hans looked Tristan in the eye, and his friend returned the glance. A moment later, Hans' forearm slammed into the ground on the opposite side.

"*Verdämmt!*" Hans swore.

"*Tristan ist der Sieger!*" Jarman announced. Tristan smiled as his squad mates patted him on the back in congratulations. Hans' face was blank in astonishment. Blaz five-starred him and his eyes focused.

"The shoe is now on the other foot," Blaz said cheerfully.

"He beat me, Blaz," Hans laughed, "Tristan Rothkirch beat me in a contest of strength."

June 6, 1943

"Are your arms sore?" Hans asked Tristan, while the two of them, Koby, Blaz, and Jaye strolled through the forest. Tristan had gotten even more muscular over the months, and impressively had kept improving at his running at the same time. His athletic shirt was no longer loose. His arms were defined and almost disproportionately big for his height. His shirt was tight against his chest, his abs were defined, and even his legs were muscular. Müller had called his work ethic "ideal" for the German youth in front of the company of boys. Not only had he surpassed Ivo, Nico, Blaz, Hans, and Jaye in strength (he could now lift more than them and had beaten all of them in boxing) but he had also beaten Gunther in boxing the past week. Not just beat, utterly decimated. Gunther had been taken off guard by Tristan's ferocity and the strength of his punches, and he never recovered from it in the fight. Tristan was just better. By the end of the fight, Gunther's nose had been broken and bloodied. And the next day, he woke up with a black eye, bruises all over his chest, and even his shoulders.

"Not too bad," Tristan answered Hans' question, "I need to up my work a bit."

"You think I should too?" Koby asked, "Some of us do push-ups and sit-ups a couple nights a week."

"I don't know, seems like it's working for you," Tristan grinned.

"*Ja*, no need to fix what isn't broken."

"How have we done? Since your last assessment?" Jaye asked Koby.

"A lot better," Koby said with wide eyes, "You've gotten much better at running Jaye. Blaz, you've gotten stronger, and Müller has really corrected your shooting. Hans, you've gotten stronger and your quick draw is a lot better now. Tristan, need I say a thing?"

"Could you?" Tristan said with a laugh.

"Well, you are damn stronger now," Koby said proudly, "Anything you guys think I need to improve on? I think my shooting could be better."

"I think you are the best, next to Jarman," Jaye said, "Guess there's always room for improvement."

"That's what Müller always says," Blaz agreed.

"Koby, your number is up next," Hans said slyly and abruptly.

"What?" Koby asked with urgency in his tone, as if he thought Hans knew something he didn't.

"Relax," Hans said, picking up on Koby's tone, "The SS hasn't drafted you."

"*Gott sei Dank.*"

"*Nein*, something worse. You are fighting Tristan next week."

Koby stiffened. "Uh, I thought I only had to once?"

"Hey, it's not Tristan telling you that you need to fight again. It's me."

"And me," Jaye seconded.
"As well," Blaz added.
"Okay, I will. This coming week's fights."
"*Ausgezeichnet*," Hans smiled.

Tristan versus Koby

June 11, 1943

The big day arrived. Hans had done a good job circulating the story among the other squad sergeants; Simon, Amon, Oswald, and Oskar and Raymond; the leaders of the two new squads to arrive. Then they had circulated it among their squad mates.

As there were now sixty-seven boys at the camp with new arrivals, Tristan was well-known by now. Mainly for being exactly what the National Socialists envisioned the Hitler Youth program accomplishing with the boys of the nation. He'd been weak, now he was strong.

Tristan and Koby took their shirts off and put their boxing gloves on. Tristan jumped up and down and shook his arms out to get loose. Koby didn't have his normal swagger today. Tristan looked invincible. Confident, energetic, and the crowd behind him.

Müller called them to the middle and laid out the rules. As always, he failed to mention rules barring cheap shots. The competitors should be aware at all times.

"*Drei, Zwei, Ein, Los!*"

Tristan and Koby circled. Koby looked less nervous now that he was moving. He stayed near Tristan while they circled. Finally, Tristan made the move that he'd been waiting for Koby to make. His attack was quick. What all the boys called '*Blitzkämpf* or "lighting fight."

The punches were low, quick, and hard. Koby adjusted to the unexpected low punches quickly, but ever so briefly left his head exposed. That was all Tristan needed. He sent one shot into Koby's nose. Blaz had never seen a punch like it. It impacted at the peak of its speed, with Tristan's arm extending perfectly to drive into Koby's nose. Drops of blood went flying. A gasp ran throughout the small crowd of boys. Everyone knew his nose had been broken. Blaz couldn't believe what happened next. Koby fell down.

There was a pause. For a good three seconds. Then Müller began counting down. He seemed just as shocked as the other boys. Tristan was shocked himself, his mouth hung open. Koby didn't even try to get up.

"*Zehn!*" Müller ended, "*Rothkirch ist der Sieger!*"

The Hitler Youths erupted into applause. Tristan still stood motionless in amazement at what he'd done. Some boys rushed out to congratulate Tristan, patting him on the back, punching him, and showering him with compliments, Jarman and Wilhelm amongst them. Blaz and Tristan made eye contact, and Blaz gave him a congratulatory nod. Tristan returned it.

Blaz's next move was toward Koby who was still laying on the ground. Ivo had noticed this as well. Müller had too. The officer was obviously beaming over Tristan but at the same time disappointed at Koby not even trying to get up.

Blaz knelt and shook Koby, "Koby, Koby stop messing with us."

Koby didn't wake up. Müller motioned for Blaz to move away, as he knelt himself. He put his head to Koby's chest, then nodded seconds later. Then he examined Koby's nose.

"Son of a bitch," the officer chuckled.

"What happened sir?" Ivo asked, not worried after hearing the officer chuckle.

Müller shook his head in awe, "Rothkirch knocked him out with that punch."

"He's unconscious?" Ivo asked in amazement.

"Indeed," Müller nodded, and picked Koby up. He flung him over his shoulders and carried him to the base.

Blaz and Ivo stood impatiently by the cot, where they waited for Koby to wake up. It didn't take long. Koby eyes flickered open. He stayed lying down, staring at the ceiling. As he did, Jarman walked in.

"What happened?" he asked after a while.

"You lost," Ivo bluntly said.

"*Ja*, I did," Koby said, "God, what happened? I don't remember what happened at all. How long was the fight? How did I lose? How did Tristan do?"

"The fight was less than thirty seconds," Jarman said, "You really got your ass handed to you."

Koby kept staring at the ceiling in disbelief.

"To be honest, you did," Blaz said, "He went on the offensive, he made a lot of low punches, and you made yourself vulnerable to block them."

"Bad mistake, brother," Jarman grinned.

Koby wasn't yet ready to laugh at this defeat, but Blaz saw his lip curl.

"What was I thinking? What did he do after that?"

"He *hammered* you in the nose," Ivo explained, reenacting the punch through the air, "I mean, blood went flying all over, everyone kind of gasped at the punch. I knew your nose had been broken."

"How many noses has that kid broken now?"

Blaz raised his hand, "To be fair, it was already broken though."

"And Gunther's," Jarman added, popping his arm.

Ivo laughed randomly.

"What's so funny?" Jarman asked him.

"Koby, if someone had told you Tristan would beat you in boxing four months ago, what would you have said?" Ivo asked.

"I probably would've shrugged it off and laughed at them. I mean, really. Tristan?"

"I would've doubted it," Blaz said.

"I assume I'm next on the hit list," Jarman said.

"We'll see," Ivo said.

"God, he beat me," Koby said again. "I'm reexamining my entire worldview."

"Is your confidence shaken?" Ivo asked.

"A little, actually."

"Koby, you didn't lose to the Tristan you knew for over two years. You lost to the new Tristan. The worker, the fighter, the talker, the *übermensch*. I know, I'm still having trouble coming to terms with it. He's just sort of been there for two years, been invisible. Now you can't help but notice him and want to talk with him. He's inspiring," Jarman said.

"I don't think I ever knew him," Koby said incredulously, "Where did this drive that he has come from?"

Blaz shrugged, feigning ignorance.

"I was sick of being weak," Tristan said from behind them.

Koby sat up. Jarman turned.

"I can't believe you beat me, Tristan," Koby breathed, "Incredible work."

Tristan smiled bashfully as he always did when complimented, "*Danke* Koby. You-"

"Don't try to sugar coat anything," Koby cut him off, "That was the most embarrassing match of my life."

"And he's had a lot of fights," Ivo winked.

"You want to start training with me?" Tristan asked him, "I think *Herr* Müller actually wants us to train more without his supervision."

"That's why we get free time?" Ivo asked.

Tristan nodded quickly.

"I'd like to train with you," Koby agreed, standing up, "I think the squad would like to. I'm sure we'll be needed up front soon. We may as well be as strong as we can."

"I'm in," Jarman said.

"Count me in," Blaz agreed.

"Me too," Ivo added.

"All right."

A New Senft

May 17, 1943

"My little brother was born! Little Erwin Siegfried Senft!"

"Little brother! How about that?" Ivo congratulated Blaz.

"When was little Erwin born?" Koby asked enthusiastically.

"On the *Führer's* birthday!" Blaz said loudly hitting his hand against the table.

"The *Führer's* birthday," Koby repeated, "How odd."

"Makes sense, father was on leave in late July."

"So?" Ivo asked.

"That's when my parents could've made the baby."

Ivo looked at the, raising an eyebrow, "What? What does that mean?"

"What do you-" Blaz began, but Ivo smirked, and Blaz realized he'd been fooled.

Ivo slapped Blaz on the back, "Well, let's look forward to seeing little Erwin Senft and little Hertz when we get back home."

The Wehrmacht's Oath

September 14, 1943

Blaz stood inside the base with no clothes on. All sixty-seven Hitler Youths did as well, in a long line as they waited to be examined for entry into the *Wehrmacht*. Everyone stood with their arms to their sides, looking straight forward, waiting for the doctor to call them in to be inspected. They were examined in groups of four to speed up the process. Neutral looks surfaced throughout the room. The Knights were in very good shape at this point after extra training with Tristan and Jarman, though many were still on the skinny side as opposed to a more muscular build that the *Wehrmacht* desired. The main issue was their height, and that went for Tristan and Ivo more so than anyone, but after and during Stalingrad, the physicals had been relaxed and younger, smaller, and shorter youths began being rushed into service. Blaz stared ahead awkwardly, as he finally neared the front of the line. The boys who'd already been inspected marched out of the room, and back to their barracks to change and prepare to take their oath of loyalty. No one had been refuted yet. The male doctor opened the door to his office and Gunther, Nico, Hans and Tristan walked out.

"Ivo Klein! Blaz Senft! Koby Hertz! Jarman Knecht!"

"All right, let's get this out of the way," the doctor said, understanding the boys' current feelings to this entire process.

The boys remained at attention. It was a humiliating moment for all four of them, made clear by their expressions, that gave a sense of perceived vulnerability. Not something they enjoyed feeling.

"Heartbeat and breathing," the doctor said, and put a stethoscope to Ivo's chest. The doctor moved the stethoscope across Ivo's chest and back, nodding several times, "*Gut, gut.*"

Then he moved over to Blaz. The cold metal caused Blaz to shiver as a natural reaction. "Deep breaths," the doctor ordered. Blaz breathed in, raising his chest while doing so. "*Gut, gut,*" the doctor said in a monotone voice, placing the stethoscope onto his back. Blaz inhaled deeply again. The doctor moved the instrument to below his shoulder blade. He took one more deep breath. "*Sehr gut,*" the doctor nodded, then moved to Koby.

"*Ausgezeichnet,*" the doctor said after hearing Koby's heartbeat and breathing, "Excellent. Good runner?" the doctor asked. Koby nodded, trying not to crack a smile.

He stepped over to Jarman and placed his stethoscope over Jarman's heart. Jarman made deep breaths and the doctor nodded several times again, "*Sehr gut.*"

He walked back to Ivo and told all of them to bend over and touch their toes. They did so. The doctor did something to Ivo, then came to Blaz. He examined Blaz's spinal cord, touching it in several places. The doctor moved on without a word. He came back to Ivo, telling the boys to straighten up. He examined the boys' eyesight, hearing, reflexes, and genitals before letting them go. Once he was released, Blaz hurried back to the barracks to change into his new *Wehrmacht* uniform. The big moment was near.

The sun shone bright when Blaz came trotting out of the barracks in his new field-gray uniform and helmet to join his squad mates. The day before, their black uniforms had been swapped out for *Wehrmacht* uniforms. The sun reflected off the damp ground, making it brighter out. Koby led them over to the flagpole where *Hauptsturmführer* Müller stood. A squad marched to behind Müller. In front of the *Hauptsturmführer*, marched another squad.

"Hertz, today you make the oath of loyalty to our *Führer* until death or until the *Führer* releases you from this oath," Müller said, "The train is at the tracks where you all arrived. You will march there once you have been sworn in.

"*Ja* sir."

"Do you swear by God this sacred oath that you shall render unconditional obedience to Adolf Hitler, the *Führer* of the German Reich, supreme commander of the armed forces, and that you shall at all times be prepared, as a brave soldier, to give your life for this oath?"

Koby thought for a moment. They had all heard and read this oath in preparation for this day, but Koby still paused. Whether about the gravity of oath or if he was remembering the words, was up to interpretation. Finally, he raised his right hand in a formal salute, then spoke, "I swear by God this sacred oath that I shall render unconditional obedience to Adolf Hitler, the *Führer* of the German Reich, supreme commander of the armed forces, and that I shall at all times be prepared, as a brave soldier, to give my life for this oath." Koby breathed a sigh of relief once he had finished saying his oath.

"And what of you?" Müller asked the squad, "Do you swear by God this sacred oath that you shall render unconditional obedience to Adolf Hitler, the *Führer* of the German Reich, supreme commander of the armed forces, and that you shall at all times be prepared, as a brave soldier, to give your life for this oath?"

The squad raised their right hands high into the air, and repeated Müller, "I swear by God this sacred oath that I shall render unconditional obedience to Adolf Hitler, the *Führer* of the German Reich, supreme commander of the armed forces, and that I shall at all times be prepared, as a brave soldier," Blaz paused at this, falling behind the remainder of the Knights who completed the words. Müller looked his way, and Blaz finished his recitation, "To give my life for this oath."

Müller nodded with approval, "Long live the Reich!"

"Long live the Reich!" the squad repeated, as well as the Hitler Youths behind Müller. Koby ushered his squad behind the *Hauptsturmführer*. They listened as the next two squads made their oath to the *Führer*. When the final group had finished, Müller turned to face all the Hitler Youth.

"Today you become soldiers," Müller said, proudly.

"Finally," Wilhelm and Jarman said.

"You know all you need to know to serve *Deutschland* now. Whether by sunshine or rain, by gun or by hand, by foot or by vehicle you will know how to most effectively fight for *Deutschland*. More importantly than this, you have undying loyalty to your people and your nation. Your honor is called loyalty," Müller gravely said, quoting not the *Wehrmacht's* motto, but the *Schutzsaffel's*. He continued with his speech. Blaz suspected he may have rehearsed it. "I do not wish to deceive you. You boys enter the war at a crucial time. The fate of the world hangs in the balance. Our people are suffering now, they are being bombed, they know no peace. But they will suffer more if we do not erase every stain of the corrupting fingers of Stalin, Churchill, and Roosevelt." The new soldiers stared at their commander with steely eyes. "But lift up your hearts! All will come right! Out of the depths of despair and loss will be restored the glory of mankind! *Heil!*"

"*Heil!*"

Now that all the soldiers had taken their oaths, Müller dismissed the squads, one by one, to go to the entrance and wait there. He left Koby's squad for last.

"Hertz, your squad is dismissed. It has been an honor to be your instructor. You have all become great soldiers, I'm confident you will serve *Deutschland* with excellence. *Heil* Hitler!"

"*Heil* Hitler!"

The Knights lowered their arms, all turned at once and began marching to the gate.

"Rothkirch!" Müller called.

Tristan halted, and cleanly spun around, "*Ja?*"

Müller waved him over. He whispered something indiscernible to Blaz, but he saw Tristan jump just a bit, then freeze. But Müller patted the new soldier on the shoulder after that. Tristan glanced up to him in admiration. Müller's gaze briefly went to the sky, then he met Tristan's eyes again, and performed the military salute, "Good luck, son."

"You too," Tristan saluted back.

Koby waited for Tristan to join the columns.

"Now we march," the sergeant commanded. The Knights goose-stepped to the gate, falling in line with the others. A song began from the front, and quickly worked its way back.

Wir standen für Deutschland auf Posten, und hielten die Große Wacht!
Nun hebt sich die Sonne im Osten, und ruft Millionen zur Schlacht!
Von Finnland bis zum Schwarzen Meer...
Vorwärts! Vorwärts! Vorwärts nach Osten du sturmen'd Heer!
Freiheit das Ziel! Sieg das Panier! Führer befiehl, wir folgen dir!
Führer befiehl, wir folgen dir!

Blaz glanced out of the corner of his eye at Tristan. He could hear it, but still looked. Tristan was singing loudly with utter determination. Blaz couldn't help but grin.

Den Marsch von Horst Wessel begonnen, im Brauen Gewand der SA!
Vollenden der grauen Kolonnen, der großes Stunde ist da!
Von Finnland bis zum Schwarzen Meer...
Vorwärts! Vorwärts! Vorwärts nach Osten du sturmen'd Heer!
Freiheit das Ziel! Sieg das Panier!

"*Führer befiehl, wir folgen dir!*" Tristan sang. Blaz sang the repeated line even louder after Tristan. It seemed all the young soldiers did the same, "*Führer befiehl, wir folgen dir!*"

Blaz sat next to Ivo and Koby inside the train, rifle in hand. Ivo held his sniper, and Koby his assault rifle. Their packs held their few personal belongings, ammunition, rations, and water. On their new uniforms, were ammo pockets and magazines, for the gun that each possessed. They sat in the middle of the train, tightly packed in with another squad. Blaz kept one hand on his rifle, while examining the bullet he'd taken from the Estonian girl in the dim light. Ivo and Koby paid no mind, assuming it to be a random bullet.

"Off to war, Blaz," Koby said, in between deep breaths.

Blaz stopped looking at the bullet. He slid it into a pocket and looked up.

"Real war," Koby continued, "The front lines."

"*Ja,*" Blaz shook his head, and his voice trailed off at the end.

"*Gott mit uns,*" Ivo said, quoting the *Wehrmacht* motto, "God with us."

First Contact

September 15-September 18, 1943

No one knew how long they were on the train, but when it came screeching to a halt, they could hear artillery. The train was on the edge of a town, south of Leningrad, presumably. The town had paved roads and was clearly a large city with many buildings of various heights and designs.

An officer ran over to the Hitler Youth and began rattling off information, "This city lays partially on a hill, so most of our defenses are there to keep us in control of the high ground. *Hitlerjugend,* your job is to guard the south side of the city to prevent Russian flanking maneuvers."

"*Ja* sir, *ja* sir," was the general reply. The young soldiers set out at a jog for the south side of the city. Rifles held across their chest, pointed away from their squad mates. Koby made sure to set the pace. The sooner they got there the better. After fifteen minutes, they came to an officer of the *Wehrmacht*.

"*Gut,* reinforcements," the officer sighed, though he seemed offset by the ages of his reinforcements. "I want you in these houses, spread out. Two men on machine guns, one to feed, other to fire," the officer instructed, "Squad snipers at windows, and riflemen at windows and roofs. *Schnell!* Quickly!"

The squads spread out across several three-storied buildings with flat roofs. Koby barked orders and the sergeant of the second squad did likewise. The artillery and flak were spread down further and operated by old soldiers in their forties. Blaz ascended to the third level with Ivo and Hans. Jarman, Tristan, and Jurgen had been ordered to the first floor, Jaye and Wilhelm to the second floor of the building next to them, and on the second building's roof, Nico, Gunther, and Koby. The floors of the buildings were concrete and had been cleared out. The back of the room was several meters from the windows to provide a fallback position. The entire floor was mainly one room, save a storage area of some kind. In their room was a small crate of rifle ammunition. A door on the level connected them, so they could move freely between the two buildings.

Hans ran into the second building to feed the machine gun alongside an officer who looked nineteen. From the other room, Dietrich, who Blaz acknowledged, and Benjamin Wiebe, who Ivo greeted. Ivo readied his sniper and waited at the window. Blaz did the same with his rifle. Outside was an open field with no trees, but a few stumps. The Germans had undoubtedly removed the trees to give attackers no cover. At the base of the homes, for hundreds of meters, was barbed wire. If the Russians did attack, it would be a bloodbath.

For days, they waited. Several times they could tell fighting was happening on the east side, where the entrenched defenses were on and inside of the hills. They'd resorted to arm wrestling, jogging in place, and push-up contests to keep their muscles from weakening. Ivo waited anxiously, tapping a foot incessantly, on their third day of inaction. Blaz glanced over at him, and Ivo stopped.

"I have to go," Ivo said.

"Then go," Blaz answered.

Ivo rose and ran down the stairs. Blaz, Dietrich, and Benjamin turned back to the window, keeping an eye out for Russians. They had only been outside for restroom breaks, and to get rations from their commanding officer during the last few days.

"What's that?" Benjamin pointed.

"Where?" Dietrich moved to Benjamin's window. Blaz stood up and grabbed Ivo's rifle to use the scope. He closed one eye and gazed through, adjusting for a clearer view.

"Russians!" he shouted, "Russians, due south!"

Benjamin, who was nearest the other room, ran in to alert the others. Blaz ran down the stairs and Dietrich up to make sure everyone knew.

"Jaye! Wilhelm! Russians from the south!" Wilhelm placed his *Panzerschreck* on the floor and squinted out the window. Jaye raised his rifle.

"I see them," Wilhelm said, "Back to your post."

Blaz sprinted back up the stairs and raised his rifle. Ivo ran right next to him seconds after he'd gotten set. The Soviets had tanks, but the number of men was incredible. A sea of brown clad soldiers came sprinting across the field at the building. The large German machine guns began firing across the line of defenses. Russians collapsed. Benjamin fired when he saw the trackers hitting men.

"They're not in range yet for our weapons," Dietrich yelled, taking command, "Hold fire!"

Some Russians exploded, body parts flying, courtesy of the mines the Germans had planted. Ivo fired his sniper rifle, which had a much further range than the normal iron sight rifles the others possessed. No Russian in view collapsed. Ivo chambered another round. He fired again. A Russian collapsed near the front of the charge. The casing bounced on the concrete floor of the building. Jarman's STG-44 unleashed lead on the enemy. Just by the sound of the gun, one could feel its power, the weight of the bullets, and the pain they would bring.

"Almost," Dietrich said with a raised voice, a Russian rifle fired towards them, "Fire at will!"

Blaz fired at a Soviet. The bullet sent dust flying up near his target, who stumbled in shock. Bullets peppered the exterior of their building. The Russians rifles were in range. They needed to keep the Russian machine gunners away. Blaz aimed at the same target, this time hitting the Russian, who collapsed on the battlefield. Blaz turned to take aim at a man on a tank who held a sniper rifle at the ready. The sniper fired in Blaz's direction. At that exact moment, a bullet sent ash from the windowsill into the air. Blaz ducked down. After a couple of seconds, he peeked over the windowsill. He prepared to fire but several bullets hit the Russian and he tumbled off the tank.

Machine guns are doing their job, thought Blaz. He refocused to aim for a Russian machine gunner. He missed again but caused the soldier to trip when the bullet impacted directly in front of him. He wasn't on the ground long, leaping to his feet, and resuming his charge. The Russian raised his machine gun. Blaz fired again, hitting the man in the head. Blaz turned to reload, taking cover away from the window. He grabbed a stripper clip and reloaded his Karabiner. The Russians came ever closer, tanks rumbling among the men. A rocket hurtled toward a Russian tank from below, leaving a thin trail of smoke behind it. It slammed into the nearest tank's treads, and the vehicle ground to a halt. The second tank fired, blasting a hole in their building. The boys fell back but scrambled to their positions in moments. Ash and smoke billowed from below them, quickly dispersing into a thin, transparent cloud.

Another rocket fired at the tank from the lower levels. Blaz faintly heard an explosion. Ivo rattled off three shots and the three nearest Russians fell. The machine gun across from them mowed down several enemy soldiers. Dietrich yelled to his comrades, "Russian bazooka, three hundred meters. Bring him down!"

Ivo immediately raised his rifle in the man's direction. Blaz fired first, missing. Once again dirt leapt up, near the man. Another bullet hit nearby, from Dietrich's rifle. The man sprinted harder, desperately trying to get in range. He raised his bazooka at a building, but blood splattered from his chest, and he fell to the ground firing into the ground ahead of him. Ivo ducked and cocked his rifle, ejecting the empty shell.

"Last tank!" Dietrich yelled, "Take out the machine gunner!"

A Soviet T-34, with a hammer and sickle emblazoned on its front chugged along, its tank commander firing the hatch-mounted machine gun.

"He's mine," Ivo grunted. Blaz aimed for men surrounding the tank. The tank's machine guns fired into their room. Blaz ducked behind the thick wall. He heard something slam into the floor. He glanced to his right. Dietrich's body lay on the ground, a bullet hole right in the center of his helmet. His eyes stared into nothingness. Blaz couldn't breathe. Benjamin scrambled over to his comrade, removing Dietrich's helmet to see if he could do anything to help him. Blaz cautiously exposed himself to take aim. He glanced in the tank's direction. Its main cannon was rotating their way. Wilhelm did his job and the tank's cannon never got to its target. By now, the thinned Russian ranks were within two hundred meters and firing their machine guns. Blaz knew ducking would only buy the Soviets more time. He had to stand and fight. He shot to his feet, took out his stick grenade and pulled the pin. He chucked it with all his might. It landed right in front of a Russian, who skidded to a stop just before the grenade exploded. The German machine guns fired away, desperately trying to halt the Russian advance. Blaz aimed his rifle, firing and cocking it, felling a Russian with at least every other shot.

The Russians were within seventy-five meters. Ivo, Benjamin, and Blaz fired as fast as their rifles would allow them to, their shots becoming more accurate with such close targets. Hundreds of Russian bodies lay across the wide front, but still they came. One Soviet ran out of view, in front of third building.

"Cover me!" Blaz shouted to his comrades. He leaned out the window and fired at the Russian, killing him instantly. Several Russians raised their rifles at Blaz's window and fired. Blaz dove to the ground, heart pounding. As he landed, he felt a sharp pain, but paid it no mind. He crawled back to the window, staying out of sight. Ivo threw a grenade, but through the dirt and ash, came dozens of Russians, who made it to the building.

"Ivo, stay here and keep sniping!" Blaz ordered, "Benjamin! Follow me!"

Benjamin glanced at Dietrich's body as he left and followed Blaz down the stairs at a frantic pace. Jaye joined them when they passed the second floor. On the first floor, Jarman, Jurgen, and Tristan stood at the back, behind two thick overturned tables with guns raised. Benjamin opened a door and took cover inside a closet that he could lean in and out of. Blaz and Jaye moved to the other side to flank the Russians. Benjamin stood behind Jurgen who knelt. Suddenly, a Russian soldier leapt through the open window, blindly spraying fire across the room. They fired back, but more Russians came vaulting in behind the soldier. Jaye and Jarman fired their machine guns, felling several, but the Russians took several bullets before they would fall. The Soviets kept coming, finally running out of men. The boys held their guns with trembling arms. Benjamin lay bleeding on the ground, but alive. Jaye warily emerged from cover to help him, while Jurgen and Jarman cautiously moved out from behind their cover. They raised their guns at a moving Russian.

"Surrender!" Jurgen shouted at the Russian in German. The Russian turned over to reveal a grenade in his hand. He pulled the pin immediately with his last strength, letting the grenade roll out of his hand.

"*Granate!*" Jurgen shouted. He lunged after the grenade, shielding his comrades, then picked it up and threw it towards the open window underhanded. The grenade made it out the window. Then it exploded. Glass in the upper window shattered. The blast sent Jurgen sprawling across the room, and into the wall.

"Jurgen!" Jarman screamed in horror. The soldiers kept their rifles raised at the window, while Jarman ran to Jurgen. He propped Jurgen against the wall, revealing to the teens what the grenade had done. The shards of glass had cut deeply into Jurgen's face. Ash covered his uniform.

"Jurgen," Jarman said loudly, "Jurgen, can you hear me?"

Jurgen unsteadily nodded, "*Ja*, I'm fine. Is-" he breathed with difficulty, "Is everyone okay?"

"*Ja*," Jarman told him, "No one else got hurt by the grenade."

"*Gut*," Jurgen said, trying to stand up by himself. He didn't make it far, before falling into Jarman's waiting arms.

Jarman propped him against the wall again, "Stay here, we'll get your wounds cleaned. Everyone else, to your posts!"

The soldiers quickly ran back to their floors, to ready for another possible attack. As Blaz walked up the stairs he felt a surge of pain in his right side. When he reached the top, he allowed himself to succumb to the pain. He went to his knees, clutching his chest, the pain growing more intense with each passing moment.

"Are you all right?" came Ivo's voice.

"I don't know, my side is hurting really bad," Blaz complained.

"Hang on," Ivo said, then sprinted up to the roof. Seconds later, Koby came down with him.

"Your side hurts?"

"*Ja*," Blaz said, still kneeling and clutching his right side.

"Let me see your hand," Koby said. Blaz removed his hand from his side, to find it covered in blood.

"Lay down," Koby ordered Blaz, "On your back."

Blaz laid down, another shot of pain surging through his side. He realized his uniform was also covered in blood, on the right side of his shirt, above his belt. Koby undid Blaz's belt, then unbuttoned his black uniformed shirt. His white undershirt was stained with blood. Koby pulled it up to examine the wound.

"*Gut, gut,*" Koby said with relief, "No bones, nothing too serious. You're going to be all right. But we need a medic to dig this bullet out."

"What?" Blaz asked in shock, "Bullet?"

"*Ja,* you got shot."

"Why didn't it go straight through me?" Blaz asked in confusion.

"Well, the Russians were firing their weapons from outside their effective range, so I would assume that's what you were hit by. Wasn't going fast enough."

"I didn't feel it until later though."

"Schlusser told us that during war, our adrenaline levels get very high during times of peril, as he described it. And that causes us to ignore or lose our feeling of pain temporarily. It's very fascinating."

"No kidding," Blaz grimaced, while more pain throbbed.

"Ivo! Get a medic! Quick!" Koby ordered. Ivo stomped his foot, then ran down the stairs.

The medic's work took some time. Digging the bullet out was painful. Once the bullet had been removed, the medic bandaged his midsection temporarily to keep the blood compressed. He told Blaz the wound would leave a permanent scar but aside from that, he would be fine.

"Feeling all right?" Koby asked.

"*Ja,*" Blaz said as he stood, "How's Jurgen?"

"He's fine."

Blaz nodded back, "That was your first battle."

"*Ja,* it was."

"How many did you shoot?"

"I didn't count."

"*Nein?*"

"*Nein.*"
"Me neither."

Four Corners

October 5, 1943

The Russians did not attack again for weeks. The young Germans were transferred during this time to the western edge of the city, outside of a bombed-out church. Two flak guns were positioned in the street outside the church and a small cemetery bordered it, surrounded by a low, stone wall. The church itself was modest, with a short steeple housing a bell and twelve rows of pews divided by an aisle. At the end of the isle was a podium. But a hammer and sickle were graffitied where the crucifix had been removed. The German commander normally ordered a sweep of the area, but today he ordered his men to take up defense of the buildings in the city.

"The Russians have broken through the northern and eastern defenses," he told squad leaders, "The southern will soon be overrun. I want you and your squads to take up defense of individual houses. Make them pay for each meter in blood."

"Sir, shouldn't we be pulling out?" one lesser officer asked, "If we lose the north, south, and east then we'll soon be surrounded."

"I have orders not to retreat."

"Sir?"

"*Nein!* Take to your defenses!"

Koby led the two squads, with the second squad leader right on his tail. At a four-way intersection, with multiple-storied buildings at each corner, Koby ordered a halt.

"All right, I want men in each of these four buildings," Koby told the boys, "We have twenty-two, so six in that one, and five in the others. Second and third floor for everyone, but one man stays on the first floor in each building to guard the stairway. Ideally, this man should have a machine gun."

The squads divided up, Blaz going with Jarman, Wilhelm, Benjamin, and Hans. Jarman remained to guard the stairway while the rest took up spots on the second floor. The second floor had several windows, which they opened, and overturned office desks littering the room.

"Koby's signaling us! Russians from the east. Two tanks, about forty men. Let them pass into the middle of the intersection. Then hit them with all you have!" Wilhelm stealthily readied his *Panzerschreck* and pistol. The others readied their rifles. Nothing but silence, and the occasional distant sound of a gun or artillery.

Then Blaz heard it. Marching. It came closer and closer. Blaz breathed in as quietly as he could, fearing they might hear him. When he'd worked up the courage, he peered into the street to see the Russians crossing with their backs to his building. The tanks followed close behind. Blaz glanced across to Koby, who nodded. Wilhelm and the second squad's heavy weapons man fired almost simultaneously, both their rockets slamming into the same tank. Fire spilled out, as the warheads had hit the more lightly armored roof. The Russians turned around to be met with bullets from four directions. Dozens were mowed down immediately. One boy threw a grenade into the panicking Russian formation, killing even more. Blaz hit his first target, then cocked his rifle with speed and felled another. The second tank fired its machine gun blindly into one building, desperately hoping to hit its attackers. Wilhelm fired again, knocking out the tank's treads. But its cannon was still operational. The cannon elevated to fire on the second floor of one building. Then the second *Panzerschreck* fired again, piercing the hatch, and the interior of the tank burst into flames. Blaz kept his own focus on the frantic Russian infantry. He fired, hitting yet another Soviet. Only a few soldiers remained, yet they kept firing hopelessly at the well-covered German youths. Some sprinted to get into the buildings, but the men Koby had ordered to guard the stairs shot them down. With only the tanks as cover, and fire from all four sides, the soldiers were finished quickly. The teenagers kept their rifles trained on the bodies.

"Send a man down from all four buildings!" Koby yelled to everyone, "Check for survivors, but stay alert!"

Everyone looked to Blaz.

"All right," Blaz begrudgingly agreed.

Blaz, Koby, Jurgen, and the second squad's commander emerged from each building, guns raised. They went from body to body, finding none alive. With only a few to go, they finally found one breathing. Koby waved the other three off. He approached cautiously, then said something in Russian to the wounded soldier. The soldier responded by pulling a pistol, but bullets riddled him from the three Germans.

Koby, just saved by his comrades, thanked his squad mates and Simon, the other squad leader.

"Move out!" Simon called to the others, "Get their ammo."

"*Ja* sir."

While they gathered ammunition, one boy yelled out, "Soldiers incoming!"

Koby and Simon sprinted over to where the boy was pointing and raised their small binoculars.

"More Russians, more tanks," Koby said, turning to the squads.

"And they see us," Simon added, lowering his binoculars.

"*Scheiße*," Koby swore, "Then we better get out of here. Fall back to the church!"

Everyone sprinted down a street, out of the Russians' view. They cut through side streets, heading west. As they approached the lines, they slowed to a march. Less men were there than when they had left. Only three or four squads. Notably, all were SS soldiers. The *Wehrmacht* was heading west in quick fashion. Hundreds, likely thousands, were marching out of the town.

"What's happening?" Koby asked the head SS officer.

"We're mounting a last defense here."

"Is this all we have?"

"These are the only men staying. The *Wehrmacht* is withdrawing," the officer said, and pointed to hundreds of soldiers marching west, tanks, horses, and trucks as well.

"Should we leave with them?" Koby asked the officer, with fake naivete.

The officer did not answer for quite some time.

"You should, son," the officer finally admitted, not looking Koby's way.

"That's what I thought," Koby nodded, "You should come with us."

The officer turned his head with uncanny speed to Koby. He frowned at the young sergeant, "We can't."

"Why not?"

"The SS will not retreat. We will destroy them all."

"*Nein, nein, nein, nein, nein,*" Koby shook his head. It was unquestionably disrespectful, but Koby didn't seem to care. "You'll be of more use if you retreat now. This position is vulnerable. You will have to defend from every way. Do you really think you'll hold out for more than ten minutes? You will all be killed! Think of your family! Think of all your men's families!"

The officer looked down, clearly thinking about all the widows and orphans a decision like this could create. Then he turned to the other SS soldiers, "We are pulling out, live to fight another day. We will bring down more in the future."

Koby smiled. Blaz gave him a pat on the back. The SS soldiers obeyed the officer without any question. Koby formed up behind them, as they marched out of the city. Heading west.

Unbreakable Spirit

October 7, 1943

The marching was long and brutal. For two straight days, the *Wehrmacht*, SS, and *Wehrmacht* youth marched, taking no breaks, even to sleep. They knew any delay could cost them if the Russians were in pursuit. The marches were uneventful, with soldiers simply conversing amongst their close comrades, but at one point, in the dark, rainy Russian evening, the *Wehrmacht* soldiers began singing, which each class of soldiers, the Hitler Youth and SS responded to by singing their own songs: *SS Marschiert* and *Es Zittern die Morschen Knochen*.

By afternoon on Thursday, morale was low. The SS commander and *Wehrmacht* commanders argued intensely, during a quick halt for water. The boys didn't know nor really care what the argument was about. They scarcely knew why they'd stopped. They were certain they would meet with a German force soon.

"I'm exhausted," Ivo complained to Blaz, "No breaks for two days, up until now."

"Chin up! We had some fun times trading songs," Blaz laughed.

"*Ja*," Ivo said, "And the SS sang a really creepy one."

"It's the SS," Blaz reasoned, "That's they're thing. I'm glad they're on our side."

"*Ja, ja*," Ivo laughed, "They've got some tough bastards in that bunch."

"But then you have your *Herr* Schlusser's."

"Then you've got him. But he's probably a tough bastard too."

Back in Line

October 8, 1943

By the end of the third day, they'd reached German lines. The Germans were defending on the edge of a forest, in thinning lines of trees. They were entrenched, with MG nests and camouflaged tanks. The SS soldiers split off while the *Wehrmacht* remained all together. Their commander contacted a general to receive new orders. But for now, they would be able to rest and recover for several days. The soldiers gathered behind the entrenchments to rest.

"Why did you tell that commander to retreat?" Simon asked Koby, curiously. A *Wehrmacht* soldier leaned against a tree nearby, listening in. The young squads spread out. Koby, Simon, Hans, Blaz, and Jurgen were in one group.

"What? The SS commander?" Koby responded with surprise, as it had happened three days ago, "Oh, well, from a tactical standpoint, the city was lost. If you can retreat and regroup, you should. That's thirty more comrades still alive now."

"Right," Simon nodded, knowing there was more to Koby's actions than simply that, but he let it go.

"Cigarette?" the soldier offered the boys.

"Sure," Simon said, taking one. Koby waved him off, but Hans darted over to get one.

"Is there a point when you can't retreat?" Simon asked, after the man had lit his cigarette.

"When you have orders to hold a position, by someone who knows more than you about the situation."

"We did have orders," the soldier reminded Koby.

"Björn, we talked to another officer. They'd recently been given permission to retreat," Simon said.

"*Oh, gut.*"

"How many do you think you killed?" Hans asked Blaz and Björn, leaving the young officers to their discussion.

"In the last few weeks?" Blaz asked.

"*Ja.*"

Hans answered his own question, as he blew a whisp of smoke, "I think three at the intersection and seven on the edge of the town."

"I didn't count," Björn said. Blaz nodded in agreement.

"*Du?*" Hans said to Jurgen, "You?"

"Four at the intersection, and six on the edge of town," Jurgen answered then continued, "These Russians don't seem to care how many men they lose, at all. It was scary, being shot at and this," he pointed to his scarred face, "But the Russians don't fight with cleverness. They're blunt and brutal. They just ran their men across a minefield. It's insane."

"In response to that," Hans began, then paused and looked up. Blaz smirked at Hans' mental break. Hans looked back down, and continued, "We can assume they've lost their best men, so they're using whoever they can. They have a hell of a lot of manpower."

Klara Hertz

October 13, 1943

"Sergeant... Hertz?" a uniformed man asked, though he was no soldier.

"*Ja*, that's me," Koby said quickly, standing up and raising a hand.

"Letters for your squad," the man said, and handed Koby several letters.

"*Danke, danke,*" Koby said, and passed the letters to whom they were addressed.

No one opened their letters with the same enthusiasm they used to. Blaz opened the letter from his father hesitantly. Seemed there was a better chance of bad news than good by now. *Please be okay, please be okay.*

He unfolded the letter to see his father's handwriting. He sighed in relief at this.

Liebe Blaz,
I am glad to hear your squad is out of harm's way now. It's comforting to know that you are away from the front lines. I pray that you are kept away from the front for the rest of the war.

Blaz gulped.

Your little brother, Erwin Siegfried Senft was born! I'm sure Cheryl wrote you months ago, I just wanted to make sure. Things are going well enough in France for now. I've mainly been on patrol for most of the time. I long for the chance to see you again son, and to see how much you've grown up. I want to speak to you in person. Three years is a lot of time to catch up on. Keep your friends close. Stay strong, son. Gott mit uns. Heil Hitler.
Mit Liebe, Ottoway Senft

Blaz smiled at the ending. But how could he respond to this? He felt exactly how his father did. They were in danger now, and he didn't need his father to have to worry about it.

"Blaz! I'm a brother now!" Koby said with an odd excitement, excitement Blaz hadn't ever seen from Koby.

"Well? Boy or girl?"

"A girl! Her name is Klara Traudl Hertz. What a wonderful name!" Koby said, his voice rising higher than usual.

Blaz patted Koby's shoulder, "Congratulations. You excited to see her or what?"

"Couldn't be more excited!"

"Looks like nothing but good news this time," Blaz added, looking across at the relief on everyone's faces.

"*Gott sei Dank,*" Koby sighed, "So many people have died already."

October 21, 1943

The boys fell in line behind the *Wehrmacht* soldiers. Orders had been given, they were to march southeast, away from Leningrad. Their last city had been further to the north, closer to Leningrad. Thousands of additional men joined their original force to hold the front lines. It would be a wide front, and more soldiers had arrived to operate all the artillery needed. The march would be for several days in the brisk October air, but it had been done before.

The Storm is Unleashed

October 27, 1943

When they arrived at the front, the squad was sent to, once again, man the artillery. There were five artillery pieces for twenty-two boys to man, so several would be available to guard their position. Koby and Simon ordered Ivo and another sniper named Oskar, to stay behind a line of sandbags that faced the Soviet lines. Five other boys defended from behind the wall of sandbags including Jurgen and Tristan. The terrain of the area was so flat, they could see the Russian lines though they were miles away. Only the occasional tree or remains of a farmstead provided any cover. Their artillery lay on flat ground, by the dirt road that ran throughout the German lines.

November 4, 1943

The storm had been building. Every day the Russians could be heard and seen approaching. Finally, they broke through. Russian artillery was now in range of the German lines.

"*Ja* sir! Understood!" Koby shouted as the artillery of both his men and the Russians in the distance fired away.

"What's the word?" Simon shouted.

"He told us we'll have to move out soon. There are some trucks coming to haul away the artillery."

"We are retreating?" Simon asked, arching an eyebrow, not wanting to fall back again.

"*Ja*," Koby answered with irritation at the other sergeant's tone, "We're retreating. I suppose that would be the term. Now we need to lower the wheels on the artillery so-"

"Got it, got it," Simon interrupted, sensing Koby's irritation, "Everyone! Don't fire another shot! Get the artillery ready for evacuation!"

Blaz, Jarman, and Jaye set to work, removing all but one restriction on the wheels. They would remove that when the trucks arrived.

"What now?" Jarman hollered to Koby.

"Wait for the trucks!"

They knelt behind the sandbags.

"Look at all that smoke!" Blaz said aloud.

"I hope it's Russian smoke," Ivo remarked sullenly.

"Trucks are here!"

Five dark green trucks, with covered backs for troops came to a halt next to the artillery.

"Get the artillery hooked up!"

Jarman, Jurgen, Blaz, and Jaye bolted to an artillery piece and pushed with all their strength up the slight incline to the road. Once they'd gotten the artillery behind the second truck in the line, Jurgen latched it on securely.

"This one's-" Jurgen was drowned out by the boom of an explosion. The first truck went up in flames. Koby, Simon, Tristan and another boy, who'd been nearest to the truck, dove to the ground.

"*Panzers*!" Blaz pointed, shouting frantically, "Russian tanks! Due east, they're coming fast!"

"Get in the trucks!" the driver in the fourth truck yelled, "*Schnell!*"

The first remaining truck rumbled away, with its artillery in tow. The boys scrambled to the backs of the other three trucks. Blaz sprinted for the middle truck and vaulted in. Several boys were already inside of the truck including Jurgen, Ivo, and Jarman. Koby came around and leapt into the back.

He leaned out of the back and yelled as loud as he could to the driver, "That's every-" His voice cracked, and he cleared his throat, ignoring the glances, and repeated himself, "That's everyone!"

The trucks accelerated. Nobody seemed to realize the tanks could still hit them until the front tire exploded. The truck skidded forward, it's momentum carrying it only a few more meters. The leading truck continued driving. The truck behind it slammed on its brakes. The tanks were closing in, two had continued pursuit. The others had pursued another target. The man on the right side of the truck leapt out. He was an older man, with whitening hair appearing under his field cap.

"My s- Jakob is dead! Get to the other two trucks! I'm holding off these tanks!" he said with rage, climbing into the back of the truck as the German youths leapt out and sprinted for the only truck they could. The soldier emerged from the disabled truck, with a *Panzerschreck* in his hands and several rockets in a backpack. Koby, Jurgen, and Blaz were the last three to climb in and the truck screeched away, sending up dust into the air. Wilhelm and Jaye sat across from them. As they passed the soldier, Blaz leaned out and yelled, "Hurry! Get in!"

The man shook his head, and sprinted the opposite way of the truck, with his *Panzerschreck*. The Russian machine guns fired.

"Get down!" Koby yelled, as he and Jurgen yanked Blaz back into the truck and to its floor. Everyone hit the floor of the truck, some on top of others. Bullets tore through the covering of the truck, right where Blaz would've been.

"*Vielen Danke,*" Blaz stammered out a thank you.

"Don't mention it," Jurgen breathed. The truck sped up, but one tank gave chase. Its machine gun fired, while the cannon lowered to aim on the truck.

"*Scheiße*! Is Wilhelm here?" Jarman swore.

His question was answered as a *Panzerschreck* appeared next to him.

"Everyone stay down," Wilhelm ordered loudly, and aimed his weapon. Then lowered it, "*Verdämmt*, out of range."

The tank's cannon fired, and Wilhelm dropped. The shell tore through the roof of the truck, ripping away the canvas cover. The driver floored the gas, but the tank was still hot on their heels.

"We've got to detach the artillery before we can outrun it!" Jurgen shouted, "Wilhelm! Give me a shot! Hit the dust far in front of the tank."

Wilhelm didn't question Jurgen's odd order. He stood up and fired a rocket into the ground, as close as he could to the Russian tank. The earth exploded and hid the tank. Jurgen climbed to the outside of the truck, trying to reach the artillery's latch. The tank came roaring through the cloud of dust, while Jurgen held onto the back of the truck with one arm and reached to unlatch the artillery with the other. The truck went into a bend in the road. The tank fired again, missing by inches. Koby and Blaz held onto Jurgen's arm as he gave a desperate reach for the latch. The machine guns of the tank fired away, as it crept closer to the truck. The bullets missed to the sides and ricocheted off the artillery piece.

Jurgen lowered himself, out of Blaz and Koby's reach, then he unlatched the artillery and the truck was free of its weight. But the free space gave the machine gunner a clear target. The guns fired and found their mark. Jurgen's fell from the truck, his momentum spinning him backwards along the dusty road. Blaz's veins turned to ice. He saw Jurgen try to push himself up, but then collapse. Jarman appeared at the back of the truck, horror on his face. The Russian tank came to a halt in front of Jurgen, recognizing the truck would be impossible to catch without the artillery weighing it down. Blaz and Koby watched as the Soviet tank commander lifted the hatch, pulled a pistol, and fired a shot.

Blaz gasped and his jaw dropped. He put his head down to the truck's trunk. Koby stared, eyes unseeing as he slid down the wall.

But Jarman kept staring. As the tank grew smaller and smaller, and Jurgen's body became invisible, Jarman stared on. Grief and astonishment, then hatred flew across his face. His eyes narrowed, and he lowered his head slightly. He stared on until the tank had disappeared into the distance. Then he turned to see the German youths, all with equally dismal and angered expressions. Jarman took a seat on the floor of the truck, between Blaz and Koby. Blaz stared blankly, with both the desire to cry, to shout in rage, and shoot the next Russian he saw.

Ivo had tear stains on his face as they climbed out of the truck. Koby and Blaz's eyes were red. Wilhelm and Jaye were in shock. Jarman remained in the back of the truck. He tapped a foot on the floor, with his hands folded together. Blaz was about to say something to him, but Koby put a hand on Blaz's shoulder and shook his head. Blaz understood. They walked in silence to the back of the German encampments where their squad mates had gone to receive orders. The German positions were dug into the side of a forested hill, with more defenses at the base of the hill, which included machine guns, tanks, and artillery. Neither said a word. Both arrived to face their commander, stomped their right foot, and fell in line. Jarman arrived minutes later.

"I understand that Hertz's squad has lost a member," the *Wehrmacht* Major said, doing his best to show as much sympathy as possible, "I'm very sorry to hear that, we will make sure he didn't die in vain. Concerning your squad, I will send for another man immediately, but it may be quite some time before anyone arrives, if ever."

Koby put a straightened hand on his forehead, formally saluting the officer.

"Moving on," the Major continued, "The *Führer* has ordered we hold this line until month's end at least. You boys will be on the artillery. Should the Russians come too close for artillery to be effective, you boys will retreat immediately, on foot to our reserve lines, about two kilometers due west. Simon Marquardt, your squad will be positioned on the artillery to the south. Koby Hertz, to the north."

"*Ja* sir," Koby and Simon nodded.

Koby led the remaining squad members north, through trees and occasional stretches of plains. On their march, they passed German tanks and machine guns. The march was done, once again, in silence. Jarman trailed behind the others.

Familiar Death

November 9, 1943

The German lines were unchallenged for days. They remained quiet for much of the next week, only occasionally starting a conversation.

Jarman sat in the grass with his knees almost in his face, Koby and Blaz beside him. Finally, he spoke, "I can't believe he's gone. I never got to say a last goodbye."

Blaz didn't know what to say, he couldn't believe it either. There was no way to make anyone feel better about the fact Jurgen was dead, or the fact that he'd been shot without mercy. "War doesn't give you a chance for last words or farewells," Blaz told Jarman, "If you get them, you're lucky."

"He would've had great last words," Jarman said in respect, "*Verdämmt*, he didn't have to do what he did."

"If he hadn't done that, there's a good chance we'd all be dead," Koby said dismally.

"At least he died a soldier's death," Jarman nodded, closing his eyes. No tears came though.

The Silence Will Shatter

December 24, 1943

The boys sat around a fire, each lost in their own thoughts.

"Feels good to be warm," Tristan said.

"It does," Hans agreed.

"*Frohe Weihnachten*, everyone," Koby had returned from speaking with a commander, "The officer gave me this," he said, holding up a chocolate bar.

"Well, that was nice of him. Where'd he get it?" Gunther asked.

"I don't know," Koby replied, "But I don't care either, we just have it."

"That's good with me," Ivo said.

Koby opened the bar and passed out a square for each of the boys. They all took their time, savoring the sweet taste.

"Wow, that was amazing," Ivo said when he'd finished.

"Tastes better when you haven't had it in, what, years?" Jaye concurred.

"Definitely years," Wilhelm nodded.

"Any news from the commander?" Blaz asked, worried for the news.

"*Ja*, I was hoping you wouldn't ask, then we could've enjoyed more of this night," Koby groaned.

"Sorry."

"It's okay, but the Russians, as we all can hear, have been getting closer. The very front lines have been beaten back. And," Koby breathed in with frustration, "It looks like the Russians are going to attack on Christmas morning, before dawn. Not sure exactly, but our scouts have done a good job. Could be in a few hours."

"Sons of bitches," Wilhelm swore.

"That's so low," Blaz shook his head in disgust, "On Christmas night."

"The Russians don't care about that," Hans said bitterly, "They want to make a bunch of widows on Christmas."

"I'm going to return that favor," Jarman claimed.

Russian Beasts

December 25, 1943

The Russians moved to attack indeed. In the peacefulness of Christmas night, they crept onto the German lines. The prepared Germans, with spotlights shining, saw them as they advanced through fields toward the defenses in the hills. Machine gun fire, tanks and artillery barraged the Russian infantry. But still they came.

"Fire again!" Jarman yelled to Blaz. The artillery fired high into the air towards the Russian advance. They'd lowered their artillery to fire directly at the Russian tanks and troops. Blaz fired the massive gun, it's impact making an equally massive crater that they scarcely saw from the spotlight.

"Load her!" Blaz yelled. Jarman lifted another shell into the artillery piece. Blaz fired for a Russian tank this time, though it was quite hard to do this in the dark. The open Russian country was rich in moon and starlight though. The incredible speed of the artillery shell pierced the tank's armor, and fire now also lit the snow-covered field.

"*Wunderbar*! Concentrate fire at the rear of their attack now!" Koby shouted as loud as he could, "Our front is holding their front at bay, let's cut off the reinforcements."

Jarman and Blaz both began adjusting the artillery, aiming further east into the field. "Hold it!" Jarman yelled to Blaz over the constant firing below them from both sides, "Russians at the rear! They're breaking off and trying a pincer movement, nearer to us. Readjust to aim that way."

Once the artillery was in optimum position to stop the pincer movement, Blaz returned to the operating side of the artillery piece.

"*Feuer*!" Jarman gave him the go ahead.

Another shell flew from the artillery barrel, into the darkness, toward the Russians.

"Attack has been stalled," Koby informed the group as he observed the Russian movement in the distance through his binoculars, "The Reds are regrouping."

"*Frohe Weihnachten, verrückt Biesten,*" Jarman growled. Merry Christmas, you mad beasts.

Russian prisoners were being marched off the former battlefield toward the back lines by German soldiers.

"Taking prisoners," Koby grumbled.

"It is Christmas," Blaz pointed out, surprising Koby, as Blaz saw him jump a bit.

"*Ja*, it is. But look what they gave us for Christmas," Koby scowled, handing Blaz the binoculars, and pointing toward the German machine guns at the base of the next hill. Blaz looked through the binoculars to see men carrying away the bodies of German soldiers, some horribly disfigured from grenades and headshots. Blaz closed his eyes at seeing one man who'd been ripped in half by some explosive and was still alive and crawling on the ground toward the medics, his blood and guts staining the snow. He handed Koby the binoculars.

"You see it?" Koby asked.

Blaz nodded, stupefied by the gore. He squatted down and put his hands on his head. Then he got down on all fours. He felt an upward surge in his stomach and started vomiting, several times into the snow.

"Worse things than that will happen if we don't resist the Reds," Koby said when Blaz began to recover, "Now come on, six of us need to help away the wounded at the base of our hill."

Koby led Blaz and four others to the bottom of the hill, where medical trucks waited. He gave no further orders, they simply helped away the wounded men. Blaz and Jaye lifted one man up and supported him on their shoulders. His friend said he'd been blinded by a grenade.

When walking away with him, a distant gunshot went off. The man reacted immediately and began groping wildly, snagging Blaz by the neck. Blaz tried to push away the man's hands, but they were the size of baseball mitts and the man as strong as a bear.

"Where are they? Where are they?!" the soldier yelled, strangling Blaz. Jaye tried to pull him off, but he was no match for a fully-grown man. The soldier only tightened his grip on Blaz.

"Bastian! Bastian!" a soldier shouted and ran over to stop his comrade. He brought the blinded man into a chokehold, restraining him while he swung uncontrollably, releasing Blaz from his grip. Blaz gasped for air, coughing several times after breathing in. Jaye helped Blaz to his feet and he shook his head when he stood up. He glanced over his shoulder to see the man finally calming down.

Russian beasts, he thought.

Reason for Hope

December 29, 1943

"*Los, los, los!*" Koby shouted. The boys sprinted down the hill, this time away from the front lines. Koby waited until everyone was in front of him, then he followed behind. Jarman led the group away from the collapsing German lines. They had been ordered to leave by a *Wehrmacht* lieutenant, who had arrived with horses to haul away the artillery. The boys jogged through the snow, raising their legs high to make it through the thick barrier. Dark clouds hung overhead, threatening to drop more onto the already covered ground. German soldiers ran to the north and south of the boys, all in retreat to the west. German tanks sped by them and horses pulling artillery trotted briskly alongside the men. Men would hitch rides on top of tanks when they got close.

"*Russisch Flugzeug!*" Koby yelled from behind, "Russian airplane! Due south!"

A fighter plane came screeching over the boys, firing its machine guns on the tank to the boys' north. The Tiger I, rotated its cannon to the north were the plane was heading. Bullets ricocheted from the tank's armor, the men hitching rides having already leapt off. Blaz kept running as fast as he could but turned his head to see the fighter pass only meters from the tank then pulling up. The tank's cannon fired, and, much to Blaz's surprise and delight, it hit the airplane, ripping its left wing off. The plane spiraled to the ground onto its belly, not exploding, but plowing through the snow for hundreds of meters.

"What a shot!" Ivo exclaimed, quite impressed.

"Keep focus ahead!" Koby yelled.

The boys ran their hearts out until they arrived at a small farming village. A German detachment was waiting for the retreating men.

"Hold up here!" an officer told all who entered the village, "My *Hauptmann* is contacting command for further orders. If the Russians near this town, we will continue to fall back."

The boys climbed onto a parked tank to rest. They watched more men, horses, trucks, and an occasional tank enter the little square. Hundreds of men crowded into the village.

"Are those our fighters?" Jaye pointed to the west.

The boys all looked in the direction Jaye pointed. Koby used his binoculars to get a better view. "Those are ours. Three Messerschmitt BF-109s. Flying low, looks like they're going to hit the Red Army."

"There's some Soviet fighters coming too," Wilhelm reported. Several Russian fighters had appeared on the horizon. They were flying low, below the clouds. Koby turned to face the Soviet fighters, gazing through his binoculars at them. By now most of the *Wehrmacht* soldiers, both *Heer* and *Luftwaffe* personnel in the small town were watching the skies.

"Looks like eighteen Soviet fighters," Koby said, turning to observe the German fighters again, "*Scheiße*, we've only got three, *nein*, two fighters. Where'd the other one go?" he said aloud, "I could've sworn I saw three."

The fighters were about to engage. The Germans widened their two-plane formation, which the Soviets proceeded to copy with their eighteen fighters. But before any of the Soviets fired, bullets came raining from the clouds, hitting two Soviet aircraft. The engines of those planes exploded, and they plummeted to the ground hundreds of meters outside the village.

The two German fighters strafed through the Soviet formation, downing two more.

"What just happened?" Wilhelm shouted. Several others echoed his astonishment. Another Soviet plane exploded, it's attacker invisible from the ground. And presumably from the air as well, because the Soviets broke formation and scattered. The two German fighters circled around and rallied to their leader who came soaring out of the clouds. The Soviet planes spread out across the sky, some heading for the village.

"Take cover!" an officer yelled. The German soldiers ran for trees, vehicles, and buildings. The boys leapt off the tank and crouched behind it. Four Soviet fighters hammered the village with machine gun fire. Bullets hit the center of the village, sending snow into the air. Some bullets hit the boys' tank, which were deflected easily by its armor.

"*Verdämmt!*" Hans yelled, "If our fighters don't do something, we're going to be target practice for the Reds!"

The Soviet fighters zoomed over the village and began a gradual circle to turn around for another pass. The four Soviet planes didn't notice this and continued their second assault on the town. The boys scrambled for the other side of the tank, but four more Soviet fighters were coming from that side now.

"*Nein, nein,*" Koby said quietly, knowing they were in trouble. The leading German plane opened fire on the four fighters that had originally attacked the town. He downed one, then two, then three, and then four, all before they had a chance to even react or fire on the German ground troops.

"Son of a-" Blaz's voice trailed off in awe. The German ace didn't stop there, firing on the leading Soviet plane on the second front. The four fighters took evasive action, and the German pilot was forced to pick a target. He went after the leader. A quick loop and he was on the Soviet's tail. The German's machine gun fired. The Soviet fighter swerved to avoid the barrage. Two Soviet fighters now trailed the masterful German fighter and his wingmen. Blaz scanned the skies. All three German fighters remained. Nine of the original eighteen Soviets remained. The German pilot seemed to ignore his pursuers, even as a third one joined the chase. He remained focused on his prey. He released a second round of fire, and the Soviet plane fell from the sky, hitting the ground in a fiery explosion. The *Wehrmacht* was completely engrossed in the dogfighting.

Seven Soviets remained. Three Germans. The lead German set a wingman to skim along the ground, while the Soviet fighters stayed above, fearful of flying so close to the ground. They fired at the wingman, but he skillfully evaded their fire. The ace circled in the air, while the Soviets continued to pursue his wingman. He disappeared into the clouds once again. When he reappeared, he was right behind the Soviets. He fired on the nearest plane with pinpoint accuracy. His other wingman fired on the next plane, missing, but forcing the plane into the ace's line of fire. Another quick burst, another plane downed. The last two Soviet planes in the formation split in two separate directions but the wingmen destroyed one immediately. The other plane began climbing into the clouds. The German ace swerved his plane after him.

Both fighters disappeared into the clouds. Seconds later a Soviet plane came hurdling towards the ground right outside of the village. A parachute opened high above the doomed plane and floated towards the village. Several German soldiers cocked their weapons, waiting to capture, or kill, the ejected pilot. Now the German ace turned his attention to the last four fighters in hot pursuit of the first German wingman. The ace dove to attack the Soviets from the front, releasing a short spray of bullets that found their mark. The leading Soviet plane exploded, as its fuel tanks had been ruptured. The last three Soviet fighters slowed, then zeroed in on their comrade's killer. They fired their guns. He evaded their fire, and ascended. The Soviet fighters pursued. All four fighters disappeared into the clouds, the other German planes headed toward the Soviet lines to open fire on the moving Red army. The Soviets fell out of the clouds, one-by-one. The lead German pilot did a flyby over the town. The ejected Soviet pilot had surrendered, and now was shouting something in Russian. Koby listened carefully.

"What is he saying?" Gunther questioned Koby.

"He keeps repeating 'It's Rudorffer! It's Rudorffer!' Who's Rudorffer?"

"Oh, I heard the men at the training camp chatting about him," Ivo exclaimed, "He's a breakout ace of *Deutschland*. Last I heard he has over one hundred kills."

"What a soldier," Hans remarked.

"Whoever it was, he saved hundreds of lives," Koby smiled, throwing a salute in the direction the ace had flown.

1944: We Stand Now, Ready to Fight Against the Red Plague

Not Retreating, Regrouping

December 31, 1943- January 3, 1944

They were sent with one hundred and forty *Wehrmacht* soldiers, two Tiger Tanks, ten horses hauling artillery, and four trucks, two armored, two not, carrying food, ammunition, and gasoline in their covered backs. The commander kept the troops on a fast pace, allowing minimal breaks. For days, they marched, only stopping to sleep once. The soldiers were showing signs of exhaustion. Their strides grew shorter; their posture fell.

"Nearly there!" came the commander's voice as they marched in the late afternoon.

Ivo yawned then shook his head to wake himself back up.

"Tired?" Blaz asked, fighting to keep his own eyes open.

Ivo nodded with little energy. His eyes were only half open while he trudged on, "What does 'nearly there' mean?"

"*Drei Uhren!*" the commander shouted from the front. Apparently, other soldiers had wondered this as well, "Three hours!"

"*Das,*" Blaz grinned as Ivo rubbed his eyes furiously at this news.

"You think we can get a ride on the tank?" Ivo asked, sounding like he was asking Blaz to allow him to.

"You really want to be the only unwounded ones on the tanks?" Blaz asked.

"*Nein, nein, nein.*"

Blaz laughed and Ivo grinned.

Three hours later, by the light of the moon, they'd entered the town they would be defending. A small Russian town with only a few houses on the main street. The roads were dirt but were covered in snow. Three massive silos stood about one hundred meters outside of the town. A line of trees ran on each side of the road linking the town and silos.

The commanding *Wehrmacht* officer, a *Hauptmann*, called for an officer meeting with all squad leaders. Koby left, and the nine boys sat down and leaned against one of the houses to rest their exhausted legs. Soon, all of them had fallen asleep, ignoring the snow.

January 5, 1944

Blaz woke to the sound of a tank treading through the street in front of him. The sun was only just rising, and the sky was a spectacular watercolor of pink, red, orange, and yellow.

"Move the *Eisenfaust* tank over to the tree line! Right behind the trees, and camouflage it!" an officer yelled, "Have *Mutig Verteidiger* take the road into the town. In between the houses, it'll shield her from the sides. When the Soviets draw near we'll lay mines on the main road and the fields."

Blaz rubbed his eyes, with numb hands. He bent his fingers several times to get his blood flowing before picking up his rifle and stumbling to his feet. Koby, Jarman, Ivo, and Wilhelm were already awake and standing by their squad mates, waiting patiently for them to rise.

"How long did we sleep?"

"Something like eleven hours, I'm not sure," Koby answered.

"Lord, we don't have nights like that often," Blaz said, grateful for that rest, "And we have marches like that more often," he added with a grin.

"You said it," Koby agreed. They stood in silence for a while, admiring the sunrise.

"Oh, what were the squad leaders meeting about?"

Koby put a hand onto his metallic STG-44. It must've been cold. "Well," Koby began, "The commander showed us where we are on a map, and where the cities and towns nearest to us are, how many men those towns have and whatnot. We set up our communications, so we'll be warned if Russians are advancing. But from the sound of things, the Russians have stalled. We should be able to regroup here. The Russians won't reach this town I've been told. We should be able to mount a counterattack at the front soon."

"How are we going to mount a counterattack?"

"More armor and troops have been sent over here, from Norway and elsewhere. They've cooperated, and we need more troops. And with the Allies' advance on Rome slowing, we may receive troops from there as well," Koby told Blaz, but sounded skeptical himself.

"Where are we on the map?" Blaz continued to ask questions, "How far from the front?"

"We're between Smolensk and Minsk," Koby said, "Closer to Minsk, though we're a bit northeast of her. I think we are about two hundred kilometers from Smolensk. And the Russian front is a few dozen kilometers west of there."

"Okay."

"We won't be on leave until the war is won," Koby informed Blaz.

"Oh," Blaz said with disappointment, but not surprise. He knew they were needed, "At least we know our siblings were both born safely. That's good enough for now."

Koby nodded solemnly, "I want to see her so badly."

"Klara?"

"*Ja*. I mean, I will keep fighting until the end, don't get me wrong, the Reds must be beaten back and defeated, they must be destroyed, they must," Koby repeated himself, with newfound contempt for the Red army after Jurgen's death and the attack on Christmas, "But, you know, I want to meet her. See my little sister. I want to see her grow up."

"I want to see Erwin too, but we have to beat back the Reds. Then we can triumphantly return home," Blaz envisioned aloud.

"It'll be great," Koby pretended to fantasize. He couldn't stop the shadow from crossing his face before Blaz saw though.

Barbarian Invaders, We'll Swiftly Strike Down

February 1, 1944

Alexander and Lukov lay side-by-side in the snow. Lukov held a sniper rifle in his hands. Alexander held binoculars in his. Both had pistols holstered at their waists. They were on high ground next to a dirt road, covered in snow. The sun hung low in the sky.

Alexander was fourteen now. He was several inches taller at five-foot-two. He was still scrawny, but his eyes weren't so sunken, his arms weren't sticks anymore. And he hadn't been sick since when he had nearly died of what Vladimir diagnosed as pneumonia.

"Make sure you don't hit the truck," Alexander whispered nervously, "That's what Vladimir needs."

"I know Xander."

"Remember to get the officer."

"I know."

Lukov exhaled out of his nose.

"Why does your father let you do it?"

"He was a soldier in the Second Patriotic War. I think he always imagined I would become a soldier like him. I always wanted to. The war came early though." Alexander looked down the road, "Vehicles! Three of them!"

Lukov aimed his weapon to the west. He set his sights on the first car's tire.

"Remember, first car."

"Hush."

The vehicles approached. Two black cars and one armored, camouflaged truck filled with the ammunition and medical supplies they wanted for partisans elsewhere. Lukov picked up some snow and shoved it in his mouth so his breath wouldn't give away his position. Alexander did the same out of curiosity. Lukov's finger rested on the trigger as the cars drove into range. But he waited. They needed to be closer. Vladimir needed to be where they would halt. The cars were nearly right below them. Alexander shook excitedly. Lukov fired. The lead car's tire exploded and it skidded to a halt. Vladimir and the other Russians fired their guns into the cars and truck. Lukov saw some bodies go limp, but SS soldiers leapt out of the back of the covered truck and took cover on the side facing Lukov. Some sprinted for trees below Lukov and Alexander. The officer himself took cover behind his car, drawing his pistol. Lukov took aim at the officer. As he was about to fire, the officer's guard pointed up at him and moved in front of the officer. The shot hit the guard instead. The officer immediately grabbed the fallen soldier's rifle and raised it toward Lukov's perch. Alexander ducked. Lukov stayed calm and pulled the trigger. His shot was good, and his bullet tore through the officer's chest. Vladimir bolted toward the truck, machine gun loaded. As an SS man emerged to meet him, Lukov fired, bringing the soldier down. Vladimir leapt up into the truck, his wife leaping in after him. The couple wasted no time, and the truck roared away. The SS soldiers and three other partisans were now exposed. But the German machine guns were better than the rifles. Alexander gasped as their three comrades, who'd they'd fought beside for the past year and a half, fell.

Lukov foolishly fired a shot, hoping to save one of his comrades. Instead, the SS soldiers all spun to face him. They spread out and charged towards them through the forest. Lukov put a hand on Alexander's shoulder and pulled him away, "Let's go, Xander. Hurry!"

Alexander and Lukov sprinted away with the SS in pursuit as the sun set below the horizon.

They arrived back at the cabin as the sun disappeared and the night sky was born. The SS was in pursuit for all they still knew. Lukov banged on the door until the old woman answered.

"What happened?" she asked, ushering them inside.

"We got the officer, Vladimir and Maria got the supplies, we lost three," Lukov quickly reported, "The SS is hunting us right now. We lost them in the snow, but they could be here at any moment."

"Lukov, under the floor," the old woman ordered, "Now!"

"What about Xander?" Lukov asked as he pulled away the bear rug.

"If they find you hiding, it's best he isn't with you," the old man replied, "He'll be our grandson. Change out of those clothes Xander."

Alexander yanked off his coat and pulled down his pants. He ran them over to a home-carved wardrobe and scanned for clothes his size. The old man got a fire going. Lukov brought his weapons and Alexander's wet clothes into the basement. As soon as the old woman shut the hatch, there was a pounding on the front door.

"Good evening, sir," Lukov heard a voice say. It was a German, but he was speaking Russian, "We have tracked two partisans to your home. Would you mind if we came in?"

"Of course not. Come in, please," the old man said, "It's really coming down out there, isn't it?"

"Indeed," the soldier replied. By the sounds above, Lukov knew at least three men had come in. Maybe more.

"Are you hungry?" the old man asked, "We have some bread right out of the oven. Nice and warm."

"Um," the SS soldier mumbled awkwardly. Lukov almost laughed but kept quiet. The SS man finally answered, "Sure." Lukov could tell they were above him now. He heard the clanking of guns as they sat down on the couches. One soldier was tapping his foot on the floor.

"*Danke,*" one soldier said. Then the original soldier spoke again, "You are old... I assume any partisans would force their way into this house."

"They could," the old man said, "But no one came here if you're wondering."

"Who is this young man, then?"

"Our grandson."

"Where's the boy's parents?" the soldier asked.

"His father died fighting years ago. His mother died in the winter of forty-one."

"Boy, come here."

Lukov heard Alexander shuffle over. It also sounded as if a soldier had stood up, from the clanking of a gun.

"How old are you, son?"

"Fourteen, sir."

"Are these your grandparents?"

"Yes."

"What's your name?"

"Alexander."

"Your hair feels wet."

"I was out chopping up some of our firewood."

"You think we're stupid?" the soldier asked, his tone shifting.

"No..." Alexander said. Lukov heard something or someone be slammed to the floor.

"Foot's the right size, he's one of them," the soldier said, "All right boy, where's your friend?"

"We split up," Alexander shot off. The soldier punched the boy. His head slammed into the ground. Lukov heard a nervous whimper from the fourteen-year-old.

"Where is he?" the soldier repeated. Alexander gave no reply. Lukov heard a weapon cock. Several sounds of feet moving away from above Lukov.

"Answer me boy!"

Another thud.

"Don't! He's only fourteen," the old man begged.

"And he shot a boy of seventeen-years-old back there, age matters not," the soldier growled. Lukov began climbing the ladder, sniper in hand. He stayed right below the hatch, waiting for another exchange of words. He heard a gun being cocked.

"Please don't kill me!" Alexander cried.

"Where is the other?!" the soldier roared. Lukov slowly opened the hatch, getting a hand on the bear rug.

"H-he and I-" Alexander stammered, "W-we-"

Lukov readied himself.

"We split up," Alexander finally said.

The SS soldier scowled and raised his gun.

Lukov sprung from the hatch, throwing the bear rug off. One soldier spun around. Lukov raised his weapon and fired. He cut down two men with one bullet, stopping the execution. The other two soldiers fired, one shooting the old man, the other shooting the old woman then they dove behind the wooden couch and overturned it. Alexander scrambled for the door of the home as the two soldiers turned on him. One fired as he closed the door. Lukov fired into the soldier's back. Then he fired another shot into the couch. Seconds passed. He kept his gun aimed on the couch and crept towards it. Right as the barrel of his gun came over the overturned couch, a bloody hand grabbed its end. Lukov was yanked over the couch, onto a wounded soldier. The soldier took a stab at his chest, which he narrowly dodged. The German kicked Lukov off himself. The two men readied themselves. Lukov raised his fists. The SS soldier adjusted his chain dagger in his right hand and charged at his enemy, swinging his dagger across Lukov's neck. The Soviet moved back. The soldier stabbed at Lukov's head. The Russian Jew grabbed the SS soldier's wrist. He swung his fist at the soldier's head. The SS man blocked the blow and gripped Lukov's fist. The two were staring right into each other's eyes as they wrestled back and forth. Lukov narrowed his green eyes and glared into the soldier's blue eyes. The SS soldier began losing ground to the Soviet Jew. At that moment, Lukov realized he was fighting a boy. Not yet eighteen. A young SS soldier. He briefly lightened his pressure on the young man. The soldier made him regret this. He sent a head butt into Lukov's forehead, the tip of his helmet hitting the Soviet. Lukov was knocked to the ground. The soldier threw the knife. It was a poor throw, missing Lukov completely. The SS soldier seemed shocked he had missed. Lukov sprung to his feet and slammed the boy to the ground. He tried to block Lukov's punches, but to no avail. Lukov finally beat the soldier until he couldn't put up any resistance. His nose was bleeding, jaw broken, and teeth were knocked out. Lukov stood up and walked over to his rifle. He picked it up and walked over to the enemy soldier. The boy's pleading eyes did not move him. He fired.

The Soviet dropped his rifle and wandered over to the door. Lukov went to the door. When he opened it, Alexander was standing outside, shivering. Lukov wrapped his arm around Alexander and they walked back into the home. A week later, the Red Army arrived. Lukov and Alexander marched off with them. Forward, to the west.

Competition

March 6, 1944

"Fifty-one! Fifty-two!" a soldier counted the last eight boys in the competition. The soldiers had been holding a push-up tournament that day, and organized it well, with two brackets; a young men's bracket and a youth bracket for the three teenager squads, two of which were seventeen and eighteen-year-olds. All were required to do push-ups at the count of a soldier. All at the same time. And they'd already faced down multiple opponents already. Blaz cheered on Koby, Tristan, and Jarman along with the rest of his squad. The seventeen-year-olds did the same for their friend.

"Sixty! Sixty-one!"

Koby gritted his teeth while he lifted himself up for his fifty-first in this round. Tristan kept cranking them out, seemingly with ease. The other two competitors continued in the muddy street.

"Sixty-two!"

Koby's left leg shook involuntarily, as he came down then up for another. But still he stayed in.

"Sixty-three!" the soldier paused, making the four competitions support themselves for several seconds to see if anyone would collapse. None did.

"C'mon Koby," Ivo whispered so only Blaz and Hans, the two boys next to him, could hear.

"Sixty-four! Sixty-five! Sixty-six!"

Somehow, Koby remained up. The seventeen-year-old began to show signs of weakness. The one facing Jarman.

"He's getting tired!" Blaz yelled to Ivo, "Our squad might have the winner!"

The four competitors pushed on, into the seventies then eighties. Koby was now breathing with difficulty every push-up. But Tristan was also getting tired.

"Eight-three!"

Jarman unexpectedly collapsed.

"Well, he'd already had the toughest competition," Ivo said, giving Jarman an excuse.

"*Ja*, he opened with one-hundred and nine against Wilhelm, then ninety, eighty-seven and now that," Blaz agreed with Ivo's explanation.

"Pretty good," Hans remarked.

"Eighty-four!"

Jarman's opponent completed a final push-up to claim victory over Koby's corporal. He stood up, shook his head in pain, then his arms appeared to go limp. He shook them to try to revive feeling.

"Eighty-five!"

"Go down already!" Tristan yelled at Koby in pain. A quick smile flashed on Koby's face but was replaced by painfully gritted teeth in moments.

"Eighty-six! Eighty-seven! Eighty-eight! Eighty-nine!"

Tristan's arms were shaking now with every push-up. Koby breathed violently through his nose and completed the push-up. The counter shook his head in astonishment.

"Ninety!"

Tristan finally went down with a groan of pain.

"Ninety-one!"

Koby lowered down, both legs quivering uncontrollably. He gritted his teeth, and suddenly shot himself back up to complete the push-up, then he immediately collapsed.

"*Ja!*" Koby said, breathlessly, raising a fist in the air from the ground. Blaz and Ivo jogged over to help Koby up.

"I got it, I got it," Koby said from the ground, "I feel terrible."

"Sit down for a second," Ivo advised, "You get fifteen minutes to the final."

"God, please *nein*," Koby moaned, not yet standing up.

Blaz and Ivo held in laughs for a moment.

"No laughing," Koby said with his face in the dirt.

"Sorry," Blaz apologized. *Shouldn't laugh at someone who's better than you.*

"How'd you do it?" Ivo asked, "You were the first one to start struggling."

"I don't, I don't know, I just fought through the pain."

"Koby, good match," Tristan said holding out a hand.

Koby lifted his arm to shake Tristan's hand, "I got you back."

"We're even now," Tristan nodded.

"What'll be the tiebreaker?" Koby asked.

"I don't know, I guess we'll have to wait and see."

"*Bist du bereit?*" the soldier counting off push-ups shouted to Koby and the eighteen-year-old, "Are you ready?"

"*Bereit,*" they both answered, still fighting pain from the last round.

"*Gut,* shake hands and drop to the ground."

Koby and the young soldier shook hands and stooped to the ground into push-up positions. They both glanced to the counter and nodded. The soldier began counting.

"*Ein! Zwei! Drei! Vier! Fünf!*"

The two boys easily started out. Their squads cheered them on wildly. There was no sign of wear until they hit the fifties. Then the recent round began to come back to haunt them. Koby's left leg shook again. He closed his eyes tight and gritted his teeth as he continued his push-ups. The eighteen-year-old looked exhausted, but he hid it better than Koby.

"Sixty!"

Koby's leg shook violently while he performed his sixtieth.

"He looks in pain," Ivo whispered.

"You think?"

"Sixty-three! Sixty-four!"

Koby breathed in loudly through his nose but stayed up. His opponent completed them with little signs of weakening.

"Sixty-five!"

"*Nein, nein, nein,*" Blaz heard Koby mutter as he performed yet another.

"Sixty-six! Sixty-seven!"

"Come on, come on," Ivo said so that Koby could hear.

"Sixty-eight! Sixty-nine! Seventy!"

Koby dropped, almost to the ground, but somehow regained his stance. His opponent kept going, red in the face. He took a deep breath and continued.

"Seventy-three! Seventy-four!"

Both competitors collapsed at the same time. They moaned in pain, breathing in to replenish themselves.

"Can't have a draw," the counter declared, "Back up! From seventy-five!"

Koby and the other young soldier raised themselves back up, begrudgingly.

"Seventy-five! Seventy-six! Seventy-seven!"

Both were unwilling to lose now, and the push-up count mounted ever higher.

"One-twenty! One-twenty-one!"

Finally, Koby collapsed in complete exhaustion. His competitor finished one more push-up to claim victory. Koby's squad mates rushed over to applaud his performance nonetheless.

"How did you do it?" Ivo asked in admiration.

"I didn't want to lose," Koby breathed with his eyes closed, and let his arms hang loosely, "But sometimes you just can't win, I guess."

"Regardless, that was quite the fight," Tristan complimented him.

Jarman added to the compliment, saying, "No one saw one hundred and twenty coming."

Koby smiled a brief and tired smile, "*Ja*, I guess the littler guys can't always get that win over the big guys though."

"Next time?" Hans grinned.

Koby raised his eyebrows and gritted his teeth, "Maybe."

Schlusser on Leave

March 21, 1944

The sun was out in full force on this spring afternoon. Everything had a silver lining. Schlusser breathed, savoring each breath of air that did not smell of death, smoke, and human waste.

In his black SS uniform and peaked cap, he strode down the streets of his beloved hometown, Dresden. Beautiful architecture around every corner, fountains in every square, interconnected housing like in Seelow, and smiling faces everywhere he walked. Whether they were women at work, Hitler Youths coming home from training, younger children at play, a mother with her child, or an occasional man at work, all wore smiles. Schlusser would've loved to have stopped and chatted, but he was eager to see the love of his life and their newborn child. He quickened his pace at the thought of them. Every step brought him closer to the woman he'd met just over four years ago, when he'd gone to Seelow to instruct. Now she waited for him, with their young child. In his right hand, he held a white flower he had just bought. His gun was slung over his shoulder. His hair was not neat, but at least it was clean. He'd had the opportunity to wash up but had missed the chance to shave.

Schlusser turned onto his street. A soccer ball rolled to his feet. He stopped it with ease. Three pairs of eyes were staring at him when he looked up. One of the children grinned widely and scampered over to the SS officer.

"Welcome back *Herr* Schlusser," the boy smiled.

"Good to be back, Adi," Schlusser said, running a hand through the boy's mop of blond hair. The little boy giggled before reclaiming the soccer ball and dribbling back to his waiting friends.

"Hi *Herr* Schlusser!" they called.

"Hello Tybalt, hello Heinz!" Schlusser waved to the brunette and ginger child.

Schlusser took another deep breath as he came into view of his door. He removed his peaked cap as he drew nearer. He stopped at the front of the door. He raised his fist to knock but paused. This was the moment. What was he waiting for? He tugged at his collar and took another deep breath. Then he knocked. Five seconds passed. Schlusser waited impatiently, involuntarily tapping a foot on the ground. Seconds later, the door opened.

"Reynald!" A lean, blond woman wearing an old blue and white dress leapt into Schlusser's arms. Schlusser dropped his cap but held onto the flower. He embraced his wife, hugging and rocking her. Tears of joy streamed down both of their faces.

"Margot," Schlusser whispered, "I've missed you, darling."

"I've missed you too, Reynald," his wife whispered back.

The two held each other for several minutes before they both let go. Reynald retrieved his cap by scooping it up on the edge of his boot and kicking it up to himself. He extended his right arm, offering the flower to his wife. She took it and wrapped her other arm around her husband. The two shared a long kiss. Reynald wrapped his arm around his wife and she held him close as they headed inside.

Reynald immediately asked Margot, "So, where is the little one?"

"He's sleeping," Margot smiled, leading Reynald into the main room. A couch, a large bed, a stove, a water pump, and a radio atop a dresser, occupied floor space. Next to the bed there was a crib. Reynald set his gun and cap on the sofa and crept over with his wife. He peered inside to see his son sleeping peacefully. When he saw him, he had to wipe his eyes.

"What's his name?" Reynald asked Margot.

"Franz," Margot smiled, "Franz Adolf Schlusser."

Reynald beamed. "A good German name."

"Let's let him sleep," Margot said, "You'll have time talk to him later."

"I'll be here for two days, *ja*," Reynald said.

"What has it been like at the front, Reynald?" Margot asked. It was always a question she asked when they saw each other. He didn't blame her.

"Oh, darling," Reynald said, in an almost whiny voice, "I don't want to talk about that while I'm on leave."

"Of course," Margot nodded.

"What's been going on here?" Reynald asked, "Everyone looks so happy."

"No bombings here, Reynald," Margot said as they sat down on the couch. Reynald put his gun on the floor. "But Dresden is just a happy city."

"I know, we are," Reynald smiled, giving his wife a kiss on the cheek, "I hope I can come home for good soon."

"Do you think you will?"

Reynald shook his head. Margot's face fell.

"Don't worry, darling," Reynald said, "I'll come back once no one will disturb *Deutschland*. For now, let's enjoy this."

Reynald and Margot kissed each other before tumbling onto the bed.

Faith in the Führer

May 23, 1944

Blaz stood outside the headquarters with his canteen, waiting for Koby. They'd just returned from the fields on a warm, humid day. Koby had been ordered to report for an officer's meeting. Another soldier, in his late thirties or early forties was standing near Blaz and Tristan with a cigarette in hand, also waiting for his squad leader.

"Blaz, why are we losing now?" Tristan asked. Blaz now understood what Tristan meant when he had told him he said a lot of stupid things.

"I don't know," Blaz quickly answered, "Why would you ask that?"

"I'm worried I may never see my mother again," Tristan admitted, shakily, "Or my sisters."

Blaz didn't respond. He glanced at Tristan uneasily.

"Blaz, aren't you ready to go home? Aren't you done with this?"

Blaz turned his head quick, like a hawk, "Tristan, we can't go home. We have to fight. Why would you even say that?"

"I want to go home more than anything," Tristan said. The other soldier nearby turned his attention to the boys. Neither Blaz nor Tristan noticed though. "Don't you want to live?" Tristan asked, "We aren't going to live if we stay."

"I'd rather *Deutschland* be better off and not live to see it, than for *Deutschland* to dissolve and maybe cease to exist and live to see it."

Tristan was defeated by this answer, "*Ja*, I guess so."

"You," the older soldier said and pointed to Tristan, "You want to leave the army?"

"I do want to live. I want to grow up before I die."

The older soldier nodded slightly and brought his cigarette up to his mouth. He puffed it and said, "Admirable sentiment, but we must secure an existence for Germans first. Extermination awaits us if we lose."

Tristan and Blaz looked at each other in terrified shock, "Really?"

"According to our good Jewish friends in America," the soldier said reaching into his pocket and pulling out a newspaper article. He handed it to them to read. Blaz and Tristan both read, becoming more horrified the further they got. The article broke down a book written in mid-nineteen forty-one by an American Jew. The book was called "Germany Must Perish!" The boys read on to discover a plan, detailed even more thoroughly in the very real book, to exterminate the German people through sterilization then immigration into their territory from foreign nations until Germans cease to exist as a people and nation. They read on to find that the author went on to say it is the Jews calling to globalize the world into one federation and that any dissenters of this plan, any race that resists, would be destroyed.

"God have mercy," Tristan murmured.

We were right about them, Blaz thought in shock, not wanting to believe it.

May 24, 1944

Blaz's hands were blistered from digging ditches for hours. Small cracks appeared on the skin on his hands and blood trickled down. The boys had been working tirelessly to barricade the town as best they could. They were now digging an anti-tank ditch at the tree line to prevent tanks from outflanking the *Eisenfaust*. But no ditch directly in front of her, in case she needed to charge the enemy.

The force of one hundred and fifty worked efficiently, to say the least. Ditches several feet deep and several real feet wide lined the moderately wide front of the town, any advance would be slowed at least. They shoveled the dirt and mud in front of the ditches, disguising them as barriers, putting barbed wire on them. If tanks attempted to go by them, the ditch would be waiting for them.

"You know," Koby said to Blaz, "I actually want the Russians to come."

"We're going to avenge him, don't worry," Blaz assured Koby. They redoubled their efforts.

June 7, 1944

"Rome has been captured by the Allies," Koby told the Knights, unrolling a small map of Europe. The command had given it to him. He pointed to Rome, drawing a line with his finger at the Allied line of advance. Koby continued, removing his cap, and pointed to Russia, east of Minsk, "And the Russian offensive is slowly moving towards us, so we will get to see them face-to-face soon. The Russian offensive in the south has been advancing, they are much further west than the northern group."

"Anything else?" Jarman asked.

Koby hesitated. Morale was too good right now.

"Nothing," he replied.

The Red Army and the Army of the Swastika

June 23, 1944

"Quiet!" a soldier hissed Blaz, "They'll be in view soon."

The sound of Russians marching in the distance grew nearer. It was a familiar sound to every soldier there. Blaz cocked his rifle and took aim out of the loft of the barn. They'd removed boards in the loft of the barn to make a machine gun nest. They then nailed the removed boards to the outside as extra reinforcement against gunfire. Both young squads had been sent to defend the silos along with a veteran squad. Machine guns had been set up across the town's east, where the Soviets were coming from.

Blaz, Jaye, Ivo, and another soldier were in the loft to guard a machine gunner and his MG-42. Wilhelm was waiting in a foxhole outside of the barn to ambush tanks. Jarman and Koby were both stationed behind sandbags they'd set up to protect an artillery behind the tree line. They would have sufficient cover, and still be able to fire through the tree line with their assault rifles. Since they were at least one hundred meters from the town, they had set up a small communications center next to the artillery using a field phone. Hans, Tristan, Nico, and Gunther were on the floor of the barn acting as cover for the machine gun there. The march ceased. Artillery appeared on the horizon. The town sat on lower ground than the Russians. But the incline at which the Russians were, was so far only artillery would be able to effectively fire on the town.

"They think they're the only ones with guns?" the soldier on the machine gun near Blaz chuckled. As if on cue, a shout from the road came, "Artillery! Open fire!"

German artillery fired on the Soviet lines. Blaz only saw dust exploding in the air where Russian artillery pieces once were.

"That'll teach them!" the soldier murmured.

Blaz kept his focus to the east, rifle held steady. The sound of tanks, trucks, and men was once again coming. Tanks rumbled over the hill, hundreds of meters from the town. The men came sprinting behind the tanks and trucks. Men with machine guns mounted on the trucks, turned to face the town.

"Machine guns! *Panzers*! *Feuer*!" an officer yelled. The machine gun next to Blaz unloaded on the Russians. The Tiger tanks fired on the nearest Soviet tanks that roared toward the town and silos with Russians creeping along behind them for cover. One Russian tank took a hit, flames spreading from the inside out as it ground to a halt. A second hit a mine, causing it to catch fire. The tanks stalled. A line of Russians ran ahead of the tanks. They locked arms and, though many were shot down, they charged forward, clearing the minefield for their comrades and armor. Explosions went up across the front, as Russians stepped on mines and their bodies flew into the air. Blaz couldn't believe the insanity of the Soviet's fighting style

"*Feuer!*" the soldier yelled to the boys.

Blaz picked a target. The tree line made it difficult to aim, but he'd trained for this with *Herr* Müller. He aimed slightly ahead of the Russian soldier, adjusting for the long range. His finger tightened around the trigger, and he fired the shot. He saw the Russian collapse, then get back to his feet. Blaz aimed again, this time hitting the Russian in the chest. The tanks were now approaching the tree line. The barbed wire mounds kept the ditches out of plain view, at least from a tank.

The machine guns fired rapidly, mowing down the charging Russians. But the tanks and trucks were almost in the town.

"Incoming!" screamed Ivo, ducking behind the wooden roof. Shreds of wood scattered across the barn, as a shell tore through the roof.

"*Scheiße!*" the machine gunner yelled, then fired a burst into the advancing Soviets. Blaz took aim through the makeshift window again. The enemy was getting close, and they didn't seem to be running out of men. Blaz fired, hitting the dirt. He worked the action his rifle, unfazed. He fired again, this time felling a Russian carrying a rocket launcher.

"*Panzer!* They're at the line!" Blaz heard someone yell. A Russian tank roared over the dirt barricade, exposing its underbelly. Wilhelm fired his launcher. Another enemy tank went up in flames. The Russians were attempting to leap the anti-tank ditches. Tanks tried to maneuver around them, but several had fallen in, where mines lay waiting.

"Hurry! Take them down!" the machine gunner shouted over the fire, "Feed it more bullets, Jaye!"

The Russians were coming through the tree line by now. Blaz fired two quick shots, not at the same man. Russians kept falling, machine gun fire mowed them down, but they pushed onward. Koby and Jarman had fallen back with Wilhelm. The Russians now ran directly at the barn. All the boys heard was machine gun fire below.

"Sir, sir!" Blaz panicked, his rifle held tight, as if it were the only thing that could keep him alive, "What do we do?"

"Cover me!" the machine gunner said, dismounting the gun, and heading down the stairs. Blaz, Jaye, and Ivo ran to the other side of the loft to cover the soldier. What they saw surprised and relieved them. Gunther, Nico, Hans, and Tristan were all fine and still shooting at advancing Russians. "What happened?" the machine gunner yelled to the officer of the barn.

"Russians almost breached us, Tiger took care of them!" came the reply, "Get back to your post!"

Blaz, Ivo and Jaye returned to find the Russians retreating.

"Why?" Jaye wondered aloud, "They could overrun us with that many men."

"We need more men on the ground!" came a call, "Some casualties. Private Pagendarm! Private Senft! Down here!"

Blaz kept his rifle loaded, now on the floor of the barn. He'd been waiting for hours but kept it aimed out the window just waiting. The Russians were coming back, no doubt.

"Here they come!" Koby shouted from outside.

The Russians came charging over the hill with a wedge of tanks and trucks. Men stayed close behind them to avoid the machine gun fire. Nonetheless, German machine guns fired away, hitting an occasional straggler.

"*Verdämmt!*" the machine gunner on the barn floor shouted in frustration, "*Panzers!* Fire on that wedge!"

The Tiger Tank *Eisenfaust* fired its cannon, piercing one tank's armor. Blaz fired a shot but the Russians were well-covered.

"That's not enough men to capture the town," the machine gunner shook his head looking in the town's direction. What he didn't see was the force coming over the hill closer to his front. A tank cannon sounded. The front of the barn exploded, sending dust and debris throughout the barn.

"On the ground, don't let them enter!" the machine gunner fired into the Russians, who now were charging full speed ahead, their tank machine guns firing. Blaz backed up from the front of the barn. The machine gunner followed them. Jaye and Ivo charged down from the loft to guard the rear.

"Guns up!" yelled Gunther, taking command. All the boys raised their rifles at the still intact wall of the barn, taking cover behind crates, even hay bales, anything.

"*Ogon'!*" shouted a Russian voice. Bullets tore through the barn wall, hitting the machine gunner in the arm.

"*Gott Verdämmt!*" the gunner screamed, grasping his arm in pain. Blaz kept his focus on the wall.

"*Zaryad!*" came a yell. The wall of the barn was ripped apart by a charging tank. The tank backed up and men poured through the newly made entrance. No one gave the order, but all the Germans fired. Blaz rapidly cocked and fired his rifle, repeating as fast as he could.

"I'm out!" he yelled, ducking below the hay bale. He ejected his cartridge, reached for another and slid it into the rifle with the grace and mastery of a veteran soldier. He raised his rifle, poked above the hay bale, and fired at the first Russian he saw. He could not miss from this range. The bullet hit the Russian in the head and blood flew out the front and back of his cranium.

"Get down!" the machine gunner yelled. Blaz ducked behind the hay bale just in time. The machine gunner sprayed fire across the barn from the hip, slaughtering the Russians. Blaz stayed down, until the firing stopped. He nodded to Gunther who nodded back. Blaz raised his cap just above the hay bale on the end of his rifle. A shot was fired, and his cap spun around on the rifle. Gunther sprung up and shot the Russian who'd fired at Blaz's cap.

"*Tot!*" Gunther shouted to the others, "Dead!" Blaz rose with his rifle raised. He turned to his back to see the machine gunner lying on the ground in his own blood. Blaz exhaled through his mouth.

"*Panzer!*" Nico shouted, "*Lauf!*"

Nico bolted to leave the barn, waving for the others to follow, as the tank that had cleared a hole hammered through the wall completely. The machine gunners dismounted their guns and fled as well. The tank unleashed a massive burst of fire, missing the last of the boys narrowly. One machine gunner was caught by the flames.

"*Panzerfaust, Panzerschreck?*" Gunther yelled once outside, "We've got a flame tank in there!"

"It's mine," Wilhelm said, and sprinted toward the barn. He aimed through the doors and fired. Smoke and fire billowed into the air as his shot slammed into the tank. But it wasn't destroyed, only immobilized. It rotated its cannon to fire on the Germans.

"Get back! Get back!" a German soldier yelled, but he was cut off as a bullet pierced his helmet. He fell to the ground, smoother than any death Blaz had witnessed.

The tank aimed on Wilhelm, who was tackled to the ground by Gunther. The shell tore by and slammed into the artillery piece, clearly its intended target. More bullets rained in, from both ways. Blaz crouched low, to stay out of the line of fire. The rest of the Knights did the same.

"Claunitzer! Get me Claunitzer!" shouted a *Wehrmacht* lieutenant to his corporal. The corporal picked up the field phone, and called to the headquarters, "No answer!" he shouted.

"The headquarters have been hit!" another soldier yelled in assumption.

"We're surrounded!" the corporal yelled, "Once the Tigers are gone, we're done for! We need to get out of here!"

"Break for the town! Get to the trucks!" the lieutenant shouted to the remaining soldiers.

"*Ja* sir!" Koby yelled back, leading the squad in a sprint away from the silos and barn. Russians had now circled their flank and rushed into the barn and silos, firing to clear out any remaining Germans. Then they began firing on the retreating youths and men.

"*Los! Los! Los!*" Koby shouted. Blaz sprinted to catch up to the front of the pack, past Nico, Hans, Jaye, Wilhelm. As he passed, he heard a shout of rage. It sounded like Gunther. "Nico!"

Blaz turned, still running, to see Nico lying on the ground with blood running from his helmet. He skidded to a halt and bolted back, but a giant German soldier, mid-sprint, scooped up Nico in his arms and flung him over his back and continued to run.

"*Los!*" he yelled to Gunther and Blaz. Neither hesitated and sprinted full force ahead. It was the longest hundred meters in history.

The *Eisenfaust* Tiger Tank rotated on the road. As the last soldiers and youths ran by the Tiger Tank, the *Eisenfaust* charged forward, firing its machine guns into the pursuing Russians. It rotated its cannon to aim at the entrance of the barn, where the flame tank was visible. Blaz didn't see how it ended. More men ahead of Blaz were being picked off, and if their friends stopped to help them, they were picked off as well.

The boys made it into the town but kept running for the garage where the trucks were parked. Blaz turned to look west; the Russians were nowhere to be seen. They would be safe that direction. The town's line was still holding, though if the *Eisenfaust* went down, the town would be lost. The *Wehrmacht* commander went from building to building, yelling of the Russians coming from the silos. The *Eisenfaust* still held the road and the *Mutig Verteidiger* rolled past the retreating youths to bring aid. When they'd passed the *Mutig Verteidiger*, a Russian tank hit her on the side, followed by a second shot from yet another, and the first German tank was defeated. Koby led the squad into the garage.

"I'll get the keys!" he shouted, though they were inside. Koby disappeared into the rooms of the building.

The soldier carrying Nico limped in. He had been shot in the leg. He laid Nico down on the garage floor. Nico's eyes were shut, he wasn't breathing, and Blaz saw a bullet hole in his helmet. But they had no time to mourn. Gunther wiped tears away, as he looked at his childhood friend lying dead on the ground.

"We'll bring him with us?" Gunther asked no one particularly.

"Of course," Jarman nodded. Blaz looked around. Only one adult survived the sprint to the town. It was a wonder the Knights had made it.

"Who's going to drive? I can't drive at all with my leg," the wounded man asked while leaning on a truck, "Do any of you know how to drive?"

All the boys raised their hands. Koby came running in with the keys to a truck.

"*Ausgezeichnet*," the man said. He would've acted impressed but now was hardly the time for such things. At that moment, the door of the garage opened and the *Wehrmacht* lieutenant limped in clutching his chest with one arm and his left leg with the other. He had bullet wounds in both places.

"We're being hit from three sides. Our troops are in full retreat. Only a few remain at their posts. The Russians are working to kill them now. It's over."

"Sir, we're taking these trucks to escape," Jarman informed the commander.

"They can all drive, by the way," the man with the wounded leg said.

"Have them take all four, pick up as many fleeing German soldiers as you can."

Koby threw his keys to Jarman and sprinted to retrieve the other keys. Jarman shouted, "Wilhelm drive this one. Jaye, shotgun," he said pointing to a lightly armored truck, "Everyone who I don't order to drive or co-pilot a truck gets in there. Unarmored will be leaving last but won't stop for men until they're out of range of the tanks. The ones driving the armor, we'll be stopping for the men you go by. Sirs," he said commandingly to the *Wehrmacht* lieutenant and private with wounded leg, "You two need to get in the back of Wilhelm's truck now."

The lieutenant raised no objections. The two soldiers limped behind Wilhelm and Jaye and climbed into the back of the covered truck.

"Hans! Tristan!" Jarman roared. The two Neuhardenberg boys instinctively shot their right arms into the air. Jarman continued, ignoring their reaction, "You two take the other unarmored truck."

"*Ja, ja*," the two nodded quickly as Koby returned, giving them the keys. The two left for the unarmored truck. Jarman looked to Koby, questioningly to know if Koby would give the orders now. Koby gave him a reassuring look and Jarman continued, "Koby, Blaz!"

Blaz stamped a foot and straightened up with his hands glued to his side.

"You two take the first armored truck," Jarman ordered.

"We'll drive out first," Koby volunteered.

"*Gut*," Jarman nodded in understanding, "Hans and I will take the other armored truck. Ivo get in the back with the lieutenant," Ivo looked disappointed and a bit insulted, but obeyed without question.

"*Los!*" Jarman shouted. Blaz and Koby vaulted into the truck.

"Blaz, you're driving. I'll cover since I've got the STG," Koby said, handing him the keys, "If any Russians are in the road, run them over."

"Got it," Blaz nodded nervously, starting the truck. Wilhelm cranked open the garage door, and Blaz floored it. The truck screeched out, drawing attention from Russians. Koby was on it though. He fired out of the window, mowing through several in seconds. Russians had advanced throughout the town, Blaz could see them heading to chase the fleeing Germans, who were sprinting across the fields as if the devil himself pursued them. He turned to the left, heading down the road out of town. Russians pursuing the Germans turned to see the truck coming full speed at them. Koby fired through the glass, causing it to rain down on the two German youths. The Russian returned fire, and Blaz ducked under the windshield, leaving his foot on the gas and keeping the wheel where it had been.

Koby fired ahead, shouting, "Eyes on the road!"

Blaz popped back up as a bullet hit the edge of seat right next to him. He glanced over at Koby in shock, but quickly returned his focus to the road. Koby mowed down Russians as they entered the fields.

"Here comes one on horseback up our rear!" Blaz yelled, "My side, in the mirror!"

"Here!" Koby shouted back, handing Blaz his Luger, "Shoot him when he gets close!"

Blaz looked out the window to see the horse coming closer. Blaz leaned out and fired a shot at the man, missing. But the startled Russian dropped his pistol, rendering himself unarmed. He kicked his horse, and it galloped right alongside the truck. Blaz fired again, hitting the horse, which collapsed. The Russian leapt from the horse, grabbing the inside of the door, trying to unlock it. Blaz raised the Luger but the Soviet grabbed at the weapon knocking it onto the floor of the truck. Blaz drew his knife.

He brought it down hard into the Russian's hand. The Russian howled and fell off the truck.

"Good work," Koby panted.

"*Ja, ja*," Blaz gasped, out of breath.

"There's some Germans!" Koby yelled pointing quite a way away, "Five Russian rifleman a couple hundred meters on their tails, they'll be massacred soon. Let's take the Russians out! Then we'll pick our comrades up."

Blaz swerved hard, heading towards the Soviets. The Russians neither saw nor heard the truck coming over their guns until the last second. Blaz bulldozed them. They were sent flying back, all dropping their rifles. Blaz slammed on the breaks, and Koby leapt out of the vehicle.

"Stay in the truck!" he shouted.

The Russians groaned in misery on the ground, one had been completely crushed. Koby approached one, and the Russian pulled his pistol. Koby fired a single shot into the man's head. Blaz watched as Koby went to the other three, firing a shot into each head. Then he sprinted back to the truck.

"All right, let's get our men!"

Blaz glanced at Koby awkwardly. Then he steered the truck after their men. The four Germans raised their weapons as the truck drove closer, but Koby leaned out the window, and put his arm on the outside of the door, so they could see his Swastika armband. The soldiers smiled in relief and lowered their weapons. Blaz recognized one as Helmut.

"Here to evacuate. Hurry, get in the back, under the cover," Koby told them. The soldiers did so quickly.

"*Bereit?*" Blaz called back, hitting the side of the truck with his arm.

"*Bereit!*" a soldier shouted back. Blaz let go of the brake, and the truck began slowly moving forward.

"Where to?" Blaz asked Koby, "Will the Russians chase us, you think?"

"*Nein*," Koby shook his head, "They've already got the town, they won't pursue any more than some eager Russians breaking formation."

Blaz nodded and pressed down on the pedal and the truck accelerated forward.

"Go get them," Koby said, pointing to four more Germans running up a hill and out of sight. Blaz made the truck go faster so it could clear the hill. He slowed as they came over the top, so he wouldn't hit his comrades.

"*Nicht scheißen!*" Koby called as they went over the hill, "Don't shoot!"

The Germans turned around to see a truck bearing the *Balkenkreuz* humming towards them. They waved for the truck. Blaz brought it to a slow stop.

"We're evacuating," Blaz told them simply.

"Three other trucks made it out, we'll be heading for a town to get further orders," Koby informed the men, "We have extra fuel in the back."

The men agreed and boarded behind the truck.

"All right Blaz, let's get out of Russkie land."

The Road of Defeat

The trucks hummed through the Russian countryside. The sky grew dark. Blaz and Koby's truck led the way with the other three following close behind. The Russians had not pursued, just as Koby had predicted.

"Our orders are to retreat all the way to Poland?" Blaz asked. It seemed such a long distance from where they were now.

"We're going to stop in a town occupied by our men, to refuel and receive more specific orders," Koby clarified, "We will take the road to Minsk, it's not too far. Then we'll head for Poland should they order us there."

Blaz looked back to the road. A massive forest lay about a kilometer ahead, "That was impressive shooting, Koby. I doubt we would've made it out if you hadn't cleared a path."

"You drove well too."

"Nico was killed," Blaz said.

"I saw," Koby said, putting a hand over his eyes. He took off his field gray helmet, then his cap, and looked at it, "If I knew the bastard who aimed at a fleeing kid."

Blaz nodded with a scowl.

Koby added bitterly, "I didn't treat Nico well enough. I never really tried to get to know him."

Blaz stayed silent and returned his focus to the road, turning the headlights on. One was shot out.

Night set in, but Blaz had practiced driving in the dark before. There was little the Hitler Youth instructors had left out of their training. A light rain fell. It kept coming, steadily growing heavier. Blaz slowed the truck, so that he wouldn't wreck. The dirt roads turned to mud. Koby had shot out of the front, so there was no windshield leading to Blaz and Koby getting wet.

"Keep going," Koby told Blaz, "We don't want to get stuck sitting in Russian mud."

Blaz kept driving, not able to see very well anymore. Every couple of seconds, rain hit him in the eye.

"You have any idea how much further Minsk is?" keeping his vision glued on the road.

"We're getting closer since we're in a forest, that's all I can say," Koby shouted over the pounding rain. Blaz glanced to Koby, and that was all it needed. The truck slid on the mud, losing traction and heading off the road. Blaz slowed down, letting the truck regain its traction, and then gently applied pressure to the gas. The truck drove on, sending up mud as it accelerated into the night.

Never Saw a Father Anymore

June 24, 1944

"Halt!" an officer yelled, lowering a roadblock, "You must wait to be investigated before passing."

"*Ja* sir," Blaz replied, exhausted. He could see the light of Minsk from this stop. Two soldiers stepped out of the small cabin-like building next to the roadblock, bearing the SS insignia on their collars. Their helmets glimmered dully in the moonlight, and they held STG-44s. Even in his exhaustion, Blaz eyed them with envy. The officer walked up to their truck with the soldiers, who moved to inspect their cargo.

"Have you your identification papers?" the officer asked.

"*Nein*, sir," Blaz answered. Everything he owned was on him right now or in his small bag that stayed closely tied to his uniform.

"Our company was forced to retreat from a town in the western Smolensk-Oblast territory in the Greater German Reich," Koby told the officer, "All the survivors are in these four trucks."

"I'm sorry to hear that your company was killed," the officer consoled the boys. He did not mean to sound insincere, but these reports were old hat to him, "Your truck certainly looks like it has been through hell. Was it quite a battle?"

"*Ja* sir," Koby answered robotically.

"Son, you have a good Berliner accent," the officer told Koby, "You come from Berlin?"

"*Nein*, Seelow," Koby replied.

"Ah, the gates to Berlin," the officer nodded, "Well, that is a convincing story, I doubt the Bolsheviks have even heard of Seelow. However, are there any adult survivors?"

"*Ja*, a lieutenant is in one of the unarmored trucks," Blaz answered before Koby. The officer thanked them for their cooperation and strode to the back of the line. Once the wounded *Wehrmacht* officer had spoken to the SS officer, they were on their way. The *Wehrmacht* officer now came to the front and sat between Koby and Blaz. He had been haphazardly treated for his wounds, and bandages were visible under his uniform, wrapped tightly around his midsection.

"Sergeant Hertz, once we arrive in Minsk, I will have to speak to a general to see what the remainder of our company should do. I will also put in a word for your squad. Who was the boy giving orders, even to myself?" the officer asked.

"That was Jarman Knecht, sir."

"Any actions of your squad you wish to brag about? Now is the time," the officer said warmly.

"Oh," Koby said with a smile, "Well, I don't want to be arrogant."

"Please do," the officer told him.

"Well, Blaz saved a lot of men, and killed some Russians during the escape. All the drivers did. Jarman Knecht, Wilhelm Kramer, and Gunther Schütz."

"Gunther stepped up and led us during the battle when we were cut off from Koby," Blaz chimed in, "And Koby led us safely to the trucks."

"*Ja*, I saw you ran close to the building on the east side of town to eliminate the Reds angle on you," the officer remembered, "I will put in a word for Jarman Knecht, Wilhelm Kramer, and Gunther Schütz."

Koby saluted the officer.

Once in Minsk, the officer directed Blaz towards the German headquarters. When they came to a halt, all four trucks unloaded, soldiers stretching sorely from the many hours in the truck. The sun was just rising in the east. It was a red dawn, and the Russkies were coming from the east.

The *Wehrmacht* lieutenant told the soldiers to fill the trucks with gasoline. He then proceeded to speak with a *Hauptsturmführer* of the SS, and from the smiles and lightheartedness beaming from both men, they were talking about not their next orders, but about what the boys had done to save thirty-one good men. The *Hauptsturmführer* sent his Hitler Youth adjutant, who looked to be the squad's age, to fetch something during their conversation. He also began taking notes during their talk, Blaz couldn't tell of what.

After several minutes of the two officers conversing, the *Hauptsturmführer* pointed to a building. The officer returned to the trucks, calling the soldiers over to the *Hauptsturmführer*.

"*Herr* Model will give me further orders now," the officer told Koby, "Remain by the trucks once the *Hauptmann* is finished speaking to you."

Koby saluted the officer. The soldiers briskly marched to the *Hauptsturmführer*. They stood erect, arms to their sides. Thirty-nine men and boys in total.

The *Hauptsturmführer* adjutant came jogging back, with a briefcase in hand. He opened it, facing the SS officer. The *Hauptsturmführer* grabbed something from the briefcase, then the Hitler Youth boy backed away, still holding the briefcase open, revealing it to hold Iron Crosses, First and Second Class.

"*Herr* Schweitzer has told me of your bravery in defending a lost town. That city was nearly encircled; you should've been pulled out. Though the town was lost, bravery must be rewarded," he looked to his notes, "Jarman Knecht and Gunther Schütz displayed leadership in the midst of battle, and thus saved many lives. They risked their lives to save retreating men, when it could have gotten them killed. They both receive the Iron Cross-Second Class."

The *Hauptsturmführer* pinned the Iron Crosses securely onto the boys' uniforms at the upper chest. He shook their hands, saying, "I'm proud of you."

He then retrieved another Iron Cross-Second Class. "Wilhelm Kramer held at the front lines, destroying multiple tanks, and receives the Iron Cross." He pinned the medal onto Wilhelm's uniform. "Adolf Hammersohn destroyed two tanks using an anti-tank rifle and receives the Iron Cross." The *Hauptsturmführer* pinned the Iron Cross onto an older soldier's uniform, "You've made the Fatherland proud," he commended them, solemnly, while saluting the soldiers and Hitler Youths, "*Danke* for your service to the Reich."

The soldiers returned the salute, but the boys returned a stiff-armed salute. The *Hauptsturmführer* lowered his hand and turned to his Hitler

Youth adjutant. He spoke to the teenager who wore the Hitler Youth armband with the white stripe, but also had an SS insignia on his collar and Death's Head on his hat. With every word, the teenager's expression turned from neutral, to confused, to dismal realization. Blaz watched it all unfold from in front of the trucks. When it looked like the conversation would end, the *Wehrmacht* lieutenant returned, striding as quickly as his wounded leg would allow him. The *Hauptsturmführer* and lieutenant exchanged words, the SS officer gesturing to the Hitler Youth teen several times and the lieutenant nodding soon after.

"What do you think they're talking about?" Ivo whispered.

"No idea," Blaz shook his head once in reply, "New orders?"

After another minute of conversation between the two officers, the *Hauptsturmführer* and lieutenant threw each other casual salutes and parted.

The lieutenant gestured for the teen to follow him, but the boy did not follow at first. He turned to the SS officer, extending his right arm to shake hands in parting. The *SS-Hauptsturmführer* obliged and pulled the teen in for a reassuring hug. Once they'd finished, the SS Hitler Youth went on his way after the lieutenant. As he came closer, his curly, reddish-blond hair and blue eyes became visible. He was built like Koby. The teen's face was stained in dirt and ash from the filthy conditions he'd been living in. He also had freckles and a noticeable scar running from his jaw to shoulder.

"Sergeant Hertz!" the lieutenant called. Koby stomped a foot and stood erect.

"At ease," the lieutenant said, "We are being sent to defend a village southeast of Königsberg, north of Warsaw on the Baltic Sea just outside of Brest to be precise. *Hauptsturmführer* Becke has informed me of the impending situation in Minsk." The Hitler Youth boy kicked at a stone in the road. The lieutenant continued, taking no notice, "Due to the danger and risk of the situation here, his *Hitlerjugend* adjutant will join your squad."

"Koby Hertz," Koby introduced himself and extended a hand, "Seelow."

"Werner von Schraeder," the teen replied, shaking Koby's hand, "Detmold."

"Welcome to the Knights," Koby said invitingly, "It's an honor to have you."

"It's an honor to serve with you," Werner responded, "The Knights?"

"It's a little nickname we have for our squad."

"All right men, you load into the back, we'll have some older soldiers drive this time," the lieutenant ordered, "First, though, I need you to load up one with weapons. They're in the boxes over there," he pointed.

"*Ja* sir," Koby respectfully, then snapped his fingers at his squad, "Knights! To work!"

Once on the road again, Koby introduced Werner to the squad, spurring a conversation.

"So Koby, Jarman, Blaz, Jaye, and Ivo are from Seelow?" Werner asked, "Hans and Tristan are from Neuhardenberg, Wilhelm is from Fürstenwalde, Gunther is from Berlin? And you call yourselves the Teutonic Knights?"

"Just the Knights," Jaye grinned, "Good memory. And you are from Detmold?"

"That's it," Werner snapped his fingers. He paused and looked around at the Knights. "You obviously have fought quite a bit, what with the Iron Crosses," he observed.

"*Ja*, we just retreated from a town in Russia, near the border," Jarman said, "We put up a fight, but we were outnumbered, outgunned, and outflanked."

"How many men were in the town to begin?" Werner asked, knowing how many had escaped.

"One-hundred and fifty, including us," Koby answered.

Werner's face fell, "Only forty of you escaped?"

"*Ja*," nodded Blaz, "That's how war can be."

"Have you been in any battles?" Ivo asked.

"*Ja*, but only one where I was being an actual soldier. When Reinhard, I mean *Hauptsturmführer* Becke fought, he normally sent me to man our artillery or something. But one time he didn't notice me follow him to the front, I think. I fought my first front line battle. I don't think he would've sent me away unless he knew he was going to die," Werner shook his head dismally, "I've been with him for over two years. He was like a new father."

Werner von Schraeder

June 25, 1944

The arrival in the town brought back a sense of security. Surely, this would be the furthest they'd move west until the war ended. Their position was favorable to defend.

Forests sat to the west and the north and trees dotted plains that lay to the east and south of the town. One kilometer east lay a wide river delta, one that would deter any vehicles from crossing. One kilometer was an easy distance for their machine guns and artillery to cover.

There were several houses in a square, the one street branching off in four directions from the roundabout. There was a mill, a single store, and a former blacksmith shop, which appeared to be the only businesses in the tiny town.

They were greeted by a pitifully small force of ten *Wehrmacht* soldiers, three Hitler Youths, a five-man tank crew and their Tiger I. There was one artillery piece in the center of the square surrounded by sandbags, manned by the three Hitler Youths in their black uniforms. This put their defenses at fifty-four men and boys, four trucks that would have to be parked outside, and two horses they'd been given to haul food.

"This is a strictly defensive force. The river delta will make this an excellent town to defend. We will keep guards at the bridge at all times, and explosives in position, prepared to destroy it at all times as well. That will stall the Russian armor for possibly days, if we keep hammering them with our machine guns and lone artillery piece," his voice betrayed irritation, "Secondly, we've been supplied with ample ammunition from Minsk and multiple machine guns. I want our best men on these. Since we have a few two-story buildings, I want them there. They can slow any rebuilding of a primitive bridge from that height. Young men, I will assign you individual positions in buildings and the square. You will also be the guards of the bridge. Four at once should make sure you see any Russians a long way off. For now, that is all. Stauffer, Schmidt, Birnbaum, Richthofen, Hammersohn. To me. The rest are dismissed."

They all scattered across the town. Werner followed Koby, Ivo, and Blaz down to the mill. They sat down under the shelter an open-air building provided, as it looked like storms were on their way.

"You are from Detmold?" Koby studiously asked.

"I am. It's somewhat small, have you heard of it?"

"I met a soldier from there a while ago, he's still with us now. Helmut Schmid. Do you know him?" Blaz asked.

"*Nein*, we're not that small," Werner laughed, "I know some 'Helmut's' and some 'Schmid's' but no one that has both in their name."

"That's fair," Ivo grinned.

"You guys are from Seelow? What's that like? Does it have anything to its name?"

"It's a farm town, in a hilly region," Blaz said, "There's a major network of defenses there and it saw increased work done on it ever since the war started."

"A lot more soldiers are there," added Ivo, "At least a division of *Wehrmacht* men when we left, and an SS battalion."

"Well, that's something."

"*Ja*, it is," Ivo said proudly, though Blaz knew he was being sarcastic.

"What sports were you into in Seelow?"

Blaz and Ivo smiled at each other at this question.

"Koby, you want to tell him?" Ivo said, holding a hand out.

"*Nein*," an embarrassed Koby told him, "You go ahead."

"*Wunderbar*," Ivo said rubbing his hands together in a burst of excitement. Werner smiled uncomfortably.

"He gets excited," Blaz explained with a grin.

"Hey, shut up," Ivo said, "Anyway, we played lots of sports, but our best was running and track. You think so?"

"*Ja*, I think so," Blaz agreed.

"What were your races?"

"Fifteen hundred, three thousand, and five thousand."

"Wow, how good were you?"

"We were fourteen the last time we ran. And now we're sixteen," Ivo said this as if he'd just realized it, "Koby's almost seventeen and-"

Blaz, Werner, and Koby waited patiently for Ivo to recover his train of thought.

"Sorry," Ivo apologized, grinning, "Blaz and I were in the high eighteens."

"That is really good! At fourteen, that is impressive!"

"And Koby was in the fifteens. He's going to the nineteen forty-eight Olympics," Ivo said.

"*Nein*! Really?" Werner exclaimed in admiration.

"I was," Koby said sadly, rubbing one of his legs, "I doubt that'll happen now."

"Why not?" Ivo asked with surprise.

"I haven't been able to train, we're in a war."

"You're in great shape, you'll be fine."

"I could, but it'll take a long time after the war. I don't know if it'll come together like that," Koby said.

"You can be ready by then," Blaz agreed with Ivo, "You've got the work ethic."

"Maybe, hopefully," Koby finally said, to humor the two.

Werner seemed to get it, and put an end to the topic, "Still, the fact that you would've is impressive. Got a backup plan? A young officer like you could go a long way.

"I want to get married."

"You don't need to worry about that. You're a handsome man."

Koby rolled his eyes. "And I'd be interested in politics, if I'm ever done with fighting."

Werner was surprised by this. He made an incriminating stare and said, "Have you any affiliation with the *Schutzstaffel*?"

"*Nein*, I'm a *Wehrmacht* Sergeant."

"Were you ever in SS education, though?"

"*Nein*," Koby said, his expression morphing into a glare. He stared back at Werner, "What are you saying?"

"You won't get into German politics ten years from now without being in the SS," Werner laughed, "At least it'll be difficult. You're young though. You could still get into the SS."

Koby thought for a moment. Blaz was sure he'd disagree with this but to his surprise Koby nodded, "*Ja*, not a bad idea."

"Really? SS?" Blaz asked, "You don't need to be in the SS to enter politics."

"If that *is* what it takes to get into politics," Koby told him, "Why not?"

"I don't know," Blaz mumbled, looked at the ground, cleared his throat, then glanced up, "I don't know."

"Other than that," Koby said with a groan, "Come on, what about *Herr* Schlusser?"

"Okay, okay."

"Who's *Herr* Schlusser?" Werner asked, completely lost.

"He was our *Hitlerjugend* instructor," Ivo told him.

"Ah, so you like him?"

"*Ja*, he was excellent," Ivo commended his former commander.

"You *liked* your instructor?" Werner said, both shocked and disgusted, "As a teacher or even as a person? I hated mine, but I obeyed him because that's only common sense."

"Definitely as a teacher," said Blaz.

"Fine, but as a person?" Werner asked, really hoping someone would reprimand Schlusser. No one answered immediately which somewhat relieved Werner.

"*Nein,* he was a fine man as far as I could tell," Ivo said.

"*Ja,* he never did anything I disagreed with or said anything I disagreed with morally. And even if he had, that wouldn't change too much of my opinion. We're all united for one cause: *Deutschland.* And that's all I need from someone," Koby answered.

"Okay, that's just odd to me," Werner said, raising his eyebrows and frowning, "You're not supposed to like them."

"Okay. Why not?"

Werner shrugged. "They're assholes, that's why."

"Ours wasn't."

"I'll have to meet him then."

To Fight for Freedom There

June 29, 1944

It took days before Blaz's shift on guard at the bridge. It was a refreshing change of pace. There were four jobs: On guard at the bridge, maintenance, on guard in the town, or on patrol in the forest.

Koby, Ivo, and Jarman took the same shift. They stood on the bridge. Ivo skipped stones, while Koby occasionally observed the gray horizon with his binoculars. The Soviets would be closing in soon.

"Minsk is expected to fall soon," Koby informed the group, "Then the next major obstacle that we must defend is the Neman River."

"Are we to the west or east of that?" Jarman asked.

Koby gulped nervously, "The east. The road that heads into the forest leads to the river several kilometers from here."

"*Scheiße.*"

"We'll stop them this time," Ivo said, "This is where we rally."

"We'll rally soon," Koby agreed, "I don't know where the *Führer* plans on that being."

"Somewhere before Warsaw is best," Blaz said, "We need the Silesian resource centers and the Danzig shipyards."

"Never thought I'd say anything in favor of Poland, but I wouldn't want to see anyone ruled by Marxists," Jarman added.

"We have to guard the freedom there," Koby said.

"Don't the democracies realize if they keep fighting us, that the Reds will overrun the Europe they claim to care about?" Jarman said, "At least the invasion of Italy has been stalled. We're mostly able to focus here."

Koby took his hat off and fingered a loose thread.

"What?" Jarman looked at Koby, "What is it?"

"Nothing, nothing."

"*Nein*, you're hiding something," Blaz agreed, "What is it?"

"You don't need to know."

"But should we know?"

Koby remained still. Then he nodded, "Probably."

"Well then?" Jarman persisted.

"Fine. The democracies have landed in France. They're driving into the Reich."

"How long ago?"

"Weeks."

"I wish they would be wiped off the face of the earth," Jarman scowled, "We've got to stop them. It's not just for Germany this time. It's for all of Europe."

Unwanted Messages

July 6, 1944

Supplies arrived and with them letters for the first time in months. The youths opened theirs, unnerved at the prospect of finding out news of their family's death.

"*Oh, Gott sei Dank*," Blaz breathed, closing his eyes in relief as he finished reading the letter from his father.

His father was still very much alive, at least he was before the invasion of Normandy. But Blaz didn't think of that. His family was alive in his mind for now.

"Ivo? Family okay?" Blaz asked.

"All alive still," Ivo smiled sadly but with gratitude, "Papa is a spy."

"What? You never told me that."

"Thought I may as well now, does the secrecy matter anymore? Now that we're here?"

Blaz shrugged. Sighs of relief passed around the circle of boys. Blaz scanned around to see his squad all had relieved looks on their faces, even traces of joy. One face did not smile. Hans crushed his letter in his hand. He covered his eyes and cried. The squad froze.

"He's dead," Hans said, "Dead." He couldn't say anything else. The crumpled letter fell to the dusty street. No one spoke.

Hans shot up and walked furiously down the road to the mill and sat down under its roof. Jarman followed him, and soon everyone else did. Hans showed no irritation at them following him. He just stayed facing the ground, sniffling, and crying.

Hans unholstered his pistol. Blaz's eyes widened. Hans flicked the safety off. Jarman inched closer to him.

Jarman sat down and Hans rubbed his eyes with his free hand and said, "I've got no one left, Jarman. I might as well meet them now. It'll happen anyway."

Hans swiftly brought his pistol up, lowered his head and opened his mouth to fire into. Jarman grabbed frantically at Hans' arm and forced the pistol away before he could fire. He pried Hans' fingers off the gun, until Hans couldn't fight him.

"What are you doing?" Jarman asked in horror.

"What did it look like?!" Hans cried.

"You can't kill yourself, Hans."

"Why not?" Hans shouted again, burying his head in his hands.

"You just can't, you're not supposed to," Jarman stuttered, "Where's the honor in that? I know your father wouldn't want that."

Hans breathed in, frustrated.

"When I give you your gun back, I need to know you'll only use it on the enemy. Never on yourself," Jarman told Hans.

Hans kneaded his fingers together but didn't reply.

"Don't kill yourself, Hans," Jaye pleaded, "You still have us. We won't just leave you once the war is over. We'll be at your side."

Hans looked at Jaye. Then he turned to Jarman.

"Give me the gun."

"I need to know first."

"Trust me."

If he didn't trust Hans, that would make it worse. He handed Hans the gun, who took it, and stared at it blankly. Jarman remained still.

Put it away, thought Blaz helplessly.

Hans slid the pistol back into his holster, stood up, and walked back to the square, "*Danke* Jarman. *Danke* Jaye," Hans said, stopping in the road, "*Heil* Hitler."

Jarman's Advice

July 7, 1944

"Jarman, watch it," Blaz said, ducking below a low-hanging branch in the forest.

"*Danke*," Jarman said, ducking under the branch as well.

"Koby!" Jarman called to Koby and Ivo, who patrolled fifty meters away, "Stay split up?"

"*Ja*, head northwest, we'll take northeast," Koby shouted back.

Ivo saluted in response. Blaz and Jarman headed northwest, knowing Koby had sent them where intruders were less likely to come from. They walked on in silence, Jarman with his assault rifle and Blaz with his rifle in hand.

"Is this war lost?" Blaz asked, kicking himself inside for doubting.

"*Nein*, it can be salvaged."

"Just because we lose a war doesn't mean we won't rise and be strong and respected again," Blaz said, "Is it best to accept defeat early?"

"Has the *Führer* accepted defeat?"

"*Nein*."

"Then we can't accept defeat. We've done that before and look what happened. We lost half our empire, so many souls. We can't go through that again. We'll never capitulate like that again."

"Hans."

"He's not the only one who will have nothing when this war is over."

"He's never going to be the same. He hasn't spoken since then."

Jarman vaulted over a branch in their way, and Blaz followed him, less gracefully.

"He has a million Reichsmarks smile. I hope he isn't done smiling."

"He'll move on," Jarman assured him, with an odd air of confidence and certainty.

"How can you move on from that?" Blaz asked, "I don't know if I could."

"You would Blaz," Jarman said, yet again with absolute confidence, "You're strong, it might take a while, but I know you would make it past that."

"But Hans? Why do you think he'll move past that? He tried to put a gun in his mouth," Blaz shuddered, "What if you hadn't stopped him?"

"*Ja*," Jarman admitted, "But I think that was just an impulsive reaction. You can't let emotions get the better of you in a war, or ever."

Blaz continued walking, thinking about that. Jarman was prone to showing emotions, but he had not done anything rash or foolhardy when Jurgen had been shot. Jarman seemed an odd person to be lecturing on controlling emotions. The only person he imagined could do that was *Herr* Schlusser.

"You've let emotions get the better of you in battle," Blaz told Jarman.

Jarman chuckled in self-awareness. "I have. But who did I take out my emotions on?"

"The Reds."

"Did I put myself in a dire situation in battle? One that was unnecessarily dangerous? Or disobeyed an order to retreat?"

"*Nein.*"

"That's what I mean."

Blaz and Jarman trudged up a short hill, further along into the forest. The trees and brush remained thick, it made them thankful for their uniforms.

"Have you seen anything?" Blaz asked.

"*Nichts*," Jarman answered.

"What did your brothers say? Yesterday?"

"*Danke* for asking. They're on the run, south of Kiev last they wrote."

"Kiev fell a while ago."

"I know," Jarman nodded, "I hope they'll be all right. I could move on, but to finish what I was saying earlier, you can move past horrible things, even deaths in the family, but you don't want to have to."

"*Ja*," Blaz agreed, "*Ja.*"

"And what about your father?" Jarman returned the question.

"He was fine. But that was before the Americans and Britons landed in Normandy."

Jarman hung his head, stopping his trailblazing. He returned his attention to Blaz. He looked down at his belt.

"*Gott mit uns. Wir alle*," he told Blaz with a hopeful smile.

"*Gott mit uns*," Blaz smiled back, repeating Jarman's words that were the *Wehrmacht's* motto.

The Siege Begins

July 14, 1944

"Tristan, Hans follow us," Koby waved to the two, "I'm taking the whole squad out to the bridge today. We're bringing some extra explosives to arm. This might be the day we destroy it." Wilhelm and Jarman carried a crate between the two of them. Jarman kept his assault rifle slung over his back, while Hans and Blaz both carried Wilhelm's heavy *Panzerschreck*, in addition to their rifles. At the bridge, the boys armed the explosives and placed them on the bridge's support struts.

"Now we wait," Koby announced, "I'm going to keep watch, when I give the word, I want Tristan to blow the bridge."

Tristan took his place next to a black box, with a bar on top to trigger the explosives.

"You guys can chat, I've got watch," Koby offered.

Jaye took off his helmet and ran a hand through his hair, "I feel like we should have some cigarettes right now, you know?"

"Like the older soldiers?" Wilhelm asked.

"*Ja*, nothing's happening, just take out a cigarette and light it up."

"Cigarettes aren't good for you, idiot," Jarman laughed, "Haven't you seen the posters before?"

"'He doesn't devour it, it devours him,'" Ivo quoted.

Jaye shrugged. Koby broke the silence, "This is it! Russian armor, due east! Massive numbers of infantry, at least three battalions, looks like fifteen hundred men," he yelled, "Ivo, Blaz, Jaye, Gunther, Hans, and Wilhelm: Get your weapons and inform *Herr* Schweitzer!"

Blaz picked up his rifle and took off at a dead sprint. The others were right behind him, but Wilhelm lagged behind, carrying his *Panzerschreck* and several rockets. They reached the town in mere minutes.

"*Herr* Schweitzer, *Herr* Schweitzer!" Blaz yelled at the top of his lungs.

"*Herr* Schweitzer!" Gunther bellowed. After he'd done so, he coughed loudly.

The *Wehrmacht* lieutenant strode out of the building looking out to the field, "*Ja?* What is it?"

"The Reds have arrived," Gunther reported. A distant explosion sounded. The bridge was destroyed.

"Battle positions! Everyone, you know where to go!"

"Lieutenant, there are at least three battalions on the other side of that river," Blaz added to Gunther's report, "Sergeant Hertz reported at least fifteen hundred men."

Schweitzer hid his terror well, before turning, "Artur, shoot a message off to command! Tell them we require reinforcements! *Sofort!* Immediately!" he shouted. "What did I just order!" Schweitzer yelled at the boys, who scrambled away to their positions.

Blaz sprinted to the second floor of one building, to his designated position. Ivo followed, sniper rifle in hand. One soldier manned the MG-42, assisted by Jaye to keep a consistent flow of bullets fed to the machine gun. Two other men, both with semi-automatic rifles, took positions to the left of the machine gun, while Blaz and Ivo took the right. The man on the machine gun looked to the adult soldiers, then the boys.

"You all owe me thirty-five dead Russians before you're allowed to die," he told them coldly.

Blaz gaped. He hadn't killed half to that many in the entire war yet.

"That bad?" one adult soldier asked.

"Three battalions, and Russian battalions are a hell of a lot bigger than German battalions. Fifteen is the low end of their numbers."

"How long can we hold out?"

"With the bridge gone, I'd say three days. We've got the ammunition. The forest protects our north, so they won't be able to build a bridge and outflank us that way. We can keep our attention to the south and east for them to flank us."

"Knowing the Russians, their men will probably charge us. They always charge small positions."

"Well, what else can they do? It's *Shtrafbat*. They can't take a step back. We'll light the bastards up if they charge."

Koby, Jarman, Tristan, and Werner came running into the town from the fields. The Russians were only about a kilometer from the river. Tristan and Gunther now manned the machine gun with a soldier next to the artillery, behind a wall of sandbags. Koby, Jarman, Werner, Wilhelm, and Hans all took positions on the second or first floors of buildings. Machine guns were on both the first and second floors too, of the buildings facing east, the Hauptmann at Minsk had supplied them well. Blaz readied his rifle, preparing for the imminent wall of death on its way.

"Hold fire!" Schweitzer yelled, "Wait till I give the order!"

The Russians were only five hundred meters from the river, tanks leading the advance with men riding atop but most marched behind. The wall of Reds continued to come closer. It was so quiet, save the distant sound of the marching and the tanks' engines rumbling. Even though Blaz knew the tanks would have to stop, he still shook. Ivo put a hand on Blaz's shoulder, "Relax. Hands on the rifle, it's your best friend right now."

Blaz took a deep breath, and gripped the rifle tighter, raising it to aim.

"Lieutenant! We have a clear shot at their infantry!"

"Concentrate fire on the closest formation to you!" Schweitzer bellowed.

The machine guns fired off short bursts into the Russian ranks. Blaz could just see the bodies collapsing in the distance. The Russians marched closer to the tanks, but with hundreds of men, many continued to make good targets. The men riding on top of tanks, fell to the backs of the line to avoid the fire laid on them from machine guns. They were now stopped at the river. Blaz kept his gun aimed on the Russians, though he was out of range. The Russian tanks raised their cannons as he looked down his rifle's sights.

"*Scheiße!*" a soldier shouted, "Incoming!"

The wall of tanks fired simultaneously. Blaz instinctively ducked below the window, though that would do him no good if a shell hit the wall in front of him. The shells tore through buildings, stone and wood splintering into the air. The building shook, and the floor under Blaz collapsed.

Blaz hit the ground, and debris showered him. He coughed as dust rose, and brought himself to his feet, pulling splinters out of his hands. Blood welled up. Jaye and the other three soldiers crawled out of debris. The other soldiers stumbled to their feet.

"Get your weapons! The rest of the building is going to collapse soon!" the machine gunner shouted. Another tank shell screamed by blowing one soldier nearly in half and hitting the building supports. The soldier screamed in agony, his blood and insides pouring out across the ground.

"Shoot me! Shoot me!" he screamed at the machine gunner. Blaz looked away, only to hear the bang of a pistol.

"Get out! Now!" the machine gunner yelled, as he and the other surviving soldier sprinted away from the building. Blaz turned to follow Ivo and Jaye out, when he saw Hans buried underneath the wood.

"Hans!"

"Get out," Hans said weakly, "You heard him, this building is about to collapse."

"Then I best get you out quickly," Blaz replied. He rushed to Hans and began lifting wooden boards and beams off his friend. His bloodied hands stung with pain whenever he lifted a heavy beam, as the splintered wood ripped his hands up further.

"*Hier, los, los, los!*" Blaz yelled when he had cleared most of the debris. Hans got to his feet, Blaz helped him out of the building. As they exited, another shell slammed into the building, collapsing the remaining walls behind them.

"*Danke* Blaz," Hans murmured with a nod.

"Back to the rubble," the machine gunner told them, "We can use it as cover. *Los!*"

Blaz followed the soldier back to the rubble, taking a position behind the remains of the front corner of the building. Ivo took the position next to him.

"The Reds aren't moving," Blaz told him, "What's happening?"

Occasional bursts from German machine guns and their Tiger Tank fired on the stationary Russian army. They remained stationary into the night.

Der Rote Pest

"*Herr* Schweitzer, command responded!" Blaz heard a voice yell.

"And?"

"Reinforcements are on their way!"

Blaz and Ivo sighed, and looked at each other.

"Are they going to attack tonight?" Blaz heard Jaye whisper.

"Maybe," the machine gunner answered, before firing a burst, his tracer shedding just a bit of light. No Russians were in the field. Seconds after the bullets had been fired, artillery sounded in the distance.

"Incoming!" A German yelled. Blaz and Ivo stayed in position. There was nothing they could do but hope for luck. Or pray for mercy. The artillery slammed into the town. Blaz heard screams from soldiers who had only been grazed by shells. Others never had the chance to scream.

Shells rained down, only feet in front of Blaz and Ivo. They both ducked and shielded their eyes as shrapnel and dust scattered. It was a good thing they did.

Blaz felt a piercing pain in his arm. He let out a cry and glanced at his right arm. He felt around, finding where he'd been hit by the debris. His sleeve had been cleanly sliced, and an equally clean slit ran through his upper forearm, below his elbow.

"Ivo, Ivo!"

"*Ja?*"

"I need you to wrap my arm. Right below the elbow, it got sliced open."

Ivo felt around in his little bag on the back of his belt and pulled out white wrapping.

"Hold it out."

Blaz held his right arm out, pain shooting through it. Ivo felt for the wound, stopping suddenly.

"That's a lot of blood, Blaz," Ivo told him nervously, as he started to wrap his arm tightly to stop the bleeding. Blaz just gritted his teeth while Ivo wrapped his arm.

"They're crossing the river! Tanks are stuck behind the river. Prepare for an infantry assault," the machine gunner yelled. Blaz checked his rifle in the late morning light. It was still cocked and loaded. The Soviets emerged from the river. About one-third of their force was charging. The German Tiger Tank fired away, and a Soviet tank burst into flames. The machine guns unleashed a torrent of bullets onto the advancing Russians. Though they were heavily outnumbered, their positions and machine guns made up for it.

Blaz kept his rifle aimed. The Russians were sprinting full speed ahead with no fear in their eyes. Ivo fired a shot, then worked the bolt on his rifle. All Blaz could do was wait. Wait for the Russians to be within effective range of his rifle. Gunshots sounded across the town. The artillery lowered to fire directly at the Russians. It's massive power tore through a Russian, blood just sprinkling to the ground where his body had been. Blaz's eyes went wide, but he refocused immediately. The Russians were almost in range. As they came, the Soviet tanks fired simultaneously. Shells hammered into the walls of German fortifications, giving the infantry several seconds to advance while the Germans recuperated. Blaz chose his target and watched the man approach. The man fearlessly charged ahead, right into range of Blaz's rifle. He fired, and the Russian fell. With every shot, Blaz's pace quickened, he reloaded in seconds and resumed shooting as the Russians grew closer. Their ranks thinned but soon that wouldn't matter.

The machine guns transitioned from quick bursts to long, sustained fire.

"Ivo, straight ahead! Bazooka for the Tiger! Target him!" Blaz yelled after he missed a shot at the man with the bazooka. Ivo scanned for the man, then crouched low to avoid Russian rifle fire. Blaz fired on a Russian rifleman who'd paused to find a target. The man fell to the ground. Blaz returned his attention to the bazooka man. Ivo fired, blood splattered into the air, and yet another man collapsed.

"Finish them!" the machine gunner yelled to his small group. Hans, Ivo, and Blaz fired faster than ever. The Russians' sub machine guns were now in range. Bullets came in massive quantities, though the Russians were firing on the run and their aim was poor. Blaz continued to fell men; every other shot hit someone. Ivo hit man-after-man, rarely missing, he seemed to be going for officers and other snipers. Hans was taking out everything he felt on the Russians. His teeth were gritted, his hands gripped his rifle, and he was shooting better than ever before. But Blaz only knew how he himself was shooting. Nothing else existed but him and the Russians right now. Because if the Russians made it to the town, nothing else might exist. They were within fifty meters, but their once massive battalion was thinned.

"Pick targets nearest you, I'll deal with the rest!" the machine gunner yelled. Blaz he peeked above the decimated wall that remained, and quickly ducked back down. He had his man.

"*Los!*"

Blaz sprung up and fired a shot cleanly into his target, the Russian fell, his momentum bringing him forward. The machine gunner unleashed a sustained burst, mowing down the remaining Russians in front of them. The other German positions did the same, no Russians from the first battalion remained to charge. The riflemen turned and ran back to the Russian lines. Hundreds of bodies lay scattered across the field.

"Jaye," the machine gunner told his aid, "Spray some fire into the bodies. Make sure they aren't pretending. Everyone else cover him."

Jaye readied his MP-40, stood up, and sprayed fire into the nearest bodies. One Russian raised his gun, but the Germans hit him simultaneously before he could do anything. The other German positions repeated this process.

The machine gunner pulled out binoculars to scan the east. Ivo looked through his scope. "The first battalion's survivors are heading back to the tanks. Second battalion is trying to build a bridge for them," the machine gunner laughed, put away his binoculars and returned to his machine gun. "This should slow the construction. He aimed his machine gun towards the men constructing the bridge, which had clearly begun at night.

"Where's the third battalion?" Ivo murmured while looking through his scope, just loud enough for Blaz to hear.

Blaz watched the bridge, and saw men falling off, or jumping off as the machine gunner pounded the soldiers building the half-completed bridge. At that moment Koby came running over, yelling frantically, "We've been outflanked! Turn to the south! They sent a battalion to cross downstream last night!" Koby yelled, "*Los!*"

Blaz ran across the square with the machine gunner in the lead. The other adult soldier was shot dead by a Russian sniper as they sprinted across.

"They're close!" Ivo yelled as they took cover in a building.

"We'll hit them from in here!" the machine gunner ordered the four and they all sprinted up the stairs.

"They're charging!" Blaz shouted.

"Give them hell!" the machine gunner screamed at the top of his lungs, "*Für Deutschland, für Freiheit!*"

The youths raised their rifles, firing into the crowd of Russians. Several fell. But they were at the edge of the town.

"Fall back! Fall back!" the machine gunner yelled to the boys, "I'll hold them-" he was cut off by a bullet piercing his helmet. The boys scrambled back in shock.

"*Los! Los!*" Jaye shouted at the others, taking command as he picked up the machine gun and slung his MP-40 over his back, "Get downstairs!"

They bolted downstairs, guns readied. The first Soviets were charging up the southern street. Every German soldier fired on them, the Tiger tank and artillery as well. As the Russians ran by, about thirty meters from their building, Blaz opened fire. Jaye fired bursts of bullets into the Soviets, mowing down rows of them. By now, the Russians were in the town, taking cover at the mill, and buildings at the southern side of the tiny town. Hans, Ivo, Blaz, and Jaye had gone largely unnoticed, but now the Russians saw them, and opened fire. They stayed on the first floor of the house, shooting through windows. The Tiger was tearing through the Russian infantry crushing men and machine-gunning them. The young Germans were hammered hard; they raised their rifles up blindly.

"We need help!" Blaz yelled to Ivo, "We're cut off from everyone else!"

A grenade came flying through the window, landing only a few feet behind them. Blaz leapt towards it, securing it in his hands and covering it with his chest. He waited, waited for the explosion, wondering what it would feel like. But it never came. Cautiously, he moved off. He picked up the grenade and threw it back out the window.

Jaye stood up, firing the machine gun across the front of Russians. Hans, seeing the Russian fire relenting, stood up and fired. Blaz followed Hans' example and quickly fired two shots before taking cover again. The other German machine guns continued to pound the ill-timed and ill-planned attack.

"They're falling back!" Ivo shouted, raising his sniper and sprinting into the streets. Blaz followed with Hans and Jaye. They all began picking off the retreating Russians, like fish in a barrel. It looked like the day might be won, as the remains of the battalion retreated with the Tiger tank giving relentless pursuit, gunning down all in its vision.

"*Panzers!*" yelled *Herr* Schweitzer, "*Panzers* due east!"

Blaz, Ivo, Hans, and Jaye ran to the artillery where two boys nursed their wounded friend. Tristan and Gunther remained on the MG-42, Gunther's hands were stained with blood. Blaz couldn't ask why.

"They're across, their armor is across," Tristan said loud enough for all in the encirclement to hear.

"Then it's over," Gunther admitted, "They've still got a thousand men."

"We'll defend this position to the last bullet," Jaye unexpectedly claimed.

Now was not the time to dissent. No defeatism. "*Für Deutschland?*" Blaz asked in the most powerful voice he could muster.

"*Für Deutschland!*" came the enthusiastic cry.

The retreating battalion discontinued its retreat when they saw their tanks crossing. Men sprinted behind the tanks in the final battalion. The tanks stopped at the town. The Tiger blocked the main road in. A tank foolish enough to take a Tiger on alone was destroyed in one well-aimed blast.

"*Feuer!*" Schweitzer shouted to the few who held anti-tank guns. No Russian tanks exploded. The Russian infantry reentered the town, spreading out to make machine guns less effective.

Blaz aimed as the Russians ran in, wishing his rifle's cartridge held more than five bullets at once. Jaye and Gunther fired their machine guns, showing no fear.

"They're entering the eastern houses!" Ivo yelled to Jaye. Germans came sprinting out of the buildings including Koby, Werner, Wilhelm and Jarman, throwing grenades in before they left.

"Jesus Christ!" one boy yelled, as a bullet sliced through the side of his helmet. His friend rose to return fire. When he raised his rifle, blood splattered out his back. The teenager dropped his rifle with a gasp of pain, then looked down. A bullet had torn through his belly. He stumbled backwards until he tripped over the sandbags and fell to the ground.

"Stay down!" Blaz shouted over the gunshots to the wounded youth. He turned back and fired two quick shots at Russians climbing over the finally destroyed Tiger tank. Schweitzer ran to the encirclement of sandbags the youths defended, exposing himself.

"Retreat! I ordered retreat! *Schnell!* Now g-" Schweitzer took a bullet to the head and fell dead to the ground. The boys hardly reacted amid the battle, but Gunther obeyed and led the retreat.

"*Schnell!* Hurry! We've got to go!" Gunther waved the boys out of the artillery position, staying behind until the last man was gone. Hans helped one boy carry his wounded friend. Ivo dashed after with his sniper slung across his back, spraying fire from Jaye's sub machine gun. Koby came sprinting back into the town, fear on his face.

"This way! *Schnell*!" he waved. Tristan and Blaz helped away the second wounded boy away, Jaye and Gunther followed both firing like mad. Most Russians had gone to clear out empty houses though. The few outside unleashed a torrent of bullets. Their spray tore through Gunther's legs, bringing him to the ground. He let out a cry as he fell. Tristan and Blaz turned to see Gunther. Jaye began back-pedaling away from the fight, but still fired.

"Gunther!" Tristan screamed and left Blaz with the wounded boy.

"Koby! Help him!" Blaz yelled, shoving his companion forward, running after Tristan. Koby took the boy and ran with him after the retreating German soldiers. Tristan made it to Gunther and hoisted his squad mate up. Blaz sprinted to them, lobbing two grenades over their heads to create a cloud of dust in the road.

"Come on!" he waved frantically, as shots flew blindly out of the massive dust cloud. He slung his rifle over his back and got under Gunther with Tristan's help. But even with their help, Gunther couldn't even manage a jog on his wounded legs. They weren't going to make it. Jaye looked at Blaz and, surprisingly, smiled. A goodbye smile.

"I swore I'd have your back," he said, taking out two grenades and pulling the pins, "I'm going to be brave."

Jaye chucked the grenades into the road towards the Russians, sending up more dust. Before Blaz could say anything, he'd sprinted for cover, firing all the way to draw attention to himself.

"Jaye!" Blaz yelled, knowing Jaye couldn't hear him over the shooting now. But he knew what Jaye was doing this for. "Come on, Gunther, Tristan, we have to go!"

When they put some distance between themselves and the town, Blaz glanced over his shoulder. He saw Jaye on his knees, still firing the gun. Finally, Jaye was shot to the point that he had no strength left. He collapsed. Blaz desperately hoped he was still alive, maybe he would be taken prisoner. But a Russian walked up to Jaye's body and drove his bayonet into him, ending any chance that he might survive. Blaz turned back around, shell-shocked. What he saw ahead added insult to injury. Russian tanks were screaming after the retreating German forces. Blaz heard cannons fire. Then he saw smoke.

"*Panzer!*" Tristan shouted. A Russian tank came roaring after them, firing its cannon. The shell exploded meters away, sending them flying. Blaz hit the ground hard, his head slamming into the grassy field. When he opened his eyes, everything was blurry. He blinked. His vision was returning, he just needed to give it some time that he didn't have. He heard a machine gun fire, a shout, an explosion followed by shouts in Russian which were cut short by machine gun fire and another explosion. His eyesight returned to normal again, but he couldn't believe what he saw. Coming from the east were Tiger and Panther tanks. Soldiers followed behind, numbering in the hundreds. Their reinforcements! The cannons fired into the town, where Russian tanks remained close together and stationary. The battle wasn't over.

"Gunther!" Tristan got to his feet, stumbled, stood up again, and bolted to his friend. Blaz pushed himself to his feet and ran over to Gunther.

"Gunther!" Tristan yelled, tears starting to wash dirt and ash off his face. Gunther's eyes were closed. Blaz looked at Gunther's chest, to the bullet hole below his armpit, in addition to three in his legs, bleeding incessantly.

"Tristan, does he have a heartbeat?" Blaz asked in a hurry.

Tristan put his head to Gunther's chest.

"*Ja, ja* he does!" Tristan said with a burst of joy, "Medic! We need a medic!" he shouted to the passing soldiers. One branched off, revealing an SS patch on his collar. Blaz looked to the other passing soldiers. They all wore camouflage of the SS combat uniforms, rather than the straight field gray of the army branch. All had the same patch on their collar; the officers' caps had the skull symbol of the *Totenkopf* 'Death's head' in the center. All young save for the highest-ranking officers.

The medic examined his patient. He removed Gunther's outer uniform to get a closer look at the wounds.

"He will live," the SS medic smiled, "But he may lose his left leg, below the knee."

Tristan's joy at the first bout of news was replaced with terrified disbelief, "His leg? But why?"

"You see where the bullets hit?" the medic said, pointing to Gunther's lower leg; the shin and ankle, "He might not have sufficient blood flow to this area anymore, not to mention nerve damage. Lot of complicated things. But I'm not certain."

Tristan nodded, "At least he will live."

"*Ja*," the medic nodded, "It looks as if we're retaking the town. We'll need every man, you two get going."

"*Ja* sir."

Jaye's Iron Cross

The SS routed the unprepared Soviet force. They hunted the Russians who fled like a herd of scattered sheep. Blaz and Tristan arrived at the town to find the Tiger Tanks lined at the eastern side of the town. Some SS soldiers stood on top of the tanks, taking potshots at the last of the fleeing Russians. Trucks full of SS soldiers, ammunition, and fuel arrived in the town, driving past Blaz and Tristan.

Blaz saw Jaye lying in the road. He inched over to Jaye and knelt. Five bullet holes riddled Jaye's corpse.

"Jaye?" Blaz whispered, shaking his friend, "Jaye?"

No response. Jaye's dark blue eyes just stared into infinity. Tristan handed Blaz his blanket from his knapsack. Blaz stared up at Tristan, and kept it held in one hand. Then he undid his Iron Cross and clipped it to Jaye's uniform.

"Jaye Baumann gave up his life to save his friends, and receives the Iron Cross," Tristan's voice came from behind Blaz, "*Heil dir*, Jaye."

"*Danke*, Jaye," Blaz whispered quietly, as he placed the blanket over his friend.

What to do with Russian Prisoners

The SS marched Russian prisoners into the center of the town. Blaz strode over to ask Koby about their squad.

"What happened? Who made it?" Blaz asked miserably.

"Ivo, Jarman, Hans, Werner, and myself. Also, the two wounded boys, their friend and seven army soldiers. Most of the army died in the town."

"Wilhelm?" Blaz asked putting his head in his hands.

"*Nein*," Koby replied, adding no more details, "What happened to you guys?"

"Tristan is all right. But Gunther might lose his leg. And Jaye died saving us."

Koby said nothing. He just looked to the ground and kicked up some dust. Then he murmured, "Lord, have mercy."

"Get down on your knees, Russian dogs!" an SS soldier shouted, beating a Russian in the back with the butt of his rifle. Seven Soviets bent down to their knees, a couple of them with tears in their eyes, but most with hatred and defiance. Koby and Blaz ran over to watch the spectacle.

"You see that? You see that!" one tall, blond-haired, blue-eyed soldier shouted. He yanked the blanket off Jaye, and pointed at his body, "You did that!" then he kicked one Russian in the ribs.

"Take them outside the town, you know what to do," an SS officer ordered the blond SS soldier. Blaz noticed a metal SS insignia clipped next to an Iron Cross.

"*Jawohl, Obersturmbannführer*," the soldier saluted, "Adi! Ottokar! Rodolfo! Come with me!" Three soldiers stepped forward. Two held bayoneted rifles, one a sub machine gun. The tall, handsome soldier casually glanced around the circle of soldiers, making eye contact with Blaz for only a moment. Blaz did a double take but the moment was over.

Erich?

The handsome soldier dismissed this and gestured to the SS soldiers he'd called. Blaz immediately looked back in the soldier's direction.

"Come on," Blaz told Koby.

"What? Where are we going?"

"Just follow me," Blaz walked to the *SS-Obersturmbannführer* and saluted.

"What can I do for you young men?" the officer asked Blaz and Koby.

"We request permission to join the-" he pointed to the four soldiers herding the Russian prisoners into the fields to the east.

"Of course, some vengeance is called for after this," the officer nodded gesturing to the dead Germans from Blaz and Koby's company, "By all means, go."

Blaz and Koby ran to catch up to the SS soldiers slowing down to stay about ten meters behind them. The young soldiers turned around warily but nodded amongst each other when they saw their uniforms. The tall SS soldier ordered a halt soon after. He gave a command to the Russians in their language. Koby showed more attentiveness, just in the slightest, when the soldier said this. The Russians knelt to the ground, hands on the backs of their heads. Blaz and Koby approached the scene quietly, though the soldiers knew they were there.

"Why are you following us?" the handsome blond asked as he turned to face them. Two of the other soldiers turned around at this as well. Though they had more height than both Blaz and Koby, their youthful faces made it clear they were all younger than eighteen.

Blaz pointed to the tall, handsome SS soldier, "Are you Erich Meyer?"

The soldier's eyes widened. "*Ja*, that's me."

"Are you from Seelow?" Blaz asked. There could be many 'Erich Meyers' in Germany.

"*Ja!*" the soldier exclaimed, grinning, "Is that you, Blaz?"

Blaz nodded with a small grin.

Erich looked Koby's way, "And you, Koby?"

Koby smiled back, "*Ja*, it's me."

Erich opened his mouth to say something else, but before any words escaped, he seemed to realize he was in the middle of an execution. He turned to his fellow SS soldiers. "Can you carry out this one?"

"*Ja*, no problem Erich," another German-looking soldier nodded.

"*Danke* Adi, guys."

Erich walked over to Koby and Blaz. He gave both of them brief hugs, with disbelief his friends were actually in front of them, "What are you doing here?"

"We've been with a company since last year. We were sent here a few weeks ago," Koby answered. The same exasperation was in his voice as Erich, only much more so.

"Come on, let's get back to the town," Erich told them.

"Okay," Koby agreed and the three of them walked away from the Russians. Seconds after they'd turned around Blaz heard gunshots. He glanced over his shoulder. All the Russians lay dead on the ground. The soldiers turned over the bodies with their feet making sure the bullets had killed the Russians.

"Why'd you kill the prisoners?" Blaz asked Erich.

"We can't keep prisoners with the mission we're on, they'd slow us down. Why do you care?"

Blaz shrugged.

"Anyway," Erich began, looking at Blaz as if he'd never heard a question of this nature before, "Where have you guys been helping and fighting since Leningrad? I haven't written in I don't know how long."

"We've been in Estonia, a training camp in, I think it was in Prussia?" Blaz looked to Koby for help.

"It was Prussia," Koby confirmed then continued the recollection of their journey across Eastern Europe, "And after that we joined the *Wehrmacht* and got these great new uniforms. We fought in a city in Russia, then they moved us back to artillery. After our army retreated, we were added to this company. And we've been with this company since the beginning of this year. What's left of it," Koby added, as only seventeen had survived the Russian assault.

"Who was that in the road? The kid that had a bayonet wound?" Erich asked.

"Jaye."

Erich kicked at the dirt mid-stride. "Is everyone else alive? Ivo, Jarman, Jurgen, everyone else from the KLV camp?"

Koby and Blaz looked at each other. Koby answered, "Jarman and Ivo are fine. So are Tristan and Hans. Jurgen was killed."

Erich took the news surprisingly calmly. "I don't suppose you want to tell me how it happened?"

"*Nein. Bitte nein*," Koby replied.

"Understandable," Erich nodded, and walked on silently until they entered the town.

Totenehrung (Honoring of the Dead)

"Let's go get Jarman and Ivo," Koby told both Erich and Blaz.

"*Ja*, let's," they agreed. Koby led them down Main Street, which was packed with SS soldiers and armor. But the trucks were pulling out to the west, in the direction of the forest.

"Jarman! Ivo!" Koby called when he saw them sitting in the rubble of a building, cleaning the barrels of their weapons. Jarman looked up, Ivo did not.

"Ivo!" Koby yelled again as they drew near, still Ivo did not look up.

"Still can't hear?" Koby asked Jarman.

"Still can't," Jarman answered with some concern, "That shell landed right next to him, explosion was loud, he hit his head hard. I hope that's the cause, then he'll get better."

Ivo looked up then, seeing them approach out of his peripheral vision.

"He'll be all right," Erich said, "It's happened to me before, it just takes some time."

"*Wer bist du? Ein Arzt?*" Jarman asked the SS soldier. Who are you? A doctor?

"*Nein*," Erich answered with an embarrassed smile, and put his hand next to the metal SS insignia, "Are you Jarman Knecht?"

"*Ja*," Jarman said, looking the SS soldier up and down. Then he saw the SS insignia he'd given Erich, still on the uniform, "Oh my God! Erich!" he exclaimed, leaping up and giving Erich a big hug, "What are you doing here, of all places?"

"You called for reinforcements, command thought this position was too advantageous to let slip away. You told us there were at least three battalions, we knew you could hold out a while with your position. They had time to call for us, we've been trained for years. One of us is worth at least ten Soviet soldiers. We're young, we're among the best. That's why they sent us."

"Do you know anything about the Russian advance, other than where we are?"

"When we left, we were given orders to wipe out resistance here, rescue your company then lay in wait for the Russians by the road. We're going to dig in in the forest, no one is going to get past. We know the small brigade you just faced was only the tip of the Bolshevik spear. There are more coming."

"We're not staying in the town?" Koby asked.

"*Nein*, we're falling back into the forest, where they won't be able to see us as they advance. They'll see their dead comrades, and our dead comrades. They'll think their men have advanced, and they will head down this road by the forest. We will have tanks, and anti-tank weapons ready to ambush them."

"All right then. How many men are in your battalion?"

"Six hundred men, twenty-two tanks, ten trucks, and twenty-five horses. Most of our armor already left for the forest," Erich said, glancing to the center of the square where SS soldiers and survivors from the original company were lining up.

The *Obersturmbannführer* was now ordering many men and tanks to head back to the forest but keeping some in the town.

Then he called over the German youths.

"Ivo," Erich said loudly, "Ivo, can you hear me?"

Ivo just looked at Erich, he still hadn't figured out who this was. Erich had changed quite a bit, and just by his looks it was hard to tell who he was. He waved awkwardly at this SS soldier, wondering why this particular person was still talking with Koby, Jarman, and Blaz. Erich gestured for Ivo to follow them. Ivo slung his rifle over his shoulder and marched after them. The only ranking adult *Wehrmacht* officer who had survived the assault stood next to the *Obersturmbannführer*. It appeared they were about to award medals. The *Obersturmbannführer* held several medals in his hands, allowing the *Wehrmacht* officer to present them to his own men who'd earned an award.

The *Wehrmacht* officer awarded the two injured German teenagers with the wound badge. He then did the same for Gunther. "Gunther Schütz was wounded bravely defending his Reich and brothers. He receives the wound badge." Gunther was held up by two SS soldiers, and the *Wehrmacht* officer attached the medal to Gunther's uniform. It was gray and circular with an engraved German helmet making up most of the award. Two swords crossed behind the helmet. On the helmet was a Swastika. Gunther nodded to the officer, though he'd much rather have his legs function again than a medal.

"Helmut Schmid destroyed two tanks late in the battle, when all appeared lost. He receives the Iron Cross-First Class."

The *Wehrmacht* officer walked past many SS soldiers, before stopping in front of a soldier who Blaz recognized as Ottokar.

"Ottokar Faust led the charge on the northern flank, wiping out Russian machine gunners. He receives the Iron Cross-Second Class."

Ottokar beamed with pride, looking Erich's way from the corner of his eye. Blaz saw Erich smile and give him a nod.

After a few more SS soldiers were decorated, the officer approached Koby, saying, "Koby Hertz returned to our crumbling positions, even after a retreat had been called and he had put a great distance between himself and the Russians. Yet he still returned. He helped away one of our wounded *Hitlerjugend* who still lives because of him. He receives the Iron Cross-Second Class. Tristan Rothkirch rescued yet another soldier, allowing his other comrades to be the first to retreat, putting himself in danger. He receives the Iron Cross-Second Class."

The officer called to all the soldiers present, "I ask for a moment of silence for our brave comrades who gave their lives to protect their brothers, their families, their nation."

The *Wehrmacht* placed their hands on their foreheads under their helmets and caps in a military salute. The SS saluted, but rather, raised their right arms high into the air.

SS will not Rest, SS will Annihilate

"You've never taken a prisoner?" Blaz asked Erich, "You?"

"We can't anymore and besides, there is no point. They do us no good, and they have been bombing our towns. They deserve what they get. Why are you so concerned with the Reds? They're our enemy."

Blaz would've loved to have said Lukov. But that was out of the question. And after the reading of 'Germany Must Perish!' Blaz's empathy for them had been shaken.

"They are people and killing is a big deal. I've done my share of killing in this war, but in war it's different. When someone surrenders, you're supposed to take them prisoner. If you show no mercy, can you expect any?"

Erich glared at Blaz. The look in his eyes said, "Did you just ask that? I'm SS," but Erich's mouth replied with, "I've seen my comrades taken captive. Some I never see again. Sometimes I'll find them dead after we've won a battle. Not dead by bullets or even daggers. They'd surrender, then the Soviets drive spikes through their heads... even their tongues, ears, and worse. Some branded by hot iron. And sometimes they're still alive after that, that's how I find them. But sometimes the Soviets shoot them on the spot, they almost shot me. But *Obersturmbannführer* Förster and his men saved me Adi, Ottokar, and Rodolfo. That's what is left of my squad. I was in school with my squad for two and a half years. Eight other young men, and they never will see their twentieth birthday. Two and a half years, and then I saw the Bolsheviks just shoot them one by one. Their pistols only hold eight bullets and the Reds ran out. I only lived because the bastard shooting us ordered us to be transferred across the city to be shipped to a camp. *Herr* Förster and his men rescued us. Damn quick work. And mercy after that? *Niemals, niemals*! Days after that I get a letter. It's a condolence letter, telling me my father died. Not even on the front lines, where he would've wanted to die. Shot by a partisan while he drove to a meeting. The Russians killed my friends, my father. I have no mercy left for them. Damn every last one."

Blaz nodded, "I'm sorry, Erich."

"Years of SS schooling. And I still thought I had some mercy left," Erich shook his head after saying this as if it was cringeworthy to speak of mercy anymore, "I've never seen humanity to warrant mercy. Not once."

Our Job

That night, Erich returned to his squad to guard the road. *Obersturmbannführer* Förster told the *Wehrmacht* soldiers to relax, they'd done enough for one day. The squad joined their comrades, deeper into the forest near the headquarters of the SS. Which were tents.

"No humanity? Have you seen any humanity?"

"Blaz, I've seen so little. So little outside of Lukov."

The two teenagers sat in silence.

"I know that Erich won't show them mercy. But I should've done more for those prisoners today. That's the problem, we just stand to the side and let things like that happen," Blaz said after a while.

Koby looked up at Blaz, "What the hell are we supposed to do about it? We can only just suggest not killing them. That's it. And Russkies will kill us if they get the chance, anyway. Lukov would kill you on the battlefield, he wouldn't show you mercy even if he recognized you. Blaz, we've got to be brutal against a brutal enemy."

"Even if we know it's not right? Is there really nothing we can do? What if... what if the Russians make it to *Deutschland*? Are they going to give us any mercy after what we've done to them?"

"We've only fought this way because of what they did to our soldiers in the opening days. *Frau* Vogel told us all about the atrocities the Russians did to us in the opening days of the war. And I have heard they have taken Poles into Siberia to freeze to death. Do you not remember the Katyn massacre? Thousands of Poles murdered! That's the enemy we are fighting. I don't understand why they even fight for a maniac like Stalin. They're barbarians from the east! They wouldn't show mercy even if we showed them mercy. And you damn well know it, Blaz," Koby saw Blaz ready to say something in response, but anticipated the rebuttal, "We've seen a lot of horrible killings in this war. And we've even taken place in some. But in war, our actions aren't always consistent with our morals. We don't kill because we enjoy it, I don't kill because I enjoy it. We are soldiers. We kill because it is our job. We kill because it's the best option we have."

Blaz nodded, yet again. It was their job. They were in a war. Yet it didn't sound like Koby.

We Hunted Them Like a Herd

July 15, 1944

Blaz walked westward through the forest. He, Koby, and Ivo all walked close together. The *SS-Obersturmbannführer* wanted men watching their rear, as it was entirely possible the Russians could move past them via another route. Ivo walked behind Koby and Blaz. He was depressed, or perhaps shell-shocked in the worst way possible. Even when they got his attention he wouldn't respond. His hearing still hadn't come back. He'd been staying close to his sergeant, so he would know what their orders were, by following Koby and duplicating him.

"You think Ivo's hearing will come back?" Blaz asked, after seeing Ivo following them with his face downcast and dismal.

"God, I hope so," Koby answered, "I've never see him so sad before, except when," Koby didn't finish.

Ivo kept his head down, shuffling behind them. Blaz and Koby marched on, some SS soldiers coming into view.

"There's where they want us, let's go," Koby pointed. Ivo followed when they gestured to him. "The Russians will be here any day. That last brigade was the beginning."

"If we're going to lay in wait, we'll need to make our attacks quick, *ja*?"

"*Ja*, if we don't finish them within half an hour, then that's too long. And no survivors, Blaz. No one can report our position," Koby said, conveying through his sternness that he meant it.

"By the *Führer's* command."

Koby, Blaz, and Ivo waited for quite some time. The sun moved across the sky, like the arm of a clock. Sometime in the later afternoon, Koby and Blaz heard tanks firing. The dozen SS soldiers spread out across the rear flank turned at the noise as well.

"That's the ambush," Koby told Blaz.

"We stay here?" Blaz asked.

"*Ja*. And that's a good thing for Ivo. If he's going to hear again we need him out of battle for at least two days."

"How much of a chance do you give him? Of hearing again?" Blaz asked, rubbing his eyes.

"Schlusser told us about all sorts of injuries and whatnot. He said deafness on the battlefield happens a lot. But normally you recover within a couple hours, if not minutes. And if Ivo can't hear after tonight-"

"*Nein*, he'll hear again," Blaz interrupted in denial, "He will."

"I hope and pray he will."

The distant shooting died down, after easily less than half an hour. There was an occasional round of shots afterwards, presumably from Russian soldiers being executed.

"Hans, Jarman, and Tristan don't have to fight yet, do they?"

"*Nein*, only the army soldiers. We get to stay in camp or defend the rear. But Jarman volunteered to go with Erich's squad."

"You don't find soldiers like Jarman every day," Blaz smiled. He respected Jarman's bravery, that was one thing no one could take away from Jarman.

"Any news from the Western Front?" Tristan called, as he made his way towards his squad mates.

"*Keiner*," Blaz shook his head, "And the Eastern Front?"

"*Sieg Heil*," Hans reported, "We wiped out a Russian infantry platoon."

"Any casualties?" Koby asked.

"The SS took them by complete and total surprise, only wounded casualties for us," Werner answered.

"How is Ivo doing?" Tristan asked as he reached their position, showing concern that Ivo had not looked up as they'd walked towards him. Ivo stood, staring into the field.

"He can't hear still," Koby said.

"Will he hear again?"

"I don't know."

"Why's his hand shaking?" Tristan asked.

"I don't know," Koby repeated.

"I think I can help answer that," a nearby, lone SS rifleman interrupted, with an odd sense of eagerness.

"*Ja*, what do you think?" Blaz asked him.

"When and how did this happen?"

"When we were retreating, Ivo and one of our friends were running side by side. A Russian tank shell exploded right next to them and sent them flying. I think he hit his head. Our friend got up after he'd hit the ground and the Russians shot him, several times," Koby breathed in bitterly and continued, "And Ivo saw it all. I saw it too. Then you guys showed up."

The SS soldier nodded, he'd seen this happen before, even though he was only months older than the boys, "Well, the shell and consequential fall is obviously what knocked out his hearing. The hand shaking, I believe he's got some head trauma or nerve damage. That may have been what made him go deaf, actually. I think it's because he hit his head, the more I think about it."

"That is very possible," Koby agreed.

"He's experiencing some head trauma and shock, and when you can't hear, that makes it worse. He knows he's in a war zone, but he can't hear anything. It makes you be on edge."

"Will he hear again?"

"This happened yesterday. If his hearing doesn't come back tonight, he probably will never hear again," the soldier answered grimly.

"*Danke*," Koby nodded to the SS teen, "Are you sure?"

"Fairly. I was training to be a doctor before the war started. Then I got drafted for an SS school. I've lost a lot of my knowledge on that, but that's how it goes," the soldier shrugged, turning away.

Blaz looked over to Ivo. The small boy in the squad was still staring across the field, enjoying the senses he had as a blood red sun set.

Gott Mit Uns

Blaz awoke in the night to see Ivo wandering around, with Koby trying to calm his friend. They were talking.

"I heard shooting, I heard shooting, Koby," Ivo frantically rattled off, breathing rapidly. The German tanks fired in the distance. Ivo put his hands on the sides of his temple as the crackle of the cannons echoed in the night. He acted as if sounds of war were a new concept to him. Blaz sat up and rubbed his eyes.

"Koby, the Russians are coming. They're coming," Ivo said with a raised voice, having no idea of his surroundings or how loud he was talking. He pointed to SS soldiers, lining the forest as if he thought they were Russians. His raised voice woke up Tristan.

"*Nein*, it's all right Ivo. The Russians aren't coming," Koby assured Ivo, "It's just us."

This turned out to be a poor choice of words. A middle-aged SS soldier had come over from his squad and approached in Koby's line of sight, behind Ivo. The raised voices had attracted attention from them.

"What's happening here?" the soldier called.

Ivo spun around with uncanny speed and pulled out his pistol.

"*Nein*, Ivo!" Koby shouted, stepping in between the SS soldier and Ivo. The SS soldier pulled his pistol in the time that Koby stepped between the two. All the squad was awake by now.

"What are you doing?" the SS soldier roared at Ivo, who tightened his grip on the pistol, his hands trembling.

"Don't yell, it'll make things worse," Koby ordered the soldier, "Ivo, put the pistol away. You're among Germans."

"Put the pistol away," the SS soldier repeated, lowering his own.

Ivo's hands shook on his pistol. Slowly, eventually, he put it back into his holster.

"He needs to come with me, immediately," the SS soldier ordered.

"I understand sir," Koby said, "Do I have your permission to accompany him? I'm his sergeant."

"Of course, you should definitely come."

July 19, 1944

Ivo's situation was straightened out well. The SS had seen cases like this before for various reasons. He was cleared to continue fighting; there was no reason to send a healthy soldier away.

But the SS was driven from their position, and the boys went with them. Their new position was a large town, where the Neman River flowed through the center. Already there were at least three battalions of soldiers there. The town was closely knit together with buildings separating streets like giant, long walls. Most of the civilians had either fled or taken shelter inside their homes.

The SS and *Wehrmacht* agreed on house-to-house fighting to limit the Russian use of tanks. They would place their few tanks in well-covered positions where they could inflict maximum casualties.

Koby's severely depleted squad was combined with three surviving soldiers: Helmut Schmid, Adolf Ingalls, and Joachim von Balasko. Helmut Schmid was made Sergeant and Koby made corporal.

God Save the Führer

July 20, 1944

Schwinghammer and his squad of SS soldiers jogged down the hallway of the *Bendlerstrasse* offices. He readied his machine gun, hearing the shooting up ahead. He came to a stop in front of a door, turning to his men.

"I want Stauffenberg alive," he ordered. He opened fire into the door, then kicked it down. The SS soldiers stormed in, two tackling a man to the ground. The other men inside quickly dropped their weapons, with soldiers now surrounding them. Schwinghammer approached the man that his troopers had restrained. The man wore a military uniform and an eye patch. His right hand was missing along with two fingers on his left hand.

"What was it, Stauffenberg?" Schwinghammer asked, looking into the man's eye, "Why did you try to kill our *Führer*?"

Stauffenberg did not answer.

Schwinghammer turned to one of his men. "Send word to Goebbels that we have captured Stauffenberg." The soldier saluted and jogged away.

Schwinghammer returned his gaze to Stauffenberg. "Greed? Power? What was it?"

"Love. For the Fatherland."

Schwinghammer nodded. "The enemy does not fight against *Führer*, but against the German people, my friend."

"They will stop fighting the German people without the *Führer*," Stauffenberg replied.

"There are other ways to wage war against a people other than bullets. You know this. The *Führer* is the guardian of our people. There will be no victory without him."

Stauffenberg did not reply.

"Take him away," Schwinghammer ordered.

"Impossible," Jarman shook his head when the German commander of the city announced that Hitler was dead. The *SS-Obersturmbannführer* and dozens of SS officers down to the corporals, had been placed under arrest. They stood behind the *Wehrmacht* commander who addressed the nearly two-thousand-man German force.

"The *Führer* died this morning, and we have been ordered to stand down while peace can be negotiated with the west while the war with the Soviet Union will be continued."

This message was met with nearly one unanimous emotion: rage. Some of the younger ones shouted, "*Heil mein Führer!*"

Blaz remained silent. Jarman was among those who shouted. Koby stared the thousand-yard stare in stupefaction.

"How did the *Führer* die?" a young voice demanded.

"We have not received that information yet."

"To hell with that!" another voice shouted, "We've fought for the *Führer* for years. We deserve to know how this happened! Who did this? Damn them to hell!"

"If I knew I would tell you," the commander shouted over the mumbling crowd of soldiers, "Now back to your posts! Immediately!"

The *Wehrmacht* soldiers obeyed this command, most begrudgingly.

"What're we gonna do without the *Führer?*" Ivo asked hopelessly, like one would ask what they would do without their father.

For the next few hours they worried and contemplated Germany without the *Führer*. Their adult counterparts stayed silent with concern, smoking cigarettes, and even breaking out a game of cards at one point. The leaderless SS squads waited, staring straight ahead. Koby's squad, on the other hand, were constantly talking and there was quite a bit of frantic pacing. Their afternoon of lamenting their *Führer* culminated when they prayed that the *Führer* still lived, and that this was only a miscommunication.

Koby led the prayer. "Dear God, we pray that you would have mercy on our nation. We need you so much now. Please protect the *Führer* through all this, if he is still alive. Allow him to be alive. We need the *Führer*, you've sent the *Führer*. Please, we beg that the *Führer* is still alive. Amen."

"Amen."

Who Says I am not Under the Special Protection of God?

As the afternoon turned into evening, and the sky turned from white clouds to red and orange clouds, the news came. The news was only the beginning of the changes the failed assassination on the *Führer* brought to Germany.

"Sergeant Schmid! Sergeant Schmid!" a young man in an SS uniform shouted while sprinting towards Schmid's squad. He nearly tripped he was going so fast.

"What is it?" Schmid asked him.

"The *Führer* lives! Our *Führer* is alive and well!"

The *Wehrmacht* and the SS erupted in cheers. Fists were raised into the air in triumph as well as stiff-armed salutes.

"The *Führer* is alive!" Hans exclaimed

"The SS officers have been restored to their positions. They'll be here any minute," the young man finished, before throwing up a salute, "*Heil* Hitler!"

In the sincerest and most enthusiastic way they ever had, everyone called, "*Heil* Hitler!"

"*Gott sei Dank*, the *Führer* is alive!" Ivo exclaimed, with tears of joy, and jumped into Jarman's arms.

"*Ja*, he's alive," Jarman smiled after catching Ivo, "*Gott sei Dank*."

Heil Hitler

July 24, 1944

Changes came quickly. On this day, in the streets of the Eastern European city on the Neman River, the *Wehrmacht* and SS were made to re-swear their oaths to the *Führer*. And each soldier was to do it individually. SS officers, from Sergeants to the *Obersturmbannführer* himself, spread out across the town to squads to ensure this happened. The SS squads nearby were sworn in first. Erich, a corporal, was the first in his squad to be sworn in a second time. All eyes in the area were on the young SS soldier. The SS officer began, asking Erich, "What is your oath?"

Erich held up his right arm, then answered, "I vow to you, Adolf Hitler, as *Führer* and chancellor of the German Reich loyalty and bravery. I vow to you and to the leaders that you set for me, absolute allegiance until death," Erich recited with sincerity, then, in a raised voice, finished the oath, "So help me God!"

"So, you believe in a God?" the officer continued. The soldiers' attention was captured by this unexpected question.

"*Ja*, I believe in a Lord God," Erich replied.

Then the officer continued, "What do you think of a man who does not believe in a God?"

Erich smiled at this question, it was particularly regarding the godless Soviets and their communist state, "I think he is arrogant, megalomaniacal, and stupid; he is not eligible for us."

"*Heil* Hitler?" the officer asked in conclusion.

"*Heil* Hitler!"

"*Ausgezeichnet*," the officer smiled, "Corporal Meyer, proceed to swear in the *Hitlerjugend* soldiers in the black uniforms and their squad mates, *verstehe?*"

"Understood."

Erich strode over to where his old friends and their sergeant were stationed outside of a building.

"Well, Sergeant," Erich said to Helmut Schmid, "Let's start with you."

"As you wish, corporal," Schmid agreed.

"What is your name, sir?" Erich asked.

"Helmut Schmid."

One-by-one the adults then teenagers were sworn in. Erich said everyone's name before asking them to swear allegiance to the *Führer*. Finally, Erich only had Blaz and Ivo left to swear in.

"Blaz," Erich said, as if he were meeting someone he'd only seen once before in his life.

"Erich," Blaz nodded in return.

"Blaz Senft, do you swear by God this sacred oath that to the *Führer* of the German Reich and people, Adolf Hitler, supreme commander of the *Wehrmacht*, that you shall render unconditional obedience and as a brave soldier you shall at all times be ready to give your life for this oath?"

Blaz took a deep breath, raised his right arm and began his oath to the *Führer*, "I, Blaz Senft, swear by, by," Blaz stopped, and nervously inhaled again, "By God this sacred oath that to the *Führer* of the German Reich and people Adolf Hitler, supreme commander of the *Wehrmacht* I shall render unconditional obedience… and as a brave soldier, I shall at all times be ready to give my life for this oath."

"*Heil* Hitler?" Erich asked with a skeptical look.

"*Heil* Hitler!" Blaz answered with unreserved energy. It was over. He would never have to take such an oath again.

Once Erich had sworn in Ivo, he turned to the entire squad, who stood erect in a line. "From now on you will no longer use the military salute," Erich said, showing them a hand-to-brow salute. The *Wehrmacht* had done this throughout the war as well up until now, "From now on you will use the Hitler salute during anytime you would be using the military salute. *Verstehe?*"

"Understood," all responded, performing a stiff-armed salute.

"*Gut.*"

"The Russians will be here in a matter of days," Schmid told the Knights. He led them down the streets to their new position: a multi-leveled asylum with windows aplenty and many rooms with thick walls. It was built right between several homes and looked just like them. The Russians could very well march right past them, making it an excellent place to ambush or defend, "Until they get here we will be laying mines, setting up sandbags to protect tanks, and hauling rubble. We will drop debris on them as they pass by us when buildings are close together and they must pass through narrow streets. Once we arrive, I will assign your positions, and you may use the rest of your time as you see fit, but you must stay in our building. We must be ready for Russian artillery and bombers."

"You sure they won't just bomb our families instead?" Hans muttered.

"What's that, Reichmann?" Schmid asked sharply.

"Nothing, sir."

The asylum was ransacked, inside and out. The walls stood strong, but most windows were shattered, and the roof was missing coverings in several places. Inside, papers littered the ground, chips of wood and bits of dirt lay around, furniture was in decay, either rotting wood or collecting dust. Metal beds were flipped over, but some still stood in their original places. The interior was mainly concrete with small crevices in places, even the occasional crater from grenades in a past fight for the city. It was a militant's palace. Schmid assigned everyone positions, always in pairs in different rooms. Once he had done so, they sat against the wall of one room, watching the sunset outside the lone window.

For Work and Bread

July 25, 1944

Setting up the defenses was on the ballot for the day. Jarman went with Erich's SS squad to carry rubble to places where it could be used as bombardment. Werner, Koby, and Hans were sent to dig anti-tank ditches across town. Tristan, Ivo, and Blaz were assigned to build protection for their own tanks. Sandbags and rubble had to be carried and placed in front of their Tigers, where they could wreak havoc on the Russians.

"Ivo, get some more over here, okay?"

"Got it," Ivo answered Blaz. He put his sand bag to the left of one of their Tiger tanks, building another wall on that side. Blaz hoisted another and carried it to the left side of the wall. Tristan followed him. Ivo came running back past them to retrieve a sandbag from the cart the horse pulled.

"Come on, faster! Get it done!" their SS overseer shouted, carrying three bags at a time. Blaz, Ivo, and Tristan shifted to two each.

"Keep working!" the SS overseer ordered. Blaz, Ivo, and Tristan had moved on to anti-tank ditches. They'd just finished one with the help of several *Wehrmacht* soldiers, but now moved on to another area in the road. Down a side street that was near the bridge they would retreat across if need be.

"Make this one a trench. Not as deep, I'll tell you when to stop," the overseer set a terrific pace. Blaz stabbed his shovel into the ground, only making a divot. Starting was the hardest part. He lined his shovel up vertically and jumped. A small cut was made in the ground. Not big enough to get started.

"Come on," Blaz muttered. He felt like an idiot more every second.

"Hey, need some help?"

Blaz jumped at the sudden, unexpected voice. He turned around to see Erich almost right behind him.

"Oh, hi Erich. When did you get here?"

"Just got let off for the night and happened to be walking this way," Erich answered, making it obvious he'd come here to see his old friends. "Need some help getting started?"

"*Nein*, I can do it," Blaz shook his head. He tried another jump. Erich watched with an amused grin. Blaz looked over his shoulder at Erich who crossed his arms with the same amused grin on his face. Blaz tried again. The ground had given way for the SS overseer and Tristan. Ivo was making as little progress as Blaz.

"Come on, Blaz. Just let me help you get it started. You're worn out, you haven't eaten much lately. Then you can keep digging," Erich smiled.

"*Nein*, I need to do this."

"All right, suit yourself," Erich shrugged. He extended the same offer to Ivo, who accepted. Then Erich asked the overseer where he could get a shovel to help out.

Blaz continued his quest to make a dent in the ground. After several jumps onto the shovel, the ground gave way.

Erich had returned and dug alongside them. "What were you working on today?" he asked Blaz.

"Setting up tank positions, with sandbags you know. And digging an anti-tank ditch. Now this. What were you up to?"

"I was probably the guy filling those sandbags this morning."

The scrape of shovels filled their silence. Ivo asked Erich about the SS school. Erich told him a good deal about it. The military aspects from shooting to tactics, the doctrine, the marching, and songs.

"How did you become a corporal?" Ivo asked, "Do you think Koby should've been in the SS, since you were a corporal?"

"*Ja,* Koby probably should have been drafted for the SS. I don't see why not. They trained us with the same men to form squads from the beginning. They looked for standout soldiers and I got noticed, being only fourteen when I got there. I was already one of the strongest in my squad. And SS training only made us stronger. But I got trained hard and got better at everything, shooting, even running. Ran a seventeen twenty-nine in a five kilometer."

"*Verdämmt,* that's fast Erich!" Ivo complimented him.

"*Danke.* Once I established myself as one of the best there, I was naturally selected to be an officer. Corporal or Sergeant, it's hard for seventeen-year-olds to sail higher than that. They made me a corporal. And I've stayed a corporal as long as we've been in combat."

"How did you get an Iron Cross?" Blaz asked.

Erich frowned. "In the battle after my squad was killed, Adi, Ottokar, Rodolfo, and I were separated from the main core of the battalion. We were cornered in a building by, I don't know, thirty Russians," Erich said. Soldiers without Iron Crosses often exaggerated their accomplishments, whereas soldiers with the prestigious award felt no need to. The Iron Cross spoke for itself. "We drew them in, the building was a few stories high, so we were able to kill them all by drawing them up a few at a time and beat them. After that, there was no one containing us, so we were able to outflank several machine gun positions. With those gone, our men advanced rapidly. The local Russian commander tried to flee, coward. We gave chase. He fled on horse, like many others. We gunned down several as we hunted down the commander and his bodyguards. Since I was the ranking officer, I received the Iron Cross. We all should have, but that's how it works."

"Wow, that's amazing," Tristan said.

"Sorry, who are you?" Erich asked, "You're in Koby's squad?"

"*Ja,*" Tristan nodded, as he knew full well this was Erich, "I've been in the squad for a few years."

Erich looked to Ivo and Blaz, who kept their faces blank. "You're not Tristan Rothkirch, are you?"

"I am."

"*Mein Gott,*" Erich murmured, "You don't look so weak anymore."

Tristan hammered the shovel into the ground, "I've been working hard."

"No kidding," Erich nodded. "You were a tiny little guy at the KLV camp."

"I know," Tristan said, his voice deepening, "Hans got me to wake up. Enough about that, you've been fighting quite a bit in the SS?"

"*Ja,* everywhere but the west. Since Normandy, most sixteen-year-olds and up in Germany have been rushed into the army, if they weren't already. And like you said, if you're in the SS, you really do never get a rest."

"We've fought a lot, but the battles are more spread out over time. We aren't just rushed from one battlefield to another," Ivo said.

"Understandable. There's a hell of a lot more people in the *Wehrmacht.* And the SS has a lot of responsibilities on and off the battlefield."

"What sort of responsibilities?" Blaz asked, "What have you had to do off the front lines?"

"Mostly we quell insurgencies. Sometimes we have to investigate people, search houses. The usual stuff that you'd imagine a police force doing. That'll be our job after the war," Erich said.

"You will stay in the military?" Ivo asked.

"The SS is paramilitary, but *ja.* You don't leave the SS," Erich jumped onto his shovel to dig deeper.

The Private on Neman's Shores

August 1, 1944

The block they were set on was shored up. Two more *Wehrmacht* squads arrived with an SS squad. Schmid gave the boys orders not to retreat until either he or Koby said. They would retreat across the bridge if it came to that. It would have to be a swift retreat. The bridge was long, and they'd be easy targets with no cover fire should their trenches fail.

Blaz closed his eyes as the metallic rumble of Soviet armor mixed with stomping Soviet boots. It almost sounded like thunder in the gray clouds that hung over the city. They could hear the outer German defenses firing away. Tristan and Blaz were stationed together in one room on the third floor of the asylum. They'd been given two *Panzerfausts*, Germany's cheap, effective, anti-tank weapon. After about thirty minutes, the sounds of fire from the outer defenses had ceased. The Russians obviously had had time to plan for this attack. Tristan was shaking, his grip on his rifle was loose.

"Calm down, Tristan," Blaz said.

Tristan took a deep breath, "Sorry, sorry," he mumbled, and looked down at his armband. He tightened his grip on his rifle. "I wish these *Panzerfausten* held more than one shot."

"They'd cost more and be heavier."

The marching and rumbling increased. The Russians were now in view. Their tanks were rolling down the street. Some broke off, going down other streets, the others went ahead. If they kept their course, they'd pass right under their position.

Come on, Bitte? Blaz thought. Hopefully, they wouldn't be spotted.

The Russians maintained course, but men were sprinting towards the building's entrance.

"*Feuer!*" came a German officer's voice. Blaz leaned out the window and took a shot at the commander of the lead tank. Apparently, many other soldiers had that same idea, because the commander was hit multiple times. Blaz ducked back into the building as the Russians returned fire.

"Tristan! Tank!"

"Got it!"

Tristan grabbed the *Panzerfaust*. He approached the window.

"I'll cover!" Blaz yelled and exposed himself to take a shot and draw attention from Tristan. His shot was a miss, but Tristan was quick on the other window, and fired a shot at the tank. The shot damaged the tank but didn't disable it.

"*Nein, nein*, they're coming in!" Tristan exclaimed as he ducked back behind cover, "Should we wait for orders?"

"I'll guard the door, you keep shooting."

"Okay."

Blaz bolted to the door, then looked down the hallway. Koby was running from door to door.

"Blaz! They're coming in! Get to the rear of the building! Hurry!" As he said this, a bullet hit the wall next to Koby. Blaz turned down the hallway and fired at the Soviet. The Russian fell to the ground but crawled behind cover.

"*Los!*" Blaz yelled to Tristan, "We need to get out of here!"

"That was quick," Tristan said picking up the unused *Panzerfaust*. They sprinted down the hallway. Schmid was holding the enemy back, firing his MP-40 in short bursts to deter them from coming down the hallway while his men retreated. Blaz turned the corner to safety with Tristan right behind him.

"There!" Blaz pointed to the door that lead to a ladder, "Let's go!"

Blaz opened the door and climbed down. Tristan followed immediately. Hans, Ivo, Jarman, and Adolf Ingalls were already at the bottom waiting for their squad with their rifles and *Panzerfausts*. Joachim von Balasko and Werner came out next, and nearly jumped down the ladder. Koby followed, falling off the ladder, but scrambled back up.

"Where is Helmut?" Ingalls asked immediately.

"He's coming! He's coming!" Koby said shaking his head up and down. Helmut opened the door and yelled as he slid down the ladder.

"Go! Now! They're coming! Get to the bridge!"

They sprinted away from the building. Helmut Schmid threw a grenade into the open door, to slow down any Russians.

"*Los! Los!*" Koby shouted to the squad leading them on the road to the bridge. As he said this, a Soviet Tank roared around the corner of the building running over Germans in their foxholes. Joachim turned to fire his *Panzerfaust*, but the tank's gunner fired first. Werner sprinted to him, but nothing could be done. Tristan and Jarman fired away, ending the new threat in a blaze of warheads. As soon as the tank went up in flames, Russians came around the corner of the building. Schmid and another squad of *Wehrmacht* soldiers came sprinting in to cut them off.

"*Los!*" Schmid screamed, "That's an order! *Lo-*" his neck exploded. Blaz couldn't breathe. Tristan hit him across the face.

"Come on, *Los!*" Tristan shouted, throwing his empty *Panzerfaust* to the ground "Werner! You too!"

Blaz shook his head and took off. They sprinted over a hill, with some German soldiers coming from side streets to join in their retreat. The shooting grew nearer and nearer.

"There's the bridge!" one soldier yelled.

Dozens of German soldiers sprinted across ahead of the Knights. Koby, Jarman, Hans, Ivo, and Ingalls had gotten a head start when Blaz froze up and were already on the bridge.

"Almost there," Blaz yelled to Werner. Some German soldiers began overtaking them, leaving fewer targets the Russians would be able to hit. Blaz's endurance kicked in, and he pulled ahead of Tristan and Werner, but the older, stronger *Wehrmacht* soldiers kept overtaking them. Blaz sprinted ahead, giving all he could, rifle clutched tight.

He was nearly on the bridge when the soldier in front of him collapsed. Blood splattered from his back onto Blaz's face. Blaz tripped over the man, dropping his rifle and scraping his hands against the concrete.

He scrambled up, ignoring the pain in his hands. He could see Russians coming, a couple hundred meters away. Tristan blew by. Blaz sprinted after him, with Werner falling in behind him. Another shot sounded in the distance. Werner shouted out in pain.

"Blaz! Help!" Werner cried after his last squad mate.

Blaz skidded to a stop with another soldier, who carried a *Panzerschreck* in gloved hands.

"*Bedecke mich*! Cover me!" the soldier yelled dropping his *Panzerschreck* and darting over to Werner. Blaz raised his rifle. He fired twice. The *Wehrmacht* soldier turned around, holding Werner in his arms, shielding as much of him from fire as he could and began sprinting away with him. And when he turned, finally revealing his face, Blaz saw he was black.

"Come on!" the soldier shouted to Blaz. Though he was a bit shocked, Blaz sprinted after the man, gaining ground.

"Hurry!" an officer yelled, "We have to destroy the bridge!"

Blaz sprinted as hard as he could to get to the German lines. A machine gun in a trench opened fire on the incoming Russians, the bullets flying past Blaz and the black soldier. Blaz made it behind the trench, and seconds later the black soldier leapt over the trench, Werner still in his arms. A massive boom sounded, and the bridge collapsed.

Koby sprinted over to meet them, giving Blaz a quick, relieved hug. Two brunette soldiers came alongside, smiling and gave the black soldier hugs as well.

"*Wo wollen sie ihm?*" the black soldier asked Koby, seeing his rank, "Where do you want him?"

Koby looked at the soldier, not hiding his surprise.

"Oh, uh," Koby stammered, "Can, can you bring him over here?"

"Sure," the soldier answered, following Koby over to where the remainder of their squad was huddled. The rest of the squad, save Adolf Ingalls, reacted in the same manner as Koby. There were many dropped jaws and all too obvious stares.

The black soldier laid Werner down next to Ivo and Jarman. Koby knelt down to examine Werner. The black soldier's two friends, who by now Blaz assumed were his squad mates, sat down amongst them.

"Jarman, come on, sit down," one of them said. Jarman turned his head, but the soldiers were looking at the black soldier who sat down next to them.

"He's going to be all right," Koby said with relief, "Broken ribs by two bullets and a twisted ankle, but that's all, it looks like."

"*Gut, gut,*" the black soldier smiled.

"Your name is Jarman?" Ivo asked the black soldier.

"*Ja,* Jarman Diallo," the soldier nodded.

"No kidding," Ivo said, "His name is Jarman too," Ivo pointed at Jarman Knecht.

"Well, pleased to meet you, Jarman," the black soldier said with a smile, extending a hand. Jarman looked at the black man's hand, he'd never seen an African in person. After several seconds, the shock wore off and he shook the man's hand with an awkward grin and nod.

"Pardon me for asking," Hans began as politely as possible, "But-"

"But how is it that I am in the *Wehrmacht*?"

"*Ja*, and-"

"And why?"

"*Ja*," Hans laughed at the man's anticipation of his questions. The black soldier's friends chuckled as well, they'd clearly heard these questions before.

Jarman, the adult Jarman, grinned at his friends and began, "First off, I am the son of an African father and mother from what was formerly German East Africa. My father was hired to be a soldier in the German army there. The French demanded all forces to pull out of East Africa at the end of *Der Krieg* and so my father and mother did as well and were brought back to the Reich. I was born in the Rhineland in November of nineteen nineteen."

"Sad year," one soldier shook his head sadly. The year Versailles was signed.

"*Ja*, not the best year in German history," Jarman Diallo agreed.

"*Bitte, weiter*," some boys said, interested in him to continue.

"Okay. The *Führer* became the Chancellor in nineteen thirty-three and *Führer* the year after, when I was fourteen."

"The year you could enter the *Hitlerjugend*," Hans said, knowingly.

"*Ja*. Exactly. My father and mother both wanted me to join. They thought it would be good to show our support for the *Führer* and get in good with the party. We had some trouble getting me enlisted. I went to an SS enlistment office to get things straightened out with my father. I was expecting the usual, a lot of staring, maybe even glares because of the intimidating reputation the SS had amongst my friends. The SS always intimidated us, with their stoic faces and stiff marching. Plus, I'm not German, very clearly. Instead, quite surprisingly, I might add, the local SS officer gave me a smile and told us to follow him to his office. We sat down, had a chat, he examined my dad's papers, confirming he'd been hired in Africa during the Great War and that was how he'd come to *Deutschland*. And then I was in. I stayed in the *Hitlerjugend* until I graduated. The war began a few months after I had finished my tenure in the *Hitlerjugend*. I was eager to join, I'm sure you can't imagine being in the *Jugend* as an African. It's uncomfortable, it's odd being the only black person, but nothing more than that. By the end of first semester everyone had stopped staring. I had some good friends," he said, while playfully grinning at one of his squad mates, "It was a good experience. I was eager to join and prove myself a real patriot to the Reich. When the war broke out, I volunteered for the SS. But they wouldn't let me in at first, said I was just under the height requirements. So I got a job elsewhere. Not the best, but enough to get by on. I kept applying to join the *Wehrmacht* or the SS, especially after we attacked the Soviet Union. In October of forty-one, my application was finally accepted. And naturally, I was sent to the Eastern Front. Where everyone wants to serve. And Helmuth shipped out with me."

"Wow," was the collective reaction from most of the boys.

"But why?" Jarman Knecht asked, "What do we stand for that you stand for?"

The adult Jarman smiled, "You're talking about what you were taught in the *Hitlerjugend?*"

"Absolutely."

"Instilling such self-confidence in the youth is a wise decision. It's part of building a strong nation," Diallo explained and did so as if this was common knowledge, "*Deutschland* is for the German. That is what Hitler fights for: the continued existence of the German people."

"You think what we've been told is-"

"A builder of society. You're all one people, one blood. The *Führer* loves *Deutschland* and wants it to be great. I understand his sentiment of Germany for the Germans, Japan for the Japanese, Africa for the Africans. As he said, he wishes each country to stick to its own sphere of influence and not play the policeman of the world. That would be great for Africa. We could at long last self-govern. If Hitler hated blacks, he wouldn't have waved at Jesse Owens even after the Olympic committee told him he could either congratulate all or none. He wouldn't have gone out of his way for that. And he wouldn't have let so many non-Aryans into the *Wehrmacht* and SS. Personally, I believe he wants the German people to live on. Which, who can argue with? Every people have a right to their homeland and their people. Wanting to maintain your culture, identity, and blood isn't wrong to strive for."

Hans smiled at this.

"The *Führer* knows who fights against the German people and indeed, all peoples. I don't think they will stop with Europe. They'll continue to Asia, the Americas, and Africa. I want the people of Africa to continue to live on, on their soil. One of my dreams is to go back to my country and help build it up, who knows, to be a civilization as impressive as Europe. Make it great for the citizens there."

"Damn good goal," Helmuth said, giving Diallo a slap on the back, "You should make it a goal of yours to stop drinking too."

Diallo shook his head, reaching into his knapsack. He pulled out a hip flask and took a swig from it. "The alcohol is too good to stop. You do it too."

"The commander's suspicious of you. When you're stumbling around at night."

"Shut up, Helmuth," Diallo laughed.

The soldiers conversed while waiting for further orders. The Russians were unable to get across with the bridges destroyed. *Obersturmbannführer* Förster eventually came around to them.

"Helmut Schmid's squad?" he asked.

"Sergeant Helmut Schmid was killed in action," Adolf Ingalls reported.

"I'm sorry to hear that," Förster said, "Well, for now, we will have all of you," he pointed to Diallo and his friends, "Join this squad. What is your name?" he asked Ingalls.

"Adolf Ingalls."

"You are the new Sergeant. Have you a corporal?"

"*Ja*," Ingalls replied, and Koby raised his hand.

"*Gut, gut*," Förster said, "That is all, then."

"Shall we introduce ourselves then?" Ingalls asked, "I am Adolf Ingalls."

"Koby Hertz."

"Jarman Knecht."

"Jarman Diallo."

"Gustav Sperlle."

"Helmuth Zweig."

"Hans Reichmann."

"Werner von Schraeder."

"Blaz Senft."

"Ivo Klein."

"Tristan Rothkirch."

Germany's Triumph in '36

August 6, 1944

Blaz marched down a street out of view of the river. Half the city was occupied by the Soviets now, but without the bridges, they could advance no further. But there were ways of moving troops into places other than by land. While the bulk of the German forces guarded the river, the boys and a few other squads patrolled the streets for any Russians who'd happened to swim across or slip past their front lines. They also kept their eyes peeled for Soviet planes carrying paratroopers.

"A black soldier," Koby nudged Blaz, "In our army. How about that?"

"And his name is Jarman," Blaz added.

"*Ja*, pretty good reaction from our Jarman when he heard. Not what I would've expected, but still amusing. It's surprising he's in the army."

"He lives in *Deutschland*, and he wants to fight for us," Blaz said.

"Oh *ja*, that's all fine. I suppose it's all right. But-"

"But every people have a homeland, and they need to protect their homeland?" Blaz interrupted, "He agrees with that."

"He's helping us do that right now. He's all right," Koby grinned after a few moments.

"*Ja*, and he saved Werner. I couldn't have picked him up. And he was still going fast with him in his arms."

"Well, they are fast sprinters," Koby laughed.

"Jesse Owens showed us that."

"*Wahr.* Damn good runner. Boy, when we won the Berlin Olympics-"

"You remember when that was considered a great victory?"

"*Ja*," Koby said, widening his eyes and raising his eyebrows, "Not so important now."

Blaz continued marching, glancing up at the sky. There were no planes in sight. He ran a hand through his light blond hair, it was long by now. And wavy. It went down over his neck and ears. Koby looked at Blaz as if for the first time, "You need a haircut, and I bet I do too."

"Sure, I'm fine with waiting anyway. It's kind of fun to have it long."

"*Ja*, it's fun to see yourself with long hair once. I haven't actually seen myself all that much," Koby nodded, "Jarman has been on top of keeping his hair short, I wonder what he'd look like with long hair."

"They tend to have shorter hair," Blaz laughed.

"What?" Koby asked, face blank, "Oh, shut up."

Blaz laughed again, "Come on, it was all right."

"It was fine," said a voice, causing them both to jump. Diallo was right behind them, holding his bayoneted rifle, marching with Tristan and Ivo.

"How long have you been behind us?" Koby asked, surprised and worried that they'd been snuck up on.

"Since the 'Jarman's been on top of keeping his hair short,' bit," Tristan answered.

"How'd you sneak up on us?" Koby asked.

"We got lucky," Tristan answered, glancing up at Diallo.

"All right," Koby said, "Why're you here? What's happening?"

"We were coming from a side street, and we saw you two walking. No Russian activity elsewhere," Diallo said, then changed the subject, "Koby, Blaz, I hear you two are quite the runners."

Koby nodded, "You could say that."

"I'm okay," Blaz agreed.

"You sounded like you were pretty good, according to Ivo," Diallo continued, looking at Koby, "You run mid fifteens for the five-kilometer?"

"Last I was timed, *ja*. I hope I can get back to training once the war is over."

"If you improve on that time, you're in the Olympics. And not just that, you'll compete at the Olympics."

"Who do you think will win the next Olympics?" Blaz asked, turning the conversation to a hopeful future.

Diallo marched along with the boys, standing just taller than Koby, the tallest of the four. Then he spoke, "I'd say either *Deutschland* or the USA."

"Sticking with the last two leaders?" asked Koby.

"No one else came close. So, *ja*, no reason that it'll change. Other countries aren't thinking about athletics right now. And *Deutschland's* got a damn good youth program still," Diallo said, pulling his sleeve up, giving his arm a flex, then giving Koby's arm a thump. Koby gave Diallo a thump in the chest, which he returned. They kept it up, each hit coming faster, until Diallo did not retaliate. They grinned and continued on.

Blaz and Koby stayed together for the rest of the day, even after Diallo branched off. When the sun had set, they returned to their squad.

"Four of us have to patrol at night from now on. Orders from the *Obersturmbannführer*," Ingalls said when they got back, they were the last to return, "Any volunteers?"

Everyone raised their hand, including Ingalls himself.

"Okay, we'll have two adults and two of you young men go tonight. I'll go, Diallo you're with me. Hertz and Senft, you come as well, before you sit down."

"Okay," Koby and Blaz nodded, giving the Hitler salute. "What's our job?" The youth sergeant asked after they lowered their arms.

"You need to keep eyes on the sky for enemy aircraft. Alert an officer if you do, they will be out there tonight, so you'll find one. Also, watch for Russians on this side of the city that may have gotten over one way or another."

"*Ja* sir."

The Darker Parts of the Sky

The night shift was never fun, especially when you were awake the day before. Blaz's eyes were rolling back in his head by midnight as they marched on, street after street. Koby was always a few feet ahead of him.

"Koby, how are you marching so fast?"

"I'm not."

"How're you marching normally? I'm exhausted."

"I'm just as tired, just try to stay with me."

Blaz caught up. At Koby's side he looked up to scan the sky. A dark object descended, and all light seemed to be blocked by it. Several more came out of the clouds while he watched the object float down.

"Koby, Koby," Blaz tapped Koby's shoulder, "What's that?"

Koby scanned the sky, then Blaz got behind him and pointed. Koby kept scanning then, he stopped suddenly, "*Scheiße*! That's a parachutist!"

Blaz's eyes went wide, "We've got to tell command!"

But the parachutists had already been spotted by Germans elsewhere in the city. A squad of *Wehrmacht* soldiers sprinted by them, as they turned around to notify someone. Then two SS squads came sprinting past, followed by their squad, Ingalls in the lead, attaching his bayonet to his Karabiner.

"Fall in!" Ingalls barked. Blaz and Koby joined in at the end of the two-by-two line.

"Zweig! Reichmann! On the roofs of those homes! The flat-roofed ones! Shoot at them as they float in!" Ingalls yelled, still running full speed with his rifle in hand, "Leipzig! Diallo! Take that side street on the left! Cover our flank. Knecht! Klein! Cover our right flank! Hertz! Sperlle! Senft! Stay with me! *Aufwärts!*"

Blaz sprinted to stay with the stronger, faster soldiers.

"There! Here they come!" Ingalls said, coming to a halt before a three-way intersection, "*Feuer!*"

Blaz raised his rifle at the floating, black dots in the sky. They were almost in range now. A flash appeared from one paratrooper, then another and another. Soon the sky was lit with flashes from rifles. Bullets rained down.

"*Scheiße!* Get to cover!" Ingalls ordered. Koby and Blaz ran to the left side of the street, while Sperlle and Ingalls made for the other side of the intersection.

"*Granate!*" Ingalls yelled, tackling Sperlle. A fiery explosion lit the night. Koby and Blaz turned to shield their faces from the grenade. Once they felt the shower of debris, they both ran to where Ingalls and Sperlle lay.

"Gustav! Adolf!" Koby yelled, "Are you all right?"

"A little burnt, but fine," Sperlle said and nodded to his comrade, "Adolf?"

"Keep shooting!" Ingalls ordered, springing to his feet, and firing at yet another parachutist, "*Feuer!*"

The paratroopers kept coming, many in the city or outside of it by now.

"Street by street! Let's go! The other squads will have the river defender's backs," Ingalls ordered, "Move swiftly."

Blaz followed at the rear of the four-man unit, glancing behind them to cover their backs every few seconds. *Where are they? I know they're here.*

The night grew still. The four Germans halted. It was the oddest sensation, but it did not last long. A shot rang out a couple hundred meters away.

Ingalls waved them on; there was no shooter in view. They crept along the side of buildings, down the street. Blaz could feel his heart beating faster by the second. It was still too quiet. Somebody had to be watching them.

"Here comes someone," Ingalls whispered, ducking down between two homes, "Three men. Check your fire. It could be our own. Let them come nearer."

"I can see them, they aren't ours. Those are Russian uniforms and Russian rifles. Let's take them out," Koby whispered back with flare in his voice.

"I'm taking your word. Pick targets, quick," Ingalls answered. Blaz raised his rifle, aiming for the man in the middle.

"*Feuer!*" Ingalls whispered.

The four rifle shots sounded, and three bodies hit the ground.

"Sperlle, with me. Hertz, Senft stay here."

Ingalls and Sperlle approached the Russian bodies, at least they hoped they were nothing but bodies. Cautiously, with rifles raised, they inched closer. The bodies remained motionless. Blaz breathed in as silently as he could when the two men were right by the Russians. Sperlle drove his bayonet through one, Ingalls copied with another. Sperlle finished the third one. They'd all been dead from the shots.

"Hertz! Senft! Come!" Ingalls hissed. Koby crept over, Blaz followed close behind.

"We need to regroup. Hertz and Senft, get to the right flank where Knecht and Klein are, we'll regroup with Diallo and Leipzig. Meet fifty meters north on this street."

"*Ja* sir," Koby answered and the two of them headed back a building and crouched down to a crawl.

Sperlle moved to the other side of the street. A shot rang out and Sperlle collapsed. Ingalls looked towards the shooter, was shot in the head, and hit the ground. Blaz leapt up to help Sperlle, who was writhing in pain on the ground, but he was yanked back by the collar.

"*Nein*, Blaz. You'll get shot!"

"We need to help!"

"*Nein*, you know we can't," Koby hissed, "Follow me."

Koby crawled between two buildings, onto the next street over. Blaz followed, knowing Koby was right.

"Here, we need to find Jarman and Ivo. I think they took this flank."

They sprinted down the street. Koby ran to a side street, waving Blaz after him. When they came to the end of the side street, Koby skidded to a sudden stop. Blaz ran full speed into Koby, when he'd glanced over his shoulder. He had heard footsteps following them. Both Koby and Blaz stumbled forward into the street. Immediately, they had guns on them. Blaz looked up to see several rifles with bayonets pointed at him. The entire street was littered with Russians. It seemed that they'd taken everything west of this place and were waiting for the parachutists who'd landed outside the town to join them. Russians began shouting at them and among one another.

"Blaz, put your hands up," Koby told him.

Blaz slowly raised his hands.

"Surrender?" he asked Koby in shock.

"We can't do a thing r-" Koby was silenced by a rifle butt to the head. He went limp. Blaz turned to the Russian in stupefaction. The Russian responded by hammering Blaz in the head with a brutal kick.

Kill, You Gallant Soldiers of the Red Army!

August 7, 1944

Blaz woke up inside of a home with one wall blown open. It was day, but clouds covered the sky. Shots rang out near and far. Four Soviets were inside, speaking amongst each other, but Blaz couldn't understand Russian. Three of them looked to be at least thirty, the other perhaps twenty. Maybe even nineteen. Blaz glanced around the home, looking for a way to escape, but the Russians were standing in the blown open wall, that would do no good.

"How're you doing, Blaz?" Koby whispered weakly. Blaz turned his head quickly, to see Koby next to him. Koby had never looked more pitiful in his life. There was a gash in his forehead, and his right eye was black and swollen.

"Koby, you're bleeding," Blaz told his friend.

"I know. Are you okay?"

"Better than you, I'd assume."

"Probably," Koby nodded, then lowered his tone to a whisper, "You see our rifles, in the corner behind us and to our right?"

Blaz glanced, ever so subtly, getting a view of the rifles. Not only their rifles were there but their pistols and knives as well. Blaz felt his pockets. He had the pocketknife, Erich had given him years ago. But that likely would do him no good against heavily armed Russians.

"*Ja*, I see them."

"We need to get to those. I understand what they're saying, and they don't plan on letting us live."

So, the Russians really don't take prisoners.

"Follow me," Koby whispered as he crawled toward the rifles.

"*Nyet! Nyet!*" one Russian said. The four men walked over to the two boys, chatting in Russian. They seemed to get into an argument, but it was quickly resolved. Two of them lifted Blaz and Koby to their knees. One Russian, huge and strong, barked something at the two Germans, going on for quite a while. He turned to one of his comrades, who began speaking in German, "We've only kept you alive this long, so you can give us information. Now, you need to tell us where your defenses are weakest, so that we can finish this battle. And it might interest you that we've captured over half of this side of the city. We'll win this battle. You'll be spared if you give us this information."

He looked at Koby and Blaz, expecting an answer.

"We're just privates, why would we know this?" Koby answered.

"We know you have information that could help us. Give us all you know. Corporal? I'd assume you know more, why don't you start?"

Koby shook his head. This was answered with a boot to the head from the tall, built Soviet. The translator said something to the burly Bolshevik.

"*Nein, Bitte?*" Koby pleaded to them as he got back on his knees, blood now trickling from his forehead. Koby looked Blaz's way, then back to the Russians, "*Bitte!*"

The built Soviet nodded to the translator, and removed his uniform, revealing a Jewish star necklace underneath. Then he ripped a wooden board from the blown open wall and walked over to Koby.

"Give us some information," the translator said. Koby replied in Russian this time, a look of defiance on his beaten face.

"You think we want to kill some kids?" the translator said in German, "Tell us what we need to know."

"*Nein*, that would put Germans in danger."

"They'll die anyway."

"At least I'll die knowing it wasn't my fault."

The translator glared at him, then ordered something to the Jew. The Soviet Jew dropped the board, drew his dagger, and moved over, where he met Blaz's eyes. The German stared up at the man in fear. His mouth hung half-open and his lip trembled. He wanted to shout for help but was too scared to even do that.

The translator said to Koby in German, "You don't fear dying, but I assume you know this young man. He dies if you don't give us information on the German positions."

"*Nein*, Koby," Blaz shook his head. He was silenced by a hard punch from the built Soviet. The translator, sensing Koby might break, laid out map of the city in front of him, "Just point and tell us the positions, what they have. That's all you need to do."

Koby looked down at the map, studying it closely.

"Koby, *nein*." Another punch to the face.

Koby began to extend his arm to the map, then stopped, and stiffened his arm. He raised it into the Hitler salute.

"I'll take that as a '*nein*,'" the translator scowled, "Nicolai, please begin."

The built Soviet returned his full focus to Blaz, stroking his dagger like a dog. Finally, he made his move. Death wasn't coming quickly. The Soviet grabbed Blaz's right arm and forced it outwards. He started to slide the dagger underneath the Hitler Youth armband Blaz had kept. Blaz instinctively recoiled. The man let him go, then smiled.

'Nicolai' grabbed Blaz by the hair, drawing him closer to his dagger. He slid the blade down across Blaz's jaw, drawing blood. Drawing a scar. Blaz screamed in agony, as the blade touched bone. The soldier gripped him tightly, so he could barely manage to struggle. After seconds that felt like an eternity, the Soviet stopped dragging his dagger across Blaz's jawbone.

Then the soldier spoke in German. "Master race," he said, looking into Blaz's blue eyes, running a hand through Blaz's light blond hair. Blaz shook. His heart felt like it might leap out of his chest, if the Soviet didn't stab it first. "All your life you've been told that, I'll bet. That you are superior," he said, with pure hatred burning in his eyes. He grabbed Blaz, turning him to face the three other Russians. Blaz felt the sharp, metal blade touch his throat. Nothing had ever felt colder. Blaz did not close his eyes. He stared straight at one Russian, the youngest one in the group. Almost pleadingly. The young Russian's expression changed from one of disinterest to one of surprise. But the built Soviet had one more thing to tell Blaz before he ended the sixteen-year old's life, "Well blondie, what good is all that going to do you now?"

As he finished saying this, four simultaneous shots rang out, and the knife fell. Blaz swiftly drew his pocketknife and ran it into the man's chest. Koby sprang into action, diving for his dagger. The soldier stumbled back, slamming into the wall near Koby. Then Koby grabbed the huge Soviet by the collar and drove his dagger repeatedly into the man's face in a fit of rage.

The other three Russians collapsed to the ground, one of the older getting up and drawing a pistol. Another shot tore through him. Blaz saw Erich. Diallo vaulted through a window, Tristan right behind. Adi and Ottokar ran in, and Rodolfo leapt in through another window. Blaz looked up to see their saviors jogging in. The young Russian tried to stand up but fell back to the floor. Erich picked him up and slammed the bleeding young man against a wall. He punched him in the face repeatedly, until the soldier was bleeding so horribly that the entire lower part of his face was red. Blaz climbed to his feet and backed away to where Koby was stabbing the man.

"Koby!" Blaz yelled, wincing at the pain in his jawbone. Blaz ignored it, pulled his friend back, and brought him into a chokehold, "Koby, he's dead, stop!"

Koby made another attempt to stab the man but stopped upon hearing Blaz's voice a second time. His breathing was rapid, and heavy. He'd unleashed all his hatred in seconds.

Diallo jogged over to Erich as he was about to throw another punch. He put a hand on Erich's shoulder, "He's had enough. Just kill him quickly, otherwise, you're no better than they are."

Erich glanced at Diallo, eyes blazing. He didn't respond. Heavy breathing filled the room.

"Breath," Diallo told him, "No torture."

Erich answered, "I don't care for the high road, he doesn't deserve it. He should suffer after that."

"Maybe he should," Diallo said.

Erich looked at Diallo. He tilted his head. Then he drew his pistol and shot the Russian in the head.

Blaz released Koby, who went down on all fours, breathing heavily. His dagger was drenched in blood, even parts of the hilt. His hands were covered as well.

"*Vielen dank*," Blaz breathed to their saviors.

Erich holstered his pistol and knelt. Diallo and the other SS soldiers remained standing. Tristan came to Koby's side.

"How'd you find us?" Blaz asked in disbelief.

"You heard shooting, throughout your interrogation, *ja*?" Erich asked.

"*Ja*."

"We combed the south side of the city, driving all the way here. This the area where Tristan and Diallo told us you were captured."

"How'd they know?"

"We were following you, trying to get your attention. Then you were captured," Tristan said.

"Anyway, our forces counterattacked this morning, and we've been driving them back all day. That interrogation would've been too little, too late."

"They said they had half of the city east of the river."

"Once we broke their front lines, the reconquest was quick. For all I know, they could've begun interrogating you as we broke through. They might've thought they had that much of the city then. We had a couple minutes to position ourselves to shoot them simultaneously."

Blaz nodded.

"Pick up your weapons, we still have a couple of streets to comb," Erich ordered the two of them. Koby stumbled over to his rifle and pistol, ignoring his red hands.

Prisoners of Their Own

The battle with the paratroopers was swift. The outgunned Russians were quickly defeated and surrendered to squads across the city. Rodolfo fell in battle. Blaz's squad captured three men. They lined them up in the street. Once the three SS soldiers had said their goodbyes to their comrade, they discussed, quite bitterly, what to do with the prisoners they'd captured.

"I say we shoot them, right now!" Erich told his SS comrades.

"*Nein*, make it slower than that," Ottokar disagreed, "Make it painful."

"I don't feel like torturing anyone," Adi said, as if he were a child debating with his play mates on what they would play next, "Let's just kill them. I'll even do it." Adi drew his pistol, and chambered a round.

"*Nein, nein*," Erich said, "Let's ask the two who were captured what they think."

Adi and Ottokar looked at each other and nodded.

"Koby, Blaz," Erich said. They turned around.

"*Ja?*" he asked.

"What do you think we should do with them? Mind you, taking prisoners is not up for discussion."

"Shoot them," Blaz answered, putting a hand up to the deep cut along his jawline, still bleeding badly, "Make it quick."

"Kill them in the same way they were going to kill us, with a knife," Koby dissented.

"All right, the knife it is then," Ottokar said immediately, drawing his chain dagger, "Koby, is it? You take one as well. Blaz? You too."

Koby drew his bloodstained dagger and walked to the Russian on the right of the row of three. Ottokar stood behind the man in the middle. Blaz slung his rifle over his shoulder, took out his knife, and walked to the man on the left. Ottokar slit the man's throat immediately. Koby looked at Blaz, then did the same. Blaz brought his knife in, closer to the man's neck. He waited, as if by waiting the action would do itself.

"Come on, kill him Blaz," Erich said.

Blaz placed the knife's blade against the man's neck. His grip tightened on the hilt. But still he did not slit the throat.

"What are you waiting for?" Ottokar asked, shaking his head.

Diallo walked over to Blaz, and stood at his side, whispering, "What's wrong?"

"I can't, sir," Blaz whispered without looking up, his hand trembling on the knife, "Not like this."

Diallo patted Blaz on the shoulder, "Step back."

Blaz stepped away from the man, knife falling to his side. Diallo drew his dagger and finished it.

Erich nodded approvingly. "Let's go," he said, and marched off down the street with Adi and Ottokar following. Tristan and Koby fell in behind those two. Diallo followed. Blaz glanced back at the bodies, shook his head, and followed his comrades.

Ivo: The Little Sniper

After a sweep of the western edge of the city, Erich led the group back to the front where the Russians had remounted their attempts to thin the German lines and use up German ammunition. The rest of the Knights were already there, save Ivo.

"*Danke*, Erich," Koby waved, as Erich went back to the front.

"Only doing my job," Erich answered, with a cruel smile, "*Auf wiedersehen.*"

"See you." Koby roughly patted Blaz on the shoulder, "I'm covering for Diallo and Zweig."

"Blaz, come on. We're going up to cover Ivo," Tristan said.

"All right. Let's go then."

Tristan led Blaz to the rear of a tall, stone building. They entered, walking up several flights of stairs and passing more than one sniper's nest on the way up. Ivo was waiting for them on the staircase, rifle in hand.

"Blaz, Tristan," Ivo nodded, "Just cover me, give me a shot or lift up your hat on your rifle when I tell you too. I'll take care of everything else."

What followed was the most impressive display of prowess in the art of killing either Blaz or Tristan had witnessed from any of their squad mates. They didn't see his targets fall but knew when he'd hit one. When he missed he was rough setting up his next shot. If he was graceful and smooth, he'd hit his man. Blaz's hat was shot at multiple times, but as far as he could tell, never twice by the same person. Whenever his hat was shot, Ivo would fire his rifle within seconds, then duck back down behind cover. Ivo never had the time to target infantrymen, it was always a duel with Russian snipers.

It was not a quick process. They were there for hours, switching floors, rooms, windows. It was a miracle none of them were fatally hit. But, as Hans had said, "We can assume they've lost their best men. So, they're using whoever they can." Ivo's shoulder was grazed, causing him to take a cautious approach for the rest of the fight.

Yet Ivo was emerging as a crack shot, in every battle he seemed to be getting better, calmer, and more accurate. His expression rarely changed. He never smiled after a shot. The closest to any form of satisfaction was a sigh of relief, in a duel that took several trips to different floors of the buildings. Ivo's agility was an advantage, along with his short build. As the sun set in the sky, they were relieved of their post by another sniper.

When at their encampment in the blasted-out building-base, Ivo dropped his rifle, and ran to just outside of the building and vomited. Tristan took a step towards Ivo, but Blaz stopped him.

"He'll be all right. Give him some time. We didn't do what he just did."

Olympia

August 21, 1944

Weeks passed, and though the Russian army crossed the Neman elsewhere, the city remained half under German control.

"The Russians have encircled us," Diallo informed the squad, "A town north of here did not destroy their bridges."

"We're low on ammo. Our machine guns haven't received ammo for days. And the Russians keep trying to cross the river. We can't hold out any longer," Zweig said.

Blaz moved away from the Knights, to the corner of the damaged building-base that they called home. Ivo was already there, sitting alone.

"Hey Ivo."

"Hey Blaz."

"You all right? You haven't been yourself."

"Myself doesn't fit into this. He was too happy."

Blaz nodded and looked at the ground. "I miss you, Ivo. We need a little levity here and there."

"Blaz, I don't-"

Before Ivo said anything else, a *Wehrmacht* commander ran over to Zweig and Diallo, attracting their attention.

"You two, we have a small opening to evacuate the city. We have maybe an hour. *Obersturmbannführer* Förster has approved my request to evacuate the city, since it serves no strategic value now. All *Wehrmacht* units, army and *Luftwaffe*, are to evacuate immediately. The tanks have pulled out already, along with the trucks and ammunition. You must cover twelve kilometers in an hour, with all your gear. Make it to the hill region, and our forces will be waiting there, we've closed off the line for kilometers. If you don't make it in under an hour, you risk being shot by snipers. Now go!"

"Hertz! Set the pace!" Diallo said.

Koby picked up his STG-44 and set off at a run. With no gear on them, they could easily make twelve kilometers that fast, but with gear, it would be tougher. Blaz and Ivo scrambled up, and followed their squad off, catching up to Koby with difficulty. They passed several *Wehrmacht* squads as they exited the city.

"Blaz, Ivo," Koby said when they pulled up alongside him.

"Hey Koby. Are you okay?"

"I'm fine."

"You don't look fine."

They passed another *Wehrmacht* squad that was retreating as well.

"Have you seen an SS squad yet?" Koby asked.

"*Nein.*"

Koby kept running, speeding ahead for a brief few seconds. Blaz and Ivo sped to his side again.

"He's not coming," Koby said under his breath.

"What? Who?" Ivo asked, slightly panicked, looking back to their squad. Diallo, Zweig, Jarman, Hans, Tristan and even the wounded Werner were following behind them, "Everyone's here Koby."

"Erich, you idiot. Erich's not coming!" Koby said, loud enough for Ivo and Blaz to hear, but no one else. Ivo recoiled, slowing down slightly.

"What? Why? We can't hold that city! The entire *Wehrmacht* is pulling out!" Blaz exclaimed. He gripped his rifle even tighter.

"They won't retreat. I tried to convince him. I even tried to convince the *Obersturmbannführer*. When the Russians come in, they'll be waiting in buildings for them. And I'm sure they'll put up a good fight. But they can't win."

Blaz blinked several times, "Why didn't you tell us? I never got to say goodbye. Jarman never got to say goodbye."

"Jarman would never have left with us if he knew. Don't you dare tell him. I'll tell him when he can't turn around. You too, Ivo."

Blaz returned his focus forward, "Fine."

"Okay," Ivo said in understanding.

"Why do we have to lose Erich too?" Koby asked no one in particular, his voice wavering, "Reinhardt, Jurgen, Nico, Wilhelm, Jaye! Now Erich! Damn you, Russia!" Blaz and Ivo ran on with Koby. "If divinity is on our side, why's this happening? We're dying, everyone's dying. Why won't God help us? Anything! Everything has gone against us. First the winter in Russia. Then we couldn't save our army in Stalingrad. Reinforcements don't do anything but delay the inevitable. Rommel couldn't stop the Allies in France."

"The *Führer* survived that bomb," Ivo pointed out.

"And yet the war hasn't turned in our favor since then, something's against us. If we have miracle weapons like Goebbels claims to, why doesn't the *Führer* use them? He must have something up his sleeve. Some strategy, weapon, plan. He's the *Führer!* We put almost all of Europe under his command. Now it's all falling apart."

"It's not falling apart, we'll stop them," Blaz reassured Koby, "We can't let them get to our home. And we never will!"

"I'll die before they step foot in our hometown. Before those beasts can reach our women, our land, they'll have to spill our blood."

"I don't think they have a problem doing that," Blaz said, remembering all their fallen comrades.

Koby sighed through the running. "I know."

"Come on!" Koby shouted to the others, who slowed in absolute exhaustion, "If you don't put in work now, the Reds will get us. *Schnell!*"

Jarman gritted his teeth, and sprinted back toward the front, inspiring Tristan and Hans to do the same. Werner gave his best effort to keep up with them, but his broken ribs slowed him down. The squad hoped he would catch up, but finally realized he wasn't going to be able to.

"Halt!" Koby ordered, and spoke immediately, "We can't all stop for one man, but there's no way we are leaving him. I'll stay and go with him."

"*Nein*, Hertz. You set the pace. None of us may escape if you aren't leading the way. You have to stay with the group," Zweig smartly said.

Koby started a light jog, so they wouldn't lose too much ground. Werner had not yet caught up, clutching his ribs.

"Then what?" Koby asked, "The longer we talk, the worse chance we have of avoiding being in range of the Russian tanks and snipers."

"I'll go with Werner," Blaz volunteered.

"*Nein*, Blaz. I'm not letting you go," Koby snapped.

"Someone has to."

"*Nein*, the adults are doing it," Zweig interrupted, "You young men have lives to live, you're going on."

"You're not that old," Tristan said.

"Doesn't matter. I'm not going to retreat, and let you do the job I should be doing. Diallo?"

"I'm with you. All the way."

"Now Hertz! Lead the rest! As fast as you can go!"

Koby's pace saved them. As they waited for Zweig, Diallo, and Werner behind German lines, it became increasingly certain they weren't going to see them again. As the window closed, though, they saw three figures running through the field towards the slapped together German lines. The Russians hadn't closed the window when they thought they would.

"There they are!" Tristan yelled to the others.

"*Gott sei Dank*," Ivo whispered next to Blaz.

The Third Branch of the SS

September 1, 1944

"Glad to have served with you boys," Diallo said, extending a hand to Koby, "But I hope that you are able to stay out of the war now."

"You know we won't," Koby smiled, shaking Diallo's hand. To the others, Diallo flashed a sad smile. The boys waved to him from inside the train they'd boarded. Zweig helped Werner in.

"*Ade*," Diallo said, before sliding the doors shut. Minutes later the train was moving out.

"Do you know where we're going?" Tristan asked Koby.

"Some small town in Poland. It's on a river, so shipping goes through the town. It's mainly agricultural though."

"Fun," Hans sighed, clapping his hands together, "Hopefully our front lines hold now."

The citizens were the most noticeable thing about the city, but also the least noticeable in a way. They were quiet, scrawny in a sickly way. They went about daily business, with little fear of their occupiers, oddly. They were lucky to have well-trained soldiers there. The *Totenkopfverbände-SS* was only twenty strong and a worn-down, Wehrmacht unit, made up of men in their late forties and early fifties, with twice that.

The *Totenkopfverbände-SS* wore the black, non-combat uniforms. Koby's squad had a negative disposition for black-uniformed SS, established during the massacre in Estonia. The SS commandant greeted them at the train with a young officer, immediately telling them of the work they would be doing during their tenure in the Eastern Polish town.

"This town supplies food to the front. You will load foodstuffs onto the train or boats on the river. You'll have relatively free reign, allowed to go into the fields to the east. Report any suspicious activity from the Poles here. And report it to an either myself, or *Scharführer* Kotze. He will show you to where you will sleep and eat and any other questions you might have." The commandant turned to the other officer. "Kotze, you take it from here."

"*Jawohl, Obersturmführer!*" the young officer, said throwing up a Hitler salute. Once the *Obersturmführer* departed, the young officer returned his attention to the new arrivals.

"*Guten tag, Wehmracht Jugend,*" the young officer said, recognizing their youth immediately, "Follow me, I'll show you around the town. We've got time."

Koby followed first, catching up to the young officer, who looked at him briefly. He was tall, about six-foot-five with a lean physique. Straight brown hair was visible below his black cap.

"What's your first name, Kotze? Where are you from?" Koby asked him.

"Jaeger. I'm from Olching. Near Buchenwald."

"How old are you?"

"Eighteen. Nineteen in a month and a half."

"What front have you fought on?"

"I, I haven't had the honor."

"Why not?" Jarman asked. None knew what the *Totenkopfverbände-SS* was; they assumed these were just *Allgemeine-SS* police forces.

"I was trained for another task. It looks like I'll be seeing action soon though. What with the Russians advancing towards us," he said, showing fear, uncharacteristic of any SS soldier the boys had come across. Erich had likely died fighting a suicide fight, a member of the esteemed, respectable *Waffen-SS*. The *Allgemeine-SS* were hard-headed, so naturally fear wasn't associated with them. People feared them, they feared nothing. Their SS Hitler Youth instructors always appeared in total control. They'd never come across the third, unknown branch of the *Schutzstaffel*.

"How does someone your age avoid combat this long?" Tristan asked, "We've been fighting for almost a full year now. And we're sixteen and seventeen."

"I was never trained for that, not front-line fighting. I was trained for something else."

"What?"

"Internment camps," Jaeger answered simply, "Someone has to do it." He lead them to a lonely house on the outside of the town in the fields. A Polish woman and what looked to be her daughter, about the boys' ages were inside, clearing an area for them to sleep and laying out blankets. "Here's the house that you'll be staying in. There's a pump outside for water and for washing up, you look like you haven't in weeks. Do that before you sleep in here."

Blaz rubbed a hand down his face and brought it in front of his eyes. His hand was filthy.

"Moving on, you'll sleep on the floor. This is someone else's home." He suddenly switched languages and raised his voice, so the boys did not understand what he said, "Though they don't mind having some soldiers stay here, do they?"

The women looked up and shook her head.

"All right, let's let them finish," Jaeger told the boys, gesturing for them to follow him out the door and back toward the town.

"What are their names?" Blaz asked Jaeger.

"The girl, I don't know, I forgot. But the women's name is Zdizława. Their last name is Oborowski."

"Okay," Blaz nodded, though he had no idea how he was going to repeat that ever.

"Hopefully the girl's name is shorter," Jarman murmured, "Or more German."

"*Ja*, no kidding."

Jaeger led them over the railroad tracks and back into town, to show them where they'd be working.

The New Guy

"What do you think of that kid?" Tristan asked Blaz and Jarman while they walked back to the house to wash up. Koby, Ivo, Hans and Werner walked a few feet ahead.

"He should be fighting by now," Jarman said with disgust, "How can you not have?"

"Well, he has a point. Someone does have to run prisoner of war camps," Blaz said.

Jarman shook his head, "He's able-bodied. Have some older men do it."

"Maybe running a prison camp isn't as easy as it seems," Tristan suggested.

Jarman frowned, "Think I could beat him in a fight?"

Blaz and Tristan exchanged a glance. Tristan said, "He's taller than you, similar build. Maybe. You'd have to be on top of your game, I would think."

Jarman grinned, "I'm going to get him to fight me."

Washing Up

Outside the house, the Knights stripped naked. Zdizława offered to wash their uniforms, and they gratefully accepted. They removed everything from their uniforms including their beloved Iron Crosses before handing them to the Polish women. Blaz removed the lone bullet and placed it into his bag.

Dirt covered their faces, arms, and legs. Their hair was filthy, especially because of its length. Blaz, Ivo, Jarman, Werner, and Hans all had wounds of some kind.

"All right, who goes first?" Koby asked the squad, "We only have one bar of soap."

"No one is just going to volunteer. That'd be selfish," Ivo said, making an attempt at his old, annoying comments.

Blaz grinned, making sure Ivo saw him.

"All right then, I'll go first to ease your conscience," Koby replied.

"Fine, fine."

Koby worked the pump, putting a rag under it. They chatted, waiting their turn. Koby had nearly finished but spoke to the group while he was washing his body, "Werner, you're next. And after you finish, come around to the other side of the house. I'm cutting everyone's hair. There is a reason they recommend short hair in the *Wehrmacht*," he said. Then he ran relatively clear water through his hair, which came out nearly black.

"It's time for haircuts," Jarman said, glancing at his long-haired squad mates after seeing Koby wash his hair.

"*Ja*." He finished washing his hair and dried off with their towel, "I'll see you over there," Koby told Werner, and slid on his boxers.

One at a time, the Knights washed themselves. They washed the dirt out of their blond hair, until a squad mate told them it was clean. Blaz cleaned himself after Werner, Jarman, and Hans had gone. Then he dried his hair as best he could, slipped on his boxers, and headed over to get his haircut.

"We've got a line," Koby said, imitating Ivo's attempt at cheerfulness. "Fifteen-minute wait, do you mind?"

"*Nein*," Blaz shook his head, "*Nein*, I have all the time in the world."

"I hope you do."

Blaz stood by in the grass, while Koby cut Werner's hair. He had nearly finished but was shaving it down into the Hitler Youth haircut. And with just a knife, this took time.

"All right, it's nice and short on the sides," Koby told Werner, "I don't have a mirror for you, but I'm sure it'll be fine.

"*Danke*, Koby."

"Hans, you're next," Koby said.

Once the boys were clean and had their haircut, they came back into the house, still in their underwear. No one was inside.

"Must be in the basement or down at that creek Jaeger showed us," Koby said, "Put on your undershirts. This is no way for our hosts to walk in on us."

"She's cleaning those too," Hans reminded him.

"You still have your *Hitlerjugend* shorts in your bags?" Koby asked, "And your *Hitlerjugend* running shirts?"

"*Ja*, it's the only backups we've got," Jarman said.

"Well, they'll do."

They put on their white tank tops with the old Hitler Youth swastika in the center of the shirt.

"Where do you think she is?" Blaz asked.

"I sure don't know. What time did they say dinner would be? We haven't had lunch, I'm starving," Jarman replied, "It's going to be great, having a home-cooked meal... sort of."

"One cooked not in a war zone," Ivo corrected him.

"They said after sunset," Koby said looking at the sun from the window, "And it looks like that'll be in about an hour."

"What do you want to do until then?" Tristan asked.

"We don't have to do anything," Koby said, "Coach Friederich always said it's good to have a day off. I'd say we just rest and talk in here."

"I second that," Jarman agreed, "I'll wait till tomorrow to do anything physical. Just got clean, I'll make it last a night."

The boys sat in silence for a few seconds, some readjusting and lying down on the floor where the blankets were laid out.

"Why is it that we can move on?" Hans asked the group, suddenly becoming very serious.

"*Wie bitte?*" Koby asked. Beg your pardon.

"Why is it that we can move on? We've lost so much in this war. We've lost Reinhardt, Jurgen, Nico, Wilhelm, Jaye. Gunther's not here anymore."

Tristan nodded slightly.

"We've lost family members. Tristan, Ivo, Jarman, Werner."

Each kept their thoughts to themselves while Hans continued.

"Whatever we return to, even a *Deutschland* led by the *Führer*, it won't be the same. We'll be missing people that we once had. We already know who some of them are. And yet we still laugh and smile and live our lives."

Blaz fiddled with his fingers.

"Jarman?" Hans said. Jarman glanced up. "I'm glad you saved me. That would've been a horrible mistake."

Jarman smiled, warmness in his eyes.

"I've got no one to return home to. But you guys keep me going. The *Führer* is great and all, but he wasn't there to stop me from shooting myself. And the thought of him didn't stop me. You guys did. If everyone who lost someone couldn't move on and live their lives, well, I figure it'd be a pretty horrible world. I don't want to be one of those people. There's always a reason to keep living. Always something or someone."

A Home Cooked Meal

The Polish woman and her daughter did not return before sunset, surprising the boys. They headed for dinner in their athletic clothes. Jarman put on his Iron Cross before they left, not wanting to miss the first chance to impress their SS and *Wehrmacht* comrades. Guard duty fell to the *Totenkopfverbände-SS* and their constant vigilance.

Inside the church when the boys arrived, half the *Totenkopfverbände-SS* were seated on benches and *Wehrmacht* soldiers were trickling in. Koby took a seat across from Jaeger, who sat alone, being the youngest in the SS, though he was somehow still an officer.

"Hello, Hertz," Jaeger smiled warmly, "How are we?"

"Better, after washing ourselves. *Frau*, uh, I can't pronounce her name."

"Zdizława." Jaeger enunciated.

"Zedieselava," Koby repeated. He corrected himself, "Zdizława offered to clean our uniforms, so we're wearing our *Hitlerjugend* clothes. That's all we have left."

"Ah. What sports were you guys good at? Back in the Hitler Youth?"

"We were okay at football. Jarman was actually pretty good, probably the best," Blaz answered, combing his hair upwards.

"Probably," Jarman said, "Blaz and Ivo are fine distance runners. Koby's legendary. In Seelow, that is."

"Really? What're you good at?"

"He's good at everything," Ivo said.

"Well-" Koby began.

"Really, he is," Blaz agreed.

"Well, let the man speak," Jaeger remarked, throwing his arm into the air energetically.

"I guess I'm good at the fifteen hundred, three thousand and five thousand meter."

"What do run them in?" Jaeger asked, getting impatient at the delay.

"Four minutes and twenty seconds, eight minutes and fifty-three seconds, and fourteen minutes and fifty-nine seconds."

"You're kidding!" Jaeger exclaimed, "Only Olympic candidates can run that fast!"

"I was going to be in the Olympics. The ones this past summer."

"You must be joking."

"I'm not."

"You must be."

"*Nein*, he isn't," Jarman said seriously with something near a glare on his face. Jaeger brushed this glance off and, for some reason, accepted Koby's word as fact when Jarman affirmed it.

"*Verdämmt*, that's amazing then!"

Koby looked down at the table, blood rushing to his cheeks.

"What were you good at?"

"I never really had much of a sports career. I mean, of course we did sports where I was trained but we had little time for it. When did you begin training?"

"I started in the *Jungvolk* at ten, back in nineteen thirty-six. In early nineteen forty-one, when I was in the *Hitlerjugend* I was taken to a camp to be trained," Jaeger said.

"Tell me Jaeger," Jarman started, acting a bit smug, which drew some quiet groans from his squad mates. Jaeger noticed, but chose to keep listening to Jarman who continued, "Why have you not fought yet?"

"Because that's not my job," Jaeger answered with a neutral expression, "I run detainment camps."

"Prison camps?" Jarman nodded, "How does that warrant using a fit, fighting age soldier like you for that purpose?"

"If you would like to trade jobs, I'd be more than happy to. I've had this conversation several times with soldiers passing through here. Since our camp was taken over by the Russkies," Jaeger calmly responded, "Trust me, you've got the better deal."

Jarman and some of the boys glared. "How so?" Blaz asked, angered by this last comment.

Jaeger played with his fingers nervously, "Well, because you might not have a noose waiting for you at the war's end. Or a firing squad if we're lucky."

"W-wait, what?" Tristan stuttered in shock, but was interrupted by the SS commandant, "You boys hungry? We have a lot of work to do tomorrow. Go get some food."

"*Ja*, of course," Koby nodded, and got up to get supper. The squad followed.

Jaeger glanced to his commander, "Would you mind helping me out here?"

"Of course, Kotze," the commandant nodded, sitting down. Jaeger followed the Knights, who all came back quickly, ready to pick up where they'd left off.

"A noose?" Hans asked.

"*Ja*, how they execute people," Jaeger clarified.

"I know that!"

Jaeger grinned, at an odd time. The SS commandant took a sip of beer, made from the town's barley.

"What are you?" Hans asked, showing fear himself.

The commandant and Jaeger glanced to each other like old friends, though the commandant had to be at least forty. Jaeger then answered, "We are the *Totenkopfverbände-SS*."

The squad glanced around at each other in confusion. "What is the *Totenkopfverbände-SS*?" Ivo asked immediately.

"We run camps. I assume you are familiar with the quarantining of Jews?" the commandant asked.

Koby nodded once with narrowed eyes. The others nodded multiple times. Werner grinned at this.

"We run those camps."

"Tell us about them," Hans said, "Why do you have a noose awaiting?"

"The Jews are being quarantined from across Europe, for partisan attacks on our troops, for their crimes against humanity in the Soviet Union and abroad, particularly what they did to our German people before Hitler's banners flew over our streets," the commandant said. The boys couldn't help but smile at hearing their nation's anthem being quoted. The commandant continued, "We did nothing wrong, I swear to you on my life. But the enemy propaganda, they say we exterminated the Jews! Down to children and babies!" The commandant shook his head in despair. "We can't prove our innocence! Not before a Jewish tribunal."

"What did you do at these camps?" Blaz asked.

"We were guards. But honestly, there was little need to have as many guards as there were," Jaeger said, playing with his fingers again, "The prisoners were given food and water. They also were required to do a lot of work. But during the last couple months… we got little food after the railroads were bombed. No medical supplies. Now they think we murdered them."

"We have to win the war. Otherwise we will be eternally cursed," the commandant declared.

A Time to Think

That night at the house, the boys laid down on the floor, ready to go to sleep. The Poles had brought back their uniforms, repaired to look as good as new. The squad all thanked them, repeatedly. The Poles said nothing in return but did crack smiles.

"That was nice of them to repair our uniforms," Ivo said blissfully.

"Don't be such a novice," Koby replied harshly, "They're doing it to get in good with us. That's it."

"Maybe they were being nice," Blaz suggested, though his head suspected Koby was correct.

"*Nein*, you know that's not why," Hans said.

"They did something nice for us, and they didn't have to. God bless them for it."

"She's a winner," Hans said after a while.

"*Wie Bitte?*" Koby asked.

"The Polish girl."

"What? What are you talking about?"

"She's so beautiful," Hans smiled.

"What are you doing?" Koby asked, annoyed by this shift in tone and disingenuous talk.

"I haven't seen a girl that beautiful ever," Hans said whimsically, almost as if no one was in the room, "So beautiful. Long blonde hair, those wonderful blue eyes, smooth skin, lean body, lovely smile."

"You're talking nonsense, Hans," Koby said, "Where did this come from?"

"From years of not seeing a female for more than a few seconds," Blaz said, knowing exactly how Hans felt.

"*Ja*, I want to talk to her so bad," Hans said into the darkness.

Ivo then said, "But she speaks Polish, and you speak-"

"I know, German."

"Have you tried to talk to her yet?"

"Well... *nein*."

"You just like her because she's the first girl we've seen, and talked to in years," Jarman said, "You'll meet a girl someday. We're busy right now."

"Maybe, I just hate to wait."

Heart of the Wehrmacht

September 2, 1944

"You want to live in Seelow?" Hans asked Blaz, "After the war?"

"It's my home," Blaz replied, "And I love and miss it. Probably will meet my wife somewhere else, though."

Hans and Blaz hoisted another crate to an older *Wehrmacht* soldier with thinning blond hair in a box car.

"*Danke*," the man said.

"I would like to live in the same city our squad ends up. I'm not going to make better friends than you guys. It's impossible," Hans smiled, while he and Blaz lifted another crate up to the *Wehrmacht* soldier.

"*Nein*," Blaz agreed, "Never."

"You boys talking about after the war?" the soldier asked.

"We are," both answered simultaneously.

"You want to get married? Or do you think that's gross?" the man asked sarcastically.

"I want to get married," Hans answered.

The man nodded approvingly. There was an awkward silence.

"How many children do you have?" Hans finally said, "I mean, do you have kids?"

"*Ja*, I have five. Three girls, two boys. Adalicia, Johanna, and Gabriele are my girls. They're twenty-three, twelve and seven. And my boys are Lewie and Swain. They're seventeen and thirteen."

"What're they like?" Hans asked, mainly to humor the soldier, "And how old are you?"

"I'm forty-seven. Adalicia, she's a beautiful young woman. Firstborns are something incredible. You just can't believe you're a parent when it happens. But it's an amazing feeling. She has the smoothest hair, blue eyes like her mother's. Prettiest face in the world too, after my wife. She's actually getting married. Her soon-to-be husband is fighting right now, bless him. And she's working in a war factory, making weapons for her man. They'll be married when he comes back."

Hans and Blaz looked at each other worriedly, as they lifted another crate to the man.

"Johanna, she's the sweetest little girl. Not like either of her sisters. Adalicia isn't shy, she's the take-charge type, but in the subtlest way. Gabriele is a bundle of energy; she likes to make jokes. Not the best of course. They can only be so funny at age seven," the man smiled to himself, "But Johanna, she's so shy, but so kind. She loves little kids, even at twelve. So adorable, so innocent. Gabriele, she can be annoying, I'll say. But that's just something you come to love. They don't know they're being annoying when they're young. They grow out of it, and you see them change. And then you look back and can't believe how much they've changed and matured. Am I boring you boys?"

"Not at all," Hans answered politely but looked at Blaz and widened his eyes, "Keep going."

Blaz put a hand over his mouth to keep from laughing.

"*Danke*," the man said, "Lewie has been fighting since forty-three. We got unlucky, I suppose. He was a standout athlete, standout shooter, and has a good mind too. Studious, he wasn't afraid of talking to girls, but he was respectful when he did. Model citizen, if I say so myself. *Deutschland's* poster child. I was so proud of him. He got sent to a KLV camp, we didn't see him for a year. Then we were sent a letter saying he and his squad were being sent to help Army Group South when he was seventeen. He's still alive. *Gott sei Dank.* But he's lost so many of his friends. I knew those kids. Some of their fathers are stationed here with me. Each letter he writes, he's dealing with some serious depression. He still has two friends left from his original squad. And it sounds like they're each other's entire world right now. I pray that he comes back with his sanity. He's such a good kid. Swain has always been trying to live up to his brother, little guy has spirit. I received a letter from my wife, saying he will be sent into military service by next year. He just turned thirteen two weeks ago. And now he's going to be fighting," the man knelt down in the boxcar, and put a sleeve up to his eyes, "He'll be all right, he must."

"I'm sorry, sir," Hans said, no one understanding better than him.

"Ah *nein*, you don't need to say that," the soldier patted Hans on the shoulder, "My family has been blessed not to lose anyone. I just hope that blessing continues."

Hans and Blaz lifted another crate up to the man.

Third Reich Cinema

September 15, 1944

Jarman sat down at the end of a table inside the church. Koby was still speaking with some officers. Jarman took out a book, a diary. He opened it up and began to write. *Every day brings us closer to the end of the war. I don't think anyone thinks of that, but the war gets shorter every minute. What opportunities we had! We'd nearly defeated Communism, almost, almost. Now matters are worse.*

Koby and Jarman returned to bring the squad to dinner, but they had news before that.

"Okay, we are moving out in three days. Us and the *Totenkopfverbände-SS*. A small town in a forest has been taken by a band of Russians separated from the main force. Scouts count twenty, it's probably more, and a tank. The town is a Polish army town, so the buildings will be concrete, we'll have to fight building to building. We're going with a detachment of the *Wehrmacht*. They'll arrive early in the morning tomorrow. Should be forty of them, and they'll have two Tiger Tanks. And an armored truck with machine guns. Most importantly, this battle is to be filmed to encourage our comrades on the home front to persevere."

"To prove we can still win battles?" Ivo asked.

"Someone always has to ask something like that," Koby muttered, "But, *jawohl*. That'd be correct. We'll sneak close enough to use the machine guns. The tanks will fire on the buildings. We will move through the town with the SS and *Wehrmacht*. The filmmakers want to include the army, SS and *Hitlerjugend* all in their film."

"Wait, are they here?"

"*Nein*, we received a message."

"Ah."

"They think that showing all three of our major ground forces in one battle will be most effective for rallying the people. The army is the most accessible part of the *Wehrmacht* and *Deutschland's* military. The SS is coming because these guys need combat experience. But people will just assume they're *Waffen-SS* in the film. And us, the teenagers, to encourage the up and coming ones that they can play their part in holding back the Reds. I was told they want two of us to burn the Soviet flag in the town. Once we retake the city, we'll march back here, and the *Wehrmacht* will take command over the town."

"Will they be filming us fighting?" Blaz asked in surprise. This was something he'd never thought happened. War was war. But the more he thought, it made sense.

"They will. They're soldiers in their own right," Koby replied, "They want to have the soldiers look particularly young. The more it appears that we can change the war, the better. If we want someone who looks young, that rules out Jarman."

Jarman spoke up. "And Koby wants you guys do be in this, not him."

Koby continued, "Werner, you look exactly your age, so let's go with someone else. Blaz, you've got a bad scar, we don't want to look beat up. Ivo, you're a little too short, in my opinion. You agree?"

"Probably."

"Hans, you're Blaz's height and you look a little healthier and less worn down. You look young, we'll have you be in the flag burning. Tristan, you look young enough to fit the part."

"You should make castings in movies," Ivo joked.

Koby laughed, "Maybe after the war."

"You think I look beat up?" Blaz inquired with a grin, "I still look better than you."

Koby rolled his eyes.

"Koby, when we go into battle are you going to shout 'action,' or just keep doing what you've been doing?" Ivo asked, grinning ear-to-ear.

"Oh, shut up Ivo."

The Reinforcements

September 18, 1944

"Wake up! Wake up!" Koby yelled, "We need to get ready for the *Wehrmacht* to arrive! They'll be here soon. The fanfares are already sounding for us to wake up!"

"Okay, okay!" Ivo said, throwing off his blanket and stumbling to his feet.

Blaz rubbed his eyes and climbed to his feet drowsily. When he'd stood up, he heard a thump and looked over to the staircase. Hans was on the ground in his underwear at the foot of the staircase. It looked like he'd fallen down the stairs. Nobody took further notice and put their uniforms on before they briskly marched to the church.

The SS and *Wehrmacht* stood at attention as a red sun rose in the east. Their field commander had arrived with a good forty men. They immediately fell in behind him and his columns without a word. The soldiers were all battle-hardened and dirty. The cameramen themselves looked nearly as worn down and filthy. Commander Dooley had strawberry blond hair, made dirty by mud. A patch with the colors of Ireland was sewn onto his right sleeve. He took off his helmet while inspecting his new troops.

He looked over the SS troops and was not shy to criticize them for their lack of medals, wounds, or scars. They looked too clean. When he came to Koby and Jarman, he was clearly pleased. At their medals, and their muscular build. At Tristan and Werner, his smile faded, though he still nodded in begrudging approval. Perhaps only because of Tristan's Iron Cross. Or Werner's *Waffen-SS* uniform. Or both. All this disappeared when he came to Ivo, Blaz, and Hans. None of whom wore an Iron Cross. Simply skinny teenagers in a war zone.

"You are the reinforcements?" he asked, glaring at the *SS-Obersturmführer* and Jaeger, "No wonder we are losing the war," he added under his breath. The SS commandant quickly looked away to avoid eye contact. He appeared terrified of this particular *Hauptmann*.

"*Jawohl, Hauptmann*," the three responded. They all expected him to ask their age, but thankfully he did not.

"Well, it looks like I'm stuck with you," he said, "Follow my orders, don't ever question them, and this battle will be won within half an hour. Follow me. Tigers, up front. SS behind one, stay close to it. *Wehrmacht*, behind the second one. Tigers, *Los!*"

The Tigers rolled forth toward the town, slow enough for the soldiers to keep up. The tank commanders kept their sights on the buildings, scanning for Russians, and the T-34 they were said to have. The truck rolled behind them, with a man in its uncovered back manning an MG-42 mounted on a swivel.

"*Vizieren nach Nord*," one said, "Aim to the north."

"*Ich sehe kein Panzer. Wo ist es?*" the second tank commander responded.

"*Vorwärts, vorwärts!*" Dooley called to the tanks, "Guns ahead!"

The tanks lowered their guns as they came closer.

"Fire into the building straight ahead!" Dooley roared, as loud as he could. When he finished saying this, a spray of fire from the buildings cut down men furthest from the back of the tanks. The Tiger Tanks fired into the buildings, doing some damage, but the walls were thick. Some SS troops were cut down by the machine gun fire.

"*Scheiße!*" Jaeger shouted in panic.

"Don't break formation! Get closer to the tanks!" Dooley roared, "Tigers! Return fire!"

The Tigers opened fire into the holes they'd blasted. Blaz saw some Russians fall, others run.

"Nearly there! Clear out the buildings, we'll take the one with the flag last! She'll be guarded heavily!"

A whistle sounded right by Blaz's ear at this moment. He spun around to see the two men standing behind him were gone, blood and body parts littered the ground. The others behind those men had stopped in their tracks.

Blaz looked to the west. "*Panzer! T-34! Neun Uhr!*"

"*Scheiße!*" Dooley swore, "Men, charge to the town! *Los!* Tigers, due west. It's the tank!"

The Tigers spun to face the T-34. Blaz fell in behind Koby and Jarman, who ran after dozens of *Wehrmacht* soldiers. The armored truck rumbled forward heading for the town.

"Spread out, sweep through the buildings!" one man screamed.

"*Los!*" Koby shouted, and the squad sprinted.

Miraculously, they made it into a building. It was close-quarters, and the concrete made it dim inside.

"Jarman, Hans, Werner. We'll take the second floor and this floor. You take the basement."

"I don't want to fight in a basement," Ivo pleaded nervously, more than he'd ever appeared in a battle.

"Just do it."

"Come on, Ivo," Blaz said, putting a hand on Ivo's shoulder, "I'll go first."

"*Danke schön*," Ivo said, with his hands shaking uncontrollably on his rifle. Blaz attached his bayonet to the rifle, took a deep breath, and creaked open the door.

"*Granate?*" Tristan whispered.

"*Ja*," Blaz nodded.

Tristan took out a stick grenade and chucked it down the stairs. They heard frantic whispers, then an explosion.

"I'll go," Blaz breathed, as quietly as possible. Blaz put a foot on the first stair. No shooting came. He decided not to risk another, though. He leapt down the stairs, tucked and rolled to a concrete wall. Two shots were fired at him, both hitting the wall of the stairs.

"I'll cover!" Blaz shouted, "Come down in five seconds!" He stood up and took a shot, but no sooner had he squeezed the trigger then a shot was returned. Blaz felt nothing but pain, and he violently slammed into the ground. Ivo made it downstairs though, and behind cover. Tristan got an angle on the Russians from the top of the stairs and shot one dead. Ivo exposed himself to draw the other one out. Tristan didn't fail his squad mate, and Ivo didn't take a bullet.

"That's it!" Tristan sighed, sliding down the wall to take a seat on the stairs.

"Blaz!" Ivo shouted. All he saw was Blaz lying on the ground, blood flowing from his head. Blaz moved an arm to his skull, where the pain was. Ivo crawled over and lifted his friend up. His eyes went wide when he saw where Blaz had been hit.

"Ivo," Blaz whimpered, "It hurts bad. Are you all right?"

"I'm fine," Ivo said.

"I want to go home," Blaz stammered, gasping for air and putting his hand to the side of his head. When he pulled it back, his hand was painted in blood. Ivo gritted his teeth.

"Your nose is bleeding, you must've fallen on it," Ivo said, "Your left ear was shot. Narrowest of misses."

"That close?"

"*Ja*, it's bleeding. I don't know how to help that."

"Koby will know," Tristan cut in, "Let's get upstairs."

Koby did know enough to stop the bleeding. He hastily wrapped Blaz's head, so that the bandage went under Blaz's jaw, up over his ears and on top of his head, under his helmet.

"Don't let the camera capture this, *ja?*" Blaz tried to joke.

Koby tried his best to smile back, but it was forced.

"Come on! We are attacking the final building. They had more than twenty," Dooley yelled to the boys, "They already repelled an attack."

"*Jawohl, Hauptmann!*" Koby saluted.

"Come on! Men, split up, groups of three and four. One *Sturmgewehr* in each group. Go with a *Wehrmacht* squad."

"*Jawohl!*" Koby saluted again, "*Hauptmann*, why don't we use the tanks?"

"This is a military base essentially, boy. The walls are meant to repel artillery and tank shells. We have to storm the building."

"*Scheiße*," Koby muttered.

"Line up! Platoon formations! Tigers! If the Russians show themselves while I speak, fire immediately."

"*Jawohl, Hauptmann* Dooley."

"We failed to take the building the first time. That's unacceptable! We outnumber them, this may be the last fight where you outnumber the enemy! Make the most of it. Make this a victory the *Führer* would be proud of. Think of your fallen comrades. Take it all out on the Russians."

"*Jawohl Hauptmann!*"

"Have you any reason to fail now?"

"*Nein, Hauptmann!*"

Dooley paced in front of his soldiers, stopping in front of Blaz, "What does it say on your belt, son?"

"*Gott mit uns!*" Blaz shouted and stamped his right foot.

"God with us," the *Hauptmann* repeated quietly, "The Lord will grant us victory."

He strode to an SS soldier. "You! What is on your belt?"

"*Meine Ehre heißt treue!*" the soldier boomed. My honor is called loyalty.

"Your honor is called victory. The *Führer* expects nothing less. SS, take the left flank and clear upstairs. My men and *Hitlerjugend*, split up into two groups. We'll advance on the center, and right flanks. Right flank will clear the top floor as well. *Für Europa!*"

"*Für Europa!*" the *Wehrmacht* shouted.

The squad advanced on the right flank with the *Hauptmann* at the front. No Russians fired as they advanced. Blaz noticed Jaeger was behind them but paid him no mind. At the door, Dooley sprayed fire through to make sure Russians at the door would be dead. Then he dropped a grenade at the doorstep.

"Move back! Move back!" Dooley commanded. No one needed to be told this. The door was blown back into the building. The soldiers inched through the dust.

"Get down!" the one at the front yelled. Bullets came flying out of the open doorway, cutting through multiple Germans. Dooley narrowly avoided being hit. The boys dropped, then barrel-rolled away from line of fire. More Germans were cut down, trying to do the same. The fire was coming from a machine gun, and the Russians had cover behind a wall of sandbags.

Dooley waved the boys over to the wall. Thirteen of them were left. Ten had been cut down, some wounded, some dead. They couldn't yet help the wounded. Dooley rolled in front of the door and lofted a grenade into the building. The toss was brilliant, exploding right above the Russians heads.

"Follow me!" Dooley shouted. The German soldiers followed him in along with the squad.

"Boys, Wilhelm, and Otto, with me! The rest, sweep this level!"

Otto and Wilhelm ran up the stairs with the Dooley, the squad chased after. Koby was up front, Ivo and Blaz behind him and Werner clutching his ribs with his left hand at the back. Tristan stayed at Werner's side helping him along. Near the top, Blaz fell, nearly onto his face, but he stopped himself before hitting the top of the staircase.

"Watch it," Ivo whispered.

"Here we go," Dooley said to his men, "They're in here."

Otto kicked open the door and was shot immediately. The others poured in. The outnumbered Russians fired into the Germans from behind overturned furniture and desks. Dooley waved the squad in behind himself while firing his pistol. Jarman and Koby charged forward, firing their machine guns viciously. Blaz and Ivo bolted in with bayonets raised. The last Russians were shot dead by the *Hauptmann*.

"Stab everyone," Dooley told the soldiers with bayonets, one cameraman came in to the room from the other side.

"The building is secure, *Hauptmann*. We won," he reported, with the camera raised.

Blaz and Ivo drove their bayonets through the Russians. Ivo walked up to the last one. He positioned his rifle and thrust it at the corpse's chest. The soldier grabbed Ivo's rifle, and forced it away from him. In his other arm, the not-so-dead-man drew a dagger. He pulled Ivo down towards him. Ivo gasped just loud enough for Blaz to hear. It all happened so quickly. Ivo fell towards the man, but he missed the dagger. The Russian had pulled so hard, expecting an adult to stab him, so Ivo was thrown just beyond and above the man's chest where the dagger was held. With Ivo out of the way, Blaz shot the soldier. Ivo scrambled to his feet, reclaiming his rifle and putting a hand on his heart. His chest moved up and down in deep breaths. He looked down. He'd pissed himself. Ivo's face turned red, and he turned away from the German soldiers in shame. Dooley patted Ivo's shoulder.

"It's all right," he said in a fatherly tone, "It's all right, son."

"*Danke Hauptmann*," Ivo breathed.

"Good?"

"*Jawohl Hauptmann*," Ivo earnestly responded throwing up his right arm.

"Let's go, then."

While Dooley led them down the stairs on the other side of the building, guns still raised, shots went off above them.

"Russians?" one soldier asked.

"I ordered those SS fools to clear out this area," Dooley said, seething with anger. A shot whistled by his head, hitting the concrete behind him.

"*Los!*" he bellowed, "Kotze, cover the exit. Keep your eyes on the stairs for Russians!"

"*Ach, Nein!*" Werner shouted from the top and came tumbling down the stairs. Jarman, Koby, Blaz, and Ivo sprinted to the exit of the building, not noticing Werner's fall. But Tristan turned back. He helped Werner to his feet, supporting him as they made for the exit where Dooley was waving troops out. Koby and Blaz covered the Hauptmann's flanks, weapons raised.

When Tristan and Werner were almost to the exit, a Russian sprinted to the stairs behind them and fired a shot into Tristan's back. Blaz turned around to see Tristan with gritted teeth, closed eyes, blood splattering out the front of his chest, and falling forward to the concrete. Jaeger's eyes went wide when he realized it had been his job to watch the stairs.

"*Nein!*" Koby screamed. He fired madly into the building, felling the Russian who was cocking his rifle to take down Werner. Koby did not stop. Koby sprinted up the stairs like a possessed man.

"Wait!" Dooley shouted and chased after Koby.

"*Russen!*" Koby yelled in rage at the top of the stairs, followed by shots. Blaz ran to Tristan's side, and turned him onto his back. Tristan's eyes stared blankly, but he was still breathing. His hand was over the bullet hole in his chest, drenched in blood. It had torn a wide hole, and blood poured from it. His breathing was shaky and fading fast.

"Medic!" Werner screamed desperately unbuttoning Tristan's uniform, "We need a medic here!"

Tristan grabbed Blaz's hand and stared at him. He seemed unable to say anything.

A German sprinted into the building, pulling out a towel from his backpack. He pressed it into Tristan's stomach, then began wrapping it. Blood kept spilling out of the bullet hole, and Tristan breathed more rapidly. Blaz held his hand, as Tristan's breathing finally slowed until he breathed no more.

"*Nein, nein*," Blaz whispered. Werner put a hand on his own forehead.

Blaz picked up his rifle, marched over to the Russian on the stairs and began bayoneting him. The one who'd shot Tristan, who still breathed.

While he viciously bayoneted the Russian, Dooley appeared at the top of the stairs. Blaz stopped and looked up at him.

"Don't, boy," Dooley said, "It won't help anything."

Koby stormed past with a Soviet knife in his hand. He ran it into the dead Russian's heart, and kept walking. Blaz looked at the Russian, whose uniform was now drenched in red.

Nein, don't you dare have thoughts of mercy. Don't, enough is enough.

"Blaz! Come on, prisoners outside!" Koby called. Blaz trotted down the stairs, and lifted Tristan's body up with Werner, as best as the battered SS youth could. They carried him outside and laid him alongside the other fallen German soldiers who were being gathered.

"We lost so many," Koby shook his head bitterly, "So, so many. *Ist Gott wirklich mit uns?*" he asked Blaz and put his face in his hands. Is God really with us?

"Of course, God is with us," Blaz assured his friend, stunned that Koby would doubt that, of all things.

"We're losing the war," Koby wiped his face of any tears, "And we're losing our friends. Why would God let that happen?"

Blaz didn't answer. Koby brought his hands down and looked at the cloudy sky. Some light reflected off his tear stained face, "He should've grown up."

"A lot of Germans should've done that," Blaz said dismally. One cameraman waved Hans and Ivo over to the Soviet flag. They walked over without hesitation.

The cameramen filmed the Germans burning the Soviet flag, which briefly distracted the soldiers from what had just happened. Jaeger was ready to move on to the Russian prisoners. He'd survived the battle, but the *Obersturmführer* had not. He kept his hand on his knife during the filming of the flag burning. As the filmmakers shut off their cameras, Dooley waved them away and strode toward the prisoners.

Sanity in War

A few SS soldiers drew their daggers near the Russian prisoners, while others waited anxiously.

"Let's make them suffer," one SS soldier suggested, looking at the bodies of fallen comrades. Dooley ordered the SS soldiers to execute the Russians with their daggers.

"Koby," Blaz whispered, "We can't allow this."

"Why not?"

"This is murder!"

"Blaz, I've had enough of you wanting to show mercy to these animals. No more."

Blaz shook his head and started making his way over to the *Hauptmann*.

"How about we have the Tigers run them over?" one *Totenkopfverbände-SS* soldier suggested.

"*Ja!*" almost every SS soldier yelled, along with several of the younger *Wehrmacht* soldiers, including Koby and Jarman. Dooley changed his mind, and ordered, "Tigers! Get in position! SS, put them in the road!"

The SS obeyed immediately, dragging the terrified men into the middle of the road.

"Tigers! Crush them!"

"*Ja* sir!" one tank commander answered enthusiastically.

"*Hauptmann*," Blaz said, not at a shout, but loud enough that those near Dooley could hear.

"What is it?" Dooley asked, looking down at Blaz. But Blaz noticed he didn't seem as tall as the officers Blaz remembered serving under. He barely had to tilt his neck to look down to Blaz's eyes. Maybe Dooley was short, but Blaz was definitely taller now. Dooley had a huge advantage when it came to weight and strength. Not that Blaz was considering fighting a superior officer, but his newly realized height gave him a surge of confidence.

"Sir," Blaz began, feeling emboldened by his supposed height, "We can't kill these men like this. It's not right."

"*Nein?*" the *Hauptmann* asked, raising an eyebrow.

"*Nein, Hauptmann.*"

"Well then," Dooley said, not showing any disapproval of Blaz's suggestion, "Who here thinks we shouldn't kill these men like this?"

No one raised their hand for several seconds. The only noise was the hum of the tank's engines. The men looked at each other, seeing if someone had raised their hand. No one appeared willing to be the first to dissent.

"Anyone?" Dooley asked again, a hint of disappointment in his tone.

Still, the soldiers did nothing. Some of the men in their thirties appeared conflicted but remained silent. The SS soldiers glared at Blaz. They wanted blood. A sixteen-year-old wasn't going to stop them. The *Wehrmacht* soldiers' expressions were mixed. Some agreed with the SS, but still some looked ready to take Blaz's side. They wouldn't be the first one to show this. They needed someone to go first.

"Ten seconds," Dooley said. Blaz looked to Koby in desperation. Koby shook his head, eyes cold. Jarman made sure not to make eye contact with Blaz. Werner wouldn't be the first to endorse mercy. Blaz looked to Hans, who kept his gaze to the ground. Ivo was the only one Blaz could turn to.

"Five!"

Ivo and Blaz made eye contact. Blaz mouthed, "*Bitte!*" to his friend. Ivo started to raise his hand but stopped halfway.

"Charge!" the Hauptmann shouted to the tanks. The tanks gradually rumbled forward, picking up speed the further they went. The SS kept guns trained on the Russians. One man jumped up and made a run for it. The SS shot him in the legs before he even got out of the Tiger's paths. Blaz closed his eyes. The tanks were only partially slowed when they ran over the men, the process slow enough that Blaz could hear screams. When the tanks had completely steamrolled the men, the dismembered bodies became visible. Blaz had seen many horrible deaths in the war. And he'd vomited several times during the war upon seeing these things. Now he added another tally to the count.

Jarman versus Jaeger

"You weakling!" Koby screamed at Jaegar at the Polish town, "You weak, pathetic bastard!"

Jaeger took the insults; it was all he could do. Jarman strode forward, shoving Koby out of the way, "Was it too hard to raise your damn rifle? Save your brother's life? You son of a bitch!"

The other SS soldiers moved away. Jarman was not finished though. Not nearly. He got into Jaeger's face, "You cowered behind us during the battle, and you couldn't even defend our backs! I should-" Jarman slammed his fist into Jaeger's face. The SS guard stumbled back, putting a hand over his nose. When he put his hand down, there was fury in his eyes.

Jaeger unbuttoned his SS tunic, to which Jarman unbuttoned his *Wehrmacht* uniform. They both threw them to the ground, and advanced toward each other. Jarman landed the first blow. The swiftest and most ferocious punch Blaz had seen since Tristan had beaten Koby in boxing. Jaeger was quick and barely dodged but lost his balance in doing so. Jarman sent a high kick into the SS guard's face right after his punch. Jaeger went to the ground but scrambled back up. He was bleeding already. But he knew he had to fight now, or he'd get no mercy from the *Wehrmacht* corporal.

Jarman swung his fists wildly at Jaeger, who blocked blow after blow. He was a fair fighter. Finally, Jaeger went on the offensive. Jarman was ready and got a grip on Jaeger's wrist. The SS guard swung his free fist. Jarman blocked the blow and grabbed this wrist too. Jaeger twisted his arms and seized Jarman's wrists so that they were in a lock. Jarman was the first to make a move. As they pushed each other back and forth, Jarman swiftly moved his head back and smashed it into Jaeger's. The head butt sent Jaeger back pedaling rapidly. Jarman sprinted at him, picked him up around the legs, and slammed him into the ground. He relentlessly punched the SS guard over and over in the face. Jaeger tried to defend against the swarm of fists, but Jarman's attack was fast and brutal. Koby watched approvingly. Finally, Ivo ran forward and grabbed Jarman by the shoulders, "Jarman! He's had enough!"

Jarman spun around and elbowed Ivo in the jaw. Ivo backed away, hands over his mouth. Jaeger stayed down, bleeding all over his face. Jarman cocked his right arm to punch again, but Hans stayed his blow. Hans shook his head, his silver-blue eyes turning to ice. The corporal backed away from Jaeger, picked up his uniform, briskly turned away, and headed back to the house. Jaeger rose to his feet once Jarman had gone, wiped his bloody nose, put his SS tunic on, and strode back into the town.

The Polish Girl

Blaz did not speak with his squad the rest of the day. He wandered around the town in silence with his rifle, staring blankly ahead. More than one soldier told him to watch where he was going. Hans had disappeared once they'd returned, but Blaz saw him kneeling in the fields at a point. At their house, late that night, Blaz remained seated against the wall near the staircase in uniform while his squad mates talked. The discussion was monopolized by Koby and Jarman. Werner was quiet. Ivo was already asleep, at least he looked asleep. He had not said a thing.

Hans sat down next to Blaz, unable to fall asleep. Blaz glanced at him out of the corner of his eye. Hans rubbed his shins. "I can't believe it, Blaz. He's gone."

Blaz exhaled. "*Ja.*"

"Just like that. After everything, he just got shot."

"Are you mad?"

"Mad? Of course not. Why would I be?"

"Jaeger."

Hans sighed. "I'm not, Blaz. I don't want to be mad at him. He's an idiot, incompetent failure. But I don't want to be angry. I'm just sad."

"Me too."

Hans looked at the ceiling as two tears streaked down his face. "He's with his father now. I'm sure he's proud of him." He and Blaz made eye contact. "I'm going outside, go on a walk," Hans said, "And get my head together."

As Hans left the house, Blaz wiped a forming tear away.

"*Guten Abend,*" a voice said. Blaz looked up the stairs. The Polish girl was standing there.

"*Guten Abend,*" he responded, "You speak German?"

"A little," the girl answered, "Germans have lived in this town for a long time. I speak with them sometimes. Not much now. But I know some German."

"You speak German pretty good," he said, impressed, "Come here."

The girl walked down the stairs and sat next to Blaz. Blaz realized he still had the wrapping over his head. He didn't know whether to remove it or keep it on.

"You are called Blaz, right?" the girl asked.

"*Ja*, Blaz Adolf Senft," he smiled.

The girl's expression changed to one of concern, "Adolf?"

"*Ja.* Problem?"

"I hate Adolf Hitler," she said quietly, so none of the other boys would hear.

"You hate-" Blaz began loudly, but she put a finger up to her mouth quickly. "Come up," the girl instructed Blaz. She led him upstairs into her room and closed the door but kept it cracked open slightly. It was the only room on the second floor, an attic turned bedroom. The girl sat down on the floor and leaned against the small bed. Other than the bed, there was one window, and a small dresser.

"So," Blaz began awkwardly and took off his cap, holding it at his upper chest, "Should I stand? Do you want me to stand? I think I should stand."

"Sure," the Polish girl shrugged, "If you want."

Blaz breathed in and leaned against the wall across from the girl. He stared straight at the other wall, then turned his head to see her looking at him.

"You hate the *Führ-* Adolf Hitler?" Blaz asked. He had never heard someone say this. Just a few angry comments from a soldier in Leningrad and a few skepticisms from Koby and Johann.

"I do," the girl said, as if it should be obvious.

"Before I ask why, what is your name?"

"Wiktoria," she said, pronouncing the 'W' as a 'V,'.

"Wiktoria? That's a lovely name," Blaz complimented her.

"You were to ask me," Wiktoria said faultily.

"Why do you hate the *Führ-* Adolf Hitler?"

"You can call him the *Führer*. Everyone in land knows him by that," the girl said.

Blaz nodded in understanding.

"I hate Hitler because he attacked my homeland. And killed my father."

"Your father?" Blaz asked.

"My father was in army. He died in a fight."

"Where?"

"Not far to the east."

"But *Fräulein*, we came from the west. The Soviets killed your father."

"*Ja?*"

"*Ja.* You don't need to hate the *Führer*. He only wants to protect his people. At home and abroad. And to spread National Socialism's message. That will make the world better. Each country will cast aside social class and unite as the one people they are. They will work on perfecting themselves. Like us Germans have."

"Does he want that?"

"*Jawohl.*"

"What if we don't want it?"

"I suppose you don't have to adopt it. But people don't always know what is best for them."

"That's, how does one say?" she motioned with her hands, raising her right hand straight up five times, then her left four times. Then she gave an approving nod to her right.

"*Demokratie?*" Blaz asked, scratching his head.

"*Ja, demokracja.* That's a good thing."

"Well, remember that people aren't always the best at choosing the best. The people chose Barabbas over Jesus Christ," Blaz said, proud at his own response.

Wiktoria glared for a moment. Blaz looked at the ground, though he didn't quite know why he was embarrassed.

"You know, my cousins were taken months ago, when the men in black arrived," she finally said.

"What? Why?"

"I'm half Jewish. My mother is a Pole, but my father was a Jew."

"*Ja, und?*" Blaz said, not catching on.

"And, my cousins of father were Jews."

"I don't understand."

"The men in black took my cousins somewhere and I haven't seen them since. They take away Jews."

"Why are you still here then?" Blaz asked.

"I-I don't know."

"I'm sure your cousins will be fine. We are just interning them. You will probably even get a postcard soon."

The girl shook her head, and, for the first time, looked away, "What did you do today? Why were you gone?"

"I fought. I lost a friend," Blaz answered, "Another friend."

Wiktoria looked startled by this, but kept her tone under control, "How many friends have you lost in the war?"

"Seven. I knew three of them since I was a kid."

"You are a kid."

"*Nein*, I am not."

"Sure you are."

"*Nein*, I am not."

"Why would you be a man?"

"I've done everything a lot of men don't do in their lives."

"That doesn't make you a man. Are you sixteen?"

"*Ja*."

"I think that is a kid."

"Okay," Blaz said.

Both of them laughed for a moment.

"Why did you tell me you were Jewish?" Blaz asked, lowering his voice, "If you hate the *Führer* and the men in black, and think we are Jew haters, why would you tell me that?"

Wiktoria continued faultily, "The men in black, they really are, what is the word, for, nice, like nice to women and children?"

"*Höflich*?" Polite.

"*Ja. Höflich*," she nodded, "They really are polite, but they took my cousins away. I need to know where they are. I think you don't trust the men in black. I don't think you would tell people I am half Jewish."

Blaz stared at Wiktoria. Then he looked down, "Fine, I won't."

Wiktoria stood up and walked around to the window. Blaz looked up at her.

"Why do you fight, Blaz? You're really young."

Blaz glared at this comment, though he again wasn't entirely sure why. "I fight for *Deutschland*, for my people, and for the *Führer*," he answered anyway.

"Why do you Germans like the *Führer* so much?" she asked, sounding irritated at the *Führer* being mentioned again.

"Has there ever been a man like him?" Blaz asked, almost laughing, "Has Poland had a *führer* like our *Führer*? Someone who brought us from starvation, degeneracy, and self-destruction to the light."

"Look where you are now," she retorted.

Blaz almost leapt up at this. His muscles were already working but he stopped before he rose, "*Fräulein*, we are-"

"Losing."

Blaz shot up now, "We've been forced to fight the world!"

"Do you think the *Führer* cares for you?" Wiktoria asked bluntly. Blaz narrowed his eyes at her. "You're all just dying in this war. What leader does that? He only wants boys to use to fight."

"The *Führer* is only doing what he must! Just imagine, for a moment if you can, if he were to call us back home. Which he would love to do if he could. The Russians would conquer all of Europe and our homeland!" Blaz shot, "Wiktoria, the end goal is never to just fight for the sake of fighting, it's to reach a goal, which is total victory over the Communists and for Germany, and the rest of Europe to live on. *Ja*, he needs boys. He needs men. You think he doesn't understand war? He fought in *Der Krieg*! He spent years in a trench! He saw people fight and die, he was wounded himself! *Ja*, it may be hard to believe for the world, especially you Poles, but the *Führer* does care about his people. Probably more than any *Führer* ever has! He worked for years to win us over, to make *Deutschland* prosperous for all. Then he united us. He helped us bring ourselves out of poverty and has given *Deutschland* a future."

"Blaz?" came a whisper from outside. Blaz recognized it as Hans, "Blaz? Are you in there?"

Blaz looked at Wiktoria, though he still had a glare on his face. She nodded nonetheless.

"May I come in?"

"*Ja*," Blaz said, "Come on in."

Hans slowly pushed the door open. He was only in his underwear. When he saw Wiktoria, his tear-stained face lit up.

"What is it?" Blaz asked.

"I was just wondering where you went. It's getting late and all. Why are you up here with her?"

"She asked me to." Hans' gaze sharpened. "*Nein. Nein,*" Blaz said in a rush.

"Okay. Okay. What were you doing?"

"Talking."

"What about?"

"Just things, the war, what's happened. Her name is Wiktoria," Blaz told Hans.

"I know."

Blaz looked at Hans in mild surprise. Hans raised his eyebrows. Both glanced at Wiktoria, then back to each other.

"What specifically did you talk about?"

"I'll tell you later," Blaz said, standing up and looking back to the Polish girl, "Wiktoria, we'll leave you alone now. It's late. *Guten Nacht.*"

"*Guten Nacht*, Hans, Blaz," Wiktoria said.

We're Young

Hans and Blaz went back down, quietly so they wouldn't wake up any of others, who had drifted off. Blaz stripped down to his underwear. Hans laid down on the floor and pulled a blanket over him.

"Sure feels nice when we get to sleep with blankets," Hans said in the darkness.

"*Ja,*" Blaz agreed, turning to face Hans, laying on his side and putting a hand on his cheek, "Nice try."

"What do you mean?" Hans asked innocently.

"You know! How you knew her name, why you raised your eyebrows. She was acting all friendly when she saw you. And you flexed when you noticed her! What on earth?" Blaz asked, keeping his voice as low as he could.

"One of man's purposes is to impress a girl," Hans stated philosophically.

"But you were acting, did you and Wiktoria–"

"Did we what?"

"You know," Blaz said painfully, "What you asked me."

"Ah, well," Hans reluctantly answered, "*Ja*, we did."

"What? You're kidding!"

"You asked, I answered."

"I know, but why? You of all people!"

"Come on, Blaz. If anyone in of the Knights would do it, it would be me."

Blaz thought for a moment. Ivo was too innocent, Werner was too disciplined, Jarman would never disobey the *Wehrmacht* code of conduct, and Koby, despite his recent attitude, had common sense more so than the rest of the squad. Hans had some flare mixed with idiocy to him.

"You would," Blaz finally agreed, "But why? Why would you do that? Why? When? How?"

"She and I have talked, most of the time when you guys are busy. When I have time to myself, I've been helping her with German. Last night after patrol, she was still awake, everyone went right to bed. I stayed up to talk with her. Pretty early in the discussion, we both decided it would be better to move the conversation upstairs so you guys could sleep. Ivo just wasn't falling asleep with us down there for some reason. I left my uniform here, so I was in my underwear and muscle shirt. We were talking for quite a while, it must've been hours, and everyone is out cold. I got my first kiss then," Hans said, and it was clear he was smiling when he said this, "It's late at night, I don't know if you have noticed but the later you stay up, the more open you are to talk about things," Hans said awkwardly.

Blaz rolled his eyes in the darkness, "I guess so."

"We started getting closer. Neither of us really planning it, it just happened. We just started coming closer, she started to, you know. I took off my shirt, I don't know why. We're kissing, a lot, our arms are wrapped around each other. Eventually, I'm on top of her, and she's staring up at me. We're both butt naked. She's beautiful. Everything about her is beautiful."

"This is getting weird," Blaz said, looking at Hans awkwardly. Hans could barely see Blaz's face but drew from his tone.

"I know, but it happened. And," Hans stopped to laugh a little, "I think that's actually the moment when we started thinking twice. She looked me in the eye and asked, 'Should we?' I didn't answer, my instincts told me to continue, but my conscience said, '*Nein*.'"

"And?"

"Since I didn't answer she said something else. She knows about what I've done in the war, we talked about that by now. I know about her father and cousins. And how she almost got taken with them. Anyway, she said, 'We're young and we're alive. What do you think?' I answered, 'I think I may never get this chance in my life.' She smiles, and says, 'Me too.' So we picked up right where we left off."

"Huh?" Blaz asked unwarily.

"You know what I'm talking about. So now I ask her, 'You sure?' And she says, '*Ja*. You're worth it.' I can only imagine she knows the Russians are coming. And if the rumors are true, I worry for Wiktoria. They won't treat a beautiful girl like her well, they couldn't."

"*Ja*," Blaz breathed.

"And we did it right then. I have no idea how long I was in her, I don't think it was more than fifteen minutes, but it felt like heaven. I forgot about everything that was happening in the world for that short time. And then we just fell asleep, naked, right next to each other. I can say, it was probably the best night of my life. We got lucky that no one figured it out. The morning fanfare woke us up, and I was out of there like a bolt of lightning. You remember, I ran down the stairs in my underwear and fell down? You remember that?"

"*Ja*," Blaz laughed.

"Well, now I know what it feels like. And I did it with someone I like and think is beautiful. I still probably shouldn't have done it, though."

"Is she the one?"

"I hope so. But I have no idea if she's the one. I'm not going to be one of those people who think someone they've known for two weeks is their future wife. She's Polish."

"She didn't mind a German," Blaz said, "The Slavs are our blood brothers."

"*Ja*," Hans murmured whimsically. Then he snapped back, "*Nein*, that's not happening. Like she said, 'We're young and we're alive.' And it'll be a miracle if both us are by the end of this war. And even a bigger miracle if I find her."

Death in the Wind

October 1, 1944

The day after the attack on the base, the graves were dug. Wooden crosses made the markers, with an Iron Cross and the *Wehrmacht* soldier's name carved onto each marker. The *Totenkopfverbände-SS* markers were inscribed not with the Iron Cross, but the SS runes. The squad said some words, Koby said nothing. Their squad finished saying goodbye with a long, stiff-armed salute while they stared at Tristan's grave. Weeks passed, and the days got colder. The days became shorter. The distance to the front got shorter. With the death of the *Obersturmführer*, there was a dispute over who would lead, though technically and clearly Jaeger was the highest ranking at *Scharführer*. They decided on a miniature high command for the town where the Sergeants, Corporals, and the *Scharführer* would debate their moves and strategies.

These men had high command meetings after dinner and sent others out to patrol the town while they did so. Their discussion was going on much longer than normal. Hans, Blaz, Werner, and Ivo were patrolling, holding their rifles closer than usual. The moon was full, the wind had picked up and whistled through the forest. It sounded as if death was speaking to them, and they all recognized his voice.

"I hope they don't reach Bieżuń," Blaz said, referring to their town, "I really hope not."

"The Red Army isn't that far," Ivo said, "Otherwise they wouldn't be discussing this for so long."

"The Red Army has been stalled for a solid month. Maybe we have them," Hans smiled, hoping beyond hope that the war's course could be reversed.

"Maybe, if we've held them for a month, maybe a little longer is possible," Blaz said, "Maybe a counterattack."

"How much time do we have left?" Werner asked, "I'd like to hear what the meeting is about."

"It's getting late, we should be allowed into the church soon and replaced out here."

"Hey, Blaz?" Hans asked.

"*Ja?*"

"When we attacked that town. Why did you ask the *Hauptmann* to not run the Russians over with our Tigers? Why do you care so much about them?"

"Should we expect mercy if we carry out revenge?" Blaz replied, "Or mercy for our people? The Russians could move into East Prussia soon... *Und das ist Deutschland.*"

"*Ja*, but you honestly think that you, what you do will change them? They don't care, they only want to see *Deutschland* burn."

"*Nein*, I guess it won't change anything, but I won't be changed. Still, we shouldn't run over privates with tanks. Do you want to get run over by a tank?"

"*Nein. Nein*, I don't," Hans answered, his voice getting quieter at the end.

The Church

"You boys!" came a call. All four turned around to see two *Wehrmacht* soldiers trotting towards them, "You boys may retire to your home now, or listen in on the meeting. We are here to take over."

"*Danke*," Hans thanked the two while saluting, and the four boys marched off to the church immediately.

Everyone in the church was in high spirits. The privates had almost all filed out. A few remained, while the ranking officers were laughing and having a good time. No reason to fear. Jarman saw the four enter and jogged over to them.

"What happened?" Ivo asked with wide eyes.

"Good news, the Russian offensive has been stalled. For now, we should be all right here. We aren't going anywhere."

"*Ja!*" Blaz and Hans exclaimed.

"What happened?" Werner asked.

"The Red Army's supply lines have been stretched thin, we believe they are regrouping before they continue their attack. We are close enough to the front that we must be prepared for any order from high command. With fresh troops needed to patrol across Poland, not to mention the front, we will be left here with the *Wehrmacht*. The *Totenkopfverbände-SS* will be moved to another town."

"How long do they think the line will hold?" Ivo asked.

Jarman squinted, trying to remember, "We honestly hope that this is as far as we retreat. But when we turn the tide we'll be back at the front. For now, we're here. Some of the ranking *Waffen-SS* and *Wehrmacht* officials hope to make peace with the West so we can focus on defeating the Soviet Union."

"But the command said sometime in the next months, if all goes according to planned, we will get to go on leave to Seelow. And Werner might be able to go to Detmold then."

"*Wunderbar!*" Ivo exclaimed with a joyous smile.

"I'll finally get to see Erwin!" Blaz grinned.

"Speaking of which, will we be able to send and receive letters now?" Ivo asked. It had been months since they'd last heard from their parents. Letters were low on the Third Reich's priorities.

"We will. They'll be months old. We could get several."

"Well," Koby said, as he walked toward the squad, "Things are changing. The Russians have halted. We'll be pushing back soon. We have four hundred thousand men available in Norway. Ready to be deployed at any time. The Home Guard is expanding. I've heard they're making a home defense force for anyone who hasn't fought yet. They'll defend their towns and be ready to come to the front when we push the Reds back. The war is going to change."

"As long as the reserve troops aren't *Totenkopfverbände-SS*," Jarman muttered glancing in Jaeger's direction.

"You're brutal to him," Ivo said seriously.

"He and his whole force. I can't stand them. Bunch of cowards, weaklings, and failures," Jarman muttered, "*Untermenschen.*"

"*Mein Wort,*" Blaz murmured.

"Don't you dare disagree," Jarman said to everyone.

Fußball

October 7, 1944

"Pass it! Pass it!" Ivo yelled to Jarman, who dribbled an old soccer ball through a grassy field outside of Bieżuń. Jarman looked Ivo's way, and Blaz sprinted to cover him. With the pass no longer there, Jarman slowed down his attack, with Koby guarding him tightly.

"*Los!*" the *Wehrmacht* soldiers yelled, rooting for whomever they felt like. They just wanted to see goals scored, "*Schnell, schießen es!* Quick, shoot it!"

Apparently, the *Wehrmacht* had done a decent job differentiating themselves from the *Totenkopfverbände-SS* and that they weren't like them because the Poles were pleased when the SS had left town, and the *Wehrmacht* soldiers joined in to reestablish a form of trust between the town and their new police force. Many parents of the Poles had come with their younger children, to see their older kids compete for the first time in years. And some for other reasons entirely.

Koby stayed on Jarman forcing him to the outside of the field. Jarman finally got Koby to overcommit and maneuvered past him. Koby spun around, nearly fell to the ground, and dragged his fingers along the grassy ground to recover. A Polish boy, about fifteen, made an attempt to slide tackle the ball away from Jarman. The German chipped it over the Polish boy and kept going. Werner, was the last obstacle, guarding the goal. Jarman slowed down as he approached the goal, which was two German helmets that the *Wehrmacht* soldiers had lent for the goal. He pushed the ball into position to shoot, and just before striking, Wiktoria swept in and stole the ball. Jarman followed through into the now vacant space and fell over, he'd tried to kick it so hard.

"Ha ha!" Koby burst out laughing and took off down the field with Wiktoria. But he fell down laughing at Jarman. The German soldiers roared with laughter.

"Wiktoria! *Idź! Idź! Idź!*" yelled a younger Polish boy, about Ivo's height but three years younger. Hans slide-tackled

Hans now tore down the field with the ball. Blaz was too far to do anything, but Wiktoria was sprinting after him. Hans heard her just in time, spun to protect the ball, then sent a pass to a Pole. Wiktoria abandoned Hans and sprinted to steal the ball. Hans nodded when she did this and took off towards the defenders. The Pole sent a pass through the line, and Hans received it perfectly. Werner sprinted out to try and stop him, but Hans sent the ball into the corner. Werner dove, having made much progress with his injuries. He missed, and the ball rolled past, lightly hitting the inside of the helmet.

"*Ja!*" he shouted and threw a stiff-armed salute into the air.

The game went on for a couple hours, everyone having a good time. The German youths, the Poles, and the *Wehrmacht*. Once the game had wrapped up, a ten-to-nine victory for Jarman, Hans, and Ivo's side, the *Wehrmacht* soldiers took the field alongside the younger Polish children and played a much shorter game while the others rested and watched them.

When the sun set, the German and Polish teenagers lined up for a hundred-meter dash. One girl volunteered to signal the command to go. She ran to the other side of the field and held up a hand. All the boys and girls lined up evenly. The Germans made sure they were further back, if anything. A victory would be an absolute victory.

The girl dropped her hand and they shot off. Koby and Jarman got out to an early lead, with Hans and Blaz close behind. Two Polish boys stayed even with Hans and Blaz while Werner and Ivo trailed their friends slightly. Wiktoria led the girls and was catching up to Werner and Ivo. She passed one Polish boy, who sped up in frustration. Ivo sprinted as fast as he could move his legs. Wiktoria challenged Werner and Ivo, nearly beating them, but came in eighth out of twenty-two. The boy she'd beaten shook her hand and complimented her.

"*Verdämmt*, she's fast," Ivo said.

"She is, I thought she was going to catch up to us," Werner said, "Can't have that."

"That would've been embarrassing," Jarman laughed, looking at Ivo and Werner.

"Hey, she's a good athlete. It's almost like she was in the League of German Girls," Ivo said.

"Almost."

"Great race, Wiktoria!" Hans called as the Poles returned home.

Allied Bombings

October 19, 1944

"We got letters, there's the truck!" Ivo pointed, while they ran into the town in heavy rain.

"Great!" Jarman shouted over the downpour. The six Germans sped up to reach the truck, right outside the mess hall. A man in the back of the truck was sorting through a box.

"Names? Dark hair, you first," he said.

"Koby Hertz."

"*Ein Moment*," the man said, scanning through the letters in the box, "Ah, here we are. You got two."

He handed Koby the letter, then pointed to Jarman.

"Jarman Knecht."

This process repeated itself until everyone had received at least one letter.

"*Gott sei Dank*," Blaz breathed when, yet again, his father, who had sent two letters, his second one becoming increasingly worried about his son. His mother's letter read:

Lieber Blaz,
Son, we are so blessed. Erwin is doing great, you and your father are all right. Our family is doing well. Seelow is not the same though, Blaz. We are on food rations now, I'm sure you know. But we are staying strong for you. We are all working hard to bring in a good harvest this year. Stay safe, Blaz.
Liebe, Mutter

The truck would be leaving in half an hour, but the man said he would take letters if they wrote them and addressed them, which they quickly set to work doing.

Blaz sat down at one of the tables to contemplate what he should write. It had been so long since his last letter, so many of his friends had fallen since then. Wilhelm, Jaye, Tristan, Erich. Blaz put his pen in position to write several times but couldn't manage to find the right words.

He was able to write: *"Dear father,"*

After several minutes, Blaz began:

Gott sei Dank you are okay, father. Our squad has lost friends; this war is horrible. I don't want anyone else to die, they deserve better. Koby, Ivo, and Jarman are still alive. But this war is changing them, especially Koby. He is struggling with being himself, you know him. He used to be kinder, and he wouldn't have thought of doing what we've done in this war. I'm worried about him. He'll come around, I'm sure. Please be okay, father. Gott mit uns. Heil Hitler.

Liebe, Blaz

Blaz finished with that. He didn't want to write about the battles. But it should be longer. He just couldn't put on paper what he wanted to say. Like his father.

Blaz instead started to draw. A bird's head. Next a body, then widespread wings. Finally, he drew the talons grasping a circle. Inside the circle, he drew the swastika. It could've been better, but it was passable. And Blaz hoped his father would like it.

He added at the bottom, *"Frohe Weihnachten, Vater."*

His letter might not even reach his father by then.

After they'd written their letters and eaten breakfast, they reported to the head sergeant for orders.

"I want you boys at the docks. You may stay under the shelter, but I need you down there until you receive further orders. *Verstanden?*"

"Sir, *ja* sir!"

"We haven't had rain like this for a while," Werner said, under the shelter at the docks, "I like the rain."

"You *like* rain?" Jarman asked, looking up from greasing his STG-44. All but Werner had started doing this after a few minutes under the shelter.

"*Ja*, I do. It's something different."

"You prefer rain or sun?" Ivo asked.

"What kind of a stupid question is that, Ivo?" Jarman grunted.

"Sun, but I like it when it rains. Do you like rain at all?"

"I guess it's refreshing," Ivo admitted.

"I like running in the rain," Koby said with a smile, reminiscing on past memories of this.

"*Ja*, me too," Blaz chimed in.

"And after a storm, when the sun starts to peak through the clouds. Half the sky is covered with clouds, then the other is all sunny," Werner said, as he sat down to grease his rifle, "That's so pretty."

No one answered this.

"What did your letters say?" Hans asked everyone.

The young men looked around, waiting for someone to begin. Jarman, Ivo, and Blaz started at the same time, stopping moments after.

"You first, Jarman," Ivo said.

"My mother told me how she's worried, how much she loves me. It warms the heart to read that, it does. My brothers are all alive and well. Amazing that they are. They fought at someplace called Kursk. You know all three of them are in a Panther tank together. Since they're each just a year or two apart from each other. They said it was insane, the battle. So many tanks, hundreds in a massive clash. But that was obviously a while ago. They've been in a Panther Tank since they were deployed in the east, and they say she's one hell of a tank. Karl drives, Heinrich loads, and Helmut is the commander."

"That is all they told you?" Hans asked.

"Ah, a bunch of stuff you wouldn't care about."

"Okay," Hans grinned, looking at the others.

"My father told me about what's going on in France right now. My mother told me about my little brother," Blaz said, "Koby?"

"Oh, just Klara is doing well. Mama says she looks like me."

"Ah," Ivo smirked. Koby looked back at his rifle and smiled at the ground.

Blaz turned. "What about you, Ivo?"

"Father got to come home. He says he's been recruited into a special commando unit led by an *Obersturmbannführer* named Otto Skorzeny. Because of his successes in spying enemy lines and whatnot, Skorzeny thought he would be of use in their unit."

"Didn't Skorzeny rescue Mussolini?" Koby asked.

"I think so." Ivo paused and looked straight ahead after saying this, and added with disappointment, "Oh, we forgot to get a newspaper from the men who came with letters."

"We can borrow one from someone else," Werner assured him.

"Have you heard anything about Jurgen or Reinhardt's fathers?"

"I don't know about *Herr* Holtzer. But *Herr* Weiss is fighting in my father's company," Blaz exhaled through his mouth, "I can't imagine how they do it."

"I can," Hans said.

"Me too," Jarman nodded, "You don't want to be able to imagine it, though."

"Did anyone get a letter from Gunther? Is he doing okay?" Ivo asked.

"*Ja*, he's recovering," Koby answered, "He'll be able to walk again. Better than that, he's expected to make a full recovery."

"*Gut*," some boys said.

Hans asked what everyone was wondering after the brief pause in the conversation, "When will he return?"

"By February."

The Beast is on His Way

"Come on, sir! Last tank, unless you want to walk!" Max called to Schlusser.

The *Sturmbannführer* gestured for Max to head out, and the *Panzer* rolled to the west. Schlusser waved the last twenty men in the dirt town square to him. All were SS.

"Let's go, men! Move out! We're heading northwest, to Polish land," he called.

The soldiers immediately formed up and marched toward him. Schlusser waited until they were right behind him, then led the march out of the farming town. It was a short march to the city limits where many Ukrainians had gathered.

"Don't leave us! Please!" was the general summary of their shouts.

Schlusser and his soldiers didn't make eye contact as they marched past the pleading Ukrainians. But one young woman ran out in front of Schlusser, grabbing him by one lapel, causing him to halt.

"Please," she begged, "Don't leave us to Stalin. Not again!"

"I am sorry," Schlusser said, putting a hand on her cheek, "We can do no more to stop them than you can."

"Please! Our children!"

Schlusser looked at the soldier nearest to him awkwardly, then back to the young woman. "We will be back someday."

"Please come back," she said, letting him go at this.

"*Auf wiedersehen*," Schlusser said, tipping his cap at her, and resumed his march.

The soldier behind him began singing as they marched past the last house, "SS marches in enemy land, and sings a devil's song."

The rest of the SS joined in the song but changed the lyrics to the next river, "A rifleman stands on Vistula's shores and quietly hums along. We whistle this song up and down. And us can the world's entirety, curse or praise us, grade as everyone will please."

Less than Six Months

October 30, 1944

The harvesting was going well. The Poles and Germans took to the field, working day in and day out. The work was at least halfway done; Bieżuń had many fields to shock, thresh, and bundle. Some of the harvest would be shipped back to Germany. Some would remain to feed Bieżuń and Poland. Days of conversation and work made for high spirits among both the Germans and Poles. For now, the Red Army was out of their minds.

"Did you send the letter?" Blaz asked, as he worked side-by-side with Wiktoria, a Pole, Koby, and Hans. They sliced down the wheat with long scythes.

"*Ja*, yesterday, when the truck came," Koby replied.

"Who did you send a letter to?" Wiktoria asked.

"A kid that I knew well, in my hometown. He recently entered a type of *Wehrmacht* service."

"What is his name?" Wiktoria continued.

"Johann Steiner," answered Koby, taking a slash through the wheat.

"Johann Steiner, that's a very German name."

"It is. It should be, he is a German."

The Polish boy working with them looked up from a bundle he was tying.

"*Was ist Ihre Name?*" he asked Koby, thinking they were talking about names in general.

"*Mein Name ist Koby Hertz.*" He pointed to Blaz and Ivo, "*Das ist Blaz Senft und Ivo Klein. Und Hans Reichmann.*"

"*Danke*," the Pole said, wrapping up the bundle.

"*Was ist Ihre Name?*" Hans asked the Pole.

"Robert Janekowski."

"*Schön, sie zu treffen*," Hans shook the Pole's hand politely.

"I speak little German," the Pole said.

"We like that," Hans said, giving the Pole a smile, "*De dobrze mówić po niemiecku.*" You speak German fine.

Hans and Wiktoria

December 19, 1944

"*Was siehst du?*" Blaz asked at a raised voice. He rubbed his hands together while heavy snow fell on the dark, empty field, "What do you see?"

"Just fields and trees. Not a soul in sight," Koby said over the howling night wind before lowering his binoculars, "Not to the east anyway."

Blaz hugged himself against the cold, drawing his hands inside of his sleeves.

"You're not cold, are you?" Koby asked, "This is nothing."

"*Nein*, just a little chilly. It's no Leningrad."

"Blaz!" a voice that belonged to Hans called. Both Koby and Blaz turned to see two figures running towards them.

"*Ja?*" Blaz shouted into the darkness.

"I need you. I need you back at the house."

"Okay, no problem."

"Hang on, why do you need Blaz?" Koby questioned, "What is it?"

"It just needs to be Blaz."

"I came to replace him," Jarman said, raising a hand.

Blaz looked his sergeant in the eye. "Come on, Koby. You trust us, right?"

"Well, sure. Fine. Go on."

Blaz ran over to Hans, and they both hurried off back to the town, while Koby kept his gaze on them. Hans kept nervously glancing over his shoulder back at Koby.

"Can he hear us?" Hans whispered just loud enough for Blaz to hear.

"*Nein*, of course not," Blaz shook his head, "Why would you think he could? We're a football field away from him in heavy snow and wind."

"I-I don't know, I don't know."

"What's the matter? You're acting really nervous."

"I should be, you'll see why," Hans said as they neared the house. When they entered, Hans shut the door behind them immediately, "I'm in trouble, Blaz. Big trouble."

"Why? Tell me what's going on!" Blaz flat out ordered Hans.

"Follow me and be quiet."

Hans led Blaz up to Wiktoria's room. She stood alone, but she had certainly been waiting for them, judging by her expression. She wore a long winter skirt, and the closest thing she had to an athletic shirt. The white sports top she'd worn during soccer. Blaz started to suspect what was going on.

Hans gestured to Wiktoria, who looked horribly nervous. Her face was pale and she took deep breaths. She turned so that Blaz saw her sideways. Then she pulled her athletic shirt skintight. She definitely had a baby bump.

"*Nein, nein, nein, nein, nein*," Blaz threw his hands in the air, "Why did you do it, Hans? *Dummkopf*! You could be court-marshaled for this! Not to mention what could happen to Wiktoria! *Dummkopf*."

"I know," Hans moaned, "I didn't mean for this to happen. I'm sorry Wiktoria."

"We have to tell Koby about this," Blaz said, and started for the door. He was stopped by two arms grabbing him, then throwing him to the ground.

"*Nein! Nein!* You can't tell him!" Hans begged Blaz, pinning him against the floor, "He's not going to understand!"

"What makes you think I do?"

"But you've kept it a secret," Hans pleaded, "Please don't."

Blaz jerked to try to throw Hans' arms off him, but Hans kept him pinned.

"Wiktoria, what do you think about all this?" Blaz asked from the floor.

"I don't know, will Koby help?" she asked, her voice shaking.

"It doesn't matter; how much longer do you think you can hide that?" Blaz asked, expecting no answer, "By the end of January, it'll be completely impossible. Koby's the third highest-ranking officer in Bieżuń. He could do something to help. *Verdämmt* Hans! Why?"

"I apologize. I shouldn't have done it. It's my fault," he said, turning to Wiktoria.

Blaz seized the opportunity and head-butted Hans as he turned around. He then kicked him off himself and stormed out of the room.

"Stay here," he heard Hans say, then footsteps behind him, "Blaz, are you going to tell him?"

"*Ja*, that is exactly what I'm going to do. I'm going to get Werner and Ivo to stay on guard with Jarman first. If you don't fess up now, you're screwed, okay?"

Hans followed Blaz into the town, silently. He knew he was screwed. The *Wehrmacht* had a code of conduct. There were ten rules they were to obey.

"You broke the seventh code of conduct. The civilian population is to be treated well and with decency," Blaz said in frustration.

"I wasn't treating her poorly," Hans defended his actions out of pathetic desperation.

"You still shouldn't have done it."

"You should have just brought me back in the first place," Koby said in annoyance.

"Maybe. But Hans should've thought of that," Blaz told him, glowering at Hans.

"What is all this about? What did Hans do? You didn't kill anyone, right?"

"*Nein*," Hans shook his head, then, maybe out of some attempt to lighten Koby's mood or as an ill-timed quip, added, "The opposite."

Koby kept walking, trying to decide what Hans could mean by this. "Saved a life?" Koby murmured, "What? Nothing wrong with that, Hans."

Hans stayed silent until they came back to the house. He led his squad mates up into the tiny room. Wiktoria was still there, still standing up.

"What is it?" Koby asked. Hans gestured to Wiktoria, who revealed her pregnant belly.

Koby stared. He looked at Hans. Hans stared blankly, and his lip trembled.

"You?" Koby stammered, "What? Hans. Not you, Hans?" he said, like his own son had done this.

"I did," Hans admitted, looking Koby in the eye.

An exasperated, confused expression made its way onto Koby's face. He put a hand over his mouth and started pacing furiously, "Hans, *nein*, why? Why?"

On a dime, Koby spun around and grabbed Hans by the throat, slamming him against the wall. Hans closed his eyes and didn't bother fighting back.

"Why? Why did you do that?" Koby whispered, eyes blazing. Hans didn't answer. He breathed shakily while Koby kept him pinned by his throat.

"Answer me!" Koby hissed behind gritted teeth.

Hans let out a whimper, like a child being scolded horribly by his father. "I'm sorry," Hans said, almost a plea for mercy, "I didn't mean for it to happen. It just did."

"That's not good enough Hans," Koby shook his head, and tightened his grip on Hans, "We can't hide this for long. They know we're in her house. You broke the German soldier code of conduct. Even Sergeant Seelenfreund won't let this slide. You realize what's going to happen, right?"

"*Nein?*" Hans stuttered.

"The SS will come. They will court martial you and God knows what could happen to Wiktoria."

"*Nein*, Koby. *Herr* Seelenfreund will not call anyone in. He is a good man," Blaz said with certainty.

"This undermines our *Wehrmacht* discipline. He wants to enforce that."

"If Hans subjects himself to any punishment Seelenfreund sees fit to brush this under the rug and maintain the face of discipline," Blaz suggested, "Maybe we can keep Wiktoria safe."

"Fine," Koby said, "Hans, I want you to report this immediately. I'll come with you, but you do the explaining. Answer every question honestly. Blaz, Wiktoria, you come with us, put on a coat. I will do what I can to make sure this doesn't warrant the SS coming."

"*Danke schön*," Hans thanked Koby, while his sergeant slackened his grip, and finally released him.

Hans headed toward the door to follow Koby's orders, "Hans," Koby said.

"*Ja?*"

"You're an idiot."

Hans nodded. "I know."

Sergeant Seelenfreund's Verdict

"You had sexual relations with this Pole?" Seelenfreund asked Hans, in the most disappointed tone imaginable.

"*Ja* sir," Hans answered.

"When did this happen?"

"Mid-September, sir."

Seelenfreund turned to Wiktoria, "Do you wish to report any mistreatment you received from Private Reichmann?"

"*Nein*, I do not."

"You realize this is a violation of the German soldier's code of conduct?" Seelenfreund said, redirecting his attention to Hans.

"*Jawohl*."

"Reichmann, I have to say, this is very disappointing."

"I'm sorry, sir, but please, *Herr* Seelenfreund. Don't report this to the SS," Hans pleaded, staring at the ground.

Unexpectedly, Seelenfreund smiled, "Son, I'm not going to report this to anyone."

Hans' gaze shot up at the Sergeant, "You aren't?"

"*Nein*, Reichmann. But this is a great disappointment from you. I will have you report here tomorrow afternoon to receive punishment."

"*Ja* sir, *danke* sir," Hans said with gratitude that Wiktoria wouldn't have to suffer.

"Now Reichmann, I want you to escort the *Fräulein* home. And Senft, you better go with him. You are all dismissed."

Blaz spun on his heel and marched away. Koby remained still. While on his way out, Blaz realized Koby had not followed. Seelenfreund waved him out. He threw up a brief salute, then turned and walked back out into the deepening snow.

Nazis

"Well, Hans, you lucky, lucky," Blaz refrained from swearing, though he wanted to, "Now that *Herr* Seelenfreund gave you a break, how are you going to explain this to Wiktoria's mother?"

"We will her together- we will tell her together," Wiktoria said, "This isn't all bad, I'm glad that I will have a kid. It's a little early, but-"

"It could've been a very bad thing," Blaz pointed out.

"Wiktoria, I feel I should stay here now, I owe it to you," Hans said, catching a cold glare from Blaz for this ludicrous suggestion, prompting him to continue, "But I have sworn an oath to the *Führer*, and I cannot abandon my squad."

"I understand. My father left for the same reason," Wiktoria patted Hans' shoulder, "What should I name her, or him?"

"Huh?" Hans asked daftly, "Oh *ja*, I guess he or she will need a name."

"*Ja*, you think?" Blaz scoffed.

"I like Wicek. It means 'conquerer.' And he will be a child of a conqueror," Wiktoria said, "If it's a girl, I really like the name Nadzia."

"What does that mean?" Hans asked.

"It means 'Hope.' And she'll be the child of a Nazi, Nadzia," Wiktoria added with a smile, more of a smirk.

"*Wie Bitte?*" Blaz inquired, having never heard this word in his life.

"You know, Nazis?"

"What is a Notsee?" Blaz asked again.

Wiktoria laughed, "You know what a Nazi is. You are one."

"I am a Nautsy?" Blaz repeated the word several times with varying pronunciation "Natsee. Nautzi. Nazi. Nazi."

"What? How do you not know what a Nazi is when you are one?" Wiktoria asked, giving Blaz's armband a tug.

Blaz readjusted his armband. "What is a Nazi?"

Wiktoria turned. "Hans, you know what a Nazi is, right?"

"*Nein*, what is it?"

Wiktoria shook her head in disbelief that neither of the two supposed Nazis she was talking to knew what a Nazi was, "You're Nazis, that's what a Nazi is."

"Do you call Germans Nazis? Or *Wehrmacht* Nazis? Soldiers? What?" Blaz pressed, "I feel like I've heard that word somewhere."

"Your leaders are Nazi."

"*Nein*, our government is National Socialist," Blaz laughed, "What are you talking about? Nazi? We have a National Socialist government and we are German soldiers. *Nazien*, Nazis? Why do you call us Nazis?"

Wiktoria shrugged.

"Is it bad to be a Nazi?" Blaz asked after several seconds of silence.

"I think so. Whenever my friends and I talk about them, we don't like them. We talk about them badly."

"Well, if Nazis are National Socialists then they must be good," Blaz argued, "National Socialism is the best system on earth. Look what it did for *Deutschland*."

"I honestly don't know what it did for *Deutschland*," Wiktoria said as they entered her home. Blaz and Hans grinned at each other. One of the most enjoyable topics to discuss was Hitler's accomplishments.

"National Socialism, but really the *Führer* brought back our pride in being German, he united the country. We cast aside class, social standing and united as Germans," Blaz explained, beaming the whole time, "Jobs were created, building roads, rearmament. The Rothschild bankers were expelled, and our currency almost immediately began to regain its value. Germans stopped starving, we had plenty. We were strong and respected again, the most powerful country on earth. The *Hitlerjugend* was created, training us to become competent, athletic young men and women. They taught us so much, and it was a really tight community."

"Still is," Hans smiled throwing up a quick Hitler salute.

"*Ja*, we got out of debt. We united Germans under one Reich. Austria is German land where Germans live. The Sudetenland is German. The Rhineland must have troops, France and we have never liked each other, because we always beat them in wars. The Seven Years War, the Franco-Prussian War, now this. They can't beat us unless they have America and their allies helping them."

Hans snickered, it was true, "We can't help that the French wave the white flag of surrender so quickly."

"You are losing the war, you know," Wiktoria said seriously.

"*Ja*, but we aren't France. We don't surrender the way they do. This war is far from its end. For every week they fight bravely, we'll fight a year," Blaz said proudly.

"You know you can't win the war?" Wiktoria asked. There was no hope if she didn't convince them that Germany was in over its head. "How will you win? You will die if you continue to fight."

"What? We're soldiers. Certainly, we have doubts about victory, but we don't question whether we should fight or not. Of course, we will fight. If we don't, *Deutschland* will be overrun by the Bolsheviks and kill our people."

"You've never voiced any concern about the war, Wiktoria. Why now?" Hans asked.

"Because you are fighting for *Deutschland*, and they will be losing side. You can't continue fighting."

Hans and Blaz looked at each other. Then they scoffed.

"Just because you're losing doesn't mean you give up. What kind of weak-willed people abandon their homeland to invaders without fighting? How despicable and pathetic is that?" Blaz told the Pole.

"Very," Wiktoria agreed, "But when all is lost, don't you surrender?"

Hans and Blaz looked once again at each other.

"I don't think so," Hans said, "Surrender never ends well."

"I think so, depending on the enemy. We can't concede to Russia. They will send *Deutschland* back to the depression," said Blaz, "So we will fight to the bitter end."

"Will you ever surrender yourself?"

"I don't know," Blaz murmured, "I did once before, and this is what I got for it," he said pointing to the scar that ran down his jawline, "I'm not sure if I should or not. I'm more scared of surrendering to Russians than dying at this point."

Wiktoria looked to Hans for disagreement with this. Hans raised his eyebrows and shrugged in agreement with Blaz, "I wouldn't surrender either. It would end worse than fighting to the death."

Hans' Confession

After quite a bit of talking, Koby returned to the house with Jarman, Ivo, and Werner as well.

"Where the hell are Hans and Wiktoria?" Koby shot at Blaz who was lying on the ground near the blankets.

"Relax, Koby," Blaz said and put his hands behind the back of his head, "He and Wiktoria are explaining to her mother."

"All right. All right," Koby said, facing his palms to the ground, trying to calm down, "He's going to get beaten tomorrow."

Blaz gritted his teeth, "That'll hurt." He faintly could remember when he'd been beaten by an SS soldier.

"He deserves it," Koby muttered.

"Oh, shut up, Koby. Shut up," Blaz went off, "You have to make that comment, don't you? Stop doing that, you're always doing that. I know he deserves it, you don't have to say it like that. You love Hans, you shouldn't want him to be beaten."

Koby glared. Jarman caught this, and in an act that shocked Blaz, gave Koby an elbow in the ribs. Not viciously, but enough to convey his disdain for Koby's attitude. Koby jumped back himself. He looked up at Jarman in surprise, "Why'd you do that?"

"You need to shake this," Jarman said, "I agree with Blaz. Why would you say that about Hans? We've fought in a war together, seen our friends die, why would you want to see anything bad happen to him? Even if he does deserve it."

Koby listened to Jarman. "Sorry. I didn't mean it like that. I don't know why I said it."

"It's not like you, Koby," Ivo murmured, "You used to be the one who would tell us not to talk like that."

Koby sighed, and sat down next to Blaz, who'd straightened up to a sitting position while Jarman was talking. Koby pushed aside his hair, which was the closest it had been to the way it was before he'd joined the Hitler Youth now. Lengthy, so that it fell over his eyes when it became unkempt, dark brown, nearly black. But he was five years older, a seventeen-year-old who'd been through hell, "I hadn't been in a war then. I'd never seen a person die then."

"What does that change?" Ivo wondered. Koby opened his mouth to respond but Hans came out of the only other room on the floor, which he shut behind him.

"How did she take it?" Werner asked.

Hans walked over to where the squad had congregated. He sat down and let his arms hang loosely, "I think she has less respect for me now."

The squad chuckled at this response.

"No shit," Jarman said.

"And?" Ivo persisted.

"Not much too say. Lots of disappointment on her face. She knew that me and Wiktoria were friends, and that's all she thought it to be. Now it's more than that. She didn't like me 'taking advantage of Wiktoria.' And I can't blame her. I should've gotten a hold of myself."

"No more of this, right Hans?" Jarman asked, "Be a soldier. Be disciplined."

"I will. I'll do better."

Hans is Beaten

December 20, 1944

Hans was apprehensive the entire day. Koby hadn't told him what his punishment was going to be, mainly because Seelenfreund had told him the mystery was part of the punishment. Hans talked briefly at breakfast and couldn't help but show a bit of nerves. During patrol, he was quieter than normal. He seemed to have let his imagination run wild on what might happen.

"Take a deep breath, Hans," Blaz told him while he and Koby walked Hans to be disciplined. Hans took a deep breath through his nose, then breathed out.

"Why are you nervous? How bad could it be?" Koby said warmly.

"I've heard about divisions in the *Wehrmacht* who discipline soldiers, where they are sent on suicide missions."

"Seelenfreund won't do that. I assure you."

Hans drew solace from this, and his nervousness died down. Seelenfreund was waiting outside the building and waved them inside.

"Private Reichmann, you will receive disciplinary measures today, for breaking the *Wehrmacht's* code of conduct. Follow me. Private Hertz, Private Senft, come as well."

Seelenfreund led them out to the side of the church, where a soldier in the field gray uniform and helmet stood, holding a wooden rod. He stood about seven feet away from a pole that was firmly planted into the ground.

"*Scheiße*," Hans muttered under his breath.

"Senft, Hertz, stand to the side. Reichmann, remove your uniform and undershirt."

Hans did so, shivering as the wind hit his bare back.

"Lean against the pole, back facing Haushofer," Seelenfreund ordered. Hans leaned against the pole, arching his back slightly.

"Haushofer, begin when you're ready."

The soldier adjusted the rod, so that he held the end giving him length to build up speed. He shuffled to the left and took a step forward. Blaz kept his eyes on Hans, who stared at the ground, waiting for the blows to begin. Haushofer raised the rod and swung hard and fast. Hans' eyes widened and he let out a short gasp of pain and surprise but wouldn't allow himself to show anymore. Haushofer swung again, equally as hard and hitting Hans in the lower back. Hans took it better the second time, but still took deep, shaky breaths. The German soldier's expression remained emotionless the entire time. A straight face, and empty eyes. But when he swung, he swung with force.

After finishing ten hits, Haushofer looked to the sergeant for orders on whether he should keep going. Seelenfreund gestured for him to continue. Haushofer nodded, with no other objections. Another arm raise, another flick of the wrist and grit of Hans' teeth as the rod struck him again. Haushofer raised the rod once more, but halted as Seelenfreund said, "That's enough. We're done. Reichmann, you're dismissed. You, I want to speak with you."

Blaz and Koby pointed to themselves, saying, "Me?" nearly at the same time.

"The two of you."

"*Ja* sir."

Hans straightened up and was handed his uniform by Blaz and Koby.

"*Danke*," Hans groaned, "How bad does it look?"

"It's pretty bad. Lots of red marks and I bet it will bruise," Koby said.

"*Ja*, that's what it feels like," Hans complained as he slid his arms into his black uniform, "See you on patrol."

The Downed Soviet Bomber

Seelenfreund walked back into the church, leading them into an empty telegraph room. No one else was there, and Seelenfreud sat down at the operator's chair. He put on a pair of reading glasses and picked up a piece of paper that lay in front of him, which he showed to Koby and Blaz.

"See this?" he asked. Both nodded, "This is a telegraph from the town nearest to our north," he began reading, though clearly it was not verbatim. He only quoted the mathematical measurements. "A Russian bomber was shot near the front, but it landed many kilometers west, between our town and the town that sent this message. The officer in charge there sent out three squads to hunt for the plane. It was found, but only five Russians were found in the plane and it has the capacity to hold ten. They have not found the Russians yet, and guess that they headed this way, or west. The machine guns of the plane were missing as well, so it is likely the last five are heavily armed."

"Sir-" Koby began.

Seelenfreund held up a hand, "The town nearest the west has sent out two squads to find the crew. So far nothing. That makes it likely they are heading east," Seelenfreund said, removing his reading glasses and looking at the boys, "My orders are to hunt them down," Seelenfreund continued,

"My squad and *Herr* Hübner's squad move out in half an hour to do just that. Hertz, your squad will maintain control of the town, and it is imperative you keep a sharp eye out for the Russians should they give us the slip. *Verstanden?*"

"*Ich verstehe,*" Koby replied.

"*Gut,*" Seelenfreud said standing up and sliding his glasses back into his pocket, "Now, on what to do with these pilots should they make it to the town. I want you to post your best shooter on the church's steeple. It is built for people to stand in with some space, it will provide an excellent view, and sniping nest. It will give you the best chance of killing them all."

"*Jawohl.*"

Red Snow

As the cold afternoon dragged on, clouds rolled in to cover the sky, and snow began to fall, adding to the many inches they'd received the past week. Blaz and Hans were stationed at the north entrance of Bieżuń, at a farmhouse that lay a few hundred feet from the center of the town. Hans sat on the house's small porch, while Blaz paced in front of him, rifle in arms.

"You think they'll get by *Herr* Seelenfreund?" Blaz asked.

"No idea."

"Koby said if he needed us there'd be a gunshot."

"That's a good signal."

"Could they be hiding anywhere, that we can't see?"

"Well, these fields aren't perfectly flat, they could be behind an incline, a ditch."

They went silent.

"But since they might be, we should find better cover," Hans suggested.

Blaz and Hans went inside, they'd ordered all families into their homes until the threat had passed. The family went about business as if they weren't there.

"Do you ever get the feeling when they speak in Polish, they're talking about you?" Hans whispered to Blaz.

"*Ja*, I do. But what does it matter? Once we leave this town we'll never see them again."

"I don't know. I was just thinking."

Blaz rolled his eyes and looked back out the window. In the snow, he couldn't see very far as opposed to if it was clear out, but he saw movement a couple hundred meters away along the ground.

"Hey, hey," Hans said and pointed, "Do you see that?"

"The five figures?"

"*Ja*, are those the Russians? Or is it Seelenfreund?"

Blaz aimed his rifle, readying it to fire. He lined up on one, examining their uniforms in the distance. Their uniforms didn't match the gray that every German who'd set out was wearing. As they continued to crawl through the snow, their guns became visible.

"Russians!" Blaz shouted and fired. His aim was true and one of the figures stopped moving. The others leapt up and began sprinting through the snow. Hans fired, and swore at his miss. The Polish family all ran for their cellar. Blaz aimed for another Russian but missed like Hans.

Nein, nein. I needed to hit him.

The Russians were running to outflank their house on the sides, where unfortunately, no windows were built.

"Stay in the house, Ivo will start picking them off," Blaz told Hans, hoping Ivo would see them.

"I'll take front, you take back?" Hans asked.

"Sure," and Blaz darted to the back of the home that faced the village. Hans was just across from him, guarding the front. Two Russians were jogging towards the village, with machine guns in hand, and had met no fire yet.

Where are the others? Where are they?

Blaz opened the window slightly. He stayed to the left of his rifle, behind the wall so a blindly firing Russian would miss him. He poked his rifle out to aim at the Russians he could see. Immediately a hand grabbed his rifle's end and yanked it, but Blaz did not let go. He tugged back, prompting a surge of strength in response from the Russian, which pulled Blaz against the glass. He was face to face with the Russian, with a half open, glass window separating them. Both thought the same thing, but the Russian acted first. The Soviet let go of the rifle causing Blaz to fall. The Russian went for his pistol while Blaz stumbled back, but another shot was fired, and the next thing he saw was the Russian falling to the ground. Blaz leapt up and fired another shot into the Russian through the window.

"*Danke* Hans."

"Don't mention it."

"I can see them entering the town. Ivo, where are you?" Blaz murmured, bouncing his leg.

"Where is that third man?" Hans said, shifting his rifle anxiously in his hands.

"Once we spot him, we're going into the village. Got it?" Blaz ordered.

"*Jawohl.*"

Both boys kept their rifles aimed out the windows, but no Russian presented himself. Shots, rapid shots began to sound from the town. Blaz saw a flash from Ivo's tower. The flash was returned by fire and Blaz saw several tracer bullets, coming from two separate places.

"Ivo's a good shot, Hans?" Blaz called.

"*Ja*, he is," Hans agreed.

"I'm trusting that he hit someone. If he did that's three of five down. Let's go. Are you with me?"

"*Ja*, let's go."

Blaz cracked open the back door. No fire. He hopped out, aiming to the right, Hans aiming to the left. No one. They made their way toward the village, across the open field. Blaz kept an eye out for the man that could still be out there. He redirected his attention ahead and saw no one but Hans. Two shots sounded behind them. Not a machine gun, consecutive shots from a rifle or pistol. Both turned immediately. Four more shots. Hans let out a cry of pain while turning and fell limply onto his back. Blood flowed into the driven snow. A Russian limped toward them, grasping his chest with one arm and holding a raised pistol with the other. Blaz turned to his left, towards the fallen Hans. Two more shots of fire, and Blaz's blood colored the snow red. He stumbled and collapsed on top of Hans, face first. The pain was intense; he knew a rib had been hit. And something in his left leg. He couldn't see what was happening anymore without moving but heard Hans whisper, "Stay still."

Blaz felt a slight movement between his legs. But after a few seconds of this, Blaz realized Hans had unholstered his pistol. Blaz remained still, not even daring to breath as he heard the Russian who'd shot them shuffling through the snow. He heard a click, that sounded like a magazine being slid into place. Blaz held his breath, staying limp. Another clicking sound, likely the man cocking his weapon. Then three consecutive shots and the light crunch of something falling into snow.

"You can move now," Hans whispered and immediately began gasping for air. Hans had shot the Russian. Blaz pushed himself up, and staggered backwards, falling next to Hans, flat on his back in the snow. He turned his head. What he saw was bone and blood. Hans left arm was gone just above the elbow. Blaz looked at Hans' uniform, where blood soaked the clothing on the right side of his chest. Hans stared into the gray sky, his chest moving up and down rapidly as he tried to breath in more. Another bullet had sliced through the side of Hans' helmet. Shrapnel from the helmet had cut through his skin.

"Hans," Blaz choked on his own blood, "We need to get you to a medic."

Blaz rolled weakly onto his chest and tried to stand up. His left leg gave out after his first step. He put a hand where the pain in his leg was. There was a long, deep cut and his hand came back covered in blood.

"Blaz, I can't breathe." Blaz crawled over to Hans and put a hand over his friend's chest, where the Reich's Eagle was. He stared into Hans' eyes who stared back at him. Hans lifted his right arm and put it on Blaz's hand. Hans gasped for air, but he couldn't breathe, as more blood flowed from his arm and chest. Blaz's eyes welled up.

Hans' looked skyward, then back to Blaz. Then he was gone.

"*Nein!*" Blaz cried, letting his tears loose.

God, don't let Hans die. Help him. Please!

That was it. Hans was dead. Blaz remained at his side, unaware of anything else.

"Private Senft? Private Senft?" came Seelenfreund's voice, "Is that you?"

Blaz didn't answer. He looked up at the approaching *Wehrmacht* soldiers who gazed at him and Hans' body with concern. And Blaz stared back with his bright blue eyes.

"Son?" Seelenfreund called. One soldier jogged over to Blaz, who still held Hans' hand. The soldier laid his rifle down and put a head to Hans' chest. Seelenfreund marched to them, and took a knee, but waved the others into Bieżuń.

"Sir, he's gone!" Blaz yelled with tears streaming down his cheeks, "Where were you?!"

Seelenfreund hung his head before answering, "They must've slipped past us somehow."

Blaz shook his head and stood up. He fell over at first. Rejecting help from his commanding officer, he managed to stand upon a second effort. He shuffled in a daze through the snowy streets, limping badly, heading for the church. Inside, Koby, Jarman, and Werner were huddled around Ivo who lay stretched out on a table that was covered in blood. Koby frantically wrapped Ivo's chest. Blaz limped over to them, "What happened?"

"He was shot pretty bad in the chest," Jarman said, "He's lost a lot of blood."

Werner surveyed at Blaz's uniform where more blood had soaked in, "Blaz. You know you're bleeding, right?"

"I know."

"That's bad. Here," Werner said, shaking his head and taking some white wrapping, "Lay down."

"*Nein*! Let a medic handle it," Koby said, "He won't bleed out. Help me with Ivo."

Ivo coughed up some blood. Koby visibly began to panic. "Jarman, we need them to come back, where are they?"

"They're back," Blaz said.

"Go get them," Koby ordered Jarman without missing a beat. Jarman sprinted out of the church in a heartbeat. Werner looked around the church after Jarman had left. He kept looking around, like he had missed something.

"Blaz," Werner said, his voice turning serious, "Where is Hans?"

Blaz locked eyes with Werner.

"*Nein*," Werner said through gritted teeth, slamming a fist into the table, "*Nein!*"

Koby's eyes narrowed as he understood what had happened, but he continued working on Ivo, "How?"

"We left the house to come back. And they were waiting for us."

Werner buried his head in his hands. Ivo got a hold of Koby's arm after missing on his first attempt to grab him.

"Ivo?" Koby whispered.

"I," Ivo said, spitting up blood onto his uniform and down his chin.

"Just a little longer," Koby told him, "He's coming."

Ivo nodded weakly, and let his head fall back against the table.

"Blaz, sit down," Koby said.

"I'm okay," Blaz said, holding a hand over his chest wound.

"That's not a suggestion, it's an order," Koby said calmly, and turned back to Ivo. Blaz sat down. It did feel better.

Jarman swung the door open, and the medic sprinted through the church that doubled as a mess hall.

"What is it? Where was he hit?" the medic shot off.

"Lower stomach, it's in there as deep as it could with his size."

"Not too deep then," the medic said, examining the wound, "I can dig it out. It'll be painful. He should be all right after a few days. Anyone else with injuries?"

"*Ja*," Koby answered for Blaz immediately, "I need you to have a look at him when you finish with Ivo, please."

"Of course," the medic replied.

Koby turned to leave, presumably to talk with Seelenfreund, but stopped during his first step.

"Jarman, Werner, come here," he waved. Jarman and Werner strode over to Koby. In a low tone, so only they heard, Koby gave an order. Both gave Koby a nod of understanding, and the squad sergeant exited the church. Jarman went to Ivo's side. Werner watched Koby leave, then sat down to Blaz's right, and laid his helmet and cap on the table behind the chair he sat on. He looked to his left, where the crucifix hung over the church.

"What do you think?" he asked when he'd sat down.

"What do I think of what?" Blaz said, following Werner's gaze.

"What do you think? What are you thinking?"

Blaz allowed tears to slide down his cheeks, thinking exactly what Koby had after Tristan's death. "How could God allow us to be losing like this? How could he allow so many to die? How could he let Hans die?"

Werner kept his gaze on the cross, "I don't know, I don't know. I guess one side must win. That is competition, that is war."

"Doesn't God want the good side to win?" Blaz asked, wiping tears from his eyes.

"The good side doesn't always win, the good guys don't always win," Werner answered. He finally turned to face Blaz, "Did Hans get any last words?"

"*Nein.*"

"Not everyone can succeed or live in a world run by evil people."

Blaz nodded. That made sense. "Could the bad side triumph?" he asked, taking a deep breath.

"I think they may have already," Werner said, leaning back against the table. He shot up when Ivo screamed in pain as the medic began digging out the bullet. Blaz and Werner shuffled over. The medic started pulling, and Ivo breathed through his teeth intensely.

"Almost, almost," the medic told Ivo, keeping his eyes on his work. Ivo pounded a fist against the table multiple times until the medic finished removing the bullet. The medic then re-bandaged Ivo's chest to prevent anymore bleeding.

"Now, I want you to lie here for a couple hours, get some sleep. You lost a lot of blood. You'll have to replenish the next couple days."

"*Ja* sir," Ivo said, finally relaxing.

The medic glanced to Blaz, "On the table."

Blaz climbed onto the table down from Ivo. The medic removed his uniform, looking at Blaz's blood-stained undershirt. He grimaced, not a good sign. Then he unbuttoned Blaz's undershirt, to see the wound.

"Broken rib. It was the very outside of your chest, went right through you. But it was at a very non-vital point, and where the bone was thin. I'll just have to bandage you up, and you'll have to recover for at least two weeks," the medic informed him.

"*Ja* sir."

The medic wrapped Blaz's chest then leg, which had been a flesh wound, and sent him on his way with Werner. Jarman remained with Ivo. Both stepped outside of the church into the snowfall to see Koby and Seelenfreund carrying Hans towards them. Werner's eyes went wide, and his mouth hung open in horror at the sight of Hans' lifeless body, his missing arm, and blood-stained neck and uniform. Koby wiped his eyes. He had no hatred on his face this time, just tears. Werner turned to Blaz and cried into his shoulder, holding tight. Blaz was taken aback but returned the hug.

Sleep in Heavenly Peace

Christmas Eve, 1944

"*Stille Nacht... Heil'ge Nacht. Alles schläft, einsam wacht. Nur das traute hoch heilige Paar, Holder Knab' im lockigen Haar,*" Blaz sang quietly on the edge of the fields to the east at the foot of Hans' grave. Koby was on watch with him, and listened to his friend sing to Hans, "*Schlaf in himmlischer Ruh, Schlaf in himmlischer Ruh...*" Sleep in heavenly peace.

"Only days before Christmas," Koby murmured.

"Why did you post us on the edge of the town?"

"Don't," Koby said, putting an end to the beginning of an impulsive accusation, "I didn't even think we'd have to fight."

"It was my fault, really. Not yours."

"Blaz, I'm sure it wasn't."

"*Ja*, it really was. If I hadn't suggested we leave our cover, then he never would've gotten shot," Blaz said, picking up some snow, and throwing it a few feet in anger before it dispersed into powder.

"That's not your fault, Blaz," Koby assured him, while he ran his finger along the snow, "That stuff just happens."

"But if we had just stayed put, if I hadn't said we should leave," Blaz imagined, as if this could be reversed, "Hans would still be here. He, he was going to be a father."

Koby looked up, just realizing this. "How is she?"

"Not well, that's all I know," Both boys looked down at Hans' grave. A cross with 'Hans Reichmann' written across the middle, and an Iron Cross carved on the top.

"*Frohe Weihnachten*, Blaz," Koby said.

"*Frohe Weihnachten*, Koby."

Christmas Day, 1945

Their Christmas was dark and snowy, nothing short of a blizzard. The German soldiers ran things as normal, men patrolled. On this night, the soldiers stayed in the church, sending five men out at a time for one-hour shifts. The Knights returned from their march, wet and shivering. Koby walked over to the next group that had been assigned, and shook one of them, "Your turn."

"Okay, okay," the soldier said through a yawn, and went about waking his men. Koby laid down next to a table to get some rest.

"You guys too," Koby said, "Get some sleep. You'll need it."

Jarman and Werner lay down to sleep, as did Ivo, who had lost all his normal energy as he recovered. Blaz laid down, exhausted. He didn't fall asleep immediately, as he wished he could. When he was about to close his eyes, someone tapped him.

"Blaz? Are you awake?"

Blaz sat up to see Werner kneeling next to him.

"Blaz?"

"*Ja*, Werner?"

Werner looked around at their sleeping squad mates, "I can't sleep. I keep thinking-"

"What? What about?" Blaz asked, trying to sound a little irritated when really, he wasn't.

"What happens when you die? What if a bomb just hit this church tonight, and, and we all died? After Hans, I can't stop thinking about it."

A good question. One Blaz wasn't confident he could answer. Even as they'd been religious for years, they'd never considered this for but a few brief moments.

"I'm not really sure, Werner," Blaz answered, "I feel like I should be asking you. You're smarter than I am."

"I know, but I have no idea about this."

"Well, I think we go to a better place," Blaz tried to give an answer.

"No matter what?"

"I don't know."

"I want to know."

Blaz nodded, "I do too."

1945: Germany, You Must Stand, Even if We May Fall

The Russkies Are Ready

January 13, 1945

"I hereby order that all troops in the east Masovian district be evacuated to Płock before being reassigned to new positions across the eastern front," read Seelenfreund aloud to all the troops.

"When is the train coming?" a private asked.

"In an hour."

"I can hear the artillery from here," another soldier said, "They better not be late."

The teenagers watched the exchange, before Koby cut in, "Are we retreating?"

Seelenfreund nodded, "Before we leave, make sure your personal belongings are with you, weapons. We will be loading any useful materials we can salvage into the train. Loading the grain and farming equipment especially. The Russians must have nothing left when they arrive," Seelenfreund said.

"With respect sir," a soldier asked, "What about the civilians? They will be left with next to nothing as well."

"We will leave enough for them," Seelenfreund assured him, "Prepare yourselves, then we get to work loading up the resources."

Only Girl I Know

In the house, the squad packed up their few possessions. Wiktoria watched them prepare to leave.

"Where are you going?" she asked them.

"We have to leave," Koby said, "The Russians are coming. We can't fight in this town. You know that."

"I do."

Blaz slid his dagger out of its sheath and examined it, "Bieżuń, right? Bieżuń, Poland?"

"*Ja*, that's right," Wiktoria said. Blaz looked around at his busy squad mates. He stood up and made his way to Wiktoria.

"I know that we aren't going to see each other again," Blaz glanced at the floor, "I know that you, I think you may have loved Hans, didn't you?"

Wiktoria nodded, "*Ja*."

"I-I," Blaz stuttered, he couldn't think of anything to say all of a sudden.

Wiktoria smiled warmly and gave Blaz a hug, "*Auf wiedersehen*, Blaz."

"In *Deutschland* that means we will see each other again. Here's a better word for this: *Ade*," Blaz smiled as they finished.

"*Ade*," Wiktoria repeated.

"Blaz, time to get to work," Koby called from the door. Blaz gave Wiktoria a last glance, before turning and strapping his helmet on.

The New Big City

Loading the train took some time but the ride took less than two hours. Their new post was not the largest city, but a city nonetheless. Blaz hopped off the train, onto the snow-covered ground. Koby ordered the squad to follow him to the town square, where hundreds of squads were dispersed about, waiting for orders, smoking, playing cards, talking around the fountain in the middle of the square. Few smiles and no laughter were had amidst the Germans as the squad came to see. Several high-ranking *Wehrmacht* and SS officers strode through the group of soldiers, chatting amongst each other. Trucks poured in from the surrounding smaller towns, from the west as well. Though the trucks coming from the west had men in their twenties rather than the men coming from the east who were in their thirties, forties, low fifties, and some weren't men at all but boys far younger than the seventeen-year-old Knights. Some that hadn't even hit puberty.

"*Was jetzt?*" Jarman asked Koby as they sat down at the edge of the encirclement, in a blasted-out home.

"Now all we do is sit and wait for orders."

"How are you doing, Ivo?" Blaz asked, while Jarman and Koby continued their conversation onto another topic of similar essence. Werner scooted over to get in on Blaz and Ivo's discussion.

"Fine, why?" Ivo answered him.

"You just looked really worn out after we got finished loading the train."

Ivo shrugged, "I was feeling a little dizzy, you know how you stumble a little and your eyes get blurry for a few seconds sometimes?"

"*Ja*," Blaz nodded. It didn't happen often, but he knew the feeling.

"Hey, Blaz, Ivo," Koby interrupted, "Could you guys just keep an eye out for young *Hitlerjugend* squads, in case Johann's squad fell back to this city? I know he was posted in our area, so he's probably somewhere in this city."

"*Ja*, of course," Blaz replied and Ivo added, "No problem."

"*Danke* guys," Koby said, "I want to see him one more time."

"Who's Johann again?" Werner asked.

"He's a kid that we ran with on our team's running squad." Blaz grinned at the good memories. "He's two years younger than us, blond hair, blue eyes, no freckles, small chin, he was a several centimeters shorter than Ivo last time we saw him."

Werner raised his eyebrows at this. Ivo let it go.

"He's no Koby, but he was a really great runner. Better than us," Ivo continued for Blaz, "He's also probably smarter than both of us," he added, looking at Blaz for affirmation.

"For sure."

"Hey, here comes a squad," Ivo said, pointing to the east, "Lots of blonds, too."

Blaz turned his attention to where Ivo pointed. The squad was about to pass by.

"Hey Johann!" Ivo shouted and shot to his feet. Multiple German soldiers in the crowd turned at the sound of their name being called, then looked away in disappointment when they realized it wasn't them being called to by who they'd hoped to have been an old friend, brother, or their son, even.

None of the boys looked up though, but Ivo yelled it again. The Hitler Youth squad all looked around at this but kept walking.

"*Scheiße*," Ivo muttered and sat back down.

Blaz leaned over to Koby and asked, "Are there any other places in the city where troops are gathering?"

"Undoubtedly."

"You want to check those?"

"I would love to, but I think we should wait to receive orders."

"Okay."

Going Home

"Guys!" Koby shouted, drawing glances from other soldiers. Some appeared irritated that anyone could show such enthusiasm at this point. Koby sprinted over to them, with the old swagger he had once had.

"What is it?" Jarman asked.

"Guess what?" Koby said excitedly, quite unusual of him to act in this way.

"We developed a super bomb?" Ivo asked, genuinely believing this might be what Koby's excitement was about.

"*Nein*, but that would be great."

"What then?"

"We're being transferred to the Berlin area defense force. And our posts are at Seelow Heights!"

"*Ja!*" Ivo and Blaz shouted, pumping their fists.

Jarman smiled but didn't celebrate. Werner looked away, his face red. A glare made its way onto his face. Seelow. Seventy kilometers from Berlin. Detmold was going to fall to the West and he could do nothing.

"When do we leave?" Blaz asked, scarcely containing his excitement.

"We leave in four days. The Eastern Front is collapsing fast. The goal now is to hold Vienna, Prague, and the Berlin area for as long as possible, and the *Führer*, *Herr* Goebbels, *Herr* Himmler, *Herr* Göring and the rest of high command will try to reach an agreement with the Western Allies. Army Group Center along with some Hungarians will defend Prague, Vienna will be defended by what's left of Army Group South, Hungarian irregulars, some SS units and the *Volkssturm*. The Western Front will use the remaining *Wehrmacht* troops they have, the *Volkssturm*, and the *Waffen-SS*. The defense of the Berlin area will be under the direct command of the *Führer*. The defense will consist of our *Wehrmacht* from Army Group North, the *Hitlerjugend*, the *Volkssturm*, and both *Waffen-SS* and *Allgemeine-SS* units. All our foreign volunteers have rallied to Berlin, including the Charlemagne-SS," Koby held up his pointer finger, "Our defense force of Berlin alone should be one million men. Vienna should be one million as well. Prague will have a couple hundred thousand. For the Western Front, I'm not sure. The Red Army has at least twelve million men. At least two million will attack Berlin, maybe more."

"*Danke* for the recap, but I had trouble following all that," Ivo said, taking a deep breath, "One million in Berlin area? Versus over two million?"

"*Ja,*" Koby nodded, "One hundred and ten thousand in Seelow. Packing armor as well."

"The Reds never get rest," Jarman said, popping his knuckles.

Blaz lay awake for most of that night. The icy ground didn't help him fall asleep. Occasionally, a soldier or Hitler Youth would walk by on patrol, or to relieve themselves. Blaz sat up against the stone wall of the building he and his squad were camped by and stared into the night sky between the two buildings that were constructed close together. It was very pretty. Like the night sky of rural Germany.

"Excuse me," a young, developing voice said, and a Hitler Youth stepped over Blaz's outstretched legs. Blaz watched him walk away and looked back up at the sky. A couple minutes later, the kid was back. Blaz saw him coming.

"Aren't you tired?" the Hitler Youth asked Blaz when he was quite close.

"A little, I suppose," Blaz answered, still staring at the sky, "I just can't sleep, too much to think about."

"It's cold out, I guess that doesn't help."

Blaz cracked a smile and glanced at the standing Hitler Youth. The boy's bright blue eyes reflected the moonlight and stared down at Blaz. "Trust me, you have no idea what cold is. This isn't anything. You want to sit down?"

The German boy stood for a few seconds with his hands behind his back. Then he answered, "Sure," and took a seat next to Blaz.

"When did you get sent to the Eastern Front?" Blaz asked the younger kid, "How old are you?"

"I'm fifteen. I left my KLV camp this past summer. After-" the young teenager cleared his throat, "After France."

"Where are you from?"

"Neuhardenberg."

"Really? I'm from Seelow. *Kleine welt*. We probably were at the KLV camp together."

"*Ja*? How old are you?" the boy asked.

"Seventeen."

"Okay, you guys were the last to leave for a while. Do you know Hans Reichmann? He went to my school, his brother was in my class, but then his brother and family moved to Berlin," the Hitler Youth asked, his legs bouncing.

"I know Hans Reichmann," Blaz answered.

"*Ja*? How's he doing? Do you happen to know how Dieter, I mean his brother is doing?" the kid said, still shaking, "He got pulled out of our KLV camp."

Blaz put his head in his hands. Had to ask. "*Ja*, I know," he answered finally.

"How are they?"

Blaz looked the boy in the eye. "They're both dead."

Though he could darkness obscured the boy's face, Blaz saw his jaw drop, "*Nein*. Dieter can't be dead. He never went into battle! He was only twelve last time, how, how could he have died?"

"Berlin was bombed."

"What about Hans? He wasn't in Berlin."

"*Nein*, he was in my squad. He fell in battle a few weeks ago."

The boy's mouth hung open.

"Have you seen anyone die before?" Blaz asked him.

"*Ja*, but they were all older guys. Not kids like Dieter."

"Well little one, it doesn't matter how old you are in a war like this. Everyone can die."

Artillery echoed particularly loud at this moment. The Hitler Youth was scared to leave now. He involuntarily, and unknowingly scooted closer to Blaz.

"Don't worry. We'll be fine here."

"You sure?"

Blaz sighed, "*Nein*, I'm not. But we can't do better."

The boy nodded. But he still didn't leave.

"You want me to walk you back to your squad?"

"*Nein*," the kid said and stood up, "I'll go myself."

January 17, 1945

The days passed with artillery growing closer every night, eventually hitting the edges of the city. The Knights were eager to leave before the Russians arrived, save Jarman, predictably. Many Germans had pulled out of the city in the passing days, all heading west to defend Prague, Vienna, or Berlin.

"*Und nun kehren wir zum Vaterland zurück,*" Koby said as he was the last to leap into the boxcar.

They were crammed in with three more squads of soldiers. All younger than them. Then the doors slid shut, and the train started chugging away. They were headed to the last line of defense between the Red Army and the German Capitol. *Wehrmacht, Hitlerjugend, Volkssturm, Schutzstaffel.*

That's the End of the Reich. Beyond that is Jewish Land.

Lukov jogged through the streets of a Prussian town. Alone. He gripped his machine gun and glanced down every side street. His battalion had moved into the town and taken most of it. Lukov had been separated from Alexander and his squad in a firefight, now he was alone in loosely controlled German land.

He sprinted around a corner and dove behind the building immediately. At the end of the street was a small flak squad. Facing away from him. Lukov readied his weapon, and snuck behind the buildings, toward the German position. Finally, he was near enough to hear the squad but still hidden behind a small house. The small flak gun was surrounded by sandbags, with four Germans manning it. They were all standing up, alert. Lukov took out his grenade, pulled the pin and chucked it over the circle of sandbags.

"*Granate!*" Lukov heard the Germans scream, in an unusually high-pitched voice. This was the Soviet's cue. He sprinted out from his cover, gun raised. The grenade exploded, then the flak gun tipped over. Lukov vaulted over the sandbag, aiming at the first person he saw. When his feet hit the ground, he was looking down at a Hitler Youth. The light blond-haired boy was on his back, burned, trying to crawl away. But his right leg and side were burnt bad, there was a gash on his forehead and his helmet had fallen off. He was no older than fourteen. Lukov's finger tightened on the trigger. The other boys groaned on the snowy ground colored red with their blood. None made a move for their pistols. Lukov brought his boot down on the boy's side and flipped him over to face him. Staring back at him were light blue eyes, like Blaz's. Eyes filled with fear. Thin, similar height to Blaz at fourteen, with a bony-face and mildly sunken eyes.

"*Bitte toten mich nicht,*" the boy begged the Russian, but by his tone, Lukov could tell the kid thought this was it. "Please don't kill me." Lukov understood. He lowered his weapon. He looked at the other boys, who were slowly getting up, but not going for their weapons.

"*Helfen ihm,*" he ordered, and stepped off the boy. All three moved forward to help, but one's leg gave out and he fell face first. Lukov made no move. The other two boys lifted the first boy. Lukov slung his rifle over his shoulder, reached into his uniform, taking out some emergency wrapping. He wrapped the boy's head, then his arm, then his chest. The German looked at Lukov in shock.

"*Warum?* Why didn't you kill me?" the boy asked him, mouth hanging partially open.

"You're a kid," Lukov answered in German, "You didn't fight me when I had a gun on you. Why would I kill you?"

"We are German. You are a Soviet," the boy answered. The two boys next to him gave a single nod. The third boy, who'd managed to stand up, nodded from behind as well.

Lukov grinned at the ground and stood up, "I guess I have a soft spot for kids."

The boys stared.

"Come on," Lukov waved them to walk ahead of him. The first three boys marched ahead, one supporting the wounded boy. Lukov got under the last boy's armpit and helped him limp along. The others slowed down to let Lukov and their comrade catch up.

"Why did you really not shoot us?" one asked.

"Because I've been shown more mercy by Germans than any soldier could ask for. And I could never live with myself if I shot an unarmed prisoner after the mercy I've been given."

The boys eyed him curiously.

"Long story," Lukov said. He led the boys down the street, "Hold your hands above your head," he ordered, "Our command is nearby."

The boys nodded and raised one or two arms, if they were able.

"What's your name?" one boy asked Lukov.

"My name? Lukov Rosovsky."

"Lukov?" the wounded blond repeated, grinning at one of his friends.

"Something funny?" Lukov asked.

"Your name ends in 'ov,'" the boy smiled awkwardly, "Seems like a lot of Russians have that. Chuikov, Zhukov, Lukov."

"*Ja*, I guess so," Lukov replied. They walked on, nearing Russian lines.

"How do you speak such good German?"

"I was with a group of partisans in Russia who taught me," Lukov answered, then asked a question that he could've looked at his own country to for the answer, "What are you boys doing fighting? You aren't the first I've encountered."

"We're fighting to keep the Reich and Europe safe from Communism. So no one will disturb *Deutschland* and her people. And in the long run, all of Europe," the tallest of the boys said, "And we'll use every man we can."

Lukov nodded.

"You needn't worry about Communism."

The boys rolled their eyes among themselves.

"*Danke* for letting us live, Lukov," the wounded blond said as they came into view of the Russian command.

"You boys may end up in a work camp, though," Lukov told them. The boys didn't seem to hear this.

"I didn't think Russians showed mercy."

"Well, now you know we do." Lukov approached an officer with the Hitler Youths, and saluted, "How goes the attack?" Lukov asked the officer.

"Ah, Sergeant Rosovsky. The attack goes well. We've taken the whole of the town, I let our men have a little fun. Search homes for any soldiers, if you know what I mean," the commander said with a chuckle.

Lukov frowned, but continued, "I have prisoners."

The officer looked at the German youths, then snapped his fingers at four guards, he nodded to them, and they each took a boy, holding them by the arms and shoulders.

"Do what you want," he said to them in Russian. One guard drew his pistol and placed its barrel on the temple of the wounded blond. All four Russians began dragging the boys away. Lukov froze. The wounded blond looked back at Lukov in horror.

"You're just like all of them!" he screamed desperately while he fought to get away. Lukov shook his head and marched after the four guards.

They brought the boys out of the main group onto an isolated bridge. Lukov sprinted onto the bridge after them. One Russian ran past Lukov back toward the town. The Germans held their hands up as they were kept at gunpoint.

"Comrades!" Lukov shouted as he neared, "Give them up, they're my prisoners. I'll do what I want with them."

The other Russians laughed, "Rosovsky, you're Jewish too. They hate us. Remember what they did to the Motherland. Why don't you join us in the fun?"

"Our ideas of fun are a lot different, I'm certain, Dimitri," Lukov answered, "I know what you did in Ukraine."

Dimitri looked oddly proud of himself. "Come on, Rosovsky. Enjoy yourself. Get some revenge on the Germans."

Lukov shook his head, "I don't want any revenge like that."

One of the three Russians looked puzzled by this but stayed quiet. Some random shots sounded in the town.

"Why not?" Dimitri growled, "Rosovsky, these boys invaded the Motherland. Their people attacked our homes. They deserve no mercy. And we will give them none."

The fourth Russian came running back, brandishing a thick, iron rod in one hand and rope in the other. He handed it to Dimitri, who held it out to Lukov, "We are gallant soldiers of the Red Army. Fierce as bears, and just as merciless. Knock that blond one's brains out. Just think of Leningrad while you're doing it, all right? Remember Leningrad. All those sick, bleeding people, Rosovsky. All our comrades."

Lukov took the rod and stepped in front of the blond boy. He put the rod against the side of the boy's temple. The wounded Hitler Youth looked back up at Lukov, shocked that the same Russian who'd just given him mercy was about to bash his skull in with a rod. Lukov closed his eyes and began thinking of Leningrad. More shots sounded. He breathed in through his nose, reviving hatred that he had for Germans. He thought back to Leningrad where his squad had been murdered. Where hundreds of thousands had died. He opened his eyes again, not seeing a child, but a person who was responsible for his people's suffering. Someone who'd killed his countrymen. The boy stared back at him, directly in the eye, and took a deep breath. He tried to look brave. Lukov inhaled. He glanced down the short row of boys. They all looked at him in horror. Like he was a monster. Something they'd never seen before that wasn't of this earth. He returned his gaze back to the wounded blond. He raised the rod over his shoulder.

"You really are all the same!" one shouted, "You dirty, Russian beasts! You-"

The boy was silenced quickly by a boot to the gut. Then the rope was fastened around his neck. The other end was tied to the bridge railing.

"Come on, Rosovsky. Leningrad, brother. Leningrad," Dimitri reminded him.

Lukov's hands shook on the rod now. He looked into the young German's eyes.

"Lukov, if you're going to do it, please do it soon," the boy pleaded, his original bold expression fading.

"Rosovsky," Dimitri said, impatiently tapping a boot on the street.

Lukov dropped the rod. "I can't," he told his comrades.

Dimitri sighed. "Fine. I'll do it," he said, picking up the rod. He raised it without a moment's hesitation, smashing it into the boy's temple. The boy fell to his side, his arms spasming. The other boys watched in terror at their friend being beaten to death. Lukov looked away. Dimitri kept beating the boy, now in the chest. He screamed in pain, as his ribs broke. Another Soviet threw the boy who had spoken off the bridge, hanging him. The other two Red Army soldiers drew their pistols and shot the others dead. Dimitri finally quit beating the boy. His breaths were rapid. He stood still, breathing for many seconds before finally dropping the rod. Lukov stared in shock at his countrymen. Dimitri nodded to the other three, then to Lukov before striding away. The rest followed. Lukov watched them walk away, none looking back. The Russian Jew took off his cap and stared at the Hammer and Sickle patch in the center. After several seconds, he shook his head and headed back to his comrades.

The Seelow Heights

"I can see Seelow!" Ivo called to Koby, Blaz, and Jarman. He peered through the lone window in the boxcar, that had bars resembling a jail cell obstructing part of the view, "There she is!"

The three hometown boys darted to the window to get a look at their home.

"There's the train stop."

"There's the hill into town center," Koby pointed out with a grin, "You remember how many times we ran up that?"

"*Ja*. It looks smaller now," Blaz said.

"Well, we were smaller last time we ran it. And it's a big world out there."

The train came to a slow halt at the same train stop they had boarded to leave for the KLV camp. They were home. Some soldiers shouted outside, and the doors swung open. The Knights jumped down out of the boxcar, onto the dirt.

"Seelow. Best place in the world." Ivo started running into the town, forgetting he was in the German Ninth Army.

"*Nein*, hold it!" an SS soldier shouted, raising his rifle, much to the squad's dismay and horror.

"Wait Ivo!" Jarman yelled. Ivo skidded to a halt. The SS soldier lowered his rifle. It was clear that this was a tightly run ship.

"Sorry sir."

"It's all right private, I shouldn't have been so quick to raise my weapon," the soldier said, removing his finger from the trigger. He turned to the hundreds of men and boys who had gotten off the train, which was already chugging away, "Once the commanders arrive and the rest of Ninth Army, we will get your posts straightened out. For now, you are to remain within the town, if you have a place to stay within town, you may. Otherwise you will lodge in the school. You are not to step foot outside of the town. Deserters will be dealt with appropriately. Rest assured the SS will be patrolling. Dismissed."

Ivo looked at his squad after the SS soldier. They couldn't help but smile even after the SS soldier's grim words. They'd been given free rein in their home.

"We'll see you at the school," Ivo told Jarman and Koby, "We'll stick with Werner."

Koby and Jarman nodded and sprinted off toward their homes. Blaz followed Ivo, wanting to see Ivo get his wish. Ivo stared down the street, scanning for his door among the connected homes.

"Go on," Blaz grinned. Ivo jogged ahead, until he was in a full sprint. Blaz and Werner followed behind him. Once there, Ivo knocked on the door, rather calmly at first. But when there was no immediate answer he anxiously knocked again. He only waited a few seconds and knocked a third time. It was a quick answer, but to Ivo it felt like an eternity. The door opened, and *Frau* Klein appeared at the door. Ivo stared up at his mother with a dirty face. She was still taller than him.

"Ivo?" she stammered in disbelief, "Ivo?"

"*Mutter*!" Ivo exclaimed, and threw himself into his mother's arms, tears poured down his cheeks. His mother cried tears of joy when she realized it was indeed her son. Footsteps approached rapidly behind them. *Herr* Klein appeared to see Blaz and Werner standing outside the door, then looked down to see his son look up to him.

"Son?" he gasped, "Ivo?"

"*Vater, Vater*!" Ivo cried, his face red from tears of joy. His father extended his right arm and picked Ivo up. Blaz noticed no movement in the other sleeve, there was no arm.

"Come on, let's let him enjoy it," Blaz smiled at Werner, blinking several times. Then he rubbed one eye. Ivo got his wish, at least part of it.

Blaz Returns Home

This was it. Blaz stood in front of the door ready to knock. Time to meet his little brother. He raised a fist and knocked on the door four consecutive times. No answer. He knocked again. The door opened, but it was no one he recognized. It wasn't his mother, this woman didn't even have the same colored hair, and was also younger. She wore a nurse uniform too. And there were a bunch of soldiers inside the home, some sitting, others lying down.

"May I help you?" the women asked kindly.

"Do you know where I could find Cheryl Senft?"

"*Ah ja*, this home belongs to the Senft's. We're using it to house sick and wounded soldiers."

"Where is Cheryl Senft?" Blaz asked, beginning to panic.

"*Frau* Senft passed away this winter."

"*Nein*," Blaz breathed, putting his hands over his eyes, "She couldn't."

"I'm afraid so. Pneumonia. Very harsh conditions in Seelow this December, little food, no sufficient doctors were available. Did you know her?"

Blaz controlled himself to give an answer, "*J-ja*. I'm her son."

"Blaz Adolf Senft?"

Blaz nodded, wiping his wet eyes with his uniform's sleeve in the cold, winter air.

"I'm sorry, Blaz," Werner consoled his friend.

Blaz sniffled, trying to regain control, and looked back to the nurse, "What about little Erwin Senft?"

"*Jawohl*, he was sent to live with a family in the area. Called the-" the woman paused, trying to remember.

"Knechts? Hertzes?" Werner asked, recalling his squad mates' last names.

"*Nein, nein*, started with an 'H,' though."

"The Holtzer's?" Werner asked again, remembering this name that had come up before.

"God," Blaz wept, falling to his knees, "Oh God."

"*Ja*, that's it," the women said. Werner waved the women back into the house and got down on a knee next to his friend. Werner put an arm around Blaz's shoulder. Blaz took notice and hugged Werner.

"*Es ist alles in Ordnung, Blaz*," Werner whispered softly, lightly hugging his friend, who hugged him back tightly with closed eyes.

The Ninth Army Command

Two trucks rumbled into the schoolyard, where classes continued. The only difference was all the Hitler Youth boys, and even some of the older girls had pistols on their belts during classes or a rifle laid at their feet. They were in the *Volkssturm*, which desperately scraped together anyone they could as the feared Red Army drew closer. The trucks attracted little attention from the students. Seelow had been turned into a town of soldiers since the New Year. Officers of many different rankings climbed out of the back of the trucks, wearing black, field-gray, and some camouflage. But all wore a field cap. The highest-ranking man led the group of officers into the school. They had arranged for a room to be cleared for their use. With the many boys off at war the school's numbers were thinned. Germany's inability to keep up the KLV camps because of excessive bombing of railroads brought the younger boys back as well. The room was prepared with a large table, several chairs and a flag hanging on the wall. The head officer laid out several maps, "Here we are men, the Seelow Heights. I have received orders from the *Führer* to defend this city. It is the gate to Berlin."

"*Oberstgeneral* Heinrici, how do you plan to defend this area?" a *Wehrmacht Hauptmann* asked.

"The Red Army is fast approaching, but our armies to the northeast have held out near Königsberg. Ultimately, Himmler is in command of Army Group Vistula, but I am the man in the field. I anticipate the Russians will halt their drive to Berlin, rather than risk encirclement. They will halt at the Oder River. I plan to dig in here. We shall absorb retreating forces into our ranks, I have been given the ability to bring them under the Ninth Army here in the Seelow Heights. These defenses have long stood dormant, they are some of the best in *Deutschland* and we will make them better. Every man will be important in a battle such as this. We have tanks and artillery. This will be a defensive battle. The *Führer* is expected to place the Ninth Army under command of General Busse," Heinrici said, gesturing to the man at his right, "Along with the *Hitlerjugend* and *Volkssturm* of Seelow. The third *Panzer* Army has been placed under command of General Hasso von Manteuffel," he gestured to the officer on his left, "He will defend our north and northeastern flanks. All officers are in charge of maintaining the men's morale. Here, in the entrenchments we will outlast them."

Heinrici turned to face the SS officers in his entourage. The officers sent their right arms into the air.

"SS, I understand you have orders from the high command."

"*Jawohl, Oberstgeneral,*" responded the leading SS officer, "*Reichsführer* Himmler and *Gruppenführer* Fegelein have issued orders to maintain order here in Seelow. Civilians and soldiers. Deserters and those unwilling to fight will be dealt with how the SS sees fit."

"Very well. I give you freedom of action."

"*Jawohl, Oberstgeneral.*"

"General von Manteuffel," Heinrici continued, "I want you at your headquarters to the north. All officers of the Third *Panzer* Army are to join him. Those officers are now dismissed. Officers defending the central and southern defenses, stay."

General von Manteuffel nodded and snapped his fingers at his officers. They followed him out of the room.

"Engel, Schlusser, Lochner, Stromschnellen, Hadler, and Kurzmann. You are the ranking SS officers that will maintain order in the town and in the defenses. We must be strict. There are many youths that will be in our ranks. But it is through their added numbers and determination that victory may be achieved. Inspire them, encourage them, motivate them. Their enthusiasm may be contagious. A confident army is the only army that can win this battle for us. If they believe they may win, then they very well may. You are dismissed."

The five officers saluted before exiting. Engel, the highest-ranking, turned to his comrades, "We must be ready to keep the troops at their posts by whatever means necessary. All of you must allow no deserters."

"Understood," the five others said simultaneously.

"All boys, ten and up, I want them in our ranks and ready to defend. If anyone wishes to join, we gladly welcome them. Women, Soviet deserters, anyone. Screen deserters, of course."

The SS officers saluted.

"Return to your platoons. *Heil* Hitler."

"*Heil* Hitler!"

Soldiers

Werner took Blaz back to the schoolyard, only just down the street from Blaz's old home. No one was there yet. They probably wouldn't return until ordered to. Blaz wandered onto the field, right next to the flagpole. The same flag flew there. The red had faded slightly, but it still waved freely in the wind. Werner cautiously approached his friend. Blaz kept walking, all the way across the soccer field, to where a small hill began behind the goals. He trudged over the hill, where new chin-up bars were. He hardly noticed, sitting down at the hill's crest. Werner sat down next to him a few seconds later. They stared at the brick wall of the U-shaped town school. Blaz didn't say a thing. He didn't want to think about it. All his fighting, all the friends lost, and he returned home to find out his mother was dead. Werner just sat with him.

The silence was broken when the children of Seelow were let out of school. The young children, the very young ones left the building, talking and running, without a care in the world. They had no idea what was coming. The Hitler Youth boys exited in a much more solemn manner. They couldn't imagine what was coming but they knew one thing: it couldn't be good. And it is hard to act like a whimsical, unaware child when you have a pistol holstered on your belt. Blaz and Werner watched. What had happened?

"You know something?" Werner asked Blaz, finally speaking.

"What?"

"I used to play with toy soldiers when I was their age," he said, breaking his normally professional tone. He pointed to the young, armed German boys, "I would pretend to have great battles, each man that I had would die during the fight, but I would reuse him as another man that I pretended was reinforcements. My German pieces would always win, and never lost all their men. One man always made it through the entire battle," Werner looked at the ground, and rubbed one eye. Blaz was still listening. "My favorite piece was the one that held a flag in one hand, and a raised pistol in the other. He always looked the most heroic, holding a flag in battle."

Blaz glanced at Werner. Werner looked back.

"What does that all mean?"

"I don't know. We just," Werner paused, and gazed skyward, "We play war when we're little. Heroes are made in war, and we all wanted to be heroes. We found out we would get to go to war, and to be honest, I was excited. But you don't truly want to be in war. Not when you see what it's like. And imagine, those kids were probably playing with toy soldiers weeks ago."

Blaz watched the last of the Hitler Youths exit the schoolyard. Werner had been an adjutant. He'd been assigned to be the assistant of a high-ranking officer. He was smart. Werner had run into battle behind his officer. But after being shot in the ribs and seeing his friends die, that enthusiasm was gone. It had taken years to garner such enthusiasm. Gone in moments.

"*Ja*, you don't want to go to war," Blaz finally agreed, "There's not much good about war, but there is good in why we fight wars. That's why they're fought. There is a reason."

Werner frowned, "I'm in the SS, Blaz. And I want this war over and done with. But I don't want to lose. I don't know if I could go on living if we lost." Werner patted his pistol, making it abundantly clear how torn he was. He kept rambling, "But I want Germany's suffering to end soon."

"If we lose, our suffering will continue for another hundred years," Blaz admitted at last. But he knew it was true. Werner nodded and stared back out across the field. His left hand shook. But he didn't seem to notice.

Koby Briefly Comes Back

Verfluchen oder auch loben,
Grad wie es ihnen gefällt.
Wo wir sind da geht's immer vorwärts!
Der Teufel der lacht nur dazu:
Ha ha ha ha ha!
Wir kämpfen für Deutschland,
Wir kämpfen für Hitler,
Der Rote kommt nie mehr zur Ruh'!

The SS song made its way to Blaz and Werner's ears. Any nearby Hitler Youths saluted as the SS marched by.

"Recruiting?" Blaz asked.

"Probably… they're so young."

"We're young."

"But they're so much younger."

"I agree."

"I wish it didn't have to happen."

"Either they fight or complete Communist takeover. We fight for the future. It'll be a sorry day if our nation comes to the point where they care not for the future of their children as long as they themselves have a comfortable life."

"*Deutschland* would never come to that," Werner said, shaking his head. The notion was absurd.

"Marxism and Capitalism. That can do it to a nation."

Werner gritted his teeth and repeatedly shook his head. At that moment, Koby came through the gate with his mother and little sister. He carried her in his arms, as the walk from the house was too long for her. Blaz and Werner ran over to meet him and see his little sister. As beautiful a baby as they come, new life, dark brown hair, and a tanner tint to her skin than Blaz and Werner but lighter than Koby. Unfortunately, she, like much of Seelow Heights, looked undernourished.

"Blaz, Werner," Koby smiled widely and put his sister down so that she stood in front of him, "Meet Klara Traudl Hertz," Koby looked down at his sister with an adoring smile, "Say '*Hallo.*' Shake their hands."

"*H-h-halo,*" Klara said, in the way only a young one can.

Blaz and Werner each put a hand out to the little girl. She took them and awkwardly shook one with each arm.

"*Nein, nein,* one at a time," Koby laughed, and demonstrated for her. The little girl nodded her head, taking Blaz's hand and shaking it. Then she turned to shake Werner's hand and fell towards the snow. Koby reacted quickly and caught her before she hit the ground. Werner knelt with a smile and gave the little girl his hand, she shook it loosely.

"*Gut, gut,*" Koby enthusiastically encouraged his little sister.

"How well can she speak?" Blaz asked Koby.

"Ask her a question. Something simple."

"What is your name?"

"K-Klara," Klara said then pointed to Koby, "*Das ist* Koby,"

"*Gut, gut.* What is Koby?"

"*Brüder.*"

"*Sehr gut, ausgezeichnet.*"

"Blaz, where's Erwin and *Frau* Senft? Why are you already here?" Werner tried to signal Koby to shut up from behind Blaz. *Frau* Hertz had clearly not told Koby either.

"Erwin is at the Holtzer's," Blaz said, "And mother is dead."

Koby jaw fell. "I'm really sorry, Blaz."

"*Danke*, Koby," Blaz sniffed, shook his head and gritted his teeth slightly to get a grip. Koby put his arms over Blaz's shoulder and gave him a reassuring hug.

"You going to be okay?"

"I'll be all right." Jarman's old advice rang through.

Reunification

By the time the sun began setting, in the early evening, the squad had gathered with their families at the Klein's home. The mood, though many loved ones had been lost, was relief and joy at seeing the boys return. *Frau* Weiss and *Frau* Meyer had come as well. *Frau* Weiss had not yet heard of her husband's death in the Battle of the Bulge, *Frau* Meyer brought her three children, two twin boys and a girl, born during the war, when *Herr* Meyer had been able to take leave. All the families brought some food, as the Kleins wouldn't be able to prepare anything without everyone chipping in. *Frau* Klein had started to prepare a home cooked meal.

Herr Klein left quickly upon the boys arriving, saying he had to be somewhere but that he would come back before dinner. Ivo hugged him as he left. Jarman had been explaining all he knew about Erich, doing the best he could to give *Frau* Meyer reason for hope. After all, surrender had still been an option. *Frau* Meyer only knew fourteen-year-old Erich, he would certainly surrender. *Frau* Weiss spoke with Koby who still stayed close to Klara. Blaz and *Frau* Knecht conversed, while Ivo helped his mother. Werner watched the conversations unfold, occasionally saying something. Koby invited him over to introduce him further to *Frau* Weiss.

The widows and fatherless and motherless were all together, simply all glad to see each other after all these years. The food's aroma filled the small room. Conversation continued; Ivo looked up at the window several times, expecting his father to return. And finally, he did. Right before the meal was ready. He came in with his rough, beardless face wet with snow that had begun to fall. *Herr* Klein was not alone. The Holtzer's came in behind, with *Herr* Holtzer holding the hand of Erwin Senft and a Karabiner 98K rifle in the other. Blaz's attention was immediately drawn to his little brother. He was walking, his light blond hair had come in and he gazed around the room with an open mouth. *Herr* Holtzer still had his beard but looked to have lost weight in recent months. He waved Blaz over to meet his little brother.

"*Schön, sie zu treffen*, Erwin," Blaz said, and knelt to eye level with his brother, "I am Blaz."

Erwin just stared blankly at this new boy who was talking to him. *Herr* Holtzer bent down and whispered something in Erwin's ear. Erwin's big blue eyes lit up in understanding.

"*Brüder*," Erwin pointed, his finger poking his brother in the eye. Blaz laughed, blinking a few times. Then he hugged Erwin tightly.

There was a knock on the door as Blaz and Erwin split. *Herr* Klein looked out the window, expecting to see soldiers. He did indeed.

"Couldn't they let us have tonight together?" he muttered, giving a nod to *Herr* Holtzer to open the door. They were soldiers, to be sure. In black, like that of the SS. But they wore Panzer uniforms with pink trim on the collars and epaulets. *Frau* Knecht immediately ran to the door followed by Jarman. The three older Knecht brothers had found their way home. A fourth, smaller figure was behind them.

"*Mutter*, Jarman," the tallest one nodded with a wide smile, who Blaz scarcely recognized to be Heinrich, the oldest of the Knecht brothers. Each brother hugged their mother and younger brother. The four of them had been gone since the Battle of France. They were barely recognizable. But *Frau* Knecht knew them.

"Helmut! Heinrich! Karl!" she cried, embracing them, "Welcome home!"

"Good to be back, *Mutter*," Karl, the middle brother said for the three of them. All were in their twenties, but the war in a tank had aged them badly. Their faces were scarred, dirtied, and stubbled. Helmut and Heinrich's blond hair was filthy, knotted and unkempt. Karl's brunette hair had dry oil in it.

"Jarman, you're taller than me now," Helmut laughed, looking up at his younger brother.

"Look at that," Jarman grinned at his now littler brother, and lightheartedly patted his head.

"May we join you?" Heinrich asked *Frau* Klein, "Oh, and we found a kid, said he was looking for Koby. He's not doing too good."

"*Absolut*," *Frau* Klein answered immediately.

"*Danke schön*," the three said, one after the other, started by Heinrich. Each man took off his boots, leaving them next to the door, but of course kept their uniforms on. The three stepped completely in, revealing the fourth soldier. Small. Koby moved forward at this.

"Koby?" a young voice said hoarsely as the small soldier walked into the light of the house.

"Johann?" Koby said in amazement at seeing his young friend again.

"Hi Koby," Johann coughed, "Good to see you."

Johann was taller, a good height for his age. But what drew everyone's attention was his face. Clearly, it had very recently been burned. The upper left part of his face was charred, and part of his hair burnt off as well. He was also missing his left eyebrow. He looked to have been through hell.

"We were just about to sit down, we don't have enough room at the table, so we'll spread out across the room," *Frau* Klein told the Knecht brothers drawing attention away from Johann, knowing Koby would have plenty of time to speak with him.

"*Na sicher, absolut*," Helmut nodded, and the three lined up on the wall. Johann followed Koby across from them.

"Shall we give thanks?" *Herr* Holtzer asked the group of German widows, orphans, motherless, fatherless, and childless.

"For this," Jarman said, gesturing to everyone in the home, "We must give thanks."

"All right," *Herr* Holtzer said holding out a hand to his wife and Blaz; the two who stood next to him. Blaz took it and extended his hand to *Frau* Weiss. It didn't take long for those gathered to join hands.

"Dear Lord," *Herr* Holtzer began, his voice not the same as the boys remembered. His old positive and encouraging tone was replaced with one of despair. "I sincerely thank you for allowing us to come together tonight.

It is a true blessing. You have been merciful to bring back this many of our boys. You are all-powerful, you can prevent further death. I pray you do so in the coming months. I thank you for the safe return of Helmut, Heinrich, Karl, Jarman, Ivo, Koby, Blaz, Johann, our new friend Werner, our old friend Ernst. Please Lord, protect them as the great battle grows near. We pray your mighty hand would shield them from the enemy," *Herr* Holtzer took a deep breath, "Those of us that have not returned, we know we will see them with you someday, but please, don't take anyone more. These young men have a future, you will do remarkable things through them, as you have done with so many in the past. Protect them, spare our boys," *Herr* Holtzer paused, remembering his son, his friend *Herr* Meyer, and *Herr* Knecht, Reinhardt, Erich, and many other men and boys who had never returned from the fighting, "God, why have you forsaken *Deutschland* and her people?"

Frau Holtzer patted her husband's back soothingly.

Johann took over for *Herr* Holtzer, "God, we've lost a lot of friends and family. I don't know why they had to be taken so young, so early. And I don't like it. But it is not my place to question you, you know more than any of us. Still, I pray you rescue us, our people, and our nation. We need you so bad now. Amen."

"Amen," some of the group echoed. No one broke hands for minutes.

Koby, Ivo, and Blaz sat on the floor with Johann. Before they ate, Koby took out some gauze and wrapped Johann's burnt face in them.

"What ha-?" Ivo began, but stopped when Koby elbowed him. Ivo glared at his sergeant.

"Don't Koby," Johann said, surprising Koby greatly.

"Sorry," he apologized.

"What happened?" Ivo immediately asked, picking up where he'd left off.

Johann looked at the ground, a quarter of his face nothing short of skinless and red. "We were retreating. The Russians overran us before the train ever arrived, a few days ago. It was so quick, how fast they moved. Our command broke down, my sergeant-"

"Your age, right?" Ivo interrupted.

"*Jawohl*," Johann answered, somewhat slowly, "He just yelled at us to start running west. We sprinted as fast as we could. I'd never run faster. We ran through the city, the Russians had artillery, tanks, soldiers, bullets, everything," Johann shot off in his hoarse voice, "I got ahead of my squad. I completely forgot about them for a while. I thought they were right behind me. When I remembered them, I couldn't even see them. I just started running, back into the city, where they'd been following me. Then I saw my best friend, Kolton. He was the last standing, and they shot him. And they kept shooting him once he was on the ground. I saw him clutching his chest with one arm, then raising his other in surrender. One Russian stepped in front of him, and shot him, not even to kill. In the arm he held up, then in the both legs, then in the chest," Johann said clenching his fists, his eyes welling up. "I raised my rifle, first time I'd shot to kill. And I wanted to kill this man." No one said a word but listened to Johann in horrified interest. "And I hit him. In the head. I hit two more men while they looked for the shooter. I shot the fourth man in the hand and missed my fifth shot. He ran at me and I couldn't reload. So I stabbed him in the leg with my bayonet," Johann said, running a finger on his rifle's bayonet, "Then I beat him to death with the back end of my rifle. I-I bashed his skull in," Johann stammered, as if he just realized what he'd done, "Then I reloaded, I'd made up my mind that I would die with my friends. A tank was coming at me, for some reason he didn't just blow me to pieces immediately. I shot at it, of course nothing happened. Then it fired, nothing but flames. Flamethrower tank. I went for the ground, but part of my face got burned up. If it weren't for the snow, I wouldn't even have a face now. But, some soldiers came, they destroyed the tank. Then we kept running, jogging, marching then trudging until we came to Seelow late last night. I fell asleep and didn't wake up until a couple hours ago. I thought, you know, it had all maybe been a bad dream, but it wasn't, now they're all gone," Johann cried. Koby wrapped an arm around Johann and hugged him tightly. "They were all fifteen," Johann said, his voice shaky, "They all had ideas for what they'd do after the war great ideas. Wolfric still wanted to play professional soccer. Rodger was going to be a pilot. Rudy thought he would have a family, and just be a farmer, and he always wanted to visit America. Kolton just wanted to help build the New Berlin. He just wanted to be a construction worker and raise a family," Johann paused to regain his composure, "You know, I try to keep faith that God has all this planned, that it is for a better purpose. I prayed that last night. But I don't know if I believe it is for a better purpose. If we are supposed to lose this war why do so many good people have to die for the *Führer*?"

"I couldn't tell you," Koby admitted, "I was hoping to talk to you about this."

Johann looked up wiping away some tears onto the burnt side of his face. He flinched at this, then returned focus to Koby, "*Ja?*"

"*Ja.*"

Ivo sighed out loud, drawing a few glances. Blaz met Ivo's gaze. Johann did not speak again. Holtzer distracted the boys from their own struggle that awaited by telling them about his own experience in *Der Krieg*. He told them stories of the depression and how he made it in Seelow. His story finished with the National Socialists and the will and work of the German people bringing back pride, spirituality, and prosperity in Germany.

The boys finished their meals in silence. But Jarman and his brothers were laughing throughout the night, and when they waved goodbye to their friends to head home with their mother, they still had grins on their faces. Blaz, Werner, and Koby remained at the house the longest, even after Koby's mother had left to put Klara to bed. Ivo changed into his old pajamas, which still fit just him. Ivo, Blaz, Werner, and Johann lightheartedly chatted for a while, until Ivo fell asleep in the middle of the floor. The other boys said goodbye and thanked *Frau* Klein, then exited into the cold, frosty night air. A light snow fell. Johann flinched as the snow hit scalded flesh, but eventually was able to suppress it.

"That was fun," Johann laughed quietly. Blaz let out a breath of laughter.

"It was," Werner said, "You guys got to see your family and friends."

"That was great," Blaz said sincerely, "Good man, *Herr* Holtzer."

"He is," Werner agreed.

"Did you know he fought in *Der Krieg*?" Blaz asked Koby.

Koby silently shook his head.

"You feel all right?"

"Could I talk to you for a second, Blaz?" Koby said abruptly, stopping in the road. Werner and Johann gestured for Blaz to go ahead. The two boys walked out of earshot before Koby spoke again. "Blaz, we've got to do something. We have to stop the Russians."

"Of course we do."

Koby glanced around, "I hate them. *Hate* them."

"Koby-"

"Blaz! They kill everyone. They've killed half my squad. They murdered Johann's squad! God damn it, why did we ever help that kike?!"

Blaz frowned. "Koby, we were young. It wasn't wrong."

"Damn it Blaz," Koby said, in an exasperated voice, "What if they get *Deutschland*?"

"It won't be good."

"How can you be so calm?"

"I just am right now. We have a short time of peace. Enjoy it."

"But all I can think about is the Russians coming. They're going to kill everyone. Blaz. I couldn't go on living if you guys all died."

"Don't say that Koby."

"Wouldn't it be better to die? *Deutschland* and National Socialism would be destroyed if we don't stop them."

"Koby. It would take a miracle for us to stop them."

Koby shook his head. "We can."

Blaz sighed. "Keep telling yourself that," he said, patting Koby on the back and walking over to the others.

Johann still had not seen his mother, so Koby took him to see her. Blaz and Werner were left to find a place to sleep in the school. Minutes later, they were lying on the stone floor, each under a blanket, that would be better described as a rag.

Deutschlandlied

January 18, 1945

"*Volkssturm*! *Hitlerjugend*! *Heer*! *Luftwaffe*! *Schutzstaffel*! Outside!" came the call in the morning over the loudspeakers, broadcasted to Seelow, "School courtyard! *Sofort*!"

Blaz and Werner shot up from the floor, put on their uniforms and grabbed their rifles. Blaz led the way out, where already dozens of troops already were organized, in tight formations.

"*Wehrmacht*?" an officer asked them, "*Volkssturm*?"

"*Wehrmacht*."

"*Hitlerjugend* age?"

"*Jawohl*."

"Please stand over there," the officer instructed pointing to a formation of Hitler Youths. Many of the Hitler Youths were Johann's age or younger. They were unofficial members of the *Volkssturm*.

More of the new arrivals from the day before streamed onto the school field. *Wehrmacht* and SS officers stood at the front, next to the flagpole. Whatever they were feeling now, the officers hid it well, keeping straight faces. Particularly the SS officers in their decorated uniforms, peaked caps, black boots and gloves. They still embodied the intimidating image the Germans had built up for years. The *Wehrmacht* officers kept their cool in their field-gray uniforms. General Heinrici remained in one place, conversing with who looked to be the highest-ranking SS officer there. Koby, Jarman, Ivo, Johann, and *Herr* Holtzer had all arrived standing in the formation they belonged. The camouflaged and black clad SS soldiers stood at the back, the field-gray clad army soldiers stood in front of them, the few Luftwaffe personnel there in front of them. The *Volkssturm* stood in front of the Luftwaffe, not even clad in uniforms, just their working clothes. The only military indication came from the black and red armbands each wore. In between two *Reichsadlers* were the words 'Deutscher *Volkssturm Wehrmacht*.' They almost all held rifles or pistols, with a few holding *Panzerfausts*. Old men wore the armbands, men that could be grandpas. Children younger than Blaz wore the armbands as well, showing no fear. They'd never been in a battle before, there was nothing to be scared of. They would win. Among these were a small handful of women who had come to join their countrymen in the fight. Wearing spare *Wehrmacht* or Hitler Youth uniforms, they added to the *Volkssturm* numbers. But the youngest fighters wore the Hitler Youth uniforms like Blaz and his squad mates had long ago. Children as young as ten. Blaz stood behind the youngest, so they could see the officers when they spoke.

"Men and women of *Deutschland*!" a helmeted *Waffen-SS* soldier boomed, so that all conversation died down, "You have gathered today to defend your great nation. You and many others, already on the defenses, have bravely stepped forward to defend Berlin. The Red Army is kilometers away. We will hold them here. None shall pass by us. Oaths you have taken. All will be fulfilled when the enemy crashes to their knees before us. All have an important part to play in this battle. You owe the Fatherland ten dead Russians in this fight. Resourcefulness, comrades! Determination yet patience, aggression yet wisdom, boldness through fanaticism, *ja*! We survived the Roman Empire, the Seven Years' War, the Napoleonic Wars, the Franco-Prussian War, even *Der Großes Krieg*! Why now do you doubt?" he shouted, looking the way of some disheartened troopers, "German blood flows in us. We are a race of great guardians. A race of workers and farmers. A race proud to defy the world that has blindly decided to fight us. A race that will defend their families and children! Defend all these now; defend the future of your people! *Hitlerjugend*, do not allow your future offspring to suffer the consequences of defeat. If you believe you can win this battle, then by God, anything can happen! If you still doubt," the officer yelled, bringing his tone up again, "If you need any more reason for faith, just look at Frederick the Great! At Otto von Bismarck!"

"*Ja!*" the hundreds of soldiers cheered simultaneously.

The SS soldier shouted, holding both hands up, palms outward, "When all was falling apart, when all appeared lost, what did they do? Did they give up? Did they lose hope?"

"*Nein!*" came the reply.

"They did not lose hope! They rallied their forces, defeating our enemies and laying the foundations of our German Reich. And now *Deutschland's* fate is in our hands. This generation, you bear *Deutschland's* destiny! *Deutschland's* future or *Deutschland's* downfall. Our enemies cry out today: *Deutschland* shall perish! But *Deutschland* can give but one answer: *Deutschland* will live! And hence *Deutschland* will win!" The soldiers roared in approval. "We will once again defy all odds, as we have done before. For all you hold dear, hold *Deutschland* dearest. Your families, your homes, your friends. You are *Deutschland*! It will stand, so long as we remain loyal to her, and do what is best for the Fatherland. Our way of life, our families, our home, our land, our people, we will defend them to our dying breath!"

"*Ja!*" the Germans roared.

"*Sieg!*"

"*Heil!*"

"*Sieg!*"

"*Heil!*"

"*Sieg!*"

"*Heil!*"

There was a short silence, then Reynald Schlusser stepped forward and began singing.

Deutschland, Deutschland über alles, über alles in der Welt!

Immediately, every soldier was singing with Schlusser.

Wenn es stets zu Schutz und Trutze, brüderlich Zusammenhalt.
Von der Maas bis an die Memel, von der Etsch bis an den Belt.
Deutschland, Deutschland über alles, über alles in der Welt!
Deutschland, Deutschland über alles, über alles in der Welt!
Germany, Germany over everything, over everything in the world,
When for protection and defense, brotherly we stand together.
From the Meuse to the Memel, from the Adige to the Belt,
Germany, Germany over everything, over everything in the world!

Now a Hitler Youth stepped forward, taking the next stanza.

Deutsche Frauen, Deutsche Treue, Deutscher Wein und Deutscher Sang.
Sollen in der Welt behalten, ihren alten schönen Klang.
Uns zu Edler Tat begeistern, unser ganzes Leben lang.
Deutsche Frauen, Deutsche Treue, Deutscher Wein und Deutscher Sang.
Deutsche Frauen, Deutsche Treue, Deutscher Wein und Deutscher Sang.

German Women, German Loyalty, German wine and German song.
Shall retain in the world, their old beautiful chime
And inspire us to noble deeds, all our lives long.
German Women, German Loyalty, German wine and German song.
German Women, German Loyalty, German wine and German song.

Then a female soldier took the lead.

Einigkeit und Recht und Freiheit für das Deutsche Vaterland.
Danach lasst uns alle streben, brüderlich in Herz und Hand.
Einigkeit und Recht und Freiheit sind des Glückes Unterpfand.
Blühe im Glanze dieses Glückes, blühe Deutsche Vaterland!
Blühe im Glanze dieses Glückes, blühe Deutsche Vaterland!

Unity and Justice and Freedom for the German Fatherland.
Then let us all strive, brotherly in heart and hand.
Unity and Justice and Freedom are the key to happiness.
Bloom in the glow of this happiness, bloom German Fatherland!
Bloom in the glow of this happiness, bloom German Fatherland!

The soldiers paused after the final verse. Reynald Schlusser held his right arm higher. Then he finished the song in a new way, in the only way appropriate.

Deutschland, Deutschland, über alles, über alles in der Welt!

Schlusser lowered his right arm, placing it on his heart. The soldiers all lowered their arms and followed his example. After a long silence, General Heinrici stepped forward. "*Volkssturm* over age fifty will remain in the town as the Home Guard. The rest of the *Volkssturm* take to the nearest defenses in the Heights. Hitler Youth will be posted in the hills surrounding the town to the east, south and near north. However, our force is primarily army soldiers who were already here or arrived before the force standing here. Hitler Youth will help to prop up our nearby defenses, you will also work our anti-tank weapons, act as watchmen, and tank hunters. Each position will have a Head Sergeant, who will give you further orders. *Allgemeine-SS*, you are to maintain order in the town. *Waffen-SS*, you know where you need to be. Sergeants, I have spoken with you, lead your men to their positions."

"*Heil!*"

"He had a good voice," Ivo whispered to Blaz.

"*Ja*, he did."

Preparations

The hundreds of soldiers dispersed across the Heights. Koby knew where the Knights were going. He led the squad through fields between two ridges to a bunker overlooking the plains. Across a short plain was another ridge where more of their comrades waited with a bunker of their own. There was a road to their position, to bring ammunition and tanks. Koby led his squad past the Tiger Tank that had dug in to guard the road, with logs and branches protecting its treads, while leaves and vines gave the tank cover. The bunker was near enough to the ridge that it's MG-42 had a wide line of fire. Sniper windows were built in, giving excellent cover to the soldiers posted. At the back of the bunker was yet another MG-42 nest to defend the rear. Trenches blocked the way to the bunker where the bulk of the troops stationed there guarded the way through the forest where Russian infantry would likely try to regroup with tanks that would travel through open fields. The bunker's position was meant to prevent that, while providing a place for *Panzerschrecks* to fire on approaching tanks. On the ridge, on either side of the concrete bunker, were flak guns, which would be used against approaching tanks. Younger Hitler Youths operated these, led by an older Sergeant. The entire Seelow Heights was busy preparing defenses.

The boys were immediately introduced to their Head Sergeant who ordered them away from the position to begin digging anti-tank ditches. While they ran towards the east, Panther Tanks, Tiger I's and II's, and *Panzer III's* and *IV's* rolled across the many fields, smashed paths through the forested areas, while Germans gathered the wood the tanks had brought to the ground to use for firewood and arranged them into traps over pits they'd dig for the Russians. The Knights worked on building traps in areas they would not walk, whether they be holes, to slow Russian advances, anti-tank ditches, barbed wire, or anti-tank barricades. As the sun set, they moved to camouflaging the tanks. The attack could come any day. The Russians were only kilometers away.

"*Herr*, anything else we can do for you?" Jarman asked the commander as they finished helping to camouflage a Panther Tank.

"*Nein*, that's good," the tank commander replied.

"Move along," Jarman nodded to Koby.

"*Gut, gut.*"

"Where to, Koby?" Johann asked, who had joined them as Koby had hoped for long ago.

"We head back now. It's dark. The Head Sergeant is going to rotate when we keep watch. Probably won't be tonight."

"Hopefully not," Johann yawned.

"You are finally here! I said report back by nightfall," Head Sergeant Schneider said as they walked up the ramp way.

"I apologize, sir," Koby responded, "We were camouflaging a tank, lost track of myself."

"Fine, fine," the Head Sergeant said, "Well, your squad will keep watch tonight."

Ivo snickered. Johann gave him a shove.

"*Ja* sir," Koby nodded taking to the trenches, where two of the other three squads were. Two squads were made up of eight men, and then the Head Sergeant's squad was made up of ten men. The squads were split up however, based on abilities.

Ivo was sent to be a sniper in the bunker, the others were in the trenches. A man, who looked forty, manned the machine gun in the trench. The Head Sergeant informed everyone he would assign tank hunters when the Red Army's attack was confirmed.

"Johann?" Blaz asked, as many soldiers slipped into sleep as the night dragged on.

"*Ja*, Blaz?" Johann replied, enthused.

"Did you talk with Koby anymore last night?"

"I did but not for long. I wanted to see my mother. Didn't get much sleep. If I hadn't slept through most of yesterday, I don't know if I could make it through tonight. Why?" Blaz began his answer, but Johann cut him off, "I know you're worried about him."

Blaz started to pick up snow and pack it, "I am. He's losing it, Johann. He cannot think rationally anymore. At least not for long. He doesn't act like himself."

"You're exaggerating," Johann said, "When did this start?"

"It started off when we started seeing our comrades go down. Jurgen, that really changed him. More often than not, he didn't sound like himself. We lost so many friends and fellow soldiers. Over time he became a different person. He just *hates* the Russians."

"I hate Russians," Johann said bluntly, to Blaz's surprise, "I absolutely understand why he hates them. You hate Russians, don't you Blaz?"

"I suppose so. I don't like them, that's for sure. I think we shouldn't match their brutality in our retaliation. We're the superior civilization, we should act in a better way. During a battle, I have no problem pulling a trigger. But when the fighting dies down, it feels more like murder. It's more personal, and when you can see their expressions, you can look into their eyes. You can tell which ones have families. But I don't *hate* Russians, I feel like I should sometimes."

"Well, saving that man probably affects how you think about it."

"How'd you-"

"Koby told me. But killing in battle feels a lot different. It's a lot easier to kill someone who's actively trying to kill you."

"It is."

"Koby, I don't know, it sounds like he has a lot of regret. Like he blames himself for those who died under his command, at least partially."

"That's what Werner said."

"I'll talk to Koby, try to figure it out. Maybe tonight."

"Okay," Blaz had packed a nearly perfect snowball by now. It was a shame he couldn't use it. "Johann? How are you dealing with losing your squad so well?"

Johann didn't make an initial response, he stared out into the forest instead. "To tell you the truth I think the killing helped. I'd never taken a life before. It felt strong avenging my friends. And I've kept a diary of what has happened."

"A diary? Since when?"

"Since we went to the KLV camp. I didn't really do it all that much until we left for the war. I take out a lot of my anger in there, and when I look back reading it, it's both fascinating and embarrassing to see what I've thought and written down. But it helps me process all this so my days aren't filled with wrestling with my thoughts."

"Do you pray? Often?"

"*Ja*, every night. That helps too. It's like having a parent to tell your sorrows to. And to ask what you can do better. After my friends were killed though, I'm confused. I don't know what God wants of me. I believe God hears my prayers and answers those who love him though. He works in ways we can't understand. Maybe that's why we're losing. Christ had to die before his message could really be spread. Maybe that's the same with our struggle."

Blaz nodded and threw his snowball at a tree ten meters away from the trench hitting it square on. "Maybe."

"How do you keep control, Blaz? You've seen so much, so much death, but you still care about mercy? Admirable, I guess."

"I don't know, Johann. It's just me, I'm just treating the Russians how I would hope they would treat my German comrades."

"What you do isn't going to change a Russian's mind," Johann said straightforwardly, shifting his tone, "That's really naive to think it would."

"Johann," Blaz groaned, "Don't start."

"Listen, I understand all you're saying, but the Russians aren't going to change their minds. They're insane. Insane!" Johann said with a rising voice. One soldier shot up from where he slept with his pistol in hand and scanned around for enemies.

"It's okay, Georg. No enemies. No Russians," Blaz assured the unnerved soldier, "Go back to sleep, we'll wake you if we spot anything suspicious."

"*Gut*," the soldier grunted and laid his head back against the trench.

Blaz and Johann picked up where they left off.

"I don't disagree with you, Johann. And I don't want to be at their mercy. I have before. It's not a good place to be," Blaz pointed to his jaw scar, "That's what they do to prisoners before they kill you. But I'm sure there's a few good ones, they deserve to be treated according to the laws of war."

"Sure, you're right. But this is kind of irrelevant to talk about. We won't be the ones taking prisoners anytime soon."

"We won't."

"We won't what?" Koby asked as he came over to check on the two.

"You want to take that, Johann?" Blaz grinned.

"*Absolut.*"

Casualties of War

January 19, 1945

"How did it go?" Blaz asked Johann as the sun rose in the red east, early in the morning.

"Better than I hoped," Johann reported, "But it *is* like talking to a new person."

"What did he say? What did you discuss?"

"I think I understand him. He hasn't moved past Reinhardt. Not at all. He told me he feels responsible. That he should've been the one dead, not them. He shouldn't think that way."

"*Nein*. But I have before."

"I have too," Johann agreed, "Koby's been doing it for years though. I can only imagine what that does to a person. But he doesn't seem to realize it. He's got more to live for."

"I think the thought of Klara at home has been keeping him together. I really do."

"He's lost a lot in this war. A lot of friends, time with his family, his childhood. He was fourteen when he took responsibility for all his friends. That's incredible of him, and he lost hope for anything else. He believes he's just going to die in the military," Johann sighed, putting his hands on his knees, "I think he's given up."

"How is he? What did he say?"

"He sounded distressed. When he was talking about everyone he should've saved, watching them die, especially seeing them dead. Especially Tristan," Johann gathered himself, "I would expect someone to cry over death, especially your friends. But what really stood out was when we started talking about how we used to run together, about how he was going to be in the Olympics. He was ready to cry at the end of that. He misses it. He told me he had ideas of what he could do once he was an Olympic athlete. But he said he'd trade the Olympics just for things to go back to the way they were. You know, when you, Ivo, and he just went running, training for a school meet."

Blaz smiled, and wrapped his arms around himself against the cold, "*Und?*"

"He was going to get to see the world while getting to do what he loved and he worked so hard to get there, but he never made it. And it was no fault of his own."

"He could still be in the Olympics, right? He's still really fast."

"Look at him right now," Johann flat out ordered Blaz, "Does he look strong? Like an Olympic athlete?"

Koby was out of the trench, with his knapsack where his spare clothing was. He was in his sleeveless undershirt, which was noticeably loose. Koby pulled out his long-sleeved undershirt and slid quickly out of his sleeveless shirt. No resistance from the shirt. No friction. His back and arms had lost muscle since September. Blaz only noticed this now. His all-too-visible ribcage was the thickest part of his chest, his washboard abs were gone. His face was more skeletal, and his eyes sallow. Koby didn't even bother unbuttoning his undershirt, and just slid into it. His *Wehrmacht* uniform, which he'd had for over a year now, looked loose too.

"Doesn't look good, does it?" Johann asked.

"He looks worse than me and Ivo," Blaz said, "He used to be really strong."

"His body is broken Blaz. He's never going to be able to get back to where he was. I bet he weighs the same now as he did at fourteen."

"He got stronger though, he was in the best shape of his life a year ago."

"*Ja*, but now look. He's a withered husk of his former self. The last thing he said when we were talking was, 'Can't anymore, I'm weak,' he rubbed his shins, '*Zu spät.*'" Too late.

"He deserved better. Hard worker, big-hearted, and a love for kids," Blaz took off his helmet.

"Have you lost weight Blaz? Are the conditions this bad all over?" Johann asked, partially hoping to change the subject.

"I have, just not as much as Koby," Blaz said, and unbuttoned his field-gray uniform. Then, like Koby, slid off his long-sleeved undershirt.

"*Ja*," Johann looked at Blaz, and sighed gravely, "Just like the rest of the German people."

"You know, I used to have a six pack," Blaz raised his eyebrows at Johann, "I was still doing ab exercises last year until November or so, around when food started to come in short supply. Can't keep that up without some fuel."

"*Nein*," Johann said, feeling his chest in his baggy uniform, "I used to have one too. We were all looking fabulous at the KLV camp," he laughed. Blaz grinned on hearing Johann's short, high-pitched laugh.

"Not anymore," Johann said, wistfully, as he leaned his head back against the trench. His head snapped forward immediately.

"What happened?"

"Face hit some dirt," Johann said, pointing to his burnt skin under the wrapping.

"Okay, are you all right?"

"I am good."

"*Gut.*"

"Are you cold?" Johann asked Blaz, who hadn't put his undershirt or uniform back on.

"It isn't that cold. It's been worse."

Johann shrugged then returned to the question of Koby, "I think he'll come around. He just needs some time."

"Do we have time?"

Johann grimaced, "We might not."

Blaz sighed, making his breath visible in the cold. He reached to touch it, knowing he would feel nothing. It didn't hurt to try, though. "Did you get to meet your mother's new husband?" he asked.

"I actually did," Johann said, and surprisingly, did so with enthusiasm.

"How did you like him? What is he like?"

"He's everything I could've hoped for. I'll never forget papa, but Rudolf is a great man."

"What did you guys talk about?"

"He told me about how my mother and he met, and about his time in the war. He's on leave from Berlin right now. He heads back any day."

"How did they meet?"

"My mother went to work in a munitions factory in Berlin. She worked there for quite a while, it was mostly women working in the factory. One day, he comes in and starts working next to her, his arm is in a sling, but he's still working. He actually demanded that they allow him to work in the factory while he was recovering from wounds he got in North Africa. I don't know how to explain how it all happened, I wasn't there. But they worked together for five months, and before he left for battle again, he proposed. And she said, '*Ja.*' He went off to fight in France, got wounded, came back, and got wounded again during a battle in the Ardennes around Christmas of forty-four. He's almost recovered so he'll be ready to fight, wherever they need him. Likely Berlin, maybe here if they order him to stay."

"Probably here. They don't want to waste any fuel getting him to Berlin."

Johann raised his eyebrows at that, "But he has a lot of awards, the Wound Badge, the Iron Cross Second and First Class, and the Knight's Cross."

"Wow," Blaz gaped.

"He's an accomplished sniper. But he really seemed to take an interest in me. Like it was something that would make his life better. I imagined he'd be disappointed, like I'd be a distraction from the two of them. He talked with me for almost four hours, all through the night. He asked me about me. The only grown-ups that have ever done that are my father and mother."

"No one else?"

"Well, *ja*. My grandparents didn't really like me, they only talked with my parents," Johann explained, "They never paid attention to me. Father told me that the depression really changed them."

"It changed a lot of people."

"Did your grandparents-"

"They did," Blaz answered, "My grandparents visited more in the early years when I was younger. They came back in thirty-eight, I think it was. My papa and grandpa moved on to a discussion about politics and the *Führer*. I didn't really understand it then, I probably would now. I think they were talking about the *Hitlerjugend*. My father was going to enter me then, but he held off, I think because he felt he had to after what he did. My father got into a shouting match with grandpa. They left when he yelled something, I can't remember quite what it was. But he insulted his father. Horribly. They got up and left. Father realized what he'd done a minute later and ran out after them, yelling, 'Father, I'm sorry!' They were gone though. And they haven't spoken to each other since."

"Wow, I'm really sorry," Johann said.

"Ah, it's all right. I never knew them all that well."

"Well, that's what I think will be different about Rudolf. He cares about us. And I'm going to have a little brother. Due in April. Mother is excited about it. She wasn't supposed to be able to have kids anymore, but we got blessed with another."

"When did they get married?"

"As soon as he came back from his second wound, last July. He got wounded in Normandy," Johann said with a yawn.

"Tired?"

"*Ja*. But who cares?"

Blaz grinned then looked beyond the trench into the forest, standing up and climbing out for a better view.

No one coming from the forest. No enemies on the plains. None in the bottleneck.

All was well.

SS Inspections

"*Eine kleines Blümelein... und das heißt: Erika! Heiß von Hunderttausend–*"

"Shut up, Hermann!"

"*Bienelein*," the singing trooper finished, getting a glare from his comrade. The eleven and twelve-year-old Hitler Youths at the flak guns had drawn much solace from the fact no attack had come and were busy goofing off, climbing on their flak guns. *Herr* Schneider had let it slide, allowing them to enjoy their last days of childhood. They weren't going to be kids for long.

"Look sharp men," Schneider told the *Wehrmacht* and *Hitlerjugend* troops at the post, "The SS is sending troops to inspect our position. Standard procedure, just keep straight faces, stay at your posts. Spread out across the trenches."

"*Jawohl, Herr* Schneider," came the answers.

"Oh," Schneider said, snapping a finger. He spun to face the Hitler Youths who were climbing on the flak guns they were posted at. "That means no climbing on the flak guns," he told them sternly.

"*Jawohl Unterfeldwebel*," the children laughed.

Blaz was cleaning his rifle when the SS arrived. He paused his maintenance to give his attention to them. Only two officers came with one additional man in the form of an *Allgemeine-SS* guard. The rest of the SS was spread out in defense or patrolling the town.

"*Heil* Hitler," the first SS officer, a lean man of fair stature saluted Schneider.

"*Heil* Hitler," Schneider saluted back. Blaz went back to maintaining his rifle. "How goes the inspections?"

"Fine enough," the officer said, then lowered his voice, "Your boys will have to perform flawlessly to win this battle. We need to give the Americans and British time to reach Berlin."

"That's what it has come to?"

"Germany may survive if that happens," the officer said lowly, "I'm Simon Stromschnellen."

"Karl Schneider."

"*Schön, sie zu treffen,*" Stromschnellen said, shaking Schneider's hand. He gestured to the officer next to him, a stocky man with red hair showing under his cap, "This is Derry Kurzmann."

Blaz looked up when he heard this name. It was one of his former instructors. If Ivo had not been in the bunker, he would have undoubtedly beaten everyone to the punch. But Johann did this time.

"*Guten tag, Herr* Kurzmann," he waved from his position. Stromschnellen turned with uncanny quickness to zero in on Johann. Unprofessional of Johann to interrupt officers, but Stromschnellen relented when he saw Johann's bandaged face. Kurzmann squinted at Johann, as he had not seen this kid in years, and the last time he had, Johann had all the skin on his face, no wrapping and all the hair on his head. And a higher pitched voice. Stromschnellen gestured for Kurzmann to speak to Johann, who did not hesitate to proceed.

"General Heinrici and Busse inspected our major positions personally. We are to maintain them daily, until our intelligence brings word of an impending attack," Stromschnellen continued, "For now-"

Blaz jumped out of his trench and strode over to where Kurzmann had leapt in to see Johann.

"*Ach ja*, you are the young kid, second to our Olympic runner. Where is he anyway?"

"Right here," Koby said, while playing with a bullet in his hand.

"*Guten tag, Herr...* Herzen?"

"Hertz."

"Near. How are you boys doing?"

"We're alive," Blaz replied.

Kurzmann managed a chuckle, "*Ja*, I suppose that's all one can say."

"And you?" Johann asked.

"Been all right. The SS has been busy, many partisans to stop, much front line fighting this past year. Got some help from a local in locating partisans in Budapest. I tell you, that eased my job."

"Why are you here now?"

"It was either Seelow, Berlin, or Prague. I'd rather face my downfall or ultimate victory earlier rather than later."

"I suppose so," Koby agreed.

"Derry! Time to give our inspection," Stromschnellen called.

"*Jawohl, Standartenführer. Auf wiedersehen jungen*," *Herr* Kurzmann waved and leapt out of the trench, with the same grace as he had leapt into the KLV camp. Stromschnellen gave him a confused sneer at why he'd called him "*Standartenführer*," instead of Simon or Stromschnellen. Kurzmann shrugged and they laughed it off. The concrete bunker was the first place they examined. Stromschnellen frowned subtlety as he left, hiding his face by removing his cap. He'd seen that most of the troops were in their forties or were teenagers. Now he moved to the flak gun crews. The young Hitler Youths had stopped climbing on the guns as ordered, and stood at attention, something they knew how to do well. Their hands were glued to their sides, backs straight, eyes forward. Stromschnellen stroked his cap nervously at the sight of what some of his troops looked like. Eleven and twelve-year-olds. Only two men in their twenties and only two or three in their late thirties. The two SS officers looked at each other before continuing.

"Well, everything seems to be in order," Stromschnellen said, "Would reinforcements help your position? Would you like to file a request?"

"*Nein, Standartenführer,*" Schneider replied.

"*Gut,*" Stromschnellen said as he turned to leave and put his cap back on over his slick blond hair, "We don't have any for you anyway."

Schneider rolled his eyes, but let it go, "Nice to have met you," Schneider said extending his hand in a parting greeting, "Good luck, Simon."

"You too. *Heil* Hitler."

Bullets

January 20, 1945

While Königsberg continued her fight, Seelow sat awaiting the Red Army. A good night's sleep, a third of a frozen loaf of bread for breakfast, and Blaz was ready for another day. Schneider and his friends had gone on a walk to get a grip on their surroundings.

Johann was over with the flak squad of one gun, chatting away with them. Ivo had finally been given leave from the bunker, as it was apparent they'd have warning if the Russians attacked. They weren't on the front line of defense, but scouts had confirmed the Russians would slow to a halt until Königsberg fell, so Ivo no longer had to be in the bunker on watch around the clock. Blaz and Ivo lay down on the edge of the ridge, rifles raised, as if they were sniping men passing through the two ridges.

"*Feuer!*" Ivo whispered and pretended that his rifle had kicked back. Blaz repeated the action.

"Too bad we can't take practice shots," Ivo said, "We aren't that far from where the shooting range was."

"You know we don't have the ammunition to burn," Blaz told Ivo, "Every single bullet counts at this point."

"*Ja*, it's a shame though."

"No one said it wasn't."

Hellstorm

February 1, 1945

"*Heil* Hitler!" a *Volkssturm* man greeted Schneider, carrying two bags over his shoulders as the sun was ending its descent in the sky, "I have letters for your company, you want to help me search for them?"

"*Na sicher*," Schneider nodded and took one bag from the man, "Read off the names to my friend here," Schneider said, gesturing to another soldier.

The older man nodded and began reading. Schneider quickly went through letters, handing the ones with a recognized name to one of his men. It took a while, and they moved into the bunker for light but letters were found for most everyone who still had people who would write to them.

Koby and Blaz received a letter from their fathers. Johann also got one. Ivo received one, from his father. He frowned when he read it but shoved the paper into a pocket nonetheless. Blaz and Koby held each other's hands to form one fist, while they slid their letters out of the envelope. Blaz breathed a sigh of relief, followed by Koby doing the same. Ottoway seemed to be lucky in war, his letter told Blaz about his squad being one of few to escape the failed Siege of Bastogne. Unfortunately, Ottoway's squad was on a long run away from the advancing Allied forces now. Peace had to be made with the West, Ottoway told Blaz.

I know, I know! It's coming soon.

Blaz looked up from the bunker's light to hear light sobbing from another trooper, who covered his face and ran out into the darkness. One of his friends got up to chase after him, but an older soldier took him by the arm, and shook his head. The soldier sat back down, putting a hand on his forehead in distress. Blaz folded his letter and slid it into his little bag, to read again another time. He turned around to hear the quietest of sobbing. Werner had his head buried in between his knees, clearly trying to hide from his squad mates. Blaz scooted toward him quietly. Werner noticed and stood up, grabbed his rifle and stormed out of the bunker. Blaz went after him. But Koby grabbed on the back of his collar. Blaz turned around and shook his head. Koby let him go.

"*Verdämmt!*" was the first thing Blaz heard Werner scream and the sound of a boot hitting bark, "*Scheiße!* God, why now? Damn Brits!"

Blaz inched closer but a hand grabbed him. This time with much more force, and it yanked him into a trench. At last Blaz was released, and the hand was revealed to be Jarman's.

"Leave him alone," Jarman whispered.

"But-"

"He won't hurt himself," Jarman assured Blaz.

"Are you sure?"

"*Ja*, I am."

"What happened?" Blaz asked.

"*Ich weiß nicht*," Jarman answered.

"Do you know anything?"

"Berlin got bombed, but that's normal at this point. The Allies are stepping up bombings. Especially on populated areas, where our families live. Swine."

"They just keep beating us down," Blaz scowled, "We're already out."

"The war isn't lost Blaz," Jarman said, though not with his usual matter-of-fact tone. This time it was a plea, "We're only a few behind."

Blaz sighed, "But how? I want to have faith in final victory, but I can't see it."

"Just trust in the *Führer*, he will do what is best for *Deutschland*."

"What if we get defeated here at Seelow?" Blaz shivered at the horrible idea, "And the *Führer* is in Berlin?"

"He will do what's best. Whether that be to die in Berlin or flee to rebuild *Deutschland* later. He'll never surrender, then we'd be helpless without him."

"But we keep dying. If we fight to the last man, the German race will cease to exist!" Blaz begged Jarman, though neither had power to do anything, "If we surrender, the German people can be restored."

"It would be better that we die off than succumb to the egalitarian Marxists and decadent Capitalism."

"One day the world will know that we were right, won't it?"

Jarman looked out of the trench, into the dark, snowy forest, "I doubt it," Jarman admitted, "Once we defeat them, only *Deutschland* will know. We used to say that 'the whole world would belong to our freedom,' now, I admit," Jarman paused, "It may not even be in *Deutschland*. The war is lo-" Jarman couldn't finish. For the first time since his father's death, tears ran down his face. "Our Third Reich…"

Werner had gotten control of himself. He climbed into the trench near two sleeping soldiers. Blaz had brought Ivo, and waved Johann over.

"How are you doing?" asked Johann.

"Do you guys have to come over here?" Werner asked, "Just leave me alone."

"Blaz told me you have some questions," Johann replied, changing Werner's focus.

"*Nein*," Werner shook his head, "I don't."

"Werner, do you think you are going to die?" Blaz spat out.

Werner's eyes darted over to Blaz.

"*Ja*, of course! Everyone dies. Even little kids. No one lives!" Werner shouted, kicking his foot against the back of the trench, "Tristan died! My half-brother, my only family left, just died! H-Hans died. Nobody lives," he said, shaking his head.

"What happens when you die?" Johann asked.

"I don't know. We go to a better place, I think?" Werner said.

"Are you a good person Werner?" Johann asked. Ivo leaned in closer.

"What?" Werner stammered, taken aback by this question, "Sure, I guess. What do you mean?"

"Do you need help sometimes? Are you perfect?"

"*Nein*," Werner shook his head, "There's better men than me out there."

"Well, only perfection can compete with perfection. And imperfection only makes it if it admits it is imperfect and asks for mercy from its superior. The strong have no necessity for the weak, but he wants to help the weak. That's all. You've been to church before, I assume? Living in Detmold?"

Werner nodded.

"Well, you know who the superior is, he's who you go to," Johann leapt out of the trench, and started walking away.

Ivo and Blaz and Werner, three *Wehrmacht* soldiers, looked back to each other in surprise. They knew they were weak.

February 2, 1945

"Whole family?" Koby whispered in shock to Blaz in the darkness, as they'd been assigned to keep watch. Blaz leaned against a tree outside of the trench, with his shirt off, holding his rifle across his chest. Koby also had taken his shirt off, it was a bit of an unspoken contest that they maintained the habit from their time in the Hitler Youth.

"All of them now. His younger siblings and parents died in an air raid," Blaz nodded, as Werner had lost much of his family already before they'd even met him, "What kind of a world is it where soldiers' families die but the soldiers live?"

Koby sighed, "I don't know."

Germany Against All

February 7, 1945

The next few days brought frigid weather. Gunther returned to the Knights, who, was disillusioned when he realized Nico wasn't there. Soldiers fell ill with fevers and rasping coughs. *Herr* Schneider briefly showed symptoms but shook them quickly. A good third of the men were ill though, unable to keep watch, and in bad condition for fighting. Some had difficulty even holding their rifles firmly. Johann was one such case, along with Ivo and, to everyone's shock, Jarman. All the sick soldiers were kept in the bunker. Koby kept up his tireless work. Even volunteering immediately to run to Seelow for a medic.

"How does he do it?" Gunther asked when Koby went bounding down the hill and into the seemingly endless fields.

"I sure don't know," Werner shook his head.

"Is it just me, or does he look a lot skinnier? And not in a good way," Gunther added.

"It's not just you. I didn't notice it until Johann pointed it out," Blaz admitted.

"He must've lost seven or eight kilograms. Maybe ten! And most of that was solid muscle!" Gunther said in disbelief.

"You look thinner too, Gunther," Werner said, and Gunther's surprised expression said everything.

"They kept us on rations. Really low ones in the hospital starting in December or so. And they said I wasn't critical enough to take off rations. I was starving half the time, just waiting for something to eat."

"Do we get more here?" Werner asked.

"Definitely, but I imagine you guys do a bit more than people in a hospital all day. I was well fed until December. All that I've lost is from mid-December to now," Gunther said, "But still not enough food here."

"Not enough for *Deutschland*," Werner corrected, "Everyone is looking badly, nowadays. Not horrible, but bad. If this has been going on for a while. I'd hate to be a prisoner to us. If we can't feed our own people, how are we going to feed them?"

Gunther shook his head, "We need help from the West quickly. I know we don't like them, but it'll save a lot of people to stop the Reds."

"Are we even able to challenge them offensively, anymore?" Werner asked, "Did you hear anything in Berlin?"

"News got worse every time. We frequently were told to limp down to the basement because of bombing raids. We lost a battle in the Ardennes. Sounded like that was our final push. Now it's up to the defense to stop them."

Frustration at High Command

February 9, 1945

Reynald Schlusser strode across the school football field with long, rapid strides in the moonlight while Russian artillery echoed in the distance. He held a briefcase and two rolled up maps under his arm, like a professor between classes. In his hand, he held a pen, a pencil, and a protractor. Another SS officer ran across the field to catch up with him, carrying a sealed envelope.

"Kurzmann," Schlusser nodded.

"Schlusser."

"How goes it?" Schlusser asked.

"I don't look forward to any reports this evening," Kurzmann said, putting a hand on his forehead.

"Neither do I."

Kurzmann opened the school door for Schlusser and the two walked at speed toward the classroom turned war room. General Gotthard Heinrici stood at the table, along with the top five *Wehrmacht* officers: Steiner, Schmidt, Fliegel, Berghoff, and Reichert. SS officers Hadler, Lochner, and Stromschnellen were also present. Engal sat on a bench at the table holding a wet cloth on his forehead, eyes closed. The room remained silent when Schlusser and Kurzmann entered. No cigarettes or alcohol were seen. Many of the officers held their canteens in their hands, filled with water.

"Gentlemen," Heinrici began, "As you are aware the Russians have halted, we discussed this, and about General Wenck, the Königsberg garrison, and whatnot. I need reports from each of you regarding the hearsay of illness in our ranks. *Hauptmann* Steiner, you first."

"*Heil* Hitler," Steiner saluted, "General, I've thoroughly swept the northern corridor and northeast defenses. There is a sickness breaking out amongst the men, should the Russians attack now these men will be slaughtered if they fight. They need time to recover. As much as we can give them."

"Schmidt!"

"Nothing differing from Steiner, sir," Schmidt modestly admitted, "At least a quarter of the men in the eastern defenses are sick in some way, I estimate."

"My estimations say the same," Fliegel added, "From the data I gathered in the southern defenses."

"I concur," Reichert said.

"General, I recommend we bring our armor near the front to intimidate the Bolsheviks and discourage them from driving through to Berlin. We need more time to rest up our men," Berghoff suggested.

"I object," Steiner dissented, "Our armor must stay hidden, we should make their aerial spying worthless by keeping the armor where they are. Camouflaged and hidden. The Soviets can only see about half our forces through the air. Let their imaginations discourage them from attacking. When they see less armor, they may believe we are hiding something. If our armor was moved and they did not buy it, an attack would devastate us. Without armor, we cannot win. Our tanks must have the high ground and distance. The Soviets have numbers, without a doubt. We estimate two and a half million men for their Berlin attack force. A good fifth of the entire Red Army! *Nein*, we must use our tanks and guns cleverly. Intimidation is not a weapon we have."

Berghoff stayed silent with a quite serious look on his face. Heinrici nodded and turned to the SS officers. "Report, *Hauptsturmführer* Schlusser."

"General," Schlusser said, unrolling each map. He laid helmets on each end. Heinrici adjusted his glasses as Schlusser began. "Here we have the Seelow Heights, and here we have the entire Berlin area. I have confirmed illnesses across the Heights. High fevers, rashes, and hacking coughs. Engal here has a mild case. Worse, it is affecting both young men, old men, and *Hitlerjugend*. We are running out of resources as the democracies advance in the West. Our medics are working around the clock. Food supplies are barely enough. Our army, too many of them look like walking skeletons with skin. Also, we have, what, hundreds?" Schlusser looked to Kurzmann who nodded after glancing down at his now open envelope. Schlusser continued, "Hundreds of serious cases. And thousands of cases overall. The men are worn down, and starving. Many of these men have been fleeing from the Reds or fighting for quite some time. Our best troops are here, alongside some our most ill-prepared. Nonetheless General, the *Volkssturm* must be deployed when the Russians attack. We have three and a half thousand from Seelow and the surrounding towns available as reinforcements," Schlusser said, pointing to several small towns in the Seelow area on the map.

"Deployed? What of the towns?" Lochner asked. As he said this, a distant artillery blast sounded.

"It is best that we keep the fight outside of the towns. The girls, women, elderly and young boys needn't suffer a battle," Schlusser answered.

The *Wehrmacht* officers all nodded at this, Steiner adding, "I second that proposal."

"I am inclined to agree. Send word to the *Volkssturm* captains," Heinrici ordered Berghoff and Steiner, who exited. "On that note, it is not in my power to do anything about this sickness. The medics must make do with what they have," he said to the remaining, quite distressed *Wehrmacht* officers, "You three are dismissed."

Heinrici redirected his attention to the *Allgemeine-SS Obersturmbannführer* and *Sturmbannführer*. "Lochner, Hadler. You have kept an iron fist on the towns, correct?"

"No attempts at desertion in Seelow or the surrounding towns, sir."

"*Gut*. Continue. *Waffen-SS*, if the battle should come I will expect you four to be up front with the troops. They will need the encouragement."

"*Jawohl*, General," the *Waffen-SS* officers nodded, expecting and embracing these orders.

"Dismissed, get some sleep. I don't want my command getting sick," Heinrici said with a faint smile. The officers thanked their general and headed out. Schlusser turned at Heinrici's voice, "Anna, Sprague, that means you too," he said to his secretary and Hitler Youth adjutant. Schlusser left behind them.

The Little Ones

February 10, 1945

As the sun rose in the east, the sick soldiers woke but remained laying on bunker floor. Jarman tried to get up, but Koby insisted he sit down. Jarman obliged his commanding officer. Several healthy soldiers sat next to ill comrades, hands over their eyes and mouths, in worriment. The younger Hitler Youths came to the entrance of the bunker with one of the rare soldiers in his twenties. He lined up the ten boys, on the three steps descending into the bunker. The sick and well soldiers watched the kids organize, each child held either a pistol, a submachine gun, or a rifle as professionally as they knew how with their Hitler Youth daggers strapped to their belts. They formed one row a five, one row of four, and one stood in the front who took out a flute from his little bag and began to play. When he restarted the same melody, another Youth stepped forward. His high voice did not match the words, but soon smiles were appearing across the room, from the ill and the well.

Siehst du im Osten das Morgenrot? Ein Zeichen zur Freiheit, zur Sonne!
Wir halten zusammen, auf Leben und Tod, Lass' kommen,
was immer da wolle!
Warum jetzt noch zweifeln, Hört auf mit dem Hadern;
Noch fließt uns Deutsches Blut in den Adern!

Do you see in the east the morning red? A sign of freedom, the Sun!
We hold together, through life and death, Let come here whatever it may be!
Why now do you doubt? Do not cast the blame,
Because still flows German blood in our veins!

The entire choir sung the next words and did so at the end of each stanza.

Volk ans Gewehr!
Volk ans Gewehr!

People to arms!
People to arms!

The flautist continued through the choir's brief pause, and many men sat up on their mats. All eyes, save the dedicated lookout were on the German boys. The first singer stepped back into his row of four at the front. A second boy stepped up, cap leaning to the side of his head revealing slick red hair.

Viele Jahren zogen dahin, Geknechtet das Volk und betrogen.
Verräter und Juden hatten gewinn, Sie forderten Opfer Legionen!
Im Volke geboren, Erstand uns ein Führer,
Gab Glaube und Hoffnung an Deutschland uns Wieder!

Volk ans Gewehr!
Volk ans Gewehr!

Many years passed here, Our people enslaved and deceived.
Traitors and Jews had profit, They demanded the sacrifice of millions!
In our people born, arose us a leader,
Who gave faith and hope to Germany again!
People to arms!
People to arms!

Some men nodded at the lyrics and tapped their feet to the tune. Not a frown remained. The last boy, bearing the signature look of the German people, stepped forward.

Jugend und Alter- Mann für Mann, Umklammern das Hakenkreuzbanner.
Ob Bürger, ob Bauer, ob Arbeitsmann,
Sie schwingen das Schwert und den Hammer.
Für Hitler, für Freiheit, für Arbeit und Brot!
Deutschland erwache, Ende die Not!
Volk ans Gewehr!
Volk... ans... Gewehr!

Youth and elderly- Man for man, Cling to the Swastika banner.
Whether farmer, civilian, or working man,
they swing the sword and the hammer.
For Hitler, for freedom, for work, and for bread!
Germany awake, end the suffering!
People to arms!
People... To... Arms!

The bunker erupted with applause and cheers. Jarman stood up to clap for them, but Blaz could see Koby's eyes dart over to Jarman every few seconds. Ivo managed to sit up for them, Johann only managed to prop himself up by leaning on his elbows. Many of the sick soldiers did their best to stand.

"Nothing like a good march song to uplift the spirit. *Ja?*" Blaz said, elbowing Koby.

"Nothing like it," Koby said, his gaze elsewhere, "Nothing like it."

"Feeling all right?" Blaz asked, in a semi-serious tone.

"What? *Ja, sicher.*"

"*Gut.*"

Ivo laid back down, exhausted from simply applauding. Johann was already fast asleep. Koby's relief that they hadn't overdone it was apparent.

"Come on, Blaz," Koby said and led the way out of the bunker past the younger boys, and out to the trenches, "Gunther, would you keep an eye on them? Just for a bit."

"*Absolut*, Koby," Gunther sprung out of the trench, leaving Werner, who watched Gunther duck into the bunker. Then he redirected his attention to the forest. Koby and Blaz leapt across the trenches and down the hill. Koby stayed close to the ridge, leading on the edge of the fields.

"What's going on?" Blaz asked, after a few minutes of walking in silence.

"Just getting away from it all. You know?" he said, lying down on his back to look straight up at the sky, "Wow."

Blaz remained standing.

"Come on, Blaz."

Blaz lay down next to Koby, staring directly into the sky. The ground was snowy.

"Just look at it. Look at that sunrise," Koby said, "You know, it really is beautiful."

"*Wunderschön*," Blaz repeated.

"You remember when we watched the sun set at the track meet?" Koby asked.

Blaz thought for a moment, "*Nein.*"

"*Nein?* Think harder. You said, 'There's a plan.'"

Blaz racked his brain, and finally it hit him, "*Ja*, I remember that. You, Ivo, and me. We got our uniforms too. How could I forget that day?"

"What happened to it all?" Koby wondered, though he clearly wasn't asking Blaz for an answer.

When Everything Falls Apart

February 11, 1945

"Jesus Christ," the medic murmured, holding a palm on Johann's forehead, "He's on fire."

"What can you do about it?" Schneider asked as he knelt next to the medic. The other soldiers in the bunker were all listening. Koby paced furiously, hand over his eyes. Stromschnellen stood above Schneider with his helmet strapped to his back and cap held at his side.

"There's not much I can do," the medic admitted, "One of the highest fevers I've ever encountered."

"What do you recommend?" Stromschnellen asked, frustrated his best medic had nothing to say.

"Keep a cold cloth on him, remove his jacket, no blankets," the medic said, "Move him closer to the bunker entrance. This bunker retains heat, especially with all the men."

Stromschnellen frowned. The medic locked eyes with him and shook his head. He had no medicine, and Stromschnellen knew it. The men moved out of the bunker, bringing Johann to the entrance. Koby knelt at Johann's side, listening intently.

"I don't know," the medic said, removing his glasses, "I've had a few cases like this in the past week, but we can't find anything effective. Send for me immediately if he gets worse. Someone as young as him can't have a fever like this for long."

"I need you to get this boy better, Roland. I don't want anyone dying from a sickness here. That is unacceptable."

"I don't know what to tell you," Roland replied, "If I had better equipment, some medicine, perhaps, I could deal with this. But we have none."

"I know," Stromschnellen glowered at the ground.

"Hold on, how bad is this fever?" Schneider asked the medic.

"I don't know if his body can take this. He hasn't eaten much as I understand it. He's lost a lot of weight in the last week and has been unconscious for a good portion of each day. It doesn't bode well. He needs to recover soon. Everything seems to be falling apart."

"Stow it," Stromschnellen grunted, his eyes gesturing to the troops.

"Sorry, sir."

Schneider kicked at the snow, and held his helmet at his belt, "*Danke* for coming personally, *Standartenführer*."

"It's my duty, *Unterfeldwebel*," Stromschnellen nodded, putting his field cap on, "*Gott mit uns!*"

"*Gott mit uns*," Schneider mumbled and waved goodbye to the two Germans.

Blaz, Werner, and Gunther huddled in a trench, and watched the *Standartenführer* and medic disappear down the hill.

"They did not look encouraging," Werner observed.

"He must get better," Blaz hoped aloud, "He has to."

Through Life and Death

February 12, 1945

Blaz woke up in the middle of the night to a shout. Koby.

He shot from the trench. Werner and Gunther followed. Blaz ducked into the bunker. Koby was crying over Johann, his head on the boy's heart. Johann's expression was eerily peaceful and even beautiful despite his burns. His skeletal arms lay limp at his sides, Koby held one of Johann's hands under his chest and with his other hand he held Johann's head.

Blaz gasped at the lifeless body. Tears ran in rivers down his face. He turned out of the bunker, Gunther just ahead of him. He dropped to a knee outside and clenched his jaw, sniffling. He slammed a fist into the snow to stop his tears.

Nein God, not Johann. Why did you take Johann?

Herr Schneider hurried to the bunker with Gunther at his side. Schneider stopped without warning at the entrance of the bunker, removed his cap, and ducked inside. At Gunther's words, Blaz came into the bunker. Schneider put a hand on Koby's shoulder. Koby shook it off. Schneider recoiled, but stayed at Koby's side through it all.

Finally, Koby released himself from Johann and removed his supporting hand from his friend's head. Johann's head gently leaned to his right, the same calm expression stayed. Koby straightened up, remained on his knees, and kept his eyes fixed on Johann. Desperately, pitifully, hoping that Johann might wake up if he just waited patiently. Minutes upon minutes passed with Johann remaining still, not a flinch. Koby's breath trembled as he came to realization: Johann wasn't coming back. And once again, he could do nothing about it.

Koby didn't leave Johann's side through the night. He remained quiet, looking to Johann every few minutes imagining he might have moved. Blaz stayed at Johann's other side, holding his hand.

"Schneider sent for his step father," Blaz said, "Shouldn't tell him this now."

Koby didn't reply.

"He looks so calm. How?" Blaz asked, staring at Johann's final, lasting expression.

"I don't know. But I guess Johann would be." Koby smiled, patting Johann's head lightly and affectionately.

"How?"

"He woke up, his forehead was burning," Koby struggled to explain, "He was breathing rapidly, his heart was racing. We held hands through it all, I thought he was going to relax, and start to breathe normal, and fall back asleep. He nodded to me, looked at me before he went, and just lost his breath and strength. I felt the life leave him when his hand slackened." Koby's face was stained with dry tears, "I loved him, Blaz. I never had a friend like him."

The squad left that morning, with Koby and Blaz carrying Johann's body. Ivo mustered the strength to come.

Rudolf, *Frau* Steiner, and Johann's siblings met them outside of Seelow. *Frau* Steiner simply broke down seeing her oldest son dead. Rudolf hugged her tightly. The Steiner children burst into tears upon realizing their older brother was dead. Rudolf took Johann in his arms, kissing the boy's forehead. *Frau* Steiner repeated the action several times over. As *Frau* Steiner knew Johann would've wanted, they took him to the church cemetery and began digging a grave. They were not the only ones there. Johann had not been the only one to fall to the plague sweeping through Germany. Another boy, older than Johann, was being lowered into a grave.

Koby shoveled slowly, still looking to Johann's body between every scoop of dirt, hoping Johann might still come back. And as the grave was finished, Koby gave a last glance.

Rudolf and Blaz wrapped Johann in cloth, as that was all they had, and lowered Johann's body into the grave, gently placing him on the ground. Koby couldn't bring himself to cover Johann in dirt, so Werner and Gunther did the job. Ivo and Jarman finished inscribing words and symbols into a white cross. When the grave was covered, they planted the cross over him. Inscribed were Johann's full name, his birthday, and day he died: *Johann Audwin Engal Steiner, November 15, 1929- February 12, 1945.* In the center of the white Christian cross was an Iron Cross and a small swastika in the middle.

Koby nodded to himself, eyes locked on the cross. As if he'd finished a debate with himself. One-by-one, the soldiers left to return to their posts as ordered. Koby, Blaz, and Ivo were the last there along with Rudolf.

"I'm sorry, sir," Koby said at last.

"I'm sorry too, son," Rudolf replied, "He was a good kid."

"*Ja*. He was. I never thought he would go like this. Never."

Blaz and Ivo turned away and trudged back through the snow.

"Johann, why Johann?" Ivo wondered.

"Nobody knows why. Johann had a future."

"*Ja*," Ivo nodded his head weakly. He stopped to regain his composure, "Even after killing those people."

"I don't know how he could have pulled the trigger. God. Johann."

"Only fifteen," Ivo shook his head.

The Final Hours Approach

Koby stood on the roof of the bunker, watching the sun disappear beyond the Heights. Blaz stood behind him.

"He was ready, Blaz. Ready to die."

Blaz stared into the distance, without replying to Koby's assertion.

"You know. We see and talk about death a lot."

Blaz nodded, though Koby's back was to him.

"We cry a lot. Why?"

"Better way of coping with loss than anger, I guess," Blaz answered. Though he'd done both and had come to hate them equally. It meant someone had gone either way.

1945: The Battle of Seelow Heights

Führer Command! We Follow!

April 15, 1945

"General, with the fall of Königsberg last week, the Russian attack should come any time," Schlusser informed the high command at the early evening meeting.

"Shall we deploy the reserves?" Steiner requested of Busse and Heinrici.

"*Jawohl*, send the Ninth Army's reserves out of the towns," Busse agreed.

"Very well," Heinrici consented, motioning to Lochner and Hadler, "*Obersturmbannführer, Sturmbannführer*. Deploy the reserves immediately. Deal with deserters how you see git."

"*Jawohl*, General," they saluted.

"*Waffen-SS* and army; pull the front lines back to our second line," Heinrici ordered.

"General?" Berghoff asked to make sure he heard correctly.

"You heard me. We are going there now to pull the troops back," Heinrici replied and motioned for the officers to follow him. He led them outside to three cars. Heinrici handed the key of one to Stromschnellen and another to Busse

"*Standartenführer*, General," Heinrici said, "Withdraw your *Waffen-SS* and all other troops from the front along the defenses in the north, I will take the central defenses, Busse, the south."

Stromschnellen jumped into the driver's seat, Fliegel, Kurzmann, and Reichert joined him. Busse waved Berghoff, Schmidt, and Engal to him. The two cars drove off.

Heinrici took the wheel of the third car, adjusted his glasses, and gazed gravely around at Schlusser, Steiner, and his Hitler Youth adjutant, "The game has begun. We cast our lot," the General said as he slowly pulled away from the school gates.

The Failed Artillery Strikes

April 16, 1945

Troops marched past the boys, taking up new positions in The Heights. Heinrici had been wise to move the troops back, because as they marched past, artillery sounded in the distance. Blaz watched as the night sky was lit with explosions. The artillery consistently hit the front lines, but steadily worked its way closer to their position.

"*Scheiße!*" Jarman shouted and leapt into the trench, covering his head when he hit the bottom. Five young Hitler Youths were on top of him in seconds, terrified of the explosions. This time it was different. The Russians were firing innumerable shells. Explosions erupted from the ground, around their position, some narrowly missing the bunker. Fortunately, it was short-range artillery. It still only took one lucky shot.

"*Nein!* Stay down!" Koby shouted dragging back Werner into the trench. A shell exploded meters away.

"Oh God," Gunther repeated several times, speaking fast, "We're dead, we're dead." He kept murmuring it, and he appeared calmer the longer he did so.

"Don't say that!" Koby commanded.

Blaz curled up next to where Koby covered Gunther, trying to take up as little space as possible. Werner sat flat against the wall of the trench, eyes closed, and murmuring words to himself. Another artillery strike landed dangerously close. Blaz faintly heard one of the kids crying in fear. Another shell hit the side of the bunker. The walls were just thick enough, the hit not direct enough. Several soldiers came sprinting out of the bunker. Schneider stood at the entrance waving them out, pointing to the west.

"Everyone, move out! We're falling back!" he screamed.

"Come on!" Koby shouted, springing from the trench. Gunther leapt out next, followed by Blaz and Werner. They hurdled over trenches on their way away from the artillery strikes.

"Wait!" Jarman called as they ran away, "Help me here!"

The others skidded to a halt. Jarman waved them back to the back trench, where the eleven and twelve-year-old Hitler Youths were holding onto Jarman and their young sergeant, the man who'd conducted them.

"Come on, guys!" Koby yelled to the children, offering a hand, "We have to move out!"

One boy took Koby's hand, and Koby lifted him out. The others saw this and some followed.

"Go with them!" Koby shouted at Blaz and Werner as another shell exploded nearby, "Gunther! Help him!"

Blaz and Werner ran away with the Hitler Youths, holding each by the hand. The Germans ran down the hill from their position into the fields. Schneider led the way, until they arrived at a new position. They crossed so many fields, hills and positions, Blaz had no idea how far they'd come. They passed a concrete bunker and stopped behind it. There was one flak gun on a much smaller hill, a wooden watchtower stood in the thick forest behind their position, and in front of the bunker, to the east, was a thin grove of trees, with trenches where troops and tanks were dug in. Koby, Jarman, and Gunther came sprinting across the final field.

More artillery strikes continued, hammering the front lines until finally, all had stopped. Troops on horseback trotted towards their old positions to retrieve guns and salvageable supplies. The rain started.

We Stand for Germany at our Posts

"*Was siehst du?*" Blaz asked Koby, while his sergeant gazed beyond the fields toward the very front lines, though those were over several hills and trench positions.

"Just the sun rising," Koby replied, as the rain had recently moved out, "But they could come from the north too." He lowered his binoculars and grinned at Blaz for the first time in months, "They could come from anywhere, really."

Blaz returned the grin, "What's that?" he asked, pointing to dots in the sky. Koby's cheerful expression remained as he raised his binoculars. It disappeared.

"Fighters," Koby muttered, before yelling a warning to their position, "Fighters! Russian! Due east!"

The Hitler Youths rotated their flak guns as fast as they could. The fighters came ever closer.

"Take the shot if you have it!" Schneider ordered.

The young soldier who'd conducted the song ran between the flak guns giving orders. Blaz and Koby ran down from the roof of the bunker back to the trenches. The hum of propellers drew nearer.

"They're in range!" the young soldier shouted, "Fire at will!"

The frightened boys fired both flak guns. They hit the lead plane, which exploded as it hit the ground. The other four fighters continued, but two broke off and began circling around.

"*Verdämmt!*" the soldier swore, "Rotate, fire again!"

The children frantically rotated the guns as the planes began their turnaround. The guns seemed to rotate in slow motion compared to the fighters, which were now coming straight on. Flak guns at another position fired away, one shot whistling by. The startled pilot swerved his aircraft, flying dangerously close to his wingman. One soldier in the bunker fired a long burst from his MG-42. The bullets pierced the glass of one plane, and into the propeller engine of the other. Fire and smoke poured from the second plane, and it hurtled into the ground. The other plane shot up into the sky and continued its flight. The Hitler Youths pumped their fists, with a new surge of confidence on seeing their enemy flee.

Stromschnellen's truck slowed to a stop in front of the bunker. He and Kurzmann climbed out, as well as their driver. Schneider rushed out of the bunker to meet them. All could hear the widespread fighting commence, and urgency was in air.

"*Heil* Hitler!" Schneider saluted.

"What?" Stromschnellen shook his head after a jab from Kurzmann, "*Ah, ja. Heil* Hitler."

"What is it?" Schneider asked quickly.

"The Russians are having trouble moving their armor, because of the rain and swampy terrain Seelow possesses to the east. Their tanks are bogged down. We can't waste this opportunity. There are roads they are using, as they can't move through the watered-down fields. We are going to send in tank hunters."

Schneider's expression turned grave, "Tank hunters, *Standartenführer*?"

"*Jawohl*. I want your most agile soldiers to come with me. Preferably small in stature. This is a dangerous assignment. They'll be going in teams of three. Give me six men. I already have three. I'm to take several roads in this area to the east."

Schneider nodded, and walked to the trenches, "Senft! Hertz! Schütz! Von Schraeder! With the *Standartenführer*!"

Schneider moved to the flak guns, calling two names.

Blaz followed his squad mates to Stromschnellen where they saluted him. Kurzmann returned the salute immediately, while Stromschnellen again seemed to pretend he had not even noticed. Two young Germans joined the mix seconds later. Stromschnellen dismissed Schneider and directed his attention to the boys.

"Men, I have *Panzerfausts* in the back of the truck. As they cannot be reloaded on the battlefield, you will be split into groups of three. One will cover, one will shoot, the other will carry two spare *Panzerfausts*. Kurzmann will organize you into teams. Into the truck."

The three men Stromschnellen had mentioned turned out to be thirteen-year-old Youths, with dirt caked faces from sleeping in trenches for weeks. None of them smiled; they knew where they were heading. Blaz nodded encouragingly to the smallest one of them, who held a lit cigarette between his fingers. The boy flashed a quick smile, looking up briefly, revealing he had no eyebrows.

"Alonzo?" Blaz coughed out, "Alonzo, what are you doing here?"

"Who are you?" the Hitler Youth asked, his expression morphing into a glare.

"I'm Blaz. You probably don't remember me. We were those kids that played football with you all those years ago."

Alonzo looked puzzled, he shook his head.

"You're Alonzo Harvey, right?"

"*Ja.*"

"Cut the chatter privates," Kurzmann snapped, "All right, we have nine *Panzerfausts*. I'm going to tell you who you're with and your job in the group and you're not going to argue or ask any questions."

"*Jawohl, Herr* Kurzmann."

"Hertz, I want you as cover fire with Christoff and Hadumar. Christoff, you will be the shooter. Hadumar, you will carry the spare *Panzerfausts*," he told the two thirteen-year-olds. Both nodded nervously, picking up their weapons from the truck floor.

"You two, what are your names?" Kurzmann asked the two eleven-year-olds.

"Koen."

"Jaecar."

"Koen, you are with Senft and Harvey. Senft, I want you to be the shooter. Koen, you'll carry the weapons, and Harvey," Kurzmann didn't like the thought of cover fire possessing a bolt-action rifle. "Here take my MP-40. Trade."

Kurzmann and Alonzo exchanged weapons and ammunition before Kurzmann assigned Gunther to cover for Werner and Jaecar.

"Hertz, your group gets off here. You can expect tanks on the road soon," Kurzmann said, as the truck began pulling away.

"Wait! Wait!" Koby called, but the truck was already moving. Blaz looked back as Koby slapped himself in the forehead. Blaz's heart pounded faster. He was very aware of his heartbeat.

"Senft, Koen, Harvey. You three get out next. Wait at the road in the trees."

Blaz nodded.

What had Koby yelled to wait for? I wonder what we do once we are out ammo?

"*Herr* Kurzmann?" Alonzo nervously asked.

"*Ja*, Harvey?"

"What do we do when we are out of ammunition?"

"Make your way back to our lines," Kurzmann put simply. Alonzo frowned, but knew better than to say anything else. Instead, he took a drag from his cigarette. The truck came to another road bordering trees, thick enough to be called a small forest. It was a part of the elaborate Seelow defenses. Even the roads, especially the roads, had to be dangerous for the enemy. The truck slowed to a stop. Blaz grabbed his *Panzerfaust* and climbed out of the truck. Alonzo did the same, then they both helped Koen out while he held two *Panzerfausts*.

"Let's go," Blaz motioned with his eyes, taking the lead.

"Good luck boys," Kurzmann said, as the truck began pulling away.

Blaz led Alonzo and Koen into the forest, a few meters from the road. Koen stayed the furthest back, keeping one *Panzerfaust* slung over his shoulder and holding the other one ready to fire. The eleven-year-old seemed to think the tanks would come within minutes. Blaz crouched in the thickly wooded and drenched area, waiting, and watching the road. The smell of wet leaves filled the air. Alonzo raised his MP-40 whenever he heard a noticeably louder shot fired in the distance.

"Where are they?" Koen whispered to Blaz.

"I'm not sure," Blaz admitted, "I know they'll come from the east. They always do," he added, trying to sound as manly as he could.

Koen accepted this answer and crept back to his cover. Blaz's legs were soaked from remaining in his crouching position. Yet he stayed ready. Many minutes, perhaps hours passed with nothing. Koen and Alonzo stayed alert, though fidgety. Blaz adjusted his position several times, making sure he stayed well concealed.

"Hey," Koen whispered, "Is that Russian or German?"

Blaz looked down the road. A Soviet T-34. And better yet, it was all alone.

"That's Russian," Blaz whispered back, "Alonzo, get ready to cover me. Stay hidden."

All three of them lay on the wet ground, weapons in hand. Blaz crawled closer to the road, staying behind trees and tall grass. The tank rolled closer, it's commander wisely watching the forest through the hatch.

Come on, a little closer, Blaz thought.

From the side, the *Panzerfaust* would have no trouble piercing the tank's armor. The commander kept his eyes on the forest, starting to look Blaz's way. But he turned to scan forward as the tank passed by. Blaz sprung from his cover, raising his *Panzerfaust*. The attuned commander spun around, cocking the mounted machine gun while he did so. Blaz fired, hitting the center of the back of the tank. The warhead pierced the armor, and flames erupted from the inside of the tank. The commander lost his grip on the machine gun as flames engulfed him.

Blaz heard screams. The commander leapt out of the tank into the field on the road's other side, and a second man followed him. Blaz threw his *Panzerfaust* to the ground, took his rifle from his back, and advanced toward them. One Russian drew his pistol, still burning. Blaz dove behind the tank, as the Russian fired a clumsy shot. Blaz attached his bayonet to the end of the rifle, wondering why he hadn't done that sooner. Alonzo ran from the forest, leaping onto the flaming tank with surprising ease, and fired a shot into each burning Russian. The two soldiers collapsed, now out of their misery. Blaz leapt onto the tank with Alonzo and slung his rifle over his back. They both stayed on the edge of the tank, away from the flames at the center.

"Get their ammo," Blaz ordered. Alonzo nodded, and searched the two bodies, careful not to burn himself. He emerged with ammunition for their pistols, giving half to Blaz.

"Keep it. You found it," Blaz said when Alonzo held out a handful of nine-millimeter bullets. Alonzo shrugged and shoved them into a pocket. Blaz gazed east. No tanks in sight. He hopped down from the tank, gesturing to Alonzo to follow him back to cover. At that moment when Alonzo jumped down, a bullet ricocheted off the area on the tank where his chest had just been.

"Sniper!" Blaz shouted sprinting to a tree, "Take cover!"

Alonzo dove to the ground of the forest and did a roll to a tree. Koen stayed where he was, the sniper couldn't have seen him. Another shot, this bullet slammed into the tree Blaz was behind. Blaz adjusted to be as thin as possible behind the tree, turning sideways.

"What do we do?" Alonzo called.

"Blaz! There's more tanks coming!" Koen pointed.

"*Ach nein*," Blaz muttered peeking to see five tanks rolling down the road, "Koen, I need you to take cover behind the destroyed tank. When the tanks get near, blast them. Alonzo we're going to draw fire while Koen sneaks to the tank."

Koen leapt up and ran for the tank. Blaz exposed himself briefly while Alonzo fired a shot with his MP-40. No shot came, and Koen made it safely behind the tank.

"Now what? We can't kill five tanks with two shots!" Alonzo yelled.

"I'm thinking, I'm thinking," Blaz said.

"Do you think we can make it to that forest?" Alonzo asked naively, pointing to a hill a good five hundred meters to the northwest, where a large tree cluster was.

"Guys?" Koen yelled nervously.

"*Nein*, we can't make it there," Blaz shouted to Alonzo.

"Guys!" Koen shouted louder this time.

"*Ja?*"

"The tanks are gonna fire!"

Blaz peeked out to see the tanks' cannons lining up on them.

"*Nein, nein, nein,*" Blaz murmured quickly unslinging his rifle, "Alonzo, get behind the tank!"

Alonzo sprinted for the back of the tank, diving behind it, as another shot from the sniper came. Blaz fired a shot at the flash, having little time to aim.

"Your turn!" Koen told Blaz, waving to the seventeen-year-old *Wehrmacht* soldier.

"Blaz, I'll cover for you," Alonzo assured him. Blaz nodded, and held up three fingers; the thumb, pointer finger, and middle finger. He counted down starting at the middle. Then he bolted for the tank. A shot sounded, and Blaz felt an echo in his head, he stumbled into the mud, sliding head first behind the tank.

"Blaz!" Alonzo yelled, turning him over. Blaz scrambled to his feet but stayed behind the tank.

"Blaz?" Alonzo asked.

"What?"

"You got hit."

"*Nein*, I'm right here."

"Look at your helmet."

Blaz removed his helmet quickly. His eyes went wide. A bullet had torn a long line through the back of his helmet. But now wasn't the time, Blaz put it back on, looking to Koen and Alonzo. The tanks were two hundred meters away. The machine gun of the lead tank fired between the Germans and the forest, some bullets ricocheting off the tank.

"What do we do?" Koen asked, tapping his foot furiously. Blaz slung his rifle over his shoulder and took the *Panzerfausts* from Koen.

"You guys get out of here," Blaz said, "Through the forest, and sprint until you get back to our lines. I'll distract them so you can make it through the forest."

"Blaz, you can't do that," Alonzo shook his head.

"*Nein*, I'm the leader here. It's my job."

Alonzo groaned in frustration and fired a burst at the lead tank. His shots were returned tenfold.

"Alonzo, this is what a soldier does. I'm not a cadet anymore. *We* aren't cadets anymore," Blaz said pulling Alonzo by the collar to look him in the eye. Only reminiscing to when he met the then eight-year-old could change Alonzo's mind here. Alonzo's lip trembled, but Blaz continued, "You run, don't you dare look back. Keep him safe," Blaz ordered, gesturing to Koen who was oblivious to their discussion. The tanks churned through the mud, coming closer to the tank.

"When I say, '*Los!*'" Blaz ordered, raising a *Panzerfaust* and moving to the other side of the tank. The lead tank moved into range. Bullets continued to periodically hammer the tank. Blaz gave Alonzo a nod. "Almost."

The tank commander was looking Blaz's way. Blaz made the *Panzerfaust* visible. The alarmed commander shouted something in Russian, and the tank's cannon rotated.

"Surrender!" the commander bellowed at Blaz over the tank's engines.

"*Niemals!*" Blaz shouted back.

The commander had heard him and responded, "*Feuer!*" saying it in German. Blaz, Alonzo, and Koen all hit the ground as a shell sent dust and mud into the air. A near miss by the tank. Blaz fired one *Panzerfaust*, hitting the bow machine gun, but not disabling the tank. Still it chugged along.

"*Los!*" Blaz shouted, his heart pounding as he jumped into the tank's view raising his *Panzerfaust*. Alonzo and Koen sprinted into the forest, no shots fired at them. The unprepared tank commander went for his pistol on seeing a loaded *Panzerfaust*, but never got the chance to raise it. The lead tank exploded, the top hatch flew right off. Smoke billowed out, making Blaz invisible to the other tanks. He sprinted back to cover. He glanced around, looking for what had fired. It hadn't been him; the *Panzerfaust* was still loaded. He looked in the direction of the forest Alonzo had thought they could flee to. Roaring around the edge of the forest was his savior: A Tiger Tank. The Tiger's main gun fired again, this time hitting the tank in the rear of the line. Blaz only saw the smoke and fire leap. The T-34s rotated, turning to face their adversary. Blaz stayed hidden, transfixed on the spectacle. The Tiger Tank fired its machine gun at the place the sniper had been. The three T-34s chugged forward with difficulty in the thick mud as Kurzmann had predicted. One fired its cannon. Blaz saw it deflect off the ground, sending mud and water into the air before continuing beyond the Tiger. The other two fired. One hit its mark. But that didn't matter, the shell ricocheted off the Tiger's armor. Blaz stared open-mouthed. He shook his head, realizing that the T-34s were completely focused on the Tiger now. He crept out from his cover.

The Tiger fired again, its shot slamming into the treads of the tank nearest to Blaz, grinding it to a halt. Blaz made to finish this one off. The Tiger commander had obviously seen him, as the Tiger's cannon rotated to the tank in the center rather than finishing the immobile tank. The two mobile T-34s initiated the classic pincer movement, both veering in opposite directions to hit the Tiger from two sides. The Tiger slowed to a stop before reversing. One T-34 fired, its shot ricocheted once again.

Blaz stopped about twenty meters behind the immobilized tank and fired. The undefended rear made for a great target, and the explosion was lethal. He made no reaction, dropped the empty *Panzerfaust*, and unslung his rifle.

One man emerged from the hatch, moving his dead commander out of the way. The man tumbled down the side of the tank, into the mud. Blaz charged with his bayonet. The Russian, not on fire, but scorched severely made no move for a weapon. And Blaz stopped in front of the wounded man. No Russians ever did this.

Kill him, kill him. Hurry. Nein, he's already dying. There's no point. Help him go faster.

Blaz positioned his bayonet to deliver the blow. The Russian's brown eyes stared back at him, without resentment but with pity. Blaz recoiled once again.

What are you waiting for?

An explosion, and the fourth T-34 went up in flames. The Tiger began rotating its main cannon to end this clash of Russian and German armor. Blaz kept the Russian at gunpoint, watching the tank battle ensue. The Russian was burnt bad. He was going to die. Blaz looked between the fighting tanks and the Russian. He stepped over the Russian keeping his eyes on the tanks. The T-34 began firing its machine gun desperately. It fired a shot at the Tiger, once again hitting the frontal armor rendering it a wasted shot. The Tiger halted, simply aiming her gun. The T-34 fired again, hitting the front and ricocheting. Blaz could almost see the German tank commander smile as the Tiger's cannon lined up. The massive cannon fired, piercing the T-34's armor on the side. Flames poured out, killing the crew. The Tiger did not head over to Blaz. The commander extended his right arm in victory. Blaz returned the salute. Both lowered their arms simultaneously, and the Tiger Tank rolled back into the woods to wait for more enemies. Blaz looked down at the Russian, who moaned in pain. He could still talk; he might be faking. Take no chances. Blaz positioned his rifle to stab the Russian. The Russian hoarsely said something, Blaz recognized a couple words. Not enough to comprehend. Blaz cracked a smile at the Russian. He shook his head.

What am I doing? He could get our men killed.

Blaz stabbed the man with his bayonet and sprinted for the forest.

Back to the Front

Blaz ran through endless fields. His good running form faded as exhaustion set in. His arms were loose, and his legs felt weak.

Where are some Germans?

Blaz tripped in a hole and face-planted in the mud. He laughed at himself, spitting out some mud as he sprung up and continued jogging.

It took a while, but Blaz found his way to his position, with the help of other troops. Alonzo and Koen were waiting nervously, looking overjoyed to see their leader return.

"Where's Koby?" Blaz asked Alonzo.

"Who's Koby?"

"Oh right, sorry," Blaz remembered Alonzo wouldn't recognize Koby by name, "My age, taller, dark brown hair, brown eyes, and tan skin."

Alonzo shook his head.

"Okay," Blaz nodded.

"Boys," Schneider said, striding toward Alonzo and Blaz, "I hate to do this, but we need to send you out again. Our front lines have inflicted heavy casualties on the Russians, but some Russian armor and infantry are slipping through. We're sending four of you to just behind the front."

"*Bitte*, don't send Koen," Blaz whispered to Schneider. Koen took no notice.

Schneider smiled, "I'm waiting for Sergeant Hertz and the rest to return. Two of them will go with you."

"*Danke schön, Herr* Schneider," Blaz said, "May I ask a question?"

"*Absolut.*"

"When Russian troops make it past the front lines, why don't we send in some men? Or tanks? Why tank hunters?"

"Because this is guerrilla warfare. Our front lines are everything. If the Russians reach this area, Senft, the battle is well and truly lost. That's why we are sending hunters forward."

Blaz looked at the trenches. They were significantly emptier than when he'd left. Jarman was still there, looking unhappy about it. Ivo was on the roof of the bunker aiming his rifle east.

"Ambushes are how we will win this battle," Schneider put simply, "With superior cover and defenses. And superior decisions by individual soldiers. And-" Schneider cut short, realizing Blaz was seventeen and not an idiot.

"We need a lot of things to win this battle," Blaz nodded.

"Many."

Koby and Blaz

With a *Panzerschreck* in his arms, a pistol on his belt, and a rifle slung on his back, Blaz followed Koby through the fields. Occasionally, German troops ran past them, toward the front lines. The Russians were kept at bay, and the battle was progressing as well as they dared hope. But the men and tanks slipping past had to be destroyed before the Russians got what they wanted: A battle with no front lines.

Koby held his STG-44 close, while Alonzo and Christoff followed with backpacks full of rockets. They headed southeast, where heavy fighting had been reported. The sounds of battle grew closer and closer.

The four Germans came to an abandoned farm, the owner likely having fled. There was a barn, a house, and a shed. A dirt road ran by the barn toward Seelow that they guarded. Flying from the porch of the farmhouse was a Swastika flag. If any Russians saw it, they'd be attracted to the house like moths to a flame.

"We're staying here," Koby said, "I'll keep watch."

"Right."

Koby opened the barn's door and found a spacious interior with a loft and window facing the house. A tree line ran between the other side of the barn and a wheat field.

"Blaz, in the loft with me. I want the *Panzerschreck* ready up there."

Blaz nodded and put his *Panzerschreck* down, "Alonzo, can I have some rockets?"

Alonzo reached into his backpack and handed three of the five rockets in his backpack to Blaz.

"*Danke.*" Blaz moved them up, creating a nest. He returned downstairs to retrieve his Panzerschreck. Alonzo and Christoff sat down on some hay bales and started chatting. Blaz took off his helmet and set it on the floor of the loft. He kept his cap on. Koby glanced down at the Christoff and Alonzo, who'd taken their caps off.

"I'm always the only one with dark hair," Koby said with a smile.

"There's lots of people with brown hair."

"Light brown, *ja.*"

"Not almost black?"

"*Ja.*"

"Well, hey, Alonzo, Christoff, and me aren't so common in the world." Koby laughed a little and looked back out the window.

"Shouldn't we surrender?" Blaz asked, knowing what reaction this might provoke.

Koby glared at Blaz, "Don't ask that."

Blaz looked at the ground, knowing he'd worded it wrong, "We'll have a second chance, if we surrender."

"Blaz, if we lose we will be eternally cursed by the world. There will be no second chance."

Koby said nothing more. Blaz knew what he thought.

Ten Men

"Quiet! Russians!" Koby hissed to Alonzo and Christoff. They dropped to their knees, readying their rifles. Blaz slid a rocket into his *Panzerschreck*. Both he and Koby stayed close to the wall, near the window.

"Switch spaces?" Blaz whispered so he could aim quicker, being right-handed.

"*Ja*," both crawled under the view of the window, transitioning flawlessly. Russians voices filled the silence.

"What are they saying?"

"They're joking about our flag there," Koby said, "I can't hear all that much." He peeked above the window and ducked back down nearly instantly.

"Did they see you?" Blaz asked, his heart beating faster at this thought.

"I don't think so. Got a grenade?"

"*Ja*."

"Throw it at them. I'll shoot."

"*Jawohl*," Blaz whispered, carefully placing his bazooka on the loft floor. He took out his grenade and pulled the pin. Koby nodded, and both sprung up. Blaz threw the grenade, right into the center of the Russians. Koby unleashed bullets on them from his assault rifle. It was a massacre. An effective piece of guerrilla warfare. Koby mowed down five before the grenade went off, which killed or wounded the rest. Koby used one bullet on each wounded man to conserve ammunition.

Seelow's Finest Hour

April 17, 1945

The German defenses repelled the attacks of the first day. No more men made it to the farmhouse all through the night. Koby and Blaz switched off keeping watch, with Blaz getting the late shift. When the sun rose, he woke everyone up for another day of tank hunting. Only minutes after, the all-too-familiar boom of artillery echoed in the distance.

"*Scheiße*," Koby muttered, "They must've moved their artillery forward last night."

Fortunately, an abandoned farmhouse was not on the Soviet hit list. Blaz leaned out the window, just enjoying the peace, if not quiet.

"Breezy?"

Blaz looked at Koby, who'd brought Christoff and Alonzo up.

"Actually *ja*," he said, "It feels nice out there."

"You'll get to feel plenty of that air once we destroy, how many rockets do we have?"

"Ten total," Christoff smiled, throwing up a playful stiff-arm salute.

Koby grinned to keep the positive morale flowing. "Once we get ten tanks, then we can go."

"You remember that we aren't supposed to fire this in the same place multiple times?" Blaz asked.

"The *Panzerschreck*?" Alonzo asked.

"*Ja*, it gives your position away and releases smoke and toxins."

"Well, you better get outside then," Koby said, "Christoff, Alonzo, you come with us. Blaz is right, there's a lot of trees around the road on both sides, so that's where we hide out. If they come, we'll see them."

"I wish we had a Tiger Tank," Alonzo said.

"Everyone wishes they had a Tiger Tank," Koby replied.

Hours passed, the Germans fought bravely at the front holding the Russians back, but breakthroughs occurred, and the fighting shifted closer to the second line of defenses.

"Someone's coming down the road!" Alonzo pointed.

Koby removed his helmet and raised his binoculars, seeing the men to be wearing field gray uniforms of the *Wehrmacht* and camouflage. Behind them rumbled a Panther tank, but the Russians had been known to steal German tanks in the past.

"Hold fire," Koby ordered, "They're German. Five of them. And a tank."

Alonzo and Christoff loosened their grip on their rifles but kept them aimed. As the men neared, Koby called, "Germans?"

"*Ja!*" one called back.

"Sounds like *Herr* Dresden, like Schlusser," Koby whispered, then shouted, "*Ja?* Then say, '*Panzerkampfwagen.*' And say it fast."

"*Panzerkampfwagen,*" the lead man said with a laugh at being asked to say, "Fighting tank."

"Someone else say, '*Eichhörnchen.*'" Squirrel.

"*Eichhörnchen!*" another man shouted back as they kept advancing, with hands up.

"All right. They're good."

"Wait, may I ask them to say something?" Christoff asked.

"You may."

"One more!" Christoff yelled, his voice cracking. Alonzo snickered, but Christoff continued, "A third man, say, '*Obergruppenführer.*'"

"*Obergruppenführer!*"

"*Danke!*"

The men lowered their arms and came to the boys' position. They held rifles only, some semi-automatic, some bolt-action. One held a massive anti-tank rifle.

"What are you young men doing here?" the lead man asked. He was older, with white hair and no indication of rank. He did, however, wear Iron Crosses. He had two, both second class. One had a swastika on it, and the year nineteen-forty-four on it. The other had no swastika, and on it was printed the year nineteen-eighteen. The man was back for a second war.

"We are tank hunters. We have orders to fight to the last rocket," Koby replied, "What are you doing?"

"Retreating to the second lines," the man answered, pointing east.

"Have the front lines been overrun?" Koby asked with concern.

"Only our position, that I know of."

"*Gut.* Well, I suppose you may move along now," Koby said, stepping out of the road.

The camouflaged *Waffen-SS* chuckled to himself, adjusted his anti-tank rifle in his hands, and stepped to Christoff's side, giving the boy a pat on the back. One soldier looked to the man questioningly. The soldier replied with the motto of the SS, "*Meine Ehre heißt Treue.*"

The tank's hatch opened and a man in a black Panzer uniform and side cap appeared.

"You want to help us out?" Alonzo asked the *Wehrmacht* soldiers and tank commander.

One kicked at the dirt, "Ah, what the hell." The man with the Iron Crosses stepped out of the road to join them. The other two followed his example. The tank commander gave a nod of affirmation.

"I assume black hair is in charge here?" the *Waffen-SS* soldier laughed, seemingly either unaware or uncaring of the dangerous odds they would face.

"I'm a sergeant. You guys?" Koby replied, pointing to the patch on his bicep.

"All privates," the Iron Cross man said.

"Well then, I'll give the orders. *Herr Panzer?*"

"*Jawohl*, sergeant?"

"Can you camouflage or conceal her well in the trees next to the house?" Koby asked.

"Absolutely."

"*Wunderbar.* You two," he pointed to the *Wehrmacht* soldiers with bolt-action rifles, "I want one of you in the house, the other use the outside of the house as cover. Crosses, can I call you that?"

"Well, the name is- you know what, you can call me that if you wish," the man agreed, perhaps not liking his real name.

"*Ausgezeichnet.* Crosses, you have a semi-automatic rifle, right?"

"I do. Stole it from the Russkies."

"You give our rocket launcher cover."

"*Sehr gut*," Crosses said.

"What's the real name?" Blaz asked.

"None of your business."

"Probably a girly name," Christoff whispered to Alonzo, grinning.

"Russkies! Coming down the road! Stay hidden," the *Waffen-SS* soldier said, aiming his anti-tank rifle on a tripod as he lay on the ground, "They don't see us. Line of tanks, at least two. They're single file, I can't tell-"

"Okay, shut up Ernest," Crosses said.

The SS soldier shot him a grin, and went back to aiming his rifle, "Sergeant Hertz, I am in range to hit their commander. Shall I fire?"

"*Nein, nein, nein.* We need to wait."

"Ten tanks!" the *Wehrmacht* soldier in the barn called quietly but still so Koby could hear.

"*Scheiße*," Koby muttered.

"This home has a basement," the *Wehrmacht* soldier inside the house said, suggesting maybe they should hide.

"Hertz, we should retreat," Crosses said thoughtfully.

"We can't retreat. They're in range, we have too many fields to cross. They'll gun us down. The Panther has a better chance with surprise. We have to stand and fight."

"Bring it," the SS soldier said, grinning like a maniac.

"Okay," Koby signaled the tank commander, "*Feuer!*"

The Panther's massive gun fired, making a deafening roar. The lead Russian tank exploded, top flying off. This gave the SS soldier a view of the second tank. He fired, hitting the alarmed tank commander in the chest with the massive ammunition. Blaz put his *Panzerschreck* on the ground and unslung his rifle. The tanks were still out of range.

"Kid!" the *Waffen-SS* soldier yelled to Alonzo, "Stand in the middle of the road. Stay still."

Alonzo looked at the soldier incredulously but didn't raise any objection. The soldier stood up and placed the barrel of the gun on Alonzo's shoulder to help aim.

"Sorry kid," the soldier said.

"*Es gut.*"

The Panther fired again, hitting the third tank in line, on the side, effectively destroying it with the superior gun of the Germans. The eight Russian tanks reversed, save the boxed in second one. Alonzo flinched as the soldier fired, hitting the second tank, but only scratching the armor. The Panther lined up on the trapped second tank.

"*Verdämmt!* Damn this Russkie weapon," he swore.

"Blaz!" Koby shouted, "Be ready with that *Panzerschreck*!"

"*Verstanden*," Blaz yelled back.

"*Feuer!*" the tank commander roared, and the Panther fired on the second tank, missing slightly.

The Russian tanks began a pincer movement, four tanks going one way three the other. Fortunately, four were going the way of the Panther.

"Ernest, get that rifle over there!" Crosses called pointing to the edge of the trees. Alonzo ran away, causing Ernest, the SS soldier, to almost drop his rifle, "We need you and the kid here to take these three tanks. The Panther will get those five." As he finished saying this, the Panther's gun fired, followed by a more distant explosion, "And keep their attention away from the Panther!"

Blaz and Ernest nodded, running closer to the field through trees. Crosses bolted to the house, taking cover at a window, opposite the man who took cover inside. Another shot from the Panther followed by another explosion. Blaz raised his bazooka but held fire, the tanks were too far away still. They fired their cannons and machine guns, the bullets sending bits of bark and mud into the air. The shells whistled by, one blasting a small tree in half.

"We have their attention!" Ernest laughed out loud.

"*Ja*," Blaz said breathlessly, after seeing the shell tear a tree in half, "*Ja*, we do." Another explosion, and another Soviet tank in flames. The Panther rolled forward from cover to confront the last two tanks opposing her. The German tank charged one head on, while aiming its gun on the other one.

Ernest lay down again to aim his rifle, staying behind the tree. Blaz stumbled backwards as a bullet ricocheted off his *Panzerschreck* from the enemy tanks. He scrambled back behind cover immediately. The Russian tanks fired again, their attention held by the two soldiers. The trio of tanks were getting close. Blaz fired a rocket, but it fizzled out, exploding into the ground just short of its target.

"Christoff!" Blaz screamed at the top of his lungs. Christoff came sprinting from his cover to Blaz's side.

"Rockets, rockets, I need rockets."

Christoff gave Blaz his backpack. The tanks fired again, a shell blowing off a low branch of the evergreen they were crouched behind.

Ernest, balancing his rifle on a branch, fired, hit the T-34's frontal armor, and it ricocheted away.

"*Verdämmt! Verdämmt!*" he swore in frustration. Another explosion boomed. Koby came running to their position, sliding behind a tree under heavy machine gun fire.

"Good thing these Russkies can't aim," Ernest yelled before firing a shot. The tracer bullet flew through the slit of one tank, where the gunner sat. The machine gun fire stopped at that moment. Christoff's mouth hung open in awe.

"Blaz!" Koby shouted, "In range! *Feuer!*"

Blaz nodded coming out of some disillusionment. He raised his *Panzerschreck*, aiming for the side of the furthest tank.

"*Feuer!*" Koby yelled.

Blaz kept aiming, then pulled the trigger. The rocket hurdled toward the tank, slamming into its vulnerable side and blasting a hole. The tank ground to a halt. Ernest aimed his rifle at the hatch, waiting for men to jump out but none did. Christoff handed Blaz another rocket, while bullets flew through by the trees. Ernest fired at a tank, having no effect. The tank returned fire, and Ernest took several hits before he collapsed. Christoff started to hyperventilate, he'd never seen a German soldier die before.

"Pull it together," Blaz jabbed him with his elbow, "Focus on the battle."

The tanks were under one hundred meters away. Blaz fired a rocket, hitting the frontal armor of one. The rocket exploded, but the armor held. Blaz frantically loaded another rocket, coughing at the smoke the *Panzerschreck* released. The tanks fired their cannons, in quick succession. The shells screamed by, slammed into the barn, causing an entire wall to collapse. Christoff fired a shot with his rifle, which bounced off the tank's armor. With another rocket loaded, Blaz aimed at the tank whose side was most vulnerable. The kickback knocked him down this time, but his shot was good and now only one tank remained. It was nearly on top of them. The tank fired again, hitting the house, where one soldier was. The machine guns fired as well, killing the man on the side of the house.

"Give me a rocket, Christoff," Koby ordered as Blaz loaded the *Panzerschreck.*

"Last one," Christoff said tossing the rocket to Koby who caught it with one hand. He took out his grenade and threw it at the tank. It landed on top, but its explosion had little effect. The tank advanced into the trees.

An explosion sounded in the distance. None of them could tell whether it was the Panther or the Russian tank. Blaz poked his *Panzerschreck* out, but bullets hammered the metal guard, as Blaz pulled it back. The tank was only meters away but had stopped advancing. It would deal with these enemies, then move on.

"Christoff, I need you to take the *Panzerschreck*," Blaz said, handing Christoff the bazooka, "Koby, give me cover!" Blaz shouted over the tank's machine guns, which ripped into the ground near Koby's tree. Koby stayed behind the tree blindly firing his machine gun one round at a time. Blaz sprinted, getting to the tank's side. He kept his rifle slung on his back and drew his pistol. He scaled the tank, purposefully trying to draw the attention of the crew by stomping as he climbed. It didn't work, the crew was not stupid enough to open the hatch now. Blaz tried to open it himself but it was sealed shut. Christoff exposed himself for a moment, drawing an uncannily swift reaction from the gunner, and he went down.

"*Nein!*" Koby screamed, leaping from his cover, throwing the rocket with one arm, and aiming his pistol with the other. Blaz ducked behind the tank's hatch. Koby's aim was perfect. The rocket hit the slit where the gunner could see out. The explosion certainly killed him, and the machine gun was destroyed. With the gun disabled, Koby boldly strutted out in front of the tank in plain view. The cannon couldn't go low enough to hit him anymore. He picked up the *Panzerschreck* and aimed it at the tank. At this range, it would be lethal.

Koby shouted something in Russian, probably ordering them to abandon the tank. "Blaz, keep them at gunpoint!" he ordered.

"*Jawohl*," Blaz said aiming his pistol down at the hatch.

"Crosses! Over here!" Koby shouted, not turning away from the tank. Crosses limped over, clutching his leg with one arm and holding his rifle in the other.

"Give Blaz your grenade," Koby ordered then shouted again in Russian. The hatch opened before Blaz was given a grenade, but that mattered not. The commander had his hands up.

"*Kommen aus, dann Händen hoch,*" Blaz ordered the Russian, but the Russian took these words the same way one would expect. He had no idea what they meant. Blaz gestured with his pistol for the Russian to leave the tank. The commander obeyed, jumping down to Crosses. The two other men in the tank followed their commander out. Blaz climbed into the tank, pistol out and ready. He saw the body of the machine gunner, but that was all. Blaz climbed back out to see Koby at Christoff's side. The boy had pulled through but was in horrible pain. His right arm had been hit twice by bullets. One on the bicep, the other the forearm. The boy's agony was expressed in a series of suppressed screams, sobs, and occasionally he would slam his heel into the ground. Blaz leapt down from the tank and walked over to the Russian bodies. He looked up at Koby.

"Crosses! I need you!" Koby called again, "Are you a medic?" he asked hopefully.

"*Nein*, but I've been in the military for two wars, so I can pass. What's the problem?" he asked.

"Bullets through the arm, at the bicep and forearm," Blaz informed him.

"Let's see," Crosses murmured, examining Christoff's arm. The thirteen-year-old kicked his heel into the ground. His teeth were gritted, his eyes tightly shut and red in the face.

"*Scheiße*," Crosses said, on seeing the wounds, "For now let's wrap it. I'll do that, you two check the barn. See if the man is alive. I never got his name."

"Okay," Blaz and Koby said, and jogged over to the barn. Blaz opened the door, and Koby walked in. A soldier lay on the floor of the barn.

"Sir?" Koby said loudly.

"*Ja?*" the man said, rolling onto his side.

"You okay?"

"Not really, I think my leg is broken."

"Blaz, let's help him out," Koby ordered, getting under the man's shoulder, prompting Blaz to do the same. The man hopped on his good leg while the boys supported him. Once at the Panther, they helped lift him so he could sit on the tank.

Alonzo kept the three Russians at gunpoint, maintaining what he imagined would be an intimidating expression.

Christoff came trudging over with Crosses at his side also holding the *Panzerschreck*. His face was red and wet, but he was no longer crying. Crosses lifted him onto the tank, where Christoff put a hand on his wrapping.

"What of the prisoners?" the tank commander said, "It would be convenient to kill them."

"I'm not going to pull the trigger," Crosses said, "If any of you are holding onto the notion that we won't be taken prisoner in the next few days, you are delusional."

"I'm not going to kill them either," Blaz said, "We can take them prisoner."

"Take them prisoner?" Alonzo questioned, aiming his rifle at one man's head, "They just killed our men!"

"I think we killed more of theirs," Crosses replied, but made no move to stop Alonzo.

"*Ja*, but-"

"That's how war works, you take prisoners sometimes. Take prisoners when possible, kill when necessary."

Koby raised his weapon at the Russians then. Blaz's eyes darted from Alonzo to Koby.

"Koby?"

Koby didn't answer. He stayed absolutely silent but kept his gun on the Russians. No one made an attempt to stop Koby, including Blaz. Koby's tan face looked redder than normal, Blaz could tell his heart was thumping fast.

"Come on, Koby. Crosses is right. Maybe we'll get mercy in a few days because of this," Christoff said.

Koby rolled his eyes but did indeed lower his rifle. He took a deep, deep breath then announced, "All right, we'll move out," then shot something at the Russians in their language. The Soviets marched forward, hands on their heads.

"*Warten*!" Blaz almost yelled, holding a hand up to signal a halt. The Russians stopped in their tracks, "That tank is completely operational?"

"*Ja*," the tank commander said.

"Shouldn't we take it with us?"

"*Ja*!" Crosses exclaimed, "It may be damaged, but the gun can do us good. I'll drive son. You get in the commander's nest. We'll have to do without a gunner."

Despite the circumstances, Blaz was excited to finally use an operational tank.

"Sergeant, can you keep the Russians at gunpoint in front of the tanks on the way back?" Crosses asked Koby.

"*Jawohl*."

"Let's go then," Crosses said to Blaz.

They jogged over to the tank, and Crosses started it up. Blaz kept the hatch open and spoke into the small microphone that allowed him to communicate.

"Can you hear me?" he said.

"Loud and clear."

"*Gut, gut.*"

The Russians marched out front, with Koby following. He kept his gun aimed at them from his hip. The Panther rumbled behind them, with Christoff and the soldier with the broken leg sitting on top. Crosses and Blaz's T-34 chugged along after the Panther. Crosses had been trying to get on the same scramble set as the Panther and had finally done so.

"You guys are one damn good tank crew," he commended them.

"I'll admit; I didn't think we were going to win that fight. Five on one," the driver of the other tank chuckled, "We have a great tank, though."

"You got a name for her?" Crosses asked.

Blaz heard the tank crew erupt with laughter.

"*Ja,*" one man snickered.

"Of course," the commander said as if this were all too obvious.

"Sorry. What is it?" Crosses asked, his tone remaining lighthearted.

"Erika," one man answered quickly.

"That's original," Crosses mumbled sarcastically, "How long have you guys been together?"

"Well Crosses," the tank commander said, "We met back when we were nineteen-year-olds in nineteen-forty after France. We were trained as a tank crew, that's how we met. We got one of those crappy *Panzer III*'s."

"Hey, don't mock Adolfina," the driver said, "She got us through two Russian winters and the offensive days of Barbarossa. Never had a breakdown with her."

Adolfina? Blaz thought with a smirk.

"Okay, fair enough. She was old reliable. But Christ, that gun! Erika's gun is infinitely better," the commander smiled, giving the tank's gun an almost affectionate pat. "Norbert just gets emotional over Adolfina," another crew member said, "Never really wanted to leave her, only after we destroyed eight tanks at Kursk and repelled three direct hits did he warm up to Erika."

"When you drive the tank, you are the tank," Norbert replied.

"I get what he means, I'm warming up to this Russkie tank," Crosses chuckled, "Kid! You want to give her a name?"

"*Nein!*" Blaz answered immediately.

Crosses and the tank crew laughed. "All right then, kid."

The boys returned to their bunker, with the Panther nearby as Stromschnellen arrived to give orders to bulk up the last lines of defense. He was quite happy to see they had salvaged an operational Soviet tank. The T-34 was posted near the bunker as well.

Gunther had returned at some point, with a wounded Jaecar and Werner. Gunther was in the bunker with them, tapping one foot nervously as Koby and Blaz entered, and Koen was talking with a barely awake Jaecar.

"Koby! Blaz!" Gunther exclaimed happily when they ducked into the bunker.

"Hey Gunther," Koby said, looking at Jaecar and Werner, "What happened here?"

"We weren't very good tank hunters," Gunther admitted, "We had one tank to deal with. We only survived by playing dead."

"*Mein Wort,*" Blaz's eyes widened.

"Jaecar missed his shot. He froze up when he missed. Werner fired our second *Panzerfaust*, and he missed too. Sort of, he skimmed the side."

Koby gritted his teeth in disappointed surprise. The tank commander opened the hatch, Jaecar started running. He shot Jaecar twice, in the leg and the back. Then Werner tried to fire the other *Panzerfaust* but he got shot in a rib-"

"Again?" Koby grimaced.

"What happened to you? How did you end up on the ground?" Blaz asked.

Gunther gave his hamstring a pat, "I got shot in the upper leg. They dug the bullet out already. I'm having trouble putting weight on it right now. I was lucky it didn't hit bone."

"How many bullets have you had in your legs?" Blaz asked with concern.

"Four," Gunther said, taking a seat. Koby and Blaz sat down on either side of Gunther, who groaned, and put a hand on his thigh.

"Wow," Gunther said with gritted teeth, "That hurt."

"You feel okay?" Blaz asked.

Gunther shook his head, "It's hurting bad. Have to grin and bear it."

"Why didn't they finish you guys off?" Koby asked.

"The tank commander, I think he showed us mercy. He walked over to Werner and me. He put a foot on my chest, at my heart. He kept it there, I stayed as still as I could. He started pushing down harder, I still stayed quiet. But I think he heard me breath in, because he stopped right after I did. He just stood over me for a few seconds, and then he knelt next to me, and put a hand on my heart. He did the same to Werner, and I think Jaecar. Then he just left. He got back in the tank. I sat up against a tree when they chugged away. He looked back several times. God bless him for it."

"No kidding," Blaz agreed. Koby appeared perplexed by this.

"So how are they doing?" Blaz asked Gunther, gesturing to Werner and Jaecar.

"They'll be okay," said Gunther, leaning against the bunker wall, "Werner will have to deal with his broken rib, doctor said a couple weeks to heal. We will need every man. Jaecar, he's taking it like a trooper. Koen has been talking with him for quite a while. Tough kid, that Jaecar. If he had started moaning or screaming when he got shot, the commander would have had to shoot us."

"Stoic little kid, then," Koby commended him.

"*Ja*," Gunther said as artillery sounded. Blaz looked out the bunker's window's slit. The sun was setting, and Blaz could see some men moving around in the trenches in the thinly forested area.

"Looks like the front lines caved," Blaz said, "Second lines now."

"It's only a matter of time," Gunther admitted, "We'll need a lot of heroes to win this one. Without reinforcements, at least."

The SS Meeting

"*Heil* Hitler!" the SS high command saluted Heinrici and Busse, who returned the salute. None of the *Wehrmacht* officers had come; they remained to command their posts. Engal, though the highest ranking of the SS, was busy at the always retreating front as well. They were at a mobile command post at the final line of defense. Under a tent.

"Generals," Lochner desperately pleaded, "We must pull out, the front lines have completely collapsed. Our second lines remain solid, but I estimate we cannot hold out until tomorrow night."

"*Obersturmbannführer*, the *Führer* gave me orders personally last month to hold at Seelow until permission was given to pull back," Busse informed Lochner, while making vague signs with his hand and arm, "My Ninth Army will not pull out."

"As commander of the Seelow Heights defense, I refuse to pull out and leave the *Volkssturm* to their fate. Schörner must put up a better defense," Heinrici agreed, "But the *Führer's* orders stand. Until we can no longer put up a legitimate defense, we stand and fight. We have been pushed back, but our front lines held for nearly two days. The longer we delay the Soviets, the longer the *Führer* has to strike a deal with the Allies."

"We can't win. What is there to fight for?" Lochner challenged.

"We are soldiers. We are German. We will stand by our *Führer* through thick and thin," Schlusser glared at Lochner, "For our future and our children's future."

"I will fight on the front lines again, with nothing but my fists before I give up on the *Führer*," Kurzmann replied savagely.

"*Reichsführer* Himmler has decided to try to negotiate with the West," Stromschnellen said, "I've been in contact with him. The longer we hold, the better chance the *Reichsführer* will have. Retreat is not an option when we still have two lines standing strong. We've suffered minimal casualties as well. This is no time to retreat when we have a fortified position."

"The Russians will overrun us within days."

"We have reinforcements from two SS *Panzer* divisions on their way," Heinrici interjected, "If we hold out until then, we can buy even more time. If not, I will assume command over them along with von Manteuffel. Then we will decide what is best."

Lochner glared at the ground. "Save some Germans and pull out. The war is lost."

"We must hold out, Lochner," Heinrici said, "The future that awaits *Deutschland* if we lose is not one of hope."

Lochner raised no objection this time, "I know," he admitted.

"*Schutzstaffel*," Heinrici saluted, "I wish you the best." With that, the general disappeared into the night.

Schlusser started laughing in disbelief, "Lochner, you, you just want to save your own skin!"

Kurzmann shot a menacing look at Lochner.

"Mine, yours, and everyone else's, *Hauptsturmführer*," Lochner retorted. Both Schlusser and Kurzmann stormed out of tent, followed by Stromschnellen.

"Wait! Reynald!" Stromschnellen called to the two.

Schlusser and Kurzmann turned around. "What is it, *Standartenführer*?" he asked ground out.

"It's Simon, Reynald," Stromschnellen asked as he came face to face with Schlusser.

"Very well Simon. What is it?"

Stromschnellen glanced to Kurzmann, deciding if this was for his ears or not.

"*Hauptsturmführer*, may I have a word with Reynald?"

"*Na sicher*," Kurzmann obediently agreed and strode away.

"Reynald, I am going to the front tomorrow. Derry is going elsewhere at the front. As a fellow *Waffen*-SS leader, I would like to make a request of you."

"Go on."

"I don't trust Lochner. I would like you to keep an eye on him. Make sure he doesn't betray the Fatherland," Stromschnellen said.

"By your command," Schlusser saluted.

Defenseless

Blaz lay in a trench to the side of the bunker, using his hands as a pillow, curled up around his helmet. Occasional bouts of gunfire and artillery dominated the otherwise quiet night. A humming intruded on the two sounds. Slowly, the humming grew louder. Blaz glanced up. Dozens of bird-like figures moved across the sky. But Blaz knew they were bombers. The air raid sirens had started up.

"Bombers!" a soldier shouted, "Russkie bombers!"

"In the trenches!" Schneider ordered, and troops came scrambling out of the bunker. Werner and Jaecar were helped by Ivo and Gunther. The bombers overshot them.

"Where are they flying?" Koby wondered aloud, watching their silhouettes fly away. The bombers flew southwest. Blaz gasped.

"Seelow," Blaz whispered, "Koby! They're going to bomb Seelow!"

Koby gasped in horror and his eyes widened. "*Nein! Nein!* They can't!"

Anti-aircraft fire soared up toward the bombers, a couple found their marks. But there were too many bombers and too few guns. The planes dropped their payloads, with every intention of hitting the town. Flames from the explosions were just visible above some trees, and the flash of their impact lit the night in the distance briefly.

"Damn you, Russkies!" Blaz heard Jarman swear, "*Fik dich, Russen!*"

Koby fell back against the wall of the trench, "*Nein.*"

Blaz and Koby couldn't fall asleep for hours. They did not speak much either. They stayed awake, glancing in Seelow's direction occasionally. As the night ran on, Blaz leaned against Koby's shoulder in exhaustion and fell asleep.

Relief of Seelow

April 18, 1945

Blaz woke up the next morning with Koby tapping his skull. He lifted his head off Koby's thighs. He rubbed his eyes and yawned.

"They sent men to help in Seelow," Koby told him.

Blaz nodded, he couldn't think of anything to say. All they could do was hope and pray that the warplanes had missed the bomb shelters and homes.

"Blaz, Jarman lost it last night. After we fell asleep, he went and shot a Russian prisoner."

"What? How did you find out?"

"*Herr* Schneider woke me up to tell me."

"What does that mean? What's going to happen?"

"He's been taken to report to the *Allgemeine-SS*. An officer came this morning." Koby said, putting his helmet on, "I doubt he'll get in trouble. We need every man we can get."

"They better not do anything to him," Blaz muttered.

Koby stood up while putting on his field gray helmet, "I hate this helplessness."

"*Wie Bitte?*"

"We have no control over anything."

"We never have."

"I know, but now I feel it."

The Officer

"I would let you get away with this," Schlusser told Jarman while he escorted him to Lochner. The young man held his Walther in one hand, but it was not cocked. "This was despicable of the Russians to do," he assured Jarman as they walked through the rubble. They had seen several bodies; women and children, being dug out of the rubble by disheartened old soldiers and women of the town. Jarman marched beside his former Hitler Youth instructor silently except for the crunch of his boots on gravel.

"It's good to see you again, Jarman," Schlusser said, trying to break the ice again. Jarman kept marching.

"Tell me, Jarman. If I could give you the chance to leave this battle would you take it? I can have you sent to a prison camp for disciplinary action. That is within my power."

This got a response. "*Nein*. I will stay in Seelow."

"Do you think any of your friends would accept this offer?" Schlusser pursued.

"*Nein*. We will stay in our hometown. We won't be cowards."

Schlusser nodded. They had absorbed his teaching well. He still wished Jarman had accepted the offer. They arrived at the school, which had been partially destroyed. Schlusser led Jarman past the former command center to the office where Lochner would be. Surprisingly, before they arrived, the door swung open. Lochner froze, seeing Schlusser standing there. He was carrying a brief case, had his MP-40 on him, and wore a trench coat.

"Ah, Reynald. What is it?" Lochner greeted his SS comrade, quickly changing his expression.

Schlusser looked Lochner up and down before responding, "Disciplinary action. This soldier executed a Russian prisoner without permission from his superior officer and had to be restrained from killing a second. As officer in charge of Seelow, the punishment is up to you."

"I see no reason to discipline him," Lochner replied.

"Are you sure?" Schlusser asked, "Do you hand over authority to me on this matter?"

"*Ja*," Lochner said, and strode down the hall.

"Where are you going?" Schlusser called.

"I have some business to attend to."

Schlusser scowled and turned to Jarman, "Follow me."

Schlusser and Jarman followed Lochner at a distance.

"You have your pistol?" Schlusser asked Jarman.

"*Jawohl.*"

"*Gut.*"

Lochner disappeared into a house where a motorcycle was parked outside. They saw Lochner's briefcase and unloaded MP-40 in the attached sidecar. Schlusser gestured for Jarman to come with him. He cocked his Walther.

"Safety off," Schlusser said, handing Jarman his STG-44, which he had slung over his shoulder.

"Sir?" Jarman asked, arching his eyebrows.

"Trust me, Jarman."

They entered the house. Lochner was speaking with Hadler, but both turned to face Schlusser and Jarman.

"What is it, Reynald?" Lochner asked, annoyance in his tone.

"I forgot to tell you. We had two *Hitlerjugend* try to desert this morning," Schlusser smiled cunningly, "What is your verdict on deserters?"

"I'd say they are the smart ones," Lochner said, striding towards the door. Hadler followed him. Schlusser acted quickly. He whacked Hadler on the head with his pistol and spun to get Lochner at gunpoint. But Lochner had also drawn his pistol and aimed it at Schlusser's head. Jarman raised his STG-44 at Hadler who had stumbled against a wall.

"You coward," Schlusser growled at Lochner, "*Feigling*!"

"I won't submit myself to any Jewish mockery of a trial," Lochner answered, both his voice and hand shaking, "I've done nothing wrong!"

"Fight like a soldier!"

"I have for years, but it's time to end this charade. The war is lost."

Jarman's grip tightened on his weapon. Hadler held his hands up in surrender.

"You are sworn to fight for the *Führer*."

Lochner scowled, "It's time to abandon that. I'm escaping with my life. I have a family to get home to. Lower your pistol, Reynald. I don't want your little boy to grow up an orphan," the officer said. Schlusser had been sent a telegraph from his wife days after Dresden was bombed that they were both okay.

"*Nein*. I must shoot you. The *Führer* forbids desertion. And so do I."

"Put the gun down!"

"*Obersturmbannführer*! Sir!" came a voice from outside and a small boy appeared at the door. He had a massive gash and a singed tear through his white, button-up shirt at the chest. Blood covered his hand that he held over his chest.

"What is it?" Lochner said without taking his eyes off Schlusser.

"Sir, I can't find my sister. She was here last night, sir. Do you know where she is?"

Lochner closed his eyes in frustration. But Schlusser didn't shoot. Jarman lowered his gun and Hadler lowered his arms.

"Where do you live?" Lochner said keeping his pistol on Schlusser, still not glancing at the young boy.

"I can show you," the boy answered, looking puzzled at why two German men were pointing pistols at each other.

"Put your pistols down," Jarman hissed at them.

Schlusser and Lochner lowered their pistols.

"Go with the kid, *Obersturmbannführer*," Jarman ordered Lochner.

"I'll deal with him, Jarman," Schlusser said, "Back to your post. *Heil* Hitler," he added at the end, to make sure Lochner heard him.

"*Heil* Hitler," Jarman replied, "See you at the front."

The Last Awards

When Jarman returned, Berghoff was pacing in front of Schneider's men among others. His steps were short, and he stared at the ground as he paced.

"The crew of Panther fourteen-eighty-eight receives the Iron Cross-First Class for destroying seven tanks." The men of the crew that Blaz had served with saluted Berghoff, who returned the salute after pinning the award to their uniforms. All had already received the Iron Cross Second Class at Kursk.

"You make all of Germany proud," Berghoff said, shaking each man's hand.

"*Danke Major*," each man replied with no trace of emotion. It was all hidden behind professionalism. Berghoff nodded and moved down the line.

"For destroying three tanks and capturing one intact, Blaz Senft receives the Iron Cross-Second Class," Berghoff said, pinning the commendation on Blaz's right chest.

"*Danke Major*," Blaz said, without smiling.

"I am proud of you," Berghoff said gravely.

Blaz stomped his right foot and thrust a salute. Berghoff returned the gesture. He moved on to the next soldier, a member of the *Waffen-SS*.

"Yaroslav Ponikarovsky moved messages to the front under heavy artillery fire and receives the Iron Cross-Second Class."

The soldier saluted, and replied, "*Spasy- Danke Major.*"

Berghoff saluted the soldier and moved on. Blaz turned to the soldier, "*Danke* for fighting for the Reich."

The soldier turned to his left to face Blaz, showing him a patch over his heart. Ukraine's flag of yellow and light blue was next to the *Reichsadler*. "The Bolsheviks we will beat back," he said faultily, holding out a hand to Blaz.

"We will," Blaz nodded, and firmly shook the man's hand.

"To your posts!" Schneider shouted, "To your posts! The Russians have broken through our second lines. To your posts!"

Blaz picked up his rifle and ran out into the trenches behind Koby. They lined up next to their comrades, weapons raised. "Watch the trees. Hold fire until you have confirmed your target," Schneider shouted to the soldiers while tanks exchanged fire in the distance.

"Don't get trigger happy, Jarman," Koby ordered, "There are trenches ahead of us."

"*Ja, ja, sicher,*" Jarman scowled.

"Werner, you feel all right?"

"*Na sicher,*" Werner answered.

Koby gave him a pat on the back, "Stay alert. Stay low."

"Knecht! Senft! Take Harvey and hunt tanks," Schneider said as he ran towards them with a *Panzerfaust* in his arms, Alonzo trailing behind. Jarman and Blaz leapt out of the trench and ran after Schneider and Alonzo. Schneider led them quite a way. Finally, he handed the *Panzerfaust* to Alonzo and headed back to his command post. Jarman took the lead, and the three Germans crept through the night to destroy the enemy.

Werwolf

April 19, 1945

Blaz crawled with his rifle through a field of growing wheat. They had run through part of the field, staying low. Now they neared the road, which was simply an area where wheat did not grow. They could hear Russian voices in the distance and the sound of engines humming.

"Halt!" Jarman called. "A truck is coming," he whispered, reaching for his grenade. "Get back."

Blaz and Alonzo slid further back into the field. The truck's headlights grew brighter and brighter as it neared. Jarman had pulled the pin, and now held the grenade as it came very near. He tossed it into the road and rolled further back into the field. The truck continued driving, right over the grenade. As the front of the truck passed over, it exploded, igniting the fuel. The truck's engine went up in flames, bringing light to the rural darkness. Jarman shot up from his hiding place as Russians leapt from the back of the flaming truck. He fired his STG-44, hitting the unprepared Russians with grim efficiency.

"Clear it out!" Jarman ordered Blaz, who leapt up and sprinted to the back of the truck with his rifle cocked and raised. The flames gave him enough light to see the Russian bodies. Jarman had killed them those who hadn't been killed in the explosion.

"*Alles gut,*" Blaz reported. Jarman and Alonzo emerged from the field. Jarman kicked each Russian in the head, to make sure they were dead. None flinched.

"Get back to cover, move further down the road."

"Towards where the truck came from?" Blaz asked.

"*Jawohl,*" Jarman answered. The boys sprinted through the field toward the Russian lines.

"When do we return?" Alonzo asked. Blaz could hear the eagerness to return to their post in Alonzo's tone.

"Before sunrise, by the cover of night," Jarman answered again. They dropped to their chests and poked their heads out of the wheat to get a view of the road. Blaz grew drowsy, but Jarman elbowed him to keep him awake. Alonzo knelt to remain alert. No Russians came by for quite a time, but it didn't last

"Soviet tank!" Jarman whispered, "Alonzo, wait for it to pass. Hit it in the rear."

"*Sicher*," Alonzo nodded, adjusting the *Panzerfaust* in his arms.

The tank rolled onward with a small spotlight lighting the way by their position. As it passed, the boys saw that Russians were marching behind. They had not heard marching with only twelve or thirteen soldiers.

"We'll take them, proceed as ordered," Jarman whispered to Alonzo.

The three youths sprung from their hiding place and raised their weapons at the backs of the Russians. Jarman fired the first shot, followed quickly by Alonzo's *Panzerfaust*. The warhead hurtled forth, pierced the armor, and flames poured from the tank.

Jarman unleashed a torrent of bullets from his weapon. Russians fell, some attempting to scatter. Blaz fired on them. Jarman's gun was fast, and the Russians appeared dead, but they approached cautiously. Alonzo dropped his now useless *Panzerfaust*. Blaz fired on one Russian who flinched on the ground.

Jarman began counting the bodies, mumbling the numbers to himself, "Twelve," Jarman finished, "Where's that last one? Circle up."

Jarman put his back to Blaz and Alonzo, so that they each faced a different direction. Alonzo drew his pistol, his only other weapon now. Blaz kept his bayoneted rifle raised. Jarman moved his STG-44, scanning the area.

"You sure there were thirteen?" Blaz asked after a while.

"Fairly sure."

"Jarman there's more vehicles coming," Alonzo whispered. Several hundred meters away, headlights lit the road. They moved slowly, this presumably being the main force of tanks, trucks, and troops.

"Let's get out of here," Jarman said, "Time to go."

The soldiers jogged northeast towards their defenses. They went past the tank, unaware of the soldier running at them on top of it. The Russian had his dagger drawn. He leapt, his shoes making a clacking sound as he jumped. Blaz spun around and raised his gun. Before he could fire, the Russian grabbed the end of the rifle. He swung his dagger at Blaz's throat but missed as the German bent backwards. Jarman raised his gun but did not fire. Blaz still had a grip on his rifle, and charged forward, trying to run the man through with the bayonet. The Russian sidestepped the attack and grabbed him by the collar. Blaz fought frantically, and the Russian's stab only nicked his shoulder. The Soviet let go of Blaz briefly, and Jarman fired. The shot was a miss, but the Russian saw Jarman and threw his dagger. Jarman didn't fire again. The enemy soldier charged at Alonzo who fired two desperate shots. Blaz heard a grunt from the Soviet, but he'd seen Russians keep fighting after getting shot. Alonzo choked out a cry for help. Blaz drew his Walther. The Russian, with uncanny senses, turned around as Blaz approached. He swung hard and socked Blaz in the nose. The German soldier went to the ground and lost his grip on his pistol.

Alonzo used this moment and sent the tip of his boot into the Russian's crotch. The man shouted in pain but managed to leap after Alonzo as he scrambled away. Blaz clambered back up, drew his knife, and stabbed the Russian in the calf. The Russian held in his scream this time and swung a fist at Blaz. This time he was ready and dodged. The Russian scowled and pulled a small pocketknife out of a shirt pocket. He held it between two fingers, so he would stab them if he punched them. Blaz stood ready with his knife. Alonzo stood across from him and had drawn his own blade.

The lights of the Russian convoy drew nearer. Blaz gritted his teeth and jabbed at the soldier, who dodged and stabbed Blaz in the shoulder. Blaz stumbled back and clutched at his new wound. Alonzo stabbed the Russian's side, but was met by a punch as well. The Russian turned back to Blaz. He punched at Blaz with both fists, but the German dodged the blows, as they were getting slower with his many wounds. Alonzo stabbed the Russian again, this time in the back. The man dropped to his knees.

Blaz picked up his rifle and bayoneted the Soviet. Alonzo picked up his pistol and Blaz's, handing the latter to its owner.

"Where's Jarman?" Blaz asked Alonzo. The lights of the convoy were near now.

"Get off the road!" Alonzo hissed and the two dove into the wheat, crawling away faster than they ever had in any drill. "Jarman!" Blaz called, hoping the engines would drown this out to the Russians. It did.

Jarman faintly answered from somewhere unseen even with the light of the fire, "Blaz."

"Jarman!"

"Over here."

Blaz followed the voice, to find Jarman lying on the ground with a Soviet dagger in one hand. He held it up.

"Feel it."

Blaz gently put his hand on the dagger and felt the warm stickiness of blood.

"He got me," Jarman said, as he sat up, "Damn good throw."

"Jarman, we need to get out of here," Blaz whispered. Russians were talking in raised and alarmed voices.

"You guys get out of here. I'm bleeding out. And I'm bringing down as many beasts as I can," Jarman said weakly, with a deep breath, "I will die like a soldier. Not on the ground hiding like this." He picked up his STG-44 and slid a new magazine into it. "Give me your grenades."

"Jarman–"

"*Jetzt!*"

Blaz and Alonzo each handed him a grenade.

"Now, you two get out of here. You stand a better chance if I do this anyway. Stay low. Run. You're small enough they won't notice you," Jarman said with a groan of pain.

"Jarman, I am not leaving you like this," Blaz answered stubbornly.

Jarman pulled Blaz close, "If you stay, Alonzo will die too. Get him out of here."

"*Aber–*"

"*Tun sie es.*" Do it.

"Okay."

Jarman kept him close. "I never deserved a friend as good as you, Blaz. I will die gladly knowing of what we have accomplished for our homeland together. Fighting for a better world. You, me, all of us." What Jarman said next must have been hard for him to say. But he said it with no hesitation. "The war is lost, Blaz. Hopelessly, hopelessly lost." He paused and smiled. "Make sure to tell that to Koby. He doesn't know."

Blaz hugged Jarman, who coughed blood up onto his uniform. "Don't you dare come back," Jarman said at a normal volume, and chambered a round, "*Heil* Hitler."

Blaz and Alonzo sprinted away, staying as low as they could. They heard an explosion followed by shooting. Blaz slowed up, but Alonzo grabbed him.

"Come on, you heard him. Come on."

"Sorry," Blaz told the thirteen-year-old, "I need to help him."

"Blaz, what did he tell you?"

"Don't you dare come back."

"He's doing this for you."

"I don't want him to die for me," Blaz said, fighting Alonzo, "I should go down with him."

"What good will that do?" Alonzo asked, echoing Blaz from earlier in the battle, "Come on."

Alonzo sprinted away. The shooting ceased then. Blaz stared at the flaming tank and line of Russians. Reluctantly, he turned away. But he stopped again, to give a last look.

"*Heil* Hitler," Blaz whispered, and sprinted after Alonzo.

My Choice

Blaz and Alonzo made it back to the trenches, in the dead of night. Koby was awake to greet them.

"What happened?"

"Jarman is dead. He was knifed."

Koby wiped one eye, kicking at the dirt. "Jarman." Koby looked up at the stars. He opened his mouth and closed it several times.

"Koby," Blaz said, making sure he had his friend's eye contact, "He told me to tell you that the war is lost. Hopelessly lost."

Koby sniffled, "The war isn't lost. Jarman would never say that."

"He said he didn't think you knew the war is lost."

Koby nodded before turning away. Blaz watched his sergeant leave. He wanted to call out to him but didn't. What good would it do?

Blaz laid down, ready for sleep.

"Blaz!" a voice whispered. No such luck. Blaz's eyes snapped open. He stared up at Ivo. The little soldier extended a hand to Blaz, who took it. Ivo lifted Blaz up and waved for him to follow out of the trenches and into the forest. Blaz stopped him after about twenty meters. "Ivo, where are we going?"

Ivo looked Blaz in the eye. His face was just visible in the moonlight, "Blaz, we need to get out of here. If we stay we're going to die. I want to grow up before that happens." Tristan's face rose in Blaz's mind at these words.

Blaz backed away. "Ivo, I can't. *We* can't-"

"Why not?" Ivo challenged, "We've served for years, now the war is lost. There is no way this ends well."

"Ivo, we can-"

"*Nein* Blaz! There is no version of this where the enemy doesn't overrun Seelow and then capture Berlin! It's over. Do I wish we had a fighting chance? *Ja*! But there is none! National Socialism is beaten! *Deutschland* is beaten! Blaz, you've said you want to have a family when you grow up. Don't you still want that? I know you still want to live after this war."

Blaz took another step away.

"Don't you?" Ivo asked, sounding unsure now.

"I do, but life after," Blaz swallowed, "I have to stay. Koby's still here."

"Koby!" Ivo exclaimed, "Blaz, Koby's lost all sense of reality! He wants to die; can't you see?"

"He's not too far gone."

"He will drag you down with him! Please, don't throw your life away like this," Ivo pleaded, "Come with me."

Blaz shook his head, "You'll be killed if you get caught."

"I'll die for sure if I stay," Ivo replied, and walked away. Blaz didn't know why, but he found himself at Ivo's side. Ivo took off his helmet, "It's been a good run, Blaz."

Blaz couldn't think of anything to say. The two made it into the forest without anyone asking where they were heading. Then a voice shouted, "Stop! What're you doing?"

Ivo and Blaz turned around. Koby and Werner were jogging towards them, weapons in hand. Gunther was behind them, but had his weapon slung over his back.

"You're deserting, aren't you?" Koby asked, disappointment dripping from his words.

"*Nein*," Ivo replied too quickly.

"Then why do you have your gear, Ivo?" Werner asked.

"I-" Ivo stammered, glancing from Blaz to Koby to Werner, "Blaz had nothing to do with it. He was trying to convince me not to go!"

"So, you were deserting?" Koby asked, aiming his weapon at Ivo. Blaz heard Gunther gasp. Koby pointed the weapon at Blaz briefly. "Get over here, Blaz."

Blaz briskly made his way behind his sergeant and to Gunther's side. Ivo backed away from Koby, further into the forest, "Koby, I want to live. I don't want any more of this."

"Ivo, wait!" Koby yelled, then said so disingenuously that Blaz knew he didn't even believe it, "It, it isn't over."

"What?!" Ivo shouted, "What?! Listen to yourself, Koby! Of course it's over! It's been over for months, we've all known it! There's no chance!" Ivo took a deep breath, his voice no longer at a shout as he resumed talking, "I'm leaving. If you want to stop me, you'll have to pull the damn trigger. If any of you stay, you'll be dead by noon. *Heil* Hitler," Ivo added, with the utmost sincerity. He gave Blaz a nod, turned away, and walked deeper into the woods. He had walked not ten meters when Koby fired. The bullet hit a tree near Ivo. He didn't even flinch.

"Ivo!" Koby called.

Ivo didn't answer or slow down. Koby fired again. This time he hit Ivo. Blaz didn't see where he shot, but he heard the bullet tear through Ivo briefly and saw his friend trip and fall to the ground, face first. Blaz looked at Koby, mouth open. Koby didn't look his way but took a step back from the shooting. His hands slackened on his gun. Werner's jaw dropped, but he recovered quickly. He shook his head and turned away, returning to the defenses. Koby stared at Ivo for several seconds before he followed suit. He turned and followed Werner as Ivo bled out. As soon as he had turned, Gunther and Blaz ran to Ivo. Gunther turned him onto his back. Ivo's chest was bleeding, on the right side. Blaz took off his uniform and shirt then wrapped Ivo's midsection with them. The blood kept coming though.

Ivo weakly lifted his head and turned to Blaz. There were tears in his eyes. "I never thought Koby would be the one to kill me."

Gunther put his hand under Ivo's head for support. They exchanged glances, Blaz and Ivo meeting eyes at last.

"I think of you as my brother Blaz. I had to say that," Ivo rasped, "And Koby too." He breathed in, and grabbed Blaz by the collar, "Bring him back. That's all that matters now." Ivo exhaled and closed his eyes.

Gunther lowered Ivo's head to the ground. The Berliner breathed rapidly on seeing Ivo dead. "How long, did Koby, know you and Ivo?"

"Since we could talk," Blaz answered, wiping his nose, "The three of us grew up together, we played together, we learned together, we trained together, we ran together." Blaz's voice trailed off, "Koby *killed* Ivo."

"Should we report this?" Gunther asked.

"Koby didn't do anything against military regulations. Deserters *are* to be shot," Blaz said.

"But this-"

Blaz looked to the east, where Koby and Werner had headed. He couldn't believe it. Koby had shot Ivo.

Schlusser's Report

"General Heinrici, Busse?" Schlusser yelled into the phone. He clutched his side, where he'd been wounded the day before in heavy fighting. Berghoff stood anxiously next to him, tapping his foot. Max was also present, pacing furiously. Outside on the soccer field, stood Schlusser and Stromschnellen's remaining men. Stromschnellen came jogging into the room to hear the conversation.

"*Jawohl*, Schlusser," Busse's voice replied.

"Busse! General, we have fallen back to the final line of defense in all positions in the center. We've lost Fliegel, Hadler, Schmidt, Kurzmann, and Reichert to bullets. Engal and Lochner have been badly wounded. Only Berghoff, Stromschnellen, and myself are in condition to manage the battle."

"Send Berghoff to manage in the north," Busse replied, "Quickly."

Schlusser nodded to Berghoff who sprinted out of the room without a word.

"Schörner's defenses have failed. You must hold out until our SS reinforcements can reach us. Stromschnellen and you take direct command in the center. To the last bullet. *Heil* Hitler."

"*Heil* Hitler!" Schlusser hung up the phone.

"That's it then," Stromschnellen nodded, put on his camouflaged helmet over his field cap, and cocked his STG-44, "Let's go, Reynald."

"I'm proud to have fought alongside you, Simon. And you Max." Schlusser shook each man's hand.

"One last SS march in enemy land," Max breathed, readying himself for death.

Then the three marched out into the early morning light to fulfill their oaths to their *Führer*, to their nation, to their people.

A Last Effort

Tanks rumbled and roared through the fields, firing their massive cannons. The Germans fired at Soviet tanks through gaps in the trees, occasionally hitting one. The men in the trenches gunned down any Russians who attempted to charge. The remnants of the squad lined up next to a machine gun. Alonzo fed bullets into the gun. Gunther and Blaz stayed side by side, keeping wary eyes on Koby and Werner. German tanks fired from the forest behind them, covering for the other German tanks engaged in hopelessly outnumbered combat. The Russians were now breaking through the flimsy defense.

German troops ran to the west, covered by their position.

"Full retreat!" Stromschnellen roared to the Germans. He ran through the trenches, telling Schneider's men, "Just a few more minutes."

"They're coming up the hill," Koby told the squad, referring to their own troops, "Rifleman, give them cover!"

Blaz, Gunther, and Werner chose targets. The Soviets were pursuing the Germans. Blaz fired, waiting until he saw the whites of the Russians' eyes.

"Run! Run!" Schneider came running by, "*Los!* Fall back to the forest! We will regroup there!"

Nobody hesitated. They climbed out of the trench and fled. The machine gunner bolted after them. As they ran, a Soviet tank came roaring up the hill. A German fired a *Panzerfaust* into its treads, immobilizing it, but the machine gun still fired. Several Hitler Youths were cut down. Koby pushed his men forward, keeping them running. Another *Panzerfaust* fired, and the Soviet tank went up in flames. They ran up a steep hill, desperately hoping to get behind their tanks. Russians were now overrunning their former position. Schneider pulled his pistol to hold for his men, killing two Russians, before being shot to death. Stromschnellen was the last man up the hill. He shouted for the tanks to fire as he slid behind a tree. The tanks responded by unleashing a burst of fire into the Soviet ranks.

"What now!" Blaz yelled to Koby, eyes blazing, as the Russians continued their push.

"Keep fighting! *Weiter!*" Stromschnellen urged the troops.

The Germans responded with a fanatic cry, firing all the more into the Russian lines. Blaz stood up, shot a Russian in the chest, and ducked behind cover. Bullets hammered into the tree behind and in front of him. The Russians tanks were rolling up the hill now. The German tanks flew into reverse.

"Artillery! Move back!" Stromschnellen screamed.

Blaz leapt up and sprinted into the forest, the remnants of the Knights behind him plus Alonzo. Artillery rained down on the Russians from the final line of German defenses.

"You two! I need you to send a message to our last line of defense. Tell them we can hold for thirty minutes here and to ready their defenses," Stromschnellen ordered the Blaz and Koby, "And we will be at their position within the hour. Run like hell."

Koby simply saluted before he sprinted off. Blaz ran after him, finger on the trigger.

"*Hauptmann!*" Koby yelled to Berghoff who was mobilizing troops at the edge of the forest. A mass retreat was occurring, enabled by a last line of defense. Concrete tank barriers were at the front of the defenses. Panther and Tiger tanks were behind mounds of dirt, so that only their guns were visible from the front. Sniper towers were all around the wide, final line, mainly to the back of the defenses. Flak and artillery were also at the rear. Troops were dug into trenches. Trucks drove to the west, heading for Berlin. Desperation hung in the air.

"*Hauptmann!*" Koby shouted, running to the officer.

"What is it?" Berghoff asked, clearly very stressed. Underneath his eyes, his skin appeared darker and it seemed to sag.

"Our third line has broken. Our forces will be here within the hour. They need your forces to be ready!"

"We are prepared already. You young men, get in the trenches. We need every soldier we can get."

"*Ja, Hauptmann!*" Blaz and Koby saluted. They took places in the trenches, side by side. Blaz turned to Koby. His sergeant looked at him. Blaz couldn't stay quiet any longer. "Koby, you killed Ivo! You killed our friend!"

Koby stared. At first with a gaze that rested on Blaz, but then went beyond into an unknown distance.

"Koby!" Blaz screamed, losing his composure, seizing Koby by his uniform's lapels. "What were you thinking last night?"

Koby looked ghostly. He stared blankly into Blaz's eyes. "I just did, Blaz. I had to."

"You've known Ivo forever!" Blaz shouted in rage, almost ready to start choking Koby.

His sergeant nodded repeatedly, "I know Blaz. I had to. I had to stop a deserter."

Blaz glared at Koby and tightened his grip, "You've lost it. I don't even know if I should call you Koby anymore, he never would've done that." Koby breathed unsteadily but didn't answer. Blaz let him go, and turned back to face the east, "But I'll follow you into battle, Sergeant Hertz."

Koby put a hand on his forehead and stared straight into the ground. Blaz raised his rifle and aimed it above the trench. The sounds of battle grew nearer.

The Final Conflict

Within the hour, Germans came marching back to the defenses. Stromschnellen limped past Koby and Blaz, with a bullet hole in his helmet, but no head wound. The *Standartenführer* was helped by his *Hitlerjugend* adjutant. His left leg bled profusely, and he clutched his chest, which was soaked in red. Koby waved over Werner and Alonzo who were supporting Gunther, who kept his right foot off the ground. Christoff had joined them at some point and carried his pistol. A handful of retreating tanks rolled past them, but that was it.

"What happened?" Koby asked, while he examined Gunther's leg. Gunther kept his eyes on his sergeant, wondering how Koby could show concern after last night.

"The Russians launched another counterattack. They got some men behind us somehow," Werner said wearily, "But you should've seen the *Standartenführer*. When he realized we'd been encircled he led the charge to break through to the west. He must've been shot five or six times."

"At one point, he was crawling on the ground, with his pistol. We got a tank to the rear then and it cleared out the Russians. Then we all started retreating," Alonzo said.

"Are we going to surrender here?" Gunther asked, as Koby wrapped up his leg.

"*Nein*. Reinforcements are coming."

Within another hour, still in the late morning, the Russians were charging the German positions. The attack was swift, and the Russians clearly wanted to end it all.

Blaz fired as they charged in behind their tanks. He aimed at the men to his left and right, who weren't shielded. Koby gunned down a tank commander, but the wall of steel kept advancing. The Soviets were hell bent on victory. The tanks approached the first trench, and the Russian troops bolted forward, all yelling an overwhelming, "*Hu-rrah!*"

When the Russians were meters from being on top of their first trench, the Germans leapt out with bayonets raised, and riflemen behind them. It was like an old Roman formation. The Germans fired, felling many Russians but they kept charging. The Russians charged right into the bayonets, some being stabbed but many trampling over their enemies. The thirst for victory burned in their eyes.

"Retreat! Retreat!" Koby ordered Werner and Blaz, "I'll be right there."

"C'mon," Blaz told him, as he followed the others away. He and Werner supported Gunther, staying as low as possible as stray shots flew past them. They made it to cover behind a machine gun nest, and Koby came sprinting back to them. A German armored truck rolled up next to them, its mounted machine gun mowing down Russians. Blaz, Werner, and Koby all joined in the shooting. But the truck had attracted attention from the Russian tanks. Three cannons boomed and the truck exploded.

"Alonzo! Christoff! Get the hell out of here! Now!" Koby shouted, "I mean it! We'll cover you!"

"But-" Alonzo began.

"That is an order!"

Alonzo saluted, and he and Christoff sprinted to the west. Koby leaned to cover. Amongst the many shots fired, one hit its mark and Christoff went down. Alonzo skidded to a halt. Gunther raised his rifle, where he seemed to think the shot had come from. Immediately, he was shot in the head.

Koby gritted his teeth and exposed himself, firing into the charging Russians. Blaz bolted from cover and tackled Koby to the ground behind the flaming truck.

"Don't Koby, don't," Blaz pleaded. Koby looked at him, mouth hanging open. Blaz looked him in the eye and said with a nod, "I'm still not gonna let you die."

Werner peeked above his cover, and a bullet hit the dust right in front of him. He ducked back behind cover, and looked to Blaz and Koby, truly terrified. A watchtower exploded only twenty meters away to add to the sense of hopelessness. One Russian charged forward, getting in range of Werner. Blaz exposed himself briefly and shot the man in the chest. But now the lines broke. The Russians charged, guns blazing. They caught one more break as a *Panzer III* roared forward from its cover to shield the boys and other fleeing Germans.

Koby pointed at Christoff and Alonzo. "Help them, we'll cover for you!" Blaz nodded, and sprinted over to them, slinging his rifle over his shoulder.

"Christoff!" Alonzo cried, shaking his friend to wake him up. Blaz shoved Alonzo out of the way and put his head to Christoff's chest.

"He's alive! *Los*! I'll get him out of here."

"*Nein*, let me help!"

"*Los*!"

"He's my best friend!"

"*Nein*, run!" Blaz said, drawing his pistol in a desperate attempt to inspire obedience. Alonzo backed away, raising his hands.

Blaz holstered the sidearm and lifted Christoff over his shoulders. He was in a weak state, but Christoff was small so he was able to lift him. Werner and Koby came sprinting back to help. They reached the rear of the final lines under cover from German soldiers. The three remaining Knights left Christoff with a medic and returned to fight. They took cover behind a mound of dirt from the trenches. The Russians were rampaging through their defenses. Even the SS troops appeared terrified, all stoicism gone. Koby's hands shook on his rifle, whether from fury or fear Blaz couldn't tell. Stromschnellen was a good twenty meters to the right of the boys and he had drawn his pistol. Russian tanks had breached the front lines and now roared toward the very last line of defenses.

"*Deutschland über alles!*" one German soldier shouted, echoed by many others.

Koby was shooting better than he ever had. He fired one bullet at a time, hitting a target with each one.

"Out of ammo!" Werner shouted to Blaz, "I need ammo!"

Blaz kept focused and fired a shot, hitting a charging Russian. He ejected his clip after.

"I'm out!" Blaz shouted back, pulling out his Walther, prompting Werner to as well. Koby's rifle clicked pathetically.

"Russian!" Koby shouted while his gun was now useless. Blaz raised his pistol to shoot the man as he charged the small mound with a machete in hand. As Blaz's bullet ended the Soviet's life, the weapon fell inches away from Koby's face.

"*Danke*," Koby gasped without breaking focus on the advancing Soviet troops. Blaz didn't bother responding but kept his sidearm aimed. Koby drew and cocked his pistol.

"Do we fight on?" Blaz asked.

"We have to," Koby answered simply. He stood up and fired two shots, hitting a Russian with both. A shot hit Koby in the shoulder. He shook his head and fired at the shooter, before ducking back behind cover. He pressed a hand to his shoulder, eyes shut.

"That hurt," Koby gritted out.

Blaz and Werner stood up and raised their pistols. The Russians were nearly on top of them. Blaz fired repeatedly, ducking down several times. The Russians were now amongst the Germans. Blaz stood up to take another shot but his legs seemed to be knocked out from underneath him and his face hit the dirt. A surging shot of pain ran throughout his stomach.

"God," Blaz groaned. He tried to push himself to his feet. More pain in his abdomen. He collapsed again. The Russians were hand-to-hand now. Koby threw his rifle at a Russian before firing a bullet into the man's skull with his pistol. He ran to Blaz's side and flipped him onto his back. Blaz's eyes were glassy and unfocused.

"Come on Blaz!" Koby yelled over the shooting, "We have to fight now!"

Koby fired, felling two Russians. He pulled Blaz to his feet and they stood their ground. They continued to gun down Russians from their cover. Then a grenade landed behind them.

"Get down!" Koby yelled, tackling Blaz. The explosion deafened both. Koby stood up in a daze. Blaz spun onto his back to see Koby be shot through the chest multiple times. He fell. Blaz's hearing slowly returned. He heard no shooting though. He turned around to see Germans, both in the SS and *Wehrmacht* with their hands raised. An SS officer stood near Blaz, with Alonzo raising the white flag to appeal to the Russians' pity. The Soviet commander made his way to the front, heading toward the SS officer. The two exchanged words and shook hands at the end. The SS officer unclipped his sheath and dagger. He handed it to the Russian commander, who accepted it proudly. The SS officer turned to the Germans and roared at the top of his lungs, "It's over! Lay down your arms. Seelow has fallen!"

Across the lines, about a dozen shots sounded, and as many bodies fell. SS soldiers had shot themselves. Blaz looked at the nearest soldier to have done so. Werner. Blaz put a hand on his pistol for a moment, but a man's hand clamped down on his arm. He glanced over his shoulder. The SS officer stood above him, "It's done Blaz. But we aren't."

"Schlusser?"

The officer nodded.

Blaz pointed to Koby. "Will he be all right?"

"Blaz," Schlusser said, seeing the wounds clearly, "Koby is gone."

Blaz's jaw dropped, only slightly. He turned back to Koby. He shook him desperately. Koby didn't wake up. His eyes stayed shut, his tan, dust-covered face still. Blaz shook his head in disbelief. Tears streamed down his cheeks, leaving rivulets of clean skin. He gave Koby a hug, as the Russians neared them. Schlusser pulled him away, but Blaz allowed him to. There was nothing he could do.

Truth Will Triumph

"Onto Berlin!" a Soviet commissar roared to his troops, who cheered in victory before bursting into the triumphant, joyous melody of the Soviet anthem. Schlusser, Alonzo, and Blaz marched with their hands on their heads behind many other German soldiers. Blood soaked Blaz's uniform, so much so that Schlusser halted to wrap his midsection tightly. They marched back east, to Seelow. Blaz saw the rubble of his home. Bodies of his countrymen and women lined up in rows. Everything gone. Soviets dragged German women into homes. It was to the German soldiers' imagination what they did inside.

"*Weiter!*" Schlusser hissed to Blaz when he slowed down on seeing Seelow. Blaz obeyed.

A train was waiting in Seelow. Germans were being loaded into the cars. Notably, as Schlusser noticed, the SS were being herded into a group away from the train. Blaz did not notice in the least. He just marched forward. None of it felt real. The war was over. Over. Schlusser glanced to both sides, seeing no Russians near. He slipped out of his SS jacket, leaving it to be trampled by the men behind him.

"Get in the train!" a Soviet guard roared in German. The guard looked in Schlusser's direction, did a double take, but didn't pay any more attention. Blaz helped Alonzo into the car and gripped Alonzo's outstretched hand to climb up. They sat down by the door. As the young SS officer climbed in behind him, Blaz thought he heard a last, "*Deutschland über alles,*" from Schlusser while the man of the SS stared across the German horizon, before sitting down next to him.

More Germans crowded in, until there was no more room at all. Blaz looked over Schlusser to see the SS officers. They were in a circle, hands raised, with Soviets aiming their weapons at them. The train doors slammed shut. A chorus of shots rang out. The train started up.

Blaz let his head fall back to the wall of the boxcar in complete realization. A tear ran down his cheek. They had lost. They had failed. The world was too much to defeat. The world had not listened. All the fighting, all the death, all the pain, all the blood. So many dying in vain.

And this was how it ended.

www.ingramcontent.com/pod-product-compliance
Lightning Source LLC
Chambersburg PA
CBHW070831160426
43192CB00012B/2171